The Sages Of Our Tradition

*Interpreters Of
The Tanakh And Talmud*

Cyril Mazansky

Mazo Publishers

The Sages Of Our Tradition:
Interpreters Of The Tanakh And Talmud
ISBN 978-1-936778-26-3

Copyright © 2013 by Cyril Mazansky

Published by:
Mazo Publishers
PO Box 10474
Jacksonville, Florida USA 32247
Tel: 1-815-301-3559

Email: mazopublishers@gmail.com
www.mazopublishers.com

Book Production
Prestige Prepress
prestige.prepress@gmail.com

All rights reserved.
No part of this publication may be translated, reproduced, stored in a retrieval system, or transmitted in any form or by any means, electronic, mechanical, photocopying, recording or otherwise, without prior permission in writing from the publisher.

To

Rabbi Dovid Shapiro
Rosh Yeshiva Emeritus
Maimonides School; Brookline, Massachusetts

The Author

Cyril Mazansky is a radiologist in Boston, Massachusetts. He immigrated to the United States of America from South Africa in the early 1970s. He is married and has two daughters and grandchildren. His interest in the traditional scholars and interpreters of the Tanakh and Talmud grew out of his personal studies in the scholarly aspects of Judaism, and in Talmud. He has a longstanding interest in military history and has published a book titled British Basket-Hilted Swords. He has also published a number of articles on aspects of British military history.

Contents

Acknowledgments   6
Introduction   8

Section I - Author Names

  Master List of Authors by Proper Last Name,
    Alternative Last Names, Epithets and Acronyms   22
  Author Listing by Proper Last Name   45
  Author Listing by First Name   60
  Author Listing by Acronym or Epithet
    Alphabetical List of Proper Names   75
    Alphabetical List of Acronym / Epithet   81
  Derivation of Acronyms and Epithets   87

Section II - Biographies

  Tannaim and Amoraim
    Pre-Tannaitic   100
    Tannaim   102
    Post-Talmudic   123

Section III - Works Of Authors And Classifications

  Authors With Categorical Listing of Their Works   266
  Categorical Listing of Works
    Categorical Listing by Author   308
    Categorical Listing by Century   358
  Primary Work and Commentaries of These   411
  Works and Authors   436

Section IV - Aspects Of The Authors

  Period Lived by Sages, Rabbis and Scholars   474
  Chronology of Selective Pre-Gaonic Sages   490
  Chronological Listing of Scholars by Birthdate   502
  Geographical Locations of Authors   518
  Shifting Centers of Output Over the Centuries   554

Selected References   557

Acknowledgments

A number of years ago a key event occurred that was a positive life-changing experience for me. A friend of mine, and fellow-synagogue-congregant, suggested I join a Tuesday night Talmud study group that he had been attending for many years. He assured me I would have no regrets. This Talmud class was taught by Rabbi Dovid Shapiro, who at the time was the Rosh Yeshiva at the Maimonides School in Brookline, Massachusetts. These *shiurim* were originally led by Rabbi Yitzhak Twersky, the Talner Rebbe and the Nathan Littauer Professor of Hebrew Literature and Philosophy at Harvard University. The classes were held at the Talner Shul. Upon the untimely death of Rabbi Twersky, Rabbi Shapiro honored the memory of his Rebbe by becoming the leader of this study group.

Rabbi Shapiro inspires his students not only with his own very special talents as a teacher, but also with his tremendous qualities as a uniquely good human being. His approach to study was one that always had a scholarly bent to the analysis of the traditional texts. This created a spiritual and intellectual environment that was for me and my co-students one of the highlights of our week. But that was not all he brought to the class. His great humility and kindness to all of us, his encouragement of our questions, his research and follow-up to those questions for which he did not have a ready answer, and his sincere interest in our personal lives, engendered in all of us not only a great respect for him but also a strong sense of endearment. Although now retired and having made *aliyah*, his strong impact on our lives remains intact.

Rabbi Shapiro's method of study involved a combination of traditional study of the original Talmudic texts together with an extensive academic and scholarly approach to incorporating into these classes the writings of the many post-Talmudic scholars who interpreted these texts. As a result of these classes I soon became interested in acquiring, in addition to the actual teachings of the rabbis and subsequent scholars, a better knowledge of the personal histories of the traditional Talmudic and post-Talmudic rabbis. I soon found there was very limited organized information in English on the history, particularly biographical and bibliographical, of these scholars. Since I have always had an interest in history I began to try to obtain information on the lives and works of these scholars. For someone who has a limited ability to read and study texts in the Hebrew language the ability to explore in any detail the few primary biographical and bibliographical works that are available in Hebrew, is severely restricted. I then tried to find written works in the English language. Such books are not substantial and only cover a few specific groups of scholars. Without much initial thought or planning I began making notes of whatever information I found. One source of information often led to another. After a while I began to organize this English-language biographical material. This book is the outcome of those years of accumulation and organization of this data. When I finally had completed the draft form of this book and reviewed it with Rabbi Shapiro, he became an enthusiastic supporter of it and strongly encouraged me to find a publisher.

It was not only from Rabbi Shapiro that I drew my inspiration and understanding of the texts. Over the years there have been a core of regular attendees to the class. They have indirectly contributed to my writing this book. My regular co-students over these years have also been and remain my teachers. I respect greatly their tremendous knowledge and learn much from them. To Michael Bohnen, David Link, Sidney Kadish, Danny Margolis, Avrom Stuchin, Elyse Friedman and Allan Gordon, I gratefully acknowledge your contributions to my ongoing education.

Michael Bohnen has shown an intense interest in this work and has provided many helpful suggestions that I have incorporated. Michael Berger, Associate Professor of Jewish Law and Ethics in the Department of Religion at Emory University, critically reviewed aspects of the introduction and made important comments and suggestions that I hope are now reflected in the final version. In the final analysis, any failings, inaccuracies and omissions in this work are solely my responsibility and maybe attributed to my limitations.

My publisher, Chaim Mazo, enthusiastically took on this project and has worked efficiently to see it to its fruition. His collaborative work and expertise in preparing the book has been much appreciated. I am indebted to him in many ways.

Finally, and for me most importantly, my enduring gratitude and boundless love go to my wife Harriet. She has always been by my side, encouraging me in my endeavors, and each week shows an intense interest in what I had learned at Talmud class. She remains my daily inspiration.

Introduction

Implicit in the title of this book is the concept of *Chachmei HaMesorah*, "the Sages of the Tradition." These Sages are the rabbis from the days of the Mishnah through our own generation who interpreted and transmitted the Written and Oral Torah. The *mesorah* encompasses the full spectrum of Jewish law and tradition. It is classically understood to cover all the legal traditions and interpretations transmitted to Moses on Mount Sinai. It contained within it numerous levels of understanding, many of which remained to be discovered over time.

The rabbis understood the task of each generation was to receive the tradition, uncover new interpretations, and transmit them to the next generation. Thus the Sages covered in this book include not only "*chazal*," the rabbis of the Talmud, but all the generations of scholars that followed them, and continue to do so. Their writings cover the Tanakh, the Midrash, the Talmud, and post-Talmudic rabbinic literature. Their subject matter encompasses Jewish law, ethics and philosophy, liturgy, commentaries and other works based on the tradition throughout the many post-Talmudic centuries. This book then attempts to cover the biographies and works of the more prominent of those individuals who, individually or collectively, produced this body of rabbinic literature.

The purpose of this book is to accomplish two major goals. The first is to create a comprehensive English language biography of these great interpreters of the Tanakh and the Talmud. The second is to categorize and classify the authors and their works.

These interpreters can be divided into two broad categories based on when they lived as well as on the nature of the interpretive work they did. The earlier group of interpreters included in this book consist of a limited selection of the great pre-Talmudic and Talmudic-era sages. The latter group of interpreters, and the ones that constitute the majority described in this book, are the rabbinic scholars from the immediate post-Talmudic era through the latter half of the twentieth century. The ones selected are predominantly those who have contributed written material. A few of these works, particularly of the earlier scholars, may no longer be extant, but even then, their work is often mentioned in other manuscripts or books, that are still extant.

Neither the contributors to the Talmud nor the subsequent interpreters were interested in the history of the Jewish people in the classical sense of the word. They certainly were not interested in the historiography of the Jewish people. Only during the period of the Second Temple destruction did the rabbis comment on aspects of this time period. Much of this they witnessed themselves and therefore it is probably historically accurate. It was not until the era of enlightenment and particularly the nineteenth century that Jewish historiography developed. The leading historian of this period was Heinrich

Graetz (1817-1891). His main work, *History of the Jews*, was among the first works to review Jewish history from a Jewish perspective. It was considered a classic. More recently Michael Brenner wrote a *Short History of the Jews*. As for the history of the Jews of Eastern Europe, Michael Polonsky wrote a multi-volume *History of the Jews of Poland and Russia*.

Thus there is only a limited detailed history of the Jews up until the second century of the common era. Apart from the major works of Josephus, not much is known of early Jewish history. Prior to the rabbinic era, most of the detailed documented information comes from the Biblical canon. In the post-Talmudic era reference to previous scholars was made only in the context of their earlier contributions to the analysis and interpretation of the texts. As a result of this paucity of any detailed Jewish history, particularly with regard to individuals, there is only limited biographical information available about the many commentators over the past 1,200 years. In only a minority of cases is there more detailed information available, and this is usually with the more famous scholars as well as the ones who lived more recently.

Perhaps the first person to provide some form of information on these scholars' works was Shabbethai Bass who wrote *Sifte Yeshenim*. This work was a bibliography written in the seventeenth century containing a list of 2,200 Jewish books. Shortly thereafter Jehiel ben Solomon Heilprin wrote his major work titled *Seder HaDorot*. It consisted of three independent volumes. The second volume was a listing of Tannaim and Amoraim in alphabetical order and chronologically. It was titled *Seder HaTannai'm weha-Amora'im*. The third volume was a listing of all authors and their works, drawn mostly from Shabbethai Bass' work, with numerous additions.

It was only in the eighteenth century that a concerted effort was undertaken to produce a categorical biographical study of the scholars and rabbis that included the post-Talmudic scholars. Haim Azulai (the Hida) gathered whatever limited historical and biographical information was available on these many scholars as he traveled throughout Europe studying the books and manuscripts in the various libraries. From these studies he produced an extensive bibliographical and biographical work titled *Shem HaGedolim*. It is a work that is still in print. To this day it is still used as a reference source. However, his work is nearly three centuries old and therefore does not cover many of the later interpreters and scholars. It has not been translated from the original Hebrew and therefore is of limited availability, particularly to the majority who cannot understand the Hebrew content. More recently in the nineteenth century Aaron Walden wrote a work on the same theme as Azulai and in fact titled it *Shem HaGedolim HeHadash*. He included material that was omitted by Azulai, specifically those scholars who lived subsequent to Azulai. However, because he was a follower of Hassidism, he emphasized the Hassidic scholars.

An important element of Jewish study of the nineteenth century was the Wissenschaft des Judentums (Judaic Studies) School. Its purpose was to utilize modern scientific methods to evaluate in a critical fashion Jewish literature and culture. A goal of this school was to place Jewish literature and culture equally with that of Western European culture. It included in its sphere of study rabbinic literature. Among its members were Leopold Zunz (1794-1886) and Heinrich Heine. The former devoted much of his study to rabbinic literature. Despite its goal of secularity the Wissenschaft des Judentums was predominantly a religious movement and was actively embraced by rabbis at Jewish seminaries.

Moritz Steinschneider (1816-1907) was another important member of this movement. He made a major contribution in the area of the biographies and bibliography of these rabbinic interpreters through the centuries. He is probably considered the father of modern Jewish bibliography. His bibliography has more than 1,400 items. Most of his works were written in German, but he was also facile in Hebrew and a few other languages. His field of interest was not related only to theological matters but also secular subjects. In one work he covered Jewish literature from the eighth to the eighteenth centuries. He compiled catalogs of collections of Hebrew manuscripts and Hebrew printed books. Much of the content of these was outside the conventional rabbinic interpretative works. He included poetry, philosophy, and astronomy. He also created a comprehensive catalog of all Hebrew books in the Bodleian Library at Oxford University, referred to as the *CB*. There were nearly 10,000 entries in this work, with over forty pages devoted just to Maimonides. Thus his *CB* and his *Hebraische Bibliographie* formed the basis for twentieth century Jewish scholarly study.

Then in the late nineteenth century Mordechai Margolioth published in Hebrew his two-volume work, the *Encyclopediyah le-Chachmei HaTalmud ve-haGeonim* (Encyclopedia of Talmudic and Geonic Literature, being A Biographical Dictionary of the Tannaim, Amoraim and Geonim) that went just beyond the Talmudic scholars to include the Geonim as well. Later he wrote another work in four volumes, *Encyclopedia le-Chachmei Yisrael* (An Encyclopedia of Great Men in Israel being A Biographical Dictionary of Jewish Sages and Scholars From the 9th to the End of the 18th century). In 1910, Aharon Heyman published his work on the Talmudic rabbis, *Toledot HaTannaim ve-haAmoraim*. Shulamis Frieman and Alfred Kolatch more recently published comprehensive English-language works of the Talmudic era rabbis and interpreters.

The Jewish Encyclopedia was possibly the culmination of the Wissenschaft des Judentums movement. It was first published in 1906 and in English, not German. It is now in the public domain. Some of the information quoted therein was obtained from Azulai's work. Subsequent sources, some in electronic form, also used Azulai's work and the Jewish Encyclopedia, but these have addressed only specific groups of these interpreters and scholars. As an example of this last group are the two books published on the Rishonim and Early Acharonim edited by Rabbi Hersh Goldworm.

Thus in a chronological fashion the development of the historical, biographical and bibliographical material on rabbinic literature from the most important individuals or movements should begin with Shabbethai Bass in the seventeenth century, followed by Jehiel ben Solomon Heilprin and then Azulai in the eighteenth century. This was followed by Aaron Walden's work in the nineteenth century that had a similar content to Azulai's work but with the later rabbis included and one that also had a Hassidic concentration. The nineteenth century also saw the development of the Wissenschaft des Judentums movement in Germany. Among its important members with regard to Rabbinic literature were Leopold Zunz and some of the work of Moritz Steinschneider. In the later nineteenth century Margolith published his first work, but restricted it to the Talmudic rabbis and the Gaonim. His later work then covered the rabbis until the end of the eighteenth century. Following this in the early twentieth century the Jewish Encyclopedia was published. Shortly after this Aaron Heyman published his work, but again restricted it to the Talmudic era. In the latter twentieth century Frieman and Kolatch also published their works on Talmudic era rabbis.

This book does not contain any new biographical information. Essentially all the biographical information used in this book repeats the already-known and published information about these scholars, often times verbatim since in the case of the earlier scholars no new information has come to light. Much of the new biographical material of the last two centuries, however, does appear for the first time in book form.

Sarah Stroumsa in her book, *Maimonides in His World* mentions how Maimonides reminds his readers about his lack of originality in his text. She quotes an excerpt from him in which he says, "Know that what I say in these chapters ... does not represent ideas which I invented of my own accord, nor original interpretations." In similar fashion there is no originality in the biographies included in this work. The author has drawn entirely from the older works as well as from information in the public domain, and has often included the language from them.

There are three new aspects to this book compared with previous biographies. It is the first comprehensive English language book on the lives of these great rabbis. It also includes for the first time the nineteenth and twentieth century interpreters and scholars. The information from the biographies is then classified and categorized in a variety of ways. The various classifications are according to the type of works authored by the scholars, the geographical locations of these authors and the centuries when they lived. Certain demographic, social, and historical information can be gleaned from this information, which are elaborated upon in each section.

Selection of Rabbis and Scholars

Neusner in his work Rabbinic Literature: An Essential Guide indicates how the Jewish religion is derived from the Written Torah (The Hebrew Scriptures or the Tanakh). However, he states that the origin of this religion must be evaluated based on the interpretation of the Tanakh by the Oral Torah, and in essence he equates that with Rabbinic literature. He goes on to state that during the last few centuries of the Second Temple era a number of communities claimed to have inherited the Tanakh. However, he stated that the one formed by the Rabbinic sages had a special position that produced writings that ultimately normative Judaism considered uniquely authoritative. He further described how these writings of the Rabbinic canon can be divided into two parts. The first is devoted to law (Halakha). It began with the Mishnah, in essence a law code. It was then accompanied by or supplemented by the Tosefta ("supplementary traditions") and thirdly includes two analytical and systematic commentaries on the tractates or selected topics of the Mishnah. The one is the Talmud of the Land of Israel or the Yerushalmi Talmud, and the other is the Talmud of Babylonia or the Talmud Bavli being completed in 400 and 600 CE respectively. Commentaries on the legal parts of the Tanakh are found in the Mekhilta of Rabbi Ishmael for Exodus, Sifra for Leviticus and Sifre to Deuteronomy. The second part of the Rabbinic canon consist of the narrative books or lore (the aggadah). These cover six different commentaries. These are the Rabbinic readings of Genesis or Genesis Rabbah, Leviticus Rabbah, Ruth Rabbah, Esther Rabbah, Lamentations Rabbah and Song of Songs Rabbah. Some of these now form an important part of the liturgy. In addition to these Halakhic and Aggadic works, there is a collection of wise sayings that include Abot (The Fathers), and Abot deRabbi Natan (The Fathers according to Rabbi Nathan).

Berger in his work on Rabbinic Authority suggested that the earliest interpreters might be considered the Sanhedrin or perhaps the Beth Din HaGadol. He presents some arguments that those within the Tradition might defend the authority of the rabbis and that over time these traditional scholars put forward arguments in favor of this authority. However, none really covers the full extent of the authority that is accorded to the Talmudic rabbis within the Halakhic system. He considered them more of a philosophical argument that is analyzed but not a true historical claim. Later in his work he provides a more historical perspective that he feels may be more helpful in accounting for why these scholars and interpreters in the subsequent centuries granted the Talmudic rabbis such authority. In his analysis of rabbinic authority, he comments that the law was analyzed, refined and developed from the time of the completion of the Talmud and for the next fifteen centuries. However, it was always done with constant reference to the Talmud that served as the basis for the vast majority of legal (Halakhic) decisions. The Babylonian Talmud was the foundation of this.

Catherine Hezser indicates (and this may be a retrospective view) that the main purpose of the rabbis who edited the Talmud and committed it to writing was not only to preserve the material for later generations but also to set in motion an ongoing process of study, explanation, and commentary. This is probably no different from the concept of *Chachmei Hamesorah* described earlier. Furthermore as Shaye Cohen points out Mishnaic law is both the product of simple (direct) exegesis as well as complex (manipulative) exegesis. It is therefore not surprising that based on the comments of these two scholars, the ongoing interpretation of both of these forms of exegesis has continued to the present day. This has produced a wealth of commentators and authors throughout the past two thousand years.

In approaching a work of this nature the first question that has to be answered is when would there have been the first accepted interpretation of the Tanakh or the Talmud? If the oral law and its transmission are to be used as the only basis for this list, then one should turn to Masechet Avot and go back to the time of Moses. As mentioned earlier and according to Goodman, Rabbinic texts and later ones reveal a complete ignorance about events from the fifth century BCE to the era of the Sages of the first century CE. Avot encapsulates the passage of a tradition from Moses to Hillel and Shammai, but with no real reference to centuries or dates. Hillel lived approximately 130 BCE and the only Hasmonean reference by the rabbis is to Salome who ruled from 76 to 67 BCE, well after Hillel. However, according to James Kugel, the earliest evidence of scriptural interpretation was during the early post-exilic era when Ezra read the Torah to the people and the Levites were there to "help them understand the law" (Neh. 8:2-8). Therefore, based on the above, a systematic selection of the scholars included in this work begins with Ezra, but then immediately advances several centuries to Hillel and Shammai.

In the latter part of the Second Temple period and in the early centuries of the Common Era, the Tannaim were the interpreters of the Tanakh, concentrating on Torah interpretation. Following them was the era of the Amoraim. Their central role was to interpret and expand on the Tannaitic literature as redacted in the Mishnah. This was accomplished through the process of debate that is recorded in the Gemara. The work of the Tannaim and Amoraim is summed up in the Mishnah and Gemarah. According to Halivni, the summation of all this was probably accomplished by the Stammaim, who finally redacted all this discussion into the Talmud.

The Talmudic Sages, mainly the Tannaim and Amoraim, cannot be categorized in the same way as the post-Talmudic interpreters. Collectively they were the primary interpreters. Only a small selection of these is included to provide a historical and chronological dimension to the process of interpretation. Complete listings and biographical material on these Talmudic sages may be found in Margolioth's famous Hebrew work that provides biographical material on all Talmudic sages, often in quite great detail. He categorizes five generations of Tannaim from 80 CE to 200/220 and eight generations of Amoraim from 220 CE to 500. In this latter group he further divides them into those in Palestine and those in Babylon. The book then lists them alphabetically beginning in the first volume with R. Abba and ending in the second volume with R. Tanchuma. Two readily available books in English by Shulamis Frieman and Alfred Koltch also provide a comprehensive list and description of these rabbis.

Finally following this long era ending with the redaction of the Talmud, the period of individual interpreters and commentators of the Tanakh and the Talmud began. The earliest of these was the Gaonim, among whom Achai Gaon was perhaps the first to leave written documentation in his *Sheilot d'Rav Achai* or *Sheiltos*. One of the last Geonim, Saadia Gaon, probably was considered the greatest and also the most prolific author of this era. Margolioth in his other major work, the *Encyclopedia le-Chachmei Yisrael* covers the period from the ninth to the end to the eighteenth centuries. He divided the work into four volumes, with the first volume covering R. Abba Mari to R. Gershon b. Shlomo, the second volume being from R. Dob Baer to R. Judah HaLevi, the third one from Rabbi Judah Liwa (Loew) to R. Levi b. Hayyim, and the fourth volume from R. Meir Abulafia to Rabbi Tanchum Yerushalmi. Again all of these were listed alphabetically, but according to the first name in Hebrew.

This book then reflects the evolution of rabbinic and scholarly interpretation in a somewhat historical way. The chronological, categorical, comparative and narrative aspects of the latter sections of the book demonstrate this development. That this extensive interpretation has taken place over the centuries, and still does, is clearly attested to by the large number of scholars who are included in this book.

Not every post-Talmudic rabbi was included in this work. No one work can be complete in that sense. The emphasis is on those rabbis who over the post-Talmudic centuries authored manuscripts or books and contributed to the large corpus of commentary, analysis or other literary aspects of the Jewish religion that are based on Biblical, Talmudic, philosophical, or practical aspects. Some of these did not write the work themselves, but either their descendants or students recorded their teachings. There are also a small number of rabbis described who may not have left anything written but who made such a mark on the Jewish religion, with many subsequent works produced, based on their teachings and philosophy, that they are also included in this work.

In addition to the famous rabbis who contributed seminal works and to the many other important scholars whose contributions were so vital to the total output of post-Talmudic literature, there are many others described who might well fit into the category of minor contributors. Yet they were important to the overall body of literature. Works of rabbis that are no longer extant have also been included. In this latter group historical information as well as reference to their work in other literature, provide enough information about these works to include them. There is a smaller group of rabbis and authors included who do not fit into the category of interpreters. However, they contributed to the religious understanding and practice of Judaism. Such authors wrote ritual works and piyyutim or liturgical works. A sample of them are also included in this work.

The listing of the rabbis and authors and the information obtained about them was derived from a variety of sources, both from previously published works as well as material that is in the public domain. Searching for these can be challenging and often one source leads to another. Electronic-based information has become an increasingly important reference source. The Global Jewish Database (of which the Responsa Project is a part) is entirely electronically-based. The latest book published on Jewish bibliography by Charles Cutter lists a number of electronic web-based sources.

When the information is available, the content of the individual biographies in this book is in general restricted to the place of birth, the family background, the education of the scholar, where he worked and then brief descriptions of the work produced. Anecdotes or myths about these scholars have been excluded from the descriptive detail. This work encompasses essentially the life and works of the traditional scholars and not those of the academic scholars who since the age of enlightenment have become a dominant force in the study and analysis of the tradition.

Identifying Rabbis by Their Names

In compiling the bibliography and index of the sages and scholars the major challenge was how to list them in a methodical fashion while at the same time provide the means for easy identification by the reader. Throughout the centuries, many rabbis were known by various names. Depending on the reference source, especially prior to a couple of centuries ago, rabbis could be identified in a variety of ways. Kessin addressed this issue in an online article related to Jewish names in medieval Islamic countries. He indicated that, at least in the Islamic world, a dualism existed in their names. They would have a classical Hebrew name, often an Arabic name, and sometimes even a Spanish name. The Cairo Genizah appears to list many in the classical Arabic form. Kessin goes on to indicate that the most common form of a full name was to add the father's name to the personal name, which then became "son of". He also described another form where a person had a by-name, which was a personal description. This was different from the surname or last name in that it was not passed on. He gave examples of these as being of a tribal nature, for example HaLevi or HaKohen. A geographical by-name was another example. A third example would be by trade, where a form of rabbi or gaon would be included. Sometimes a personal trait was utilized. He gives the example of Shimon HaTzaddik. Only rarely would an actual surname or last name be used. The use of a hereditary last name or family name came into use at different times in different cultures. For example in Britain among the aristocracy it was used as early as the thirteenth and fourteenth centuries. Until the family name came into use among the Jews, the most frequently used last name was that of the father, with the ben or bar prefix. Jewish scholars were also often given acronyms, epithets or abbreviations, leading to further confusion with the names. This then became the form of identification for that particular rabbi. This practice of naming a traditional scholar by the acronym or epithet is still in wide use.

In approaching the listing of a rabbi's name in the book, all these variations had to be taken into account. They also had to be correlated in a way such that the reader would always be able to find the name of the scholar with the correct link to the biographical and analytical material.

Sections of the Book

The book is divided into four sections. The first one includes the listings of all the scholars included in this work, according to their various names or titles. The second and major part of the book consists of the individual biographies. The third part is that which contains the classification and categorization of the authors and their works in various ways. This is done in tabular form. The fourth part, also in tabulation, lists when and where the rabbis lived throughout the many centuries.

In the first section the approach taken in identifying the scholar is to list the last component of the name first, unless the individual had only a single name. The aim is to both standardize the names and also to relate this with modern practice, whereby an individual is identified by the last name first and then by the personal names. However, because most interested readers will either identify the individual by using the first name or the acronym as the starting reference point for a search of the list, a system of cross-reference of the various names was created that adequately covers all ways of searching for the individual. There are therefore four different alphabetical listings of the scholars. First there is the master list that combines all the ways of how a scholar can be identified through his various names. This list is alphabetically created with the formal last name highlighted. It is this highlighted name that then is used in organizing alphabetically the biographical and tabulated sections. Where an individual is known by more than one name, there is cross-reference to these. The second list is by the scholar's first name and then last name with the latter listed alphabetically and highlighted. The third listing is according to the alphabetical sequence of their first name with the last name highlighted. The final list is alphabetically of the acronym or epithet with the associated formal full name of the individual. Finally there is a list of the derivation of the acronym or epithet. Thus by using the master list alone, every rabbi and scholar can be found no matter how that individual is known to the reader.

The second section of the book then provides in alphabetical order the brief biographies of all the scholars as well as listing and sometimes briefly describing their works.

Solomon Freehof in the introduction to his work, *The Responsa Literature*, comments on how the greatness of a book may be judged by the number of works written about the original work. In that context he briefly mentions the Biblical-related works and then goes on to describe the extensive Talmudic-related literature that has been produced over a fourteen-century period. In the Biblical-related literature he describes two broad categories; explanations of the Biblical texts, where Rashi was the pre-eminent scholar, and the commentaries. As for the commentaries of the Talmud he divided these into three broad categories; direct commentaries of the Talmud; a review of all aspects of the Codes of Law; and the Responsa literature. The first two of these categories were further subdivided.

As for the commentaries on the Talmud, these were subdivided into three groups: The first was the explanations or direct commentaries of the Talmud where Rashi, writing in the eleventh century, was the most famous of these authors. The second was the harmonizing literature or Tosafot literature that was a body of twelfth and thirteenth-century work, and was one of the earliest forms of analysis of the Talmudic explanations. Rashi's grandson, Jacob ben Meir Tam (Rabbeinu Tam) was a leader in this field in the era of the Tosafists. It raised questions both on the content and the explanations of the Talmud and drew conclusions that were all based on the principle that the Talmud contained all the laws given by God. The third group was the Novellae or Hiddushim ("new notes"). Freehof classifies all the remaining post-Talmudic literature in this broad group. He considers this literature both an extension of and a deeper analysis of the type of work begun by the Tosafists.

The Talmudic text was so complex so that the practical application of the large body of laws contained therein was not easily apparent. This resulted in the codification of the law. Here perhaps the *Shulkhan Arukh* is the most famous code, written in the sixteenth century by Rabbi Joseph Caro (Karo). There were the extensive commentaries on the codes. Just as there were commentaries on the Talmud as a whole, so too was there the development of a body of literature of commentaries on the various codes.

The post-Talmudic literature may be more extensive than that described by Freehof. Therefore in the third section of this work there is a more extensive subdivision of these categories. In the Biblical-related literature, additional sub-groups are used. The Midrashic literature is one such sub-group. There is another sub-group, that would fall into Freehof's larger explanation section, and that is of commentaries on previous commentaries or explanations. These are termed super-commentaries. Since Glosses are explanations of a single word or phrase, these too technically would fit into the explanatory section, but could also warrant their own sub-group. Then there are various works that cannot be specifically classified in the above two categories and should be in a general or miscellaneous category. In the literature related to the Talmud this can be subdivided into those parts directly related to the Mishnah and the Talmud and then the commentaries on these. They would also include Talmudic interpretative super-commentaries. There is also the subgroup of the glosses. There is a large literature on the discussions of and commentaries on the laws as derived from the Talmud and also comments on the Codes. The category of novellae (Hiddushim) covers mainly the Talmudic ones, both direct Talmudic as well as those in the category of Codes of Law. However, it also includes a few Biblical novellae. Therefore it is in a category of its own.

There are other works that require their own classification. Besides the above three broad categories that cover the vast majority of post-Talmudic rabbinic literature, there is a significant body of work that may be classified under other categories. In some of these groups, for example the Hassidic literature, there is obviously overlap with the various divisions of Biblical and Talmudic literature. This group includes the categories of ethics, Hassidic literature, Kabbalah, liturgical works, ritual works, philosophy, and also piyyutim.

Finally there is a group that cannot be clearly categorized. A table summarizes these various groups.

The fourth section of the book approaches this information from a quasi-historical perspective.

Historical Aspects

Rabbinic literature seamlessly interspersed fact and fiction. The rabbis were not interested in recording history. Subsequently traditional scholars were more interested in providing their own interpretations of the Talmud or that of preceding scholars' interpretations than of recording the history of the Jews. Consequently the information is sparse. When it comes to biographies and historical information on these scholars, Haim Azulai, in the eighteenth century, made the first major and systematic effort to document this aspect.

Solomon Freehof indicates that in studying the responsa over the centuries, it maybe possible to gain much knowledge on the history of the Jews, the social and political as well as religious aspects. He further indicates that in different centuries political upheavals against the Jews led to disruption of the quality and productivity of responsa. As the Jews settled in new territories, after a while the pace of high quality responsa picked up again. This concept could probably be equally applied to other areas of traditional scholarly literary output.

In an attempt to demonstrate the historical aspect of the output of the post-Talmudic rabbis and scholars the data has been organized in a variety of ways based on the chronological sequence of centuries and geographical regions. Therefore there are geographical tables and tables that correlate the genre of work and the centuries when these were produced. These tables highlight some of the historical aspects.

Tables

An important section of the book consists of the multiple tables that were created to categorize the information extracted from the biographies of the individual rabbis and scholars. These tables cover many aspects.

There are tables that list the rabbis by their various names. An important group of tables are those that categorize the work according to a classification system or genre. This is done in several ways. One table lists the rabbi alphabetically and the work they produced and then categorizes each of these. Two tables categorize the work according to the major categories, but also chronologically through the centuries. These are done in slightly different ways. Another important table is one that lists the primary work of interpretation and then includes the listing of commentaries on these primary works. There is a table that lists alphabetically the title of every work included in the book with its respective author. There are two tables that list when the rabbis lived. The first one lists the rabbis alphabetically and when they were born and died. The second one lists all the rabbis who were born in a particular century. Then there is a table that is geographically based. Freeman pointed out that in different periods during the last two millennia rabbis congregated in different regions of Europe, North Africa and the Middle East. The reason for this was often related to persecutions and expulsions in a particular country. Those tables listing the works by century and genre indicate to some extent this phenomenon. Following these relocations there would be a major outpouring of work from these new regions of settlement by these scholars. Also if the rabbi was famous he would have been invited to lead various communities, often in more than one place, during his career. From the biographical data a table was therefore created that shows, according to countries and centuries, first where the rabbi was born and then where he may have worked. This provides additional sociologic and historic information as well.

What this book may also demonstrate is that, as Berger in his article *The Centrality of The Talmud*, points out, beginning with the Moslem conquests mainly in the eighth century and then beyond that, Rabbinic interpretation of Judaism spread into everyday Jewish life. The interpretations, particularly of the Babylonian Talmud, determined the everyday practices of all aspects of Jewish life.

It is hoped that the combination of the biographical material and the analytical aspects of this information will provide the general reader and student with a comprehensive, but admittedly incomplete, English language reference book on the great scholars and religious authors of the Biblical and Talmudic interpretive tradition throughout the centuries.

Section I
Author Names

Alphabetical List Of Sages, Talmudists and Authors

Proper Last Name, Alternative Last Names, Epithets and Acronyms

This list is the master list that correlates all the various names and spellings by which the individual author and scholar may be known. Since the standard form of identification used in this book is by the proper last name, it is highlighted in bold. From this one list all the other names can be found, since in all those situations where there is more than one name or spelling, these are cross-referenced.

A

Aaron of Pesaro
Aaron, Samuel ben, of Schlettstadt
Abarbanel (See **Abravanel**)
Abba Arika (See **Arika**, Rav)
Abba, Hiyya bar (See Hiyya)
Abba the Surgeon
Abba Mari ben Joseph (See **Mari**)
Abba Mari, Yitzhak (See **Mari**)
Abba, Samuel bar (See Samuel of Nehardea)
Abba, Tanhuma bar
Abba, Yirmiyahu bar (See Jeremiah)
Abbahu
Abbahu, Hanina bar
Abbaye
Abel, Solomon ben Kalman HaLevi
Abenezra (See Ibn Ezra, **Ezra**)
Aboab (Abuhab), Isaac (See Menorat HaMaor)
Aboab, Samuel (See Rasha)
Abraham, Isaac ben, of Dampierre (See Riba)
Abraham, Jonah ben
Abraham, Obadiah ben, of Bertinoro (See Bartenura, Obadiah)
Abraham, Samson ben, of Sens (See Rash)
Abravanel, Don Isaac ben Judah (See Abarbanel)
Abuchatzeirah, Israel (See Baba Sali)
Abudraham, David ben Joseph ben David
Abuhab (See **Aboab**)
Abulafia, Abraham ben Samuel
Abulafia, Meir ben Todros HaLevi (See Ramah)

Abuyah, Elisha ben
Aceda, Shmuel
Adarbi, Isaac (See Adribi)
Adels (See **Eidels**)
Adeni, Solomon ben Joshua (M'Lekhet Shlomo)
Aderet, (See **Rabinowitz-Teomom**, Teomim)
Aderet, Shlomo ben (See Rashba)
Adribi (See **Ardarbi**)
Ahai of Sabha (See Achai **Gaon**)
Ahavah, Adda bar Aidels (See Maharsha, **Eidels**)
Akavya ben Mahalel
Akiva, Rabbi (See **Joseph**)
Alami, Solomon
Alashkar, Moses
Albargeloni, Isaac ben Reuben
Albo, Joseph
Alegri, Abraham
Alfasi, Yitzhak ben Yaakov HaKohen (See RIF)
Algazi, Yom Tov
Al-Hakam (See **Chaim**)
Alharizi (al-Harizi), Judah ben Solomon
Alkabetz, Solomon ben Moses HaLevi
Alkalai, Judah ben Solomon Chai
Almosnino, Joseph
Almosnino, Moses ben Baruch
Alshich, Moshe
Alter, Avraham Mordechai (See Imrei Emes)
Alter, Pinchas Menachem (See Pnei Menachem)
Alter of Kelm (See **Ziv**)
Alter, Simchah Bunim (See Lev Simcha)
Alter, Yaakov Aryeh
Alter, Yehuda Aryeh Leib (See Sfas Emes, Leib)
Alter, Israel (See Beis Israel)
Alter Rebbe (See GRaZ, Shneur Zalman **Baruch**, Zalman, GRaZ)
Alter, Yitzhak Myer (See Chiddushei Harim)
Alter of Novardok (See **Hurwitz**, Horwitz)
Altschul, Naphtali (Hirsch) ben Asher
Altshuler (**Altshul**), David ben Aryeh Loeb
Amemar I
Amemar II
Ammi ben Nathan
Amnon, of Mainz
Amram, Gaon, (See Gaon, **Sheshna**)
Anaw (**Anav**) **Family**
Anaw (**Anav**), Benjamin ben Abraham

Anaw (Anav), Nathan ben Jehiel (Yechiel)
Anaw (Anav), Zedekiah ben Abraham (See **HaRofei**)
Ankava, Abraham
Arach, Eleazar ben
Arama, Isaac ben Moses (See Ba'al Akedah)
Ari, The (See **Ashkenazi, Luria,** Arizal, He-Ari)
Arika, Abba (See Rav)
Arizal, The (See **Ashkenazi, Luria,** Ari, He-Ari)
Aruch Hashulchan (See Yechiel Michel HaLevi **Epstein**)
Aruch LaNer (See **Etlinger**)
Asevilli, Yom Tov Ibn (Ritva)
Ash, Meir (See Meir **Eisenstadt,** Maharam Ash, Panim Me'irot)
Asher, Aryeh ben Leib (See **Gunzberg**)
Asher, Aaron ben Moses ben
Asher, Bahya ben (See Halawa, Rabbeinu Behaye or Bachya, Bachya)
Asher, (See Isaac ben Asher **HaLevi,** Riva)
Asher, Jacob ben (See Ba'al HaTurim)
Ashi, Hiyya bar
Ashi, Rav
Ashi, Tabyomi bar (Mar bar Rav)
Ashkenazi, Bezalel
Ashkenazi (See **Isserlein,** Petahiah)
Ashkenazi, Gershon
Ashkenazi, Mordechai ben Hillel (See The Mordechai)
Ashkenazi Moses (Johann Peter Spaeth)
Ashkenazi, Tzvi Hirsch ben Yaakov (See Chacham Tzvi)
Ashkenazi, Yehuda ben Shimon
Ashkenazi, Yisroel ben Shmuel, of Shklov (See Shmuel)
Ashkenazi, Yitzhak Luria (See The Ari)
Ashlag, Yehuda Leib HaLevi (See Ba'al HaSulam)
Assi
Attar, Hayyim ibn (Ohr HaChaim HaKadosh)
Auerbach, Menachem Mendel ben Meshulam Zalman
Auerbach, Shlomo Zalman
Avin, Yose bar
Avina
Avraham of Trisk
Avtalyon
Ayyas, Judah
Azariah, Elazar ben
Azaryah, Menachem of Fano (See Rama of Fano, Emanuel)
Azikri, Elazar ben Moshe (See Ezkari)
Azulai, Abraham
Azulai, Haim Yosef David (See Chida or Hida)
Azzai, Shimon ben

B

Ba'al Akedah (See **Arama**)
Ba'al HaLevushim (See **Jaffe**, Yoffe, Levush)
Ba'al HaMaor (See Gerondi, HaLevi, ReZaH, RaZBI)
Ba'al HaNesivos (See **Lorberbaum**, Lisser)
Ba'al HaSulam (See **Ashlag**)
Ba'al HaTurim (See **Asher**,)
Ba'al Shem Tov, (See **Eliezer**, the Besht)
Baba, Judah ben
Baba Sali (See **Abuchatzeirah**)
Babad, Yosef ben Moshe
Bach (See **Sirkis**)
Bachrach, Abraham Samuel
B**acharach**, Yair Chaim
Bachya (See Rabbeinu Behaya or Bachya, **Asher**)
Barfat, Isaac ben Sheshet (See Perfet, RiBaSH, Sheshet)
Bar Kappara (See Berebi, **HaKappar**)
Bartenura, The (See **Abraham**)
Baruch, Joseph ben (Joseph of Clisson)
Baruch, Joshua Boaz (See **Mevorakh**, Shiltei Gibborim, Shimon)
Baruch, Meir ben (See Rothenburg, MaHaRaM)
Baruch (Borukovich), Shneur Zalman, of Liadi (See Zalman, Alter Rebbe, GRaZ)
Barzillai, Judah ben
Bass, Shabbethai ben Joseph
Bechofen (See **Reischer**)
Behag, The
Behaye, Rabbeinu (See **Asher**, Halawa)
Beis Israel (See **Alter**)
Bei HaLevi (See Yosef **Soloveitchik**)
Ben Ish Chai (See **Chaim**, Al-Hakam)
Benet, Mordechai ben Abraham
Benveniste, Chaim
Ber, Dov of Mezritch, (See Dov Ber, Maggid)
Berab (Berav), Jacob (See Mhari Beirav)
Berabi (See Roba, **Rabbah**)
Berebi (See Bar Kappara, **HaKappar**)
Berechyah, Aharon, of Modena
Berezovsky, Sholom Noach
Berlin, Isaiah ben Judah Loeb (Isaiah Pick Berlin)
Berlin, Naftali Tzvi Yehuda (See The Netziv)
Besht (See Ba'al Shem Tov, Israel **Eliezer**)
Bezalel (See **Loew**, Levai and Maharal / Maharal of Prague)
Bibago, Abraham ben Shem Tov
Blaser, Isaac ben Moses Solomon (Rav Itzele Peterburger)
Boruch of Kosov
Bouton, Abraham ben Moses de

Boya'a, Shlomo ben
Brisker, Reb Chaim (See **Soloveitchik, Chaim**)
Bruna, Israel
Buber, Solomon

C

Campanton, Isaac ben Jacob
Caro, Joseph ben Ephraim (See Karo, Mechaber / HaMechaber)
Castro, Jacob de
Chacham Tzvi (See Tzvi **Ashkenazi**)
Chafetz Chaim (See Chofetz Chaim)
Chaim, Aharon ibn
Chaim, Hakham (Chacham) Yosef (See Ben Ish Chai, All-Hakam)
Chaim of Volozhiner (See **Volozhin,** Isaac, Ickovits, Reb Chaim)
Chajes, Zvi Hirsch (See Maharatz Chajes)
Chacham Tzvi (See **Ashkenazi**)
Chama, Rav (See Hama)
Chama, Rabbi Chanina bar
Chama, Rami bar (See Hama)
Channeles, Yehuda Leib ben Meir
Chananyah, Abraham ibn
Chatam Sofer (See **Sofer,** Schreiber)
Chaviv, Levi ben Jacob ibn (See Habib, Ralbach)
Chaviv, Moses (See **Habib**)
Chaviv, Yaakov ibn (See **Habib**)
Chaviva, Yosef
Chayei Adam (See Chochmat Adam, Abraham **Danzig,** Jehiel,
Chayon, Avraham
Chayon, Joseph
Chida, The (See **Azulai,** Hida)
Chiddushei Harim (See **Yitzhak Myer Alter**)
Chinuch The (See Aaron **HaLevi**)
Chisda (Hisda), Rav
Chizkuni (See **Manoah,** Hizkuni)
Chochmat Adam (See Abraham **Danzig,** Jehiel, Chochmat Adam)
Chofetz Chaim (See **Kagan,** HaKohen, and Meir)
Chorin, Aron
Chuli (See **Culi**)
Chushiel, Chananel ben (See Rabbeinu Chananel)
Cohen, Abigdor (of Vienna)
Colon, Joseph (See Maharik, Solomon, **Trabotto**)
Cordovero (also Kordovero) (See Ramak)
Coucy, (See Jacob)
Crescas, Hasdai ben Abraham
Culi, Yaakov (See Chuli, Kuli)

D

Danzig, Abraham ben Jehiel (See Jehiel, Chayei / Chochmat Adam)
Danzig, Samuel
Daud, Ibn (See Ravad 1, **HaLevi**)
David (See Aaron ben Jacob ben David **HaKohen**, Jacob)
David, Abraham ben (See Ravad III)
David, Baruch ben
Delacrut. Mattithiah ben Solomon
Dessler, Eliyahu Eliezer
DiSilo, Hezekiah ben David
Donolo, Shabtai
Dosa, Hanina ben
Dov Ber (See **Ber**, Maggid)
Duran, Simeon ben Zemah (See Rashbatz / Tashbetz)
Duran, Solomon ben Simon (See Rashbash)
Dvinsk, Meir Simcha of (See **HaKohen**, Kalonymus, Meir, Simcha)
Dvir, Yehuda Meir

E

Eger (Eiger), Akiva
Eibenschutz, David Solomon
Eidels (Edels, Adels), Samuel Eliezar ben Judah (See Maharsha)
Eisenstadt, Abraham Zwi Hirsch ben Jacob
Eisenstadt, Benjamin
Eisenstadt, Meir ben Iszak (Meir Ash) (See Maharam Ash / Panim Me'irot)
Eisenstadter, Meir (Meir Ash) (See Maharam Ash)
Elchanan, Naftali Hertz ben Yaakov
Eleazar, Isaac ben Eleazar (See **HaLevi**)
Eliakim, Hillel ben
Eliezar, Tobiah ben
Eliezer, Israel (See Ba'al Shem Tov and Besht)
Eliezer of Toul
Eliezer of Touques
Eligdor, Abba Mari ben
Elijah, (Abigdor ben Elijah **HaKohen**)
Elijah, Gaon of Vilna (See **Zalman**, Shlomo, Gra, HaGra)
Elijah, Perez ben (See Rap / RaPaSh / MaHaRPaSh)
Elisha, Ishmael ben (See Ishmael)
Ellenburg, Yissachar Ber
Emanuel (See **Azaryah**, Rama of Fano)
Emden, Jacob Israel ben Zvi Ashkenazi (See Yabets)
Enoch, Judah ben
Ephraim, Moshe Chaim, (of Sudilkov)
Epstein, Avraham
Epstein, Baruch HaLevi
Epstein, Moshe Mordechai

Epstein, Yechiel Michel HaLevi (See the Aruch Hashulchan)
Escapa, Joseph
Etlinger, Yaakov (See Aruch LaNer)
Ettinger, Hayyim Judah Lob
Ettinger, Isaac Aaron
Even HaEzel (See **Meltzer**)
Eybeschutz, Jonathan
Ezekiel, Judah ben (See Rav Yehuda)
Ezkari, Elazar (See **Azikri**)
Ezobi, Joseph ben Hanan ben Nathan
Ezra
Ezra, Abraham ben Meir ibn (See Ibn Ezra, Meir, Abenezra)
Ezra, Moses ibn (See HaSallah)

F

Faibesh, Samuel ben Uri Shraga (See Fayvish, Phoebus)
Falk, Joshua ben Alexander (Katz) HaKohen
Falk, Jacob Joshua (See **Hirsch**)
Faibesh (Fayvish) (See Faibesh, Phoebus)
Feinstein, Moshe (See Reb Moshe)
Fradkin, Shneur Zalman, of Lublin
Freehof, Solomon Bennett

G

Gabirol (See Gvirol), Solomon ben Judah ibn
Gafeh (See **Quafih**, Qafeh, Kapach, Kafich)
Galante, Abraham
Gamliel I (The Elder) (See Rabban)
Gamliel II (of Yavne)
Gamliel III
Gamliel IV
Gamliel V
Gamliel VI
Gamliel, Shimon ben
Gamliel II, Shimon ben
Ganzfried, Solomon ben Joseph
Gaon, Achai (See Ahai of Sabha)
Gaon, Amram bar Sheshna (See **Sheshna**)
Gaon, Hai (See Hai Gaon, **Sherira**)
Gaon, Nissim (See **Jacob,** HaMafteach)
Gaon, Saadia ben Joseph Al-Fayumi (See **Josef,** Sa'adia)
Gaon, Shem Tov ben Abraham ibn
Gaon, Sherira ben Hanina (See **Hanina**)
Gaon, Hai ben Sherira (See Hai Gaon, **Sherira**)

Gaon, Amram bar Sheshna, (See Amram, **Sheshna**)
Gaon, Yehudai (See **Nahman**)
Gaon of Vilna (See **Zalman**, Solomon, Gra, Vilna Gaon)
Gedaliyah, Meir ben (See **Lublin**, Maharam)
Gediliyah, Abraham
Gerondi, Yonah ben Avraham (See Rabbeinu Yonah)
Gerondi, Zerachiah ben Isaac HaLevi (See HaLevi, ReZaH, RaZBI, Ba'al HaMaor)
Gershom, Levi ben (See Ralbag, Gersonides)
Gershom, Rabbeinu Me'Or HaGolah (See **Judah**)
Gersonides (See **Gershom**, Ralbag)
Ghiyyat (Ghayyat), Isaac ben Judah ibn
Gias, Isaac ibn
Gikatilla, Joseph ben Abraham (Joseph Ba'al HaNissim)
Ginzberg, Louis
Golinkin, David
Gombiner, Abraham Abele ben Chaim HaLevi
    (Magen Avraham) (See Abraham HaLevi)
Gorion, Joseph ben
Gra (See **Zalman**, Solomon, Vilna Gaon)
GRaZ (See Shneur Zalman **Baruch**, Zalman, Alter Rebbe)
Greenwald, Eliezer David
Grodzinski, Chaim Ozer
G'rash, The (See **Lieberman**)
Gunzberg, Arey Leib (Loeb) ben Asher
Gvirol, Solomon ibn (See **Gabirol**)

H

Habib (See Levi ibn Yaakov ibn **Chaviv**, Ralbach)
Habib (Chaviv), Moses ibn (See Chaviv)
HaDarshan, Moses
HaGadol, (Nechynya (See Nechunya ben **HaKanah**)
HaGadol, Shimon ben Yitzhak
Ha Gaon, (See Rav Hai Gaon, **Sherira**)
Hagiz, Jacob
Hagiz, Moses
Hai, Gaon (See Gaon, **Sherira**)
HaKanah, Nechunya ben (See Nechuniah HaGadol)
HaKappar, Eleazar ben Eleazar (See Berebi, Bar Kappara)
Hakinai, Hanina ben
HaKohen, Aaron ben Jacob ben David (See Jacob, David)
HaKohen, Abigdor ben Elijah (See Elijah)
HaKohen, Abraham ben Eliezer
HaKohen, Israel Meir (See **Kagan**, Meir and Chofetz Chaim)
HaKohen, Joseph ben Joshua Meir (See Meir)

HaKohen, Meir Simcha Kalonymus of Dvinsk
 (See Simcha, Dvinsk, Meir, Kalonymus)
HaKohen, Shabbatai ben Meir (See Kohen, Shach)
HaLaban, Isaac ben Jacob
Halafta, Jose ben (See Yose)
Halawa, (See **Asher,** Behaye)
Halberstam, Chaim, of Sanz
HaLevi, Aaron (of Barcelona) (See The Chinuch)
HaLevi, Aaron Abraham ben Baruch Simeon (See Simeon)
HaLevi, Abraham Abele ben Chaim (See **Gombiner**)
HaLevi, Abraham ben Isaac (See Isaac)
HaLevi, Abraham ibn David (See Ibn Daud, Ravad I)
HaLevi, Aharon (See RaAH)
HaLevi, David ben Samuel (See **Segal,** Taz)
HaLevi, Eliakim ben Meshullam (See Meshullam)
HaLevi, Eliezer ben Joel (See Joel, Raviah)
HaLevi, Isaac ben Asher (See Asher, Riva)
HaLevi, Isaac ben Eleazar (See Eleazar)
HaLevi, Jacob ben Isaac (See Isaac, Jabez)
HaLevi Segal, (See **Segal,** The Taz)
HaLevi, Judah ben Samuel (See Samuel, RiHa'l)
HaLevi, Zerachiah (See **Gerondi,** ReZaH, RaZBI, Ba'al HaMaor)
Halivni, David Weiss
HaMeiri, Menahem ben Solomon (See **Meiri**)
Hama, Rav (See **Chama**)
Hama, Rami bar (See **Chama**)
HaMafteach (See **Jacob,** Nissim Gaon)
HaMechaber (See Mechaber, **Caro,** Karo)
Hamnuna
Hamnuna Saba (The Elder)
Hananiah, Joshua (See **Hannanya**)
HaNasi, Judah (Rabbeinu HaKadosh) (See Judah)
HaNagid, Samuel (See **Naghrela**)
Hanina, Sherira ben, (See Gaon)
Hannanya (Hananiah), Joshua ben
Haparchi, Ishtori ben Moses, (Kaftor Vaferech)
HaPenini, Yedayah
HaRaAYah or HaRav (See Abraham Isaac **Kook**)
HaRav (See Joseph Ber **Soloveitchik**)
HaRofei, Tzidkayah ben Avraham Anav (See **Anaw**)
HaSallah (See Moses ibn **Ezra**)
HaSardi (See HaSefaradi, Samuel ben Isaac **Sardi**)
HaVif (See **Palaggi,** Maharhaf)
Hayyim, Joel (See Mahariah)
Hayyun, Samuel

Hazaken, Yeshayah ben Mali (See Mali)
He-Ari (See Ari, Arizal, **Ashkenazi, Luria**)
He-Hasid (See Sameuel ben **Kalonymus**)
Heilprin, Jehiel ben Solomon
Heller, Aryeh Leib HaKohen (See Ketzos)
Heller, Yom Tov Lippman (See Tosefos Yomtov)
Herrera, Abraham
Heschel, Abraham Joshua
Hezekiah (See Hizkuni, **Manoah**)
Hida, The (See **Azulai**, Chida)
Hillel, The Elder
Hillel, Son of Gamliel III
Hillel II
Hillel, Mordechai ben (See **Ashkenazi**, The Mordechai)
Hillel, Shimon ben
Hirsch, Abraham Tzvi (See **Eisenstadt**)
Hirsch, Yaakov Yehoshua ben Zvi (See Falk)
Hisda, Rav
Hisma Eleazar
Hiyya bar Abba, (See **Abba**)
Hizkuni (See Hezekiah, **Manoah**)
Hoffmann, David Zevi
Horowitz Family
Horowitz, Abraham ben Shabtai Sheftel
Horowitz, Isaiah HaLevi (See Shaloh, Shelah)
Horowitz, Shabtai Sheftel
Horwitz (See **Hurwitz**, Alter of Novardok)
Hoschel, Judah Aryeh Lob ben Joshua
Hoshayya (See **Rabbah**, Berabi)
Huli (See **Culi**, Chuli, Kuli)
Huna, Rav
Hurkanos, Eliezer ben
Hurwitz, Shabbethai Sheftel ben Akiba
Hurwitz, Yosef Yozel (See Horwitz, Alter of Novardok)
Hushiel, (See **Chushiel**)
Hutner, Yitzhak

I
Ibn Ezra, Abraham ben Meir (See Meir, **Ezra**, Abenezra)
Ickovits, Chaim (See **Volozhin**, Reb Chaim, Isaac Chaim of Volozhiner)
Ilai, Judah ben
Ikriti, Shemariah ben Elijah, of Negropont
Imrei Emes (See Avraham Mordechai **Alter**)
Isaac, Abraham ben, of Narbonne (See Ravad II)
Isaac, Baruch ben

Isaac, Chaim ben (See **Volozhin**, Reb Chaim, Isaac Chaim of Volozhiner, Ickovitz)
Isaac, Elhanan ben, of Dampierre
Isaac, (See **Samuel**, Ri)
Isaac, Jacob ben (See **HaLevi**)
Isaac, Joseph ben (See **Shor**)
Isaac, Kalonymus ben
Isaac, Nahman bar (See Yitzhak)
Isaac Or Zarua (See **Moses**, Isaac ben of Vienna, Or, Zarua, Riaz)
Isaac the Blind (See **Nehor**)
Isaac, Samson ben, of Chinon (MaHaRShak)
Isaac, Solomon ben
Ishmael ben Elisha, (See **Elisha**)
Israel of Bramburg
Israel of Krems
Israel, Menasseh ben
Isserlin, Israel ben Petahiah (See Petahiah, Ashkenazi)
Isserles, Moses ben Israel (See Rema, Ramo)

J

Jabez (See Jacob **HaLevi**)
Jacob of Chinon
Jacob (See Aaron ben Jacob ben David **HaKohen**, David)
Jacob, Menahem ben (Solomon ben Simson) (See Simson, Solomon)
Jacob, Meshullam ben
Jacob, Moses ben (of Coucy) (See Moshe ben Yaakov)
Jacob, Nahman bar (See Nachman)
Jacob, Nissim ben (See HaMafteach, Nissim Gaon)
Jacobson, Yissachar
Jaffe (Yoffe, Yafeh), Mordechai ben Abraham (See Ba'al HaLevushim, Levush)
Jam'a, Samuel ben Jacob
Janach, Yonah ibn (Merinos)
Jehiel (See Abraham **Danzig**, Chayei / Chochmat Adam)
Jehiel, Asher ben (See Rosh, Yehiel)
Jeremiah (See Yirmiyahu, bar **Abba**)
Joel, (See Eliezer ben Joel **HaLevi**, Raviah)
Jonah, (Rav)
Jose, Jose bar
Jose, Eliezar ben (See Yose)
Joseph, Akiva ben (See Akiva)
Joseph, Enoch Zundel ben
Joseph Isaac ben, of Corbeil (See Yitzhak ben Yossef)
Joseph, Jehiel ben, of Paris
Joseph, Joshua Hoschel ben
Joseph, Jehiel ben (Jehiel of Paris)

Joseph, Jacob (See Jacob Joseph ben Tzvi HaKohen **Katz**, of Polonnoye)
Joseph, Moses ben, of Trani (See Trani)
Joseph, Sa'adia ben (See Gaon, Sa'adia)
Joseph, Samson ben, of Falaise
Josiah (Yehoshiyahu), Ahai (or Achai) ben
Joshua (Yehoshua) (ben Chananyah), Rabbi
Judah, Daniel ben
Judah, Gershom ben
    (See Rabbeinu Gershom or Rabbeinu Gershom Me'Or HaGolah)
Judah (See **HaNasi**)
Judah II
Judah III
Judah IV
Judah, Eleazar ben (See Rokeach, **Kalonymus**)
Judah, Solomon ibn (See **Gabirol**)

K

Kaf HaChaim (See Yaakov Chaim **Sofer**)
Kafich (See Gafeh, Kapach, Qafehh, **Qafih**)
Kagan, Israel Meir (HaKohen) (See HaKohen, Meir and Chofetz Chaim)
Kahana, Rav
Kaidanover, Aaron Samuel ben Israel
Kaidenover, Zevi Hirsch
Kalir, Eleazar
Kalischer, Zvi Hirsch
Kalonymus Family (liturgical poets)
Kalonymus, David ben, of Munzenberg
Kalonymus, Eleazar ben Yehuda ben, of Worms (See Rokeach)
Kalonymus, Elijah ben
Kalonymus, Meir Simchah (See **HaKohen**, Dvinsk, Meir, Simcha)
Kalonymus, Samuel ben (He-Hasid), of Speyer
Kamenecki, Jacob (Yaakov Kamenetsky)
Kapach (See Gafeh, Kafich, Qafeh, **Qafih**)
Kappara, Bar (See **HaKappar**, Berebi)
Kara, Abraham ben Abigdor
Kara, Simeon, of Frankfurt (HaDarshan)
Karelitz, Abraham Isaiah (Chazon Ish)
Karo, Joseph (See **Caro**)
Kasher, Menachem Mendel
Katz, Jacob Joseph ben Tzvi HaKohen, of Polonnoye (See Jacob Joseph)
Katzenellenbogen, Meir ben Isaac (See Maharam Padua, Meir of Padua)
Kayyara, Simeon
Kelin, Samuel ben Naftali HaLevi
Ketzos, The (See **Heller**)

Kimchi (Kimhi) family
Kimchi, Joseph ben Isaac
Kimchi, Moses
Kimchi, David (See Radak)
Kli Yakar (See Shlomo Ephraim **Lunshitz)**
Kluger, Solomon ben Judah Aaron
Kohen, Shabbatai (See Shabbatai **HaKohen,** Shakh, Shach)
Kook, Abraham Isaac (See HaRaAYaH or HaRav)
Kordovero, Moshe (See **Cordovero,** Ramak)
Kotzker Rebbe (See Menachem **Mendel)**
Krochmal, Menachem Mendel ben Abraham
Krochmal, Nachman Kohen
Ksav Sofer (See Abraham **Sofer)**
Kuli (See **Culi)**

L
Labi, Joseph ben David (See **Lev)**
Labrat, Dunash HaLevi ben
Lakish, Shimon ben (See Resh Lakish)
Lampronti, Yitzhak Hezekiah
Landau Family
Landau, Ezekiel (Yechezkel) (See Nodah B'Yehuda)
Landau, Yaakov Baruch ben Yehuda
Lapapa, Aaron ben Isaac
Leib, Yehuda (See Sfas Emes, **Alter)**
Leibowitz, Boruch Ber
Leibush, Meir (See **Michel,** Malbim, Weiser)
Leifer, Mordechai, of Nadvorna (See Mordechai)
Lema (See **Lima)**
Leon, Judah ben Isaac Messer
Leon, Moses de (See Moshe ben Shem Tov)
Lev, Joseph ibn (See Labi)
Lev Simcha (See Simchah Bunim **Alter)**
Levai, Judah ben Bezalel (See **Loew,** Bezalel, Maharal / Maharal of Prague)
Levi, Joshua ben
Levin, Joshua Hoschel ben Elijah Zeeb
Levita, Shabbatai Carmuz
Levovitz, Yerusham
Levush (See Ba'al HaLevushim, **Jaffe,** Yoffe)
Lida, David
Lieberman, Saul (See G'rash)
Lieblein, Avraham
Lima (Lema), Moses ben Isaac Judah:
Lipschitz, Baruch Mordechai ben Jacob

Lipschutz, Hayyim ben Moses
Lipschutz, Israel
Lipschutz, Moses ben Noah Isaac
Lipschutz, Noah ben Abraham (Noah Mindes)
Lipkin, Israel (See **Salanter**)
Lissa Rav (See **Lorberbaum**, Ba'al HaNesivos)
Lisser (See **Lorberbaum**, Ba'al HaNesivos)
Loanz, Yosef (Yoselman), of Rosheim
Loew, Samuel ben Nathan
Loew, Judah ben Bezalel (See Bezalel, Levai, Maharal / Maharal of Prague)
Lonzano, Menachem di
Lorberbaum, Jacob ben Jacob Moses, of Lisser
    (See Lisser, Ba'al HaNesivos / Lissa Rav)
Lublin, Meir ben Gedaliyah (See Gedaliyah, Maharam)
Lunshitz, Shlomo Ephraim (See Kli Yakar)
Luria (Ashkenazi), Isaac (See Ari, Arizal, He-Ari)
Luria, Solomon (See Maharshal, Rashal)
Luzzatto, Moses Chaim (See Ramchal)

M
Maggid (of Mezritch) (See **Ber**, Dov)
Maharhaf (See **Palaggi**, HaRif)
Maharal / Maharal of Prague (See Bezalel, Levai, **Loew**)
Maharam (See Gedaliyah, **Lublin**)
MaHaRaM (See **Baruch**, Rothenburg)
Maharam Ash (See Meir **Eisenstadt**, Meir Ash, Panim Me'irot)
Maharam Ash (See Meir **Eisenstadter**)
Maharam Schick (See Moses **Schick**)
Maharatz Chajes (See **Chajes**)
Mahariah (See **Hayyim**)
Maharik (See Colon, Solomon, **Trabotto**)
Maharil (See **Moelin**)
Mahariv (See Jacob **Weil**)
MaHaRPaSh (See **Elijah**, Rap / RaPaSh)
Maharsha (See Aidels, **Eidels**)
Maharsham (See **Schwadron**)
Mhari Beirav (See **Berab**)
Marharshal (See **Luria**, Rashal)
Maimonides (See **Maimon**, Rambam)
Maimon, Moses ben (See Maimonides and Rambam)
Malbim, (See Leibush, **Michel**, Weiser)
Mali (See **Hazaken**)
Mali (See di **Trani**, RI'D)
Manoah, Hezekiah ben (See Hizkuni / Chizkuni)

Margolis / Margolioth Family
Margolis, Abi Ezra Zelig
Margolis, Alexander
Margolis, Ephraim Zalman (Solomon)
Margolis, Hayim Mordechai
Margolis, Meir ben Zvi, Hirsch
Mari, Abba, ben Moses ben Joseph Don Astruc of Lunel (See Abba Mari)
Mari, Abba, Yitzhak ben, of Marseilles (See Abba Mari, Yitzhak)
Mechaber (See HaMechaber, **Caro**, Karo)
Mecklenberg (Mecklenburg), Jacob, Tzvi
Medina, Moses de
Medina, Samuel ben Moses de, (See RashDaM)
Medina, Shemaiah de
Medini, Chaim Chizkiya
Megash (See **Migash**, Ri Migash)
Meir of Padua (See **Katzenellenbogen**)
Meir, Ba'al HaNes (See Nahori)
Meir (See Ibn Ezra, **Ezra**, Abenezra)
Meir, Isaac (Yitzhak) ben (See Rivam)
Meir (Tam), Jacob ben (See Rabbeinu Tam and Tam)
Meir, (See Joseph ben Joshua **HaKohen**)
Meir, Moses ben, of Ferrara
Meir, Samuel ben (See Rashbam)
Meir, Simcha of Dvinsk (See **HaKohen**, Kalonymus, Simcha, Dvinsk)
Meir, Yisroel (See **Kagan**, HaKohen, Chofetz Chaim)
Meiri, Menachem ben Solomon (See HaMeiri)
Meltzer, Isser Zalman (See Even HaEzel)
Mendel, Menachem of Kotzk (See Kotzker Rebbe)
Mendelssohn, Moses
Menorat HaMaor (See **Aboab**)
Me'Or HaGolah (See **Yehuda**)
Meshullam, Asher ben
Meshullam, Eliakim ben (See **HaLevi**)
Meshullam, Moses ben
Meshullam, Yerucham ben
Mevorakh, Joshua Boaz (See Baruch, Joshua Boaz ben Shimon, Shiltei Gibborim)
Mharsheishoch (See **Schotten**)
Michel, Meir Leibush ben Yechiel (See Leibush, Malbim, Weiser)
Migash, Joseph ben Meir HaLevi ibn (See Megash, Ri Migash)
Minchat Yaakov (See **Weiss**)
Mindes, Noah (See **Lipschutz**)
Minz, Abraham ben Judah HaLevi
Minz, Judah ben Eliezer HaLevi (Mahari Minz)
Mitteler Rebbe (See **Schneuri**)
Mizrachi, Elijah (See Re'em)

Modena, Samuel ben Moses di (Maharshdam)
Moelin, Jacob ben Moses Levi (See Maharil)
Mordechai, The (See Mordechai ben Hillel, **Ashkenazi**)
Mordechai, Isaac ben, of Regensburg
Mordechai of Nadvorna (See **Leifer**)
Mos, Moshe, of Premysl
Moses of Evreux
Moses, Isaac ben, of Vienna (See Isaac, Or Zarua, Riaz)
Moses, Joseph ben
Moses, Meshullam ben
Moses, Meshullam ben

N
Nachman of Breslov
Nachman, bar Jacob (See **Jacob**)
Nachman (See **Yaakov**)
Naghrela, Samuel ibn (See Samuel Hanagid)
Nahman, Moses ben (See Nahmanides, Ramban)
Nahman (Nahmani), Samuel ben
Nahman, Yehudai ben (See Yehudai Gaon)
Nahmani, Rabbah bar (See Rabbah)
Nahmanides (See Ramban, **Nahman**)
Nahori (See **Meir**)
Nappacha, Yochanan bar
Nathan
Nathan, Abraham ben
Nathan, Eliezer ben (Raavan)
Nathan, Judah ben (See Riban)
Nathanson, Joseph Saul
Nehor, Yitzhak Saggi (See Isaac the Blind)
Nehorai, Meir ben Isaac (See Meir ben Yitzhak)
Netziv, The (See **Berlin**)
Nissim (See Ran, **Reuven**)
Nissim, Jacob ben (See **Shahin**)
Nodah B'Yehuda (See **Landau**)

O
Obadiah, Rabbi Bertinoro (See **Abraham**)
Onkelos
Ornstein, Jacob Meshullam ben Mordechai Ze'ev
Or Zarua (See Isaac, **Moses**)

P
Palaggi, Hayyim (See Maharhaf, HaVif)

Panim Me'irot Ash, (See Meir Ash, Meir **Eisenstadt**, Maharam Ash)
Pappa, Rav
Pappa, Chanina ben
Paquda, Bahya ben Joseph ibn
Parta, Eleazar ben (See Elazar ben Perata)
Pedat, Eleazar ben
Pallier, Moshe, of Kobrin
Perfet, Isaac ben Sheshet (See **Barfat**, Isaac bar Sheshet, Rivash / Ribash)
Perata, Elazar (See **Parta**)
Petahiah, Israel Isserlein ben (See **Isserlein**, Ashkenazi)
Phoebus (See **Faibesh**, Fayvish)
Plat, Joseph ibn
Pnei Menachem (See **Alter**)
Popperos, Meir
Price, Avraham Aharon

Q
Qafih, Yosef (See Kafich, Gafeh, Kapach, Qafeh)

R
Raavan (See Eliezer ben **Nathan**)
Rabad III (See Raavad, Ravad III, **David**)
Rabbah (See **Nahmani**)
Rabbah, Hoshayya (See Roba, Berabi)
Rabban (See **Gamliel**)
Rabbeinu Chananel (See **Chushiel**)
Rabbeinu Gershom Me'Or HaGolah (See **Judah**)
Rabbeinu Nissim (See **Shahin**)
Rabbeinu Tam (See Jacob ben **Meir**, Tam)
Rabbeinu Yonah (See **Gerondi**)
Rabinowitz, Chaim Shalom Tuvia (See Reb Chaim Telzer)
Rabonowitz-Teomim, Eliyah David (See Aderet, Teomim)
RaDaK (See **Kimchi**)
Radvaz (See **Zimra**)
Ralbag (See **Gershom**, Gersonides)
Ralbach (See Habib, Levi ibn **Chaviv**)
RAM (See **Samuel**)
Ramah (See **Abulafia**)
Rama of Fano (See **Azaryah**, Emanuel)
Ramak (See **Cordovero / Kordovero**)
Rambam (See Maimonides, **Maimon**)
Ramban (See **Nahman**, Nahmanides)
Ramchal (See **Luzatto**)
Ramo (See **Isserles**, Rema)

Ran (See Nissim, **Reuven**)
Rap (See Elijah, RaPaSh / MaHaRPaSh)
Rapash (See Elijah, Rap / MaHaRPaSh)
Rapoport, Solomon Judah Loeb
Rash (See **Abraham**)
Rasha (See Samuel **Aboab**)
RashDaM (See Samuel **Medina**)
Rashal (See Maharshal, **Luria**)
Rashash (See **Strashun**)
Rashash (See **Sharabi**)
Rashba (See **Aderet**)
Rashbi (See **Yohai**)
Rashbam (See Samuel ben **Meir**)
Rashbash (See Solomon **Duran**)
Rashbatz (See Tashbetz, Simeon **Duran**)
Rashbi, The (See **Yohai**)
Rashi (See **Yitzhaki**)
Rav (See **Abba Arikha**)
Rav, The Brisker (See Brisker, Chaim **Soloveitchik**)
Rav Yehuda (See Judah ben **Ezekiel**)
Rava (Abba bar Yosef bar Chama)
Ravad I (See ibn Daud, **HaLevi**)
Ravad II (See Abraham ben **Isaac** of Narbonne)
Ravad III (See **David**)
Raviah (See Eliezer **HaLevi**)
Ravina I
Ravina II
Ra'Za'H (See **Zerachiah** HaYavani)
RaZBI (See **Gerondi,** HaLevi, ReZaH, Ba'al HaMaor)
Reb Chaim (See **Volozhin,** Isaac, Chaim of Volczhin, Ickovits)
Reb Chaim Telzer (See **Rabinowitz**)
Reb Meir Ba'al HaNes (See **Meir**)
Reb Moshe (See **Feinstein**)
Rebbe (See Menachem Mendel **Schneerson**)
Rebbe Maharash (See Shmuel **Schneerson**)
Rebbe Rayatz (See Yosef Yitzhak **Schneerson**)
Rebbe Rashab (See Dovber **Schneerson**)
Re'em (See **Mizrachi**)
Reggio, Isaac Samuel (See Yashar)
Reischer (Richer), Jacob ben Joseph (Backofen)
Rema (See **Isserles,** Ramo)
Resh Lakish (See **Lakish**)
Reuben, Jacob ben
Reuben, Jacob ben
Reuven, Nissim ben, of Gerona (See RaN)

ReZaH (See **Gerondi**, HaLevi, RaZBI, Ba'al HaMaor)
Ri (See Isaac ben **Samuel** of Dampierre)
Riaz (See **Moses**, Isaac ben of Vienna, Isaac, Or Zarua)
Riba (See Isaac ben **Abraham**)
Ribam (See Mordechai, Isaac)
Riban (See **Nathan**)
RiBaSH (See **Barfat**, Isaac bar Sheshet)
RI'D (See **Trani**)
Ridbaz (See Ridvaz, **Wilovsky**)
Ridvaz (See Ridvaz, **Wilovsky**)
RIF (See **Alfasi**)
RiHa'l (See Yehuda **HaLevi**, Samuel)
Ri Migash (See **Migash**, Megash)
Ritvah (See **Asevilli**)
Riva (See **HaLevi**)
Rivam (See Isaac ben **Meir**)
Rivash (See Perfet, Ribash, **Barfat**, Isaac bar Sheshet)
Rivkes, Moses ben Naftali Hertz
Roba (See **Rabbah**, Berabi)
Rogatchover Gaon (See Rosen, Tzafnach Paneach)
Rokeach, Eleazar (See **Kalonymus**)
Rosanes, Judah ben Samuel
Rosen, Yosef (See Rogatchover Gaon, Tzafnach Paneach)
Rosh (See **Jehiel**, Yehiel)
Rothenburg, Meir of (See **Baruch**)
Ruderman, Yaakov Yitzhak

S

Sa'adia ben Josef (See **Joseph**, Gaon)
Saba, Avraham ben Yaakov
Safra, Rav
Sahula, Meir ben Solomon Abi
Salanter, Israel Lipkin (See Lipkin)
Samuel of Nehardea (See Samuel bar **Abba**)
Samuel, Aaron ben
Samuel, Eliezer ben, of Metz
Samuel, Isaac ben, The Elder, of Dampierre (See Ri)
Samuel, Isaac ben (Hasefardi)
Samuel, Judah ben (See **HaLevi**, RiHa'l)
Samuel, Judah ben, of Regensburg (He-Hasid)
Samuel, Meir ben (See RAM)
Samuel, Simha ben, of Speyer
Samuel, Simhah ben, of Vitry
Sardi, Samuel ben Isaac (See HaSardi, HaSefaradi),

Sarug, Israel
Saruq, Menahem ben Jacob ibn
Sasportas, Jacob ben Aaron
Schick, Moses (See Shik, Maharam Schick)
Schmelkes, Isaac
Schneerson, Levi Yitzhak
Schneerson, Menachem Mendel (See Tzemach Tzedek)
Schneerson, Shmuel (See The Rebbe Maharash)
Schneerson, Menachem Mendel, (See The Lubavitcher Rebbe)
Schneerson, Sholom Dovber (See Rebbe Rashab)
Schneerson, Yosef Yitzhak (See Rebbe Rayatz)
Schneuri, Dovber (See Mitteler Rebbe)
Schotten, Samuel (See Mharsheishoch)
Schreiber, Moses ben Samuel Sofer (See **Sofer**, Chatam Sofer)
Schwadron, Sholom Mordechai (See Maharsham)
Segal, David ben Samuel HaLevi (See HaLevi, Taz)
Sfas Emes (See **Alter**)
Sforno, Obadiah ben Jacob
Shabbethai, Kalonymus ben
Shahin, Jacob ben Nissim ibn (See Nissim, Rabbeinu Nissim)
Shakh (Shach) (See Kohen, **HaKohen**)
Shakna, Shalom
Shaloh, The (See Shelah, **Horowitz**)
Shammai
Shamua, Elazar ben
Shapira (Szapira), Kalonymus Kalman
Shapiro, Eliyahu ben Benjamin Wolf
Shapiro, Yehuda Meir
Sharabi, Shalom (See Rashash)
Shatz (See **Zvi**)
Shelah (See Shaloh, **Horowitz**)
Shem Tov, Shem Tov ibn
Shem Tov, Moshe (See de **Leon**)
Shemuel (Shmuel)
Sherira, Hai ben (See Gaon, Hai)
Sheshet
Sheshet, Isaac bar (See Perfet, Rivash, Ribash, **Barfat**)
Sheshna, Amram bar, Gaon (See Amram, Gaon)
Shik (See **Schik,** Maharam Shik)
Shila of Kefar Tamarta
Shiltei Gibborim (See **Mevorakh**, Baruch, Shimon)
Shimon, Elazar ben
Shimon, Yehoshua Boaz ben (See **Mevorakh**)
Shkop, Shimon
Shlomo, Elizah ben (See **Zalman**, Solomon, Vilna Gaon, Gra)

Sh'maya (Shemaiah)
Shmuel, Yisroel ben, of Shklov (See **Ashkenazi**)
Shor, Joseph ben Isaac Bekhor (See Joseph ben Isaac)
Simcha, Meir, of Dvinsk (See **HaKohen,** Kalonymus, Dvinsk, Meir)
Simlai
Simeon, Aaron Abraham ben Baruch (See **HaLevi**)
Simson, Menahem ben Jacob ben Solomon ben (See **Jacob,** Solomon)
Sirkis, Yoel (See Bach)
Slonik, Benjamin Aaron ben Abraham (See Solnik)
Sofer, Abraham Samuel Benjamin (See Ksav Sofer)
Sofer, Moses (See Schreiber, Chatam Sofer)
Sofer, Yaakov Chaim (See Kaf HaChaim)
Solnik (See **Slonik**)
Solomon (See Colon, Maharik, **Trabotto**)
Solomon, Elijah ben (See **Zalman,** Vilna Gaon)
Solomon, Menahem ben (See Simson, **Jacob,** Solomon)
Solomon, Menahem ben
Solomon, Samuel ben, of Falaise
Soloveitchik, Chaim (See Brisker)
Soloveitchik, Joseph Ber (See HaRav)
Soloveitchik, Yosef Dov (See Beis HaLevi)
Somekh, Abdalla
Spektor, Yitzhak Elchanan
Spira, Chaim Elazar
Steinhardt, Aryeh Leib
Steinhardt, Menahem Mendel ben Simeon
Steinhart, Joseph ben Menachem
Strashun, Samuel ben Joseph (See Rashash)
Szapira, Elimelech

T

Taitazak, Joseph ben Solomon
Tam, (See Jacob ben **Meir,** Rabbeinu Tam)
Tarfati, Abraham (See **Treves**)
Tarfon, Rabbi
Tashbetz (See Rashbatz, Simeon **Duran**)
Taubes, Aaron Moses ben Jacob
Taz, The (See **Segal,** HaLevi)
Teomim Eliyah David (See Aderet, **Rabonowitz-Teomim**)
Teradion (Teradyon), Hananyah (Hanina) ben
Tibbon, Moses ibn
Tibbon, Samuel ben Judah ibn
Tolosa, Vidal di
Torizer, Mordechai Gimpel Yaffe (See Yaffe)

Tosefos Yomtov (See **Heller**)
Trabotto, Joseph Colon ben Solomon (See Color., Maharik, Solomon)
Trani, Isaiah (ben Mali), di (See RI'D, Mali)
Trani, Moses ben Joseph di (See **Joseph**)
Treves (Tarfati), Abraham ben Solomon
Tukachinsky, Yechiel Michel
Tur (See Jacob ben **Asher**, Ba'al HaTurim)
Twersky Family
Twersky, Isadore (Yitzhak)
Twersky, Menachum Nachum
Tyrnau, Isaac
Tzaddik, Joseph ibn (See **Zaddik**)
Tzadok
Tzafnach Paneach (See **Rosen**, Rogatchover Gaon)
Tzahalon, Yom Tov ben Moshe (Maharitz)
Tzemach Tzedek (See **Schneerson**, Menachem Mendel)
Tzvi, Chacham (See Tzvi **Ashkenazi**)

U
Ulla
Uzeda, Samuel de
Uziel, Ben-Zion Meir Hai
Uzziel, Jonathan ben

V
Veltz, Israel
Vidas, Eliyahu de
Vilna Gaon (See **Zalman**, Solomon, Gra)
Vital, Hayyim ben Joseph
Volozhin, Chaim ben Izchok
       (See Isaac, Chaim of Volozhiner, Ickovits, Reb Chaim)

W
Walden, Aaron
Walkin, Aaron
Wallerstein, Abraham ben Asher
Weil, Jacob ben Judah (See Mahariv)
Weil, Jedidiah
Weil, Nethaneel ben Naftali Tzvi
Weinberg, Yechiel Yaakov
Weiser (See Leibush, **Michel**, Malbim)
Weiss, Isaac Hirsch
Weiss, Yitzhak Yaakov (See Minchat Yaakov)

Wilovsky, Yaakov David (See Ridbaz, Ridvaz)

Y

Yaakov, Moshe ben (See Moses **Jacob**)
Yaakov, Rav Nachman bar (See Nachman)
Yabets (See Jacob **Emden**)
Yaffe, Mordechai (See **Jaffe**, Yoffe, Ba'al HaLevushim, Levush)
Yaffe, Mordechai Gimpel (See **Torizer**)
Yashar (See Samuel Isaac **Reggio**)
Yechiel, Nathan ben (See Nathan ben Jehiel **Anaw**)
Yehiel (See Asher ben **Jehiel**, Rosh)
Yehuda, Eliezer ben, of Worms
Yehuda, Gershon ben (See Me'Or HaGolah)
Yehudai Gaon (See **Nahman**)
Yitzhak, Baruch ben, of Worms
Yitzhak, Meir ben (See **Nehorai**)
Yitzhak, Nahman bar (See **Isaac**)
Yitzhaki, Shlomo (See Rashi)
Yohai, Shimon bar (See Rashbi)
Yohai, Rabbi Shimon bar (Palestinian Tanna)
Yoffe (See **Jaffe**, Levush, Ba'al HaLevush)
Yose, (See **Halafta**)
Yose I, Eliezer ben (See **Jose**)
Yosef, Ovadia
Yosef, Yitzhak
Yossef, Yitzhak ben (See Jacob ben **Joseph**)

Z

Zaddik, Joseph ben Jacob (See Tzaddik)
Zaddok, Eliezar bar
Zakai, Yochanan ben
Zalman, Elijah ben (See Vilna Gaon, Solomon, GRA)
Zalman, Schneur of Liadi (See **Baruch**, Alter Rebbe, GRaZ)
Zerachiah HaYavani (The Greek) (See Ra'Za'H)
Zerah, Menahem ben Aaron ibn
Zevi, Hillel ben Naphtali
Zimra, David ben Solomon ibn Abi (See Radvaz)
Ziv, Simcha Zissel (See Alter of Kelm)
Zoma, Simon ben

Alphabetical List Of Sages, Talmudists and Authors

In this list the last name of the scholar, based on the methodology described in the introduction, is listed alphabetically and is highlighted in bold.

A

Aaron of Pesaro
Samuel ben **Aaron** of Schlettstadt
Abba **Arika** (Rav)
Hiyya bar **Abba**
Abba the Surgeon
Samuel bar **Abba** (Samuel of Nehardea)
Tanhuma bar **Abba**
Yirmiyahu bar **Abba**
Abbahu
Hanina bar **Abbahu**
Abbaye
Solomon ben Kalman HaLevi **Abel**
Isaac **Aboab (Abuhab)** (Menorat HaMaor)
Isaac **Aboab**
Samuel **Aboab** (Rasha)
Isaac ben **Abraham** of Dampierre (Riba)
Jonah ben **Abraham**
Obadiah ben **Abraham** of Bertinoro
Samson ben **Abraham** of Sens (Rash)
Isaac ben Judah **Abravanel**
Israel **Abuchatzeirah** (Baba Sali)
David ben Joseph ben David **Abudraham**
Abraham ben Samuel **Abulafia**
Meir ben Todros HaLevi **Abulafia** (Ramah)
Abusa
Elisha ben **Abuyah**
Shmuel **Aceda**
Isaac **Adarbi** (Adribi)
Solomon ben Joshua **Adeni** (M'Lekhet Shlomo)
Shlomo ben **Aderet** (Rashba)
Adda bar **Ahava**
Akavya ben Mahalel
Solomon **Alami**
Moses ben Isaac **Alashkar**
Abraham **Alegri**

Isaac ben Reuben **Albargeloni**
Joseph **Albo**
Yitzhak b**en Yaakov HaKohen Alfasi**
Yom Tov **Algazi**
Judah ben Solomon **Alharizi** (al-Harizi)
Solomon ben Moses **Alkabetz**
Judah ben Solomon Chai **Alkali**
Joseph **Almosnino**
Moses ben Baruch **Almosnino**
Moshe **Alshich**
Avraham Mordechai **Alter** (Imrei Emes)
Pinchas Menachem **Alter** (Pnei Menachem)
Simchah Bunim **Alter** (Lev Simcha)
Yaakov Aryeh **Alter**
Yehuda Aryeh Leib **Alter** (Sfas Emes)
Yisrael **Alter** (Beis Yisrael)
Yitzhak Myer **Alter** (Chiddushei Harim, Reb Itche Myer)
Naphtali (Hirsch) ben Asher **Altschul**
David ben Aryeh Loeb **Altshuler (Altshul)**
Amemar I
Amemar II
Ammi ben Nathan
Amnon of Mainz (Mayence)
Anaw (Anav) Family
Benjamin ben Abraham **Anaw (Anav)**
Nathan ben Jehiel (Yechiel) **Anaw (Anav)**
Zedekiah ben Abraham **Anaw (Anav)**
Abraham **Ankava**
Isaac ben Moses **Arama**, (Ba'al Akedah)
Yom Tov Ibn **Asevilli** (Ritva)
Aaron ben Moses ben **Asher**
Bahya ben **Asher** (Rabbeinu Behaye)
Jacob ben **Asher** (Ba'al HaTurim, Tur)
Hiyya bar **Ashi**
Rav **Ashi**
Tabyomi bar **Ashi,** (Mar bar Rav Ashi)
Bezalel **Ashkenazi**
Gershon **Ashkenazi**
Mordechai ben Hillel **Ashkenazi** (or Mordechai ben Hillel)
Moses **Ashkenazi** (Johann Peter Spaeth)
Tzvi Hirsch ben Yaakov **Ashkenazi** (Chacham Tzvi)
Yehuda ben Shimon **Ashkenazi**
Yisroel ben Shmuel, **Ashkenazi** of Shklov
Yitzhak **Ashkenazi (Luria)** (Ari, Arizal, He-Ari)
Yehuda Leib HaLevi **Ashlag** (Ba'al HaSulam)

Rabbi **Assi**
Hayyim ibn **Attar** (Ohr HaChaim HaKadosh)
Menachem Mendel ben Meshulam Zalman **Auerbach**
Shlomo Zalman **Auerbach**
Avina
Avraham of Trisk
Avtalyon
Judah **Ayyas**
Elazar ben **Azariah**
Menachem **Azaryah** of Fano
Elazar ben Moshe **Azikri** (Ezkari)
Abraham **Azulai**
Haim Yosef David **Azulai** (Hida)
Shimon ben **Azzai**

B
Judah ben **Baba**
Yosef ben Moshe **Babad**
Abraham Samuel **Bachrach**
Yair Chaim **Bachrach**
Isaac ben Sheshet **Barfat (Perfet)** (RiBaSH)
Joseph ben **Baruch** (Joseph of Clisson)
Joshua Boaz ben Simon Baruch / Joshua Boaz **Mevorakh** (Shiltei Gibborim)
Meir ben **Baruch** (Meir of Rothenburg) (MaHaRaM)
Shneur Zalman **Baruch** (Borukovich), of Liadi (Alter Rebbe, GRaZ)
Judah ben **Barzillai**
Shabbethai ben Joseph **Bass**
Behag
Mordechai ben Abraham **Benet**
Chaim **Benveniste**
Dov **Ber** of Mezritch, Rabbi (See Dov, Ber, Maggid)
Jacob **Berab** (Mhari Beirav)
Aharon **Berechyah** of Modena
Sholom Noach **Berezovsky**
Isaiah ben Judah Loeb **Berlin**
Naftali Tzvi Yehuda **Berlin**
Abraham ben Shem Tov **Bibago**
Isaac ben Moses Solomon **Blaser** (Rav Itzele Peterburger)
Boruch of Kosov
Abraham ben Moses de **Bouton**
Shlomo ben **Boya'a**
Israel **Bruna**
Solomon **Buber**

C

Isaac ben Jacob **Campanton**
Joseph ben Ephraim **Caro**
Jacob de **Castro**
Aharon ibn **Chaim**
Hakham (Chacham) Yosef **Chaim** (Ben Ish Chai)
    (Joseph Hayyim ben Elijah Al-Hakam)
Zvi Hirsch **Chajes** (Chayes) (The Maharatz Chajes)
Chama, Rav
Chanina bar **Chama**
Rami bar **Chama**
Abraham ibn **Chananyah**
Yehuda Leib ben Meir **Channeles**
Levi ben Jacob Ibn **Chaviv** (Habib)
Yaakov ibn **Chaviv** (Habib) (Ralbach)
Yosef **Chaviva**
Avraham **Chayon**
Joseph **Chayon**
Rav **Chisda** (Hisda)
Aron **Chorin**
Chananel ben **Chushiel** (Hananel ben Hushiel)
Abigdor **Cohen** (of Vienna)
Moses ben Jacob **Cordovero**
Hasdai ben Abraham **Crescas**
Yaakov **Culi**

D

Abraham ben Jehiel **Danzig** (Chayei / Chochmat Adam)
Samuel **Danzig**
Abraham ben **David** (Ravad III)
Baruch ben **David**
Mattithiah ben Solomon **Delacrut**
Eliyahu Eliezer **Dessler**
Hezekiah ben David **DiSilo**
Shabtai **Donolo**
Hanina ben **Dosa**
Simeon ben Zemah **Duran** (Rashbatz / Tashbetz)
Solomon ben Simon **Duran** (Rashbash)
Yehuda Meir **Dvir**

E

Akiva **Eger**
David Solomon **Eibenschutz**
Samuel **Eidels**

Abraham Zevi Hirsch ben Jacob **Eisenstadt**
Benjamin **Eisenstadt**
Meir ben Iszak **Eisenstadt** (Meir Ash) (Maharam Ash / Panim Me'irot)
Meir **Eisenstadter** (Meir Ash) (Maharam Ash)
Naftali Hertz ben Yaakov **Elchanan** (Bachrach)
Hillel ben **Eliakim**
Israel ben **Eliezer** (Ba'al Shem Tov / Besht)
Tobiah ben **Eliezer**
Eliezer of Toul
Eliezer of Touques
Abba Mari ben **Eligdor**
Perez ben **Elijah** (Rap / RaPaSh / MaHaRPaSh)
Ishmael ben **Elisha** (Rabbi Ishmael)
Yissachar Ber **Ellenburg**
Jacob Israel ben Zvi Ashkenazi **Emden** (Yabets)
Judah ben **Enoch**
Moshe Chaim **Ephraim** (of Sudilkov)
Avraham **Epstein**
Baruch HaLevi **Epstein**
Moshe Mordechai **Epstein**
Yechiel Michel HaLevi **Epstein** (the Aruch Hashulchan)
Joseph **Escapa**
Yaakov **Etlinger** (Aruch LaNer)
Hayyim Judah Lob **Ettinger**
Isaac Aaron **Ettinger**
Jonathan **Eybeschutz**
Judah ben **Ezekiel** (Rav Yehuda)
Joseph ben Hanan ben Nathan **Ezobi**
Ezra
Abraham ben Meir ibn **Ezra** (Abenezra)
Moses ibn **Ezra** (HaSallah)

F
Samuel ben Uri Shraga **Faibesh** (Phoebus)
Joshua ben Alexander (Katz) HaKohen **Falk**
Moshe **Feinstein** (Reb Moshe)
Shneur Zalman **Fradkin** of Lublin
Solomon Bennett **Freehof**

G
Solomon ben Judah, ibn **Gabirol** (Gvirol)
Abraham **Galante**
Gamliel I (The Elder) (Rabban)
Gamliel II (of Yavne)

Gamliel III
Gamliel IV
Gamliel V
Gamliel VI
Shimon ben Gamliel
Solomon ben Joseph Ganzfried
Achai Gaon
Hai Gaon
Shem Tov ben Abraham ibn Gaon
Abraham Gediliyah
Yonah ben Avraham Gerondi (Rabbeinu Yonah)
Zerachiah ben Isaac HaLevi Gerondi (ReZaH, RaZBI, Ba'al HaMaor)
Levi ben Gershom (Gersonides, Ralbag)
Isaac ben Judah ibn Ghiyyat (Ghayyat)
Isaac ibn Gias
Joseph ben Abraham Gikatilla (Joseph Ba'al HaNissim)
Louis Ginzberg
David Golinkin
Abraham Abele ben Chaim HaLevi Gombiner (Magen Avraham)
Joseph ben Gorion
Eliezer David Greenwald
Chaim Ozer Grodzinski
Aryeh Leib ben Asher Gunzberg (Shaagat Aryeh)

H
Moses ibn Habib (Chaviv)
Moses HaDarshan
Shimon ben Yitzhak HaGadol
Jacob Hagiz
Moses Hagiz
Nechunya ben HaKanah
Eleazar ben Eleazar HaKappar (Bar Kappara, Berebi)
Hanina (Hananyah) ben Hakinai
Aaron ben Jacob ben David HaKohen
Abigdor ben Elijah HaKohen
Abraham ben Eliezer HaKohen
Joseph ben Joshua Meir HaKohen
Meir Simcha Kalonymus of Dvinsk HaKohen
Shabbatai ben Meir HaKohen (Shach)
Isaac ben Abraham HaLaban
Jose ben Halafta
Chaim Halberstam of Sanz
Aaron HaLevi (of Barcelona)
Aaron Abraham ben Baruch Simeon HaLevi
Abraham ben Isaac HaLevi

Abraham ben David **HaLevi** (Abraham ibn Daud, Rabad / Ravad I)
Aharon **HaLevi** (Ra'AH)
Eliakim ben Meshullam **HaLevi**
Eliezer ben Joel **HaLevi** (Raviah)
Isaac ben Asher **HaLevi** (Riva)
Isaac ben Eleazar **HaLevi**
Jacob ben Isaac **HaLevi** (Jabez)
Judah ben Samuel **HaLevi** (RiHa'l)
David Weiss **Halivni**
Hamnuna
Hamnuna Saba (The Elder)
Judah **HaNasi** (Rabbeinu HaKadosh)
Sherira ben **Hanina**, Gaon
Joshua ben **Hannanya**
Ishtori ben Moses **Haparchi** (Kaftor Vaferech)
Yedayah **HaPenini**
Tzidkayah ben Avraham Anav **HaRofei**
Joel **Hayyim** (Mahariah)
Samuel **Hayyun**
Yeshayah ben Mali **Hazaken**
Jehiel ben Solomon **Heilprin**
Aryeh Leib HaKohen **Heller** (The Ketzos)
Yom Tov Lippman **Heller** (Tosefos Yomtov)
Abraham **Herrera**
Abraham Joshua **Heschel**
Hillel the Elder
Hillel, Son of Gamliel III
Hillel II
Mordechai ben **Hillel**
Shimon ben **Hillel**
Yaakov Yehoshua ben Zvi **Hirsch** (Jacob Joshua Falk)
Rav **Hisda**
Eleazar **Hisma**
David Zevi **Hoffmann**
Horowitz Family
Abraham ben Shabtai Sheftel **Horowitz**
Isaiah HaLevi **Horowitz** (Shelah, Shaloh)
Shabtai Sheftel **Horowitz**
Judah Aryeh Loeb ben Joshua **Hoschel**
Rav **Huna**
Eliezer ben **Hercanus** (Hyrcanus) (Eliezer HaGadol)
Shabbethai Sheftel ben Akiba **Hurwitz**
Yosef Yozel **Hurwitz** (Alter of Novardok)
Yitzhak (Isaac) **Hutner**

I

Judah ben **Ilai** (Rabbi Judah)
Shemariah ben Elijah **Ikriti** (of Negropont)
Abraham ben **Isaac** of Narbonne (Ravad II)
Baruch ben **Isaac**
Elhanan ben **Isaac**, of Dampierre
Kalonymus ben **Isaac**
Nahman bar **Isaac**
Samson ben **Isaac**, of Chinon (MaHaRShak)
Solomon ben **Isaac**
Israel of Bamberg
Israel of Krems
Menasseh ben **Israel**
Israel ben Pethahiah Ashkenazi **Isserlein**
Moses ben Israel **Isserles** (Rema)

J

Jacob of Chinon
Menachem ben (ben Solomon ben Simson) **Jacob**
Meshullam ben **Jacob** (Yaakov)
Moses ben **Jacob** of Coucy
Nahman bar **Jacob**
Nissim ben **Jacob** (HaMafteach) (Rav Nissim Gaon)
Yissachar **Jacobson**
Mordechai ben Avraham **Jaffe** (Yoffe) (Ba'al HaLevushim)
Samuel ben Jacob **Jam'a**
Yonah ibn **Janach** (Merinos)
Asher ben **Jehiel** (Rabbeinu Asher / Rosh)
Nathan ben **Jehiel**
Rav **Jonah**
Jose bar **Jose**
Eliezer ben **Jose**
Akiva ben **Joseph** (Rabbi Akiva)
Enoch Zundel ben **Joseph**
Isaac ben **Joseph** of Corbeil
Jehiel ben **Joseph** of Paris
Joshua Hoschel ben **Joseph**
Moses ben **Joseph**, of Trani
Saadia ben **Joseph**, Gaon (Saadia Gaon)
Samson ben **Joseph**, of Falaise
Ahai (or Achai) ben **Josiah** (Yehoshiyahu)
Joshua (Yehoshua) (ben Chananyah)
Daniel ben **Judah**
Gershom ben **Judah** (Rabbeinu Gershom or Rabbeinu Gershom Me'Or HaGolah)

Judah II
Judah III
Judah IV

K
Israel Meir **Kagan** (HaKohen) (Chofetz Chaim)
Kahana
Aaron Samuel ben Israel **Kaidanover**
Zevi Hirsch **Kaidenover**
Eleazar **Kalir**
Zvi Hirsch **Kalischer**
Kalonymus Family
David ben **Kalonymus** (of Munzenberg)
Eleazar ben Yehuda ben **Kalonymus** of Worms (Rokeach)
Elijah ben **Kalonymus**
Samuel ben **Kalonymus** (He-Hasid), of Speyer
Jacob **Kamenecki** (Yaakov Kamenetsky)
Abraham ben Abigdor **Kara**
Simeon **Kara** of Frankfurt (HaDarshan)
Abraham Isaiah **Karelitz** (Chazon Ish)
Menachem Mendel **Kasher**
Jacob Joseph ben Tzvi HaKohen **Katz**, of Polonnoye
Meir ben Isaac **Katzenellenbogen** (Maharam Padua)
Simeon **Kayyara**
Samuel ben Naftali HaLevi **Kelin**
Joseph ben Isaac **Kimchi**
Moses **Kimchi**
David **Kimchi**
Solomon ben Judah Aaron **Kluger**
Abraham Isaac **Kook** (HaRaAYaH / HaRav)
Menachem Mendel ben Abraham **Krochmal**
Nachman Kohen **Krochmal**

L
Dunash HaLevi ben **Labrat**
Shimon ben **Lakish** (Resh Lakish)
Yitzhak Hezekiah **Lampronti**
Landau Family
Ezekiel (Yechezkel) ben Judah **Landau**
Yaakov Baruch ben Yehuda **Landau**
Aaron ben Isaac **Lapapa**
Boruch Ber **Leibowitz**
Mordechai **Leifer** of Nadvorna
Judah ben Isaac Messer **Leon**

Moses de **Leon** (Moshe ben Shem Tov)
Joseph ibn **Lev**
Joshua ben **Levi**
Joshua Hoschel ben Elijah Zeeb **Levin**
Shabbatai Carmuz **Levita**
Yerusham **Levovitz**
David **Lida**
Saul **Lieberman** (Gra'sh)
Avraham **Leiblein**
Moses ben Isaac Judah **Lima** (Lema)
Baruch Mordechai ben Jacob **Lipschitz**
Hayyim ben Moses **Lipschutz**
Israel **Lipschutz**
Moses ben Noah Isaac **Lipschutz**
Noah ben Abraham **Lipschutz** (Noah Mindes)
Yosef (Yoselman) **Loanz** (of Rosheim)
Samuel ben Nathan **Loew**
Judah ben Bezalel **Loew** (Maharal / Maharal of Prague)
Menachem di **Lonzano**
Jacob ben Jacob Moses **Lorberbaum** (of Lisser) (Ba'al HeNesivos / Lissa Rav)
Meir ben Gedaliyah **Lublin** (Maharam)
Shlomo Ephraim **Lunshitz** (Kli Yakar)
Isaac **Luria** (**Ashkenazi**) (Ari, He-Ari, Arizal)
Solomon **Luria** (Maharshal, Rashal)
Moses Chaim **Luzzatto** (Ramchal)

M
Moses ben **Maimon** (Maimonides) (Rambam)
Hezekiah ben **Manoah** (Hizkuni / Chizkuni)
Margolis / Margolioth Family
Abi Ezra Zelig **Margolis**
Alexander **Margolis**
Ephraim Zalman (Solomon) **Margolis**
Hayim Mordechai **Margolis**
Meir ben Zvi, Hirsch **Margolis**
Abba **Mari** ben Moses ben Joseph Don Astruc (of Lunel)
Yitzhak ben Abba **Mari** of Marseilles
Jacob Tzvi **Mecklenberg** (Mecklenburg)
Moses de **Medina**
Samuel ben Moses de **Medina** (RashDaM)
Shemaiah de **Medina**
Chaim Chizkiya **Medini**
Meir Ba'al HaNes (Nahori)
Isaac (Yitzhak) ben **Meir** (Rivam)
Jacob ben, **Meir** (Tam) (Rabbeinu Tam)

Moses ben **Meir** of Ferrara
Samuel ben **Meir** (Rashbam)
Menachem ben Solomon **Meiri** (HaMeiri)
Isser Zalman **Meltzer** (Even HaEzel)
Menachem **Mendel** of Kotzk (Kotzker Rebbe)
Moses **Mendelssohn**
Asher ben **Meshullam**
Yerucham ben **Meshullam**
Joshua Boaz **Mevorakh** / Joshua Boaz ben Simon Baruch (Shiltei Gibborim)
Meir Leibush ben Jehiel **Michel** (Malbim)
Joseph ben Meir HaLevi ibn **Migash** (Ri Migash)
Judah ben Eliezer HaLevi **Minz** (Mahari Minz)
Abraham ben Judah HaLevi **Minz**
Elijah **Mizrachi** (Re'em)
Samuel ben Moses di **Modena** (Maharshdam)
Jacob ben Moses Levi **Moelin** (Maharil)
Isaac ben **Mordechai** of Regensburg (RiBaM)
Moshe **Mos** of Premysl
Moses of Evreux
Isaac ben **Moses** of Vienna (Or Zarua, Riaz)
Joseph ben **Moses**
Meshullam ben **Moses**
Meshullam ben **Moses**

##
Nachman of Breslov
Samuel ibn **Naghrela** (Samuel HaNagid)
Moses ben **Nahman** (Nahmanides) (Ramban)
Samuel ben **Nahman** (Nahmani)
Yehudai ben **Nahman** (Yehudai Gaon)
Rabbah **Nahmani**
Yochanan bar **Nappacha**
Nathan
Abraham ben **Nathan**
Eliezer ben **Nathan** (Raavan)
Judah ben **Nathan** (Riban)
Joseph Saul **Nathanson**
Yitzhak Saggi **Nehor** (Isaac the Blind)
Nehorai, Meir ben Isaac **Nehorai**

O
Onkelos
Jacob Meshullam ben Mordechai Ze'ev **Ornstein**

P

Hayyim **Palaggi** (Maharhaf, HaVif)
Rav **Pappa**
Chanina ben **Pappa**
Bahya ben Joseph ibn **Paquda**
Eleazar ben **Parta** (Elazar ben Perata)
Bahya ben Joseph ibn **Paquda**
Eleazar ben **Pedat**
Moshe **Pellier** of Kobrin
Joseph ibn **Plat**
Meir **Popperos**
Avraham Aharon **Price**

Q

Yosef **Quafih** (Qafeh, Kafich, Gafeh, Kapach)

R

Hoshayaa **Rabbah** (Roba, Berabi)
Chaim Shalom Tuvia **Rabinowitz** (Reb Chaim Telzer)
Eliyahu David **Rabinowitz-Teomim** (Aderet)
Solomon Judah Loeb **Rapoport**
Rava (Abba bar Yosef bar Chama)
Ravina I
Ravina II
Isaac Samuel **Reggio** (Yashar)
Jacob ben Joseph **Reischer** (Backofen)
Jacob ben **Reuben**
Jacob ben **Reuben**
Nissim ben **Reuven**, of Gerona (RaN)
Moses ben Naftali Hertz **Rivkes**
Judah ben Samuel **Rosanes**
Yosef **Rosen** (Rogatchover Gaon, Tzafnach Paneach)
Yaakov Yitzhak **Ruderman**

S

Avraham ben Yaakov **Saba**
Safra
Meir ben Solomon Abi **Sahula**
Israel Lipkin **Salanter**
Eliezer ben **Samuel** of Metz
Aaron ben **Samuel**
Isaac ben **Samuel** of Dampierre (Ri)
Isaac ben **Samuel** (Hasefardi)

Judah ben **Samuel** of Regensburg (He-Hasid)
Meir ben **Samuel** (RAM)
Simha ben **Samuel** of Speyer
Simhah ben **Samuel** of Vitry
Samuel ben Isaac **Sardi** (HaSardi, HaSefaradi)
Israel **Sarug**
Menahem ben Jacob ibn **Saruq**
Jacob ben Aaron **Sasportas**
Moses **Schick** (Maharam Schick)
Isaac **Schmelkes**
Levi Yitzhak **Schneerson**
Menachem Mendel **Schneerson** (Tzemach Tzedek)
Menachem Mendel **Schneerson** (The Lubavitcher Rebbe)
Shmuel **Schneerson** (The Rebbe Maharash)
Sholom Dovber **Schneerson** (Rebbe Rashab)
Yosef Yitzhak **Schneerson** (Rebbe Rayatz)
Dovber **Schneuri** (Mitteler Rebbe)
Samuel **Schotten** (Mharsheishoch)
Sholom Mordechai **Schwadron** (Maharsham)
David ben Samuel HaLevi **Segal** (Taz)
Obadiah ben Jacob **Sforno**
Kalonymus ben **Shabbethai**
Jacob ben Nissim ibn **Shahin**
Shalom **Shakna**
Shammai
Elazar ben **Shamua**
Kalonymus Kalman **Shapira** (Szapira)
Eliyahu ben Binyamin Wolf **Shapiro**
Yehuda Meir **Shapiro**
Shalom **Sharabi** (Rashash)
Shem Tov ibn **Shem Tov**
Shemuel (Shmuel)
Hai ben **Sherira**, Gaon
Sheshet
Amram bar **Sheshna**, Gaon
Shila of Kefar Temarta
Elazar ben **Shimon**
Shimon **Shkop**
Sh'maya (Shemaiah)
Joseph ben Isaac Bekhor **Shor**
Meir **Simcha** of Dvinsk
Simlai
Yoel **Sirkis** (Bach)
Benjamin Aaron ben Abraham **Slonik**
Abraham Samuel Benjamin **Sofer** (Ksav Sofer)

Moses **Sofer** (Chatam Sofer)
Yaakov Chaim **Sofer** (Kaf HaChaim)
Menahem ben **Solomon**
Samuel ben **Solomon** of Falaise
Chaim **Soloveitchik** (The Brisker Reb)
Joseph Ber **Soloveitchik** (HaRav)
Yosef Dov **Soloveitchik** (Beis HaLevi)
Abdalla **Somekh**
Yitzhak Elchanan **Spektor**
Chaim Elazar **Spira**
Aryeh Leib **Steinhardt**
Menahem Mendel ben Simeon **Steinhardt**
Joseph ben Menachem **Steinhart**
Samuel ben Joseph **Strashun** (Rashash)
Elimelech **Szapira**

T
Joseph ben Solomon **Taitezak**
Tarfon
Aaron Moses ben Jacob **Taubes**
Hananyah (Hanina) ben **Teradion** (Teradyon)
Moses ibn **Tibbon**
Samuel ben Judah ibn **Tibbon**
Vidal di **Tolosa**
Mordechai Gimpel Yaffe **Torizer**
Joseph Colon ben Solomon **Trabotto** (Maharik)
Isaiah ben Mali di **Trani** (RI'D)
Abraham ben Solomon **Treves** (Tarfati)
Yechiel Michel **Tukachinsky**
Twersky Family
Isadore (Yitzhak) **Twersky**
Menachem Nachum **Twersky**
Isaac **Tyrnau**
Tzadok
Yom Tov ben Moshe **Tzahalon** (Maharitz)

U
Ulla
Samuel de **Uzeda**
Ben-Zion Meir Hai **Uziel**
Jonathan ben **Uzziel**

V

Israel **Veltz**
Eliyahu de **Vidas**
Hayyim ben Joseph **Vital**
Chaim ben Itzchok **Volozhin** (Reb Chaim)

W

Aaron **Walden**
Aaron **Walkin**
Abraham ben Asher **Wallerstein**
Jacob ben Judah **Weil** (Mahariv)
Jedidiah **Weil**
Nethaneel ben Naftali Tzvi **Weil**
Yechiel Yaakov **Weinberg**
Isaac Hirsch **Weiss**
Yitzhak Yaakov **Weiss** (Minchat Yaakov)
Yaakov David **Wilovsky**

Y

Eleazar ben **Yehuda** (of Worms)
Gershon ben **Yehuda** (Me'Or HaGolah)
Baruch ben, **Yitzhak** of Worms
Shlomo **Yitzhaki** (Rashi)
Shimon bar **Yohai** (Rashbi)
Ovadia **Yosef**
Yitzhak **Yosef**

Z

Eliezer bar **Zadok**
Yochanan ben **Zakai**
Elijah ben Solomon **Zalman** (Vilna Gaon, Gra)
Menahem ben Aaron ibn **Zerah**
Zerachiah HaYavani (The Greek) (Ra'Za'H)
Hillel ben Naphtali **Zevi**
David ben Solomon ibn Abi **Zimra** (Radbaz)
Simcha Zissel **Ziv** (Alter of Kelm)

Alphabetical List Of Sages, Talmudists and Authors

Many rabbis are often known by their first name and this would be their form of recognition. In this list the scholar's first name is therefore listed alphabetically, but the last name is highlighted in bold according to the methodology described in the introduction.

A

Aaron of Pesaro
Aaron Abraham ben Baruch Simeon **HaLevi**
Aaron ben Isaac **Lapapa**
Aaron ben Jacob ben David **HaKohen**
Aaron ben Moses ben **Asher**
Aaron ben **Samuel**
Aaron **HaLevi** (of Barcelona)
Aaron Moses ben Jacob **Taubes**
Aaron Samuel ben Israel **Kaidanover**
Aaron **Walden**
Aaron **Walkin**
Abba the Surgeon
Abba **Arika** (Rav)
Abba Mari ben **Eligdor**
Abba **Mari** ben Moses ben Joseph Don Astruc (of Lunel)
Abbahu
Abbaye
Abdalla **Somekh**
Abi Ezra Zelig **Margolis**
Abigdor ben Elijah **HaKohen**
Abigdor **Cohen** (of Vienna)
Abraham Abele ben Chaim HaLevi **Gombiner** (Magen Avraham)
Abraham **Alegri**
Abraham **Ankava**
Abraham **Azulai**
Abraham ben Abigdor **Kara**
Abraham ben Asher **Wallerstein**
Abraham ben **David** (Ravad III)
Abraham ben David **HaLevi** (Abraham ibn Daud, Ravad I)
Abraham ben **Isaac** of Narbonne (Raavad II)
Abraham ben Eliezer **HaKohen**
Abraham ben Isaac **HaLevi**
Abraham ben Jehiel **Danzig** (Chayei / Chochmat Adam)
Abraham ben Judah HaLevi **Minz**
Abraham ben Meir ibn **Ezra** (Abenezra)

Abraham ben Moses **de Bouton**
Abraham ben **Nathan**
Abraham ben Samuel **Abulafia**
Abraham ben Shem Tov **Bibago**
Abraham ben Solomon **Treves** (Tarfati)
Abraham **Galante**
Abraham **Gediliyah**
Abraham **Herrera**
Abraham ibn **Chananyah**
Abraham Isaac **Kook** (HaRaAYaH / HaRav)
Abraham Isaiah **Karelitz** (Chazon Ish)
Abraham Joshua **Heschel**
Abraham Samuel **Bachrach**
Abraham Samuel Benjamin **Sofer** (Ksav Sofer)
Abraham Zevi Hirsch ben Jacob **Eisenstadt**
Achai **Gaon**
Ahai (or Achai) ben **Josiah** (Yehoshiyahu)
Adda bar **Ahava**
Aharon **Berechyah** of Modena
Aharon ibn **Chaim**
Aharon **HaLevi** (Ra'AH)
Akavya ben Mahalel
Akiva **Eger**
Akiva ben **Joseph** (Rabbi Akiva)
Alexander **Margolis**
Amemar I
Amemar II
Ammi ben Nathan
Amnon of Mainz (Mayence)
Amram ben Sheshna, Gaon
Aron **Chorin**
Aryeh Leib ben Asher **Gunzberg** (Shaagat Aryeh)
Aryeh Leib HaKohen **Heller** (The Ketzos)
Aryeh Leib **Steinhardt**
Asher ben **Jehiel** (Rabbeinu Asher / Rosh)
Asher ben **Meshullam**
Avina
Avraham Aharon **Price**
Avraham ben Yaakov **Saba**
Avraham **Chayon**
Avraham **Epstein**
Avraham **Lieblein**
Avraham Mordechai **Alter** (Imrei Emes)
Avraham of Trisk
Avtalyon

B

Baba Sali (**Abuchatzeirah**)
Bahya ben **Asher** (Rabbeinu Behaye)
Bahya ben Joseph ibn **Paquda**
Bar Kappara (Eleazar ben Eleazar **HaKappar** (Berebi)
Baruch ben **David**
Baruch ben **Isaac**
Baruch ben, **Yitzhak** (of Worms)
Baruch HaLevi **Epstein**
Baruch Mordechai ben Jacob **Lipschitz**
Behag
Bezalel **Ashkenazi**
Benjamin ben Abraham **Anaw (Anav)**
Benjamin **Eisenstadt**
Benjamin Aaron ben Abraham **Slonik**
Ben-Zion Meir Hai **Uziel**
Boruch Ber **Leibowitz**
Boruch (of Kosov)

C

Chacham (Hakham) Yosef **Chaim** (Ben Ish Chai)
    (Joseph Hayyim ben Elijah Al-Hakam)
Chaim ben Itzchok **Volozhin** (Reb Chaim)
Chaim **Benveniste**
Chaim Chizkiya **Medini**
Chaim Elazar **Spira**
Chaim **Halberstam** of Sanz
Chaim Ozer **Grodzinski**
Chaim Shalom Tuvia **Rabinowitz** (Reb Chaim Telzer)
Chaim **Soloveitchik** (The Brisker Reb)
Chama
Chananel ben **Chushiel** (Hananel ben Hushiel)
Chanina bar **Chama**
Chanina ben **Pappa**
Chisda (Hisda)

D

Daniel ben **Judah**
David **Abudraham**
David ben Aryeh Loeb **Altshuler (Altshul)**
David ben **Kalonymus** (of Munzenberg)
David ben Samuel HaLevi **Segal** (Taz)
David ben Solomon ibn Abi **Zimra** (Radbaz)
David Solomon **Eibenschutz**

David **Golinkin**
David Weiss **Halivni**
David Zevi **Hoffmann**
David **Kimchi**
David **Lida**
Dov **Ber** of Mezritch (See Dov, Ber, Maggid)
Dovber **Schneuri** (Mitteler Rebbe)
Dunash HaLevi ben **Labrat**

E

Elazar ben **Azariah**
Elazar ben Moshe **Azikri** (Ezkari)
Elazar ben **Shamua**
Elazar ben **Shimon**
Eleazar ben **Arach**
Eleazar ben Eleazar **HaKappar** (Bar Kappara, Berebi)
Eleazar **Hisma**
Elhanan ben **Isaac**, (of Dampierre)
Eleazar ben Yehuda ben **Kalonymus** of Worms (Rokeach)
Eleazar ben **Parta** (Elazar ben Perata)
Eleazar ben **Pedat**
Eleazar **Kalir**
Eliakim ben Meshullam **HaLevi**
Eliezer ben **Hercanus** (Hyrcanus) (Eliezer HaGadol)
Eliezer ben Joel HaLevi (Raviah)
Eliezer ben **Jose**
Eliezer ben **Nathan** (Raavan)
Eliezer ben **Samuel** of Metz
Eliezer bar **Zadok**
Eliezer of Toul
Eliezer of Touques
Eliezer David **Greenwald**
Elijah ben **Kalonymus**
Elijah ben Solomon **Zalman** (Vilna Gaon, Gra)
Elijah **Mizrachi** (Re'em)
Elimelech **Szapira**
Elisha ben **Abuyah**
Eliyahu ben Binyamin Wolf **Shapiro**
Eliyahu David **Rabinowitz-Teomim** (Aderet)
Eliyahu de **Vidas**
Eliyahu Eliezer **Dessler**
Enoch Zundel ben **Joseph**
Ephraim Zalman (Solomon) **Margolis**
Ezekiel (Yechezkel) ben Judah **Landau**
Ezra

G

Gamliel I (The Elder) (Rabban)
Gamliel II (of Yavne)
Gamliel III
Gamliel IV
Gamliel V
Gamliel VI
Gershom ben **Judah** (Rabbeinu Gershom or Rabbeinu Gershom Me'Or HaGolah)
Gershon **Ashkenazi**
Gershon ben **Yehuda** (Me'Or HaGolah)

H

Hai **Gaon**
Hai ben **Sherira**, Gaon
Hamnuna
Hamnuna Saba (The Elder)
Hananyah (Hanina) ben **Teradion** (Teradyon)
Hanina (Hananiah) bar **Abbahu**
Hanina ben **Dosa**
Hanina (Hananyah) ben **Hakinai**
Hasdai ben Abraham **Crescas**
Hayyim Judah Lob **Ettinger**
Hayyim ben Joseph **Vital**
Hayyim ben Moses **Lipschutz**
Hayyim ibn **Attar** (Ohr HaChaim HaKadosh)
Hayyim Mordechai **Margolis**
Hayyim **Palaggi** (Maharhaf, HaVif)
Haim Yosef David **Azulai** (Hida)
Hezekiah ben David **DiSilo**
Hezekiah ben **Manoah** (Hizkuni / Chizkuni)
Hillel ben **Eliakim**
Hillel ben Naphtali **Zevi**
Hillel the Elder
Hillel, Son of Gamliel III
Hillel II
Hiyya bar **Abba**
Hiyya bar **Ashi**
Horowitz Family
Hoshayaa **Rabbah** (Roba, Berabi)

I

Isaac Aaron **Ettinger**
Isaac **Aboab** (**Abuhab**) (Menorat HaMaor)
Isaac **Aboab**

Isaac ben **Abraham** of Dampierre (Riba)
Isaac **Adarbi** (Adribi)
Isaac ben Asher **HaLevi** (Riva)
Isaac ben Eleazar **HaLevi**
Isaac ben Jacob **Campanton**
Isaac ben **Joseph** of Corbeil
Isaac ben Judah **Abravanel**
Isaac ben Judah ibn **Ghiyyat** (Ghayyat)
Isaac ben Reuben **Albargeloni**
Isaac (Yitzhak) ben **Meir** (Rivam)
Isaac ben **Mordechai** of Regensburg (RiBaM)
Isaac ben Moses **Arama** (Ba'al Akedah)
Isaac ben **Moses** of Vienna (Or Zarua, Riaz)
Isaac ben Moses Solomon **Blaser** (Rav Itzele Peterburger)
Isaac ben **Samuel** of Dampierre (Ri)
Isaac ben **Samuel** (Hasefardi)
Isaac ben Sheshet **Barfat** (Perfet) (RiBaSH / Rivash)
Isaac Hirsch **Weiss**
Isaac ibn **Gias**
Isaac **Luria** (Ashkenazi) (Ari, He-Ari, Arizal)
Isaac Samuel **Reggio** (Yashar)
Isaac **Schmelkes**
Isaac **Tyrnau**
Isadore (Yitzhak) Twersky
Isaiah ben Mali di **Trani** (RI'D)
Isaiah ben Judah Loeb **Berlin**
Isaiah HaLevi **Horowitz** (Shelah, Shaloh)
Ishmael ben **Elisha** (Rabbi Ishmael)
Ishtori ben Moses **Haparchi** (Kaftor Vaferech)
Israel **Bruna**
Israel (of Bamberg)
Israel ben **Eliezer** (Ba'al Shem Tov / Besht)
Israel (of Krems)
Israel ben Pethahiah Ashkenazi **Isserlein**
Israel Lipkin **Salanter**
Israel **Lipschutz**
Israel Meir **Kagan** (HaKohen) (Chofetz Chaim)
Israel **Sarug**
Israel **Veltz**
Isser Zalman **Meltzer** (Even HaEzel)

J

Jacob of Chinon
Jacob ben Aaron **Sasportas**

Jacob ben **Asher** (Ba'al HaTurim, The Tur)
Jacob ben Isaac **HaLevi** (Jabez)
Jacob ben Jacob Moses **Lorberbaum** of Lisser (Ba'al HeNesivos / Lissa Rav)
Jacob ben Joseph **Reischer** (Backofen)
Jacob ben Judah Weil (Mahariv)
Jacob ben, **Meir** (Tam) (Rabbeinu Tam)
Jacob ben Moses Levi **Moelin** (Maharil)
Jacob ben Nissim ibn **Shahin**
Jacob ben **Reuben**
Jacob ben **Reuben**
Jacob **Berab** (Mhari Beirav)
Jacob de **Castro**
Jacob **Hagiz**
Jacob Israel ben Zvi Ashkenazi **Emden** (Yabets)
Jacob Joseph ben Tzvi HaKohen **Katz**, of Polonnoye
Jacob Joshua Falk (Yaakov Yehoshua ben Zvi **Hirsch**)
Jacob **Kamenecki** (Yaakov Kamenetsky)
Jacob Meshullam ben Mordechai Ze'ev **Ornstein**
Jacob Tzvi **Mecklenberg** (Mecklenburg)
Jedidiah **Weil**
Jehiel ben **Joseph** of Paris
Jehiel ben Solomon **Heilprin**
Joel **Hayyim** (Mahariah)
Jonah ben **Abraham**
Jonathan **Eybeschutz**
Jonathan ben **Uzziel**
Jose bar **Jose**
Jose ben **Halafta**
Joseph **Albo**
Joseph **Almosnino**
Joseph ben **Baruch** (Joseph of Clisson)
Joseph ben Abraham **Gikatilla** (Joseph Ba'al HaNissim)
Joseph ben Ephraim **Caro**
Joseph ben **Gorion**
Joseph ben Hanan ben Nathan **Ezobi**
Joseph ben Isaac **Kimchi**
Joseph ben Isaac Bekhor **Shor**
Joseph ben Joshua Meir **HaKohen**
Joseph ben Meir HaLevi ibn **Migash** (Ri Migash)
Joseph ben Menachem **Steinhart**
Joseph ben **Moses**
Joseph ben Solomon **Taitezak**
Joseph Ber **Soloveitchik** (HaRav)
Joseph **Chayon**
Joseph Colon ben Solomon **Trabotto** (Maharik)

Joseph **Escapa**
Joseph ibn **Lev**
Joseph ibn **Plat**
Joseph Saul **Nathanson**
Joshua ben Alexander (Katz) HaKohen **Falk**
Joshua (Yehoshua) (ben Chananyah)
Joshua Boaz **Mevorakh** / Joshua Boaz ben Simon Baruch (Shiltei Gibborim)
Joshua ben **Hannanya**
Joshua Hoschel ben **Joseph**
Joshua ben **Levi**
Judah Aryeh Loeb ben Joshua **Hoschel**
Joshua Hoschel ben Elijah Zeeb **Levin**
Judah **Ayyas**
Judah ben **Baba**
Judah ben **Barzillai**
Judah ben Bezalel **Loew** (Maharal / Maharal of Prague)
Judah ben Eliezer HaLevi **Minz** (Mahari Minz)
Judah ben **Enoch**
Judah ben **Ezekiel** (Rav Yehuda)
Judah ben Isaac Messer **Leon**
Judah ben Samuel **HaLevi** (RiHa'l)
Judah ben **Samuel** (of Regensburg) (He-Hasid)
Judah ben Samuel **Rosanes**
Judah ben Solomon **Alharizi** (al-Harizi)
Judah ben Solomon Chai **Alkali**
Judah **HaNasi** (Rabbeinu HaKadosh)
Judah ben **Ilai** (Rabbi Judah)
Judah ben **Nathan** (Riban)
Judah II
Judah III
Judah IV

K
Kahana
Kalonymus Family
Kalonymus ben **Isaac**
Kalonymus ben **Shabbethai**
Kalonymus Kalman **Shapira** (Szapira)

L
Landau Family
Levi ben **Gershom** (Gersonides, Ralbag)
Levi ben Jacob ibn **Chaviv** (Habib) (Ralbach)
Levi Yitzhak **Schneerson**
Louis **Ginzberg**

M

Meir Ba'al HaNes (Nahori)
(Mar bar Rav **Ashi**) Tabyomi bar **Ashi**
Meir ben **Baruch** (Meir of Rothenburg) (MaHaRaM)
Meir ben Gedaliyah **Lublin** (Maharam)
Meir ben Isaac **Katzenellenbogen** (Maharam Padua)
Meir ben Isaac (Yitzhak) **Nehorai**
Menachem ben Solomon **Meiri** (HaMeiri)
Meir ben Iszak **Eisenstadt** (Meir Ash)
    (Maharam Ash / Panim Me'irot)
Meir ben **Samuel** (RAM)
Meir ben Solomon Abi **Sahula**
Meir ben Todros HaLevi **Abulafia**
Meir ben Zvi **Margolis**
Meir **Eisenstadter** (Meir Ash) (Maharam Ash)
Meir Leibush ben Jehiel **Michel** (Malbim)
Meir **Popperos**
Meir Simcha Kalonymus **HaKohen** (of Dvinsk)
Menachem **Azaryah** (of Fano)
Menachem ben (ben Solomon ben Simson) **Jacob**
Menahem ben Aaron ibn **Zerah**
Menahem ben Jacob ibn **Saruq**
Menahem ben **Solomon**
Menachem di **Lonzano**
Menachem Mendel ben Meshulam Zalman **Auerbach**
Menahem Mendel ben Simeon **Steinhardt**
Menachem Mendel **Kasher**
Menachem Mendel ben Abraham **Krochmal**
Menachem **Mendel** of Kotzk (Kotzker Rebbe)
Menachem Mendel **Schneerson** (The Lubavitcher Rebbe)
Menachem Mendel **Schneerson** (Tzemach Tzedek)
Menachem Nachum **Twersky**
Menasseh ben **Israel**
Meshullam ben **Jacob** (Yaakov)
Meshullam ben **Moses**
Meshullam ben **Moses**
M'Lekhet Shlomo (See **Adeni**)
Mordechai ben Abraham **Benet**
Mordechai ben Avraham **Jaffe** (Yoffe) (Ba'al HaLevushim)
Mordechai ben Hillel **Ashkenazi** (or Mordechai ben Hillel)
Mordechai Gimpel Yaffe **Torizer**
Mordechai **Leifer** (of Nadvorna)
Mattithiah ben Solomon **Delacrut**
Moses **Ashkenazi** (Johann Peter Spaeth)
Moses ben Baruch **Almosnino**
Moses ben Isaac **Alashkar**

Moses ben Isaac Judah **Lima**
Moses ben Israel **Isserles** (Rema)
Moses ben Jacob **Cordovero**
Moses ben **Jacob** of Coucy
Moses ben **Maimon** (Maimonides) (Rambam)
Moses ben **Meir** of Ferrara
Moses ben **Nahman** (Nahmanides) (Ramban)
Moses ben Naftali Hertz **Rivkes**
Moses ben Noah Isaac **Lipschutz**
Moses Chaim **Luzzatto** (Ramchal)
Moses of Evreux
Moses de **Leon** (Moshe ben Shem Tov)
Moses de **Medina**
Moses **HaDarshan**
Moses **Hagiz**
Moses ibn **Ezra** (HaSallah)
Moses ibn **Habib** (Chaviv)
Moses ibn **Tibbon**
Moses **Kimchi**
Moses **Mendelssohn**
Moses **Schick** (Maharam Schick)
Moses **Sofer** (Chatam Sofer)
Moshe **Alshich**
Moshe Chaim **Ephraim** (of Sudilkov)
Moshe Mordechai **Epstein**
Moshe **Feinstein** (Reb Moshe)
Moshe **Mos** (of Premysl)
Eleazar ben **Pedat**
Moshe **Pellier** of Kobrin

N
Nachman (of Breslov)
Nachman Kohen **Krochmal**
Naphtali (Hirsch) ben Asher **Altschul**
Naftali Tzvi Yehuda **Berlin**
Naftali Hertz ben Yaakov **Elchanan** (Bachrach)
Nahman bar **Jacob**
Nahman bar Isaac (Yitzhak)
Nathan
Nathan ben Jehiel (Yechiel) **Anaw** (Anav)
Nechunya ben **HaKanah**
Nethaneel ben Naftali Tzvi **Weil**
Nissim ben **Jacob** (HaMafteach) (Rav Nissim Gaon)
Nissim ben **Reuven**, of Gerona (RaN)
Noah ben Abraham **Lipschutz** (Noah Mindes)

O

Obadiah ben **Abraham** of Bertinoro
Obadiah ben Jacob **Sforno**
Onkelos
Ovadia **Yosef**

P

Perez ben **Elijah** (Rap, RaPaSh, MaHaRPaSh)
Pinchas Menachem **Alter** (Pnei Menachem)

R

Rabbi **Assi**
Rabbi Ishmael (Ishmael ben **Elisha**)
Rami bar **Chama**
Rav **Ashi**
Rav **Hisda**
Rav **Huna**
Rav **Jonah**
Rav **Pappa**
Rav Yehuda (Judah ben **Ezekiel**)
Rava (Abba bar Yosef bar Chama)
Ravina I
Ravina II

S

Saadia ben **Joseph**, Gaon (Saadia Gaon)
Safra
Samson ben **Abraham** of Sens
Samson ben **Isaac**, of Chinon (MaHaRShak)
Samson ben **Joseph**, of Falaise
Samuel **Aboab** (Rasha)
Samuel bar **Abba** (Samuel of Nehardea)
Samuel ben **Aaron** of Schlettstadt
Samuel ben Isaac **Sardi** (HaSardi, HaSefaradi)
Samuel ben Jacob **Jam'a**
Samuel ben Joseph **Strashun** (Rashash)
Samuel ben Judah ibn **Tibbon**
Samuel ben **Kalonymus** (He-Hasid) (of Speyer)
Samuel ben **Meir** (Rashbam)
Samuel ben Moses de **Medina** (RashDaM)
Samuel ben Moses di **Modena** (Maharshdam)
Samuel ben Naftali HaLevi **Kelin**
Samuel ben **Nahman** (Nahmani)
Samuel ben Nathan **Loew**

Samuel ben **Solomon** (of Falaise)
Samuel ben Uri Shraga **Faibesh** (Phoebus)
Samuel de **Uzeda**
Samuel ibn **Naghrela** (Samuel HaNagid)
Samuel **Danzig**
Samuel **Eidels**
Samuel **Hayyun**
Samuel **Schotten** (Mharsheishoch)
Saul **Lieberman** (Gra'sh)
Shabbatai ben Meir **HaKohen** (Shach)
Shabbatai Carmuz **Levita**
Shabbethai ben Joseph **Bass**
Shabbethai Sheftel ben Akiba **Hurwitz**
Shabtai **Donolo**
Shabtai Sheftel **Horowitz**
Shalom **Shakna**
Shalom **Sharabi** (Rashash)
Shammai
Shemuel (Shmuel)
Shem Tov ben Abraham ibn **Gaon**
Shem Tov ibn **Shem Tov**
Shemaiah de **Medina**
Shemariah ben Elijah **Ikriti** (of Negropont)
Sherira ben **Hanina**, Gaon
Sheshet
Shila of Kefar Temarta
Shimon bar **Yohai** (Rashbi)
Shimon ben **Azzai**
Shimon ben **Gamliel**
Shimon ben **Lakish** (Resh Lakish)
Shimon ben Yitzhak **HaGadol**
Shimon **Shkop**
Shlomo ben **Aderet** (Rashba)
Shlomo ben **Boya'a**
Shlomo Ephraim **Lunshitz** (Kli Yakar)
Shlomo **Yitzhaki** (Rashi)
Shlomo Zalman **Auerbach**
Sh'maya (Shemaiah)
Shmuel **Aceda**
Shmuel **Schneerson** (The Rebbe Maharash)
Shneur Zalman Fradkin (of Lublin)
Shneur Zalman **Baruch** (Borukovich), (of Liadi) (Alter Rebbe, GRaZ)
Sholom Dovber **Schneerson** (Rebbe Rashab)
Sholom Mordechai **Schwadron** (Maharsham)
Sholom Noach **Berezovsky**

Simchah Bunim **Alter** (Lev Simcha)
Simcha Zissel **Ziv** (Alter of Kelm)
Simeon ben Zemah **Duran** (Rashbatz / Tashbetz)
Simeon **Kara** of Frankfurt (HaDarshan)
Simeon **Kayyara**
Simha ben **Samuel** of Speyer
Simhah ben **Samuel** of Vitry
Simlai
Solomon **Alami**
Solomon ben **Isaac**
Solomon ben Joseph **Ganzfried**
Solomon ben Joshua **Adeni** (M'Lekhet Shlomo)
Solomon ben Judah Aaron **Kluger**
Solomon ben Judah, ibn **Gabirol** (Gvirol)
Solomon ben Kalman HaLevi **Abel**
Solomon ben Moses **Alkabetz**
Solomon ben Simon **Duran** (Rashbash)
Solomon **Buber**
Solomon Bennett **Freehof**
Solomon Judah Loeb **Rapoport**
Solomon **Luria** (Maharshal, Rashal)

T
Tabyomi bar **Ashi** (Mar bar Rav Ashi)
Tarfon
Tanhuma bar **Abba**
Tobiah ben **Eliezer**
Tvi Hirsch ben Yaakov **Ashkenazi** (Chacham Tzvi)
Tzadok
Tzidkayah ben Avraham Anav **HaRofei**

U
Ulla

V
Vidal di **Tolosa**

Y
Yaakov Aryeh **Alter**
Yaakov Baruch ben Yehuda **Landau**
Yaakov ben Bezalel **Loew** (Maharal / Maharal of Prague)
Yaakov Chaim **Sofer** (Kaf HaChaim)
Yaakov ben Yaakov Moshe **Lorberbaum** of Lisser (Ba'al HeNesivos / Lissa Rav)

Yaakov David **Wilovsky**
Yaakov **Etlinger** (Aruch LaNer)
Yaakov ibn **Chaviv** (Habib)
Yaakov **Culi**
Yaakov Yehoshua ben Zvi **Hirsch** (Jacob Joshua Falk)
Yaakov Yitzhak **Ruderman**
Yair Chaim **Bachrach**
Yechezkel (Ezekiel) ben Judah **Landau**
Yechiel Michel HaLevi **Epstein** (the Aruch Hashulchan)
Yechiel Michel **Tukachinsky**
Yechiel Yaakov **Weinberg**
Yedayah **HaPenini**
Yehoshua (**Joshua**) (ben Chananyah)
Yehuda Aryeh Leib **Alter** (Sfas Emes)
Yehudai ben **Nahman** (Yehudai Gaon)
Yehuda ben Shimon **Ashkenazi**
Yehuda Leib HaLevi **Ashlag** (Ba'al HaSulam)
Yehuda Leib ben Meir **Channeles**
Yehuda Meir **Dvir**
Yehuda Meir **Shapiro**
Yerucham ben **Meshullam**
Yerusham **Levovitz**
Yeshayah ben Mali **Hazaken**
Yirmiyahu bar **Abba**
Yisrael **Abuchatzeirah** (Baba Sali)
Yisrael **Alter** (Beis Yisrael)
Yisroel ben Shmuel, **Ashkenazi** of Shklov
Yisroel Lipkin **Salanter**
Yissachar Ber **Ellenburg**
Yissachar **Jacobson**
Yitzhak ben Abba **Mari** (of Marseilles)
Yitzhak (Isaac) ben **Meir** (Rivam)
Yitzhak ben Yaakov HaKohen **Alfasi**
Yitzhak Elchanan **Spektor**
Yitzhak Hezekiah **Lampronti**
Yitzhak **Luria** (**Ashkenazi**) (Ari, Arizal, He-Ari)
Yitzhak Myer **Alter** (Chiddushei Harim, Reb Itche Myer)
Yitzhak (Isaac) **Hutner**
Yitzhak Saggi **Nehor** (Isaac the Blind)
Yitzhak (Isadore) **Twersky**
Yitzhak Yaakov **Weiss** (Minchat Yaakov)
Yitzhak **Yosef**
Yochanan bar **Nappacha**
Yochanan ben **Zakai**
Yoel **Sirkis** (Bach)

Yom Tov **Algazi**
Yom Tov ben Moshe **Tzahalon** (Maharitz)
Yom Tov ibn **Asevilli** (Ritva)
Yom Tov Lippman **Heller** (Tosefos Yomtov)
Yonah ben Avraham **Gerondi** (Rabbeinu Yonah)
Yonah ibn **Janach** (Merinos)
Yosef ben Moshe **Babad**
Yosef **Chaviva**
Yosef Dov **Soloveitchik** (Beis HaLevi)
Yosef (Yoselman) **Loanz** of Rosheim
Yosef **Quafih** (Qafeh, Kafich, Gafeh, Kapach)
Yosef **Rosen** (Rogatchover Gaon, Tzafnach Paneach)
Yosef Yitzhak **Schneerson** (Rebbe Rayatz)
Yosef Yozel **Hurwitz** (Alter of Novardok)

Z
Zedekiah ben Abraham **Anaw (Anav)**
Zerachiah ben Isaac HaLevi **Gerondi** (ReZaH, RaZBI, Ba'al HaMaor)
Zerachiah HaYavani (The Greek) (Ra'Za'H)
Zevi Hirsch **Kaidenover**
Zvi Hirsch **Chajes** (Chayes) (The Maharatz Chajes)
Zvi Hirsch **Kalischer**

Acronyms And Epithets Of Rabbis And Scholars

This listing covers only those rabbis who in addition to their proper name had acronyms or epithets by which they were also known. The first section lists the scholar alphabetically by his last name first and then provides the acronym or epithet.

In the second section the scholar's acronym or epithet is listed alphabetically, followed by the proper name.

Alphabetical List of Proper Names

A

Aboab, Isaac	Menorat HaMaor
Aboab, Samuel	Rasha
Abraham, Isaac ben	RIBA, Abraham of Dampierre
Abraham, Obadiah ben, of Bertinoro	The Bartenura
Abraham, Samson of Sens	The Rash of Sens
Abravanel, Don Isaac ben Judah	The Abarbanel
Abuchatzeirah, Harav Israel	Baba Sali
Abulafia, Meir ben Todros HaLevi	Ramah
Aderet, Shlomo ben	Rashba
Adeni, Solomon ben Joshua	M'Lekhet Shlomo
Alfasi, Yitzhak ben Yaakov HaKohen	RIF
Alter, Avraham Mordechai	Imrei Emes
Alter, Pinchas Menachem	Pnei Menachem
Alter, Simchah Bunim	Lev Simcha
Alter, Yehuda Aryeh Leib	Sfas Emes
Alter, Israel	Beis Israel
Alter, Yitzhak Myer	Chiddushei Harim
Arama, Isaac ben Moses	Ba'al Akedah
Arika, Abba	Rav
Asevilli, Yom Tov Ibn	Ritva
Asher, Bahya ben	Rabbeinu Behaye / Bachya
Asher, Jacob ben	Ba'al HaTurim, the Tur
Ashi, Rav	Rav
Ashi, Tabyomi bar	Mar bar Rav Ashi
Ashkenazi, Tvi Hirsch ben Yaakov	Chacham Tzvi
Ashkenazi, Mordechai ben Hillel	The Mordechai
Ashkenazi, Yitzhak Luria	Ari, Arizal, He-Ari
Attar, Rav Hayyim ibn (Also Chaim ben Atar)	Ohr HaChaim
Azaryah, Menachem, of Fano	Rama of Fano
Azulai, Haim Yosef David	Chida or Hida

B

Barfat (Perfet), Isaac ben Sheshet	RiBaSH / Rivash
Baruch, Meir ben (Meir of Rothenburg)	MaHaRaM
Baruch (Borukovich), Shneur Zalman, of Liadi	Alter Rebbe, GRaZ
Ber, Dov (of Mezritch)	The Maggid (of Mezritch)
Behag	Author of Halakhot Gedolot
Berab, Jacob	Mhari Beirav
Berlin, Naftali Tzvi Yehuda	The Netziv
Blaser, Isaac ben Moses Solomon	Rav Itzele Peterburger
Bruna, Israel	Mahari Bruna

C

Caro (Karo), Joseph ben Ephraim	Mechaber / HaMechaber
Chaim, Hakham (Chacham) Yosef (Ben Ish Chai) (Joseph Hayyim ben Elijah Al-Hakam)	Ben Ish Chai
Chajes (Chayes) Zvi Hirsch	The Maharatz Chajes
Chushiel, Chananel ben	Rabbeinu Chananel
Cordovero, Moses ben Jacob	Ramak

D

Danzig, Abraham ben Jehiel	Chayei / Chochmat Adam
David, Abraham ben	Ravad III
Duran, Simeon ben Zemah	Rashbatz / Tashbetz
Duran, Solomon ben Simon	Rashbash

E

Eidels, Samuel	Maharsha
Eisenstadt, Meir ben Iszak	(Meir Ash) Maharam Ash / Panim Me'irot
Eisenstadter, Meir (Meir Ash)	Maharam Ash
Eliezer, Israel ben	Ba'al Shem Tov / Besht
Elijah, Perez ben	Rap / RaPaSh / MaHaRPaSh
Elisha, Ishmael ben	Rabbi Ishmael
Emden, Jacob Israel ben Zvi Ashkenazi	Yabets
Epstein, Yechiel Michel HaLevi	Aruch Hashulchan
Etlinger, Yaakov	Aruch LaNer
Ezra, Abraham ben Meir ibn	Abenezra
Ezra, Moses ibn	HaSallah

F

Feinstein, Moshe	Reb Moshe

G

Gamliel I (The Elder)	Rabban
Gerondi, Yonah ben Avraham	Rabbeinu Yonah
Gerondi, Zerachiah ben Isaac HaLevi	ReZaH, RaZBI, Ba'al HaMaor
Gershom, Levi ben	Gersonides, Ralbag
Gikatilla, Joseph ben Abraham	Joseph Ba'al HaNissim
Gombiner, Abraham Abele ben Chaim HaLevi	Magen Avraham
Gunzberg, Aryeh Leib ben Asher	Shaagat Aryeh

H

Habib, Levi ben Jacob ibn	Ralbach
HaKappar, Eleazar ben Eleazar	Bar Kappara, Berebi
HaKohen, Shabbatai ben Meir	Shach
HaLevi, Abraham ben David (Abraham ibn Daud)	Ravad I / Rabad
HaLevi, Aharon	Ra'AH
HaLevi, Eliezer, ben Joel	Raviah
HaLevi, Isaac ben Asher	Riva
HaLevi, Jacob ben Isaac	Jabez
HaLevi, Judah ben Samuel	RiHa'al
HaNasi, Judah	Rabbeinu HaKadosh
Haparchi, Ishtori ben Moses	Kaftor Vaferech
Hayyim, Joel	Mahariah
Heller, Aryeh Leib HaKohen	Ketzos, The
Heller, Yom Tov Lippman	Tosefos Yomtov
Horowitz, Isaiah HaLevi	Shelah, Shaloh
Hurcanus (Hyrcanus), Eliezer ben	Eliezer HaGadol
Hurwitz (Horwitz), Yosef Yozel	Alter of Novardok

I

Isaac, Abraham ben, of Narbonne	Ravad II
Isaac, Samson ben, of Chinon	MaHaRShak
Isserles, Moses ben Israel	Rema, Ramo
Israel, Menasseh ben Joseph ben	MB'Y

J

Jacob (Yaakov), Meshullam ben	Rabbeinu Meshullam HaGadol
Jaffe (Yoffe) Mordechai ben Avraham	Ba'al HaLevushim
Jehiel, Asher ben	Rabbeinu Asher / Rosh
Joseph, Saadia ben, Gaon	Saadia Gaon
Judah, Gershom ben	Rabbeinu Gershom / or Rabbeinu Gershom Me'Or HaGolah

K

Kagan, Israel Meir (HaKohen)	Chofetz Chaim
Kalonymus, Eleazar ben Yehuda ben, of Worms	Rokeach
Kalonymus, Samuel ben, of Speyer	He-Hasid
Kara, Simeon Ashkenazi, of Frankfurt	HaDarshan
Karelitz, Abraham Isaiah	Chazon Ish
Katzenellenbogen, Meir ben Isaac	Maharam Padua
Kimchi, David	RaDaK
Kook, Abraham Isaac	HaRaAYaH / HaRav

L

Lakish, Shimon ben	Resh Lakish
Landau, Ezekiel (Yechezkel) ben Judah	Nodah B'Yehuda
Loew, Judah ben Bezalel	Maharal / Maharal of Prague
Lorberbaum, Jacob ben Jacob Moses, of Lisser	Ba'al HeNesivos / Lissa Rav
Lublin, Meir ben Gedaliyah	Maharam
Lunshitz, Shlomo Ephraim	Kli Yakar
Luria, Isaac (Ashkenazi)	Ari, He-Ari, Arizal
Luria, Solomon	Maharshal, Rashal
Luzzatto, Moses Chaim	RaMCHaL

M

Mahari Beirav	Jacob Berab
Maimon, Moses ben (Maimonides)	Rambam
Manoah, Hezekiah ben	Hizkuni / Chizkuni
Medina, Samuel ben Moses de	RashDaM
Meir, Isaac (Yitzhak) ben	Rivam
Meir (Tam), Jacob ben	Rabbeinu Tam
Meir, Samuel ben	Rashbam
Meiri, Menachem ben Solomon	HaMeiri
Meltzer, Isser Zalman	Even HaEzel
Mendel, Menachem of Kotzk	Kotzker Rebbe
Mevorakh, Joshua Boaz / Baruch, Joshua Boaz ben Simon	Shiltei Gibborim
Michel, Meir Leibush ben Jehiel	Malbim
Migash, Joseph ben Meir HaLevi ibn	Ri Migash
Minz, Judah ben Eliezer HaLevi	Mahari Minz
Mizrachi, Elijah	Re'em
Moelin, Jacob ben Moses Levi	Maharil
Mordechai, Isaac ben, of Regensburg	RiBaM
Moses, Isaac ben, of Vienna	Or Zarua, Riaz
Modena, Samuel ben Moses di	Maharshdam

N

Nahman, Moses ben (Nahmanides) — Ramban
Nathan, Eliezer ben — Raavan
Nathan, Judah ben — Riban

P

Palaggi, Hayyim — Maharhaf, HaVif

R

Rabinowitz-Teomim, Eliyahu David — Aderet
Reggio, Isaac Samuel — Yashar
Reischer, Jacob ben Joseph — Backofen
Reuven, Nissim ben, of Gerona — RaN
Rosen, Yosef — Rogatchover Gaon, Tzafnach Paneach

S

Samuel, Isaac ben, of Dampierre — Ri
Samuel, Judah ben, of Regensburg — He-Hasid
Samuel, Meir ben — RAM
Schick, Moses — Maharam Schick
Schneerson, Menachem Mendel — Tzemach Tzedek
Schneerson, Menachem Mendel — The Lubavitcher Rebbe
Schneerson, Shmuel — The Rebbe Maharash
Schneerson, Sholom Dovber — Rebbe Rashab
Schneerson, Yosef Yitzhak — Rebbe Rayatz
Schneuri, Dovber — Mitteler Rebbe
Schotten, Samuel — Mharsheishoch
Schwadron, Sholom Mordechai — Maharsham
Segal, David ben Samuel HaLevi — Taz
Shahin, Jacob ben Nissim ibn — Rabbeinu Nissim, HaMafteach

Sharabi, Shalom — Rashash
Sirkis, Yoel — Bach
Sofer, Abraham Samuel Benjamin — Ksav Sofer
Sofer, Moses — Chatam Sofer
Sofer, Yaakov Chaim — Kaf Hachaim
Solomon, Joseph Colon ben — Maharik
Soloveitchik, Chaim — The Brisker Rav
Soloveitchik, Joseph Ber — HaRav
Soloveitchik, Yosef Dov — Beis HaLevi
Strashun, Samuel ben Joseph — Rashash

T

Trabotto	Maharik
Trani, Isaiah ben Mali di	RI'D
Tzahalon, Yom Tov ben Moshe	Maharitz

V

Volozhin, Chaim ben Itzchok	Reb Chaim

W

Weil Jacob ben Judah	Mahariv
Weiss, Yitzhak Yaakov	Minchat Yaakov
Wilovsky, Yaakov David	Ridvaz

Y

Yehuda, Gershon ben	Me'Or HaGolah
Yitzhaki, Shlomo	Rashi
Yohai, Shimon bar	Rashbi

Z

Zalman, Elijah ben Solomon	Vilna Gaon, Gra
Ziv, Simcha Zissel	Alter of Kelm
Rabinowitz, Chaim Shalom Tuvia	Reb Chaim Telzer
Zerachiah HaYavani (The Greek)	Ra'Za'H
Zimra, David ben Solomon ibn Abi	Radbaz

Alphabetical List of Acronym / Epithet

A

Abarbanel, The	Don Isaac ben Judah Abravanel
Abraham of Dampierre (Riba)	Isaac ben Abraham
Abenezra	Abraham ben Meir ibn Ezra
Aderet	Eliyahu David Rabinowitz-Teomim
Alter of Kelm	Simcha Zissel Ziv
Alter of Novardok	Yosef Yozel Hurwitz
Alter Rebbe (GRaZ)	Shneur Zalman Baruch, of Liadi
Ari (Arizal, He-Ari)	Isaac (Ashkenazi) Luria
Aruch Hashulchan, The	Yechiel Michel HaLevi
Aruch LaNer	Yaakov Etlinger

B

Ba'al Akedah	Isaac ben Moses Arama
Ba'al HaLevushim	Mordechai ben Avraham Jaffe (Yoffe)
Ba'al HaNesivos (Lissa Rav)	Jacob ben Jacob Moses Lorberbaum of Lisser
Ba'al HaMaor	Zerachiah ben Isaac HaLevi Gerondi (ReZaH, RaZBI, Ba'al)
Ba'al HaTurim (The Tur)	Jacob ben Asher
Ba'al Shem Tov (Besht)	Israel ben Eliezer
Baba Sali	Harav Israel Abuchatzeirah
Bach	Yoel Sirkis
Backofen	Jacob ben Joseph Reischer
Bar Kappara (Berebi)	Eleazar ben HaKappar
Bartenura, The	Obadiah ben Abraham, of Bertinoro
Behag	Author of Halakhot Gedolot
Beis HaLevi	Yosef Dov Soloveitchik
Beis Israel	Yehuda Aryeh Leib Alter
Ben Ish Chai	Chaim, Hakham (Chacham) Yosef (Joseph Hayyim ben Elijah Al-Hakam)
Berebi	Eleazar ben Eleazar HaKappar (Bar Kappara,)
Besht (Ba'al Shem Tov)	Israel ben Eliezer
Brisker Reb	Chaim Soloveitchik

C

Chacham Tzvi	Tvi Hirsch ben Yaakov Ashkenazi
Chatam Sofer	Moses Sofer

Chayei / Chochmat Adam — Abraham ben Jehiel Danzig
Chazon Ish — Abraham Isaiah Karelitz
Chida (or Hida) — Haim Yosef David Azulai
Chizkuni / Hizkuni — Hezekiah ben Manoah
Chochmat / Chayei Adam — Abraham ben Jehiel Danzig
Chofetz Chaim — Israel Meir Kagan (HaKohen)

E

Eliezer HaGadol — Eliezer ben Hurcanus (Hyrcanus)
Even HaEzel — Isser Zalman Meltzer

H

HaDarshan — Simeon Kara of Frankfurt
HaMafteach (Rabbeinu Nissim) — Shahin, Jacob ben Nissim ibn
HaMechaber / Mechaber — Joseph ben Ephraim Caro (Karo)
HaMeiri — Menachem ben Solomon Meiri
HaRav — Joseph ber Soloveitchik
HaSallah — Moses ibn Ezra
HaRaAYaH / HaRav — Abraham Isaac Kook
HaVif (Maharahaf) — Hayyim Palaggi
He-Ari (Ari, Arizal) — Isaac Luria (Ashkenazi)
He-Hasid — Samuel ben Kalonymus of Speyer
He-Hasid — Judah ben Samuel of Regensburg
Hida (or Chida) — Haim Yosef David Azulai
Hizkinu / Chizkuni — Hezekiah ben Manoah

G

Gersonides — Levi ben Gershom
Gra (Vilna Gaon) — Elijah ben Solomon Zalman
Gra'sh — Saul Lieberman
GRaZ (Alter Rebbe) — Shneur Zalman Baruch, of Liadi

I

Imrei Emes — Avraham Mordechai Alter

J

Jabez — Jacob ben Isaac HaLevi
Joseph Ba'al HaNissim — Joseph ben Abraham Gikatilla

K

Kaf HaChaim — Yaakov Chaim Sofer
Kaftor Vaferech — Ishtori ben Moses Haparchi

Ketzos, the	Aryeh Leib HaKohen Heller
Kli Yakar	Shlomo Ephraim Lunshitz
Kotzker Rebbe	Menachem Mendel of Kotzk
Ksav Sofer	Abraham Samuel Benjamin Sofer

L

Lev Simcha	Simchah Bunim Alter
Lissa Rav (Ba'al HaNesivos)	Jacob ben Jacob Moses Lorberbaum of Lisser
Lubavitcher Rebbe	Menachem Mendel Schneerson

M

MB'Y	Menasseh ben Joseph ben Israel
M'Lekhet Shlomo	Solomon ben Joshua Adeni
Magen Avraham	Abraham Abele ben Chaim HaLevi Gombiner
Maggid, The (of Mezritch)	Dov Ber (of Mezritch)
Maharal / Maharal of Prague	Judah ben Bezalel Loew
MaHaRaM	Meir ben Baruch (Meir of Rothenburg)
Maharam	Meir ben Gedaliyah Lublin
Maharam Ash	Meir ben Iszak Eisenstadt (Meir Ash) (Panim Meirot)
Maharam Ash	Meir Eisenstadter (Meir Ash)
Maharam Padua	Meir ben Isaac Katzenellenbogen
Maharam Schick	Moses Schick
Maharatz Chajes	Zvi Hirsch Chajes (Chayes)
Maharhaf (HaVif)	Hayyim Palaggi
Mahari Bruna	Israel Bruna
Mahari Minz	Judah ben Eliezer HaLevi Monz
Maharia	Joel Hayyim
Maharik	Joseph Colon ben Solomon Trabotto
Maharil	Jacob ben Moses Levi Moelin
Maharitz	Yom Tov ben Moshe Tzahalon
Mahariv	Jacob ben Judah Weil
MaHaRPaSh	Perez ben Elijah
MaHaRShak	Samson ben Isaac of Chinon
Maharsha	Samuel Eidels
Maharshal (Rashal)	Solomon Luria
Maharsham	Sholom Mordechai Schwadron
Maharshdam	Samuel ben Moses di Modena
Malbim	Meir Leibush ben Jehiel Michel
Mar bar Rav Ashi	Tabyomi bar Ashi
Mechaber / HaMechaber	Joseph ben Ephraim Caro (Karo)

Menorat HaMaor	Isaac Aboab
Me'Or HaGolah	Gershon ben Yehuda
Mharsheishoch	Samuel Schotten
Minchat Yaakov	Yitzhak Yaakov Weiss
Mitteler Rebbe	Dovber Schneuri
Mordechai, The	Hillel ben Mordechai Ashkenazi

N

Netziv, The	Naftali Tzvi Yehuda Berlin
Nodah B'Yehuda	Ezekiel (Yechezkel) ben Judah Landau

O

Ohr HaChaim	Rav Hayyim ibn Attar
Or Zarua (Riaz)	Isaac ben Moses of Vienna

P

Panim Me'irot	Meir ben Iszak Eisenstadt (Meir Ash) (Maharam Ash)
Pnei Menachem	Pinchas Menachem Alter

R

Ra'AH	Aharon HaLevi
Raavan	Eliezer ben Nathan
Rabban	Gamliel I (The Elder)
Rabbeinu Asher / Rosh Jehiel	Asher ben Jehiel
Rabbeinu Behaye / Bachya	Bahya ben Asher
Rabbeinu Chananel	Chananel ben Chushiel
Rabbeinu Gershom or	Judah ben Gershom
Rabbeinu Gershom Me'Or HaGolah	Judah ben Gershom
Rabbeinu HaKadosh	Judah HaNasi
Rabbeinu Meshullam HaGadol	Jacob (Yaakov), Meshullam ben
Rabbeinu Nissim (HaMafteach)	Shahin, Jacob ben Nissim ibn
Rabbeinu Tam	Jacob ben Meir (Tam)
Rabbeinu Yonah	Yonah ben Avraham Gerondi
Rabbi Ishmael	Ishmael ben Elisha
RaDaK	David Kimchi
Radbaz	David ben Solomon ibn Abi Zimra
Ralbag	Levi ben Gershom
Ralbach	Levi ben Jacob ibn Habib
RAM	Meir ben Samuel
RAMA	Meir ben Todros HaLevi Abulafia
Rama of Fano	Menachem Azaryah of Fano

Ramak	Cordovero, Moses ben Jacob
Rambam	Moses ben Maimon (Maimonides)
Ramban	Moses ben Nahman (Nahmanides)
RaMCHaL	Moses Luzzatto
RaN	Nissim ben Reuven, of Gerona
Ramo (Rema)	Isserles, Moses ben Israel
Rap / RaPaSh	Perez ben Elijah
Rash of Sens, The	Samson ben Abraham of Sens
Rasha	Samuel Aboab
Rashal (Maharshal)	Solomon Luria
Rashba	Shlomo ben Aderet
Rashbam	Samuel ben Meir
Rashbi	Shimon bar Yohai
Rashash	Shalom Sharabi
Rashash	Samuel ben Joseph Strashun
Rashbash	Solomon ben Simon Duran
Rashbatz / Tashbetz	Simeon ben Zemah Duran
RashDaM	Samuel ben Moses de Medina
Rashi	Shlomo Yitzhaki
Rav	Abba Arika
Rav	Rav Ashi
Rav, The	Joseph ber Soloveitchik
Rav Itzele Peterburger	Isaac ben Moses Solomon Blaser
Ravad I / Rabad	HaLevi, Abraham ben David (Abraham ibn Daud)
Ravad II	Abraham ben Isaac of Norbonne
Ravad III	Abraham ben David HaLevi
Raviah	Eliezer, ben Joel HaLevi
Ra'Za'H	Zerachiah HaYavani (The Greek)
RaZBI	Zerachiah ben Isaac HaLevi Gerondi (ReZaH, Ba'al HaMaor)
Reb Chaim	Chaim ben Itzchok Volozhin
Reb Chaim Telzer	Chaim Shalom Tuvia Rabinowitz
Reb Moshe	Moshe Feinstein
Rebbe Maharash	Shmuel Schneerson
Rebbe Rashab	Sholom Dovber Schneerson
Rebbe Rayatz	Yosef Yitzhak Schneerson
Re'em	Elijah Mizrachi
Rema (Ramo)	Moses ben Israel Isserles
Resh Lakish	Shimon ben Lakish
ReZaH	Zerachiah ben Isaac HaLevi Gerondi (RaZBI, Ba'al HaMaor)
Ri	Isaac ben Samuel of Dampierre
Riaz (Or Zarua)	Isaac ben Moses of Vienna

RIBA	Isaac ben Abraham (Abraham of Dampierre)
RiBaM	Isaac ben Mordechai of Regensburg
Riban	Judah ben Nathan
RiBaSH (Rivash)	Isaac ben Sheshet Barfat
RI'D	Isaiah ben Mali di Trani
Ridvaz	Yaakov David Wilovaky
RIF	Yitzhak ben Yaakov HaKohen Alfasi
RiHa'l	Judah ben Samuel HaLevi
Ri Migash	Joseph ben Meir HaLevi ibn Migash
Ritva	Yom Tov Ibn Asevilli
Riva	Isaac ben Asher HaLevi
Rivam	Isaac (Yitzhak) ben Meir
Rogatcher Gaon	Yosef Rosen
Rokeach	Eleazar ben Yehuda ben Kalonymus of Worms
Rosh / Rabbeinu Asher	Asher ben Jehiel

S

Saadia Gaon	Joseph, Saadia ben Joseph
Sfas Emes	Yehuda Aryeh Leib Alter
Shaagat Aryeh	Aryeh Leib ben Asher Gunzberg
Shaloh (Shelah)	Isaiah HaLevi Horowitz
Shach	Shabbatai ben Meir HaKohen
Shelah (Shaloh)	Isaiah HaLevi Horowitz
Shiltei Gibborim	Joshua Boaz Mevorakh / Joshua Boaz ben Simon Baruch

T

Tashbetz / Rashbatz	Simeon ben Zemah Duran
Taz	David ben Samuel HaLevi Segal
Tur, The	Jacob ben Asher
Tosefos Yomtov	Yom Tov Lippman Heller
Tzafnach Paneach	Yosef Rosen
Tzemach Tzedek	Menachem Mendel Schneerson

V

Vilna Gaon (Gra)	Elijah ben Solomon Zalman

Y

Yabets	Jacob Israel ben Zvi Ashkenazi Emden
Yashar	Isaac Samuel Reggio

Derivation Of Acronyms And Epithets

The purpose of this list is to indicate how the rabbi obtained his acronym or epithet. The scholar's acronym or epithet is listed in alphabetical order followed by the proper name and then the basis for the acronym or epithet.

Acronym / Epithet	Name	Basis Of Acronym / Epithet
A		
Abarbanel, The	Don Isaac ben Judah Abravanel	From name
Abenezra	Abraham ben Meir ibn Ezra	From name
Aderet	Elijah David Rabinowitz-Teomim	Acronym of Hebrew name – Aliyahu David Rabinowitz Teomim
Alter of Kelm	Simcha Zissel Ziv	Founder of Kelm Talmud Torah
Alter of Novardok	Yosef Yozel Hurwitz	After town of yeshiva
Alter Rebbe / GRaZ	Schneur Zalman Baruch of Liadi	The "old" Rabbi Rabbeinu HaGadol Zalman
Ari (Arizal, He-Ari)	Isaac Luria Ashkenazi	Alohi Rabbi Itzhak / AriZal (+ Zikhrono Livrakha)
Aruch Hashulchan, The	Yechiel Michael HaLevi	Title of work
B		
Rabbeinu Bachya	Beyha / Bachya ben Asher	Title of work
Ba'al Akedah	Isaac ben Moses Arama	Title of work
Ba'al HaLevushim	Mordechai ben Avraham Jaffe (Yoffe)	Title of work
Ba'al HaNesivos (Lissa Rav)	Jacob ben Jacob Moses Lorberbaum of Lisser	Title of work

Acronym / Epithet	Name	Basis Of Acronym / Epithet
Ba'al HaMaor, ReZaH, RaZBI	Zerachiah ben Isaac HaLevi Gerondi	Title of work, ReZaH – After Hebrew name – Reb Zerachiah HaLevi
Ba'al HaSulam	Yehuda Leib HaLevi Ashlag	From title of work HaSulam (Sulam)
Ba'al HaTurim	Jacob ben Asher	Title of work – The Tur
Ba'al Shem Tov (Besht)	Israel ben Eliezer	Nickname – "Master of the Good Name". Besht is an abbreviation
Baba Sali	Israel Abuchatzeirah	Arabic for "our praying father"
Bach	Yoel Sirkis	Title of work
Backofen	Jacob ben Joseph Reischer	Alternate last name
Bar Kappara (Berebi)	Eleazar ben HaKappar	Son of Kappara
Bartenura, The	Obadiah ben Abraham, of Bertinoro	"From Bartenura"
Behag		Author of Halakhot Gedolot
Beis HaLevi The Rav	Yosef Dov Soloveitchik	Title of major work. "The Rabbi"
Ben Ish Chai	Hakham (Chacham) Yosef Chaim	Title of work
Berebi	Eleazar ben Eleazar HaKappar	Bar Kappara
Besht (Ba'al Shem Tov)	Israel ben Eliezer	Besht – Abbreviation.
Brisker Reb	Chaim Soloveitchik	From Brest (Brisk in Yiddish)

C

Acronym / Epithet	Name	Basis Of Acronym / Epithet
Chacham Tzvi	Tzvi Hirsch ben Yaakov Ashkenazi	Title of work
Chatam Sofer	Moses Sofer	Acronym for **Ch**iddushei **T**orat **M**osher **Sofer**
Chayei / Chochmat Adam	Abraham ben Jehiel Danzig	Title of work

Acronym / Epithet	Name	Basis Of Acronym / Epithet
Chazon Ish	Abraham Isaiah Karelitz	After signing his writings "the ish", "the young man"
Chida (or Hida)	Haim Yosef David Azulai	Acronym – **H**aim **Y**osef **D**avid **A**zulai
Chiddushei Harim	Yitzhak Myer Alter	Title of work
Chizkuni / Hizkuni	Hezekiah ben Manoah	Title of work
Chochmat / Chayei Adam	Abraham ben Jehiel Danzig	Title of major work
Chofetz Chaim	Israel Meir Kagan (HaKohen)	Title of first book "Chafetz Chaim"

E

Acronym / Epithet	Name	Basis Of Acronym / Epithet
Eliezer HaGadol	Eliezer ben Hurcanus (Hyrcanus)	Eliezer The Great
Even HaEzel	Isser Zalman Meltzer	Title of commentary on Mishneh Torah

G

Acronym / Epithet	Name	Basis Of Acronym / Epithet
Gersonides, RaLBaG	Levi ben Gershon	Latinized name – **Ra**bbi **b**en **G**ershon
Gra (Vilna Gaon)	Elijah ben Solomon Zalman	Abbreviation of **Ga**on **R**abbi **E**liyahu
Gra'sh	Saul Lieberman	**Ga**on **R**abbeinu **Sh**aul
GRaZ / Alter Rebbe	Schneur Zalman Baruch of Liadi	**Ga**on **R**abbeinu Ha**Z**aken

H

Acronym / Epithet	Name	Basis Of Acronym / Epithet
HaDarshan	Simeon Kara of Frankfurt	Rabbi Simeon HaDarshan (the preacher)
HaMafteach (Rabbeinu Nissim)	Jacob ben Nissim ibn Shahin	Title of work
HaMechaber Mechaber	Joseph ben Ephraim Caro (Karo)	HaMechaber – The author
HaMeiri	Menachem ben Solomon Meiri	After last name

Acronym / Epithet	Name	Basis Of Acronym / Epithet
HaRav	Joseph ber Soloveitchik	"The Rabbi"
HaSallah	Moses ibn Ezra	"Writer of penitential prayers"
HaRaAYaH / HaRav	Abraham Isaac Kook	Acronym – **HaR**av **A**vraham **Y**itzhak **H**aKohen Kook
HaVif (Maharhaf)	Hayyim Palaggi	?
He-Ari (Ari, Arizal)	Isaac Luria (Ashkenazi)	See under "Ari"
He-Hasid	Samuel ben Kalonymus of Speyer	"The pious one"
He-Hasid	Judah ben Samuel of Regensburg	"The pious one"
Hida (or Chida)	Haim Yosef David Azulai	See under "Chida"
Hizkinu / Chizkuni	Hezekiah ben Manoah	Based on the title of his work

I

Acronym / Epithet	Name	Basis Of Acronym / Epithet
Imrei Emes	Avraham Mordechai Alter	Title of work

J

Acronym / Epithet	Name	Basis Of Acronym / Epithet
Jabez	Jacob ben Isaac HaLevi	Based on his name
Joseph Ba'al HaNissim	Joseph ben Abraham Gikatilla	Based on his ability to perform miracles

K

Acronym / Epithet	Name	Basis Of Acronym / Epithet
Kaf HaChaim	Yaakov Chaim Sofer	Title of work
Kaftor Vaferech	Ishtori ben Moses Haparchi	Title of work
Ketzos, the	Aryeh Leib HaKohen Heller	Based on title of work "Ketzot HaChoshen"
Kli Yakar	Lunshitz, Shlomo Ephraim Lunshitz	Title of major work
Kotzker Rebbe	Menachem Mendel of Kotzk	Where he lived

Acronym / Epithet	Name	Basis Of Acronym / Epithet
Ksav Sofer	Abraham Samuel Benjamin Sofer	Title of work

L

Lev Simcha	Simchah Bunim Alter	Title of work
Lissa Rav (Ba'al HaNesivos)	Jacob ben Jacob Moses Lorberbaum	The city where he was chief rabbi / Title of work
Lubavitcher Rebbe	Menachem Mendel Schneerson	Leader of Hassidic Jews

M

MB'Y	Menasseh ben Joseph ben Israel (Yisrael)	Hebrew acronym of name – **Me**nasseh **b**en **Yi**srael
M'Lekhet Shlomo	Solomon ben Joshua Adeni	Title of work
Magen Avraham	Abraham Abele ben Chaim HaLevi Gombiner	Original title of work
Maggid, The (of Mezritch)	Dov Ber (of Mezritch)	The Preacher of Mezritch
Maharal / Maharal of Prague	Judah ben Bezalel Loew	Acronym – **M**oreinu **HaRa**v **L**oew
MaHaRaM	Meir ben Gedaliyah Lublin	Acronym – **M**oreinu **Ha**Rabbeinu **M**eir
Maharam Ash (Panim M'eirot)	Meir Ash / Meir Eisenstadt	Acronym – **M**oreinu **HaRa**v **M**eir **Ash**
Maharam of Padua	Meir ben Isaac Katzenellenbogen	Acronym – **M**oreinu **HaRa**v **M**eir **of Pa**dua
Maharam Schick	Moses Schick	Acronym – **M**oreinu **HaRa**v **M**oishe **Sch**ick
Maharatz Chajes	Zvi Hirsch Chajes (Chayes)	Acronym – **M**oreinu **HaRa**v **Tz**vi
Maharhaf (HaVif)	Hayyim Palaggi	Acronym – **M**oreinu **HaRa**v **H**ayyim

Acronym / Epithet	Name	Basis Of Acronym / Epithet
Mahari Bruna	Israel Bruna	Acronym – **Ma**hareinu **hara**v Israel **Bruna**
Mahari Minz	Judah ben Eliezer HaLevi Minz	Acronym – **Ma**hareinu **hara**v **Minz**
Maharia	Joel Hayyim	Acronym – **M**oreinu **hara**v Joel
Maharik	Joseph Colon ben Solomon Trabotto	Acronym – **M**oreinu **hara**v
Maharil	Jacob ben Moses Levi Moelin	Acronym – **M**oreinu **hara**v Yaakov Levi
Maharitz	Yom Tov ben Moshe Tzahalon	Acronym – **M**oreinu **hara**v **Tz**ahalon
Mahariv	Jacob ben Judah Weil	Acronym – **M**oreinu **hara**v **W**eil
MaHaRPaSh	Perez ben Elijah	Acronym – **M**oreinu **hara**v **RaPaSH** (Rabbi Perez)
MaHaRShak	Samson ben Isaac of Chinon	Acronym – **M**oreinu **hara**v **Shak** (Samson of Chinon)
Maharsha	Samuel Eidels	Acronym – **M**oreinu **hara**v **Sh**muel
Maharshal (Rashal)	Solomon Luria	Acronym – **M**oreinu **hara**v **Sh**lomo
Maharsham	Sholom Mordechai Schwadron	Acronym – **M**oreinu **hara**v **Sh**lomo **M**ordechai
Maharshdam	Samuel ben Moses di Modena	Acronym – **M**oreinu **hara**v **Sh**muel **d**i **M**odena
Malbim	Meir Leibush ben Jehiel Michel	Acronym – **M**eir **L**eibush **b**en Jehiel **M**ichel
Mar bar Rav Ashi	Tabyomi bar Ashi	Mar ("my lord")
Mechaber / HaMechaber	Joseph ben Ephraim Caro (Karo)	"The author"
Menorat HaMaor	Isaac Aboab	Title of work
Me'Or HaGolah	Gershon ben Yehuda	"Light of the Diaspora"

Acronym / Epithet	Name	Basis Of Acronym / Epithet
Mharsheishoch	Samuel Schotten	**M**orein **Har**av **Sh**muel Schotten Cohen. Also name of collection of responsa
Minchat Yaakov	Yitzhak Yaakov Weiss	Title of work
Mitteler Rebbe	Dovber Schneuri	"Middle rebbe". Was second of first three generations of Chabad leaders
Mordechai, The	Hillel ben Mordechai Ashkenazi	Title of work

N

Acronym / Epithet	Name	Basis Of Acronym / Epithet
Netziv, The	Naftali Tzvi Yehuda Berlin	Acronym - **Na**ftali **T**zvi
Nodah B'Yehuda	Ezekiel (Yechezkel) ben Judah Landau	Title of work

O

Acronym / Epithet	Name	Basis Of Acronym / Epithet
Ohr HaChaim	Rav Hayyim ibn Attar	Title of work
Or Zarua (Riaz)	Isaac ben Moses of Vienna	Title of work

P

Acronym / Epithet	Name	Basis Of Acronym / Epithet
Panim Me'irot (Maharam Ash)	Meir ben Isaac Eisenstadt	Title of work
Pnei Menachem	Pinchas Menachem Alter	Title of work

R

Acronym / Epithet	Name	Basis Of Acronym / Epithet
Ra'AH	Aharon HaLevi	Acronym of name - **A**haron **H**aLevi
Raavan	Eliezer ben Nathan	
Rabad / Ravad I	Abraham ben David (Abraham ibn Daud) HaLevi	Acronym - **R**abbeinu **A**vraham **b**en **D**avid

Acronym / Epithet	Name	Basis Of Acronym / Epithet
Rabban	Gamliel I (The Elder)	"Master" – Rabbinic title given to head of Sanhedrin
Rabbeinu Asher Rosh Jehiel	Asher ben Jehiel	"Our teacher Asher" / Acronym – **Ra**bbeinu **Asher**
Rabbeinu Behaye	Bahya ben Asher	"Our teacher Bayha"
Rabbeinu Chananel	Chananel ben Chushiel	"Our teacher Chananel"
Rabbeinu Gershom / Me'Or HaGolah	Judah ben Gershom	"Our teacher Gershom" / "The light of Exile"
Rabbeinu HaKadosh	Judah HaNasi	"Our holy teacher"
Rabbeinu Meshullam HaGadol	Meshullam ben Jacob (Yaakov)	"Our teacher Meshullam the Great"
Rabbeinu Nissim / (HaMafteach)	Jacob ben Nissim ibn Shahin	"Our teacher Nissim" / Title of work
Rabbeinu Tam	Jacob ben Meir (Tam)	"Our teacher Tam"
Rabbeinu Yonah	Yonah ben Avraham Gerondi	"Our teacher Yonah"
RaDaK	David Kimchi	Acronym – **Ra**bbi **D**avid **K**imchi
Radbaz	David ben Solomon ibn Abi Zimra	Acronym – **Ra**bbi **D**avid ibn **A**bi **Z**imra
Ralbach	Levi ben Jacob ibn Habib	Acronym – **Ra**bbi **L**evi ibn Ha**b**ib (**Ch**aviv)
RalBaG	Levi ben Gershon	Acronym – **Ra**bbi **L**evi **b**en **G**ershon
RAM	Meir ben Samuel	Acronym – **Ra**bbi **M**eir
RAMA (Ramah)	Meir ben Todros HaLevi Abulafia	Acronym – **Ra**bbi **M**eir **A**bulafia
Rama of Fano	Menachem Azaryah of Fano	Acronym – **Ra**bbi **M**enachem **A**zaryah of **Fano**
Ramak	Moses ben Jacob Cordovero	Acronym – **Ra**bbi **M**oshe **C**ordovero
Rambam	Moses ben Maimon (Maimonides)	Acronym – **Ra**bbeinu **M**oshe **b**en **M**aimon

Acronym / Epithet	Name	Basis Of Acronym / Epithet
Ramban	Moses ben Nahman (Nahmanides)	Acronym – **Ra**bbeinu **M**oshe **ben** **N**ahman
RaMCHaL	Moses Luzzatto	Acronym – **Ra**bbeinu **M**oshe **Ch**aim **L**uzatto
RaN	Nissim ben Reuven, of Gerona	Acronym – **Ra**bbeinu **N**issim
Ramo (Rema)	Moses ben Israel Isserles	Acronym – **Ra**bbeinu **Mo**she
Rap / RaPaSh	Perez ben Elijah	Acronym – **Ra**bbi **P**erez
Rasha	Samuel Aboab	Acronym – **Ra**bbeinu **Sh**muel
Rashal (Maharshal)	Solomon Luria	Acronym – **Ra**bbeinu **Sh**lomo **L**uria
Rashash	Shalom Sharabi	Acronym – **Ra**bbeinu **Sh**alom **Sh**arabi
Rashash	Samuel ben Joseph Strashun	Acronym – **Ra**bbeinu **Sh**muel **S**trashun
Rashbash	Solomon ben Simon Duran	Acronym – **Ra**bbi **Sh**lomo **ben** **Sh**imon
RashDaM	Samuel ben Moses de Medina	Acronym – **Ra**bbeinu **Sh**lomo **de** **M**edina
Rash of Sens, The	Samson ben Abraham of Sens	Acronym – **Ra**bbeinu **Sh**lomo of Sens
Rashba	Shlomo ben Aderet	Acronym – **Ra**bbeinu **Sh**lomo **b**en **A**deret
Rashbam	Samuel ben Meir	Acronym – **Ra**bbeinu **Sh**muel **b**en **M**eir
Rashbi	Shimon bar Yohai	Acronym – **Ra**bbeinu **Sh**imon **b**ar **Y**ohai
Rashbatz / Tashbetz	Simeon ben Zemah Duran	Acronym – **Ra**bbeinu **Sh**imon **b**en **Tz**emakh
Rashi	Shlomo Yitzhaki	Acronym – **Ra**bbeinu **Sh**lomo **Y**itzhaki

Acronym / Epithet	Name	Basis Of Acronym / Epithet
Rav	Abba Arika	Common usage by contemporaries – "The Master"
Rav, The	Joseph ber Soloveitchik	Common usage by contemporaries.
Rav Itzele Peterburger	Isaac ben Moses Solomon Blaser	Named after his period in St. Petersburg
Ravad I / Rabad	Abraham ben David (Abraham ibn Daud) HaLevi	Acronym – **Ra**bbeinu **Av**raham **b**en **D**avid
Ravad II	Abraham ben Isaac of Norbonne	Acronym – **Ra**bbeinu **Av**raham
Ravad III	Abraham ben David	Acronym – **Ra**bbeinu **Av**raham **b**en **D**avid
Raviah	Eliezer ben Joel HaLevi	Acronym of Hebrew name – **Ra**bbeinu **Av**i **E**zri **H**aLevi
Ra'Za'H	Zerachiah HaYavani	Acronym – **Ra**bbeinu **Z**erachiah **H**aYavani
RaZBI (ReZaH)	Zerachiah ben Isaac HaLevi Gerondi	Acronym – **Ra**bbeinu **Z**erachiah **b**en **I**saac
Reb Chaim	Chaim ben Itzchok Volozhin	After his personal name
Reb Chaim Telzer	Chaim Shalom Tuvia Rabinowitz	After the Telz Yeshiva where he taught
Reb Moshe	Moshe Feinstein	Yiddish Reb (honorific title) and first name
Rebbe Maharash	Shmuel Schneerson	Rebbe and Acronym – **M**oreinu **Ha**rav **Sh**muel
Rebbe Rashab	Sholom Dovber Schneerson	Rebbe and Acronym – **Ra**bbeinu **Sh**olom **D**ovber
Rebbe Rayatz	Yosef Yitzhak Schneerson	Rebbe and Acronym **Ra**bbeinu **Y**osef **Y**itzhak
Re'em	Elijah Mizrachi	Acronym – **R**abbi **E**lijah **M**izrachi

Acronym / Epithet	Name	Basis Of Acronym / Epithet
Rema (Ramo)	Moses ben Israel Isserles	See Ramo
Resh Lakish	Shimon ben Lakish	Nickname
ReZaH (Razbi)	Zerachiah ben Isaac HaLevi Gerondi	See Razbi
Ri	Isaac ben Samuel of Dampierre	Acronym – **R**abbi **I**saac
Riaz (Or Zarua)	Isaac ben Moses of Vienna	Acronym of name and title of work – **R**abbi **I**saac **Z**arua
RIBA	Isaac ben Abraham (Abraham of Dampierre)	Acronym – **R**abbi **I**saac **b**en **A**braham
RiBaM	Isaac ben Mordechai of Regensburg	Acronym – **R**abbi **I**saac **b**en **M**ordechai
Riban	Judah ben Nathan	Acronym – **R**abbi **Y**ehuda **b**en **N**athan
RiBaSH (Rivash)	Isaac ben Sheshet Barfat	Acronym – **R**abbi **I**saac **b**en **Sh**eshet
RI'D	Isaiah ben Mali di Trani	Acronym – **R**abbi **I**saac **d**i Trani
Ridvaz	Yaakov David Wilovsky	Acronym – **R**abbi **Y**aakov **V**ilo**vz**ky
RIF	Yitzhak ben Yaakov HaKohen Alfasi	Acronym – **R**abbi **Y**itzhak al **F**asi
RiHa'l	Judah ben Samuel HaLevi	Acronym – **R**abbi **Y**ehuda **HaL**evi
Ri Migash	Joseph ben Meir HaLevi ibn Migash	Acronym – **R**abbi **Migash**
Ritva	Yom Tov ibn Asevilli	Acronym – **R**abbi **Y**om **T**ov ibn Asevilli
Riva	Isaac ben Asher HaLevi	Acronym – **R**abbi **I**saac **Ha**Levi
Rivam	Isaac (Yitzhak) ben Meir	Acronym – **R**abbi **I**saac **M**eir
Rogatcher Gaon	Yosef Rosen	After birthplace – Rogachev

Acronym / Epithet	Name	Basis Of Acronym / Epithet
Rokeach	Eleazar ben Yehuda ben Kalonymus of Worms	Title of work
Rosh / Rabbeinu Asher	Asher ben Jehiel	Rosh – "The Head"

S

Acronym / Epithet	Name	Basis Of Acronym / Epithet
Saadia Gaon	Joseph, Saadia ben Joseph	After personal name
Sfas Emes	Yehuda Aryeh Leib Alter	Title of work
Shaagat Aryeh	Aryeh Leib ben Asher Gunzberg	Title of work
Shach	Shabbatai ben Meir HaKohen	Abbreviation of title of work
Shaloh (Shelah)	Isaiah HaLevi Horowitz	Abbreviation of title of work
Shiltei Gibborim	Joshua Boaz Mevorakh / Joshua Boaz ben Simon Baruch	Title of work

T

Acronym / Epithet	Name	Basis Of Acronym / Epithet
Tashbetz / Rashbatz	Simeon ben Zemah Duran	Acronym – **Ra**bbi **Sh**imon **ben T**zemach
Taz	David ben Samuel HaLevi Segal	Abbreviation of title of work
Tur, The	Jacob ben Asher	Title of work
Tosefos Yomtov	Yom Tov Lippman Heller	Title of work
Tzafnach Paneach	Yosef Rosen	Title of work
Tzemach Tzedek	Menachem Mendel Schneerson	Title of work

Y

Acronym / Epithet	Name	Basis Of Acronym / Epithet
Yabets	Jacob Israel ben Zvi Ashkenazi Emden	Acronym – **Ya**akov **b**en **Z**vi Also title of collection of responsa.
Yashar	Isaac Samuel Reggio	Acronym – **Y**itzhak **Sh**muel Reggio

Section II

Biographies

Selective Tannaim And Amoraim

Pre-Tannaitic

Avtalyon

Avtalyon (spelled also Abht'alyon and Abtalyon) was the vice-head of the Sanhedrin in Jerusalem in the first century BCE. According to various sources in the Talmud he was of heathen descent. However, together with his colleague Sh'maya (Shemaiah), who was the head of the Sanhedrin, he was one of the most influential and respected men of his time. He used this influence to convince the leaders of Jerusalem to open its gates to Herod the Great in 37 BCE.

According to Josephus, Herod rewarded Avtalyon. However, this author refers to a Pollion, which he perhaps meant Ptollion, which would have been closer to Avtalyon's correct name. There is another reference corresponding to the year 19 BCE to a Pollion, the Pharisee, and a Sameas, but Avtalyon had died many years before. Hillel, who was a disciple of Avtalyon, had assumed the latter's position following his death before 30 BCE. Thus Josephus could have been confused with Shammai and therefore wrote Pollion and Sameas instead of Hillel and Shammai.

There is little known of the life of Avtalyon. He was a pupil of Judah ben Tabbai and Simon ben Shetach. He also studied under Judah. He probably spent some time with Judah in Alexandria, having fled when Alexander Jannaeus persecuted the Pharisees.

Shemaiah and Avtalyon were the first to hold the title *darshan* and their pupil Hillel was thus the first to lay down the hermeneutic rules for Midrashic interpretation. They are also the first two scholars whose sayings are recorded in the Haggadah. Their method of *derush* (biblical interpretation) was opposed by the Pharisees. Avtalyon and Shemaiah's halakhot (legal decisions) are also the first to be handed down to later times.

Gamliel I (The Elder – Hazaken) (Rabban)

Gamliel the Elder was the grandson of Hillel the Elder and lived in the first century, dying nine years before the destruction of the Temple. He was a leader in the Sanhedrin. In the Talmud he is referred to as Rabban, given to him as a result of his being the head of the Sanhedrin. According to the Mishnah, he was the author of legal rulings relating to the community welfare and certain conjugal rights. According to the Mishnah he was considered one of the greatest teachers of Judaism.

Gamliel, Shimon ben

Shimon ben Gamliel was the son of Gamliel I and lived from approximately 10 BCE to 70 CE. He succeeded his father as Nasi in 50 CE and held this position until just before the destruction of the Temple in 70 CE. Tradition indicates that he was one of the Ten Martyrs killed by the Romans.

Gamliel II (of Yavne)

He was the son of Shimon ben Gamliel, a leader in the war against the Romans, and a grandson of Gamliel I. To differentiate him from his grandfather he is referred to as Gamliel of Yavne. After the destruction of the Temple, he was appointed Nasi of the Sanhedrin, a position he held from 80 to approximately 120 CE.

He was a part of the group of rabbis under Yochanan ben Zakai that had gone to Yavne during the siege of Jerusalem and became his successor. In this role he ended the divisions between the schools of Hillel and Shammai and enforced his authority with a view to uniting the Jews after the destruction of the Temple.

He is said to have directed Simeon HaPakoli to edit the Amidah and instructed that it be recited three times daily. He was a controversial leader, having excommunicated his brother-in-law, Eliezer ben Hyrcanus, and embarrassing Rabbi Joshua ben Hananiah in a dispute over fixing the calendar. This led to a rabbinic revolt in the Sanhedrin.

Hillel, The Elder

He lived during the period from the end of the first century BCE to the early first century CE. He was considered one of the greatest of the late second temple sages. He was the founder of the Beit Hillel school of Tannaim. He was born in Babylon, but virtually nothing is known of his background. According to the Mishnah, Hillel went to Jerusalem to study and in the tractate Yoma (35B) it describes how he overcame hardships and suffering while studying to achieve his goal. He ultimately received a degree of authority that resulted in a number of decrees being handed down in his name. He was also responsible for the introduction of the *Pruzbul*, the law dealing with debt cancellation and loan repayment. A number of sayings of his have been handed down. Many of these reflect the type of life he led, most of which are preserved in the Babylonian Talmud. He is also credited with the creation of the "sandwich" or *Korech* from the Haggadah.

His colleague and adversary was Shammai under whom the opposing School of Shammai (Beit Shammai) developed. Beit Shammai generally tended to follow a more restrictive route, whereas Beit Hillel was more of a moderate route. Of the over 300 controversies that are preserved in the Talmud, in only fifty-five the House of Shammai presented the lenient view.

Shammai

Shammai lived from about 50 BCE to about 30 CE. He was considered one of the pre-eminent rabbinic figures in establishing the material for the Mishnah. He was a contemporary and generally a halakhic opposite of Hillel. Shaimmai's school of thought was known as the House of Shammai (Beit Shammai), as opposed to Hillel's which was Beit Hillel. After Hillel's death, Shammai became the president of the Sanhedrin. During his presidency eighteen ordinances were passed according to his views. His halakha took on a more strict view.

Sh'maya (Shemaiah)

He was a pre-Tannaitic sage who lived in the first century BCE and was a contemporary of Avtalyon. He was a leader of the Pharisees and president (Nasi) of the Sanhedrin before and during the reign of Herod. Nothing is known of his private life. He was a pupil of Judah ben Tabbai.

Tannaim

Abba, Hiyya bar

Rav Abba was born in the middle of the second century CE at Kafri, near Sura in Babylonia. He later emigrated to Tiberius where he established a successful business. He was close to Judah I whom he visited in Sepphoris (Tzippori) on a number of occasions. He was active in teaching, creating schools for children and often teaching them himself.

He was active in halakhot, redacting those that Judah did not include in the Mishnah. These go under the names of *Baraitot de-Rabbi Hiyya*, *Mishnat de-Rabbi Hiyya* or *Mishnayot Gedolot*. Some of these halakhot are introduced into the Talmud as "Tanna Rabbi Hiyya." He was considered the author of the Tosefta. He spoke about early Christianity and in the midrash, Pesikta Rabbati, he refers indirectly to Christ's blasphemy, with regard to the latter calling himself the son of God. He was an uncle of Abba Arika (Rav).

Abuyah, Elisha ben

Abuyah was an early Tanna, born in Jerusalem sometime before the destruction of the Temple. Since he had somewhat of a world view of matters he was ostracized by Talmudic rabbis, was referred to as the Acher (Other One) and his teachings were not referred to by his name. A clear picture of his personality and beliefs is very difficult to obtain from rabbinical sources. It seems that he was the son of a well-respected and wealthy Jerusalem citizen and trained as a scholar. He studied Greek. The only single quotation of his in his name in the Mishnah can be found in Avot 4:20. He had a reputation as an authority on halakhic matters and in Mo'ed Katan 20a there is a record of one of his decisions. There is a baraita (Hagigah 14b, Jerusalem Talmud) that makes reference to his views. The Jerusalem Talmud has a statement which indicates that he was an informer during the Hadrianic persecutions. He seems to ultimately have abandoned the Jewish religion. His life was fictionalized in Milton Steinberg's 1939 novel, *A Driven Leaf*.

Akavya ben Mahalel

Virtually nothing is known about this sage. He was a Tanna who is known for a saying of his in the tractate Avot. "Reflect upon three things and you will never come to sin. Know from where you came, to where you are going and before whom you are destined to give an accounting." He then goes on to describe these.

Arach, Eleazar ben

He was a second generation Tanna and was a disciple of Yochanan ben Zakai. He was considered to be a very accomplished scholar. He also excelled in the mystical interpretation of the Tanakh. His name is associated with only a few halakhot. This was probably because after Yochanan ben Zakai's death and his disciples moved to Yavne, Arach went to Emmaus, from where his wife came and there his study was very limited.

Azariah, Elazar ben

Elazar ben Azariah was a Tanna who lived after the destruction of the Second Temple in 70 CE. He studied at Yavne under Rabban Gamliel the Second who succeeded Rabbi Yochanan ben Zakai as the second head of the Academy. Elazar is said to have come from a long line of a prominent and wealthy family tracing itself back to Ezra the Scribe. He was a contemporary of Rabbi Eliezer ben Hyrcanus, Rabbi Joshua ben Hananiah, Rabbis Akiva and Tarfon. Rabbi Elazar ben Azariah's teachings can be found in many places in the Talmud.

Dissatisfied with the leadership of the Sanhedrin and the Academy, under Gamliel II, the leadership among the scholars decided to depose him and selected Rabbi Elazar ben Azariah to replace him. This was despite his youth. He was only eighteen years of age at the time of his selection. Out of this event comes the famous legend that overnight he turned gray and grew a beard.

His first action as the new head of Yavne was to open its doors to a wider selection of students, a process that his predecessor had kept very exclusive. However, after a short while, Rabban Gamliel was re-instated as the Nasi or President as well as head of the Academy, but on condition that Rabbi Elazar presided over the Academy one week in the month. On one occasion he was sent to Rome together with several other leading scholars to make a representation to the Emperor to ease the conditions of the Jews.

Azzai, Shimon ben (Ben Azzai)

Shimon ben Azzai was a second century Palestinian Tanna. He was also known as Ben Azzai. This last name is an abbreviation of Azaryah. He was such a well thought of rabbi, that when the Talmud uses the generic term "before the sages" it is frequently referring to him. He believed that one is obligated to teach one's daughter Torah. Several of his sayings are recorded in Avot.

Baba, Judah ben

He was a second century rabbi in Palestine. He ordained a number of rabbis, despite the Roman prohibition, including Judah ben Ilai. He was killed by Hadrian's soldiers when seventy years old, and is known as one of the Ten Martyrs.

His comments and sayings appear many times in the Talmud. He was responsible for several halakhic decisions. Rabbi Akiva, who was another of the Ten Martyrs, was his main opponent on halakhic issues.

Dosa, Hanina ben

Hanina ben Dosa was a sage from the first century CE. He lived in the Galilee and was a student of Yochanan ben Zakai. Although he is considered to be one of the Tannaim, technically this is not so, since there are no halakhot and only a few aggadot preserved from him. However, he is popularly remembered and has been made immortal, especially among mystics, not for his scholarship, but for his saintliness and his miraculous powers. He is considered to be among the ancient Hassidim. His life was in fact seen as a succession of miracles.

Elisha, Ishmael ben (Rabbi Ishmael)

Ishmael ben Elisha was a third generation Tanna who lived from 90-135 CE. He was descended from a wealthy priestly family of the Upper Galilee. In his youth he was taken away by the Romans, but Joshua ben Hananiah secured his release and installed him in Judea where he became an accomplished scholar.

Elisha was a prominent member of the Sanhedrin at Yavne. In his halakhic work he established principles of logical methods whereby laws maybe deduced from laws and other phraseology in the Bible. He formalized a set of thirteen hermeneutic rules whereby halakha was derived from the Torah. He took the seven rules of Hillel and elaborated on these and built his own system. Elisha also laid the foundation for the Mekhilta, the halakhic midrash on Exodus, as well as a good portion of the similar midrash, the Sifre on Numbers.

Gamliel II, Shimon ben

Shimon lived in the second century CE. He was a youth during the Bar Kokhba revolt and was in Betar at the time, but managed to escape the massacre. He was a third generation Tanna. He succeeded Gamliel II as Nasi of the Sanhedrin. In the Mishnah there are a number of sayings of his which reflect a knowledge of biology, anatomy and dealing with diseases, for example in Berakhot and Shabbat. During his term as Patriarch he organized the functions of the Sanhedrin and added another administrative position. His aim was to increase the authority of the college of which the Nasi was the head and also to increase its respect as a place of learning. In halakhic matters he tended towards the more lenient interpretation of the laws.

HaKanah, Nechunya ben (Nechunya HaGadol)

Nechunya ben HaKanah lived in the first to second century. He was sometimes known as Nechunya HaGadol. He was a Tanna and probably was a student of Yochanan ben Zakai. He was known to pray before entering and when leaving the academy and this is recorded in Berakhot 28b. He is quoted several times in the Mishnah.

Hakinai, Hanina ben

Hanina or Hanania ben Hakinai was a second century Tanna. It is not known exactly who his earlier teachers were, but from the Tosefta, Tarfon might have been one of them. Rabbi Akiva was his main teacher. He was a contemporary of Ben Azzai. Although not ordained he was allowed to regularly argue cases in front of the sages. Several halakhot have been preserved in his name. He also left some halakhic midrashim, as found in the Sifra. A later source indicates that he was one of the Ten Martyrs.

Halafta, Jose ben

Jose or Yose ben Halafta was a fourth generation Tanna, living in the second century CE. He was a student of Rabbi Akiva and teacher of Yehuda HaNasi. Although his family was of Babylonian origin, he was born in Sepphoris. He was ordained which required him to flee to Asia Minor because of the temporary Roman decree against this. He later settled in Usha, which was then the seat of the Sanhedrin. Later he returned to Sepphoris where he established a school which attracted many students. He died there.

His halakhot are mentioned many times in the Mishnah. His opinion was usually a compromise between the schools of Hillel and Shammai. He generally took a more liberal view.

Seder Olam Rabbah is the earliest chronicle preserved in Hebrew following the expulsion from Judea. It has traditionally been viewed as having been written by Jose ben Halafta, but probably supplemented by later commentators. This view is based primarily on the comment by Rabbi Yochanan's statement in Yeb 82b and Nidah 46b, "The Tanna of 'Seder Olam' was Rabbi Jose." It is a chronological record extending from Adam and Eve through to the Bar Kokhba Revolt. It was written with a view to establishing the timeline of the creation. The Talmud both quotes from *Seder Olam* as well as alluding to it.

Hannanya, Joshua ben

He was one of the most prominent disciples of Yochanan ben Zakai. He studied at Yavne after the destruction of the Second Temple. A close colleague of his was Eliezar ben Hyrkanos with whom he frequently took the opposite opinion on halakhic matters. He became head of the Sanhedrin while Rabbi Gamliel was the Nasi at Yavne. He was considered one of the greatest Tannaim of his generation in the second century, and is often referred to in the Mishnah just as Rabbi Joshua. He had contact with the Roman emperor Hadrian, meeting him in Athens.

HaNasi, Judah (Yehuda) (Rabbeinu HaKadosh)

Judah HaNasi, Judah the Prince or more correctly translated, Judah the President, lived in the second century CE. Like the other Mishnaic rabbis, there is little detailed historical information on his life. He was born about 135. He was a descendant of Hillel. He spent his youth in Usha, which was then the seat of the academy and probably studied under his father, Rabbi Gamliel II. He also studied under Yehuda ben Lai and Yaakov ben Kurshai. Later he studied under Shimon bar Yohai, Yose ben Chalafta and Elazar ben Shamua. He was taught Greek which served him well later in life in that as Patriarch of Palestinian Jewry, he communicated with the Romans.

He was so highly regarded that he was given the title of Rabbeinu HaKadosh. In the Talmud he is simply referred to as "Rabbi."

He established his first academy in Sh'faram and then moved to Beit She'arim where he spent many years. For health reasons he finally moved for the last seventeen years of his life to Tzippori (Sepphoris). Among his students were Rabbi Chia and Abba Arika (Rav).

He is best known for being the redactor / editor of the Mishnah in about 200. He died about 220. He was succeeded by his eldest son Gamliel III.

Hisma, Eleazar

He was a Tanna of the first third of the second century and one of the sages of Yavne. He was a pupil of Joshua ben Hananiah and possibly of Akiva. Some think Hisma was his father's name and therefore refer to him as Eleazar ben Hisma, but this is generally not accepted. He transmitted most halakhot in the name of Hananiah rather than Akiva. Some of his statements can be found in Mishnah, in Baraita and in the Halakhic Midrashim. He was also proficient in astronomy and mathematics.

Hurcanus (Hyrcanus), Eliezer ben (Eliezer HaGadol)

Eliezer ben Hurcanus was one of the most important Tannaim. He was a disciple of Yochanan ben Zakai. He married the sister of Gamliel II. It appears that he only began to study when an adult. He was in Jerusalem during the Roman siege, but survived it. He then went to Yavne and later became a member of the Sanhedrin under Gamliel II. He went on to establish his own academy at Lydda. Akiva studied at his school.

In his teaching he strictly adhered to the tradition. He was thus more inclined to the school of Shammai, even though Yochanan ben Zakai was a student of Hillel. This ultimately brought him into conflict with his colleagues, who felt that his conservative approach prevented the full development of the oral law. It led to his ultimate excommunication.

Ilai, Judah ben (Rabbi Judah)

Rabbi Judah was a second century Tanna. He was born in Usha in the Galilee and studied under Rabbis Eliezer and Akiva. His halakhic interpretations of the Bible and the legal deductions from it followed the method of Rabbi Akiva.

Jose, Eliezer ben

Eliezer ben Jose lived in the second century in Judea and was the son of Jose the Galilean. He was a Tanna and a pupil of Rabbi Akiva. His fame rests mainly on his knowledge and development of the aggadah. He is believed to have been responsible for drawing up a baraita of thirty-two rules whereby the Bible is interpreted.

Joseph, Akiva ben (Rabbi Akiva)

Rabbi Akiva was born in about 50 CE and was a Tanna of the latter part of the first century and second century. He was one of the most important contributors to the Mishnah and the Midrashic halakha. Despite his great fame as an early rabbi, and possibly the "father of rabbinic Judaism", there is little factual information available on his life, with most of it being based on legend. He probably only started studying later in life, attending the academy in his hometown of Lydda and studying under Eliezer ben Hyrcanus. His other teachers were Joshua ben Hananiah and Nahum of Gimzo. Rabbi Tarphon was a great admirer of him.

He married the daughter of a wealthy farmer, who disowned his daughter. She encouraged Akiva to study. He lived apart from her for over twenty years while pursuing his study. By that time he was a very famous scholar.

The greatest Tannaim of the middle of the second century were his disciples. These included Jose ben Halafta, Judah ben Ilai, Rabbi Meir, Rabbi Nehemiah, Eleazar ben Shammai and Shimon bar Yohai.

His exact relationship to Bar Kokhba and the revolt is unclear, but Akiva did consider Bar Kokhba as the promised Messiah.

Akiva's greatest accomplishment was in the area of halakha. At this stage and with the onset of Christianity there was no systematization or even any logical or exegetical study of the halakha. It was most likely Akiva who systemized the coding of the halakha in the Mishnah as well as the Midrash or exegesis of the halakha.

During the Bar Kokhba revolt he was imprisoned by the Romans and ultimately executed by them about 132-135.

Josiah (Yehoshiyyahu), Ahai (or Achai) ben

He was a late second and early third century Tanna, one of the last generation Tannaim. After studying in Israel he returned to his native Babylonia. His comments appear in Berakhot 2b regarding the proper time to recite the evening Shema. In Erubin 13a he comments on the ritual to be performed when a woman is suspected of infidelity.

Joshua (Yehoshua) (ben Chananyah), Rabbi

Rabbi Joshua or Yehoshua was a Tanna of the first to second century and is one of the most distinguished of the Tannaim. Only occasionally is he also known as Yehoshua ben Chananyah. He is quoted in this way in only Chagighah 5b, Kiddushin 30a and Sukkah 53a.

Joshua studied Torah at the academy of Yochanan ben Nuri and later established his own one in Beki'in, between Yavne and Lydda. He was also a student of Yochanan ben Zakai. He is quoted in Nedarim 50a as having taught Akiva ben Joseph. He was also a member of the Beth Din under Gamliel II. The two had their disagreements and over one of them Gamliel was temporarily removed from his position.

Joshua was an independent thinker whose ritual practices would sometimes deviate from the standard. He is quoted in many places throughout the Talmud.

In 95 CE together with several other rabbis he visited Rome to raise funds. He also visited Athens. He debated with Christians and came to the attention of Hadrian with whom he also debated on several topics.

Meir, Rabbi Ba'al HaNes (Nahori)

Rabbi Meir was considered one of the greatest second generation Tannaim. His real name was probably Misha or Nahori. In the Babylonian Talmud, in tractate Erubin there is a discussion on his real name. His principal teacher was Rabbi Akiva.

There is a Mishnaic rule which states that all anonymous Mishnahs are attributed to Rabbi Meir. He was called Ba'al HaNes (The Master of Miracles) because of an episode of how he managed to save the life of his sister-in-law, a daughter of Rabbi Hananyah ben Teradyon.

Nathan

Rabbi Nathan was a third generation Palestinian Tanna. He lived in the second century. He was the son of a Babylonian exilarch, but settled in Palestine where he became head of the school at Usha. Many halakhic decisions and haggadic sayings by him are recorded. His views were mainly opposed by the Patriarch Rabbi Judah. Nathan also was a strong proponent of ritual observance.

Parta, Eleazar ben (Elazar ben Perata)

Eleazar ben Parta or Elazar ben Perata was an early second century Tanna. He is described as a colleague of Judah HaNasi in Pesachim 119b and Sukkah 39a, although this would not correspond with his period of the early second century. He was arrested by the Romans for contravening Hadrian's ban on the public reading of the Torah. He was a co-prisoner with Hananyah ben Teradyon who was put to death. He had the ability to make practical deductions from the Scripture. This was demonstrated in Midrash Rabbah. He is mentioned only once in the Mishnah (Gittin 3:4), but he was known as an aggadist.

Shamua, Elazar ben

Rabbi Elazar ben Shamua lived in the second century CE. He was the son of Rabbi Shimon bar Yohai and a student of Rabbi Akiva. He was one of the five students entrusted with the transmission of the Torah after Akiva lost his original students in a plague. According to Rashi in Tractate Shabbat 19b whenever a Rabbi Elazar is mentioned in the Mishnah and Baraitot, it refers to Elazar ben Shamua. He was the teacher of Rabbi Yehuda HaNasi. He lived to an old age.

Shimon, Elazar ben

He was a Tanna of the second century. His father was Shimon bar Yohai, under whom he studied. He was a noted scholar who engaged in halakhic controversies with his contemporary Judah HaNasi, as well as with other scholars. He is quoted three times in the mishnah, but later Amoraim ascribe several anonymous mishnayot to him. He is frequently quoted in baraitot as well as many times in the tosefta.

Tarfon

Rabbi Tarfon lived in the late first and second centuries of the common era. He lived in Yavne and probably Lydda as well. He was from a priestly family. He was a follower of the School of Shammai, but he did tend towards leniency in the interpretation of the halakhot. He would engage in controversies with Rabbis Akiva, Simeon and Elazar ben Azaryah. He was strongly against the Jews who converted to Christianity. In Justin Martyr's *Dialogue with Trypho*, it has been thought that his dialog was with Tarfon, although this was probably just a literary device. There are several of his quotations in *Pirkei Avot*. He is also mentioned in the Passover Haggadah.

Teradion, Hananyah ben (Teradyon)

Hananyah ben Teradion was a second century Tanna. He lived in Siknin where he established a distinguished academy, mentioned in a baraita. Under Hadrian, decrees were passed with severe penalties for those observing and teaching Jewish law. He continued to teach and was thus condemned to death, being wrapped in a scroll and burned alive.

Tzadok

Tzadok was a Palestinian Tanna who lived in the first century CE. He was a pupil of the School of Shammai, although he often ruled according to the School of Hillel. He was very influential in the Sanhedrin of Gamliel II, by whose side he always sat. It is stated that he predicted the fall of Jerusalem (Gittin 5a-b). When it occurred he was elderly and frail but through the help of Yochanan ben Zakai, Titus released him.

Uzziel, Jonathan ben

Jonathan ben Uzziel was a student of Hillel the Elder. He is known as the author of Targum Jonathan. He is said to be buried in the Galilee where his tomb according to tradition is located in Amukah, near Tzfat.

Yohai, Simeon (Shimon) bar (Rashbi)

Rabbi Shimon bar Yohai was a Tanna who lived during the Roman rule and after the destruction of the Second Temple. He was one of Rabbi Akiva's most famous disciples. He was a vocal critic of the Romans. This forced him to go into hiding with his son for many years. He is accredited with the authorship of the *Zohar* ("The Brightness"). Moses de Leon, who scholars believe wrote this work, ascribed it to Shimon bar Yohai.

Zadok, Eliezer bar

Eliezer bar Zadok was a first century Tanna. He lived during the time of the destruction of the Second Temple, after which he went to Acre. He then went on to Yavne. He died in Ginzak in Media.

Based on Talmudic excerpts he was most likely the compiler of the treatise on mourning called *Ebel Zutarta*.

Zakai, Yochanan ben

Yochanan ben Zakai was a Tanna who was born about 30 CE. He was a major contributor to the Mishnah.

The Mishnah divides his life into three components: his commercial life as a merchant, then as a student and finally as a teacher. He was probably a student of Hillel, but was the major source for passing on the teachings of both Hillel and Shammai.

During the revolt against Rome, he supported peace, but since this was not the popular view, he left Jerusalem, supposedly in a coffin in order to negotiate with Vespasian. Apparently he correctly predicted the elevation of the Roman leader to that of emperor. Vespasian then granted the right to establish a center at Yavne (Jamnia) for the sages. After the destruction of Jerusalem, the school performed functions previously the responsibility of the Sanhedrin. He died in 90 CE and was buried in Tiberias.

Amoraim

Abba the Surgeon

This is an individual first mentioned in the Talmud as an example of Jewish piety. There is a Talmudic legend where he received daily greetings from heaven.

Abba, Samuel bar (Samuel of Nehardea)

He was a first generation Babylonian Amora born in about 165 in Nehardea. He was the son of Abba bar Abba who was his main teacher. He is frequently associated with Abba Arika with whom he debated. He had an interest in and knowledge of astronomy. He spent time in Palestine studying, mainly under the students of Yehuda HaNasi. He subsequently returned to Nehardea with his father, who had also gone there.

After the death of Rav Shila, Samuel became the head of the Academy at Nehardea and helped to establish Babylon as a center of learning. At that time it was the only academy and Samuel was recognized as the greatest authority in Babylon. His good relations with the Persian king helped to establish a secure position for the Jews in Babylonia. He died in 257.

Abba, Tanhuma bar

Tanhuma bar Abba lived in Palestine probably in the fourth century. He was a fifth generation Amora. His teacher was Huna bar Abin, whose halakhic and haggadic sayings he transmitted. There are a few halakhic teachings attributed to him in the Jerusalem Talmud. However, his haggadic sayings are frequently quoted. He is known for providing the scriptural basis for his sayings. He often had disputations with Christian scholars.

As for the Midrash Tanhuma, which consist of three Pentateuchal haggadot, although having the name of R. Tanhuma associated with it, it cannot be ascribed to him.

Abba, Yirmiyahu bar

There were two scholars known by this name. The first was a third century Babylonian Amora referred to as Yirmiyahu ben Ammi in Mo'ed Katan 9a. He was a disciple of Rav. Elsewhere (Ta'anit 11b) he is mentioned as a student of Shimon ben Lakish. He is famous for a statement in Sotah 42a referring to people who would not be admitted before God.

The second was a fourth century Babylonian Amora who went to Palestine and studied with Abbahu and Ze'ira.

Abbahu

Abbahu belonged to the third generation of Amoraim from the Land of Israel. He lived from the late third century into the early fourth century. He received his education in the academy in Tiberias under Rabbi Yochanan bar Nafcha (Nappah), and was a younger contemporary of Resh Lakish. He established an academy in Caesarea and was therefore also known as Abbahu of Caesarea. His interests and influence went beyond Talmudic matters. He had a good knowledge of Greek, having taught himself and encouraged Jews to study this language. This gave him the opportunity to be politically connected with the Roman proconsuls, which he would use to intercede for his fellow Jews. He was an authority on weights and measures.

Abbahu was known as an eminent halakhist. He regulated the sounding of the shofar, which subsequently became universally accepted. This latter enactment was referred to by medieval scholars as 'Takkanat R. Abbahu". He was also well-known as a haggadist. He would engage Christians in disputes as well. He studied the Bible extensively so as to argue effectively against those who misinterpreted it. In the Palestinian Talmud he is attributed to a midrash referring to Jesus as a blasphemer.

He had two sons, Ze'ira and Hanina, the latter also studying at an academy in Tiberias.

Abbahu, Hanina (Hananiah) bar

A fourth generation Palestinian Amora. He was the son of the third generation Amora, Abbahu, and was also known as Hanina of Caesarea. There are no original halakhic rulings by him preserved.

Abbaye

Abbaye was a third generation Babylonian Amora, living from approximately 280-340 CE. In the latter part of his life he was head of the academy at Pumbedita, having succeeded Rav Joseph, under whom he had studied. According to Sherira Gaon, Abbaye was not his real name, but rather it was Nachmani, after his grandfather. Rashi, however, disputed this. His father died before he was born and his mother in childbirth. Therefore he was brought up by his uncle Rabbah bar Nachmani.

Little is known of Abbaye's personal life. Rava was his close friend from childhood. The two participated in legalistic discussions and the Talmud often quotes them jointly. In most situations though, later sages in deciding opinions ruled in favor of Rava on most occasions.

Ahavah, Adda bar

Ahavah was a second generation Amora (250-290 CE) who lived in Babylonia. He is frequently quoted in both the Jerusalem and Babylonian Talmuds. He was a disciple of Abba Arika (Rav). He had many students at his academy in Pumbedita. In tractate Taanit he gives an autobiography of his personality that indicates someone who is constantly thinking about halakha and was very sensitive about others. He never became angry.

There is another Rav Adda bar Ahavah who studied under Rava, Rav Papa and Rav Nachman ben Isaac.

Amemar

There are two Babylonian rabbis who go by this name. It is actually a compound word.

Amemar 1: He was a third generation Amora in Babylon and a contemporary of Rabbi Judah ben Ezekiel and of Rav Sheshet. He combined halakhic and scriptural studies, using the latter to support legal decisions and sayings.

Amemar II: A contemporary of Rav Ashi. He re-established the college at Nehardea, which had been destroyed a century earlier, and restored its reputation. He was also president of the court there and introduced several changes in ritual.

Arika, Abba (Rav)

Abba Arika was a famous Babylonian Amora and the founder of the Academy at Sura, which flourished in the third century He died in Sura in 247. He is known mostly as Rav, although in the Tannaitic literature he is referred to as Rabbi Abba. He claimed to be descended from King David's brother and his uncle was Rav Hiyya. He was a scholar in the circle of Judah I. His arrival in Babylon in 219, after spending time in Palestine, is considered the onset of the Talmudic era. He first chose Nehardea as his base but subsequently moved to Sura where he established his own school. Rav's work and status there made Babylonia independent of Palestine. Samuel, another disciple of Judah I taught at Nehardea.

Rav established the method of Talmudic discourse by taking the Mishnah as the text or basis and adding to it other Tannaitic traditions and from all of these developed the theoretical explanations and the practical applications of halakha. The legal and ritual opinions recorded in Rav's name and his disputes with Samuel form the basis of the Babylonian Talmud. His disciples then amplified on these. The Palestinian Talmud also records a number of his haggadic and halakhic statements. His haggadic statements all have a moral basis to them.

Rav is also attributed with being the author of a composition that forms a part of the Musaf service of Rosh Hashanah.

Little is known of his personal life. He appears to have been wealthy and was involved in commerce and agriculture and was highly respected by the Gentiles of Babylonia. He died at an advanced age. He was succeeded as head of the Academy by Rav Huna and then after that two of his grandsons occupied that post.

Ashi, Rav

Rav Ashi was a Babylonian Amora who lived from 352 to 427. He re-established the Academy at Sura, originally founded by Abba Arika, but closed after the death of Rav Chisda in 309. He was the first editor of the Babylonian Talmud. Preserved Academy tradition indicated that he was born in the same year as Rava. Ashi was taught by Rav Kahana at the College of Naresh near Sura, which was headed by Rav Papa. Kahana later became the head of the Academy at Pumbedita.

Rav Ashi's standing in the community was such that he was compared to Yehuda HaNasi in his learning and social distinction. In fact it is traditionally believed that Rav Ashi did for the Babylonian Talmud what Judah I did for the Mishnah. He is said to have collected and critically scrutinized the explanations of the Mishnah, which had been handed down in the Babylonian academies since Rav (Abba Arika), together with all the other halakhic and haggadic material discussed in the schools, and compiled these under the name of Gemara. A combination of factors, including the support of King Yazdegerd I, the respectful recognition of his authority by the Nehardea and Pumbedita academies, and the over fifty-year tenure as head of the Sura Academy, all contributed to the successful completion of this enormous task.

After his initial preparation of the work, he subsequently spent many years revising it, actually twice, as is mentioned in the Talmud. There is no documentation anywhere as to whether Rav Ashi committed it to writing or whether this was done later.

There are, however scholars, among them Kalmin, Julius Kaplan and Avraham Weiss who dispute this authorship. Kalmin maintains that a number of mid-generational Amoraim were the main editors of the Babylonian Talmud.

Rav Ashi elevated the status of Sura such that it became the intellectual center for Babylonian Jews. He rebuilt both the academy and the associated synagogue, supervising the reconstruction. As a result of his work, Sura retained its status as the leading academy for several centuries.

It is believed that Rav Ashi is buried on a hill overlooking Kibbutz Manara.

Ashi, Tabyomi bar (Mar bar Rav)

He was the son of Rav Ashi and was known as Mar (Master). He was also a recognized scholar. However, it was not until 28 years after the death of his father that he became head of the Academy of Pumbedita.

Assi, Rabbi

Assi was a third generation Palestinian Talmudic Amora, living in the third and fourth centuries. His close companion with whose life he was closely associated at a professional level was Rabbi Ammi. Assi was a disciple of Rabbi Yochanan under whom he distinguished himself. Rabbi Eleazar called him a prodigy of his age. Rabbi Assi is frequently quoted in the Talmud and Midrashim.

Avina, Rabbi

Avina was a third to fourth century Amora who emigrated from Babylon to Israel. His name appears in the Talmud in several places.

Chama (Hama), Rav

Rav Chama lived in the fourth century. He was a Babylonian Amora who followed Nahman bar Yitzhak as the head of the Pumbedita academy. He was considered an outstanding scholar as is attested to in Sanhedrin 17b. He also had a good relationship with the king of Persia.

Chama, Chanina bar

Rabbi Chanina bar Chama was one of the great Talmudic sages. He was of the first generation of Palestinian Amoraim although he was a native of Babylon. However, he came to Israel to study under Judah HaNasi. Among his other teachers were disciples of Rabbi Judah, especially Rabbis Chiya, Ishmael bar R'Yossi and Bar Kappara. Among his contemporaries were Rabbi Joshua ben Levi, Rav Yochanan and Resh Lakish.

Rabbi Chanina would represent Yehuda HaNasi in appearances before the Roman governor in Caesarea in pleas for the Jewish people. After Yehuda HaNasi's death, his son, Rabban Gamliel became the Nasi and appointed bar Chama as the senior sage, a position he only took after the death of an older sage, Rabbi Efes.

Chanina was a gifted healer, using natural herbs and sound advice in his actions as a doctor. He was also famous for his knowledge of Torah.

Rabbi Chanina lived a very long life and died in Tiberias.

Chama (Hama), Rami bar

He was a third generation Babylonian Amora, living in the fourth century. He was a pupil of Rav Hisda (Chisda) and Raba, although somewhat junior to him, was a fellow student. He was associated with Rav Nahman with whom he frequently disagreed. He married Rav Hisda's daughter. He died prematurely.

Chisda (Hisda), Rav

Rav Chisda was a third generation Babylonian Amora who died about 308 CE. He was descended from a priestly family. He studied under Abba Arika. His contemporary and companion was Rav Huna. He married at sixteen and he had seven sons and two daughters. Chisda's halakhot are frequently found in the Talmud. He deduced these in a casuistic way. He also had expertise in the Haggadah. His main opponent in these rulings was Rav Sheshet. Chisda was also an authority on aggadah.

Chisda was a casuist and his sharp mind helped to increase the fame of Huna's academy at Sura. Although this brought him into conflict with Rav Huna over the obligations of a disciple to be a master, they held each other in high esteem. After Huna died, he presided over the academy for ten years.

Ezekiel, Judah ben (Rav Yehuda)

Judah ben Ezekiel, better known as Rav Yehuda, was a second generation Babylonian Amora who lived from 220 to 299 CE. His most prominent teacher was Abba Arika (Rav). After the latter's death he went to Samuel of Nehardea. Following this he opened his own school in Pumbedita.

As a result of his great retentive memory he managed to collect and transmit most of Rav's and Samuel's sayings. As a result, the Talmud has about 400 of Rav's haggadic and halakhic sayings and many of Samuel's.

Rav Yehuda introduced a new method of instruction at his school. It emphasized the need for both careful differentiation as well as critical examination of the subjects treated. He was thus the originator of Talmudic dialectics. Pumbedita became famous for this form of Talmudic instruction. However, he also paid attention to the interpretation of the Mishnah, but did not pay much attention to the aggadah.

Gamliel III

He lived during the third century CE and was the son of Rabbi Yehuda HaNasi (Judah I). He succeeded his father as Nasi, a position he held from about 220 to 230. It is probable that the completion of the Mishnah occurred during his era. In tractate Avot there are records of several of his sayings.

Gamliel IV

He probably lived in the late third century and was the son of Rabbi Judah II. He was Nasi from 270 to 290. The Jerusalem Talmud has a story regarding his humility relative to his knowledge compared with Abbahu.

Gamliel V

He lived during the fourth century and was the son of Hillel II. He is known for having perfected the Jewish calendar in 359. He was Nasi from 365 to 385.

Gamliel VI

He was the last Nasi of the Great Sanhedrin and died in 425. The position of Nasi was disbarred by Emperor Theodosius II. Gamliel VI was also known as a physician.

Hamnuna Saba (The Elder)

This title is often used to separate him from Hamnuna (the younger). He was a Babylonian Amora of the third century. Among his teachers in the latter part of the third century were Adda bar Ahavah, Judah ben Ezekiel and Ulla. His most prestigious teacher was Rav Hisda. Later Huna became his teacher. He ultimately became a recognized rabbinic authority. He believed that the study of the halakha should even precede good deeds. He also is credited with being a liturgical author, one of which is still recited before studying Torah (Ber. 11b). He died at the same time as Huna and both were buried in Palestine.

Hamnuna

Hamnuna was a Babylonian Amora of the third to fourth centuries and a disciple of Rav (Abba Arika) from whom he received training in both halakha and ethics. He was prominent among his fellow students and honored Rav's memory both by quoting him and preventing deviations from Rav's teachings.

HaKappar, Eleazar ben Eleazar (Bar Kappara, Berebi)

Bar Kappara or Berebi are the abbreviated forms for the late second early third century Palestinian rabbi, Eleazar ben Eleazar HaKappar. He fell somewhere in the timeline between a late Tanna and early Amora.

Bar Kappara was a student of Rabbi Yehuda HaNasi, but was also taught by Rabbi Nathan of Babylonia and the Rabbi Jeremiah ben Eleazar mentioned in the Mekhilta and Sifre. A split with the Patriarch's house led to a move to Caesarea where he established an academy. Its most prominent students included Hoshayya, famous for his explanations of the Mishnah and Joshua ben Levi who transmitted the Haggadah of Bar Kappara.

Bar Kappara was known as a great halakhist, but also as a humanitarian. He had a liberal view of things and appreciated broader secular knowledge as well. However, the irreconcilable split with Yehuda HaNasi led to him never being ordained by the latter. Yet when Yehuda HaNasi died Bar Kappara went to Sepphoris because of his deep appreciation of and obligation to his teacher.

Bar Kappara was known to the later Amoraim because of his mishnah called the *Mishnah of Bar Kappara*, but this has not survived. However, many of its passages can be found in the Talmud. Meiri considered it a supplement to Yehuda HaNasi's Mishnah. The redactor of the Tosefta made use of his Mishnah.

Hillel, son of Gamliel III

Hillel was a third century CE sage and brother of Judah II. He has not been quoted in the Talmud on any halakhic ruling but apparently Origen, an early Christian theologian consulted him on biblical passages.

Hillel II

Hillel HaNasi, or simply known as Hillel, and therefore confused with Hillel the Elder was a religious authority about 330-360 CE. He was the son of Judah III and his successor. He is credited, in his position as head of the Sanhedrin with creating the permanent calendar that reconciled the lunar and solar year by intercalating additional days and months in an organized and permanent fashion into the Jewish lunar calendar.

Hillel, Shimon ben

Shimon was the son of Hillel the Elder. Very little is known about him. He succeeded his father as Nasi, but did not live long and was soon succeeded by his son Gamliel I.

Huna, Rav

Rav Huna was a second generation Babylonian Amora. He was thirty when Rav died, but out of respect for Shmuel, who was then head of the yeshiva at Nehardea, Rav Huna was not appointed as a successor to Rav until after Shmuel's death seven years later. He then became head of the academy at Sura. In this capacity he was highly acclaimed as a Torah authority. Rav Chisda (Hisda) was one of his pupils. Rav Huna died when over eighty years old.

Isaac, Nahman bar

Nahman bar Isaac was a fifth generation Babylonian Amora. He was a student of Rav Nahman bar Jacob. He first went to Sura where Rav Nahman bar Hisda was and then after the death of Raba Naman bar Isaac succeeded him as head of the academy at Pumbedita. He held this position for four years. There he collected, arranged and so saved the halakhic teachings of his predecessors. He utilized mnemonic sentences to remember these halakhot. In this way he was one of the first to redact the Talmud. He is quoted in the Haggadah. He died in 356.

Jacob, Nahman bar

Nahman (Nachman) bar Jacob was a third generation Amora and was a pupil of Mar Samuel. He was the head of the school at Nehardea and after that town was destroyed he moved his pupils to Shekanzib. He was also the chief justice of the Jews under the exilarch. In this capacity he was the author of the important ruling that if a defendant absolutely denies his guilt he must take the rabbinic oath of "shebu'at hesset" (Shebu. 40b). He died in 320.

Jonah, (Rav)

Jonah was a leading fourth generation, fourth century Palestinian Amora. He studied under Ze'ira I and Rav Ela. He also studied under Rav Yirmeyahu (Jeremiah) bar Abba. Beginning as a student at the academy in Sepphoris in Tiberias, he ultimately became a leader there. In this capacity he took care of his students, both materially and with advice. He was said to have mystical inclinations.

Judah II

Judah II was a third century Palestinian Amora. He was the grandson of Judah HaNasi. He was also known as Judah (Yehuda) Nesi'ah. He was the son of Gamliel III. He was not considered as a great scholar, but he is known for three ordinances, one dealing with the reform of the divorce laws. Another was on permission to use oil prepared by pagans.

Judah III

Judah III was a third-century Amora. He was the son of Gamliel IV and grandson of Judah II. He held the position of Nasi from the end of the third to the early fourth centuries. He was a student of Yochanan who died in 279. He was associated with Ravs Ammi and Assi with whom he worked to develop elementary education in many Palestinian towns. His son, Hillel II succeeded him as Patriarch.

Judah IV

He was a fourth century Palestinian Amora. He succeeded Gamliel V as the Nasi, a position he held from 385 to 400. He was succeeded by his son Gamliel VI.

Kahana, Rav

He was a third to fourth century Babylonian Amora and the teacher of Rav Ashi, as mentioned in Sukkah 7a, 19a and elsewhere. He was a member of the college at Nasrah, near Sura and subsequently became the president of the academy at Pumbedita for twenty years.

Lakish, Shimon ben (Resh Lakish)

Shimon or Simeon ben Lakish, who is better known as Resh Lakish, was a second generation, third century Palestinian Amora. He was born about 200 and lived most of his life in Sepphoris. He was considered as one of the most prominent Amoraim of his generation. He was apparently a student of Judah Nesi'ah (Judah II). Many of Lakish's sayings were transmitted in the name of Judah. He could also have been a student of Bar Kappara, since he also transmitted sayings in the latter's name.

His knowledge was said to be the equivalent of his senior, Rabbi Yochanan bar Nappacha whom he accompanied to open an academy in Tiberias. There are many debates recorded in the Talmud between these two, and with the exception of three situations, the rulings follow those of Yochanan. Lakish was an independent thinker and would even revoke decisions of his colleagues. This independence was manifest in both halakhic and aggadic matters.

There were contemporary stories that for a time he had been both a gladiator and even a bandit before studying Torah.

Levi, Joshua ben

Joshua ben Levi was a Palestinian Amora from the first half of the third century. He was born in Lydda where he established an academy. He was an elder contemporary of Resh Lakish. He studied under Bar Kappara, but his greatest mentor was Judah ben Pedaiah.

He was tolerant of the then emerging Christian theology. Joshua was recognized as a representative of Palestinian Jewry and was connected with the Patriarchal family through the marriage of his son Joseph.

His legal interpretations were considered valid, even when disputed by Resh Lakish. Aggadic exegesis was very important to him. He was influential in this sphere.

Nahman (Nahmani), Samuel ben

Rabbi Samuel Nahmani was an Amora who lived in Palestine in the third century to the beginning of the fourth century. He was a disciple of Jonathan ben Eleazar. He went to Babylon in an official capacity to determine the intercalation of the calendar year. Together with Judah II he went to Tiberias on the orders of the Roman Emperor, Diocletian, whom he later met. Nahman was one of the foremost haggadists of his time.

Nahmani, Rabbah

Rabbah Nahmani was a third generation Babylonian Amora, who was born in about 270 and died in about 330. He was a student of Rav Huna at Sura and Judah ben Ezekiel at Pumbedita. Rav Huna was so impressed with his student that he always consulted him. He and his family lived a life of poverty.

He was not a prolific haggadist, and only a few of these have been preserved. Many more of his halakhic comments have been preserved.

On the death of Judah he became a leader in the Academy at Pumbedita, where his lectures were very popular.

Nappacha, Yochanan bar

Yochanan bar Nappacha, also known as Nafcha or ben HaNapach (the blacksmith) was born in Sepphoris (Tzippori) in the latter years of Yehuda HaNasi's life (early third century). His father died prior to his birth and his mother shortly after. He was raised by his grandfather. He studied first under Yehuda HaNasi and then later in Caesarea under Oshaya Rabbah, Yannai and Chanina bar Chama.

Yochanan was an active Amora in his generation. He is quoted in Chullin 84b, 137b, in Pesachim 3b, Shabbat 15b, 114a, Berakhot 5b, Sanhedrin 22a. His halakhic method was to establish broad rules that had wide applicability. He taught mostly in Tiberias and was considered the greatest rabbi in Palestine during his life. He was succeeded in Tiberias by Eleazar ben Pedat. His colleague and brother-in-law was Simeon ben Lakish. He died in about 279.

Nathan, Ammi ben

There were several Talmudists by the name of Ammi, but the most distinguished one is a third generation Amora, probably from Babylonia, who gave himself the full name of Ammi ben Nathan. He had a lifelong friendship, possibly even a blood relationship with Rav Assi or Rav Assi ben Nathan who was Babylonian.

Ammi received his early education in Caesarea under Hoshayya Rabbah and then went to Tiberias where he studied under R. Yochanan. There he associated with Ravs Abbahu, Hanina, Pappi, Isaac and Samuel ben Nahman. His most enduring relationships though were with R. Hiyya bar Abba and R. Assi. Abba, Assi and Ammi were Av Beit Din. Ammi eventually became the head of the college at Tiberias.

Apart from his great knowledge of halakha and aggadah, he also had a good knowledge of the sciences. Both R. Ammi and Assi are frequently quoted in both the Jerusalem and Babylonian Talmuds and in Midrashim.

Pappa, Rav

Rav Papa or Pappa, also known as Pappa bar Chanan was a fifth generation Babylonian Amora. He was born in about 300. He was a student of Rava and Abbaye at Pumbedita. After Rava died, Papa established an academy at Nehardea. His long time friend and associate Rav Huna bar Rav Joshua accompanied him there.

Rav Papa was also a successful businessman. He used his wealth to support poor students and also the poor of the city.

He produced significant legal opinions in the Talmud, but he was also superstitious and this is seen in Pesachim 110a where he describes the powers of demons. He died in about 375.

Pappa, Chanina ben

Chanina ben Pappa was a Palestinian Amora and lived in the third to fourth centuries. He was a younger contemporary of Samuel ben Nahman. He is frequently quoted in the Talmud and Midrash, suggesting he was a person of great learning. He was also associated with Abbahu and Isaac Napacha. Many legends surround his life.

Pedat, Eleazar ben

Eleazar ben Pedat was a Babylonian Amora where he studied under Samuel (Erubin 66a) and under Rav (Hullin 111b). After Rav's death he went to Palestine. He studied further there under Hanina in Sepphoris, and in Caesarea under Hoshayya Rabbah. Many of Eleazar's quotations are in the name of Hanina. He was one of the scholars entrusted with intercalating the calendar. In his later years he was seen as the master legal authority in Palestine and many of his rulings were sent to Babylon. Eleazar was also a prolific aggadist. He died in 279.

Rabbah (Roba, Berabi), Hoshayya

Rabbah was a first generation Palestinian Amora, living in about 200 CE. He wrote a number of baraitot relative to the Mishnah. For many years he lived in Sepphoris. He taught there. Later in life he moved his academy to Caesarea. He was known as the father of the Mishnah, not because he had any role in compiling it, but because of the important role he had in explaining and interpreting it. Most of his haggadic comments are found in Midrash Rabbah. He is also quoted in Genesis Rabbah.

He was in contact with the early Christians, especially Origen who lived in Caesarea.

Rava (Abba bar Yosef bar Chama)

Rava was a great Babylonian Amora born in 270. He married the daughter of Chisda (Hisda). He is one of the most frequently quoted rabbis in the Talmud. He studied at the Pumbedita Academy. His reputation was established because of his famous debates with his good friend and colleague, Abbaye. These debates are classical Talmudic discourse. They almost invariably disagreed and even though Abbaye's opinion is quoted first, the sages ruled in Rava's favor in all but six cases. The reason Abbaye was quoted first was because after Rabbah bar Nahmani died Abbaye became the head of the academy at Pumbedita. At this time Rava went to Mahuza where he opened his own academy.

Rava had two sons who were also great scholars, Rav Joseph and Rav Mesharashay. He died in about 350.

Ravina I

Ravina or Rav Avina was a fifth generation Babylonian Amora. He was the uncle of Ravina II and was his guardian after his father died. Ravina I was a pupil of Raba bar Joseph bar Hama. Even when young Ravina was recognized as a teacher. He was a colleague of Rav Aha with whom he disagreed frequently. Ravina generally gave a more liberal interpretation, and in almost all cases this opinion prevailed.

When Rav Ashi became head of the Academy at Sura, Ravina I became a student there. He participated in the redaction of the Talmud with Rav Ashi and others. He died in about 470.

Ravina II

Ravina II or Ravina bar Huna was a fifth generation Babylonian Amora. He was the nephew of Ravina I. He is most famous for having worked with Rav Ashi to redact the Babylonian Talmud and then to complete this task of editing it after Rav Ashi's death.

He died in 499 and his death marked the end of the Amoraic period.

Safra

Rav Safra was a fourth century Babylonian Amora. He studied under Abbaye and Amni ben Natan. He visited Palestine, studied there and brought the teachings back to Babylon. He was a successful businessman who was known for his honesty. He is quoted in an early post-Talmudic code of law as an example of practicing high business ethics.

Shemuel (Shmuel)

Shemuel was a second / third century (first generation) Babylonian Amora and one of the most famous scholars of his era. His major expertise was in the Torah, especially in the area of monetary law. He also was a physician and astronomer. He was the son of Abba bar Abba. He was known to be liberal in his interpretation of the law. He cared for Yehuda HaNasi when the latter was ill. He also consulted with Rav Nahman bar Yaakov, his most famous student.

Sheshet

Rav Sheshet was a third generation Babylonian Amora during the third century. He first lived in Nehardea and then in Shilhe where he founded an academy. His contemporary with whom he had many opposing halakhic debates was Nahman bar Jacob. He also frequently disagreed with Rav. He relied on the tradition that he knew very well quoting from the Mishnah. He particularly transmitted the sayings of the Tanna, Elazar ben Azariah. He concentrated on biblical exegesis and did not study the aggadah. Some of his Haggadic interpretations have been preserved.

Shila of Kefar Temarta

Shila was a third century Palestinian Amora. An older Babylonian Amora also bore the name Shila and he was therefore differentiated in the Babylonian Talmud, but not the Jerusalem one with the name of his home in Judea. Although he is only mentioned with regard to Talmudic aggadah, he would lecture in public on the halakha, but only the former have been preserved.

Simlai

Simlai was a third century Palestinian Amora, although he was born in Nehardea, Babylonia. His strength was in the aggadah. He was one of the earliest scholars to recognize that the 613 commandments were revealed to Moses at Mount Sinai and that there are 365 negative and 248 positive commandments (Makkot 23b). He stated that these correspond respectively to the days in the year and the bones in the body.

Ulla

Ulla was a third to fourth century Palestinian Amora. He studied under Eleazar II. He transmitted nine of the latter's halakhic teachings. He also transmitted teachings of several other rabbis. His teachings in turn were transmitted by Aba bar Adda. He frequently visited Babylonia where he was invited to speak. He followed a strict interpretation of the halakha. He commented in the Talmud on Jesus' crucifixion.

Post-Talmudic Sages

Aaron of Pesaro

Very little is known about Aaron of Pesaro, a rabbi and author. He possibly lived in Germany somewhere after 1400. However, his name, "of Pesaro", indicates a significant Italian connection. He is best known for his work *"Toledot Aharon"*. The title is taken from Numbers 3:1, "The Generations of Aaron". Aaron died prior to its publication, which was in 1583.

Aaron, Samuel ben, of Schlettstadt

Samuel ben Aaron was born in Schlettstadt, Germany in the second half of the fourteenth century and lived in Strasburg, where he was the head of a major yeshiva. Because of a conflict with certain members of this community, he was nearly killed by the knights of Andlau, but managed to flee, ultimately arriving in Babylonia for a while. He then returned to Germany, but in a subsequent massacre of the Jews of Strasburg he was probably killed as well.

He is known for his abridgement of Mordechai ben Hillel's *Sefer HaMordekai*. It was called *Kizzur Mordekai* or *Mordekai HaKaton*. In his work he changed some of the content of Hillel's work and therefore it was considered an independent work by which it was quoted. Israel Bruna and Israel Isserlein quoted from it. Jacob Weil and Jacob Moelin also quoted from it.

Abel, Solomon ben Kalman HaLevi

Solomon Abel was born in Novomyesto-Sugin (Neustadt) in the district of Rossieny, Kovno, Russia (Lithuania) in 1857 and died in 1886. He was one of the founders of the famous Telz Yeshiva and his success there as a teacher made it one of the highest-ranking educational institutions of Lithuania.

He is known for his posthumously published work *Beit Shlomo* which was considered an outstanding literary work applying rabbinic ideas for then current everyday life and business. It was written for popular use.

Aboab (Abuhab), Isaac (Menorat HaMaor)

Isaac Aboab was a Talmudic scholar in the fourteenth century, living in Spain. He is also known by his pen name of Menorat HaMaor. He combined philosophy with rabbinical knowledge in his writings and quoted from Aristotle and Plato. His writings were aimed at the average reader with a view to making the knowledge easily accessible to lay people.

He wrote three books, *Menorat HaMaor*, *Aron HaEdut* (The Ark of Testimony) and *Shulkhan HaPanim* (Table of Showbread).

Aboab, Isaac

Isaac Aboab was born in Toledo in 1433. He is a different Isaac from Menorat HaMaor. He was a pupil of Isaac Companton. With the expulsion order of 1492 he went with thirty other respected Jews to the king of Portugal to negotiate permission for Jews to settle there. He and his companions were allowed to settle in Porto.

He was the author of a super-commentary on Nahmanides' Pentateuch commentary and also a super-commentary on Rashi's Pentateuch commentary. He died in 1493 a few months after going to Portugal.

Aboab, Samuel (Rasha)

Samuel Aboab was born in Venice in 1610. At age thirteen he became a pupil of David Franco, whose daughter he later married. He was appointed the rabbi of Verona where he gained a reputation. At this stage he became known as Rasha, based on the initials of his Hebrew name. He was also accomplished in other languages besides Hebrew. In 1650 he became the rabbi of Venice. He became involved in the controversy of Shabbetai Tzvi.

A number of personal misfortunes struck him in his old age, forcing him to temporarily leave Venice, but was allowed to return there shortly before his death.

He was the author of two works. *Devar Shemuel* was a collection of rabbinical decisions. *Sefer HaZikranot*, which was published anonymously, was a treatise on ethical conduct. He died in Venice in 1694.

Abraham, Isaac ben, of Dampierre

Isaac ben Abraham is known by the acronym of RIBA. He was the brother of Rabbi Samson ben Abraham of Sens. He grew up in Troyes. After the death of the head of the school, Isaac ben Abraham became head of the school at Dampierre. He died there in 1210.

He wrote tosafot to several Talmudic treatises, one that was well known, was on Berakhot. He is also known as a biblical commentator and his ritual decisions and responsa were quoted by other Talmudists.

Abraham, Jonah, of Gerona

A fourteenth century rabbi who wrote *Sefer haYashar*, a book that a number of authors, as well as a midrashic work of unknown origin, used the same title.

Abraham, Obadiah ben, of Bertinoro

Obadiah ben Abraham was born in the second half of the fifteenth century where he spent most of his life. He was the rabbi of Bertinoro and Castello. He immigrated to Israel in 1488, living in Jerusalem. Rabbi Abraham was a pupil of Rabbi Joseph Colon Trabotto.

In Jerusalem, he encouraged the study of Talmud and other rabbinic literature among the youth. After the expulsion of Jews from Spain in 1492, many fled to Jerusalem and Abraham became their leader. He founded the first yeshiva in Palestine one thousand years after the extinction of the previous one there.

Bertinoro is best known as a commentator of the Mishnah. Almost all editions of the Mishnah contain his commentaries. It is based mainly on

Rashi and the Rambam (Nahmanides). He is also the author of a supercommentary on Rashi and had some liturgical productions. He died in Jerusalem in 1500.

Abraham, Samson ben, of Sens

Samson ben Abraham of Sens was born about 1150. He was also known as the Rash of Sens. He was one of the leading Tosafists of this period and the student and spiritual heir of the Ri. He was born in Falaise, Calvados where his grandfather, Samson ben Joseph, the Tosafist lived.

Abraham studied under Rabbeinu Tam (Rabbi Jacob ben Meir), David ben Kalonymus of Munzenberg, and attended the yeshiva of the Ri (Rabbi Isaac ben Samuel) for ten years. He took an opposing view, together with Rabbi Meir Abulafia, over the Rambam's rationalistic views on bodily resurrection and Talmudic Haggadah, as well as some of his halakhic views.

As a result of papal persecution by Innocent III, he immigrated with 300 other rabbis to Palestine in 1211.

Abraham was the author of many tosafot that were later abridged by Elezar of Touques. He also was the author of commentaries on the Mishnaic orders Zeraim and Tohorot. Reference is made to him in the Jerusalem Talmud. He also wrote a commentary on the Sifra. He died in Acre about 1250.

Abravanel, Isaac ben Judah

Rabbi Don Isaac ben Judah or Yitzhak ben Yehuda Abravanel was the scion of an aristocratic Sephardi family known as Abravanel, Abrabanel or Abarbanel. He was born in Lisbon in 1437.

He is referred today as "The Abarbanel". After completing his study with Joseph Chaim, he spent his early years on Jewish philosophy. He became the treasurer of King Alfonso V of Portugal. He used his great family wealth to help secure the release of Jewish inhabitants of Arzila in Morocco, after they were sold into slavery by the Moors. After this monarch's death, he was accused by King John II of involvement in conspiracy with the Duke of Braganza and was forced to flee to Castile in 1483, his personal fortune having been confiscated.

In Toledo he devoted himself to biblical studies and produced commentaries on books of the prophets. After the Jews were banished from Spain in 1492 he went to Naples, where he served the king until that city was taken by the French forcing him to flee with the king to Messina in 1495, then went on to Corfu, then Monopoli and finally to Venice in 1503.

His writings covered three general themes. In the field of exegesis he composed commentaries on the book of Prophets, especially on the books of Kings then on Deuteronomy and later on the other books of the Torah. His works on philosophy dealt with the sciences and in the area of apologetics he defended the Jewish concept of the Messiah. He died in Venice in 1508, but was buried in Padua next to Rabbi Judah Minz.

Abuchatzeirah, Harav Yisrael

A Sephardic Talmudist, Yisrael Abuchatzeirah was born in Tafillalt, Morocco in 1890. When still young he had established for himself a reputation and people used to come to him for his blessings. He thus became known as "Baba Sali" (our praying father). He came from a family of kabbalists and was himself very knowledgeable in this area.

He became Rosh Yeshiva at nineteen after his father's death (Rav Massoud). When most of the Moroccan Jewry emigrated to Israel after the second world war, Abuchatzeirah also followed in 1964 settling in Yavne. In 1970 he moved to Netivot, where he was consulted by Sephardim, Ashkenazim and Hassidim. He had a close relationship with the Lubavitcher Rebbe.

Although he gave many lectures on Torah and kabbalah he did not permit his students to write down his teachings. Thus there is nothing from him in written form. He died in 1984.

Abudraham (Aburdaham), David ben Joseph ben David

David Abudraham was a rishon who lived in Seville Spain probably in the fourteenth or early fifteenth centuries. He is thought by Azulai to have been a student of the Ba'al HaTurim (Jacob ben Asher), however, it has been argued otherwise. He is known for his commentary on the Synagogue liturgy, published as a book, popularly called *Sefer Abudraham*, although the official title seems to be *Tzibbur Perush HaBerakhot ve-ha-Tefillot* (Commentary on the Blessings and the Prayers). His goal for this book was to allow the population to use the liturgy intelligently. It was an important and comprehensive work in the history of prayer and the meaning and laws of tefilah.

Abulafia, Abraham ben Samuel

Abulafia was born in Saragosa, Spain in 1240 and died just after 1290 on the Maltese archipeligo. His parents took him to Tudela, near Navarre where he studied Bible and Talmud with his father. After his father died when Abraham was eighteen years old he wandered through different countries, including Palestine, Capua and then returned to Spain. He immersed himself in kabbalah and studied *Sefer Yetzirah* and its commentaries. This book had a great influence on him and his kabbalistic views.

He again left Spain and went to Greece where he wrote the first of his prophetic books, *Sefer HaYashar* in 1279. In 1280 he went to Rome with a mission to convert the Pope! He next went to Sicily. Abulafia had prophetic and messianic visions there, but his conduct was condemned by Rabbi Solomon ben Aderet. He wrote two further works on Comino near Malta, *Sefer HaOt* (The Book of the Sign) between 1285-1288 and in 1291 he wrote his last book, *Imrei Shefer* (Words of Beauty).

Abulafia called his kabbalistic system a prophetic kabbalah. His influence on kabbalah was felt to be of retarding nature.

Abulafia, Meir ben Todros HaLevi (Ramah)

Abulafia was also known as the Ramah. Abulafia was a significant Sephardic Talmudist and halakhic authority who lived in Spain from 1170 to 1244. He was of the famous wealthy and scholarly family, whose rabbinic descendants had an impact from the sixteenth through to the nineteenth centuries. He was the most well-known Spanish rabbi of the first half of the thirteenth century. When still only in his thirties he was appointed to the Toledo Beth Din. He played an important role in establishing ritual regulations for Spanish Jewry.

He is probably best known as being one of the first to oppose Maimonides' disbelief in physical resurrection.

He wrote extensively on subjects to do with the Talmud, various responsa, a poem and a book of regulations on writing a Torah.

Aceda, Shmuel

Shmuel Aceda was born in 1538. In 1578 he became the head of a major yeshiva in Safed, known for its Talmud and kabbalah study. He was the author of a classic commentary on *Pirkei Avot*, titled *Midrash Shmuel*. He died in 1602.

Adarbi (Adribi), Isaac

Isaac Adarbi was born in about 1510 and was a student of Rabbi Joseph Taitatzak. He was the preacher to the Shalom Congregation in Salonika during most of his career. He wrote a work of 430 responsa called *Divrei Rivot*, His *Divrei Shalom* consisted of thirty sermons and commentaries on the weekly Pentateuch readings.

Adeni, Solomon ben Joshua (M'Lekhet Shlomo)

Solomon ben Joshua lived in the first half of the seventeenth century in Saana and Aden in Southern Arabia, from where he got his name Adeni. He moved to Palestine where he spent most of his time in Hebron. He was a Talmudist and author. He was a pupil of Bezalel Ashkenazi and the kabbalist Hayyim Vital. Either in 1622 or 1624 he wrote a commentary on the Mishnah, called *M'lekhet Shlomo* (The Work of Solomon), only small portions of which have been published. It was first printed in the Vilna-Romm editions of the Mishnah. His analysis of the Mishnah is quite modern and scientific in its approach. Menasseh ben Israel made use of it in the latter's edition of the Mishnah in 1632.

Adeni also wrote *Dibre Emet* (Words of Truth) that according to Azulai contain notes on the Mesorah. This latter work has been lost.

Aderet, Shlomo ben (Rashba)

Known as the Rashba, Aderet lived all his life in Barcelona, Spain. He was born in 1235. His reputation is based on being a Talmudist who wrote a prolific number of responsa on halakha. He was considered one of the greatest of Rishonim.

Aderet was a student of the Ramban (Nahmanides) and taught Rabbi Yom Tov ibn Asevilli (Ritva). He also wrote a work on kashrut and other religious laws to be observed in the home titled *Torat HaBayit*. Aderet died in 1310.

Alami, Solomon

Solomon Alami was an author who lived in Portugal during the fourteenth and fifteenth centuries. He wrote an ethical work titled *Iggeret Mussar*. It was written in the form of a letter to one of his disciples. He believed that the persecutions that befell the Jews of Spain were as a result of their religious and moral decadence. He precedes each section of the work with a related biblical verse.

Alashkar, Moses ben Isaac

Moses Alashkar was a prominent rabbi who lived from the late fifteenth into the sixteenth centuries in Italy. His two most important works are *Hassagot* (Critical Notes) in which he argues against the theme of Shem Tov ibn Shem Tov's book *Sefer HaEmunot*. The second work is a collection of 121 of his responsa. They were printed in Italy and used in many distant Jewish communities.

Albo, Joseph

Joseph Albo was a Spanish rabbi during the fifteenth century, living probably in the town of Monreal in Aragon. He was probably born in the late thirteen hundreds. He is known best for his work on the Jewish principles of faith – "*Ikkarim*". This was first published at Soncino under the title "*Ohel Ya'acov*" in 1485 and again in 1584 in Freiburg and in 1618 in Venice. It was translated into German in 1844. All these editions had commentaries or introductions in them by others.

This book summed up his own personal philosophy and principles of faith. Albo believed there were three fundamental principles of faith: 1. The belief in the existence of God; 2. The belief in revelation; and 3. The belief in divine justice, as related to the idea of mortality. These selections were made with the idea of correcting Maimonides' scheme on these aspects that seemed to support Christian contentions. He died in approximately 1430.

Albargeloni, Isaac ben Reuben

Isaac ben Reuben Albargeloni was born in Barcelona in 1043. He was a Talmudist and liturgics poet. His grandson was Nahmanides. He wrote commentaries to several sections of the tractate Ketubot. His most famous liturgical poem is *Azharot*.

Alegri, Abraham

Abraham Alegri was a sixteenth to seventeenth century rabbi who lived in Constantinople. He wrote a commentary on Maimonides' *Sefer HaMitzvot* titled *Lev Sameach*. He also wrote a work of responsa with the same title. He died in 1652.

Alfasi, Yitzhak ben Yaakov HaKohen (RIF)

Rabbi Alfasi, also known by the acronym of RIF (Rabbi Isaac Fasi) was born in Kalat ibn Hamad, near Fez in North Africa in 1013. He was one of the greatest and most well-known of codifiers of the halakha. Alfasi or Alfes implies an inhabitant of Fez. He was a student of the RaN (Rabbi Nissim ben Reuven of Girona) and Rabbi Hananel in Kirwan near Fez. He was considered a second generation Rishon after the Geonic era had ended. At the age of 75 he was forced to flee from Fez to Spain, because of groundless accusations of being a traitor. There he established a Yeshiva at Lucena, succeeding Rabbi Yitzhak ibn Giyyat. One of his students was Rabbi Joseph ibn Migash.

Alfasi's great work was his "*Halachoth*", known as the "*Alfes*" or "*RIF*" which abbreviates and follows the Mishnaic tractates, but restricts itself to the practical rulings and laws in the Mishnah. Thus it is restricted to that portion of the Talmud which has only post-Temple relevance and therefore deals with only three of the six orders and several other tractates. In the presence of the large amount of information from both the Jerusalem and the Babylonian Talmuds, as well as the Geonic work, Alfasi had to decide on conflicting opinions. Using the rules for decision making in the Talmud as well as later authorities, Alfasi made his determinations. Although he frequently quoted the Jerusalem Talmud, Alfasi usually followed the Babylonian Talmud when there was a conflict.

His work was widely accepted and became the basis for future codes of law. Maimonides, who was a pupil of Rabbi Migash, spoke of the RIF as "my teacher". Rabbi Joseph Caro, centuries later used the Alfes, in combination with Maimonides' and Asher ben Yechiel's (the Rosh) as the fundamental sources of his own great code of law. The first printed edition appeared in Constantinople in 1509. The best edition was printed in Wilno by Romm in 1881 and now appears in standard editions of the Talmud. He died in 1103.

Algazi, Yom Tov

Algazi was born in 1727. He was a kabbalist and student of Shalom Sharabi (Rashash). He wrote several books on Jewish law. Algazi studied at the famous Beit El Synagogue, also known as the Midrashim Hassidim or Yeshivat haMekubalim in Jerusalem. He is buried on the Mount of Olives close to the grave of the Rashash. He died in Jerusalem in 1802.

Alharizi (al-Harizi), Judah ben Solomon

Judah Alharizi was a Spanish rabbi, born in 1160, translator and poet who lived in Spain. He was a rationalist and translated some of Maimonides' work. He wrote his own poetic work, *Takhemoni*, which is written in a witty style using scriptural verse. It contains fifty chapters. He died in 1230.

Alkabetz, Solomon ben Moses HaLevi

Solomon Alkabetz was born about 1505 and made his way towards the Land of Israel in 1529. He went to Safed in 1535 where he met Joseph Caro and was probably instrumental in the latter's development of kabbalah. He is most famous for being the author of the *Lecha Dodi*, the prayer chanted during the Sabbath Eve service.

Although little is known about details of his life, he wrote extensively both from the Bible and of a kabbalistic nature. Very little of these survive.

He is attributed with starting the ritual of going out into the fields just before Erev Shabbat to welcome the *Shechinah* or the Sabbath bride. His brother-in-law and disciple was Moses Cordovero.

Alkali, Judah ben Solomon Chai

Rabbi Alkali was a Sephardi rabbi born in 1798. He studied in Jerusalem and was influenced by kabbalah. He became the rabbi in Semlin, Croatia. He is known for his promoting the return of the Jews to Palestine and hence was a precursor of modern Zionism. Theodor Herzl's grandfather attended his synagogue and the two were friendly.

His major work was *Goral la-Adonai*. It was published in Vienna in 1857. It was a treatise on the restoration of the Jews in Palestine. It was both religiously based as well as practical. His *Shalom Yerushalayim* was a response to the critics of his first book. He died in 1878.

Almosnino, Joseph

Joseph was the son of Isaac and the grandson of Moses ben Baruch Almosnino. He was born in 1642 and lived in Belgrade, Serbia. He authored many responsa that were published by his son, Isaac, in Constantinople in 1711 and titled *Edut bi-Yehosef*. Joseph died in Nikolsburg, Moravia in 1689.

Almosnino, Moses ben Baruch

Moses Almosnino was born in Thessalonika in about 1515. He became the rabbi of the Neveh Shalom community of Spanish Jews in that city in 1553. He wrote a lengthy commentary on the biblical "Five Rolls" – the books of Ruth, Lamentations, Canticles, Esther and Ecclesiastes called *Yede Mosheh*. His *Pirkei Moshe* was on the Talmudic tractate Avot. His *Meammez Koah* was a collection of his sermons. He died in Constantinople in 1580.

Alshich, Moshe

Rabbi Moshe Alshich was born in Adrianople, Turkey in 1508, but spent most of his life in Safed. He studied with Joseph Caro in Adrianople, by whom he was ordained, and with Yosef Taitatzak in Salonica. He went to Israel with Rabbi Caro.

Alshich was most well-known as a great sermonizer. These sermons were compiled into a book, *Torat Moshe* based on the Torah. Among his most famous students was Rabbi Hayyim Vital. Alshich also served on the rabbinical council of Safed. He died in 1593.

Alter, Avraham Mordechai (Imrei Emes)

Avraham Alter was born on December 25, 1866. He succeeded his father Aryeh Leib as the third Gerrer Rebbe from 1905 until his death on June 3, 1948. He was also known by the title of his book on the Torah, the *Imrei Emes*. In Poland he was influential in establishing the Agudat Israel movement, which was the political arm of Ashkenazi Torah Judaism (a Judaism based on strict adherence to the Torah mitzvot and halakha) in Eastern Europe. He promoted setting up Talmud Torah schools as well. He had eight children by his first marriage and after his wife died, he remarried in 1922 and had another child, Pinchas Menachem.

In 1940, he managed to escape from Poland to Palestine with several of his sons where he started rebuilding the Ger dynasty. He died during the siege of Jerusalem in 1948.

Alter, Pinchas Menachem (Pnei Menachem)

Pinchas Menachem was born in Falenits, near Warsaw on June 9, 1926. He came from a long line of Ger Hassidic Jews in Poland. He was also known as the Pnei Menachem after his Torah work. He escaped with his extended family from the Holocaust to Palestine and after World War II, he married his cousin Tsippora Alter. They had seven children.

In the 1950s he was appointed Rosh Yeshiva of Sfas Emes. In 1992 he became the sixth rebbe of this largest Hassidic group in Israel. He was very active politically. He authored a work on the Torah called *Pnei Menachem*. He died on March 7, 1996.

Alter, Simchah Bunim (Lev Simcha)

Simchah Bunim Alter was born on April 6, 1898. With his family he fled from Poland during the Holocaust and went to Palestine. He was a Ger Hassid and was the fifth rebbe in Israel from 1977 to 1992, having succeeded his brother Yisrael. Once the State of Israel was founded the Ger Hassidim grew rapidly. Like his brother he was also active politically leading the Agudat Israel of the Israel party, whose interest in parliament was Haredi Judaism in the Jewish state. He instituted the daily learning of a page of Talmud, similar to the Daf Yomi of the Babylonian Talmud.

He wrote a work on Torah titled *Lev Simcha*, by which he was also known. Alter died on August 6, 1992. After his death he was buried in the cave of the Gerrer Rebbes on the Mount of Olives cemetery.

Alter, Yaakov Aryeh

He was born in Lodz Poland in 1939 and is the seventh rebbe of the Gerrer Hassidim in Israel. He succeeded his uncle, Pinchas Menachem. His major contribution in the movement has been the introduction of significant innovations into the curricula offered by the Gerrer Hassidim, opting for a broader expanse of Talmudic study, rather than focusing in-depth in narrow areas of study. He and his wife have nine children.

Alter, Yehuda Aryeh Leib (Sfas Emes)

He was the son of Rabbi Abraham Mordechai Alter of the Ger Hassidim dynasty. He was born in 1847 in Gor Kalwaria (Ger), Poland. He was also known as the Sfas Emes after the name of his book. At age nineteen he became the head of the Beth Din after the death of his grandfather.

He was known for his biblical interpretations that were recorded in his book *Sfas Emes al HaTorah*. There is a project underway to translate it into English. He died in 1905.

Alter, Yisrael (Beis Yisrael)

Rabbi Yisrael Alter was born on October 12, 1895 in Gora Kalwaria (Ger for short) in Poland. He escaped from there and went to Palestine in 1940, but his wife and children were killed in the Holocaust. He remarried but had no further children. In 1948 he became the sixth rebbe of the dynasty on the death of his father Avraham Mordechai Alter. He became very active politically in the Agudat Israel to further the Haredi causes in the State of Israel. His work on the Torah was called *Beis Israel*. He died on February 20, 1977.

Alter, Yitzhak Myer (Chiddushei Harim)

Yitzhak Myer was the founder of the Ger Hassidic dynasty. He was also known alternatively as Rothenburg. He was born in 1799. He was the founder of the Ger Hassidic dynasty within Hassidic Judaism. The term Ger is an abbreviation for the town from where he lived, Gora Kalwaria in Poland, although he was born in Magnuszew, Poland. He was of a long line of distinguished rabbis, dating his ancestry back to Rashi and Rabbi Meir ben Baruch of Rothenburg. His work on the Torah was titled Chiddushei Harim, by which he was also known. He was also referred to as Reb Itche Myer by his followers. He was a disciple of Rabbi Menachem Mendel of Kotzk (The Kotzker Rebbe), later becoming his brother-in-law. He died on March 10, 1866.

Altschul, Naphtali (Hirsch) ben Asher

Naphtali Altschul lived in Russia and Poland towards the end of the sixteenth and early seventeenth centuries. He traveled widely and in 1607 was in Constantinople.

He wrote two works. The first was titled *Ayyalah SheluHah* (A Swift Deer) that was a commentary on the Prophets and Writings (Nevi'im and Ketuvim). His second work was titled *Imrei Shefer* (Beautiful Words) which listed alphabetically all matters likely to be discussed by rabbis in their sermons.

Altshuler (Altshul), David ben Aryeh Loeb

David Altshuler lived in the latter part of the seventeenth century in Prague. He wrote a commentary on Nevi'im and Ketuvim (The Prophets and The Writings). It was titled *Metsudot* and consists of two components: *Metsudot Zion* (Fortress of Zion) that is a glossary of difficult words and completed and edited by his son Jehiel (Yehiel) Hillel ben David Altshuler. Many editions of these works were published.

Amnon of Mainz (Mayence)

Rabbi Amnon is the subject of a medieval legend related to the origin of the Rosh Hashanah and Yom Kippur prayer "*U-netanneh Tokef*". The story behind this prayer relative to this legendary figure, Rabbi Amnon, is that he was a wealthy and respected Jew of Mainz, who refused to convert to Christianity, but one day under pressure from the Archbishop, he asked for three days to consider this. Relenting his momentary indecision he did not appear before the Archbishop who then had him brought before him and as a punishment cut off both his hands and feet. This occurred on Rosh Hashanah. Rabbi Amnon then asked to be taken to the synagogue where he then recited this prayer just before the Kedushah. He then died and his body disappeared. However, three days later he re-appeared in a dream to Rabbi Kalonymus (Meshullam ben Kalonymus) and taught him the dream, asking him to spread it. This story appears in a Mahzor published in 1541.

Anaw / Anav Family

The Anav family, which was known as the Anaw family in Rome, was an ancient Italian Jewish family. According to their tradition they were one of four aristocratic Jewish families deported to Rome at the time of the destruction of the Second Temple. They founded a yeshiva in Rome in the eighth century together with the Kalonymus family. In the ninth century the latter family moved to Germany. Yechiel ben Abraham Anaw / Anav was the head of the yeshiva in the mid-eleventh century. His son Nathan wrote the *Arukh*. His other sons, Daniel and Abraham were also Talmudic scholars. Tzidikayah ben Avraham Anav HaRofei wrote glosses to the Talmud. There were a number of other members of the family as well.

Anaw (Anav), Benjamin ben Abraham

Benjamin Anaw was a thirteenth century liturgical poet, Talmudist and commentator who lived in Rome. He was the elder brother of Zedekiah ben Abraham Anaw. He also had a great knowledge of mathematics and astronomy. He began writing liturgical poetry after Pope Gregory IX ordered the destruction of many Talmudic manuscripts in Paris and Rome. Many of his poems formed part of the Roman mahzor, part of which is still extant in manuscript form.

Anaw (Anav), Nathan ben Jehiel (Yechiel)

Nathan ben Jehiel was born in Rome, probably about 1035. He belonged to a famous Roman family of scholars. He first studied under his father, Rabbi Jehiel ben Abraham and then went to Sicily to study under Mazliah ibn al-Bazak, who had just returned from Pumbedita where he in turn studied under Hai Gaon. In this way Nathan obtained his Babylonian knowledge. He then went to Kerwan in North Africa and studied under Chananel ben Chushiel and Nissim ben Jacob Gaon. After that he went to Narbonne and studied under Moses HaDarshan. He returned to Rome and after the death of his father in 1070, Nathan and his two brothers, Daniel and Abraham became co-presidents of the rabbinic college.

He had a sad personal life. Four of his five sons died when young.

He is known for his famous work the *Arukh*. He drew on numerous sources to compile it, much based on his teachers work. It is a lexicon. It contains many old readings, interpretations as well as titles of old, mostly lost books. It also contained, and therefore preserved, old rabbinic works of great value. This work, together with Alfasi's code and Rashi's commentary, contributed to the spread of rabbinic study. Jehiel died in 1106.

Anaw (Anav), Zedekiah ben Abraham

Anaw was the younger brother of Benjamin. He received his training in both Rome and Germany. His reputation is based on his great work, while not original, was a compilation on the ritual. It was titled *Shibbole HaLeket* ("Ears of Gleaning"). It is divided into twelve sections, consisting of 372 paragraphs. Added to the work are several treatises and responsa on various religious and legal matters. A complete edition of the book was published by Solomon Buber in Vilna in 1886.

Ankava, Abraham

Abraham Ankava lived in the nineteenth century, probably in Italy. In 1871 he published a collection of responsa in Leghorn (Livorno) titled *Kerem Hemed*.

Arama, Isaac ben Moses (Ba'al Akedah)

Arama was a Spanish rabbi and author born in about 1420. He first headed the rabbinical assembly in Zamora. He then became the rabbi at Tarragona and then at Fraga in Aragon. He finally became the rabbi and head of the Talmudic Academy in Calatyaud. After the expulsion of the Jews from Spain in 1492 he settled in Naples where he died.

Arama is most well known for his works on the Tanakh. He is known for his work on the Akedat Yitzhak (*Sefer HaAkedah*) and is therefore referred to as the Ba'al Akedah. He wrote a commentary on the five books of the Torah and a commentary on proverbs called *Yad Absholom*.

He was the classical fifteenth century Spanish-Jewish Scholar. He commented on Maimonides and wanted to pay more attention to the synagogue services, so as to possibly change their format. He died in 1494.

Asevilli, Yom Tov Ibn (Ritva)

Rabbi Yom Tov Ibn Asevilli, also known as the Ritva lived in Spain from the second half of the thirteenth century to the first half of the fourteenth century. He was the rabbi and head of the Yeshiva of Seville. "Asevilli "is sometimes pronounced as "Ishbilil" meaning "from Seville." He was the leading student of the Rashba (Shlomo ben Aderet).

Asher, Aaron ben Moses ben

Aaron ben Moses ben Asher was from a long family of Masoretes. He lived in Tiberias in the tenth century. His father, Moses ben Asher was responsible for the Cairo Codex of the Prophets.

Shlomo ben Baya'a was the scribe for this most authoritative Masoretic text of the Hebrew Bible that has now come to be known as the *Aleppo Codex*. However, it was Aaron ben Moses ben Asher who was responsible for refining the Tiberian system of vowels. He added these vowels to this text as well the cantillation notes which are still in use.

Maimonides, in writing his *Mishneh Torah*, relied on this Codex. He had great confidence in it because according to him it was worked on, analyzed and proofread many times over the years by this famous Masorete.

Asher was also the first grammarian of the Hebrew language. His *Sefer Dikdukei HaTe'amim* ("Grammar of the Vocalizations") consisted of grammatical principles and masoretic information. He had a major influence on subsequent biblical grammar and scholarly work.

Asher, who died about 960, was thought to have been a Karaite.

Asher, Bahya (Bachya) ben (Rabbeinu Behaye)

Bahya or Bachya ben Asher, or Bahye ben Asher ben Halawa, also known as Rabbeinu Behaye (Bachya) was born in the mid-thirteenth century in Saragossa. He ranks among the most distinguished of biblical commentators in Spain and was also noted for introducing kabbalah into Torah study. In this aspect he followed and used as his role model Nahmanides (Moses ben Nahman). Asher was a pupil of Rabbi Shlomo ben Aderet (the Rashba) who in turn was a student of Nahmanides.

Bahya is best known for his commentary on the Torah, *Midrash Rabbeinu Bachya*, that is extant and has been translated into English. A number of commentaries on his work have also been written. The first printing of his work was in Naples in 1492. He wrote several other works titled *Kad HaKemah* ("Receptacle of the Flour"), *Shulkhan Arba* ("Table of Four"), probably *Hoshen HaMishpat* ("Breastplate of Judgment") and *Ohel Moed*. Several other works have been erroneously attributed to him. He died in 1340.

Asher, Jacob ben (Ba'al HaTurim, The Tur)

Jacob ben Asher was a famous Talmudic authority and was from a family of accomplished Talmudists. He was born in 1270. He was not born in Spain but went there from Germany with his family at a young age. His father and main teacher was Rabbi Asher ben Jehiel (Rosh). It is not certain whether he or his brother Judah ben Asher, succeeded their father as head of the Jewish community of Toledo (Zacuto). Due to his dual Ashkenazi and Sephardi backgrounds he could give a wider range of interpretations of customs and halakha than most others.

Asher is known for his famous work on halakha, *Arba'ah Turim*, after which he was known as the Ba'al HaTurim or more frequently just the Tur. He also authored several other works, *Sefer HaRemazim* or *Kitzur Piske HaRosh*, *Rimze Ba'al HaTurim* and *Perush Al HaTorah*.

Joseph Caro's work, *Beit Yosef* is a commentary of the *Arba'ah Turim*. Other commentaries of ben Asher's main work were by Rabbi Joel Sirkis (*Bayit Chadash*), Moses Isserles (*Darkhei Moshe*), Joshua Falk (*Beit Yisrael / Perishah u-Derishah*) as well as works of other Acharonim. Most of these defend the views of ben Asher against Caro. He died in 1343 while on a visit to the Island of Chios off the coast of Turkey.

Ashkenazi, Bezalel

Descended from a German family, Bezalel Ashkenazi was born probably in Palestine in the sixteenth century. He spent most of his life though in Egypt where he was educated in Talmud by David ben Solomon ibn Abi Zimra and Israel de Curial. He was one of the most highly regarded Talmudic scholars of the Orient and counted among his disciples Isaac Luria and Solomon Adeni. In 1587 he moved to Palestine and settled in Jerusalem. The situation was bad for Jews at that time and it was mainly due to his efforts that the congregations did not dissolve. He managed to get the Ashkenazi Jews to support the taxes in Jerusalem and so relieve the burden on the impoverished Sephardi Jews there. Unfortunately after Ashkenazi's death, this solution disintegrated.

Ashkenazi is best known for being the author of *Shittah Mekubetzet*, that was a commentary on the Talmud, consisting of collection of glosses on most of the Talmud. It combined his own original material plus that of others. These are Nahmanides, Shlomo ben Aderet and Yom-Tov of Seville (Asevilli) and the Frenchmen Abraham ben David, Baruch ben Samuel, Isaac of Chinon and others.

Ashkenazi, Gershon

Gershon Ashkenazi was a Polish rabbi who was born, probably in Cracow, in the second decade of the seventeenth century. He studied under Joel Sirkis and Joshua Harif. He was the rabbi respectively of Prossnitz, Hanau, and Nikolsburg. Then he went on to Vienna and finally Metz.

During his lifetime he became a recognized authority on Talmudic lore and was consulted from afar. His influence was significant. He was also a highly respected teacher. Ashkenazi died in 1693.

He wrote *Avodat HaGershuni*, which was a series of 124 responsa. These provide much information on the lives and conditions of the Polish Jews of that time, especially after the Cossack persecutions. *Tifferet HaGershuni* consisted of Midrashic and kabbalistic discussions on the Pentateuch. *Hiddushe HaGershuni* consists of explanations of the third and fourth parts of the *Shulkhan Arukh, Even HaEzer* and *Choshen Mishpat*.

Ashkenazi, Mordechai ben Hillel (or Mordechai ben Hillel)

He is often referred to just as Mordechai ben Hillel. He was from a family of famous scholars, including Rabbi Eliezer ben Joel HaLevi and Rabbi Jehiel. He was born in 1250 and died in 1298. He spent most of his life in Nuremberg, Germany. He was a disciple of Rabbi Meir of Rothenburg. He also studied with Rabbi Abraham ben Baruch, the brother of Meir of Rothenburg and Rabbi Jehiel ben Joseph of Paris. He also spent time with rabbis Ephraim ben Nathan, Jacob HaLevi of Speyer and Dan Ashkenazi.

After the death of Emperor Rudolf of Hapsburg, disorder ruled and many Jewish communities were attacked. In the town of Sinzig, seventy-two Jews were locked in the synagogue which was burnt. In response to this Rabbi Mordechai wrote Lamentations, which included the Selichot to mourn the death of the martyrs.

A fanatical anti-Semite, Rindfleisch, head of a band of ruffians, attacked many towns in southern Germany, leaving thousands of Jews dead in his path. When he attacked Nuremberg in 1298, Rabbi Mordechai ben Hillel, his wife and five children were murdered.

Mordechai ben Hillel is well known for his work *Sefer Hamordechai* or in abbreviated form *The Mordechai* that was published posthumously by his disciples. It was included in the first printed Talmud and Joseph Caro and Moses Isserles drew heavily upon it for their works. Super-Commentaries were written on *The Mordechai*, of which the most famous one was *Gedulath Mordechai* (The Greatness of Mordechai) by Rabbi Baruch ben David.

Ashkenazi, Moses

Moses Ashkenazi or Moses Germanus was born with the name of Johann Peter Spaeth and converted to Judaism. He was born in the first half of the seventeenth century. He was raised a Catholic, converted to Lutheranism and then returned to Catholicism. However, doubts about the church remained with him. He studied Hebrew, kabbalah, finally renounced Christianity and then vehemently attacked it.

His publications were many. The first ones were obviously of a Christian content, but his later ones included translations of Judah HaLevi's (Judah ben Samuel) poem *"Mi Kamoka"*. He died in 1701 in Vienna.

Ashkenazi, Tzvi Hirsch ben Yaakov (Chacham Tzvi)

He was born in 1656, a descendant of a well-known line of rabbis. He studied in Salonica under Elihu Cobo. After that he studied for a while in Constantinople. After the death of his wife and child when the Austrians invaded Alt-Ofen in 1686, he fled to Sarajevo for a few years and then went to Germany. There he married the daughter of Meshullam Zalman Mirles Neumark, the chief rabbi of a German region. By 1710 he had moved to Amsterdam where he was appointed the chief rabbi of the Ashkenazi congregation. Because of his independent personality he soon came into conflict with the leaders there. By 1714 he had gone to London where he had many Ashkenazi friends. Finally in 1717 he became the rabbi in Lemberg, but died four months later.

Ashkenazi was a keen intellect, who did not have time for the wealthy. He was held in high regard. His work, *Responsa Chacham Tzvi*, represented only a portion of his responsa. It was first published in 1712 in Amsterdam. They have been frequently re-published.

Ashkenazi, Yehuda ben Shimon

Rabbi Yehuda ben Shimon Ashkenazi was born in Germany in 1730 and died in 1770. He wrote *Be'er Heitiv* ("Explain Well") that consists of summaries of halakhic rulings and responsa relative to decisions made from the *Shulkhan Arukh*. It concentrates on the *Orach Chaim* and the *Even HaEzer*.

Ashkenazi, Yisroel ben Shmuel, of Shklov

Yisroel ben Shmuel Ashkenazi was born in about 1770. He was one of a group of Talmudists who went to Vilna as disciples of Elijah (the Vilna) Gaon (1720-1797).He was selected by Elijah to arrange for the publication of the Gaon's commentary to the first two parts of the *Shulkhan Arukh*. That and the *Orach Chaim* (the second part of the *Arba'ah Turim* of Jacob ben Asher) were published in Shklov in 1803.

Ashkenazi later emigrated to Palestine where he was head of the German and Polish congregations in Safed. It was there that he assumed the last name "Ashkenazi" (the German) as a distinction from the Sephardim from Spain and Portugal. He returned briefly to Europe to collect funds to support the poor Palestinian Jews.

His main work was *Pe'at HaShulchan* that was meant as a supplement to the *Shulkhan Arukh*. It also included other material. He also published a collection of responsa called *Nachalah u-Menuchah*.

Ashkenazi died in Tiberias on May 13, 1839.

Ashkenazi, Yitzhak Luria (The Ari)

The ARI (Eloki Rabbi Yitzhak) was born in Jerusalem in 1534. After his father died when he was still young, his mother moved to Egypt and his uncle Rabbi Moshe Francis took care of the family. He later married his daughter. Rabbi Ashkenazi studied under David ibn Zimra (the Radbaz) and Rabbi Bezalel Ashkenazi.

At 36, he returned to Israel to Safed where he taught kabbalah and was a contemporary of Rabbi Moshe Cordovero (the Ramak). Although he never wrote down any of his kabbalistic teachings, these were all recorded by his student, Rabbi Hayyim Vital. He did write some piyyutim and zemirot that are sung on Shabbat. He died at 38 years of age in 1572.

Ashlag, Yehuda Leib HaLevi (Ba'al HaSulam)

Yehuda Ashlag was born in Lodz in Congress Poland, which was then a part of the Russian Empire, in 1885. He came from a family of Hassidic scholars. He apparently began studying kabbalah on his own when he was seven, using Isaac Luria's (Arizal) book *Etz Chaim*. By the age of twelve he was independently studying Talmud. So great was his knowledge that by age nineteen he was granted s'micha by the Warsaw rabbis. In Warsaw he became a judge of the court as well as training other judges. While still in Poland he studied under a kabbalist.

In 1921, he began a journey to Palestine, settling there by 1922. Once there he began to write commentaries and in 1924 he was appointed the rabbi of Givat Shaul in Jerusalem. He became friendly with chief rabbi Abraham Kook. In 1926, he went to London for two years where he wrote his commentary on Luria's *Etz Chaim*, titled *Panim Meirot Umashbirot*.

In 1928, he returned to Palestine and in 1932 went to Jaffa. While there he began his main work, *Talmud Eser Sefirot*, which was a commentary on all of the Arizal's writings. It was divided into sections. *Mamot Elyonim* was an explanation of the sequence of the upper world creation and *Olam Hazeh* dealt with the earthly world.

In 1943, he went to Tel Aviv and began work on his next book, *HaSulam (Sulam)* that was a collection of commentaries on the *Zohar*. It took him ten years to complete this major work. He died on Yom Kippur in 1954.

Attar, Hayyim ibn (Ohr HaChaim HaKadosh)

Hayyim ibn Attar was born in Sale, Morroco in 1696 and was taught in his youth by his grandfather. After the death of his great-uncle Shem Tov, he moved to Meknes to manage his business with Shem Tov's son. He married his daughter, studied and worked there. However, after the economic situation deteriorated he decided to settle in Palestine. He went to Livorno, Italy in 1739 with his closest disciples Rabbi David Hasan and Rabbi Shem Tov Gabbai. He rapidly developed this as a center for study. He believed the redemption was imminent and with this in mind he sent proclamations to Jewish communities throughout Italy as well as visiting there, urging immigration to Palestine.

In 1741, he sailed from Livorno to Palestine reaching Acre in the late summer, where he established a temporary yeshiva. A year later he moved to Peki'in. He then went on to Jerusalem where he established the Midrash Knesset Israel Yeshivah. There he concentrated on the codes and their relationship to the Talmud, especially reconciling decisions of Maimonides with the Talmud. Rabbi David Hasan is said to have been the author of the work *Rishon Le-Ziyyon* that was the result of this work.

Attar's most important work was the *Ohr HaChaim*, a commentary on the Torah. It was republished many times and was very popular with the Hassidim in Poland and also in Germany. The original text is found in most editions of *Mikraot Gedolot*. It has recently been published in English. In many communities it is still used today. Rabbi Attar died in 1743.

Auerbach, Menachem Mendel ben Meshulam Zalman

Rav Menachem Mendel was born in Vienna in 1620. He was a student of the Bach (Rabbi Joel Sirkis). His major work was *Ateret Zekeinim*, that appears in the margins of current printings of the *Shulkhan Arukh*. He died in 1689.

Auerbach, Shlomo Zalman

Rabbi Shlomo Zalman Auerbach was born on July 20, 1910 in Jerusalem. He became the Rosh Yeshiva of Kol Torah Yeshiva. He was an erudite teacher and a prolific author. He was a pre-eminent Haredi leader in his time and was the major halakhic authority of his time. His first book, *Meorei Esh*, addressed the halakhic issue of the use of electricity on Shabbat for the first time. He also wrote several other books. He was married to Chaya Rivka Ruchamkin and had seven sons and several daughters.

Rabbi Auerbach died on February 20, 1995.

Avraham of Trisk

He was one of eight sons of Rabbi Mordechai of Chernobyl. He was born in 1802. His book *Magen Avraham* contains guidelines for yeshiva students on the Torah readings and the festivals. He died in 1889.

Ayyas, Judah

Judah Ayyas was born in North Africa in 1690 and died in Jerusalem in 1760. He studied Talmud in Algiers where he later served as dayan. He was very strict in his interpretation of the halakha. In 1756, he went to Jerusalem, probably because of the progressive approach that was taking hold in Algiers.

He wrote several works. *Lehem Yehuda* was a commentary on Maimonides' *Yad HaHazakha* (*Mishneh Torah*). *Bet Yehuda* consisted of responsa on the *Arba'ah Turim*. It gives insight into the social and economic conditions of the Jews of North Africa at that time. *Mateh Yehuda* and *Shebbet Yehuda* were novellae on the *Shulkhan Arukh*, *Orach Chaim* and *Yoreh De'ah*.

Azaryah, Menachem, of Fano (Rama of Fano)

Menachem Azaryah was born in Farno, Italy in 1548. He was also known as Rabbi Emanuel. He studied under Yishmael Chanina and then Ezra of Fano, who taught him kabbalah. He became an ardent kabbalist. He corresponded with Moses Cordovero. When Israel Saruk came to Italy he was introduced to the works of Luria (the Ari). This proved a turning point in his life. He disseminated these teachings throughout Italy.

He wrote many kabbalistic works, but his best known is *Assarah Ma'amarot*. It is a compendium of various treatises. He died in Mantua in 1620.

Azikri (Ezkari), Elazar ben Moshe

Rabbi Elazar Azikri, alternatively known as Elazar Ezkari, was kabbalist, poet and author. He was born in Safed in 1533 to a Sephardi family that had fled from Spain. He studied under Rabbis Yosef Sagis and Yaakov Berab. He was counted among the great intellectuals of his time, Alkabetz, Caro and Isaac Luria.

His major work, printed only after his death was *Sefer Hareidim*. It is considered the major work on Jewish deontology, the ethical theory dealing with duties and rights. Another work on ethics that he authored was *Divrei Kivushim*. He also wrote a commentary on Tractate Bezah in the Jerusalem Talmud. He is the author of the famous Shabbat Piyyut, *Yedid Nefesh*.

Azikri died and was buried in Safed in 1600.

Azulai, Abraham

He was the great-grandfather of Haim Yosef David Azulai and was born in Fez Morocco in 1570. He was significantly influenced by kabbalah and while in Morocco he wrote a number of works, all of which were subsequently lost when he moved to Palestine. His work on kabbalah was titled *Chesed L'Avraham*, which was a three-part commentary on the *Zohar*.

He also wrote separately other books on the *Zohar*, *Ohr HaChama* (Light of the Sun) *Ohr HaGanuz*. He wrote two books respectively on the *kavanot* of prayer and Mitzvot according to Rabbi Yitzhak Luria Ashkenazi (the Ari) called *Knaff Renanim*. Further he wrote a commentary on the Tanakh; *Baalei Brit Avraham*. He wrote two other books of commentary on the Mishnah and on halakha respectively called *Perush Yakar Al Shisha Sidrei Mishnah* and *Perush Yakar Al HeLevush*. He died in 1643.

Azulai, Haim Yosef David (Hida)

Rabbi Azulai was born in Jerusalem in 1724. He was the great grandson of Rabbi Abraham Azulai. He kept extensive diaries that cover all aspects of his life and these have been translated into English. He studied under Rabbi Chaim ben Atar (Ohr HaChaim) and became a great scholar and prolific author. For a while he studied at the Beit El Synagogue in Jerusalem. In 1753 he traveled as an emissary to Europe representing the communities of Palestine and he did so again to both North Africa and Europe in 1772 on behalf of Hebron. He also served as the rabbi of Cairo for five years. On his visits to Europe he inspected the libraries and became familiar with many of the manuscripts. He even owned some of those written by Isaac Luria, the kabbalist.

Out of these visits and studies he created an extensive bibliography and biographical work called *Shem HaGedolim* ("Name of the Great"), which was his best known work. It consists of two parts, the first giving the names and some brief information on about 1,500 scholars and the second part, titled *Vaad Lachachamim* provides the names of about 2,000 works, both published and unpublished and their contents.

Azulai became an expert in kabbalah and wrote several treatises on this subject. He also copied and published many Torah compositions that had disappeared for many centuries. He also wrote several books on various aspects of the Torah, halakha and history. He died in Livorno, Italy in 1806.

Babad, Yosef ben Moshe

Rabbi Babad was born in Przeworsk, Poland in 1801. He studied under Chaim Halberstam, whose sister he later married. He was the rabbi of several cities in Galicia and in 1857 became the Av Beit Din of Tarnopol.

He is best known for his work, the *Minchat Chinuch*, which was a commentary on the *Sefer HaChinuch*. He died in 1874 in Safed.

Bachrach, Abraham Samuel

Abraham Samuel Bachrach was born in 1575, probably in Worms. In 1600 he married the granddaughter of the chief rabbi of Prague, Judah Loew ben Bezalel. He became a rabbi in Turbin, Koln in Bohemia and in Pohrlitz (Moravia) and then in Worms. After riots there he fled the city and died in exile in Alsbach.

He wrote responsa, collected by his son, Yair Chaim in the collected work, *Hut HaShani*. He died in 1615.

Bachrach, Yair Chaim

Rabbi Yair Chaim Bachrach was born in 1639. He was a German rabbi who spent most of his life in Worms and Metz. He was a descendant of the

Maharal of Prague.

He was the author of *Havvot Yair* (Villages of Yair) that was a collection of responsa. His other work, and the major one, although it was only published posthumously in 1982, was his *Mekor Chaim*. It was a principal commentary on the *Shulkhan Arukh*. He was a very cultured individual and was considered one of the pioneers in the Jewish renaissance. He died in 1702.

Barfat (Perfet), Isaac ben Sheshet (RiBaSH)

Isaac Barfat was a Spanish rabbi who was born in Valencia in 1326. In Barcelona, where he went early in life, he studied under Perez HaKohen, Hasdai ben Judah and Nissim ben Reuben (RaN). Early on he established a reputation as a Talmudic authority. He earned his livelihood in commerce and then practicing as a rabbi after fifty. He had a troubled existence, being falsely accused and imprisoned for a while in Barcelona. He then went to Saragossa, but both the deaths of his brother, Judah ben Sheshet and his son-in-law, together with dissension in the community, caused him further grief.

In 1391 with the Spanish persecution of the Jews resulting from the preaching of Fernandes Martinez, he fled Spain and ultimately ended up in Algiers. Despite his veneration by the Jews of Algiers, he found much opposition by certain leaders there. He died in 1408 in Algiers and for centuries after that Jews made pilgrimages to his grave.

Barfat was the author of 417 responsa, which were of the highest quality, being valued by Caro, Berab and others. They also have a historical value because they reflect the conditions of Jews in the fourteenth century. These responsa were first published in Constantinople in 1546, titled *She'elot u-Teshubot*. They were re-published in the nineteenth century under the title *She'elot u-Teshubot HaRibash HaHadashot*. Barfat also wrote Talmudic novellae that are no longer in existence.

Baruch, Joseph ben (Joseph of Clisson)

Joseph ben Baruch or Joseph of Clisson was a Tosafist who lived in France in the twelfth and thirteenth centuries. For a while he was in Paris where he associated with Judah Sir Leon. In 1211 he emigrated with his brother, Meir, to Palestine. In Jerusalem he met Joseph Alharizi, the Spanish poet and author of Takhemoni.

Joseph's explanations are quoted in the *Shittah Mekubbetzet* of Bezalel Ashkenazi and in various Pentateuch commentaries. He also wrote piyyutim and selichot for the Day of Atonement, one of which has been preserved in the service.

Baruch, Meir ben (Meir of Rothenburg) (MaHaRaM)

Meir ben Baruch was born in Worms in about 1215. He was a Tosafist, but was also known for being a codifier and liturgical poet. He came from a family of scholars, noted for their contributions to Talmudic interpretation. He was also known as the MaHaRaM (Moreinu Harav Reb Meir). His formal education was primarily under that of Isaac ben Moses of Vienna in Wurzburg. He also studied in France under Samuel ben Solomon of

Falais, Jehiel ben Joseph of Paris and Samuel of Evreux. He then returned to Germany.

It is not certain, but he is thought to have been the chief rabbi of Germany, but there is no definite proof for this. However, he did officiate in a number of communities – Kosnitz, Augsburg, Wurzburg, Rothenburg, Worms, Nuremberg and Mayence. His stay was probably the longest at Rothenburg, from where he gained his title of Meir of Rothenburg.

While on a journey abroad, he stopped at Lombardy, where through the Bishop of Basel, he was informed upon to the lord of the city, who handed him over to Emperor Rudolph, who had him imprisoned. The reason for this imprisonment is not clear, but the safety of Jews overall in the thirteenth century in Germany was at great risk. The ransom for his release was so great, that Meir ben Baruch prohibited its payment. He therefore languished in prison from 1286 until his death in 1293. While in prison he wrote and revised most of his work, which was voluminous.

His literary output included tosafot to several Talmudic treatises. The printed ones are in Yoma. He wrote a number of responsa that were published in various centers over the next few centuries. These are highly respected and were quoted by other scholars in their work. He wrote in a number of areas of halakha. He published regulations for formulae for various blessings called *Hilkot Berakhot* or *Seder Berakhot*. This maybe identical to *Birkot MaHaRaM* issued in Riva di Trento in 1558. His work, *Hilkot Shehitah* the manuscript that is now located in the Bodleian Library, covered regulations for the ritual slaughtering of animals and their subsequent examination. *Hilkot Abelut* or *Hilkot Semahot* covered customs of mourning. *Halakot Pesukot*, another manuscript in the Bodleian, covered a variety of subjects. *Piske Erubin* was a short summary on the regulation of the *erub*. Another manuscript with copies in the Bodleian and Vatican, covered customs of ritual ceremonies in the synagogue. *Hiddushim* were novellae of some treatises in the Talmud. He wrote a treatise on the marital duties of a husband and wife. He wrote a commentary on the sixth order of the Mishnah that appears in Romm's edition of the Talmud, as well as several other Mishnaic commentaries.

Meir was also a prolific liturgical poet, with a number of his poems appearing in the German Mahzor.

Among Meir's famous pupils were Mordechai ben Hillel and Meir HaKohen.

Baruch (Borukovich), Shneur Zalman, of Liadi (Alter Rebbe, GRaZ)

Shneur Zalman of Liadi, the founder of Chabad Hassidism, was born in 1745 in Liozna in the Polish-Lithuanian Commonwealth that at that time was a part of Russia. He was descended from Judah Loew (the Maharal of Prague). He was a disciple of the Maggid of Mezritch. He first studied under Rabbi Issachar Ber in Lyubavichi. At age fifteen he married the daughter of Yehuda Leib Segal who was wealthy and therefore allowed him to devote himself to full time study. He also studied the secular subjects of mathematics, geometry and astronomy. He also became familiar with Isaac Luria's form of kabbalah.

After the death of Dovber, together with Menachem Mendel of Vitebsk, he became the leader of Hassidism in Lithuania. He attempted unsuccessfully to interact with the Vilna Gaon, the head of the *mitnagdim*, who were powerful in Lithuania.

His Chabad Hassidic philosophy was to create a rational and practical system out of Hassidism and kabbalah. He stressed mind over emotions.

After the death of the Gaon in 1797 he was falsely accused of subversive activity. He was arrested but released a few weeks later on the order of Paul I of Russia. He was arrested once again but released by Alexander I and was then given permission to freely practice his religious teachings. He then moved the headquarters of Chabad to Liadi in Vitebsk in Russia.

Shneur Zalman wrote extensively. His major work was the *Tanya* or *Likkutei Amarim*. It is a systematic explanation of Hassidic Jewish philosophy. It deals with Jewish spirituality from a kabbalistic perspective. His other major work was the *Shulchan Aruch HaRav*, based on the *Shulkhan Arukh*. It gives the underlying reasons for the halakha. It is the authoritative work for Hassidim but is also quoted in the *Mishnah Berurah* and the *Ben Ish Chai*. He also edited the first Hassidic siddur, *Siddur Torah Or*, based on Isaac Luria's *Ari Siddur*. He also wrote *Likutei Torah* that were explanations of the weekly Torah readings. Rabbi Zalman died in 1812.

Barzillai, Judah ben

Barzillai was a Spanish Talmudist of the late eleventh and early twelfth centuries. Very little is known of his life except that he came from a distinguished family.

He was considered one of the great codifiers of the Middle Ages, but unfortunately most of this type of work of his has been lost. His works are often cited authoritatively by other Talmudists. His work was superseded by that of Maimonides and Judah ben Asher.

His *Sefer HaIttim*, of which fragments still exist, is quoted by name by many other authors and halakhists. Besides his halakhic work he also wrote a detailed commentary on *Sefer Yezirah*, that was first published in the nineteenth century.

Bass, Shabbethai ben Joseph

Shabbethai was born in Kalisz, Poland in 1641, but because of the persecutions there, in 1655 he went to Prague, where he studied Talmud and singing. Between 1674 and 1679 he traveled in Poland, Germany and Holland, finally settling in Amsterdam. There he became a printer of Jewish books. He subsequently moved his business near Breslau. However because of continued anti-Jewish feelings attempts were made by several Christians to stop his work, and he was even arrested once.

His most important work was *Sifte Yeshenim* a bibliography containing a list of 2,200 Jewish books and printed in Amsterdam in 1680. It was divided into two major groups, biblical and post-biblical. Each group was then subdivided into ten divisions. It included dictionaroes, grammars, translations, commentaries and novellae. It also included a list of the authors. He was also the author of *Sifsei Chachamim,* which was a commentary on the Pentateuch. Bass died in 1718.

Behag ("Author of Halakhot Gedolot")

The term Behag is an acronym for what is probably an anonymous work. It stands for "author of the *Halakhot Gedolot.*" However, when reference is made to this work there is often a statement such as "So and so cites the Behag and explains." Thus it seems to be attributed to in the same way as reference is made to a particular scholar and his work. It is a work of probably the eighth century and has been attributed by different scholars mainly to various Gaonic authors. These are essentially Sherira Gaon and Hai Gaon, whereas other scholars attribute it to Simeon Kayyara who, according to Abraham ibn Daud preceded Yehudai Gaon, the author of *Halakhot Pesukot,* whom one authority indicates he quotes from the *Halakhot Gedolot.* However, this, as well is disputed by other scholars who place Simeon Kayyara in the ninth century, following Yehudai Gaon.

Benet, Mordechai ben Abraham

Mordechai Benet was born in Csurgo in the county of Stuhlweissenburg, Hungary in 1753. At age five he was sent to his grandmother in Nikolsburg to study under Gabriel Markbreiter. From there he was sent to Ettingen, Alsace for further study.

Over the course of nearly forty years he devoted himself to the study of the Tanakh utilizing commentaries, as well as Talmudic Haggadah and Midrash. Later on he went to study halakha. He went on to Prague where he married and then became the Av Beth Din of Nikolsburg. Later he became the rabbi of Schossburg, Hungary and then the rabbi of that same city and the chief rabbi of Moravia.

He wrote several works that were considered classics of that time. *Biur Mordechai* was a commentary on Mordechai ben Hillel Ashkenazi's compendium, *Sefer HaMordechai. Magen Abot* was a treatise on prohibited acts of the Sabbath. *Parashot Mordechai* was a collection of responsa. *Tekelet Mordechai* consisted of halakhic and aggadic discourse.

He died in Carlsbad in 1829 where he had gone for treatment of a nervous affliction.

Benveniste, Chaim

Chaim Benveniste was born in 1603 and lived in Constantinople. He was a student of Rabbi Joseph Trani. In 1644 he became the rabbi of Tire.

His major work, for which he is most well-known, is *Knesses HaGedolah.* It is a compilation of all the known halakha from a variety of sources dating from Caro's work and including all other available sources. It was considered a major work and was cited by many other authorities. He used the same order as the *Shulkhan Arukh*. He later added to this work called the latter *Sheyarei Knesses HaGedolah*.

His other works included a commentary on *Semag* (Moses ben Jacob of Coucy), called *Dina DeChaye*. He published a three-volume set of responsa called *Ba'ei Chaye*, novellae on the tractate Sanhedrin, called *Chamra VeChaye*. He also wrote a work on the laws of the Pesach Seder called *Pesach MeUvin*.

Rabbi Benveniste died in Smyrna (Izmir) in 1673.

Ber, Dov (of Mezritch) (The Maggid)

Dov Ber of Mezritch, also known as the Maggid or the Maggid of Mezritch was born in 1710 in Volhynia, Russia, although this date is questioned. He was a student of Rabbi Yisrael Ba'al Shem Tov, the founder of Hassidism, and was viewed as his successor. Dov Ber was in fact the first proponent of Hassidism and was principally responsible for its propagation.

Dov Ber was an admirer of the kabbalistic system of Rabbi Isaac Luria, whose work was becoming known in Poland. He also knew the writings, available in manuscript form, of Rabbi Moshe Chaim Luzzatto. He followed the ascetic Lurian life himself and his health suffered as a result.

At some point he went to see the Ba'al Shem Tov, where he was struck by the latter's application of his knowledge to everyday life. Dov Ber ultimately stayed with him and studied under him. He learned from the Ba'al Shem Tov the value of everyday things and events and also his emphasis on the way to study Torah.

After the death of the Ba'al Shem Tov in 1760, his son, Rabbi Tzvi became the next rebbe, but soon gave this up. Dov Ber then assumed the leadership of this new movement of Hassidism. He appointed disciples to spread these teachings. Hassidism spread rapidly, but did meet with opposition, most prominently by the Gaon of Vilna, who issued an excommunication edict against Hassidism in 1772. This ban however, had the opposite effect for the movement.

Although the Maggid did not personally author any books, there are two major works of his, that were excerpts of his sermons, written down by his relative, Rabbi Solomon ben Abraham of Lutzk. These were *Likkutei Amarim* (Collected Sayings) or *MaggiD DebarO le-YaakoV* (DOV), and *Likkutei Yesharim* (Collected Gems). These were published in 1780 and 1790 respectively.

Dov Ber died in 1772.

Berab, Jacob (Mhari Beirav)

Jacob Berab, variously spelled as Berav or Bei Rav was born in Moqueda, near Toledo, Spain in 1474. He was a pupil of Isaac Aboab. In 1492 he fled to Tlemcen in the Barbary States (Algeria) where he was appointed rabbi. At some stage before 1522 he went to Jerusalem. Then by 1527 he had moved to Damascus. In 1533 he became the rabbi of Cairo. Several years later he finally settled in Safed. It was there that he developed his famous idea of establishing a central spiritual Jewish power.

Berab also planned to reintroduce the old form of "Semichah." He also had plans to re-establish the Tannaitic form of the Sanhedrin. Maimonides had taught, and which was opposed by Nahmanides, that if the sages in Palestine could agree among themselves, that one person could ordain himself, then that person could ordain others. The scholars in Safed accepted this. In 1538, twenty-five rabbis met in Safed and ordained Berab. He thus could ordain any number of other rabbis who could then form a Sanhedrin. Most Palestinian scholars accepted this.

Although Berab had had many disputes with Levi ibn Habib, the chief rabbi of Jerusalem, he still ordained him. However, ibn Habib took this as a personal insult and went so far as to send a letter to the scholars of Safed pointing out the illegality of this. Berab had to flee to Egypt for a while. Ibn Habib's following increased such that upon Berab's return, his plans were rendered ineffective. He died a few years later in Safed in 1546.

Among famous scholars ordained by Berab were Joseph Caro and Moses di Trani. Caro in turn used his privilege to ordain Moses Alshich and Hayyim Vital.

Berechyah, Aharon, of Modena

He was a sixteenth to seventeenth century Italian rabbi who trained under Hillel of Modena and Menachem Azaryah. He is known because of his work *Maavar Yabok* that consists of the laws and ritual for the preparation for death and the regulations for the burial society for the subsequent internment of the body. It was a widely used book and re-published many times. His other works were *Me'il Tzedakah* and *Bigdei Kodesh* that were used for devotional prayer. He died in 1639.

Berezovsky, Sholom Noach

Rabbi Berezovsky was born in 1911 in Baranovitsch, Belarus. On his maternal side he was descended from the first Slonimer Rabbi, known by the title of his work, *Yesod HaAvoda*. He studied at the Slonimer Yeshiva Toras Chesed. When only twenty the current Slonimer Rebbe, Avrohom Weinberg, instructed Shalom Noach to write up all his discourses that were then published under the title of *Beis Avrohom*. In 1933, he married a daughter of Rabbi Avrohom.

In 1940, Rabbi Berezovsky was appointed Rosh Yeshiva of Achei Temimim, a Lubavitch yeshiva in Tel Aviv. With the destruction of the Slonimer dynasty and movement in the Holocaust, its revival was begun in Jerusalem. Rabbi Berezovsky assumed responsibility for collecting the oral traditions of previous Slonimer rebbes and became the Slonimer Rebbe. Again Rabbi Berezovsky wrote up his discourses that was published as *Birkath Avrohom*. After the death of Rabbi Avrohom in 1981, Sholom Noach assumed the title. He served in that position until his death in 2000. Rabbi Sholom Noach's teachings were published in a book titled *Nesivos Sholom*.

Berlin, Isaiah ben Judah Loeb

Rabbi Berlin was born in 1725. He must not be confused with the great twentieth century political philosopher of the same name. He was also known as Isaiah Pick Berlin.

He adopted a moderate approach to the vehement debate between traditional and reform Judaism in Germany in the eighteenth century.

He is known for his Talmud glosses (additional short comments to the text or cross-references) that first appeared in the Dyhernfurth publication of the Talmud. These glosses mostly supplement the *Mesoret HaShas*, adding also to the lexicon the *Arukh* by Rabbi Nathan ben Jehiel of Rome from the tenth century. He died in 1799.

Berlin, Naftali Tzvi Yehuda (The Netziv)

Naftali Berlin was born in 1817 to a family of Talmudic scholars. He was the head of the yeshiva at Volozhin (presently a part of Belarus) from 1854 to 1892 when it was closed down by the authorities. This yeshiva produced a number of prominent rabbis who led Eastern European Jewry until the second world war.

While in Volozhin his leadership was contested by Rabbi Joseph Dov Soloveitchik, who had a different style of Torah study. Rabbi Soloveitchik was the founder of the rabbinical dynasty that bears his name. He went on to become the rabbi of Slutsk, Warsaw and Brisk. Rabbi Berlin's approach to Torah study was traditional, as opposed to the analytical style known as *lombdus* (learned intellectual analysis) pioneered by Soloveitchik. The Netziv's approach to Talmudic study was to examine all the relevant passages in the Tannaitic literature, attempting to go back to the earliest sources and paying especial attention to the Geonic and early Rishonim literature.

He was in favor of the resettlement of Israel by the Jews and was supportive initially of Rabbi Zvi Hirsch Kalisher's Chovevei Tzion movement.

He wrote a number of works which included a collection of responsa (*Meishiv Davar*), a halakhic work which was a commentary on Achai Gaon's geonic work *Sheiltos*, and titled *HaEmek She'ela* (The Depth of the Question), *HaEmek Davar* (The Depth of the Word) which was a Torah commentary and a commentary on *Nevi'im* and *Ketuvim* titled *Meromeih Sadeh* (Heights of the Field). Berlin died in 1893 from the complications of diabetes.

Bibago, Abraham ben Shem Tov

Abraham Bibago was born in Saragossa, Spain in the fifteenth century. He was a religious philosopher and preacher who had an excellent knowledge of Arabo-Judean philosophy as well as Christian theology.

His main work was *Derek Emunah* ("Path of Faith") that was written towards the end of his life and published in Constantinople in 1521. It was a defense of the Jewish religion that would lead a person to the highest appreciation of God. It is divided into three parts; the doings of God, the intellect and the fundamentals of faith. Another work, *Ez Hayyim* deals with creation.

Blaser, Isaac ben Moses Solomon (Rav Itzele Peterburger)

Isaac Blaser was born in Vilna in 1837. He was the most prominent disciple of Israel Salanter, and a major proponent of the Mussar movement. He won over many people to this movement that stressed an ethical and moral way of life. He lived in St. Petersburg, Russia from 1864 to 1880. Following this he lived in Kovno (Kaunas), Lithuania until 1904 where he was head of the kollel which trained many rabbis for Lithuanian and Russian Jewish communities.

He was the author of *Peri Yitzhak*, a collection of responsa. In 1904, he settled in Jerusalem and died in 1907.

Boruch of Kosov

Rabbi Boruch was born in the eighteenth century. He was an important disciple of Dov Ber of Mezritch, the Maggid of Mezritch. He worked actively to propagate the teachings of Hassidism. He was the author of two works, *Yesod HaEmunah* and *Amud HaAvodah*. He died in 1782.

Bouton, Abraham ben Moses, de

Rabbi Abraham de Bouton lived in the sixteenth century in Salonika Turkey. He was born about 1560. He was a pupil of Samuel de Medina.

De Bouton is known for his commentary on Maimonides' *Mishneh Torah*. His work is titled *Lehem Mishneh*, the title being taken from Exodus 16:22. In it he traces the origins of Maimonides' rulings and tries to resolve apparent contradictions between the *Mishneh Torah* and the Talmud. After he became aware of Caro's work, *Kesef Mishneh*, he tried not to duplicate material. Rabbi de Bouton died in about 1605.

Boya'a, Shlomo ben

Shlomo ben Boya'a was a tenth century scribe responsible for having produced what has been viewed as the most authentic manuscript of the Hebrew Bible according to the Tiberian mesorah. It was edited then by Aaron ben Asher. This manuscript has come to be known as the *Aleppo Codex*, after its last location. Maimonides in his *Mishneh Torah* considered this codex to be the most authoritative source for his work.

Bruna, Israel (Mahari Bruna)

Rabbi Bruna was born in Brno, Moravia in 1400. He studied under Rabbis Jacob Weil and Israel Isserlin. He was elected the rabbi of his town, but when the Jews were expelled from there he went to Ratisbon, Bavaria where he started a yeshiva. While there he had controversial interactions with the authorities over taxation on the Jews and he was imprisoned for a short while.

He was one of the greatest Talmudic authorities of his time He wrote a number of responsa collected in his best-known work, *Teshuvot Mahari Bruna*. He died in 1480.

Buber, Solomon

Solomon Buber was born in Lemberg, which is now the Ukraine, on February 2, 1827. His father, Isaiah Abraham Buber, was his philosophy teacher, while his biblical and Talmudic studies were assigned to professional teachers. He married when twenty years old and entered business becoming a banker. He was also active in public life.

He devoted himself to learned research of which midrashic literature was a particular interest of his. He edited a major work on this Aggadic collection with an extensive commentary, called *Pesikhta de-Rab Kahana*. He also edited other midrashic works. However, by the rigorous scholarly standards of today, his work is considered somewhat flawed.

He was the grandfather and teacher of Martin Buber. He died in 1906.

Campanton, Isaac ben Jacob

Isaac Campanton was a Spanish rabbi, born in 1360. He was designated as the "Gaon of Castile." Isaac Aboab was one of his pupils.

His one work was *Darche HaGemara* or *Darche HaTalmud* that provides a practical guide for teaching Talmud. It is considered an important work. It has been published several times over the centuries. He died in 1463.

Caro (Karo), Joseph ben Ephraim (HaMechaber, Mechaber)

Rabbi Caro, sometimes referred to as Yosef Caro, and often spelled as "Karo", was one of the most important leaders in rabbinic Judaism and the author of the *Shulkhan Arukh*. Thus he was also known as the Mechaber or HaMechaber ("the author of the *Shulkhan Arukh*"). He was born in 1488, probably in Spain. The family left for Portugal after the Spanish expulsion and then in 1497 they were expelled from there.

Around 1520, Caro settled in Adrianople and then in 1535 he emigrated to Palestine. During the latter years of his life his reputation was considered to be the greatest since Maimonides. He established a yeshiva at Safed. He wrote many responsa to halakhic questions coming from all over the diaspora.

Caro was also a kabbalist, believing in a heavenly mentor called a "maggid." He was married three times (his first two wives died) and had six children. He is particularly known as a great codifier. Like Maimonides, he based his code, the *Beit Yosef* and its abbreviated form, the *Shulkhan Arukh*, on the Talmud.

The other work of his published during his lifetime was *Kesef Mishneh*, which was a commentary of the *Mishneh Torah* of Maimonides. After his death a number of other writings of his were published. These were *Bedek HaBayit, Kelalei HaTalmud, Avkath Rochel, Maggid Mesharim* and *Derashot*.

Caro died in Safed on March 24, 1575.

Castro, Jacob de

De Castro was a rabbinic authority who lived in Egypt during the sixteenth century. He met Joseph Caro on a pilgrimage to Safed.

He was the author of several works: *Erek Lehem, Ohole Ya'akob, Kol Ya'akob, Nazir* and *Erech HaShulchan*. He died in 1610.

Chaim, Aharon ibn

Aharon ibn Chaim was born in Fez, Morocco in 1560. He studied under his father Avraham ibn Chaim and Joseph Almosnino. He first served on the Beth Din in Fez under Rabbi Vidal Tzarfati and then went on to become the rabbi first in Cairo, then Smyrna and finally in Venice.

His most important contribution was his commentary on the halakhic midrash, *Sifra*. It was titled *Korban Aharon* and was published in Venice in 1609. It was widely quoted by other authorities.

He also wrote *Midos Aharon* (Rules of Aharon) which was a commentary of the baraita of Rabbi Yishmael. This work listed the thirteen rules that the Sages used to derive their teachings from the Bible. Rabbi Horowitz referred to it in his *Shelah*.

Late in life Chaim went to live in Jerusalem where he died in 1632.

Chaim, Hakham (Chacham) Yosef (Ben Ish Chai) (Joseph Hayyim ben Elijah Al-Hakam)

Chacham Yosef Chaim was born in 1832 in Baghdad. Until age ten he studied in his father's library but then went to study under his uncle David Chai Nissim. He married in 1851 and also spent some time studying under his brother-in-law Abdalla Somekh.

His father died when he was twenty-five and the Jewish community made him rabbi of Baghdad. He established a reputation for himself as the major religious authority in the Middle East, and his opinions were considered of significance, even outside of the Sephardi community. On his advice his patron Joseph Shalom established the highly regarded Sephardic yeshiva, Porat Yosef, in Jerusalem.

Chaim authored many works on halakha and aggadah, but his most famous work was the *Ben Ish Chai* ("Son of Man who Lives"), by which title he is also known. It is considered the "Sephardi Kitzur Shulkhan Arukh."

He published about thirty other works of which the best known are: *Me-Kabtziel*, which gives more detailed explanations for certain decisions found in the *Ben Ish Chai*; *Ben Yehovada* and also responsa collections called *Rav Pe'alim* and *Torah Lishmah*.

He was also known for his stories and parables that were later collected and published. His *Qanan-un-Nisa* consists of parables concerning self-improvement, directed towards women.

Chaim died in 1909 and is buried on the Mount of Olives in Jerusalem.

Chajes (Chayes), Zvi Hirsch (The Maharatz Chajes)

Zvi Hirsch was born in Boridy on November 20, 1805. He was considered one of the most prominent Galician scholars. He was also known as The Maharatz Chajes. He studied under a number of great scholars, but in particular Rabbi Ephraim Zalman Margulies. He also had a modern secular education in languages, literature, geography and history.

At 22, he was appointed to an important rabbinical post in Zolchiv, Galicia. Twenty-five years later he was appointed to the important position as rabbi of Kalisz in Poland.

Chajes' work covered aspects of Judaism that, while being faithful to the tradition, were scientific in their approach. He was thus closely associated in this context with the work of Nachman Krochmal and S.L. Rapoport. He left his mark thus on most modern works dealing with halakha and the aggadah.

Mevo HaTalmud was both about the halakhic and aggadic aspects of the Talmud. It covers the history and classification of the Talmud. It is the first modern work to evaluate the extent and the authority of the tradition.

Torat Nevi'im concentrated specifically on the authority of the Talmudic tradition.

Darkhei Hora'ah dealt with the rules that were applied during the Talmudic times to decide on practical religious issues. There are *Glosses* to the Talmud published in the Romm-Vilna edition. *Imrei Binah* was on aspects of the Babylonian and Jerusalem Talmuds, Rashi's commentary on Taanit and on the Targumim. Chajes died at the age of 50 in October 1855.

Chananyah, Abraham ibn

Rabbi Abraham ibn Chananyah was born in 1605 in Salonica, which was then a part of Turkey. He was a student of Joseph Trani. He later moved to Palestine in about 1651, settling in Safed where he became a leading authority. As was a common situation, he went back to Europe to raise funds and while in Belgrade he befriended the rabbi there, Simchah HaKohen. On his return he settled in Jerusalem.

Rabbi Avraham wrote novellae on the Talmud and a major work on the *Shulkhan Arukh* and other works which were not published. However, in 1984 some of these, including a portion of the *Shulkhan Arukh* commentary on *Even HaEzer*, were published under the title of *Beit Avraham*.

He died in Jerusalem in 1665.

Channeles, Yehuda Leib ben Meir

Rabbi Yehuda Channeles was born in Posen (at that time a part of Poland) in the early 1500s. He wrote a commentary on the *Arba'ah Turim* of Jacob Asher titled *Vayigash Yehuda* that complemented Caro's *Beit Yosef*. He died in 1596.

Chaviv (Habib), Levi ben Jacob ibn (Ralbach)

Rabbi Levi ibn Chaviv or Habib was the son of Yaakov ibn Chaviv (Habib). He was born in Zamora, Spain about 1480.

Under King Manuel of Portugal, where he went after the Spanish expulsion, he was forced to be baptized, but then fled to Salonika. He permanently settled in Jerusalem in 1525.

He edited his father's book, *Ayn Yaakov*. He also wrote many responsa that were collected in a book, *She'elot u-Teshubot*. His other works were *Kontres HaSemikah* and *Perush Kiddush HaChodesh*. He died in Jerusalem, where he was the rabbi, in about 1545.

Chaviv (Habib), Yaakov ibn

Rabbi Yaakov ibn Chaviv or Habib lived in Spain until the expulsion in 1492 when he went to Portugal. He finally settled in Salonika where he had access to the complete Talmud as well as commentaries by Ramban, Rashba, Ritva, Raan and Baalei Tosfot. These were in the home of Judah Benveniste of the famous scholarly family and also an exile from Spain. This opportunity allowed him to compile his work, Ayn Yaakov, and print two orders (Zeraim and Moed) before he died. His work addressed the aggadic portion of the Talmud and he even incorporated the aggadah portion of the Jerusalem Talmud together with his own commentaries. The book was edited by his son Rabbi Levi ibn Chaviv. After Yaakov's death more parts were added to it and it is in this expanded form that it is known today.

Chaviv died in 1516.

Chaviva, Yosef

Rabbi Chaviva lived in Spain in the late fourteenth to early fifteenth centuries. His teacher was Rabbi Chisdai Crescas II.

He wrote a halakhic commentary on Alfasi's (RIF) *HaHalachot*, titled *Nimukei Yosef*. In it he quoted many of the Talmudic authorities of the previous generations.

Chayon, Avraham

He was a fifteenth century rabbi who was born in Portugal. He was a student of Yosef Chayon. He was forced to leave Portugal at the time of the expulsion and went to Constantinople. He wrote *Amorot Tehorot* which dealt with ethics and repentance. He died in 1510.

Chayon, Joseph

Rabbi Joseph Chayon was born in Portugal about 1425 and was a leading figure of his time. He wrote a commentary on the tractate Avot called *Milei DeAvot*. He also wrote a commentary on Psalms. He died in Constantinople in the early sixteenth century.

Chorin, Aron

Aron Chorin was born in Weisskirchen (or Hranice), Moravia in 1765. He first studied at a yeshiva in Mattersburg, Hungary and then in Prague under Ezekiel Landau. In 1789 he became the rabbi of Arad where he remained until his death.

Chorin was one of the pioneers of religious reform.

In 1803, he published *Emek HaShaweh* (Vale of the Plain), which was a three-part work. The first and most important, *Rosh Amanah* (Head of the Perrenial Stream) provided guidance on the modification of traditional laws to be adaptable to the then current requirements. He also dealt with Maimonides' thirteen articles of faith, the aggadah and the *Zohar*. This work brought strong opposition from Mordechai ben Abraham Benet. An attempt was made to have the book burned as heretical, but the congregation of Arad stood by Chorin. This issue ultimately led to a penalty being pronounced by the religious authority of Assod. An appeal to the imperial government led to the annulment of the judgment.

He also wrote a number of articles on reforming the religious practices, including prayers in German, the use of the organ, and other liturgical modifications. These were published as a collection *Nogah HaBedek* (Light of Righteousness). He died in 1844.

Chushiel, Chananel ben (Rabbeinu Chananel)

Chananel ben Chushiel or Hananel ben Hushiel was one of the last of the Geonim, best known for his commentary on the Talmud and referred to as Rabbeinu Chananel. He was born in Tunisia in 990 and studied under his father, the head of the Kairouan Yeshiva, and also via correspondence with Hai Gaon. He was also closely associated with Nissim ben Jacob.

Chananel's major work was a complete commentary on the Talmud, which is today embedded in the Talmud. It consists mainly of paraphrased summaries of the gemara arguments. It includes parallel passages from the Palestinian Talmud, and in this way it contributed to the revival of this Talmud. The RIF (Isaac Alfasi) made use of it. Manuscripts of this summary are found in Munich, the Vatican and the Codex Almanzi in London. His other significant work was a commentary on the Torah, only fragments of which survive, and which have recently been published.

Cohen, Abigdor (of Vienna)

Abigdor Cohen lived in Vienna in the twelfth century and was considered the first of the great Austrian Talmudists. He was a pupil of Rabbi Simha of Speyer. He wrote tosafot to the treatise of Ketuvot, which is no longer in existence. A commentary of the Pentateuch and five Megillot exists in manuscript form. One of his famous pupils was Rabbi Meir of Rothenburg.

Cordovero, Moses ben Jacob (Ramak)

Moses ben Jacob Cordovero, known as the Ramak (from the first letters of his title, Rabbi Moshe Cordovero), was one of the most prominent of the early scholars of modern kabbalism in sixteenth-century Safed. There is some debate as to his birthplace and date of birth. One source indicates that his birthplace was Cordoba, Spain, and he probably fled the inquisition of 1492. Another source indicates his family was from there and that he was born in 1522. This latter is probably more accurate.

Besides his significant knowledge of kabbalah, which he did not involve himself with until age twenty, he was also a great Talmudist, a philosopher and prolific writer. He was the head of the yeshiva at Safed for the Portuguese immigrants.

According to his own writings he heard a "heavenly voice" urging him to study kabbalah with his brother-in-law, Rabbi Shlomo Alkabetz, who composed the *Lecha Dodi*. He rapidly mastered the contents of the *Zohar*. The philosopher Spinoza was influenced by his writings.

Cordovero soon embarked on organizing kabbalistic themes, resulting in his first book, *Pardes Rimonim* ("Orchard of Pomegranates") that he completed in 1548. It was an attempt at reconciling the various early schools with the conceptual teachings of the *Zohar*, and so try and find a unifying theme. His second and major work was *Ohr Yakar* ("Precious Light") which was a multi-volume commentary on the *Zohar*. A modern publication of this work began in the mid-nineteen sixties and was completed in 2004. Some of his other books are, *Tomer Devorah* ("Palm Tree of Deborah"), *Ohr Neerav* ("A Pleasant Light"), *Elimah Rabbati*, and *Sefer Gerushim* ("The Book of Banishments"), *Shiur Komah* ("Measurement of Height").

About 1550 he founded a kabbalah academy in Safed that he led for twenty years until he died in 1570. He was survived by his wife and son, Gedaliyah, who published some of the Ramak's books. Among his disciples were Rabbi Eliyahu de Vidas and Rabbi Hayyim Vital.

Crescas, Hasdai ben Abraham

Hasdai Crescas was born in Barcelona, Spain about 1340. He was philosopher and well-known halakhist. As a philosopher he took a rationalist approach. He came from a family of scholars and was a disciple of Nissim ben Reuven (The RaN). He had a significant effect on Baruch Spinoza and the latter's philosophy.

Crescas never held the position of an official rabbi, but included among his friends Isaac ben Sheshet (the Ribash). Joseph Albo was his student.

He was imprisoned in 1378 with false accusations and his son died in 1391 during the anti-semitic persecutions.

His work on halakha does not survive in writing. His philosophical work *Or Adonai* ("The Light of the Lord") was the classical work on the refutation of medieval Aristotelianism. He wrote three other works: *The Refutation of the Christian Principles*, *Passover Sermon* and *Letter to the Congregations of Avignon*. He died in about 1411.

Culi (Chuli, Huli, Kuli), Yaakov

Rabbi Culi was a biblical commentator and Talmudist who was born in Jerusalem in 1689. He was from an exiled Spanish family living in his early years in Safed. His father was Rabbi Machir Culi who was the scion of one of the leading Jewish families of Crete. His grandfather and teacher was Moses ibn Habib.

His first literary work was the publication of his grandfather's work called *Ezrat Nashim*. He went to Constantinople to do this work. Just a short while after the death of Judah Rosanes in 1727 he organized the latter's work and published first his *Parashat Derakim* and then Rosanes' important commentary on Maimonides' *Mishneh Torah* called *Mishneh la-Melek*.

Culi's most important work was his commentary on the Pentateuch called *Me'am Loez*. It was considered one of the most important commentaries among the Sephardim and was written in Ladino. It covered all aspects of Jewish life. He took his material from the Talmud, Midrash and early rabbinic works. He died before completing his work, only doing Genesis and a part of Exodus. So important was this work considered to be that the task was then taken up and completed by other prominent rabbis in Turkey. Yitzhak Bechor Agruiti did Deuteronomy, Yitzhak Magriso did

Leviticus and Numbers, Rachamim Menachem Mitrani did the commentary on Joshua, and Esther was done by Raphael Chiya Pontremoli. Shmuel Yerushalmi translated the work into Hebrew. In the twentieth century a Hebrew translation was made by Shmuel Kravitzer called *Yalkut Me'am Loez*. An English translation called *Torah Anthology* was written by Aryeh Kaplan. This latter introduced the work to the Ashkenazi world.

He also wrote a halakhic work called *Simanim le-Oraita* which exists only in manuscript form. Culi died in Constantinople on August 9, 1732.

Danzig, Abraham ben Jehiel (the Chayei / Chochmat Adam)

Abraham Danzig was born in Danzig in 1747/8. At the age of fourteen he was sent to Prague where he studied under Ezekiel Landau and Joseph Lieberman. At eighteen he left there as an accomplished Talmudist and settled in Vilna, Lithuania. Originally he did not accept a position as a paid rabbi, but many years later, after losing his fortune, he accepted the position as dayan (judge).

Danzig was the author of *Hayye Adam: Nishmat Adam* ("The life of Man: the Soul of Man"), *Hokmat Adam: Binat Adam* ("The Wisdom of Man: the Understanding of Man"), *Sha'are Zedek* ("The Gates of Justice"), *Zikru Torat Moshe* ("Be Mindful of the Teachings of Moses"), *Toledot Adam* and *Bet Abraham* ("The House of Abraham"). *Kitzur Sefer Hareidim* is an abridgement of Rabbi Elazar Azikri Ezkari's *Sefer Hareidim*.

The first two books are his most well-known. These were considered very important codification works after that of Caro. His codex was directed mainly at the layman. His *Hayye Adam* was very successful during his lifetime and in many cities societies were formed to study his work. These works have become standard sources for halakhic study. Later Shlomo Ganzfried based his rulings in the *Kitzur Shulkhan Arukh* on Danzig's work. This latter work, together with the *Mishnah Berurah*, have mostly superseded Danzig's code.

All Danzig's works were based on a highly ethical conduct of religious precepts. He died in Vilna, Lithuania on September 12, 1820.

Danzig, Samuel

He was the grandfather of Abraham Danzig. However nothing is known of his life, except that he was the author of a commentary on Isaiah called *Nehamot Ziyyon*.

David, Abraham ben (Ravad III)

Rabbi Abraham ben David was born in Provence, France in 1125. He was the son-in-law of Abraham ben Isaac of Narbonne (Ravad II). His most important teachers were Rabbi Moses ben Joseph and Rabbi Meshullam ben Jacob of Lunel. After completing his studies under the latter rabbi, he stayed in Lunel and ultimately became one of the rabbinical authorities there. He subsequently moved on to Montpellier for a short while and then on to Nimes for a longer period. However, he spent his most important time in Posquiereres, after which he is often called.

Among his disciples there were Rabbi Isaac HaKohen of Narbonne, the first commentator of the Yerushalmi Talmud, Rabbi Abraham ben Nathan of Lunel, the author of *HaMinhag*, Rabbi Meir ben Isaac of Carcassonne, the author of *Sefer HaEzer* and Rabbi Asher ben Meshulam of Lunel.

Ravad III was a prolific author. He wrote many responsa, some of which are partially preserved in the collections *Temim De'im*, *Orot Hayyim* and *Shibbole HaLeket*. He also wrote a commentary on the whole Talmud. Most of his work has been lost, but *Sefer Ba'ale HaNefesh* (The Book of the Conscientious), a treatise on the laws relating to women and his commentary on *Torat Kohanim* have been preserved.

He opposed the Rambam's *Mishneh Torah*, being concerned that such a guide would replace the study of Talmud itself. He is probably best known for his glosses to Maimonides' *Mishneh Torah*. He essentially was opposed to the codification of the halakha. The Ravad had a certain mystical view of the Deity and thus many kabbalists view him as one of the fathers of the system. He also wrote *HaSagot HaRaavad* where he supports Alfasi's *Sefer Halacoth* (RIF) against Zerachiah HaLevi Gerondi's *Ba'al HaMaor* criticism.

The Ravad III died in Posquieres on November 27, 1198.

David, Baruch ben

He wrote a super-commentary on Mordechai ben Hillel's *Sefer HaMordechai*, called *Gedulah Mordechai* ("The Greatness of Mordechai").

Dessler, Eliyahu Eliezer

Dessler was an influential rabbi and Talmudic scholar of the first half of the twentieth century. He was born in Libau, Latvia in 1892. He studied at the yeshiva in Kelm and received s'micha from his uncle, Rabbi Chaim Ozer Grodzinski, the spiritual head of Lithuanian Jewry. In the late twenties he accompanied his father to London for medical treatment and decided to remain in the United Kingdom, where he served in the rabbinate.

In the late nineteen forties he was invited to assume the role of mashgiach ruchani (spiritual counselor and lecturer on ethical issues) at the Ponevezh Yeshiva in Bnei Brak. He died in 1953.

Posthumously his pupils edited his collected correspondence and ethical writings into a five volume set, *Michtav me-Eliyahu* ("Letter from Elijah"), which was subsequently translated to English with the title "*Strive for Truth.*" It is widely studied and used.

DiSilo, Hezekiah ben David

Rabbi DiSilo was born in Livorno Italy in 1659 and died in 1698 His major work was the *Pri Chadash*, a commentary on the *Shulkhan Arukh*.

Donolo, Shabtai

Shabtai Donolo was born in Oria, Italy in 913. His family was captured by the Arabs, and after his release he was separated from them. He studied and was interested in astrology, which he was taught by an Arab, named Bagdesh. He practised as a physician.

He wrote a commentary to *Sefer Yetzirah* ("The Book of Creation") titled

Chachmuni which was based on astronomy. He also wrote a medical treatise called *Sefer HaYekar*. He died in about 982.

Duran, Simeon ben Zemah (Rashbatz / Tashbetz)

Simeon ben Zemah Duran was born in Adar on the island of Majorca in 1361. He was a relative of Levi ben Gershon. He studied under Ephraim Vidal. He also gained an expertise in medicine, philosophy, astronomy and mathematics. After the 1391 persecutions he went to Algiers where he both practised medicine and continued his Talmudic studies. After Isaac ben Sheshet's death he became the rabbi of Algiers, a position he held until his death. He wrote commentaries on several tractates of the Mishnah and the Talmud. He also wrote a number of piyyutim and secular poems. He wrote a number of responsa. He died in 1444.

Duran, Solomon ben Simon (Rashbash)

Solomon ben Simon Duran was born in Algiers in about 1400. His father was Simeon ben Zemah Duran. As a youth he studied Talmud and rabbinical literature. He had strong negative views of kabbalism. Similar to his father, he was the author of many responsa. He died in 1467.

Dvir, Yehuda Meir

Rabbi Yehuda Meir Dvir was a twentieth century scholar. He provided a contemporary commentary and editing of Nahmanides' *Torat Hashem Temima*, which praised the benefits of the Torah.

Eger, Akiva

Rabbi Akiva Eger was born in Eisenstadt, Hungary in 1761 and died in 1837. He was descended from a family of scholars and rabbis. Although the family name was Gins, he was named after his maternal grandfather. He attended his uncle Rabbi Benjamin Wolf Eger's yeshiva in Breslau. Later he became the dean of the yeshiva in Lissa, Poland.

After his marriage he was elected the rabbi of Markish Friedland, in Prussia. Twenty-five years later he was invited to become the rabbi in Posen. Eger was recognized as a great authority on the halakha. His legal decisions (teshuvot – responsa) are still valuable. These were published in part during his lifetime. His tosafot (additions or glosses) to the Mishnah and to the *Shulkhan Arukh* consist mainly of brief cross-references to other works that elaborate the specific passage in these works.

Eger was staunchly opposed to assimilation and the Reform movement.

Eibenschutz, David Solomon

He was a Russian rabbi occupying a position in Buzhanov and Iasi, Romania, from where he went to the Land of Israel and remained in Safed until his death in about 1812. He studied under Rabbi Moses Tzvi Heller. He authored Talmudic and kabbalistic works which are in manuscript form. He wrote *Lebushe Serad* which was a two-part commentary on the *Shulkhan*

Arukh, the first on the *Orach Chaim* with comments on Samuel's work, *Ture Zahab* and Gombiner's *Magen Avraham*. The second was on the *Yoreh De'ah*. His book of 138 responsa is called *Ne'ot Deshe*. He also wrote *Arbe Nahal* that is in two parts, the first a treatise on the Pentateuch and the second a compilation of his sermons.

Eidels (Edels), Samuel Eliezer ben Judah (Maharsha)

Samuel Eidels (Edels) was born in Cracow, Poland in 1555. He was a descendant from both parents of rabbinic families, his mother being the cousin of Rabbi Yehuda Loew, the Maharal of Prague. After marrying Edel Lifschitz of Posen, he moved there and established a yeshiva, which was supported by his mother-in-law. Later he served as rabbi in Chelm, Lublin and Ostrog.

His major work, *Hiddushei Halakhot* ("Novellae in Jewish Law"), was an analytical commentary on the Talmud, Rashi and the tosafot, concentrating on the latter. It was rapidly accepted and printed in all editions of the Talmud. His other work, *Hiddushei Aggadot* ("Novellae in Aggadah") was an extensive commentary of the Aggadot of the Talmud and reflected his deep knowledge of kabbalah and philosophy. Eidels died in 1631.

Eisenstadt, Abraham Zevi Hirsch ben Jacob

Abraham Eisenstadt, who was born in 1813 in Bialystok, was a halakhic authority. He was rabbi first of Berestovista in the district of Grodno, appointed to this position in 1836, and then in 1856 of Utina in the district of Kovno. His major work, *Pithei Teshuvah*, was aimed at collecting, digesting and supplying the missing link in the enormous literature of halakhic material present throughout the responsa literature. He then related it to the relevant laws in Joseph Caro's *Shulkhan Arukh*. In addition to then stating what the halakha should be, he also gave the reason for the particular halakha and a summary of the arguments used in the various responsa. This allowed rabbis to then render opinions on various issues and matters that had changed since the publication of Caro's work.

The *Pithei Teshuvah* on *Yoreh De'ah* and *Even HaEzer* was published in 1836 and 1861 and the one on *Hoshen Mishpat* in 1875, after his death.

Eisenstadt died in 1868 in Koenigsberg, where he had gone for medical treatment.

Eisenstadt, Benjamin

He was the son of Abraham Eisenstadt and lived from 1846 to 1920. He filled his father's post in Utina, serving there for 52 years. He was the author of *Masot Binyamin*, which consisted of Talmudic novellae.

Eisenstadt, Meir ben Iszak (Meir Ash) ### *(Maharam Ash / Panim Me'irot)*

Meir Eisenstadt, who was also known as Meir Ash, was born in 1670. He served as the dayan in Posen and then the rabbi in Szydlowiec, Poland. He then settled in Worms, Germany where he became the Rosh Yeshiva. From there he went to Prosnitz, Germany for a while, moving back to Szydlowiec for three years and finally going to Eisenstadt, where he adopted the name of the town for his last name.

He was the author of several works. His major work was *Panim Me'irot*, a collection of responsa and various Talmudic novellae in four parts. *Or HaGanuz* consisted of novellae on the marriage laws. *Kotnot Or* was a commentary on the Pentateuch. He died in 1744.

Eisenstadter, Meir (Meir Ash) (Maharam Ash)

Meir Eisenstadter was born in 1780 in Schossburg (Sastin). He was also known as Meir Ash and the Maharam Ash. While still a youth he moved to Eisenstadt and also adopted this name for his own. He studied under Moses Sofer (Chatam Sofer). He served as rabbi of Baja for twenty years until 1835. He was then appointed the rabbi of Ungvar, Hungary where he was also the head of a large yeshiva.

He is best known for his work *Imrei Esh* (Words of Fire) that was a collection of responsa in two parts. He also wrote *Imrei Yosher*, a collection of sermons and *Imrei Binah*, which consisted of novellae on a number of tractates. He died in 1852.

Elchanan (Bachrach), Naftali Hertz ben Yaakov

Naftali Hertz was a seventeenth century German rabbi born in Frankfurt. His major work was *Emeq HaMelekh* ("Valley of the King") that was about Lurianic kabbalah. It was based largely on Israel Sarug's *Limmudei Azilut*. It had major impact on later kabbalah and was viewed as the authoritative work on Lurianic kabbalah, especially by the Hassidim and the followers of the Vilna Gaon. Contemporaries like David Azulai and Moses Hagiz disapproved of it.

Eliakim, Hillel ben

Hillel ben Eliakim was of Greek birth. He lived during the eleventh and twelfth centuries. Hillel was a student of Rashi. He wrote commentaries to the Midrash Sifra and Midrash Sifre. Both of these were known to the Tosafists. Both of these works were mentioned or quoted in other works.

Eliezer, Israel (Yisroel) ben (Ba'al Shem Tov / Besht)

Rabbi Yisroel ben Eliezer was born in Okopy, which was a small village in the Ukraine on the border of Poland and Russia, on August 27, 1698. He is considered the founder of the Hassidic movement. He was known by most Jews as the Ba'al Shem Tov ("Master of the Good [Divine] Name"). The acronym Besht was used more in writing than in speech.

There is little factual biographical information known about him. Most of what is known is tied in with legend. He was apparently orphaned early and the community cared for him. As a teenager he was given the job as a teacher's assistant. He then became the caretaker of the synagogue where he had the opportunity to study and during this period gained a high level of knowledge and eventually even studied kabbalah.

He was of a gentle disposition and apparently had a sentimental nature. This aspect of his personality led him to act as an arbitrator and mediator. He married Chana, the daughter of Ephraim of Brody, whose son was the well-known kabbalah authority, Abraham Gershon of Kitov, although the latter did not accept his brother-in-law.

Eliezer then moved to a village in the Carpathian mountains where he worked as a laborer. During this time he further enhanced his knowledge. He later became a ritual butcher in another village and his economic status improved somewhat. He then went on to run a village tavern that his brother-in-law had purchased for him. His years in the countryside taught him the use of plants and their healing powers and he put this knowledge to use. This gained him the reputation as a miracle healer and hence the name of Ba'al Shem Tov. He started appearing in public and expound his teachings.

The Besht moved to the village of Medzhybizh about 1740 and many people would come to listen to him. This ultimately became the seat of the Hassidic movement and of the Medzhybizh Hassidic dynasty. His efforts were supported by the brothers, Meir and Isaac Dov Margolis, prominent Talmudists. Later Rabbi Dov Ber of Mezritch was won over and it was this latter rabbi who in fact, in somewhat altered form introduced the Besht's teachings to a wider learned circle.

Rabbi Yisroel ben Eliezer did not write any books or other works His basic philosophy was that the whole universe, both physical and mental was a manifestation of the Divine Being and it is not an emanation from God, as the Mitnagdim viewed kabbalah. He also opposed Lurianic kabbalism which had contempt for the physical world. He considered the care of the body as important as the care of the soul. His teachings were recorded by his students.

His direct legacy was on the teachings he imparted to his students, many of whom went on to form their own Hassidic dynasties. The Ba'al Shem Tov died on May 22, 1760 in Medzhybizh, where he was buried and where his gravestone is still present. Although technically his grandson Boruch of Medzhybizh was his designated successor, the true succession fell to Dov Ber of Mezritch.

Eliezer, Tobiah ben

Eliezar ben Tobiah was an eleventh century Talmudist and poet, proved by Martin Buber to have been born in Castoria, Bulgaria in the latter part of the eleventh century. His father was Eliezer ben Isaac HaGadol, probably one of the teachers of Rashi. He was a Talmudist and poet, best known for his midrashic work.

His midrashic work was the *Lekah Tob* or *Pesikhta Zutarta* (the "Lesser Pesikta"). It is a midrashic commentary on the Pentateuch and the Five Megillot. The second title to this work comes from the sixteenth century to differentiate it from the *Pesikta Rabbati* (the "Greater Pesikta"). A number of later commentators, including Rashi's pupils, Menahem Solomon Jacob

Tam, Rashbam, Isaac ben Abba Mari and several others quoted from him.

He was also known as a poet, having written four poems that are still extant. Two are as a commentary and epilogue to the *Pesikta*, a third forming an epilogue to Leviticus and the other one is a seliha.

Eliezer of Toul

He was a Tosafist from the beginning of the thirteenth century. His work is mentioned by Zedekiah Anaw in his *Shibbole HaLeket*.

Eliezer of Touques

He was a French Tosafist of the second half of the thirteenth century. He abridged the tosafot of many others and added marginal notes of his own which were titled *Gilyon Tosafot* and *Tosafot Gillayon*. This abridgement with his notes was called *Tosafot Tuk*. It is the basis for the tosafot that are now printed in the Talmud. Eliezer was also the author of a commentary on the Pentateuch that was appended to the manuscript of Ibn Janah's *Sefer HaRikmah* which is in the Bibliotheque Nationale in Paris.

Eligdor, Abba Mari ben

In addition to being a distinguished thirteenth and fourteenth centuries Talmudist from Salonica, he was also a philosopher, physicist and astronomer. He wrote many commentaries on the Pentateuch, Job and parts of the Talmud, but there are only fragmentary manuscripts that are extant. His manuscripts on Job can be found in several European libraries. Abba Mari questioned the existence of Job. He was a loyal student of Maimonides.

Elijah, Perez ben (Rap, RaPaSh, MaHaRPaSh)

Perez ben Elijah of Corbeil was a French Tosafist of the thirteenth century. He is known by the acronyms Rap (Rabbi Perez), RaPaSh (Rabbi Perez, may he live) and MaHaRPaSh (our master Rabbi Perez may he live). He was a student of Rabbi Jehiel of Paris and Samuel of Evreux. On a trip to Germany he met Meir of Rothenburg. He was widely known as a Talmudic authority and his commentaries were widely studied.

Perez wrote several glosses. He had commentaries on a majority of the Talmud and he wrote a Masoretic work, *Sefer Peretz* which is no longer in existence. He died about 1295.

Ellenburg, Yissachar Ber

Rabbi Yissachar Ber was born in Posen, Poland in 1570. He was a student of the Maharal. He studied kabbalah under Israel Seruk. In 1600, he became the rabbi of Gorizia in Italy and then later of Austerlitz, which was then a part of Czechoslovakia.

He is most well known for his Talmud commentary, *Be'er Sheva*, which provides commentaries on some of the tractates for which no tosefot exist. He also authored a super-commentary on Rashi's Pentateuch commentary, called *Tzeidah LaDerech*. He died in 1623.

Emden, Jacob Israel ben Zvi Ashkenazi (the Yabets)

Jacob Emden or the Yabets was born in 1697 in Altona (then a part of Denmark and now in Germany) and died in 1776. Until age seventeen he studied under his father, Rabbi Tzvi Ashkenazi, and after his marriage, under his father-in-law Mordechai ben Naphtali Kohen at his yeshiva. Later he also studied kabbalah, philosophy and grammar. He opposed Maimonides' *Guide for the Perplexed* since he felt it favored a non-Jewish theology. He spent most of his life in various commercial endeavors and did not function as a rabbi.

He was an anti-Shabbethian. This brought him into conflict with Eybeschutz that ultimately led to legal proceedings. He wrote several articles on the conflict.

He authored *Lehem Shamayim*, a commentary on the Mishnah. *She'elat Yaabez* was a collection of 372 responsa. His *Siddur Tefilah* contained, in addition to the ritual prayers, commentary, grammatical notes and ritual laws.

Mor u-Kezi'ah were novellae on the *Orach Chaim* of Asher's *Arba'ah Turim*. *Zizim u-Ferahim* was a collection of articles on kabbalah. He also wrote a number of other smaller works, some of which were published.

Enoch, Judah ben

Judah ben Enoch lived in the latter half of the seventeenth and first part of the eighteenth centuries. He was the chief rabbi of Pfersee, Bavaria. A collection of his responsa, titled *Hinnuk ben Yehuda*, was published by his son Enoch ben Judah.

Ephraim, Moshe Chaim (of Sudilkov)

Rabbi Moshe Chaim Ephraim was born in 1748 in Medzhybizh in Poland. He was the grandson of Israel ben Eliezer, the Ba'al Shem Tov. He was brought up in the latter's household. After the death of his grandfather, he studied under Rabbi Dov Ber, the Maggid of Mezritch and under Rabbi Yaakov Yosef of Polonoye. Following this he settled in Sudilkov where he served as Maggid from 1780 to 1785. He then returned to Medzhybizh where he served as rebbe until his death in 1800.

Ephraim's major work was *Degel Machaneh Ephraim* that was published by his son Yaakov Yechiel in 1810. It is considered a classical work of Hassidic literature. It contains discussions of the weekly Torah portions based on the teachings of the Ba'al Shem Tov. It is considered a primary source for understanding the ideology of the Ba'al Shem Tov.

Epstein, Avraham

Nothing can be found on his life. He wrote a work, *Ma'aseh Hageonim* that consists of the responsa and laws of Rashi and the Geonim.

Epstein, Baruch HaLevi

Rabbi Epstein was a Lithuanian rabbi born in 1860. He grew up in Novardok where his father, Rabbi Yechiel Michel Epstein the author of the *Arukh HaShulkhan*, was the community rabbi. He studied at the Volozhin Yeshiva under his uncle Naftali Zvi Yehuda Berlin. After his marriage he moved to Pinsk where he stayed for the remainder of his life. He was in the United States from 1923 – 1926.

Epstein never practised as a rabbi, but was a bookkeeper. He authored a number of books, but he is most well-known for his work *Torat Temimah* ("The Perfect Torah"), a commentary on the Torah. There has recently been an English translation of the work by Rabbi Shraga Silverstein called "The Essential Torah Temima". He also wrote *Baruch she-Amar* ("Praised he who Spoke"), a commentary on the siddur, *Mekor Baruch* ("Source of Blessing"), which was an autobiographical work and *Tosefet Berakhah* ("Added Blessing") that were novellae on the Torah. He died in Pinsk in 1941.

Epstein, Moshe Mordechai

Rabbi Epstein was born in Bakst, in the Vilna district of Lithuania in 1866. He began his studies at the Volozhin Yeshiva at the age of sixteen under the guidance of Rabbi Chaim Soloveitchik. There he met his future brother-in-law, Rabbi Isser Zalman Meltzer. In 1889 he married Menucha Frank whose father was Rabbi Shraga Feival Frank of the illustrious Frank family.

After his marriage he moved to Kovno where, with his brother-in-law, he studied under Rabbi Yitzhak Blazer, Rabbi Yisrael Salanter's pupil. It was there that Moshe Epstein became interested in the study of Mussar.

In 1894 both these rabbis started teaching at the famous Slabodka Yeshiva, and in 1897 Rabbi Nosson Tzvi Finkel invited Rabbi Epstein to become the Rosh Yeshiva there. Under both these famous rabbis the yeshiva flourished.

In 1924 the yeshiva relocated to Hebron, Palestine where it thrived until the 1929 massacre there by the Arabs, where sixty-eight Jews were killed. The yeshiva then relocated to the Geula section of Jerusalem.

Rabbi Epstein authored the *Levush Mordechai*, which contained his hiddushim or novellae of the entire Talmud. He died in Jerusalem in 1933.

Epstein, Yechiel Michel HaLevi (the Aruch haShulchan)

Yechiel Michel Epstein was born in Lithuania in 1829 into a wealthy family of contractors to the Czarist army in Babruyak (Belarus). He was often called the *Aruch haShulchan*, after his main work.

He studied in his hometown and later married the sister of Naftali Zvi Yehuda Berlin. He obtained s'micha after his marriage and became the rabbi of Novozhypkov near Minsk. This was a town of mainly Chabad Lubavitch followers. He forged a close relationship with Rabbi Menachem Mendel Schneerson, the *Tzemach Tzedek*. He later assumed a position of rabbi in Novogrudok, where he served for thirty-four years until his death. It was here that he composed his writings.

Epstein's most well-known work was his *Aruch HaShulchan*, which traces the origins of each law and custom, provides the view of the Rishonim, and arrives at a decision, which could be in agreement with or disagree with those decisions of the Acharonim. His *Aruch HaShulchan he'Atid* ("Laying the

Table of the Future"), summarizes and analyzes the laws that will apply in the Messianic times. Many agricultural laws that are applicable to Israel only are described here. Hence this work did have later relevance. His *Or li-Yesharim* is a commentary on *Sefer HaYashar*, the classical work of the Tosafist, Rabbi Yaakov ben Meir (Rabbeinu Tam), not the anonymous one. Then he wrote a commentary on the Talmud titled *Mical HaMayim* and a commentary on the Haggadah, *Leil Shimurim*. Rabbi Epstein died in 1907.

Escapa, Joseph

Joseph Escapa was born in 1572, possibly in Uskap, Turkey. He became head of the yeshiva in Salonika and then at Smyrna. His student was Shabbetai Tzvi.

His major work was *Rosh Yosef*, which was a commentary and novellae on the *Arba'ah Turim* of Jacob Asher. Only a portion of this was published. He also wrote a number of responsa, some of which were published under the title of *Teshubot Rosh Yosef*. He died in 1662.

Etlinger, Yaakov (Aruch LaNer)

He was born in 1808 in Germany. He studied under his father and then under the son of Aryeh Leib ben Asher Gunzberg (Shaagat Aryeh). At age twenty-eight he became the rabbi of Altona. Among his predecessors in this position were Rabbis Jonathan Eybeschutz and Isaac Horowitz. He was considered an authority on halakha. His eponym indicated that he was "Carrying the Torch and Passing the Torch." He was vehemently against the Reform Movement in Germany. He wrote a work called *Responsa Binyan Tzion*. He also wrote a commentary on the Mishnah titled *Aruch LaNer*. Rabbi Etlinger died in 1871.

Ettinger, Hayyim Judah Lob

An Austrian rabbi, he was born in the latter half of the seventeenth century. He was the rabbi of Hollesschau and the head of the Talmudic school. Later he became the head of the Talmud school and then the rabbi of Lemberg. He wrote many responsa, but none were published as a collection. He died in 1739.

Ettinger, Isaac Aaron

He was a Galician scholar and rabbi born in Lemberg in 1827. Being independently wealthy he declined several offers to the rabbinate until in 1868 he became the rabbi of Przemysl. His responsa had significant influence on both Hassidim and Mitnagdim. Some of these were published by his children. He died in 1891.

Eybeschutz, Jonathan

Eybeschutz was an eighteenth-century Talmudist and kabbalist who was born in Krakow in 1690. With Jacob Emden, he is known for the Emden-Eybeschutz controversy where the former accused the latter of heresy concerning amulets that he was suspected of issuing and which recognized the false messianic claims of Shabbetai Tzvi. He also angered the rabbis of Prague because of his friendly relations with Cardinal Hassebauer from whom he got permission to print the Talmud as long as he omitted all passages contradicting the principles of Christianity. The rabbis responded by revoking his printing license.

Eybeschutz was a child prodigy in Talmud. In 1715 he settled in Prague where he became the well-respected head of the yeshiva. In 1741 he became rabbi of Metz and then in 1750, he was elected the rabbi of the "Three Communities" of Altona, Hamburg and Wansbek.

He was recognized as an authority in Talmud, halakha and kabbalah. A number of his works in these areas have been printed. These included works on homiletics, for example *Ya'arot Devash*, *Tiferet Yehonatan*, and *Taryag Mitzvot*. His works on halakha and Talmud included novellae on the *Shulkhan Arukh*, notes on Maimonides' *Mishneh Torah* called *Binah la-Ittim* and *Chiddushim al Hilkot Yom Tov*. On kabbalah, he published a collection of letters called *Shem Olam*. Eybeschutz died in 1764 in Altona.

Ezobi, Joseph ben Hanan ben Nathan

Joseph ben Hanan Ezobi was a thirteenth century liturgical poet. He lived in Perpignan, France. He is known to have written poems for the Festival of Shavuot, for the Ten Martyrs under Hadrian, for his son's wedding and also some that were found in the Barcelona Haggadah.

Ezra

Ezra lived in the sixth century BCE. He led a contingent of Israelites back from exile in Babylon in 459 BCE. He was a descendant of Seraiah, the high priest who was taken captive by the Babylonians. During the reign of Artaxerxes I, he was given permission to lead the Israelites back to Jerusalem. Upon his return to Jerusalem he took measures against intermarriage, and insisted on the dismissal of the non-Hebrew women. He introduced the reading of the Torah of Moses to the assembly.

According to the text in Nehemiah (8:7) he, other scholars, and the Levites explained the meaning of what was being read to the people so that they could understand what was being read. He was thus the first interpreter of the law.

Ezra is thought to have established the Great Assembly, the forerunner of the Sanhedrin, and which was responsible for establishing the practices which form the basis of traditional Judaism, including prayer and the reading of the Torah.

Ezra, Abraham ben Meir ibn (Abenezra, Ibn Ezra)

Ibn Ezra, also known as Abenezra was born in about 1092 at Tudela in Spain and died in 1167. He was one of the greatest men of letters and writers of the Middle Ages, excelling in philosophy, astronomy, medicine, poetry, linguistics and exegesis. The Abenezra crater on the moon is named after him.

Abenezra spent most of his life wandering Europe and North Africa.

After leaving Spain he resided for several years in Rome, Lucca, Mantua, and Verona. He also made journeys to Egypt as well as traveling to Palestine and Baghdad. He also spent time in Provence as well as several years in northern France and London. It was while sojourning in these various countries that he produced the majority of his large corpus of written work. His work first and foremost covered the fields of philology and biblical exegesis. These works together with his other work were written in Hebrew and thus made available to the Jews of Christian Europe many treasures written in Arabic. His mission was to introduce to the non-Arabic Jews the science of Judaism, an aspect of which they were unfamiliar.

His grammatical works, especially *Moznayim* ("Scales") and *Zahot* ("Correctness") were the first to present Hebrew grammar. But of even greater value than these works were his commentaries on most of the books of the Bible, especially the Pentateuch. The importance of his biblical exegetic work lay in it arriving at the simple sense of the text, the *Peshat*. His work produced much on the philosophy of religion. In this field, *Yesod Mora* ("Foundation of Awe") was particularly important. It covered the divisions and reasons for biblical law.

Ibn Ezra left his mark on Jewish thought through his philosophical legacy. He was much influenced by Saadia, the Jewish thinker. His list of doctrines can be summarized as the deity rules the terrestrial world by means of heavenly bodies and that humans live under astral destiny, although the stars are subservient to God. The precise structure of the human soul or the way it is bonded to the body is not known. However, nurturing this spiritual component is the hope of refuge from this world.

The resume of his religious and Hebrew work maybe divided as follows:

Commentaries

Biblical Exegesis: His main work is a commentary on the Pentateuch. Like Rashi, this work subsequently produced many super-commentaries. This work, more than any other, established his reputation. The complete commentary, published just before his death is titled *Sefer HaYashar*. The commentary on Exodus is an independent work.

Hebrew Grammar
1. *Moznayim* is a work examining the terms used in Hebrew grammar.
2. Translation of the work of Judah ben David Hayyuj, the Spanish-Jewish grammarian into Hebrew.
3. *Sefer HaYesod* or *Yesod Dikduk* which is on linguistic correctness.
4. *Safah Berurah*

Smaller works
1. *Sefer Yeter* which was a defense of Saadia Gaon.
2. *Sefer Ha-Shem*
3. *Yesid Mispar*, on numerals and Babylonian-Hebrew punctuation.
4. *Iggeret Shabbat*, a responsum on the Sabbath.

Religious Philosophy
Yesod Mora which describes the divisions of and reasons for Biblical commandments.

Ezra, Moses ibn (HaSallah)

Moses ibn Ezra was known as HaSallah ("writer of penitential prayers"). He was born in Granada somewhere between 1055 and 1060. He was related to Abraham ibn Ezra.

Moses was also a distinguished philosopher, linguist and poet. In the religious sphere he is known for his sacred poems or piyyutim, which are selichot and found in the Mahzor. He died after 1138.

Faibesh (Phoebus), Samuel ben Uri Shraga

Rabbi Faibesch, also known as Phoebus or Fayvish was a Polish rabbi and Talmudist in the second half of the seventeenth century. He served several communities in Poland and Germany.

He is known for his commentary, *Beit Shmuel*, on the *Shulkhan Arukh*, the section *Even HaEzer*. He frequently disagreed with the decisions of Caro and Isserles. His commentary is distinguished by its clarity and individuality of opinion.

Falk, Joshua ben Alexander (Katz) HaKohen

Rabbi Falk was born in 1555 in Lvov (Lemberg), Poland and died in 1614. He studied under rabbis Solomon Luria and Moses Isserles (Rama). He became head of the yeshiva in Lemberg. Among his pupils was Joshua Hoschel ben Joseph, the author of *Maginne Shelomoh*. Falk opposed the study of codes of law to the exclusion of the original sources.

He devoted most of his time to analyzing and then writing commentaries on Jacob ben Ashur's *Tur* and Caro's *Shulkhan Arukh*. His work was titled *Beit Israel* ("House of Israel"). It is subdivided into two parts, the *Perishah*, which is a straightforward explanation of the Tur aimed at clarifying the rulings, and the *Derishah* that has more in depth discussion, analysis and comparison of various interpretations offered by different Talmudic authorities.

Feinstein Moshe (Reb Moshe)

Moshe Feinstein was born in Uzda, Belarus on March 3, 1895. He was the son of Rabbi David Feinstein who was the rabbi of Uzdan and under whom he studied as a youth, before going to yeshivas in Slutsk, Shklov and Amistlav. He was then appointed rabbi of Luban where he served for sixteen years before emigrating to the United States. He settled in New York where he became the Rosh Yeshiva of Mesivta Tifereth Jerusalem.

He belonged to the Haredi division of Hassidism and in later life came to be viewed as the supreme rabbinic authority of Orthodox Jewry in North America. As a result, he was called upon to answer difficult halakhic questions from around the world, providing more than 2,000 responsa.

Feinstein published several works during his life and some were published posthumously. Among these are *Igrot Moshe* which is an eight-volume work containing most of his responsa. *Dibros Moshe* is an eleven-volume work of Talmudic novellae. *Darash Moshe* consists of novellae on the Torah that was published posthumously.

Rabbi Feinstein died on March 23, 1986 and is buried on Har HaMenuchot in Jerusalem.

Fradkin, Shneur Zalman, of Lublin

Rabbi Shneur Zalman Fradkin was born in 1830 and died in 1902. He was a follower of Menachem Mendel Schneerson, the Tzemech Tzedek. He was the chief rabbi first of Polotsk and then of Lublin. He subsequently immigrated to Palestine. He is best known for his important scholarly work, *Toras Chesed*.

Freehof, Solomon Bennett

Solomon Freehof was born in London in 1892. He was a well-known Reform rabbi and scholar. He was a descendant of the Alter Rebbe, the founder of Lubavitcher Hassidism. In 1903, he immigrated to the USA. He studied halakha with a number of rabbis.

He studied at the University of Cincinnati and was ordained by the Hebrew Union College in 1915. He was an army chaplain in the first world war and then went on to become a professor of liturgy at HUC. He was the rabbi of Congregation Kehillath Anshe Maarav in Chicago. After that he moved to Pittsburgh.

His major work was in the area of Reform responsa. He wrote a number of works on responsa on this denomination of Judaism, but his best known is *The Responsa Literature* published in 1955. It gives a scholarly history of responsa, the major contributors as well as important examples of this aspect of biblical and Talmudic interpretation. Freehof died in 1990.

Gabirol (Gvirol), Solomon ben Judah, ibn

Solomon ibn Gabirol was born in Malaga in 1021. Little is known of his life. His parents died when young and he became a protégé of Jekuthiel Hassan, who was assassinated. He soon showed his poetic capabilities composing a poem on Hassan's death as well as that of Hai Gaon. He wandered around Spain. Samuel ibn Naghrela was another patron and friend.

At twenty, he wrote a Hebrew grammar work in verse called *Anak*. Many of his writings were of a philosophical nature and Moses ibn Ezra recognized him as such. He was the first teacher of Neoplatonism in Europe. Gratz referred to him as the Jewish Plato. In his most well known philosophical work, *Mekor Chaim* or in Latin, *Fons Vitae*, he states his philosophy in three terms; There is the first substance – God; there is matter and form – the world; and then there is the will as the intermediary. Judaic monotheism is found in Gabirol's doctrine of "material universalis." In the twelfth century Abraham ibn Daud opposed Gabirol's philosophy in his work, *Sefer HaKabbalah*. However, some of Gabirol's philosophy is found in thirteenth century kabbalistic literature.

He was also well-known as a poet which also reflected his philosophical ideas. *Keter Malkut* ("Royal Crown") is one of the better known of his philosophical poems. His liturgical poems were considered of a lofty nature. His *Keter Malkut* did not follow the payetanic form. However, in many places it was used as part of the Yom Kippur service. His other well known poem *Azharoth*, which was based on the *Taryag* (613) commandments of the Torah, was included in Shavuot services in many congregations. His *Shir Hakavod* ("Song of Glory") and *Shir Hayichud* ("Song of Unity) were included in the prayer book.

Gabirol also wrote an ethical treatise called *The Improvement of the Moral Qualities* or more commonly known as *Ethics*.

He died in about 1058 in Valencia, the circumstances of his death being a mystery, but shrouded in a legend that he was trampled to death by an Arab horseman, like Rabbi Judah HaLevi.

Galante, Abraham

Abraham Galante was born in Rome and studied under his elder brother, Moshe Galante. Both immigrated to Palestine where Rabbi Abraham studied kabbalah under Moses Cordovero. He wrote a commentary on the *Zohar* titled *Yare'ach Yakar*, which was a short version of Cordovero's *Ohr Yakar*. He died in Safed in 1588.

Ganzfried, Solomon ben Joseph

Rabbi Shlomo Ganzfried was born in Uzhorod (Ungvar) in the Carpathian region of what is now the Ukraine, in 1804. His father died when he was eight and the Rosh Yeshiva, Rabbi Zvi Hirsch Heller became his legal guardian. He studied under him for a decade until he was ordained and got married. He was a Haredi Orthodox Jew.

In 1843, he became the rabbi of Brezevitz and then returned to Ungvar as a judge in the religious court. It was while he was there that he wrote his well known work, the *Kitzur Shulkhan Arukh* that summarized Caro's *Shulkhan Arukh*, and added Hungarian customs to include the nineteenth century. He also wrote several smaller works; *Kesses Hasofer*, *Pnei Shlomo* and *Toras Zevach*. Ganzfried died in 1886.

Gaon, Achai

Achai Gaon, who was also known as Ahai of Sabha, was one of the eighth century Geonim, and was a renowned Talmudist. He is the first rabbinic author following the close of the Talmud.

After being passed over by the exilarch to be the next Gaon of Pumbedita, Achai settled in Palestine in about 752. It was there that he wrote his book *Sheilot d'Rav Achai* or *Sheiltos*. The book consisted of treatises of biblical and Talmudic precepts written for the thoughtful layman. It was written with a view to the practice of moral duties and was based on the weekly parashot. It was first published in Venice in 1546. A later edition was published by Isaiah Berlin with a short commentary. Hebrew manuscripts of this book are in the Bodleian Library, Oxford and in the Bibliotheque Nationale, Paris. Simeon Kayyara used his work in compiling his own *Halakot Gedolot*.

Gaon, Hai

Hai Gaon lived from 969 to 1038. He was head of the Academy at Pumbedita and was the last of the Geonim. His father was Rav Sherira Gaon. He was the author of a commentary on the Talmud as well as a collection of responsa.

Gaon, Shem Tov ben Abraham ibn

Shem Tov was born in Spain in about 1283. His name Gaon was probably based on it being the proper name of one of his ancestors. He studied Talmud under Solomon ben Aderet and kabbalah under Isaac ben Todros. After completion of his studies he went to Palestine, first to Jerusalem and then settled in Safed, where he advanced his kabbalistic meditation.

He wrote many works of which only two were published. The first was *Migdal Oz* that was a commentary on Maimonides' *Yad*, and *Keter Shem Tov* that was a super-commentary on Nahmanides' commentary on the Pentateuch. He died in 1330.

Gediliyah, Abraham

Rabbi Abraham Gediliyah was born in Jerusalem in 1590. He later moved to Hebron. He authored a commentary on the *Yalkut Shimoni* titled *Bris Avraham*. He went to Leghorn to publish the book there as well as a new edition of the *Yalkut Shimoni*. He stayed in Leghorn as a printer and proofreader. He later returned to Jerusalem where he died in 1672.

Gerondi, Yonah ben Avraham (Rabbeinu Yonah)

Yonah ben Avraham Gerondi, also known as Rabbeinu Yonah was a Catalan rabbi and a cousin of Nahmanides. He was a student of Solomon of Montpellier, a fierce opponent of Maimonides' philosophical work. Gerondi was apparently the instigator of burning of Maimonides' work as ordered by the Parisian authorities. He later apologized for this act. He went on to Toledo where he became a great Talmudic teacher. He would always quote Maimonides.

Gerondi is most well known for his ethical writings. It is assumed that these were written both to atone for and to stress his repentance for his earlier attacks on Maimonides. The *Iggeret HaTeshuvah*, the *Sha'are Teshuvah* and the *Sefer HaYirah* are among the standard Jewish ethical works from the Middle Ages. They are still quoted from currently.

His hiddushim to Alfasi's *Berakhot* was probably written by his disciples. He wrote novellae on aspects of the Talmud. A commentary on Proverbs exists in manuscript. He died in 1263.

Gerondi, Zerachiah ben Isaac HaLevi (ReZaH, RaZBI, Ba'al HaMaor)

Zerachiah HaLevi was born in about 1125 in the town of Gerona in Spain. He was a member of the rabbinic family called Yitzhari of Gerona. His father was Isaac HaLevi, his grandfather was Zerachiah HaLevi (his namesake) and his great-grandfather was the great Talmudic scholar Shem

Tov HaLevi from Provence.

In his youth Zerachiah moved to Provence to study. One of his teachers was Moses ben Joseph ben Merwan HaLevi, who headed the yeshiva at Narbonne. He later went to Lunel where he studied with Meshullam ben Jacob of Lunel.

Zerachiah was a great Talmudist who had an analytical mind and he devoted himself to halakhic problems. He was a gifted poet and was also versed in Arab literature, in philosophy and astronomy.

His most famous work is *Sefer HaMaor*, which he spent nearly forty years writing. The book is divided into two parts, *HaMaor HaGadol* (the Great Light) and *HaMaor HaKaton* (the Small Light). The first part discusses the tractates Berakhot, Mo'ed and Chullin and the second part discusses Nashim and Nezikin. He also wrote *ReZaH* that critically objects to the RIF's views while holding him in high esteem. His other major work was *Sefer HaTsava* that explained the thirteen principles of drasha used in the Gemara. He also wrote several other works as well as many piyyutim.

Zerachiah HaLevi had a great influence on other rabbis and scholars, some, including Nahmanides, writing responsa in support of his views. He died in Lunel in 1186.

Gershom, Levi ben (Gersonides, Ralbag)

Levi ben Gershom, who was better known as Gersonides or the Ralbag, was born in Bagnol in Languedoc, France in 1288 and died in 1344. He was not only a well-known Talmudist but also an astronomer and mathematician. Not much is known of his life and he never seems to have occupied a formal rabbinical position. His father was probably Gershom ben Solomon de Beziers. He was either a grandson or great-grandson of Nahmanides (Ramban). He might have married a distant cousin, although there are no known offspring.

His works covered philosophical, religious, mathematical and astronomical subjects. In the religious and philosophical sphere his most important work was *Sefer Milkhamot Ha-Shem* ("The Wars of the Lord"). It was modeled after Maimonides' *Guide for the Perplexed*. This work covers the doctrine of the soul, prophecy and God's knowledge of facts and providence, celestial subjects and creation and miracles. However, overall his philosophical ideas went against mainstream traditional Jewish thought. His scientific work was *Sefer Ma'aseh Hoshev* ("The Work of a Counter").

His religious works were *Perush al Sefer Iyob* that have been translated into English by Abraham Lassen ("The Commentary of Levi ben Gersom on the Book of Job") and *Perush al Sefer HaTorah* (Commentary on the Pentateuch). Several other works have also been translated into English: Providence and the Philosophy of Gersonides by David Bleich, Creation of the World according to Gersonides by Jacob Staub, The Wars of the Lord by Seymour Feldman, and the Commentary on Song of Songs by Menachem Kellner. Gersonides' views of philosophy have only recently come to be well received, but his commentaries have always been important in Jewish theology.

Ghiyyat (Ghayyat) Isaac ben Judah ibn

Isaac Ghiyyat was a Spanish rabbi who was born in 1038 in Lucena where he also lived. Some authorities believe his teacher was Isaac Alfasi. Moses ibn Ezra was one of his pupils.

He was the author of *Sha'areh Simhah* that covered the ritual laws of the festivals. *Hilkot Pesahim* was a separate publication regarding the laws of Passover. He was the author of many piyyutim, many of which can be found in the Mahzor of Tripoli under the title of *Sifte Renanot*. He died in 1089 in Cordoba.

Gias, Isaac ibn

Isaac ibn Gias was born in Lucena, Spain in 1020. He studied under Samuel ibn Naghrela (Samuel HaNagid). After the death of Samuel HaNagid's son, Joseph, Gias became head of the yeshiva.

He started writing many works, but these were left unfinished due to the demands of his educational role. The only manuscript that has survived is that of his halakhic compendium, *Meah Shearim* that was published, with a commentary in the nineteenth century under the title of *Yitzhak Yeranen*. This work was arranged according to Talmudic topics and not according to the sequence of the Talmud. Ibn Gias described the halakha in his own words and then gave a series of sources and discussed the various positions taken. He also used the Jerusalem Talmud extensively.

He went to Cordoba to receive medical care when he became ill, but died there in 1089. He was buried in Lucena.

Gikatilla, Joseph ben Abraham (Joseph Ba'al HaNissim)

Gikatilla was a Spanish kabbalist who was born in 1248 at Medinaceli, Old Castile. He was a pupil of Abraham Abulafia who praised him highly for his knowledge. His work was seen as a progressive development of philosophical insight into mysticism.

His two major works on kabbalah were *Ginnat Egoz* ("Garden of Nuts") that deals with the names of God, and *Sha'areh Orah* or *Sefer Orah* that also deals with the names of God. He died at Penafiel after 1305.

Ginzberg, Louis

Rabbi Ginsberg was born in Kovno, Lithuania in 1873. His lineage can be traced back to the Vilna Gaon. Like the Gaon, he mixed academic knowledge with Talmudic study.

In 1899 he immigrated to the USA and accepted a position at the Hebrew Union College. He also wrote articles for the Jewish Encyclopedia. A few years later he began teaching at the Jewish Theological Seminary. His major area of interest was in writing responsa.

He was the author of a number of scholarly works. He wrote a commentary on the Talmud Yerushalmi. His *Legends of the Jews* consisted of hundreds of legends and parables, covering both the midrashic literature, other classical rabbinic literature and also the apocryphal, pseudo-epigraphical and early

Christian literature. *Geonica* that was published in 1909 described the Babylonian Gaonim with extracts from their responsa. Many of his responsa were collected and edited by David Golinkin and titled *The Responsa of Professor Louis Ginzberg*. He died in 1953.

Golinkin, David

David Golinkin was born in 1955. He is a major halakhic authority in the Conservative movement. He studied under Louis Ginzberg. He lives in Israel and is head of the Schechter Institute of Jewish Studies.

He is an authority on the halakha and has written many responsa. He has also been responsible for uncovering and re-publishing many of the past responsa of the Committee on Jewish Law and Standards of the Rabbinical Assembly. These are now available in a three-volume set. He also edited *The Responsa of Professor Louis Ginzberg*. In 2000, his book *Responsa in a Moment: Halakhic Responses to Contemporary Issues* was published.

Gombiner, Abraham Abele ben Chaim HaLevi (Magen Avraham)

Abraham Gombiner, who was also known as the Magen Avraham, was born about 1633 in Gabin (Gombin), Poland. His parents were killed in the Chmielnicki massacres of 1648 and he then went to live and study with a relative, Jacob Isaac Gombiner, in Lithuania.

He is known for his important work, *Magen Avraham*, which is a commentary on the *Orach Chaim* of Caro's *Shulkhan Arukh*. It was only published after his death. There was originally debate over the name of the book since this is one of the names of God. It was therefore called *Ner Israel*, but the book was eventually published under its original title.

His book incorporated the local customs of Poland. It was a difficult book to follow and required explanations of it by later commentators, particularly Samuel Neta HaLevi Loew titled *Mahatsit HaShekel* and one by David Solomon Eibenschutz titled *Lebushe Serad*. He also incorporated kabbalistic customs of Safed, particularly those which could be found in Isaiah Horowitz's *Shnei Luhot HaBrit*.

Gombiner's work also influenced Rabbi Yechiel Michel Epstein's *Arukh HaShulkhan* and the Chofetz Chaim's (Israel Meir Kagan) *Mishnah Berurah*.

His other works included *Zayit Ra'anan*, a commentary on the Midrashic collection *Yalkut Shimoni*, and also a commentary on the work of the Tosafists on the tractate Nezikin which was published by his grandson as a part of the work of Moshe Yekutiel Kaufman, *Lehem Hapanim*.

Gombiner died in about 1683.

Gorion, Joseph ben

Joseph ben Gorion was probably a medieval historian who lived in southern Italy in the tenth century. He is the most likely author of *Sefer Yossipon*, which is a history of the Jews. One source considers it to be from the time of Creation, whereas the Jewish Encyclopedia considered it from the time of the return from Babylonia in 539 BCE. It ends with the destruction of the Second Temple in 70 CE.

Until a few centuries ago the work was widely known as the "Hebrew Josephus" or the "smaller Josephus", compared with that of the later Second Temple era Jewish historian Josephus who wrote in Greek. *Yossipon* is written in almost pure biblical Hebrew. It was widely read and respected by the Jews of the Middle Ages and considered an accurate historical source. It was first published in Mantua in 1476 by Abraham Conat. A later Yiddish edition was very popular.

Greenwald, Eliezer David

He was born in the nineteenth century and later lived in Jerusalem where he was the dean of Satmar. He wrote a collection of responsa titled *Keren L'David*. He died in 1928.

Grodzinski, Chaim Ozer

Rabbi Grodzinski was born in 1863 in Iuje, Belarus, near Vilna. His father and grandfather had been rabbis there for many years. At age fifteen he went to study at the Volozhin Yeshiva where he came to the attention of Rabbi Chaim Soloveitchik. He married the daughter of Rabbi Eliezer Eliyahu Grodzinski, the son-in-law of Rabbi Salanter.

After his father-in-law's death two years later the Vilna community approached him to take his father-in-law's position as one of the dayanim who formed the rabbinical leadership of Vilna. He served in this capacity for fifty-five years. There he created a group of students who would study independently and on Shabbat come together in his home for discussions. Many great rabbis emerged from this group.

Grodzinski was one of the founders of Agudat Israel. He also established a network of schools in Poland. He was the author of a three-volume collection of responsa called *She'elot uT'eshuvot Achiezer*. He died in 1940.

Gunzberg, Aryeh Leib ben Asher (Shaagat Aryeh)

Rabbi Gunzberg was born in Lithuania about 1695. In about 1720 he became a rabbi of the upper Minsk district acting as an assistant to his father. In 1733 he founded a yeshiva that attracted students from Belorussia and Lithuania.

Jehiel Heilprin, the author of *Seder HaDorot* was the head of another yeshiva in Minsk. There was friction between Aryeh Leib and him over their methods of instruction. Gunzberg was considered one of the most eminent casuists of his time and thus Heilprin was opposed to the pilpulistic method used by Gunzberg. However, the latter was also critical of this approach to establishing "the truth of the Torah" as he described it in the introduction to his most noted work, *Shaagat Aryeh*. His long-standing dispute with Heilprin forced him to leave Minsk in 1742.

In 1750, he became the rabbi at Volozhin. One of his disciples was Hayyim Volozhiner. It was here that he prepared *Shaagat Aryeh*. In 1765, he became the rabbi of Metz, although because of a dispute he only gave four sermons a year there. In addition to his major work, he also wrote *Turei Even*, novellae on several tractates, *She'elot u-Teshuvot Shaagat Aryeh HaHadashot* and *Gevurot Ari*, a novella on tractates of the Talmud. He died in Metz, France on June 23, 1785.

Habib (Chaviv), Moses ibn Yitzhak

He was a seventeenth century Palestinian rabbi. His teacher was Jacob Hagiz. He married one of his daughters. He wrote a work on the laws of divorce called *Get Pashut*. Another work on matrimonial laws was *Ezrat Nashim*. He also wrote Talmudic novellae called *Shammot ba-Arez*. Some of his responsa may be found in Abraham HaLevi's *Ginnat Weradim*.

HaDarshan, Moses

Moses HaDarshan lived in the eleventh century and was head of the yeshiva at Norbonne. He is considered the first exegesist in France. Together with Tobiah ben Eliezer he is considered the most prominent proponent of midrashic-symbolic biblical exegesis. His work on the Bible, sometimes called *Yesod* is known only through quotations in Rashi's commentaries. The midrash *Bereishit Rabbah Major* took much from the *Yesod*.

HaGadol, Shimon ben Yitzhak

He was born in Mainz, Germany in about 950. He served on the Beth Din of Mainz together with Gershom Me'Or HaGolah.

He is best known for his liturgical compositions that included selichot (supplication prayers) and the krovot (prayers said during repetition of the Amidah). These were published in the twentieth century under the title of *Piyutei Rabbi Shimon ben Yitzhak*. A number of them are included in the Mahzor. He died in Mainz in about 1020.

Hagiz, Jacob

Jacob Hagiz was born to a Spanish family in Fez in 1620. He studied under David Karigal. In 1646 he went to Italy to publish his book and remained there, teaching for ten years. He then went to Jerusalem where he became a member of the rabbinical college. In about 1673 he went to Constantinople to publish his book *Lehem HaPannim* but died there before this was accomplished. This book and other writings have all been lost.

Hagiz, Moses

Moses Hagiz was born in Jerusalem in about 1671 and died in 1750. He received his education from his maternal grandfather, Moses Galante. After the death of the latter he went to Safed for a while, returned to Jerusalem and then went on to Europe, wandering through Italy, spent some time in Venice and then went on to Amsterdam where he taught and published his works. He later returned to Palestine and ultimately settled in Safed.

Hagiz was a well-known Talmudic scholar in his era as well as being a kabbalist. He also had a wide secular knowledge. He wrote several minor works, including *Leket HaKemah*, novellae on the *Shulkhan Arukh* and *Eleh HaMitzvot* on the 613 commandments.

HaKohen, Aaron ben Jacob ben David

Aaron ben Jacob was a thirteenth century French scholar from Narbonne. After the expulsion of Jews in 1306 he went to Majorca. It was here that he published his great work, *Orhot Hayyim* ("The Paths of Life"). It is a ritual work. It slightly preceded Jacob ben Asher's *Arba'ah Turim*, which in fact replaced his one because of its more practical nature. An abridged version under the name of *Kol Bo* was later published, most likely by a German scholar, Shemeriah ben Simhah. It was more commonly used.

HaKohen, Abigdor ben Elijah

He was one of the Tosafists from the middle of the thirteenth century. His work is mentioned in Ketubot 63B.

HaKohen, Abraham ben Eliezer

Abraham ben Eliezer HaKohen was a seventeenth and eighteenth century darshan or preacher in Poland. He published his book *Ori We-Yish'i* ("My Light and my Salvation") that was a compilation of certain of his sermons and the treatment of repentance, prayer, and charity.

HaKohen, Joseph ben Joshua Meir

Rabbi Joseph HaKohen was born in Avignon, France in 1496, after his family was forced to flee from Spain. The family had once again to flee and settled in Genoa, where other family members had previously settled. He was taught by his father, Joshua Meir HaKohen. He not only studied traditional Jewish texts but also Greek. He went on to become a physician and had a successful career in this field in Genoa until the community was expelled. He was invited to practise in Voltaggio. A number of years later he went back to Genoa where he lived the remainder of his life.

He wrote a general historical book, but his most important contribution was his *Emek Habachah* ("Valley of Weeping"). It was a history of Jewish martyrdom through the ages. It used to be the custom in many communities to read this work on Tisha B'Av. Rabbi HaKohen died in Genoa in 1577.

HaKohen, Meir Simcha Kalonymus, of Dvinsk

Meir Simcha of Dvinsk was born in 1843 in Butrimonys (Baltrimantz), Lithuania. He obtained his education locally and after marriage at age seventeen he moved to Bialystok, Poland, where he continued his studies. In his late thirties he accepted the rabbinate of Dvinsk (Daugavpils) in Latvia. His contemporary there was the Hassidic Rabbi Yosef Rosen, the Rogatchover Gaon.

Rabbi Simcha wrote *Ohr Somayach* which was a collection of novellae on Maimonides' *Mishneh Torah*. It was a very popular work. His major contribution was to Jewish philosophy. His work, *Meshech Chochma*, was published posthumously by his pupil Menachem Mendel Zaks. It contains novellae on the Torah, but branches off into Jewish philosophy. He is said to have predicted the Holocaust by the presence of a statement in his work, "they think that Berlin is Jerusalem." He died in Riga in 1926.

HaKohen, Shabbatai ben Meir (Shach)

Shabbatai HaKohen, known as Shach (Shakh) after his work, was born in 1621 in Vilna. He entered yeshiva in 1633 and later studied at Cracow and Lublin as a student of Rabbi Heschel ben Yaakov. Following this he married and then was appointed an assistant to Rabbi Moshe Lima ben Isaac, the author of *Chelkat Mechokek*.

In 1646, he went to Cracow where he published his most well-known work, *Sifte Kohen* ("Lips of the Kohen") or *Shakh*, which was a commentary on the *Yoreh De'ah* and *Choshen Mishpat* of the *Shulkhan Arukh*. This work was very well received by the great scholars of the time. He also wrote a work on a collection of his responsa called *Gevurat Anashim*.

The Shach also often contested the opinions of his predecessors and provided a fresh interpretation of the halakha. He also disagreed with decisions of his contemporaries, David ben Shmuel HaLevi (The Taz) and Aaron Samuel Kaidanover.

Shabbatai HaKohen was also well-versed in kabbalah. He wrote selichot in commemoration of the Chmielnicki (Kmelnytsky) Uprising and the significant losses suffered by the Jews. He died in 1662.

HaLaban, Isaac ben Abraham

He was one of the earliest Tosafists and a pupil of Jacob Tam. He lived in the twelfth century. He was the author of a commentary on Ketubot and is frequently quoted in edited tosafot.

Halberstam, Chaim, of Sanz

Chaim Halberstam was born in 1793 in Tarnogrod, Poland. He studied under Rabbi Moshe Yehoshua Heshl Orenstein and Rabbi Naftali Zvi of Ropshitz. He was the first rebbe of the Sanz-Klausenberg Hassidic dynasty in Austria-Hungary (now Poland).

His extensive and wide-ranging writings covering Talmud, kabbalah and Torah responsas were all published under the title of *Divrei Chaim*.

He died in 1876 in Sanz, Austria-Hungary.

HaLevi, Aaron (of Barcelona)

Little is known about this rabbi, but much research has been done on him, primarily because scholars, particularly, Rosin, believe he is the author of the well-known work *Sefer HaChinuch*. Most accept this view. He must not be confused with the Aharon HaLevi who lived slightly earlier in the same century and was a colleague of the Rashba (Shlomo ben Aderet). Aaron was most likely a student of the Rashba and lived in the latter half of the thirteenth century.

Aaron HaLevi's landmark work is *Sefer HaChinuch* ("Book of Education") or simply "the *Chinuch.*" HaLevi wrote it as an anonymous work. It is a work that discusses the 613 commandments, based on Maimonides' system of counting as in his *Sefer HaMitzvot*. Each mitzvah is listed chronologically according to its appearance in the weekly parsha. Each mitzvah is discussed from the legal and moral perspective with each one being linked to the biblical source. He describes the root or the underpinnings of the commandment and then gives a brief overview of the halakha that governs the observance of each commandment. He also discusses the applicability of each one. Thus it summarizes in a simple, clear and practical way all the halakhot. It remains a popular work and is taught in yeshivot. Yosef ben Moshe Babad wrote a commentary on the legal aspects, called *Minchat Chinuch*.

The intention of the book was to impart to youth a knowledge of the law and to present the principles of Judaism in a simple way. Some thought the author wrote it for his own child.

HaLevi, Aaron Abraham ben Baruch Simeon

Rabbi Aaron HaLevi was born in the first quarter of the sixteenth century. He wrote a minor work on kabbalah, *Iggeret HaTe'amim* ("Letter of Accents"). It indicates how each accent and its specific name are supposed to contain references to the Ten Sefirot and to the people of Israel. Shabbethai Hurwitz wrote a commentary on this work.

HaLevi, Abraham ben Isaac

Abraham HaLevi was born in Barcelona in the early fourteenth century. He was a Talmudist and author, known for his religious poetry, one being for Passover that is preserved in manuscript form. He died in Narbonne in October 1393.

HaLevi, Abraham ben David
(Abraham ibn Daud, Rabad / Ravad I)

Abraham ibn Daud was born in Toledo, Spain about 1110. He was a philosopher and historian as well as being an astronomer. His philosophy, which was similar to but slightly preceded Maimonides, was of a more systematic form which was derived from Aristotle.

Hi philosophical work, *Al-Akidah Al-Rafiyah* ("The Sublime Faith") was completed in 1168. It was written in Arabic, but has been preserved in Hebrew translation, the one by Solomon ben Labi titled *Emunah Ramch*.

Ibn Daud died in about 1180, reportedly as a martyr.

HaLevi, Aharon (Ra'AH)

The Ra'AH was born in Gerona, Spain in 1235 and died in about 1290. He came from a prestigious family of rabbis on both his mother's and father's side, the former including the Rabbeinu Meshullam of Lunel and the latter Rabbeinu Zerachiah HaLevi, the Ba'al HaMaor, who was therefore Aaron HaLevi's great-great-grandfather. He studied under his father, his brother Pinchos HaLevi and under Nahmanides. He was also a colleague of the

Rashba (Shlomo Aderet).

He was the author of *Bedek HaBayit* that consisted of critical notes on the Rashba's *Torat HaBayit*. Some think he is the author of the possibly anonymous *Sefer HaChinuch*, but most doubt it, thinking it was another Aaron HaLevi who lived later in the thirteenth century and was a student of the Rashba.

HaLevi, Eliakim ben Meshullam

Eliakim ben Meshullam was a German Talmudist who was born in about 1030 and died at the end of that century in Speyer in Bavaria, where he founded a respected yeshiva.

He wrote commentaries on all the tractates of the Talmud, except Berakhot and Niddah. These were used by scholars up to the fourteenth century. Rashi, who was a fellow student, mentions his ritual decisions. Only the manuscript of Yoma still exists and is in the Codex Munich. He also composed a piyyut that is read when a circumcision is performed in the synagogue on the Sabbath.

HaLevi, Eliezer, ben Joel (Raviah)

Eliezer HaLevi was a German Tosafist born in 1140 and died in 1225. He was taught by his grandfather Rav Eliezer ben Natan (Raavan). His students included Eleazar Kalonymus (Rokeach) and Isaac ben Moses (Or Zarua). He is known mainly for his compendium of halakha originally called Avi HaEzri or later *Sefer HaRaviah*. It follows the sequence of the Talmudic tractates. He used both Sephardic and Ashkenazi authorities and was the first to try and synthesize the two.

HaLevi, Isaac ben Asher (Riva)

The Riva is the earliest known Tosafist. He was the son-in-law of Eliakim ben Meshullam HaLevi and a student of Rashi. He lived in the eleventh century in Speyer. He is frequently quoted under the name of Tosafot Riva in Abraham ben David's (Ravad) collection of responsa, *Temim De'im*. He also wrote a commentary on the Pentateuch that is no longer in existence, but was quoted by Rabbeinu Tam in his *Sefer HaYashar*.

HaLevi, Isaac ben Eleazar

Isaac ben Eleazar HaLevi was an eleventh century German Talmudist who flourished in Worms. He was a student of Gershom ben Judah (Me'Or HaGolah). He was also one of Rashi's teachers, and is often mentioned by the latter in his Talmud commentary (e.g. Yoma 39a, Sukkot 35b) and twice in his biblical commentary. HaLevi, the author of four wedding piyyutim, died in 1070.

HaLevi, Jacob ben Isaac (Jabez)

He lived in the first half of the twelfth century. He was a student of Kalonymus ben Isaac the Elder. He was the author of a tosafot, *Haggahot Maimuniyot*.

HaLevi, Judah (Yehuda) ben Samuel (RiHa'l)

Yehuda HaLevi was a Spanish philosopher and poet. He was born in Tudela, Navarre, Spain in about 1075. He studied under Isaac Alfasi, but became a physician, although his real interests lay in philosophy and poetry. He was a friend of Moses ibn Ezra. Because of his intense interest in his religious philosophical work he went to the Holy Land. He died in about 1141 shortly after arriving in Palestine.

His writings were devoted to philosophy and poetry. His philosophical work is the *Kuzari*, which is divided into five essays and deals with the conversion of a pagan king of the Khazars to Judaism. The essays deal with the superiority of Judaism, discussion of detailed theological questions, the various names of God and attacks against other forms of philosophy.

As for his poetry, it was firstly of a purely secular nature, but then later it became religious. He wrote about 750 poems. The latter type of poetry took the form of patriotism, and poetry for the synagogue, many of which were subsequently included in the liturgy as piyyutim (poetry), selichot (penitential hymns) and kinot (lamentations). Centuries later these had a profound effect on kabbalism and Hassidism.

Two of his most famous poems were "My Heart is in the East and I am at the ends of the West" and "Zion – thou art anxious for news of thy captives." In the twentieth century Naomi Shemer selected a phrase from the latter poem for her famous song "Jerusalem of Gold".

Halivni, David Weiss

David Halivni was born in 1927 in Ruthenia, a part of Czechoslovakia at the time and currently in the Ukraine. He grew up in the home of his grandfather, who taught him Talmud, in Sziget, Romania. During the Holocaust he was in several camps, first Auschwitz, then Gross-Rosen, followed by Al Wolfsberg and finally Mauthausen. After the war he came to the United States of America where he came to the attention of Saul Lieberman, the leading Talmudist at the Jewish Theological Seminary He first studied at the Yeshiva Chaim Berlin, then obtained a secular education and ultimately obtained a doctorate in Talmud.

Following a career at the JTS, he went on to become the Littauer Professor of Talmud and Classical Rabbinics at Columbia University. After retiring from there is 2005, he moved to Israel.

He is the author of a number of works. *Mekorot u'Mesorot* is a projected ten-volume commentary on the Talmud. He uses the method of source-critical analysis of the Talmud. He also believes that the Stammaim who followed the Amoraim, redacted the Gemara.

His other work is the volumes in English of *Peshat and Derash: Plain and Applied Meaning in Rabbinic Exegesis* that discusses both halakha, exegesis and theology. *Revelation Restored: Divine Writ And Critical Responses, Introductions to Sources and Traditions; Studies in the Formation of the Talmud, Midrash, Mishnah, and Gemara: The Jewish Predilection for Justified Law* that elaborates more on the Stammaim and *Breaking the Tablets: Jewish Theology After the Shoah* are some of his other works.

Hanina, Sherira ben, Gaon

Sherira Gaon lived in the tenth century. He was perhaps the most famous head of the Pumbedita Academy, being appointed to that position in 968 and holding it for thirty years. He was a descendant of prominent families from both parents. He was the father of Hai Gaon.

He authored the epistle *Iggeret Rav Sherira Gaon*, that was a history of the composition of the Talmud. It was written in response to an enquiry from the Jews of Kairouan, located in Tunisia and considered one of the holy cities of Islam. However, in the early middle ages Judaism flourished in Kairouan. Rabbeinu Chananel and the RIF (Rabbi Isaac Alfasi) came from there. Their query related to the authorship and composition of the Mishnah and Talmud. It existed in two forms – an Arabic one which was believed to be the original one and a Spanish version. There was a slight difference between the two with regard to whether the Mishnah was recorded in writing by Judah HaNasi. The Arabic one indicated that it was not while the Spanish one that it was.

Haparchi, Ishtori ben Moses, (Kaftor Vaferech)

Haparchi was born in Provence, France in 1280, although his family originated in Florence, Italy.

After the Jews were expelled from France in 1306 he went to Spain, then Egypt and settled In Israel where he was a physician in Bet Sha'an.

He was the author of a travelogue, written in Hebrew, called *Sefer Kaftor Vaferech* ("Book of Bulb and Flower"). It described the topography of the Land of Israel. He died in Bet Sha'an in 1345.

HaPenini, Yedayah

A thirteenth century Provencal rabbi. He studied under his father Rabbi Avraham of Bezier and Rabbi Meshullam of Bezier.

He wrote several minor works but is best known for his *Bechinot Olam*. It is a philosophical work that in a poetic way addresses the value of spiritual advancement and downplays worldly pursuits. He died in 1315.

HaRofei, Tzidkayah ben Avraham Anav (Anaw)

Tzidkayah ben Avraham Anav HaRofei was an Italian Talmudist born in 1230. He is known for his work, *Shibbole HaLeket* that were glosses to the first part of the Tur, particularly describing the ritual followed in Italy. He died in Rome in 1300.

Hayyim, Joel (Mahariah)

He was an eighteenth century rabbi who wrote novellae that were published by his son. The title of this was *Hiddushei Mahariah*. It was a super-commentary, the aim of which was to resolve difficulties of Abraham of Bertinoro's Talmudic commentary, in the presence of objections raised in the tosefot of Rabbi Yom Tov Lippman Heller.

Hayyun, Samuel

Samuel Hayyun was born in the sixteenth century. He was the grandson of Samuel ben Moses de Medina. He was the author of a work of novellae and responsa titled *Bene Shemuel*.

Hazaken, Yeshayah ben Mali

Yeshayah ben Mali Hazaken was born in Trani, Italy in 1180. He was one of the Tosefists and the author of *Piskei HaRid* which was a complete compendium of the halakhic rulings of the Talmud, similar to that of Isaiah ben Mali of Trani (RI'D). It also contained novellae on over nineteen Talmudic tractates. He died in 1260.

Heilprin, Jehiel ben Solomon

Jehiel ben Solomon Heilprin was a Lithuanian rabbi who was born about 1660. He was a descendant of Solomon Luria. He was first a rabbi in Glusk but was then called to Minsk where he was the head of the yeshivah for the remainder of his life.

He opposed casuistry, which was then strongly advocated by Aryeh Leib ben Asher Gunzberg, who also had founded a yeshivah at Minsk. There was also an antagonism between them related to their teaching methods and this antagonism even spread to the pupils.

Heilprin devoted time as well to the study of kabbalah, He wrote his work *Seder HaDorot* on this subject. It consisted of three independent volumes; *Yemot Olam* that was a history of creation to his time, *Seder HaTannaim wehaAmora'im* that contains a list of Tannaim and Amoraim in alphabetical order and with their dates, and the third part was of authors and their works also arranged in alphabetical order. He drew on Shabbethai Bass' *Sifte Yeshenim*, but added many more of his own. He also published a dictionary of synonyms and homonyms found in the Bible called *Erke HaKinnuyim*.

He died in about 1746.

Heller, Aryeh Leib HaKohen (The Ketzos)

Aryeh Leib was born in 1745 in Kalush, Galicia, which is currently in the Ukraine. He died in 1813. He was a fourth generation descendant of Rabbi Yom Tov Lippman Heller. Recognizing him as a prodigy, his father sent him at a young age to study under Rabbi Meshullam Igra in Tysmenieca, Poland, who was an outstanding authority of that age. He was the rabbi of Stry from 1788 to 1813. This position was later held by his halakhic opponent, Rabbi Yaakov Lorberbaum of Lisser (Jacob Lisser).

Rabbi Heller was critical of the Hassidic movement. Despite this many Hassidic leaders held him in high regard because of his Talmudic knowledge.

He wrote three significant works of which his *Ketzot HaChoshen* ("Ends of the Breastplate") was his greatest. It is a halakhic work that clarifies difficult passages of the *Shulkhan Arukh*, *Choshen Mishpat*. It is considered a classic.

He introduced novel ideas. It is often studied in conjunction with Rabbi Lorberbaum's *Netivot HaMishpat*, which takes the opposite view in many situations. His second important work is *Avnei Milluim* ("Filling Stones"), that follows the format of his first work, except covering the *Even HaEzer* of the *Shulkhan Arukh*. His third major work is the *Shev Shema'atata* ("Seven Passages") that is also a halakhic work covering many intricate topics. It is divided into seven sections with twenty-five chapters. It is a work on Talmudic logic and methodology. Heller's analytical methods used in deriving decisions is the basis for the methods used in modern times.

Heller, Yom Tov Lippman (Tosefos Yomtov)

Rabbi Heller was born in 1579 according to records, but according to his own biography it was in 1577, just days after the death of his father Nathan HaLevi Heller. He was raised by his grandfather, Moses Wallerstein Levi Heller, in Vienna. At the age of thirteen he went to Prague to study with the Maharal (Rabbi Yehuda Loew) at his yeshiva. At age eighteen he was appointed to the Maharal's judicial court in Prague. He held this position for twenty-seven years. In 1622 he was called to serve as the chief of the Beth Din in Vienna. In 1627 he was chosen for a similar position in Prague, but after only six months he was imprisoned for forty days and then banned. The ban was lifted in 1631. He then became the rabbi in Nimerov and then Ludmir. Finally in 1641 he became the head of the Beth Din and the Rav of the Jewish community in Krakow, succeeding Yaakov Yehoshua and Joel Sirkis in these two positions respectively. He stayed there until his death in 1654.

Rabbi Heller is known for his major commentary on the Mishnah, the *Tosefos Yomtov*.

Herrera, Abraham

Rabbi Abraham Herrera was born in Spain in 1570 to an influential Marrano family. They later settled in Italy. He was both a successful businessman as well as studying philosophy and kabbalah. Through a business contact he met Rabbi Israel Seruk in Raguza, Dubrovnik. He became his disciple and an accomplished kabbalist. Later he was sent to Cadiz, Spain by the Sultan of Morocco, where he was captured by the English and taken to London. After his release he settled in Amsterdam.

He wrote two works on kabbalah. These were in Spanish, but he left money to have them translated into Hebrew. These were later translated and published by Rabbi Yitzhak Abohab III under the titles of *Sha'ar HaShamayim* and *Beit Elohim*.

Abraham Herrera died in Amsterdam in 1635.

Heschel, Abraham Joshua

Abraham Joshua Heschel was born in Warsaw, Poland on January 11, 1907. He was a descendant in a long line of famous Polish Hassidic rabbis, from both parents. After having a traditional yeshiva education and receiving ordination he went to the University of Berlin to obtain his doctorate. He stayed on to teach Talmud there. Joining a poetry group there, in 1933 he published a volume of Yiddish poems, *Der Shem Hamefoyrosh: Mensch*.

In 1938, he was deported to Poland by the Nazis. Six weeks before the German invasion of Poland he went to London. He subsequently came to the USA in 1940. He lost his family in the war. In 1946, he joined the Jewish Theological Seminary as professor of Jewish Ethics and Mysticism, a position he held until his death. Also in 1946, he married Sylvia Strauss. His daughter Susannah Heschel is an accomplished Jewish scholar as well.

Heschel used the Hebrew prophets as the basis for his social action and worked for the Black Civil Rights Movement as well as being against the Vietnam War.

His most influential works are *Man is Not Alone*, *God in Search of Man*, *The Sabbath*, and *The Prophets*. *Man Is Not Alone: A Philosophy of Religion* gives the author's views on how man can appreciate God. He describes repetitively the theme of radical amazement that many experience when aware of the presence of God. He explores the issues of both faith and doubt. He then gives his views on how Judaism can fit into a pattern of life.

God in Search of Man: A Philosophy of Judaism is a companion volume to *Man is not Alone*. In this book Heschel follows a logical progression of what is the nature of religious thought, how this then, in turn, becomes faith, and finally how this faith results in certain responses by the believer. The book is divided into several sections dealing with the Jews as the chosen people, revelation, how a Jew should understand the nature of the Jewish religion and the need to correlate ritual observance with spirituality and love when performing mitzvot.

The Sabbath: Its Meaning For Modern Man is a work on the celebration of the Sabbath, which Heschel sees as a manifestation of Judaism being a religion of time, with the Sabbath sanctifying time.

In *The Prophets*, which began as his Ph.D. thesis Heschel covers the lives and the historical contexts in which their prophetic missions were set. He then puts forward the idea that the prophetic view of God is best understood from the perspective that God has human feelings.

He also wrote a series of essays that were published as *Prophetic Inspiration After the Prophets: Maimonides and Others*. It describes his view of the existence of prophesy in Judaism after the destruction of the Second Temple.

Considered by many to be his most accomplished work, *Torah min HaShamayim BeAspaklariya shel HaDorot* (Torah from Heaven in the Light of the Generations) is a work of classical rabbinic theology and aggadah. The book explores the views of the rabbis in the Mishnah, Talmud, and Midrash. It has been translated into English under the title of *Heavenly Torah: As Refracted Through the Generations*. Heschel died on December 23, 1972.

Hirsch, Yaakov Yehoshua ben Zvi (Jacob Joshua Falk)

Yaakov Yehoshua ben Tzvi Hirsch was also known as Yaakov Yehoshua Falk or Jacob Joshua Falk. He was born in Cracow 1680 and was a German and polish Talmudist. He died on January 16, 1756. He was the grandson of Rabbi Yehoshua Hoschel, the author of *Maginne Shelomoh*. He was first the chief rabbi in Lemberg and then in 1731 assumed a position in Berlin. Following this he became the rabbi of Metz and then the chief rabbi of Frankfurt am Main.

His work, *Pene Yehoshua* is considered one of the classical Talmudic commentaries and novellae of the era of the Acharonim. It is a book in four parts. He also wrote an unpublished commentary on the Pentateuch.

Hoffmann, David Zevi

David Hoffmann was born in Verbo (Slovakia) in 1843. He first studied at several Hungarian yeshivot, then at Hildesheimer Seminary in Eisenstadt before going off to universities in Vienna, Berlin and Tuerbingen. He was then invited to teach Talmud at the recently established Hildesheimer Seminary in Berlin. He also became a member of the Beth Din of Berlin. In later years he was considered the pre-eminent halakhic authority for Orthodox German Jewry. In 1918 he was awarded a governmental professorial title and taught in public.

Hoffmann was pro-Zionist, but did not publish his writings on this subject. His halakhic responsa took into account contemporary conditions and they tended towards leniency. His writings on the *Shulkhan Arukh* and his biblical writings took the form of a polemic against criticisms of these. In this way he was very traditional. He encouraged though Talmudic criticism without veering from the halakha. His Talmudic writings applied a critical method and concentrated on the Tannaitic period. His most important work, however, was the study of halakhic Midrashim. He established that there were two schools of anonymous baraitot in the halakhic Midrashim, one originating in the school of Rabbi Akiva and the other in the school of Rabbi Ishmael. This explanation has been rejected since then. Most of his writing was in German. Rabbi Hoffmann died in 1921.

Horowitz Family

It is one of the largest and most prominent Ashkenazi families that have existed since the fifteenth century. The family took its name from the town of Horovice in Bohemia. They dominated life in Prague in the sixteenth century. Through marriages they formed alliances with other famous families.

The Horowitz family traces its roots to the Golden Age of Spanish Jewry. Zerachiah HaLevi Gerondi is mentioned with possible family connections. They came to central and Eastern Europe after the Spanish expulsions. Karl Marx was one of the descendants.

Horowitz, Abraham ben Shabtai Sheftel

Abraham ben Shabtai Sheftel was born in the first half of the sixteenth century. He lived and worked in Cracow and Lvov. He was a student of Moses Isserles (Rema). He originally had Maimonidean rationalistic beliefs but later turned to kabbalah.

He wrote several works of a halakhic and ethical nature. One was titled *Emek Berakhah*. His most famous work was *Yesh Nohalin*, which was a treatise written in the form of an ethical will. He died in about 1615.

Horowitz, Isaiah HaLevi (Shelah, Shaloh)

Isaiah Horowitz, also known as the Shelah or Shaloh after his most well-known work, was born in Prague in 1565. He studied under Rabbi Meir Lublin (the Maharal) and under Rabbi Joshua Hirsch or Falk. He was a wealthy person and an active philanthropist, especially for Torah study in Jerusalem. He held many prestigious rabbinic posts in different European cities, ultimately ending up as the rabbi of Prague. After the death of his wife he moved to Palestine, remarried and settled in Jerusalem. He then moved to Safed.

Horowitz was both a great Talmudist and a kabbalist. He stressed in his works the joy of every action and the need to convert the evil inclination into good. His teachings had a great influence on the development of the Hassidic movement.

His most important work was the *Shnei Luchos HaBris* ("Two Tablets of the Covenant"), abbreviated to the better known *Shelah*, from the initials of the work. It was an exhaustive compilation of ritual, ethics and mysticism. This work had tremendous influence on the Hassidic movement and on Rabbi Shneur Zalman of Liadi. The work was first published by his son, Rabbi Shabtai Sheftel Horowitz, in 1648. He also composed a prayer book, *Sha'ar HaShamayim*. The Shelah died in Safed on March 24, 1630.

Horowitz, Shabtai Sheftel

Shabtai Sheftel Horowitz was born in about 1590, probably in Ostroh, Volhynia. He was the son of Isaiah HaLevi Horowitz and grandson of Abraham Horowitz. He later went to Prague where he became a preacher. Later he moved to Furth and from there he was invited to become the rabbi of Frankfurt am Main. He finally went to Vienna in about 1650.

Shabtai wrote several works. He compiled additions to his grandfather Abraham's work, *Emek Berakhah*. His most famous work was on religious ethics, titled *Vave HaAmmudim*. He considered this as an introduction to his father's famous work *Shnei Luchos HaBris*. This introduction is always printed as an appendix with his father's work. He also wrote another ethical work containing charitable teachings and strictness in ritual practice as well as kabbalistic teachings and titled *Zuwwa'ah*. He wrote additions to his father's prayer book *Sha'ar HaShamayim*. He died in 1660.

Hoschel, Judah Aryeh Loeb ben Joshua

Little is known of Judah Hoschel. He was a rabbi in Slutsk, Mintz in the eighteenth century. He was the author of *Torah Or*, published in Berlin in 1745. It is a work of halakhot relating to the reading and writing of the Law and with Hebrew Grammar.

Hurwitz, Shabbethai Sheftel ben Akiba

He was a late sixteenth / early seventeenth century physician and kabbalist who wrote a voluminous commentary, *Shefa' Tal* on Aaron HaLevi's book on kabbalah called *Iggeret HaTe'amim*.

Hurwitz (Horwitz), Yosef Yozel (Alter of Novardok)

Yosef Yozel Hurwitz was born in 1849 in Russia. He died in Kiev in 1919. He was a student of Yisroel Salanter. In 1896, he established his famous yeshiva at Novardok where it became a center for the Mussar movement. He was the author of *Madragat Adam* ("Stature of Man"), the basic theme of the book being that of trust and concern for only spiritual matters.

Hutner, Yitzhak (Isaac)

Yitzhak Hutner was born in 1906 in Warsaw into a family that had both Ger-Hassidic and non-Hassidic Lithuanian roots. As a teenager he was enrolled in the famous Slabodka yeshiva under Rabbi Nosson Tzvi Finkel. He was then sent to the Palestine extension of the yeshiva in Hebron. There he became a disciple of Abraham Isaac Kook, the first chief rabbi of Israel.

After the pogroms in 1929, Hutner traveled as a wandering scholar. During this period he wrote *Torat HaNazir* on the laws of the Nazarite. Years later he repudiated this work.

In 1932, he married Masha, who was American. They went back to Palestine where he studied further and completed his research and writing of *Kovetz Ha'aros*, on Hillel ben Eliakim's commentary on *Midrash Sifra*. In 1935 he immigrated to Brooklyn, New York. He soon became the Rosh Yeshiva of Yeshiva Rabbi Chaim Berlin. In this capacity he grew the yeshiva into a place of great prominence. He was a firm proponent of secular education as well, so that people could support themselves. In fact his daughter, Bruria Hutner David obtained her Ph.D. at Columbia University in Philosophy and then went on to become the dean of a major women's seminary in Jerusalem, Beth Jacob of Jerusalem.

In the 1950s he established a post-graduate school in Talmudic studies for married scholars, the Kollel Gur Aryeh. It produced many prominent educational and pulpit rabbis.

Hutner's major work was *Pachad Yitzhak* ("Fear of Isaac"). The book contained his ideas that were a synthesis of different schools of Jewish thought, but was to a large extent based on the teachings of the Maharal of Prague. He called his ideas *Hilchot Deot Vechovot Halevavot* ("Laws of Ideas and Duties of the Heart"). Hutner is credited with opening up the ideas and writings of the Maharal.

In his later years he went back to Israel where he ultimately established a yeshiva called Yeshiva Pachad Yitzhak in Jerusalem. He died in 1980.

Ikriti, Shemariah ben Elijah, of Negropont

Shemariah was an Italian philosopher and biblical exegete who was born in about 1275. He came from a long line of Roman Jews. He was a contemporary of Dante. After studying Tanakh, he studied Talmudic aggadah and philosophy.

In 1346, he wrote *Sefer HaMora* wherein he refuted the philosophical views of the Creation. He believed this work placed Rabbinic Judaism on a more sure footing. He also wrote *Elef HaMagen*, a commentary on the aggadah of Megillah. He also wrote some piyyutim.

Isaac, Abraham ben, of Narbonne (Ravad II)

Abraham ben Isaac, also known as Ravad II was a French rabbi born in 1110, probably in Montpelier. He was a student of Moses ben Joseph ben Merwan HaLevi and Meshullam ben Jacob of Lunel. He spent some time in Barcelona where he familiarized himself with the work of Rabbi Judah ben Barzillai. Ravad II was appointed the Av Beth Din of Narbonne and was head of the academy there.

He composed many commentaries on the Talmud, all of which have been lost, except for one on *Baba Batra* in manuscript form kept in Munich. Many of his Talmudic interpretations can be found in his responsa that are quoted by other scholars, Gerondi, Nahmanides and others.

He is best known for his primary work which was ultimately published in the nineteenth century, called *HaEshkol* ("The Cluster"). It was modeled after Alfasi's work and was the first attempt of a French rabbi to create a legal code. He also drew from the traditions in Barzillai's *Sefer HaIttim*. The arrangement of the contents and subject matter made it of practical value. He drew extensively on the Babylonian Talmud and the Geonic literature.

Abraham ben Isaac died in 1179.

Isaac, Baruch ben

Baruch ben Isaac, was a Tosafist who flourished at the beginning of the thirteenth century. He was born in Worms, but lived at Regensburg. He was a student of Isaac ben Samuel of Dampierre. He wrote tosafot for several treatises (Nashim, Nazir, Shabbat, Hullin).

He authored a book that was a legal compendium of the laws of slaughter, of permitted and forbidden foods, of the Sabbath and several other subjects, titled *Sefer HaTerumah* ("Book of the Heave-Offering"). It was a popular and important German code.

Isaac, Elhanan ben, of Dampierre

Elhanan ben Isaac was a twelfth century Tosafist. He was martyred in 1184. He left many tosafot, to which his father, who outlived him, added glosses. Among these are tosafot to Nedarim, Megillah and Avodah Zarah. He wrote a work *Tikkun Tefillin* that was a casuistic study on tefillin. He also wrote pizmonim (non-liturgical songs of praise of God) for the eight evenings of Passover.

Isaac, Kalonymus ben

Kalonymus ben Isaac was a German halakhist who lived in Speyer in the eleventh and twelfth centuries. For a while he was the rabbi of Mayence, but with the First Crusade he had to flee to Speyer.

He is quoted in the tosafot to Hullin 47b. A responsum of his is also quoted in the collection of responsa of Meir of Rothenburg.

He died in December 1127.

Isaac, Samson ben, of Chinon (MaHaRShak)

Samson ben Isaac was a French Talmudic scholar who was born in 1260 and died in 1330. He was the author of several works. *Sefer Keritut* was a methodological study of the Talmud and was divided into five parts. It was considered a classic because of its easy style and the Talmudic status of Isaac. *Kontres* was a commentary on Eruvin and Avodah Zarah. *Biur HaGet* discussed the laws of divorce. He was also probably the author of the super-commentary on Ibn Ezra's commentary on the Pentateuch.

Isaac, Solomon ben

He was a twelfth century Tosafist and a colleague of Joseph ben Isaac Bekhor Shor of Orleans. He signed responsa with the latter as quoted in *Sefer HaYashar*. He also corresponded with Rabbeinu Tam (Jacob ben Meir).

Israel of Bamberg

He was a Tosafist who lived in the middle of the thirteenth century in Bamberg, Germany. He was the author of tosafot on *Mordekai* and *Haggahot Mordekai*.

Israel of Krems

He was an Austrian rabbi who lived in the fourteenth and fifteenth centuries. In 1407 the German Emperor Rupert appointed him chief rabbi of all German communities.

Israel was the author of *Haggahot Asheri* that consisted of notes on Jacob ben Asher's Talmudic compendium, *Arba'ah Turim*.

Israel, Menasseh ben Joseph ben (MB'Y)

He was born as Manoel Dias Soeiro in 1604 in Madeira one year after his parents had left Portugal. The family moved to the Netherlands in 1610. He not only became a rabbi and author but also established the first Hebrew printing press in Amsterdam in 1626, named Emeth Meerets Titsma'h. One of his earliest works was *El Conciliador*, which was an attempt at reconciling apparent discrepancies in the Bible. His major work was *Nishmat Hayim*, a treatise on the Jewish concept of reincarnation of the souls.

His student was Spinoza, who was excommunicated by the rabbis in 1655 while he was in London where he went to appeal to Oliver Cromwell to repeal the law expelling the Jews from England. His rationale was laid out in his *Humble Addresses* to the Lord Protector. He was a friend of Rembrandt, who painted his portrait.

Menasseh ben Israel died on November 20, 1657.

Isserlein, Israel ben Pethahiah Ashkenazi

Israel Isserlein (Isserlin) was born in 1390 and was the leading German

(Austrian) Talmudic authority of his time. Isserlein died in 1460. He came from a long line of scholars. His grandfather was Israel of Krems. His maternal uncle, Aaron Blumlein, who had a yeshiva in Neustadt, was his primary teacher. After the persecutions at Neustadt, where his mother and uncle were victims, he left Austria for Italy. Years later he returned to Neustadt where he remained until his death.

As a result of his reputation, Isserlein attracted many students to Neustadt. Isserlein revived basic Talmudic study and the works of the Rishonim.

His two printed works are *Terumat HaDeshen* that was a collection of responsa related to the synagogue, ritual and various legal aspects, and *Pesakim u-Ketabim* that was also a collection of responsa, mainly related to marriage laws. Other responsa can be found in the works of Israel Beuna, the MaHaRaSh (Shmuel Schneerson), and Jacob Weil. These responsa were very important for the Jews of Germany and Poland and filled gaps from Caro's *Shulkhan Arukh*. Still extant in manuscript form is a super-commentary (*Be'urim*) on Rashi's commentary on the Pentateuch.

Isserles, Moses ben Israel (ReMA, Ramo)

Moses Isserles (Isserlis) was born in 1520 in Cracow. His father, Israel, was a prominent Talmudist and his grandfather was the first rabbi of Brisk. Moses studied in Lublin under Rabbi Shalom Shachna (Shakna). One of his co-students was Solomon Luria (the Maharshal).

In 1550, he returned to Cracow and established a yeshiva there. He supported the students from his own funds. His emphasis was not on pilpul (more intense analysis of text), but on the simple interpretation of the Talmud. In 1553, he was appointed as dayan. His fame as a Talmudist was such that his opinion was sought by many rabbis, including Yosef Caro.

The Rema was also accomplished in kabbalah, as well as in various secular areas such as history, astronomy, and philosophy.

Isserles' writings were in two broad categories. The first was halakhic, based on the codes of law. The other is of a kabbalistic and philosophical nature. Thus he is most well-known for his famous work of halakha called *HaMapah* ("The Tablecloth"). It was a commentary and component of the *Shulkhan Arukh*. His other important work was *Darkhei Moshe*, that was a commentary on the *Tur*.

His other works were *Torat Hattat*, also called *Issur we-Hetter* (*Torat Hattat*), which is mainly on the laws of kashrut, and *She'elot u-Teshubot ReMA*, consisting of 132 of his responsa. He also had some unpublished works.

Felix Mendelssohn was a descendant of his. He died in 1572 in Cracow and was buried next to his synagogue. On his tombstone is engraved "From Moses (Maimonides) to Moses (Isserles) there was none like Moses. Up until the second world war, his grave was the location of an annual pilgrimage by thousands on Lag B'omer, his yahrzeit.

Jacob of Chinon

He was a French Tosafist who lived from about 1190 to 1260. He was a pupil of Isaac ben Abraham of Dampierre. He wrote tosafot on Sanhedrin and a commentary on Gittin.

Jacob, Menahem ben (ben Solomon ben Simson)

Menahem ben Jacob was a twelfth century synagogue poet. His family was from Worms, and were well-known scholars. He has been documented as producing 31 poems or piyyutim for the synagogue services as well as a number of selichot. He died in Worms in 1203.

Jacob (Yaakov), Meshullam ben

Meshullam ben Yaakov who was also known as Rabbeinu Meshullam HaGadol was a twelfth century Talmudist. He had a yeshiva in Lunel. His Talmudic decisions are quoted in *Sefer HaTerumot*, written by Samuel ben Isaac Sardi. His son was Asher ben Meshullam and his students were the Ravad (Abraham ibn David HaLevi) and the Ba'al HaMaor (Zerachiah ben Isaac HaLevi Gerondi).

Jacob, Moses ben, of Coucy

Moses ben Jacob was a thirteenth century French Tosafist, who came from a long line of scholars. He studied under Judah ben Samuel of Regensburg (Yehuda He-Hasid).

He is best known for his work *Sefer Mitzvot Gadol* ("Large Book of Commandments"), abbreviated to *SeMaG*. It is one of the earliest codes of law. It deals with the 248 positive and the 365 negative commandments.

In 1240, he was one of four rabbis who was required to defend the Talmud in a public disputation in Paris.

Jacob, Nissim ben (HaMafteach) (Rav Nissim Gaon)

Nissim ben Jacob, also known by his work, HaMafteach or as Rav Nissim Gaon was born in 990. He died in 1062. He studied at the Kairouan yeshiva in Tunisia, North Africa, first under his father Jacob ben Nissim (Rav Yaakov Gaon) and then under Chushiel ben Elchanan, who tradition maintains was one of four rabbis captured by pirates and then ransomed by the Jewish community. Jacob later became head of this yeshiva, where he was then associated with Chushiel's son, Chananel. He also had an active literary interaction on halakhic matters with Hai ben Sherira Gaon. His most famous student was Isaac Alfasi. Jacob ben Nissim and Chananel are considered by some to be the first Rishonim.

Rav Nissim's most famous work was the *Sefer Mafteach Manulei HaTalmud*, more commonly known as *HaMafteach* ("The Book of the Key of the Talmud"). It is a Talmudic cross-reference. He correlated Mishnaic quotes with other places in the Talmudic literature. He also quoted from the Tosefta, Mekhilta, Sifre and Sifra as well as the Jerusalem Talmud. The second part of the work had fifty subdivisions providing a collection of halakhot in the Talmud, often found in unexpected places.

He also wrote other works of which only a siddur, *Siddur Tefilah*, a collection of notes on halakhic decisions, explanations and midrashim called *Megillat Setarim*, and a collection of tales called *Sefer Ma'asiyyot HaHakhamim*, are still extant.

Jacobson, Yissachar

Yissachar Jacobson was a German scholar. He is known for two works he wrote. These are *Binah Mikrah* ("Meditations on the Torah") and *Netiv Binah*, which is a five-volume work on prayer.

Jaffe (Yoffe) Mordechai ben Avraham (Ba'al HaLevushim)

Rabbi Mordechai ben Avraham Yoffe or Jaffe was born in Prague in about 1530. He died in 1612. His father, Abraham ben Joseph was a pupil of Abraham ben Abigdor Kara. Jaffe's teachers were Moses Isserles and Solomon Luria in rabbinics and Mattithiah ben Solomon Delacrut was his teacher in kabbalah.

Jaffe was head of the yeshiva in Prague until 1561 when the Jews were expelled from Bohemia. He then went to Venice until 1571 where he studied astronomy, mathematics and philosophy. In 1572, he became the rabbi of Grodno, in 1588 the rabbi of Lublin and later he moved on to the rabbinical position in Kremenetz. In 1592, he went back to Prague and in 1599, he became the chief rabbi of Posen where he remained for the rest of his life.

He was the author of *Levush Malkhut*, a ten-volume code of laws most applicable to the customs of Eastern European Jews. His other work, *Levush Orah* is a commentary on Rashi's Pentateuch. He also wrote several other minor works.

Jam'a, Samuel ben Jacob

Samuel ben Jacob Jam'a was a rabbi in the North African community of Kabez in the twelfth century. He had a very close relationship with Abraham ibn Ezra.

He wrote a supplement to the *Arukh* of Nathan ben Jehiel, titled *Elef HaMagen* or *Agur*, which was his Arabic name. It is still extant in manuscript form and excerpts from this supplement were published by Solomon Buber. He also authored novellae on Sanhedrin which are mentioned by Isaac ben Abba Mari in his *Sefer HaIttur*.

Janach, Yonah ibn (Merinos)

Rabbi Merinos was born in 983 and died in 1040. He was the greatest Spanish philologist. He was the author of *Sefer HaShorashim*, a Hebrew dictionary.

Jehiel, Asher ben (Rabbeinu Asher / Rosh)

Asher ben Jehiel was born between 1250 and 1259 in Germany. He died in 1328. He came from a prominent Talmudic family. His main teacher was the Tosafist, Rabbi Meir ben Baruch of Rothenburg and then of Worms. Asher succeeded him in this latter position. He was forced to emigrate from

Germany and first went to the south of France and then on to Toledo, Spain. He had eight sons of whom the most famous was Jacob ben Asher (Ba'al HaTurim).

Rabbeinu Asher's approach to Talmudic study was a methodical and systematic one. He generally took a more strict approach to halakhic interpretation. However, his legal interpretations were of an independent nature. His best known work is an abstract of Talmudic law, which specifies practical halakha, concisely giving the final decision on any law. It also omits those laws that apply only to Eretz Israel. His work was compiled by his son Jacob under the title of *Piskei HaRosh*. The work was similar to the RIF's (Isaac Alfasi) *Hilchot*, but soon came to supersede it. Caro used Jehiel as one of the major deciders in his *Shulkhan Arukh*.

He also authored *Orchot Chaim*, an essay on ethics, and commentaries on the first and sixth orders of the Mishnah and tosafot.

Jose, Jose bar

Jose bar Jose lived about 700 CE. He is the first known liturgical poet (payyatan), known for his New Year Day and Day of Atonement pieces. Many of his writings were ultimately included in the Siddur.

Joseph, Enoch Zundel ben

Joseph was a Russian Talmudist of the nineteenth century. He wrote a number of commentaries covering *Midrash Rabbah* of the five Megillot and *Mibhar Mi-Peninim*, a commentary on the *Midrash Rabbah* of the Pentateuch. He also wrote *Olat HaChodesh*, prayers for the new moon and novellae on the Haggadah of the Talmud. He died in 1867.

Joseph, Isaac ben, of Corbeil

Isaac ben Joseph of Corbeil was a thirteenth century French Tosafist. He was the son-in-law of Rabbi Jehiel ben Joseph of Paris, and studied under him. He was also a student of Samuel of Evereux.

In 1277 he published an abridgement of Moses ben Jacob of Coucy's work, *SeMaG* (*Sefer Mitzvot Gadol*), titled *Ammude HaGolah* or *Sefer Mitzvot Katan* (*SeMaK*). It was a popular work.

Joseph, Jehiel ben, of Paris

Jehiel ben Joseph or Joseph of Paris was born at the end of the twelfth century. He was a French Tosafist and was a disciple of Judah Sir Leon or Judah ben Isaac Messer Leon whom he succeeded as the head of the yeshiva in Paris in 1224. A number of well-known rabbis and Tosafists attended the school while under his direction, including Isaac of Corbeil and Meir of Rothenburg.

As head of the Parisian Jewish community he had many controversial interactions with Christians, although he was favorably received at the French court. Among these, the most notorious was the dispute over the content of the Talmud which resulted in the burning of many of the manuscripts. As a result of these interactions, as well as the unjust imprisonment of his son, he left for Palestine and settled in Acre, where he spent the rest of his life.

He was the author of tosafot on a number of tractates in several orders of the Mishnah and are mentioned by later Tosafists. None exist today, however. Jehiel died in 1286.

Joseph, Joshua Hoschel ben

Joshua Hoschel ben Joseph was a Polish rabbi born in Vilna in about 1578. As a youth he was sent to Galicia to study under Rabbi Samuel ben Faibesh. He then returned to Poland and studied further under Rabbi Joshua Falk. He first became the rabbi of Grodno, but was then called to the rabbinate of Tiktin (Tykotzin), and after that to Przemysl. He later became the rabbi of Lemberg in the Ukraine. Following this he was appointed the head of the yeshiva at Cracow. He was considered an eminent Talmudist during his era.

He had several published works. *Maginne Shelomoh* was a series of novellae on various tractates of the Talmud. This work supported the commentaries of Rashi against the refutations of the Tosafists. His other work was a collection of responsa called *She'elot u-Teshubot Pene Yehoshua*. Other works exist in manuscript form. He died in Cracow in 1648.

Joseph, Moses ben, of Trani

Moses ben Joseph was born in Salonika in 1505. His father sent him to Adrianople to study with his uncle. While still a teenager he went to Safed where he was a student of Rabbi Yaakov Beirav (Jacob Berab), the Mhari Beirav, who ordained Joseph, and was known for attempting to re-introduce the Sanhedrin in 1538. In 1525 Joseph was appointed rabbi of Safed and in 1535 he moved to Jerusalem. He was a teacher of Yom Tov Tzahalon, the Maharitatz.

Rabbi Joseph's major work was *Kiryat Sefer*, a major commentary on Maimonides' *Yad Chazakah*. He died in Jerusalem in 1585.

Joseph, Saadia ben, Gaon (Saadia Gaon)

Saadia Gaon was one of the last and greatest of Gaonim. He was born in 892 in Dilaz in Upper Egypt. His first name is a Hebrew creation of his Arabic name Sa'id. Nothing is known of his youth or education. There is just one reference to him being a student of Abu Kathir.

At age twenty he created his first significant work, a Hebrew dictionary called *Agron*. At age twenty-three he settled in Palestine. While still young he established a reputation for himself, the most important incident being the dispute with Aaron ben Meir and between the Palestinian and Babylonian authorities regarding the Jewish calendar. It was the depth of his knowledge that impressed the Babylonian authorities and resulted in his being called to Sura in 928. There David ben Zakai, the exilarch of the ancient academy, made him a gaon.

Saadia was a prolific author and was considered, after Philo, to be the first great post-biblical writer on Judaism. He fused Arabic culture and language with the Jewish spirit and it had a lasting influence. He also worked and wrote much in the scientific field. Most of his primary writings have disappeared and most of what is known is through quotations in other writings. A start was made by Joseph Derenbourg in the late nineteenth century to bring together all the extant writings, but only five of the ten-volume proposed work had been completed by the end of that century. His work covered biblical exegesis, a translation of the Bible into Arabic, Hebrew linguistics of which *Agron* was his first book. He also wrote a commentary to *Sefer Yezirah*. He wrote short monographs on halakha that were in the form of responsa. Saadia also wrote a siddur. His great philosophical work on religion was *Emunot v'Deot* ("Beliefs and Opinions"). He also had a number of polemical writings. Saadia died in 942.

Joseph, Samson ben, of Falaise

He was a twelfth century Tosafist who was the grandfather of Abraham of Dampierre and Samson ben Abraham of Sens. He authored tosafot for the tractates Shabbat, Erubin, Yebamot and Hulin. He also wrote ritual decisions under the title of *Pesakim*.

Judah, Daniel ben

Judah ben Daniel lived in Rome in the middle of the fourteenth century. He was a liturgical poet who was the author of the hymn *Yigdal Elohim Hai*, which consists of the thirteen articles of belief of Maimonides. It forms part of both the daily and the Sabbath eve prayers.

Judah, Gershom ben (Rabbeinu Gershom)

Gershom ben Judah, commonly known as Rabbeinu Gershom, and also by scholars as *Rabbeinu Gershom Me'Or HaGolah* ("Our teacher Gershom the light of exile") was born about 960 in Metz. His teacher was Judah ben Meir HaKohen.

After the death of his first wife, he married a widow and he devoted himself to the study of Talmud. He established a yeshiva at Mainz and had students from different countries, including Eleazar ben Isaac HaLevi and Jacob ben Yakar, the teacher of Rashi. He was also the spiritual guide for the developing Ashkenazic communities.

He is famous for his religious ordinances (*takkanot*) banning polygamy, the prohibition of divorcing a woman against her will and the prohibition of reading private mail.

He wrote a number of commentaries on the Talmud and on the Bible. These were apparently written down by his disciples. Commentaries to nine Talmudic tractates have been preserved. They probably were sources for Rashi's commentaries. Most of his commentaries have been lost. He also provided a number of responsa as well as composing piyyutim, some of which are part of the standard selichot for the High Holidays.

Rabbeinu Gershom died in 1040.

Kagan, Israel Meir (HaKohen) (Chofetz Chaim)

Israel Meir Kagan, who was popularly known as the Chofetz Chaim was born in Zhetl in modern Belarus on February 6, 1838. His father died when he was young and the family moved to Vilna to continue his studies. There he became a student of Rabbi Jacob Barit. He married the daughter of his step-father at age seventeen and moved with the family to Radun where after a short term as the rabbi he went on to establish a yeshiva there. During the late nineteenth and early twentieth centuries he became one of the most influential orthodox rabbis. A number of Jewish religious institutions around the world carry his eponym.

He produced a number of works of which his most famous is the *Mishnah Berurah* ("Clarified Teachings"). It is a six-volume commentary on the *Orach Chaim* section of Joseph Caro's *Shulkhan Arukh*. It consists of both clarifications as well as opposing opinions with those of earlier commentators. It is therefore not a code per se, but more likely a gloss to the *Orach Chaim*. His *Beiur Halacha* ("Explanation of the Law") is a commentary that goes with the *Mishnah Berurah*. It provides complex analysis of rulings by earlier scholars. *Sha'ar HaTziyyum* ("Gates of Distinction") documents sources for the laws and customs quoted in the *Mishnah Berurah* as well as clarifying ambiguous legal statements. Another important work was *Ahavat Chesed* ("Love of Kindness") dealing with the mitzvah of lending money and other aspects of human relationships.

His first book, *Chafetz Chaim* ("Seeker of Life") was a code dealing with the biblical laws of gossip and slander. *Sh'mirat HaLashon* is a discussion of the philosophy behind the power of speech. Kagan also wrote a number of other works that are quoted in the book *The Chofetz Chaim* by Moses Yosher. Kagan died in Radun on September 15, 1933.

Kaidanover, Aaron Samuel ben Israel

Aaron Samuel Kaidanover was a Polish / Lithuanian rabbi who was born in Vilna in 1614. Jacob and his son Joshua Hoeschel were among his teachers.

During the Chmielnicki revolution (1648-1649) Kaidanover's possessions were plundered by the Cossacks and his two daughters killed. He then moved to Moravia. He was elected rabbi first in Lower Austria and then in Frankfurt am Main. He returned to Poland in 1671 to become the rabbi of Cracow, where he lived until his death on December 1, 1676.

Kaidenover wrote several works. *Birkat HaZebah* was a series of annotations to the Talmudic tractate of Kidushin. *Birkat Shemuel* was a series of derashot on the Pentateuch. *Emunat Shemuel* consisted of sixty responsa on marriage cases. *Tifferet Shemuel* were novellae to various tractates. The last two were edited by his son Zevi Hirsch.

Kaidanover, Zevi Hirsch

Zevi Hirsch Kaidanover was born in Vilna in the seventeenth century. He was the son of Aaron Samuel Kaidenover. He studied under Joseph ben Judah Jeidel, who was the rabbi of Minsk. From this teacher he mostly developed his kabbalistic views. His straight halakhic views came mainly from his father's teachings. He was also imprisoned at the time of his father based on false charges. After his release he settled in Frankfurt am Main.

It was in Frankfurt that he pursued his literary interests. He first published his father's works, *Birkat Shemuel* and his works on responsa and novellae. He added notes to these. He is best known for his work *Kav HaYashar*. It became a very popular work and has been published many times. It is an ethical collection of stories, customs and moral guidance with a kabbalistic bent. After the Chmelnitzky Massacres of 1648-1649, this work helped to elevate the spirits of the Jewish communities. Kaidanover died on March 23, 1712.

Kalir, Eleazar

Eleazar Kalir was one of the earliest and most prolific liturgical poets (payatanim). The period when he lived is not clearly known, but is given somewhere between the sixth and tenth centuries. Many of his hymns are included in festive prayers among Ashkenazi Jews. His material came from the Talmud and Midrashic compilations.

Kalischer, Zvi Hirsch

Zvi Hirsch Kalischer was a German rabbi born either in Lissa or Thorn, Prussia, depending on the reference, on March 24, 1795. He was one of the pioneers of Zionism. He received his Talmudic education under Jacob of Lissa (Jacob ben Jacob Moses) and Rabbi Akiva Eger. He returned to Thorn where he spent the rest of his life.

While still a youth he wrote *Eben Bochan* which was a commentary on several legal themes in the *Choshen Mishpat* of the *Shulkhan Arukh*. He also wrote *Sefer Moznayim la-Mishpat* that was a three-part commentary on the whole of the *Choshen Mishpat*. He wrote glosses to the *Yoreh De'ah* of the *Shulkhan Arukh* which were published in the new Vilna edition of that work. His *Sefer HaBerit* was a commentary on the Pentateuch. The *Sefer Yitziat Mitzrayim* was a commentary on the Passover Haggadah. *Chiddushim* was a commentary on several Talmudic tractates. His *Sefer Emunah Yesharah* was a study in Jewish philosophy and theology.

Among all this literary work, he managed to devote a significant amount of time to the idea of recolonizing Palestine in order to provide a home for Eastern Jews and transform the many beggars in the Holy Land into an agricultural population. His Zionistic ideals were expressed in his *Derishat Ziyyon* that had three themes of colonization of Palestine, self-help and re-introduction of sacrifices into Palestine. As a result of his influence Hayyim Lurie formed the first society of this kind in 1861, followed by others.

Kalischer died on October 16, 1874.

Kalonymus Family

This was a famous family that originated from Lucca but then settled in

Mayence and Speyer and for a number of generations were leaders in the development of Jewish learning in Germany, mainly during the eleventh and twelfth centuries. Other descendants lived later and contributed as well. The eleventh and twelfth century members were mainly liturgical poets, writing a number of piyyutim. These members will be listed as a group, and others will be described individually.

1. Hananeel I lived in the eleventh century and wrote piyyutim for the last day of Passover.

2. Jekuthiel ben Moses lived in the eleventh century and wrote piyyutim for the New Year.

3. Kalonymus II ben Moses flourished in Lucca about 950. He authored piyyutim for feast days. He was also a halakhist and twelve of his responsa were included in a collection compiled by Joseph ben Samuel Alam Tob.

4. Meshullam III ben Kalonymus flourished at the beginning of the eleventh century. He features in the legend of Amnon of Mainz (Mayence) (See under Amnon) and the "u-Netannah Tokef". It is said that Amnon appeared to him in a dream and revealed this poem to him, which he then wrote down.

5. Kalonymus ben Judah or Kalonymus the Younger. He flourished about 1160. Thirty of his poems have been incorporated into the Mahzor. He also wrote selichot.

6. Moses ben Kalonymus. He flourished in Mayence in 1020. He wrote various poems that were incorporated for the seventh day of Passover.

Kalonymus, David ben, of Munzenberg

David ben Kalonymus flourished at the end of the twelfth and early thirteenth centuries in Germany. He was a rabbi of Munzenberg, Hesse. He was a Tosafist and liturgical poet. He is quoted in the tosafot and also in the work of his pupil Samson of Sens and in the responsa of Meir of Rothenburg. He also wrote some selichot.

Kalonymus, Eleazar ben Yehuda ben, of Worms (Rokeach)

Eleazar Rokeach was born in Germany in about 1176 probably in Mayence. He was a descendant of the famous Kalonymus family. In 1196 his wife and three children were murdered by the Crusaders. In 1233 he participated in the great synod of Mayence that enacted the set of regulations known as the *Takkanot Shum*.

Not only was he a great Talmudist, but he also wrote a number of piyyutim, particularly directed at Israel's suffering and hope for redemption and revenge against her tormentors. He was also involved in kabbalah. He applied arithmetical criteria to his kabbalistic philosophy.

Eleazar wrote a number of ethical works: *HaRokeach* which was divided into 497 paragraphs of halakhot and ethics; *Adderet Ha-Shem* which is in manuscript form in the Vatican; *Sefer HaKapparot* which is on penitence and confession, has been published many times under various titles; *Sefer HaHayyim* and *Sha'are HaSod HaYihud weha-Emunah* deal with the unity and incorporeality of God.

He also wrote a large number of kabbalistic works. These covered various topics such as psalms, certain other biblical passages, the five megillot, on Ruth and the Song of Songs, on the kabbalistic aspects of the various names of God and the angels. Rokeach also wrote tosafot to various Talmudic tractates. He died in Worms in 1238.

Kalonymus, Elijah ben

Elijah ben Kalonymus was a Talmudic scholar who lived in Lublin in the seventeenth century. He was the author of a commentary on the Pentateuch called *Adderet Eliyahu*.

Kalonymus, Samuel ben (He-Hasid), of Speyer

Samuel ben Kalonymus lived in the twelfth century, probably in Spain and France. He was named He-Hasid ("The Prophet") by Solomon Luria. He was a tosafist, liturgical poet and a philosopher.

He was the author of a commentary to the Talmudic tractate Tamid, where it is mentioned by Abraham ben David in his commentary. He wrote a liturgical poem *Shir HaYihud* that had seven parts, one for each day of the week. It is a philosophical hymn on the unity of God.

Kamenecki, Jacob (Yaakov Kamenetsky)

Rabbi Jacob Kamenecki was born in Kalushkove, Lithuania in 1891. His family then moved to Dolhinov. He then studied in Minsk and after that spent twenty-one years at the Slobodka yeshiva under Rabbi Nosson Tzvi Finkel. While there he also spent time at the Kelm Talmud Torah. In 1926 he was appointed the rabbi of Tzitavyam and then in 1937 moved to North America. He ultimately ended up at the Mesivta Torah Vodaath in Brooklyn, New York. Together with Rabbi Moshe Feinstein, he led American Jewry on halakhic and spiritual matters. He was the author of two works. *Emes leYaakov* was a multi-volume commentary on the Torah and the Talmud, with grammatical points on the Torah. *Iyunim BaMikra* was a commentary on the Chumash. He died in 1986.

Kara, Abraham ben Abigdor

Abraham ben Abigdor Kara was a fifteenth and sixteenth century Bohemian rabbi and liturgist. He wrote a super-commentary on Rashi's commentary to the Pentateuch, as well as glosses to all parts of the *Arba'ah Turim* of Jacob ben Asher, but he might have also written glosses to the other three parts. He also wrote a selikhah called *Ana Elohe Abraham*, the verses being in alphabetical order. Kara died in Prague on October 7, 1542.

Kara, Simeon, of Frankfurt (HaDarshan)

Simeon Kara was a rabbi who flourished in southern Germany in the early part of the thirteenth century. This rabbi is of interest because several scholars, based on an extensive analytical approach, believe him to be the most likely author of the *Yalkut* or *Yalkut Shimoni*. The title HaDarshan was probably conferred on him at a later date.

The *Yalkut* is a haggadic compilation of the Pentateuch. The author collected various interpretations and explanations from earlier works that were available to him and arranged them in a sequential fashion. The work is divided into sections, mostly according to the various books and sections of the Pentateuch. Thus the sources are mainly from the ancient and Gaonic periods, as well as including the twelfth century works. The author also incorporated Midrashic works.

Karelitz, Abraham Isaiah (Chazon Ish)

Abraham Isaiah or Avrohom Yeshayahu, known as the Chazon Ish was born in Kosava in the Belarus in 1878. He received his education from his father who was the head of the Beth Din there. In 1920, he moved to Vilna where he became closely associated with Rabbi Chaim Ozer Grodzinski. In 1933, he settled in Palestine in Bnei Brak.

He married but never had children. His wife supported him while he devoted his life to Torah and Talmud study, but he was also very knowledgeable in the various sciences, believing that a good understanding of these was necessary for a full appreciation of aspects of Jewish law and practice. Although he did not hold any official position he became recognized as an international authority on all aspects of halakha and Jewish life.

He belonged to no official movement, but was loved and respected by all. David Ben-Gurion consulted with him and today in Israel in many towns streets are named after him.

In 1911, he published his first work, the *Chazon Ish* on the *Orach Chaim* and other parts of the *Shulkhan Arukh*. His approach to the halakha and Jewish life was a very practical one. Overall he wrote forty works in his lifetime. Karelitz died in 1953.

Kasher, Menachem Mendel

Kasher was born in Poland in 1895 but settled in Palestine. When only nineteen he became the editor of the periodical Degel HaTorah that represented the opinions of Agudat Israel. During the second world war he brought the Ger Rebbe to Palestine. For the first two years after it was formed, he was the Rosh Yeshiva of the Yeshivas Sfas Emes of Gur. He was awarded an honorary doctorate from Yeshiva University.

Kasher's major work was *Torah Shelemah*. It was divided into two parts. The first part was an encyclopedia that included all of the Pentateuch and the Talmud and Midrashim arranged side-by-side. The second part consisted of annotations and addenda, based on his extensive personal knowledge, to clarify many obscure points in the Talmud and the explanations of Maimonides. He also published *Divrei Menachem Responsa*, that consisted of responsa from many of the major scholars of the day. He died in 1983.

Katz, Jacob Joseph ben Tzvi HaKohen, of Polonnoye

Jacob Joseph was born in about 1710 in Volhynia, which at that time was a part of the Polish-Lithuanian Commonwealth. He led the large Jewish community of Shargorod in Podolia. While the rabbi there he came under the influence of the Ba'al Shem Tov (Besht, Israel ben Eliezer). When his Hassidic leanings became known, he was expelled from his rabbinate. He then assumed an active role in promoting Hassidism from Nemirov. Later he succeeded Aryeh Leib of Polonnye as the preacher there. After the passing of the Ba'al Shem Tov, he clashed with Dov Ber, the Maggid of Mezritch, over the succession of the former. However, Jacob Joseph is best remembered as Hassidism's first theoretician and the direct transmitter of the Besht's teachings. He was banned by the Vilna Gaon because of his teachings.

Rabbi Joseph wrote biblical commentaries where he combined general biblical principles with Hassidic doctrine. His wrote three works. The first one was *Toledot Yaakov Yosef*, published in 1780, where he was critical of the traditional rabbinical concept of Torah study and exalted the Tzaddik as the means whereby God's influence flows to the common people. His other two biblical commentaries were *Ben Porat Yosef*, published in 1781 and *Tsafenat Pane'ah* published in 1782. He died in about 1784.

Katzenellenbogen, Meir ben Isaac (Maharam Padua)

Meir ben Isaac Katzenellenbogen, also known as Meir of Padua or Maharam Padua was an Italian rabbi born at Katzenellenbogen in Germany in 1482. He was the founder of the family with this last name. He studied in Prague under Jacob Pollak and then went to Padua to study in the yeshiva of Judah Minz, whose granddaughter he later married. He became the chief rabbi of Padua after his father-in-law, Abraham ben Judah Minz, and held this position until his death.

Meir was considered a great Talmudic authority and among the rabbis who consulted him were Moses Alashkar, Obadiah Sforno and his relative Moses Isserles.

He self-published a book of ninety responsa called *She'elot u-Teshubot*, which indicated a liberal leaning. Many of his responsa are also to be found in the collection of Moses Isserles. Katzenellenbogen died January 12, 1565.

Kayyara, Simeon

Simeon Kayyara was a Babylonian halakhist from the first half of the ninth century. His major work was the *Halakot Gedolot* or as later Spanish scholars called it *Halakot Rishonot* to distinguish it from later codes. It is the first such work to give all the halakhic and practical material from the Talmud in a code-like form. It concentrates on the content rather than on the tractates. It is probably the greatest and most comprehensive code of law from the Geonic period. The author of this work has also been referred to as Behag (see earlier description under this name).

Although there was originally some controversy as to whether Kayyara wrote this work or whether Yehudai Gaon (Yehudai ben Nahman) wrote it, it is now well-accepted that Kayyara wrote *Halakot Gedolot* and drew on Yehudai Gaon's *Halakot Pesukot* and Achai Gaon's (Ahai of Sabha) *Sheiltos*.

Over the next few centuries the *Halakot Gedolot* underwent a number of changes as it was used in Spain, North Africa and then later in Italy, France and northern Germany.

Kelin, Samuel ben Naftali HaLevi

Rabbi Kelin was born in Germany in 1724. He wrote a super-commentary, titled *Mechatzit HaShekel*, on Abraham Abele Gombiner's *Magen Avraham*, that was a commentary on Joseph Caro's *Orach Chaim* section of the *Shulkhan Arukh*. He died in 1806.

Kimchi (Kimhi) Family

This was a famous Jewish family of scholars of Spanish descent but who flourished in France during the twelfth and thirteenth centuries. There was the father, Joseph ben Isaac, and his two sons, Moses, the elder and David, the younger. The latter, also known by the eponym Radak, is perhaps the most famous of the family.

Kimchi, Joseph ben Isaac

Joseph was born in southern Spain about 1100. He emigrated to southern France at the time of the Moslem persecutions under the Almonade Moorish dynasty, and settled in Narbonne. It was about the same time that Maimonides and his family left Spain. Kimchi was known as a grammarian and wrote several works on this subject. His *Sepher Zikkaron* ("Book of Remembrance") was the first description of the types of Hebrew vowels. *Sepher Haggalui* ("Book of Open Evidence") was a criticism of Menahem ben Saruk's (Saruq) dictionary and its defense by Jacob ben Meir. He also wrote commentaries on the Pentateuch. These stressed the peshat or straightforward explanations of the Pentateuch. He also wrote some of the earliest anti-Christian polemics in Europe. He died in Narbonne in about 1175.

Kimchi, Moses

Moses Kimchi was the older son of Joseph. He is known for his work *Mahalakh Shevile Hadda'ath* ("Guide to the Paths of Knowledge") which was a Hebrew grammatical work. It was a brief work and was popular for a long time. In the early sixteenth century it was translated into Latin and used by Christian Hebraists. His other grammatical work, *Sepher Tahbosheth*, which was quoted by his brother David, has been lost. He died about 1190.

Kimchi, David (RaDaK)

David Kimchi, also known as RaDaK, was born in Narbonne, Provence in 1160. His father, Joseph died when he was young and his elder brother Moses undertook his upbringing and education.

His primary contribution was a commentary of the entire Tanakh, called the *RaDaK*. It is considered by students to be the commentary of choice because of its ability to clearly explain the text, making connections clear as well as clarifying Christian misrepresentations of the text. Of the Pentateuch commentaries only that of Genesis is extant. His psalms commentaries are particularly well-known, and his commentaries on the Prophets are particularly well-received. He elucidated much Midrashic material in his work. His commentaries are similar to those of Rashi. His commentaries were translated into Latin by Christian scholars.

His first book was an encyclopedia of Hebrew grammar, *Michlol* or *Sefer Michlol* ("Completeness"), whereby he established his reputation. He distilled and summarized the best of the grammatical works of previous scholars, particularly Jehuda of Fez and Jonah ibn Janah. It was also later used by Christian Hebraists.

Another work was *Teshuvoth LaNotzrim* ("Refutation to the Christians") which refuted attacks by Christian theologians. It was used extensively by later Jewish scholars in disputes with the Church. *El HaSofer* ("Pen of the Scribe") dealt with the writing of Torah scrolls according to masoretic tradition.

In later life he became involved in the defense of Maimonides' *Moreh Nevuchim* ("Guide for the Perplexed"). He died in 1235.

Kluger, Solomon ben Judah Aaron

Solomon Kluger was born in Komarow, Poland in 1783. He became the chief dayan of Brody, Galicia, then rabbi of Rawa in Poland, Kulikow in Galicia and Jozefow in Lublin. He then went to Breznay in Galicia and finally back to Brody.

He was a very prolific author in a wide variety of subject matter. Only some were published. *Sefer HaHayyim* consisted of novellae on the *Shulkhan Arukh*, the *Orach Chaim*; *Me Niddah*, haggadic and aggadic novellae on *Niddah*; *Shenot Hayyim*, *Sefer Setam* and *Moda'a le-Bet Yisrael* were collections of responsa; and several other works. He died in 1869.

Kook, Abraham Isaac (HaRaAYaH / HaRav)

Abraham Isaac Kook, known in Hebrew as HaRav Avraham Yitzhak HaKohen Kook or by the acronyms HaRaAYaH or HaRav was born in Griva, Latvia in 1865. Rabbi Kook died in 1935. He entered the Volozhin Yeshiva in Lithuania in 1884 where he became close to the Rosh Yeshiva, Rabbi Naftali Zvi Yehuda Berlin (the Netziv). He married Batsheva, the daughter of Rabbi Eliyahu David Rabinowitz-Teomim (the Aderet). After his wife's premature death he married her cousin, Raize-Rivka. In 1895, he became the rabbi of Bausk. During the years there he wrote a number of works, most of which were published posthumously.

In 1904, Rabbi Kook moved to Palestine and became a rabbi in Jaffa. He involved himself in outreach programs, thus bringing to the many immigrants a religious involvement. He was in Europe at the outbreak of the first world war and did not return until after the war. While in London he became the rabbi of an immigrant community in Whitechapel. He was involved in the activities leading to the Balfour Declaration in 1917.

After the war he became rabbi of Jerusalem and then in 1921 its first chief rabbi. He founded a yeshiva, Mercaz HaRav in 1924. Although a strict halakhist he was open to new ideas and thus attracted many non-religious individuals to him. He communicated and created political alliances among the various Jewish sectors. He believed deeply in the theological significance of the movement to re-establish Israel as a Jewish state. He related well to anti-religious elements as well.

Kook was a prolific author of halakha and Jewish thought. His writing include *Ayin Aiyah*, a commentary on *Ayin Yaakov*, the Aggadic sections of the Talmud; *Igorot HaRaiyah*, which were his collected letters; *Olat Raiyah* which was a commentary on the siddur.

Krochmal, Menachem Mendel ben Abraham

Menachem Mendel Krochmal was born in Cracow in about 1600. He was taught Talmud by Joel Sirkis. He soon distinguished himself and he opened a yeshiva, whose graduates included Mendel Auerbach and Gershon Ashkenazi.

In 1636, he left for Moravia and became the rabbi of Kremsir. He also started a yeshiva there. In 1645, he returned to Cracow and the next year became the rabbi of Prossnitz. Then in 1650 he took up his final rabbinate in Nikolsburg. His collection of responsa, *Tzemach Tzedek (Zemah Zedek)*, was posthumously published by his son, Aryeh Leib Krochmal.

Menachem Krochmal died in 1661.

Krochmal, Nachman Kohen

Nachman Kohen Krochmal was born in Brody, Galicia on February 17, 1785. He studied Talmud at an early age, got married at fourteen and went to live with his in-laws where he continued his studies. He also studied German and the German philosophers. After his parents-in-law died he became a merchant. Twelve years later his wife died and his business was a failure. He then became a bookkeeper in Zolkiev. He retired in poor health in 1838 and he went to live with his daughter in Tarnopol.

Krochmal wrote one book in Hebrew, *Moreh Nebuke HaZeman* ("Guide for the Perplexed of the Time"). It is a philosophical work of seventeen chapters dealing with several subjects, including a desire for seeking God, a philosophical Jewish history and Jewish religious philosophy. It was written as a guide for students of Jewish science of the nineteenth century.

Krochmal died in Tarnopol on July 31, 1840.

Labi, David ben Joseph ibn

David ben Joseph ibn Labi was a sixteenth century Turkish scholar born at Monastir. He was descended from a family of Spanish scholars. In about 1540 he became the rabbi of Salonica and then took the position of rabbi at Constantinople where he lived for the rest of his life.

He was the author of a collection of responsa that was published in four parts. He also wrote novellae to a number of Talmudic treatises.

He died in about 1600.

Labrat, Dunash HaLevi ben

Dunash ben Labrat was born in Fez, Morocco in 920. He was a

commentator, poet and grammarian. He was a student of Saadia Gaon. His poetry introduced Arabic meter into Hebrew poetry, which interspersed long and short vowels. It then formed the basis for all future Medieval Jewish poetry. His classic poem was *Dror Yikra*. He also wrote a book on grammar that was controversial for a long time. Labrat died in 990.

Lampronti, Yitzhak Hezekiah

Yitzhak Lampronti was born in Ferrara, Italy in 1679. Orphaned at age eight, he shortly thereafter began his Hebrew and Talmudic studies, first under the local rabbi, Shabbatai Elchanan Recanati. He was then sent to the yeshiva of Rabbi Manoah Provencal in Lugo and after that he went to Padua where he studied to become a physician. Following his education he returned to Ferrara where he taught Talmud as well as developing a medical practice. After the death of Rabbi Recanati, Lampronti was appointed the Rosh Yeshiva of Ferrara.

Lampronti wrote a single work of great significance. It was titled *Pahad Yitzhak* ("The Fear of Yitzhak"). It is an encyclopedia of the Talmud, where all the Talmudic subjects are discussed in alphabetical order. It also includes Midrashic material and ethical teachings of the sages. He died in 1756.

Landau Family

This family name is said to have derived from the name of a city in western Germany, but is found mainly among Polish Jews. They were probably expelled from that city in the middle of the sixteenth century.

The earliest recorded member of this family name is that of **Jacob ben Judah Landau** who lived in Italy about 1480-1490. He was the author of the ritual work, *Agur*, (See below).

After that, the name is then found in Poland from the latter part of the sixteenth century. A number of these family members were involved in various Jewish communal affairs, but were not scholars. These were Judah Landau, Ezekiel Landau (not the famous one), Zebi Hirsch Landau, and a later Judah Landau. There was also Hermann Landau who lived in Prague and died there about 1890.

Landau, Israel Jonah was a rabbi in Kempen, a province of Posen. He died in 1824 and was the author of *Me-on HaBerakhot*, that contain novellae to the tractate Berakhot.

Another rabbi of Kempen was **Samuel Joseph Landau** who died in 1837 and was the author of *Mishkan Shiloh*, that contain novellae and responsa.

Landau, Eleazar ben Israel was the rabbi of Brody and died in 1831. He wrote *Yad HaMelek*, that contain novellae to Maimonides' *Yad*.

Isaac Landau was born in Opatow and died in Cracow in 1768. He was a rabbi.

Landau, Isaac Elijah ben Samuel was born in Vilna in 1801 and died in 1876. He was a prolific author on both biblical and Talmudic subjects.

Isidor Landau was a newspaper editor.

Landau, Israel ben Ezekiel lived towards the end of the eighteenth century. He was a scholar and the author of *Hok Le-Yisrael*, a compendium of Maimonides' *Sefer HaMitzvot*.

Marcus Landau was an Austrian literary historian born in Brody, Galicia in 1837.

Landau, Moses Israel was an Austrian printer and publisher born in 1788 and died in 1852. He was the superintendent of the Jewish school in Prague. His book, *Marpe Lashon*, which was a collection of the foreign words found in Rashi, the Tosafot, Maimonides and the Rosh (Asher ben Jehiel), are considered invaluable.

Landau, Samuel ben Ezekiel was the chief dayan of Prague in the first half of the nineteenth century. His responsa were published under the title of *Shibat Ziyyon*.

Landau, Ezekiel (Yechezkel) ben Judah (Nodah B'Yehuda)

Yechezkel ben Yehuda Landau was born in Opatow, Poland on October 8, 1713. He was the scion of a famous Jewish family that originated in Western Germany. His father was Judah ben Zevi Hirsch Segal Landau. His first teacher was Rabbi Isaac of Vladimir (Ludmir). At age fourteen he was sent to Brody to study further. He married Yakelko of Dubno at age eighteen.

In 1734, he was appointed a dayan in Brody and in 1745 became the rabbi of Jampol (Yampole). He was involved in the mediation of the controversy between Jacob Emden and Jonathan Eybeschutz. In 1755 he was appointed the rabbi of Prague, where he established a yeshiva. Abraham Danzig was his most prominent student.

Landau is best known for his important halakhic work, *Nodah B'Yehuda* ("Known as Judah") that was a book of responsa and one of the most authoritative works on halakha. He also wrote *Tziyyon Lenefesh Hayyah* ("Memorial to a Living Soul") that were notes and commentaries on various Talmudic tractates, *Dagul Merevavah* ("Pre-eminent Above Ten thousand") that were notes on the *Shulkhan Arukh*. He also wrote several other minor works. Rabbi Landau died on April 29, 1793.

Landau, Yaakov Baruch ben Yehuda

Rabbi Yaakov Landau was born in Italy in the early 1400s. He wrote a compendium titled *Agur*. It contained a collection of laws (halakha), customs (minhagim) as well as a collection of responsa on the *Orach Chaim* and *Yoreh De'ah* based on the *Arba'ah Turim* of Jacob ben Asher. He died in 1493.

Lapapa, Aaron ben Isaac

Aaron Lapapa was born in c. 1590 and died in c. 1674. He studied in Salonika and Constantinople under Rabbi Mortal and Rabbi Joseph Trani. His rabbinic career began in the poor community of Manissa, Turkey. When advanced in age he was called to Smyrna as a civil judge.

He wrote a number of responsa and novellae, many of which were published titled *Bnei Aharon*.

Leibowitz, Boruch Ber

Rabbi Boruch Ber Leibowitz was born in Slutsk, Belarus in 1870. At a young age he went to study at the Volozhin Yeshiva, but disagreed with the Talmudic methods of the Rosh Yeshiva. He then embraced the approach of the Brisker Reb, Chaim Soloveitchik, and became one of the latter's main students. He became known for his Talmudic lectures. In 1904, he was appointed the head of the Keseth Beis Yitzhak Yeshiva in Slobodka. During the first world war he went to the yeshiva in Minsk, then to Kremenchug and Vilna. In 1926 he re-established the yeshiva in Kaminetz where he attracted many students.

His major work was *Birkas Shmuel*, named in memory of his father, Shmuel Leibowitz. It covered unrecorded teachings of the Brisker Reb as well as his own interpretations of Torah topics on the Talmud. His students recorded and published his lectures under the title of *Shiurei Reb Boruch Ber*.

He went to Vilna in 1939 and died there in 1940.

Leifer, Mordechai, of Nadvorna

Mordechai Leifer was born in the nineteenth century in the Austro-Hungarian Empire in the province of Galicia. Orphaned at an early age, he was raised by his great uncle, Rebbe Meir'l of Premishlan. He formed the Nadvorna Hassidic dynasty.

His teachings are collected in *Gedulas Mordechai*. He died in 1895.

Leon, Judah ben Isaac Messer

Judah ben Isaac Messer Leon was a French Tosafist. He was born in Paris in 1166. He might have been a descendant of Rashi. He was a student of Isaac ben Samuel of Dampierre. He also trained under Simson of Sens, Simson of Coucy, Solomon of Dreux and Abraham Nathan of Lunel.

Leon probably composed tosafot to most tractates of the Talmud. The only published one is to Berakhot and a long manuscript of tosafot to Avodah Zarah existing in manuscript form. Some responsa of his are found in parts of the *Mordechai*. Leon died in Paris in 1224.

Leon, Moses de (Moshe ben Shem Tov)

Moses de Leon, who was known in Hebrew as Moshe ben Shem Tov was born in Guadalajara, Spain in 1250. He was considered a kabbalist. He is most famous for probably, but not with certainty, being considered the author of the *Zohar*. De Leon studied the Middle Ages philosophers, Solomon ibn Gabirol, Judah HaLevi and Maimonides.

In 1287, he wrote, and which is still in existence in manuscript form, *Sefer HaRimonim*. It was a mystical approach to the ritual laws. In 1290, he wrote a further mystical work, also still extant in manuscript form, *HaNefesh HaHakhamah*. *Shekel HaKodesh*, written in 1292, was a similar work. In 1293, he wrote *Mishkan HaEdut* or *Sefer HaSodot* which dealt with heaven and hell. At the end of that century he probably wrote a kabbalistic midrash on the

Pentateuch. It was filled with mystical allegories and he ascribed it to the great Tanna, Shimon bar Yohai. This was titled *Midrash de Rabban Shimon ben Yohai* or the *Zohar*. Moses de Leon died in 1305.

Lev, Joseph ibn

Joseph ibn Lev was born in Monastir, Turkey in 1500. He studied under Rabbi Isaac Tzaddik ibn Lev. He later settled in Salonica. There he filled the position of dayan. He later went to Constantinople as the head of the yeshiva there.

He was considered a great halakhist and his responsa are collected in a work called *She'elot U'Teshubot R'Yosef ibn Lev*. It also contains novellae to many tractates. He died in 1580.

Levin, Joshua Hoschel ben Elijah Zeeb

Joshua Levin was a Lithuanian Talmudist and author. He was born in Vilna on July 22, 1818. He studied under Elijah Kalischer. Following this he settled in Volozhin where he taught Talmud. In 1871 he became the rabbi of Praga, near Warsaw. In later life he went to Paris where he became the preacher to the Polish-Russian community there.

A number of Levin's works were published. *Haggohot* was notes on the *Midrash Rabbah*. *Ma'yene Yehoshua* was a commentary on Pirke Avot. *Ziyyun Yehoshua* was a complete concordance to both the Jerusalem and Babylonian Talmuds. *Tosefot Sheni le-Ziyyon* contained glosses to the Mishnah and *Dabar b'itti* consisted of discussions on halakhic matters. Levin died in Paris on November 15, 1883.

Levita, Shabbatai Carmuz

Levita was a fourteenth century rabbi who wrote a moral treatise titled *Sefer HaYashar*. It is preserved in the Vatican in manuscript form.

Levovitz, Yerusham

Rabbi Levovitz was born in Lithuania in the nineteenth century. He was one of the great masters of the Mussar movement. His work *Daas Chochmah U'Mussar* was a collection of essays on Mussar. He died in 1936.

Lida, David

Rabbi David was born in Zwolen, Poland in 1625. He was a pupil of Rabbi Joshua Heshel of Cracow. After marrying he settled in Lemburg, but subsequently held various positions elsewhere in Poland, then Lithuania, Mainz, Germany, and then in Amsterdam. After a controversial stay in Amsterdam he returned to Lemburg.

He wrote several works. *Ir Miklat* was a listing of the 613 commandments with cross-reference to various sources. *Ir David* was on the laws of the Sabbath, *Sod Hashem Ver Sharvit HaZahav* covered the laws of circumcision, and *Chalukei Avanim* was on Rashi's Pentateuch commentary. Rabbi Lida died in Lemburg in 1698.

Lieberman, Saul (Gra'sh)

Saul Lieberman was born in Motol, Belarus in 1898. He studied at the Slobodka Yeshiva. His contemporaries included Yitzhak Ruderman and Yitzhak Hutner. Following this he studied at the University of Kiev. After studying further in France he went to Jerusalem where he studied at the Hebrew University. In 1940, he went to the Jewish Theological Seminary as Professor of Palestinian Literature. In 1949, he was appointed dean, and rector in 1958.

He is well-known for his "Lieberman clause" which is a clause added into the ketubah which allowed for arbitration in the case of a divorce when the woman was refused a *get* from her husband. Both must go to a rabbinic court of the Jewish Theological Seminary of America and heed their directives. The Orthodox leader Joseph Soloveitchik approved of this, but most of Orthodox Judaism rejected it.

Lieberman wrote a number of works. *Al HaYerushalmi* was a book recommending corrections to errors in the text of the Jerusalem Talmud and also included a variant reading of the tractate Sotah. He also wrote articles on a series of text studies of the Jerusalem Talmud. Later he published a four-volume text, *Tosefet Rishonim*, that was a commentary on the entire Tosefta with corrections to the text and brief explanatory notes.

Between 1955 and 1967, a new ten-volume edition appeared which included the entire Tosefta text with the brief commentaries. His work *Sifre Zuta* suggested that this halakhic Midrash was most likely edited by Bar Kappara in Lydda. His book *Sheki'in* was on Jewish legends, customs and literary sources found in Karaite and Christian polemical writings. *Midreshei Teiman* describes how Yemenite Midrashim preserve exegetical material that the rabbis had omitted. Rabbi Lieberman died in 1983.

Lieblein, Avraham

Rabbi Avraham Lieblein lived in Lemberg, Poland in the nineteenth century. He was the author of *Kesef Mezukak* that was a super-commentary of Nahmanides' (Ramban's) commentary on the Pentateuch.

Lima (Lema), Moses ben Isaac Judah

Moses Lima was a Lithuanian rabbi born about 1615. Lima was not the family name, but rather a nickname for Yehuda / Judah.

He became the rabbi of first Brest-Litovsk and then Slonim while still young and established a reputation for himself. He was then later called to be the chief rabbi of Wilna in 1650.

He wrote a manuscript commentary on the *Shulkhan Arukh, Even HaEzer* that was published by his son in 1670 under the title of *Helkat Mehokek*. It was so concise in format that the editor had to add explanatory notes. The work only covered the first 126 chapters of *Even HaEzer*. Lima died in about 1670.

Lipschitz, Baruch Mordechai ben Jacob

He was a Russian rabbi born in about 1810. His Talmudic decisions were sought after and recognized worldwide. He officiated in a number of cities for forty-three years. He wrote *Berit Ya'akob* that contained responsa to the four parts of the *Shulkhan Arukh*. He also wrote *Minhat Bikkurim* that contained novellae on the *Shulkhan Arukh*, and novellae on the Jerusalem Talmud. He died in 1885 at Siedlce, Poland.

Lipschutz, Hayyim ben Moses

He was a Polish rabbi born at Ostrog in 1620. He wrote a book of prayers and ritual laws for travelers called *Derek Hayyim*.

Lipschutz, Israel

He was born in 1782 and became a rabbi first of Dessau and then Danzig. He wrote a significant commentary on the Mishnah called *Tiferet Yisrael*. It includes interpretation of the text, philosophical aspects as well as practical halakha. There are also discussions on aggadic aspects. He died in 1860.

Lipschutz, Moses ben Noah Isaac

He was a sixteenth century Polish rabbi who wrote a commentary on several orders of the Mishnah titled *Lehem Mishneh*.

Lipschutz, Noah ben Abraham (Noah Mindes)

He was a Polish rabbi who lived in Vilna. He was the author of two kabbalistic works that were published anonymously and called *Parpera'ot le-Hokmah* and *Nifla'ot Hadashot*. He died in 1797 in Vilna.

Loanz, Yosef (Yoselman), of Rosheim

Rabbi Yoselman was born in Germany in 1480. In 1510, he was appointed as the leader of the Jewish communities of Alsace. This was predominantly an administrative role. He was also a prominent Torah scholar.

He was the author of an ethical and philosophical work called *Sefer HaMiknah*. It has recently been published. It is a two-part work, the first on the ethics of evil, particularly that as a result of informers. The second part is a philosophical work based on the Sephardi tradition and is a review of *Derech Emunah* of Abraham Bibago. He died in Alsace in 1554.

Loew, Samuel ben Nathan

Samuel ben Nathan Loew (in Hebrew, HaLevi), was born in about 1720 in Kolin, Bohemia and died in 1806. He is known for his major work that was a super-commentary on two scholars' commentaries on the *Shulkhan Arukh*. One was on Abele Gombiner's *Magen Avraham* commentary and the other was on Shabbatai ben Meir HaKohen's (Shach) commentary on the *Shulkhan Arukh*, called the *Shach*. The title of this super-commentary was *Machatsit HaShekel*.

Loew, Judah ben Bezalel (Maharal / Maharal of Prague)

Judah Loew was born in Poznan (now Poland) in 1525. He was the son of R' Bezalel Loew. He spent his youth studying in various yeshivot. He became the rabbi of Mikulov (Nikolsburg), Moravia in 1553. In 1588, he accepted a rabbinical position in Prague. In 1592, he moved to Posen as chief rabbi of Poland. Towards the end of his life he moved back to Prague. One of his most famous students was Yom Tov Heller.

His intellect and approach were such that he had a great influence on both the religious approach of the Gaon of Vilna (Elijah Zalman) and on Rabbi Shneur Zalman, the founder of a branch of Hassidism and a descendant of the Maharal. His philosophical work also inspired modern scholars, especially Eliyahu Dessler, Abraham Kook and Isaac Hutner.

The Maharal is also known for or is accredited with the fictitious creation of a golem (a human figure created from clay and brought to life by the use of one of God's names).

He was the author of many works. His most famous work was the *Gur Aryeh* ("Young Lion"), that is a super-commentary on Rashi's commentary of the Pentateuch. He wrote two works covering all aspects of Passover, called *Gevurot Hashem* ("God's Mighty Acts") and *Divrei Negidim* (Words of Rectors"), the latter being a commentary on the Seder. He also wrote works on the minor holidays of Hannukah, *Ner Mitzvah* ("The Candle of the Commandment") and Purim, *Or Chadash* ("A New Light"). He wrote novellae on the aggadic portion of the Talmud called *Chiddushei Aggadot* ("Novellae on the Aggadah"). *Derech Chaim* ("Way of Life") was a commentary on the tractate Avot. His overall collection of works, a sixteen-volume set, is titled *Kol Kitvei Maharal*. The Maharal died in 1609.

Lonzano, Menachem di

Menachem di Lonzano was born either in Turkey or Italy in the sixteenth century but went to Jerusalem as a child. He traveled extensively with his parents in Turkey, Italy and Syria.

He was the author of a collection of works called *Shtei Yadot* ("Two Hands"). It consisted of ten separate works divided into two parts, the first, consisting of five works, originated from him and the second was based on other work. The first part titled *Yad Ani* ("The Pauper's Hand") comprised of *Or Torah*, an analysis of matters related to the Torah; *Maarich* consisting of additions to the *Aruch*; *Avodat Mikdash* that was a description of the Temple service set in rhyme; *Derech Chaim* relating to daily laws and ethics; *Tovah Tochachot* was also on ethics. The second part was titled *Yad Melech* that contained rare midrashim and was the only one of this part that was published. The other four parts consisted of improved editions of other works or filling in missing parts of some works. He also wrote a short treatise on parts of the *Zohar*, titled *Omer Man*. *Sefer Maasiyot* was a collection of stories from the Jerusalem Talmud as well as midrashim. Lonzano died in the early seventeenth century.

Lorberbaum, Jacob ben Jacob Moses, of Lisser (Ba'al HaNesivos / Lissa Rav)

Jacob Lorberbaum or Jacob Lisser was born in 1760. He was related to

Jacob Emden. He was a pupil of Rabbi Meshulam Igra. In 1809 he became the rabbi of Lissa, which was previously known as Leszno in Poland, until Germany annexed it and it became part of the province of Posen. While there the yeshiva grew, attracting many scholars. In 1822 he moved to Kalish where he was head of the Beth Din. He was considered an authority by many of his contemporaries.

He wrote many works on the Tanakh and the Talmud. His most famous work was *Nesivos HaMishpat* that was a commentary in two parts on the *Choshen Mishpat* of the *Shulkhan Arukh*. It has been published many times and as a part of the *Shulkhan Arukh*. It became famous because of the strong opposing views in it to those of Aryeh Leib Heller's *Ketzot HaChoshen*. Another popular halakhic work was his *Derech Chaim* on the *Orach Chaim*. It is a compendium that has been reprinted in Hebrew prayer books.

Lorberbaum died in 1832.

Lublin, Meir ben Gedaliyah (Maharam)

Meir ben Gedaliyah, also known as the Maharam was born in Lublin in 1558. He came from a family of rabbis. His teacher was Isaac HaKohen Shapiro, the rabbi of Cracow. By thirty he became a part of the rabbinate of Cracow. Subsequently he became the rabbi of Lemberg. Later he became the rabbi of Lublin, where he remained until his death. Joshua Hoschel and Isaiah Horowitz were among his pupils.

He wrote novellae on the Talmud, Rashi and the tosafot called *Meir Einei Hakamim (Chachamim)*, that is now printed in editions of the Talmud under the heading of *Maharam*. *Manhir Einei Hakamim (Chachamim)* consisted of 140 responsa. He wrote several other smaller commentaries, called *Maor HaGadol, Maor HaKaton, Ner Mitzvah* and *Torah Or*. He died in Lublin in 1616.

Lunshitz, Shlomo Ephraim (Kli Yakar)

Ephraim Lunshitz was born probably in Lenshiz, Poland in the sixteenth century. The name Shlomo was added after an illness. He studied under Solomon Luria. He became the Rosh Yeshiva in Lemburg and after that he went to Prague in 1604 where he served as the rabbi until his death.

He was considered to be expert in the field of homolitics, the study of the composition of sermons and other religious discussions. To this end he wrote a number of works, most of which are considered classics. These were: *Ir Gibborim, Sifsei Daas, Orach LeChaim* and *Amudei Sheish*. *Kli Yakar* is a Torah commentary, widely used. He died in Prague in 1619.

Luria (Ashkenazi), Isaac (Ari, He-Ari, Arizal)

Isaac Luria was born in 1534 in Jerusalem. His family originated in Germany and had previously the name Ashkenazi, thus the initials of Ari (Ashkenazi Rabbi Isaac). His father died when he was young and he lived with an uncle in Cairo who encouraged him in his religious studies. He studied under Bezalel Ashkenazi, the author of *Shittah Mekubetzet*. He married his cousin when fifteen years old. He immersed himself in the study of the *Zohar* in his early twenties, becoming a recluse for seven years as he meditated extensively.

He moved back to Jerusalem in 1569 and after a short while moved to Safed. There he formed a group of other kabbalists, including Jacob Cordovero, Solomon Alkabetz, Joseph Caro, Moses Alshech, Eliyahu de Vidas, and several others. His most famous pupil was Hayyim Vital.

Arizal did not write much, but lectured extensively. His pupil Hayyim Vital collected the notes of other students of Luria's lectures. Vital then produced many works of which the most important one was an eight-volume set called *Etz Chaim*, the non-systematized collection of discourses of the Ari.

He introduced his mystical system (Lurianic kabbalah) into religious observance. The Sabbath was viewed as the manifestation in daily life of the Divine. His teachings have gained wide acceptance among Orthodox groups. He also introduced many holy customs. Many of his songs and prayers have been included in the prayer book. Rabbi Luria died in 1572.

Luria, Solomon (Maharshal, Rashal)

Solomon Luria was born in Posen in 1510. His father was the rabbi of Slutsk, Lithuania. The family could trace its origins to Rashi. He studied under Shalom Shachna in Lublin and then went to Ostrog yeshiva to study under Kalonymus Haberkasten, whose daughter he later married. Luria became the head of this yeshiva when the former went to Brisk. Later Luria succeeded Shachna as head of the Lublin Yeshiva. Subsequently he started his own yeshiva. The building in which it was contained was called the Maharshal's Shul and this remained intact until World War II.

Solomon Luria's major work was a halakhic one. It is called *Yam Shel Shlomo*. It consisted of an analysis of sixteen Talmudic tractates, although only seven are extant. It evaluated the various authorities and he then decided on what should be the practical halakha. His other significant work was *Chochmat Shlomo* consisting of glosses and comments on the actual Talmudic text. The abridged version of this appears in most editions of the Talmud, being placed at the end of each tractate. His other works were *Yeri'ot Shlomo*, a super-commentary on Rashi's Pentateuch commentary, but where he also make reference to Mizrachi's similar super-commentary; *Amudie Shlomo*, a commentary on Jacob of Coucy's *Semag* (*Sefer Mitzvot Gadol*); and a collection of responsa. Solomon Luria died in 1574.

Luzzatto, Moses Chaim (Ramchal)

Moshe Chaim Luzzatto was born in Padua, Italy in 1707. After a standard Jewish education he probably went to the University of Padua where he dabbled in mysticism and alchemy. Because of his extensive Jewish knowledge he soon became a leader of this group. At age twenty he claimed to receive direct instruction from a mystic called the Maggid, although the rabbinical authorities were skeptical. Because of his beliefs he was threatened with excommunication.

In 1735, he went to Amsterdam where he earned his living as a diamond cutter while studying kabbalah. It was here that he produced his major work *Mesillat Yesharim* ("Path of the Just"), an ethical treatise with mystical aspects. It was a practical book of how a person can overcome the inclination to sin and used rabbinic language. He also wrote *Derekh Hashem* that was a philosophical work on God's role in Creation, justice and ethics. *Da'at Tevunoth* was a work bridging kabbalah and rationality. *Derekh Tevunoth* described the logic which forms the structure of the Talmud to understand the world. His work was praised by the Vilna Gaon. Later the Mussar Movement adopted his ethical works as a result of the great Torah ethicist, Israel Salanter's support. *Messilat Yesharim* was core to the study program in the Mussar yeshivot in Eastern Europe. The Haskalah movement adopted his secular writings.

In 1743 Luzzatto went to Palestine and settled in Acre. In 1746 he and his family died in a plague.

Maimon, Moses ben (Maimonides) (Rambam)

Moses Maimonides was born in Cordoba, Spain in 1135. As a youth he showed a great interest in secular subjects, studying the sciences and philosophy. He also studied the Greek philosophers. With his pragmatic mind he had no interest in mysticism or poetry. This was in keeping with his rationalist approach to religion. He also had a traditional Jewish education, studying under his father, Maimon.

Following the Almohades conquest of Cordoba, most of the Jews left and Maimonides' family first moved elsewhere in Spain, but then moved on to Morocco, settling in Fez. It was here that he studied at the Al Karaouine University. It was while in Morocco that he produced his commentary on the Mishnah.

After leaving Morocco, he spent a short while in Palestine before finally settling in Forstat, Egypt. During his early years there he experienced personal misfortune. First his father died and then his brother, David, who supported the family by trading, died at sea and most of the family fortune was lost. Maimonides was compelled to seek his own livelihood. He became a physician. It was not long after that he achieved his great status as a physician to the Sultan Saladin and Grand Vizier Alfadhil. Most of his subsequent work was done in Forstat. Between 1158 and 1190 he produced a number of minor works, but also his great work.

Maimonides' first major work was his *Commentary on the Mishnah* (*Perush Hamishnayot*). It was written in Arabic. It was one of the first such commentaries. It condenses many of the Talmudic debates and also provides conclusions to a number of issues not decided on in the Mishnah. His introduction to the work, as well as introductions to the various sections, have been widely quoted in works by other scholars.

The Rambam's *Sefer HaMitzvot* ("Book of Commandments") lists all 613 laws in the Pentateuch. The book contains fourteen principles that he used to guide his selection of these laws. For example, rabbinical laws were excluded, laws that were not of a permanent nature historically were excluded and the details of how a law is applied are not counted. It is considered the most authoritative source for the enumeration of the laws.

Probably his most famous work is his *Mishneh Torah* (*Yad HaHazakha*). It was the first Code of Jewish law. The work consists of fourteen books that are divided into various sections, chapters and paragraphs. These fourteen books cover all aspects of religious law. Some examples are the laws of the Sabbath and Holidays, laws specific to women, agricultural laws, laws of offerings, tort and civil law etc. The book is known for its brevity of description and the information was drawn from both the Jerusalem and the Babylonian Talmuds, the Tosefta and the Halakhic Midrashim, of which the latter were mainly from the Sifra and Sifre. He also included responsa of the Geonim. He also drew from unnamed other Palestinian, French and Spanish authorities as well as from some non-Jewish sources. Although the work initially drew much criticism, it has come to be recognized and studied as one of the greatest sources of halakha. Many commentaries on it have been written by various authorities over many centuries.

The *Guide for the Perplexed* (*Moreh Nevuchim*) is another major work by the Rambam. It was the main source of his philosophy and was written in the form of a three-volume letter to a student. According to Maimonides there is no contradiction between the Divinely revealed truths and those truths that the human mind has discovered. He was a religious rationalist.

His *Epistle to Yemen* (*Iggeret Temam*) was a letter of support to the Jewish population of Yemen that was suffering religious persecution at the time.

In the twentieth century Yosef Quafih translated Maimonides' *Commentary on the Mishnah*, the *Mishneh Torah*, *Sefer HaMitzvot* and *Guide for the Perplexed*.

Maimonides also wrote several scientific works on astronomy and medicine. He died in Egypt in 1204.

Manoah, Hezekiah ben (Hizkuni / Chizkuni)

Hezekiah ben Manoah was a thirteenth century French scholar. He wrote a commentary on the Pentateuch called *Hazzekuni*. It was a kabbalistic commentary. It was based mainly on Rashi's commentary, but he used many others as well. It was first printed in Venice, but then there were several other editions over the centuries.

Margolis / Margolioth Family

This was a Polish family of Talmudists who trace their origins to Rashi and Samuel Edels. The first of these was a Samuel Margolis who lived in the mid-sixteenth century in Posen. His son was Moses Mordechai Margolis whose daughter married a relative Mendel Margolis. They had eight children, all of whom were Talmudists. One was Judah of Potok. A descendant of his was Mordechai ben Menahem Monis who was a kabbalist. The most famous Margolis was Ephraim Zalman (Solomon). There are many other scholars named Margolis where the relationship to the original family cannot be directly linked.

Margolis, Abi Ezra Selig

He was a German Talmudist during the first half of the eighteenth century. He later went to live in Palestine. He wrote a commentary on the Pentateuch called *Kesef Nivvar*, and a collection of novellae and responsa called *Hivvure Likkutim*.

Margolis, Alexander

He was a Polish rabbi who lived in the eighteenth century. He wrote a collection of responsa, published over half a century after his death and titled *Teshuvot HaRam*. He died in Satanov, Podolia in 1802.

Margolis, Ephraim Zalman (Solomon)

He was born in 1762 in Brody, Galicia and studied Talmud in several yeshivas. He died in 1828. He corresponded with Ezekiel Landau and soon achieved a great reputation. He became a very successful banker. In 1785 he published his responsa titled *Bet Hadash HaHadashot*. After that he was made a rabbi by the other rabbis of Brody. He then opened a yeshiva.

Ephraim published a number of other works. These were:

Bet Ephraim; a two-part commentary on the *Yoreh De'ah* of the Shulkhan Arukh.

Bet Ephraim; a four-part set of responsa on the four parts of the Shulkhan Arukh.

Yad Ephraim; commentaries on the *Orach Chaim* of the *Shulkhan Arukh*.

Sha'are Ephraim; on the rules of reading the law.

Shem Ephraim; a commentary on the Torah.

Matteh Ephraim; on the ritual laws from Elul to after Sukkot and also on regulations for Kaddish for orphans. This is perhaps his most popular work.

Zera Ephraim; a commentary on the *Pesikta Rabbati*.

Margolis, Hayyim Mordechai

He was an eighteenth century Polish rabbi and brother of Ephraim Zalman. He became the rabbi of Brestitski and then Dubno. He was the author of *Sha'are Teshubah*, a commentary on the *Orach Chaim* of the *Shulkhan Arukh*. He died in Dunajowce in 1818.

Margolis, Meir ben Zvi Hirsch

He was an eighteenth century Polish rabbi born in Galicia. He was the rabbi of Lemberg for over forty years. He then went to Ostrog where he spent the rest of his life. He was a student of Israel Ba'al Shem Tov (Besht), the founder of Hassidim. He authored a work of responsa and novellae titled *Meir Netivim*, a work on kabbalah titled *Sod Yakin u-Voaz* and a commentary on the *Shulkhan Arukh* called *Derek HaTov veha-Yashar*. He died in 1790.

Mari, Abba, ben Moses ben Joseph Don Astruc of Lunel

Abba Mari was a French rabbi born towards the end of the thirteenth century. He was a descendant of Meshullam ben Jacob. He studied theology and philosophy as well as the works of Maimonides and Nachmanides. He was against the then current popularity of Aristotelian rationalism and hence he was against Maimonides, particularly since he felt it undermined the authority of the Pentateuch. He preferred the mystical approach of Nahmanides.

With the expulsion of the Jews from France by Philip IV in 1306 he went to live in Perpignan in the Pyrenees. It was here that he wrote all his letters to Solomon ben Aderet regarding his concerns with philosophy, Aristotelian rationalism and the allegorical interpretations of the Bible. These were later published under the title of *Minhat Kenaot* ("Jealousy Offering").

Mari, Abba, Yitzhak ben, of Marseilles

Rabbi Yitzhak ben Abba Mari was born in Provence in about 1122. He wrote a major code called *Sefer HaIttur* ("Book of Separation") or *Ittur Soferim* ("Scribal Separation"). It drew its information from the Talmudic and Gaonic periods. It consisted of three parts dealing with civil matters, religious aspects of tefillin, circumcision and forbidden foods as well as on the festivals. It was widely used until the appearance of the *Arba'ah Turim*. Abba Mari died in about 1193.

Mecklenberg (Mecklenburg), Jacob Tzvi

Rabbi Mecklenberg was born in Germany in 1785. He was the rabbi of Koenigsberg. He was involved in the struggle against the religious reformers. He wrote a biblical commentary titled *HaKetav V'ha-kabbalah* (*K'sav V'ha-kabbalah*). Rabbi Mecklenberg died in 1865.

Mendelssohn, Moses

Moses Mendelssohn was born in Dessau, Germany in 1729. His early teacher was David Frankel who taught him Tanakh, Talmud and the philosophy of Maimonides. When Frankel went to Berlin, Moses joined him there a short while later. He also studied secular subjects, including Latin and mathematics. He already became famous as a German philosopher while still young.

Although he maintained his traditional Jewish religious upbringing, Mendelssohn is known as the "father" of the Haskalah (the Jewish Age of Enlightenment). Yet in the end he was not recognized by the Reformers, and he engendered bitterness by the Orthodox being labeled as a Reformer.

He wrote two major works. The first was *Biur* that was a German translation and commentary on the Torah. It was met with controversy among the Jewish leadership because it would force teachers to spend more time explaining German grammar than concentrating on the content. In the commentary aspect, however, the book stuck to traditional rabbinic interpretation even though at that time there was the developing scholarship in critical historical study of the Bible. His second major work was *Jerusalem* that was Mendelssohn's summary of his philosophy of Judaism. Its aim was to try and reconcile the potentially conflicting aspects of Jewish life – adapting to a full European culture in public while maintaining the strict parochial religious practice at home. He died in 1781.

Medina, Moses de

Moses de Modena was born in the late seventeenth century, probably either in Turkey or Egypt. He wrote two works on kabbalah. The one was a commentary on the Pentateuch titled *Nefesh David* and the other was a commentary on the *Iddera Rabba* section of *Zohar* titled *Ruach David v'Nishmat David*.

Medina, Samuel ben Moses de, (RashDaM)

Rabbi Samuel Medina was born in 1505. He was taught by Joseph Taitazak and Levi ibn Chaviv. Among his contemporaries were Moses Almosnino and Isaac Adarbi. He later became head of the Talmudic college of Salonica that produced many great scholars. Abraham de Boton and Joseph ibn Ezra were his disciples. His grandson was Samuel Hayyun, who wrote *Bene Shemuel*.

The RashDaM wrote *Ben Shemuel*, that consisted of thirty sermons, *Hiddushim*, which were unpublished Talmudic novellae and a collection of 956 responsa titled *Piske RashDaM*. He died in Salonica in 1589.

Medina, Shemaiah de

Shemaiah de Medina was the son of Moses de Medina. He was born in Salonica. He later moved to Venice following a quarrel with influential citizens of Salonica. He was the author of many liturgical poems. He died in 1648.

Medini, Chaim Chizkiya

Chaim Chizkiya was born in 1832 in Jerusalem where he grew up. He spent many years in Turkey, Buchara and the Crimea. He returned to Palestine in 1878 and became the Rosh Yeshiva in Hebron.

He is best known for his eighteen-volume Talmudic and Halakhic encyclopedia, *S'Dei Chemed*. He died in 1904.

Meir, Isaac (Yitzhak) ben, (Rivam)

Yitzhak ben Meir was born in 1090 in Ramerupt, France. He was the grandson of Rashi and brother of Jacob (Rabbeinu Tam) and Samuel (Rashbam) ben Meir. He was one of the Ba'alei Tosafot. In his short life he contributed to the tosafot and he is quoted. He died in 1130, preceding his father, Shmuel.

Meir (Tam), Jacob ben, (Rabbeinu Tam)

Jacob ben Meir, who is always referred to as Rabbeinu Tam, was born in Ramerupt, France in 1100. He was one of the most famous of the Ba'alei Tosafot, whose commentaries appear in all editions of the Talmud opposite

Rashi's commentaries. He was Rashi's grandson.

The name Tam is based on the comparison of his first name with the biblical Jacob who was described as "tam", being straightforward and truthful.

He was the son of Meir ben Shmuel, who together with his brother, Samuel ben Meir (Rashbam) were his primary teachers. His other brothers were Yitzhak (Rivam) and Solomon.

He disagreed with Rashi on the contents of the head-piece of the tefillin and to this day both Rashi and Rabbeinu Tam tefillin are available.

He was a prolific author of piyyutim and composed pieces for Sukkot and Shemini Azeret and several others.

Rabbeinu Tam is best known for his work called *Sefer haYashar* that consists of novellae and responsa to explain and resolve problems with many Talmudic texts. This work shares the same title as works by Ibn Ezra, Abraham Abulafia and Shabbatai Levita as well as the anonymous Midrash of the same name, which is also known under the title *Toledot Adam*.

He died about 1171 and is buried with his brothers, the Rashbam (Shmuel ben Meir) and the Rivam (Yitzhak ben Meir) in Ramerupt.

Meir, Moses ben, of Ferrara

Meir was a French Tosafist who flourished in the thirteenth century. He was probably a pupil of Judah ben Isaac of Paris. His tosafot appear in the *Haggahot Maimuniyot* of Jacob ben Isaac HaLevi (Jabez).

Meir, Samuel ben (Rashbam)

Samuel ben Meir was born in Ramerupt near Troyes, France in 1085. His mother Yocheved was the daughter of Rashi. He was a leading French Tosafist and like his grandfather, a biblical commentator. His younger brothers were Yitzhak (Rivam) and Jacob (Rabbeinu Tam). He studied under Rashi and Riva (Isaac ben Asher HaLevi).

His biblical commentaries are known for stressing the *peshat* (plain meaning) of the text. Parts of his comments have been preserved and appear in Bava Batra and Pesachim. He died in 1158.

Meiri, Menachem ben Solomon (HaMeiri)

Menachem Meiri was born in Provence, France in 1249. He was an essentially unknown scholar until the discovery of, and subsequent publication of his major work, *Beit HaBechirah*. It is now considered a classical work on the Talmud, covering several orders and a number of tractates. It is not a typical Talmudic commentary but more of a digest of the Gemara commentaries to the Mishnah. It also includes many of the various interpretations by the great preceding and contemporary scholars.

Meiri also wrote a number of novellae to various tractates of the Talmud. He also produced various other works. *Chibbur HaTeshuvah* was on repentance and *Kiryat Sefer*, on the laws of writing a Torah scroll. He died in 1306.

Meltzer, Isser Zalman (Even HaEzel)

Isser Zalman Meltzer was a Lithuanian rabbi born in 1870 in Mir (which is now part of Belarus). He studied under Rabbi Yom Tov Lippman at the Mir Yeshiva. He then went on to the Volozhin Yeshiva, studying under Naftali Berlin (the Netziv) and Rabbi Chaim Soloveitchik. He was also a disciple of the Israel Meir Kagan (Chofetz Chaim).

In 1897 he moved to Slobodka and from there he went to head a yeshiva in Slutsk, which had been started by Rabbi David Wilovsky (Ridvaz / Ridbaz). He held this position for twenty years. He then immigrated to Palestine where he became the head of the Etz Chaim Yeshiva in Jerusalem.

He wrote a commentary on the *Mishneh Torah* of Maimonides, titled *Even HaEzel*. Rabbi Meltzer died in 1953.

Mendel, Menachem of Kotzk (Kotzker Rebbe)

Menachem Mendel was born in Goray, near Lublin, Poland in 1787. He is best known as the Kotzker Rebbe. He received his education from his father Leibus Morgenstern, who also introduced him to Hassidim. He became a pupil of Rabbi Simcha Bunam. He then became the rabbi of Kotzk. Here he attracted many brilliant young scholars. He had an analytical approach to study and pursued justice. He made Kotzk a center of Hassidut.

His thoughts and commentaries were published in two books titled *Ohel Torah* and *Emet Ve'emunah*. His wisdom was also recorded in the book *Amod HaEmet*. He died in Kotzk, Poland in 1859.

Meshullam, Asher ben

Asher ben Meshullam lived in the second half of the twelfth century in Lunel, France. He was the son of Meshullam ben Jacob. He studied under Joseph ibn Plat and Abraham ibn Daud HaLevi (Ravad).

He wrote two Talmudic works that are not extant. These were *Hilcoth Yom-Tov* ("Rules for the Holidays") and *Sefer HaMatanah* ("The Book of Gifts").

Meshullam, Yerucham ben

Yerucham ben Meshullam was born in Provence, France in 1280. He wrote a code of law divided into two parts, *Meisharim* which was on civil law and *Adam V'Chava* that deals with laws of lifecycles. It was quoted frequently in the *Beit Yosef* of Joseph Caro. He died in Spain in 1350.

Mevorakh, Joshua Boaz / Baruch, Joshua Boaz ben Simon (Shiltei Gibborim)

Joshua Boaz Mevorakh was also known as Joshua Boaz ben Simon Baruch or Shiltei Gibborim, after one of his works. He was descended from a Spanish family that settled in Italy after the Spanish Inquisition. He first lived in Sabbineta and then later in Savigliano. He lived during the sixteenth century.

He was only twenty-three when he began publishing his important Talmudic works.

Masoret HaShas or *Massoret HaTalmud* ("Tradition of the [Six orders of the] Talmud"). It consists of cross-references to other passages in the Talmud where the same quote appears. It first appeared in the third Venice printing of the Talmud.

Ein Mishpat ("The Wellspring of Justice") contains references to the main codes of Jewish law; The *Mishneh Torah* of Maimonides; *Arba'ah Turim* of Jacob ben Asher; *Shulkhan Arukh* of Joseph Caro; and *Sefer Mitzvot Gadol* of Moses ben Jacob of Coucy. It is an index of the Talmudic laws quoted by these authors.

Ner Mitzvah ("Lamp of Commandment") lists chronologically all the codified laws as they appear in each chapter of the Talmud as indexed in the *Ein Mishpat*. These two works also first appeared in the third printing of the Venice Talmud.

Torah Ohr was an index of the biblical passages mentioned in the Talmud. It also appeared in the Venice printing of 1546-1551.

He also wrote two other works.

Siddur Mordechai Ve-Simanav (or *Siddur Dine Mordekai*) was a compendium of Mordechai ben Hillel Ashkenazi's halakhic work.

Shiltei HaGibborim (or *Sefer HaMakloket*) ("Shields of Heroes") was a selection of notes on Alfasi's work and the Mordekai. He died in 1557.

Michel, Meir Leibush ben Jehiel (Malbim)

The Malbim was born in 1809 in Volochisk, Volhynia, which was then part of the Russian Empire. He was educated first by his father, who died when he was thirteen and then by his stepfather. He then went on to further study in Warsaw. He also obtained an education in the secular sciences.

He first became the rabbi of Wreschen in Posen in 1838 and then in 1845 of Kempen. In 1860 he became the chief rabbi of Bucharest, Rumania. There he had a major conflict with the German Jews who wanted to introduce Reform Judaism. This episode resulted in him being thrown into prison. Through the mediation of Sir Moses Montefiore, he was released and went to Constantinople, then Paris, Kalisz, Kherson, Moghilef and Konigsberg. In each of these places he came into conflict with certain personalities of the community because of his uncompromising attitude towards Reform Judaism.

He had a modernistic approach to his writing that caused some initial suspicion in the Hassidic community. This was particularly so with his modern interpretations of the Tanakh. The Chatam Sofer (Rabbi Moses Sofer) supported his approach.

He is known for his novel commentary to the Bible. *HaTorah vehaMitzvah* is an analytical and innovative commentary on the Pentateuch and the midrash halakha. He published a commentary on Megillat Esther. *Mikra'ei Kodesh* was a commentary on the Prophets, Job, Proverbs and Psalms, and the five Megillot. He also wrote *Artzoth HaChaim* that was a commentary and novellae on the *Shulkhan Arukh, Orach Chaim* section. *Artzoth HaShalom* was a collection of sermons. He died in Kiev in 1879.

Migash, Joseph ben Meir HaLevi ibn (Ri Migash)

Joseph ibn Migash was probably born in Seville, although possibly in Granada in 1077, based on a comment by Moses ibn Ezra. At age twelve he went to Lucena to study under Isaac Alfasi for fourteen years who then ordained him. He also appointed him the successor head of his yeshiva, a position he held for thirty-eight years. His appointment was commemorated by the poet and his contemporary, Judah (Yehuda) HaLevi. His most famous student was Maimonides' father, Maimon.

Ri Migash was the author of a collection of over 200 responsa titled *She'elot uTeshuvot Ri MiGash*. He quoted Chananel ben Chushiel and Alfasi as his authorities. He also authored novellae on tractates Baba Batra and Shevuot, that were quoted by other Rishonim. His other works have not survived. One of these is mentioned by Zerahiah HaLevi, called *Megillat Setarim*. He also wrote extensive commentaries on the *Sefer HaHalachot* of Alfasi (RIF), but these have all been lost. He died in Lucena in 1141.

Minz, Abraham ben Judah HaLevi

Abraham ben Judah Minz was a late fifteenth-sixteenth century Italian rabbi. He lived in Padua and studied under his father Judah Minz, whom he succeeded as the head of the Padua yeshiva. He was the author of *Seder Gittin ve-Halizah*, which was a treatise on divorce and haliza. It was printed by his son-in-law, Meir Katzenellenbogen, together with the latter's own responsa and the surviving responsa of his father, Judah ben Eliezer Minz. These were later edited with additional commentary by Moses Preschel in 1898.

Minz, Judah ben Eliezer HaLevi (Mahari Minz)

Judah ben Eliezer Minz was a prominent Italian rabbi who was born in about 1408. The latter half of his life was spent as the rabbi of Padua. He wrote a number of responsa, of which only sixteen survived the sack of Padua. These were later published by Meir Katzenellenbogen together with the latter's responsa, as well as Judah Minz's son's work. He died in about 1508.

Mizrachi, Elijah (Re'em)

Rabbi Mizrachi was born in Constantinople in 1455. His family was originally from Turkey and not Spain. He studied under Elijah HaLevi and also Judah ben Eliezer Minz of Padua. He also studied the secular sciences of mathematics and astronomy. On the death of Moses Kapsali (Capsali) he succeeded the latter as the Grand Rabbi of the Ottoman Empire.

Mizrachi is best known for his work *Sefer HaMizrachi* which is a super-commentary on Rashi's commentary of the Pentateuch. The work describes Rashi's Talmudic and midrashic sources and also clarifies obscure passages. He wrote it partly to defend Rashi's positions against Nachmanides. Solomon Luria made reference to it in his super-commentary.

His other works were *Tosefe Semag* that were novellae on Moses ben Jacob of Coucy's *Semag*, and mathematical works. He died in 1525-6.

Modena, Samuel ben Moses di (Maharshdam)

Samuel ben Moses di Modena was born in Salonika in 1506. He was the student of Maharalbach, the chief rabbi of Jerusalem. He was the teacher of Moses de Bouton, the author of *Lehem Mishneh*. He was the author of a collection of responsa. He died in 1590.

Moelin, Jacob ben Moses Levi (Maharil)

Rabbi Moelin was born in 1365 and died in 1427. He was the son of Rabbi Moshe Levi Moelin. He studied under Shalom of Wiener Neustadt. He became the Rosh Yeshiva at Mayence where his most famous pupil was Jacob Weil, who produced a number of authoritative responsa. Moelin survived the massacre of Austrian Jews in 1420 as well as the Hussite wars which created much misery for the Jews of Bavaria, the Rhine and Thuringia.

Jacob Moelin was considered the greatest authority of his time. He is most well-known for his discourses and responsa. His opinion was sought from far and wide. His responsa were published after his death by his student, Zalman of St. Goar, under the title of *Minhagim* ("Book of Customs") or *Minhagei Maharil* or *Sefer HaMaharil*. This work is frequently quoted in the codes of law and other commentaries. It contains details of religious observance within and out of the synagogue, as well as rites, regulations of ceremonial laws and comments on the texts. Moses Isserles (Rema) quoted from it in his *HaMapah*. It was very influential on the Jews of central Europe.

Mordechai, Isaac ben, of Regensburg (RiBaM)

Isaac ben Regensburg was a twelfth century Tosafist. He was a student of Isaac ben Asher HaLevi. His tosafot are quoted by Eliezer ben Joel HaLevi and Meir of Rothenburg. He is also frequently quoted in the edited tosafot.

Mos, Moshe, of Premysl

Rabbi Moshe Mos was born in Premysl, Poland in 1540. He served as the rabbi of Bez, Premysl and finally Apta (Opatow).

He was the author of *Matteh Moshe* that was a compendium of halakha related to prayer, benedictions, holidays and several other subjects. He also wrote *Ho'il Moshe* that consisted of two parts, *Be'er Moshe*, a commentary on Rashi's commentary of the Pentateuch and *Ba'er Heitev*, consisting of his sermons. It also included his Talmudic novellae. *Taryag Mitzvos* was his work that listed the 613 commandments in rhythmic form and accompanied with a commentary. He died in Apta in 1606.

Moses of Evreux

Moses of Evreux was a French Tosafist who lived in the first half of the thirteenth century. He was the elder brother of Samuel of Evreux. He authored a much-used work titled *Tosafot of Evreux*. He is quoted in the tosafot on Berakhot. He wrote his glosses on the margin of Alfasi's *Halakot*, probably at the time of the burning of the Talmud.

Moses, Isaac ben, of Vienna (Or Zarua, Riaz)

Isaac ben Moses was probably born in Bohemia and lived from about 1200 to 1270. He moved to Vienna and became one of the greatest rabbis of the Middle Ages. His two teachers were Bohemian rabbis, Jacob HaLaban and Isaac ben Jacob HaLaban. In his youth he studied in famous yeshivas in France and Germany. In Paris Judah ben Isaac Messer Leon became his teacher. In Germany he studied under Eleazar ben Yehuda of Worms and at Speyer under Simchah ben Samuel and Eliezer ben Joel HaLevi.

He went to Wurzburg to be the head of the yeshiva there. Meir of Rothenburg was his pupil. He went to Vienna to become the Av Beth Din as well as the Rosh Yeshiva. He finally went to Saxony and Bohemia.

In the latter part of his life he wrote his ritual work, *Or Zarua*. It covered the whole of the ritual, arranged according to the Talmudic tractates, but also kept the halakhot together. He cited the passage in the Talmud, explained it and then developed the law from it. Thus it is a combination of law as well as a Talmud commentary. It also contains explanations from the Bible.

Moses, Joseph ben

Joseph ben Moses was born in 1423 in Hoechstaedt, Bavaria. He was a pupil of Jacob Weil of Augsburg, Judah Minz of Padua and Joseph Colon of Mestre. However, his main Talmud teacher was Israel Isserlein.

He wrote his work, *Leket Yosher*, which was a collection of Israel Isserlein's customs, responsa and other halakhic decisions. It was the first work to be based on the *Arba'ah Turim*, although only parts are extant. Its value lies in the responsa that give important information about the lives of the Jews and the scholars of Germany of that period. He died in about 1490.

Moses, Meshullam ben

He was a German poet who lived in Mayence in the eleventh century. He wrote a number of piyyutim, including for a Sabbath marriage and a kedushah for the Musaf service.

Moses, Meshullam ben

There was a Meshullam ben Moshe who lived in Provence. He was born in 1175. He wrote a commentary on the *Sefer HaHalachot* of Alfasi (RIF), called *Sefer HaHashalamah*. It also complements the RIF in areas that were not covered by it, and then these parts were incorporated into *Sefer HaHalachot*. He died in 1238.

Nachman of Breslov

Rebbe Nachman was born in 1772 in Medzibizh. He was the founder of the Breslov Hassidic dynasty. He was the great-grandson of the Ba'al Shem Tov. He combined the kabbalistic aspects of Hassidut with detailed Torah study. His concepts attracted many followers in his lifetime and this continued after his death.

In 1798, he traveled to Palestine where he visited with the various

Hassidic communities. In 1800, he became the rabbi of Zlatipolia but shortly thereafter he moved to Bratslav. There Nathan Sterhartz (Reb Nusn) became his student. He became the Rebbe's scribe and recorded all his teachings in what became the main work of the Rebbe, *Likutei Moharan*. Reb Nusn also recorded all the informal conversations and teachings of the Rebbe and published these after Nachman's death. These were *Sefer HaMiddot*, a treatise on morals; *Tikkun HaKlali*, which was Nachman's order of ten psalms which were to be recited for various problems; and *Sippurei Ma'asiyyot* that were stories in Hebrew and Yiddish with mystical secrets.

He died at the young age of 38 in 1810 from tuberculosis. He was buried at the cemetery in Uman where 20,000 Jewish martyrs were buried following the Haidemack massacre of 1768.

Naghrela, Samuel ibn (Samuel HaNagid)

Samuel ibn Naghrela, also known as Samuel HaNagid, was born in Merida, Spain in 993. He was a poet, statesman, warrior and Talmudic scholar. He represented the symbol of the successful Jew in the early golden era of Spanish Jewry. When the Berbers took control of the city in 1013 he went to Cordoba and then moved to Granada where he rapidly became very influential in the court of the Berber king.

He founded a yeshiva that educated scholars like Isaac ibn Gias and Maimonides' father. His main poetic works were *Ben Tehillim* ("Son of Psalms") that were devotional poems, *Ben Koheleth* ("Son of Ecclesiastes") which was a philosophical work and *Ben Mishlei* ("Son of Proverbs") which contained maxims. He also wrote *Mavo HaTalmud* that described the approach of the Talmud and its terminology. *Hilchata Gevurta* was a digest of Talmudic laws aimed at the layperson. The actual book was lost but many other scholars quoted from it. These quotes have been collected and in 1962 were published as *Hilchos HaNagid*. He died in 1056.

Nahman, Moses ben (Nahmanides) (Ramban)

Nahmanides was born in Gerona in 1194. He was the grandson of Isaac ben Reuben of Barcelona. He studied Talmud under Judah ben Yakar and Meir ben Nathan of Trinquetaille. He also studied kabbalah under Azriel of Gerona. His secular studies covered philosophy and medicine, the latter providing him with his livelihood. He became the chief rabbi of Aragon and Catalonia. In the Disputation of 1263 he successfully defended the Jewish religion.

His Talmudic philosophy was a conservative one in that he believed the Mishnaic, Talmudic and Geonic rabbis words were unquestionable. He disagreed with Maimonides although he had great respect for him. This related mainly to his *Guide for the Perplexed*, because in a letter to French rabbis, Nahmanides strongly supported the Rambam's *Mishneh Torah*. He also disagreed with Abraham ibn Ezra's biblical commentary.

In 1263, Ramban was involved in the Disputation of Barcelona. This consisted of a debate between Nahmanides and the Dominican Friar Pablo

Christiani who was a Christian convert from Judaism. The debate centered around whether the Messiah had arrived yet or not, whether according to Scripture the Messiah is divine or a human being and whether the Jews or the Christians believed in the true faith. Ultimately the disputation ended in Nahmanides' favor, but despite this he was ultimately exiled from Spain.

In 1267, Ramban left for Palestine and settled in Jerusalem. There he established the Ramban Synagogue, which still is in existence He was instrumental in re-establishing Jewish life there, which remained uninterrupted until 1948. He later settled in Acre.

His most important work was his commentary on the Torah. It frequently cites Rashi and also gives alternative interpretations. His interpretations include aggadic and mystical aspects. He also wrote glosses on the whole of the Talmud. He wrote a number of small, minor works on halakha. These were *Mishpetei HaCherem* on excommunication, *Hilkhot Bedikah* on the examination of slaughtered animals, *Torat HaAdam* on mourning and burial, *Sha'ar HaGemul* on escatology. His *Milhamot HaShem* was a halakhic defense against the critics of Alfasi's decisions. *Torat Hashem Temima* praised the benefits of the Torah. Nahmanides died in Palestine in about 1270.

Nahman, Yehudai ben (Yehudai Gaon)

Yehudai Gaon was an eighth-century Gaon. He was the head of the Academy at Sura from 757 to 761 following the death of Mar Aha. His brother Dodai ben Nahman was the Gaon of the Pumbedita Academy.

He was the author of a work, *Halakhot Pesukot* that discussed those halakhot which were practiced in the diaspora since the destruction of the Second Temple. It was organized according to the tractates in the Babylonian Talmud. Simon Kayyara in his *Halakhot Gedolot* quoted from this work. He also wrote a number of responsa, dealing with prayers, the Torah readings, various laws of the Sabbath and holidays, tefillin, dietary laws, and divorce.

Nathan, Abraham ben

Abraham ben Nathan was born in Lunel, France in the second half of the twelfth century. He studied in Dampierre in northern France in the academy under Rabbi Isaac ben Samuel. In 1204 he left France and settled in Toledo, Spain where his knowledge quickly gained him a reputation with wealthy patrons.

There he wrote his work *HaMinhag* ("The Guide"), or as he called it *Manhig Olam*. The book consists of two parts. The first is a collection of responsa. The second part contains extracts from various halakhic works, including those of Alfasi, Ibn Giyyat and Abba Mari. The book also contains exact quotations from the two Talmuds and most of the halakhic and haggadic Midrashim, collections from the Haggadot, which had mostly been lost. It also gives insight into special synagogue customs.

Nathan, Eliezer ben (Raavan)

Eliezer ben Nathan was a Tosafist and was born in Mayence in 1090. He was a contemporary of Jacob ben Meir (Rabbeinu Tam) and Samuel ben Meir (Rashbam). He was the son-in-law of Eliakim ben Joseph. His great-grandson was Asher ben Jehiel (Rosh), the father of Jacob ben Asher, author of *Ba'al HaTurim*.

His major work was *Even HaEzer* that consists of two parts. The first covers aspects of complicated legal matters, ritual observances and explanations of traditional customs. The second and larger part has extensive halakhic discussions on subjects that follow the tractates of the Talmud. He also wrote a number of liturgical poems, but very few of them were incorporated into the German liturgy. He died in 1170.

Nathan, Judah ben (Riban)

Judah ben Nathan lived in Troyes, France in the eleventh century. He was the son-in-law and disciple of Rashi. He was one of the earliest Tosafists. He completed Rashi's commentary on Makkot, wrote the commentary to Nazir, and also wrote commentaries to the tractates Erubin, Shabbat and Yebamot. He is often quoted in the edited tosafot.

Nathanson, Joseph Saul

Joseph Nathanson was born in Berezhany, Galicia in 1808 and died in 1875. He studied Talmud in Lemberg. There he later established an informal study group that attracted many students from Galicia. In 1857 he became the rabbi there. Considered a major authority of his time, he was called upon to provide many rulings on a number of then contemporary subjects. Many of these are still widely quoted.

He wrote a number of works, but he is best known for his responsa. These were of a practical nature and he based these directly on the Talmud and the Rishonim. He tended towards the lenient view. One of his well-known rulings was on the use of machinery to produce matzo. This view was in opposition to that of Solomon Kluger. His responsa are collected in a six-volume work titled *Sho'el u-Meshiv*. He also wrote works on the Pentateuch, kabbalah, the Mishnah, the aggadah of the Talmud, and the *Shulkhan Arukh*.

Nehor, Yitzhak Saggi (Isaac the Blind)

Rabbi Yitzhak Nehor was born in Provence, France in about 1160. He was the son of Abraham ben David of Posquieres. He was well known as a writer on kabbalah and is attributed with being the author of the *Bahir*, an important work on kabbalah. This work discussed many aspects of kabbalah. He died in 1235.

Nehorai, Meir ben Isaac

Rabbi Meir ben Yitzhak was an eleventh century cantor in Worms, Germany. He composed a mystical liturgical poem, *Akdamut* (Akdamut Millin, "The Introduction"). It is recited on the first day of Shavuot in the Diaspora during the Torah service. It is a poem entirely in praise of God. It has a total of forty-five two-line verses.

Onkelos

Onkelos was the name of a convert to Judaism during the immediate pre- and post-Second Temple destruction. He is most likely the author of the famous *Targum Onkelos* of about 110 CE. He is also mentioned in the Talmud several times.

The *Targum Onkelos* or Unkelus is the official Babylonian targum of the Torah. It is an Aramaic translation and reflects rabbinic or midrashic interpretation of the Tanakh. According to tradition, Onkelos authored his Targum based on Rabbi Eliezer's basic interpretation of the Torah.

Ornstein, Jacob Meshullam ben Mordechai Ze'ev

Jacob Meshullam Ornstein was a Galician rabbi who was born in Lemberg in the eighteenth century. His father died when he was too young to accept the rabbinate of Lemberg, that had been in the family for 150 years. He became the rabbi at Zolkiev, in Galicia. When the rabbinate at Lemberg became vacant he went there and filled this position until his death.

His most important work was *Yeshuot Ya'acob* which was a multi-volume commentary on the *Shulkhan Arukh*, covering the *Orach Chaim*, *Yoreh De'ah* and *Even HaEzer*. The commentary is divided into a short section and a long one. The short commentary explains the *Shulkhan Arukh* and the long one combines the comments from other works and tries to simplify difficult aspects and resolve contradictions. He also wrote a commentary of the Pentateuch under the same title of *Yeshuot Ya'acob*. He died in 1839.

Palaggi, Hayyim (Maharhaf, HaVif)

Hayyim Palaggi was a Turkish rabbi. He was born in 1788 in Smyrna where he spent his life. He was held in great veneration during his lifetime. He was a prolific author of numerous minor works, most of which contained his name, Hayyim. Twenty-six were published. These works included responsa, various halakhic rulings and a variety of miscellaneous subjects. He died in 1869.

Pallier, Moshe, of Kobrin

Moshe Pallier was born in 1784. In 1833 he became the first Rebbe of the Kobrin Hassidic dynasty. Many of his followers moved to Israel. His teachings are collected in *Imros Taharos*. He died in 1858.

Paquda, Bahya ben Joseph ibn

Bahya ibn Paquda lived in Saragossa, Spain in the first half of the eleventh century. He was a philosopher and rabbi. He wrote the first Jewish book on ethics. It was written in Arabic, but translated into Hebrew by Judah ibn Tibbon a century later under the title of *Chovot HaLevavot* ("Instruction in the Duties of the Heart"). He wrote this work, because as he stated in the introduction, he felt that neither the Talmudic sages nor subsequent rabbis had created a coherent system of Jewish ethical teachings. His concern centered around the emphasis on the physical observance of Jewish law without regard to the inner sentiments. The book is divided into ten sections termed Sha'arim (gates), corresponding to the ten principles that constitute a spiritual life. It became a popular work and extracts were read in the days leading up to the High Holidays.

Plat, Joseph ibn

Joseph ibn Plat was a twelfth-century rabbi who probably was born in southern Spain but then went to Lunel, Provence. He also spent some time in Rome. He taught Asher ben Meshullam and Zerahiah HaLevi Gerondi, also of Lunel. He corresponded with Maimonides and Abraham ben Isaac of Narbonne. He wrote a work on prayers titled *Tikkun Soferim*, of which a fragment is still in existence. He wrote halakhic treatises on various tractates. His date of death is given by various authorities between 1198 and 1225.

Popperos, Meir

Rabbi Meir Popperos was born in Prague, Bohemia (modern day Czech Republic) in 1624. He descended from a distinguished family of rabbis. While still young he immigrated to Jerusalem. There he studied kabbalah under Israel Ashkenazi and Jacob Tzemach. Through Hayyim Vital's son he had access to the father's papers that he studied. He also studied Isaac Luria's (The Ari) work that had been edited by Tzemach.

Vital's writings, *Etz Chaim*, were in no systematic fashion since he wrote these after each discourse of Rabbi Luria. Rabbi Popperos undertook to systematize these. He also called his work *Etz Chaim*. It was divided into three parts. These were *Derech Chaim*, containing the fundamentals of kabbalah; *Pri Etz Chaim*, that consisted of ritual information for prayers and holiday; and *Nof Etz Chaim*, that had the treatises on souls, reincarnation and biblical and *Zohar* commentaries. These works would serve as the basis for instruction in Luria's kabbalah for many generations.

Rabbi Meir also wrote other works on kabbalah. The more important ones were *Meorei Or*, a kabbalistic encyclopedia; *Or Tzaddikim* on kabbalistic customs and ethics; *Or Rav*, and a commentary on the *Zohar*. He died in Jerusalem in 1662.

Price, Avraham Aharon

Avraham Aharon Price was born in 1900 in Poland. He went to Berlin but in 1931 fled to Paris and in 1937 went to Toronto, Canada. On arrival there he established a yeshiva that soon flourished. Many professionals received their Talmudic and Hebrew education there. During the second world war he helped bring many refugees to study at his yeshiva. He developed over the years an extensive library of rabbinic literature. These are now in the Price collection of Rabbinics at the University of Toronto.

Rabbi Price was the author of four sets of books. *Mishnat Avraham* in two volumes and *Imrei Avraham*, also in two volumes contain his speeches and writings on the weekly Torah portion. *Sefer Hasidim* is a three-volume commentary on the same title of the work of the thirteenth century scholar Judah ben Samuel of Regensburg. *Mitzvot Gadol* is a two-volume commentary on the early halakhic codification of Moses ben Jacob of Coucy's *Sefer Mitzvot Gadol* (SeMaG). The latter was the student of Judah ben Samuel. Rabbi Price died in 1994.

Quafih (Qafehh, Kafich, Gafeh, Kapach) Yosef

Rabbi Quafih was born in 1917 in Sana'a, Yemen. His parents died when he was very young and he was taught by his grandfather. He married his eleven-year-old cousin to avoid being imprisoned, because under Yemeni law an orphan had to convert to Islam. In 1943 he immigrated to Palestine and studied at the Merkaz HaRav Yeshiva. He was then appointed dayan of the Harry Fischel Institute, then the Jerusalem district court and finally the Supreme Rabbinical Court. He presided over the Yemenite community in Jerusalem. In 1969 he won the Israel Prize for Torah literature.

Quafih translated a number of works of Sephardi Rishonim. These included the *Emunot ve-Deot* of Saadia Gaon, *Kuzari* of Judah HaLevi, *Chovot HaLevavot* of Bahya ibn Pakuda and others. However his main work was his translations of Maimonides' *Commentary on the Mishnah*, the *Mishneh Torah*, *Sefer HaMitzvot* and *Guide for the Perplexed*. He also published *Siach Yerushalayim* that was a Yemenite prayer book reflecting the views of Maimonides. He died in 2000.

Rabinowitz, Chaim Shalom Tuvia (Reb Chaim Telzer)

Chaim Rabinowitz was born in Lithuania in 1856 and died in 1930. He studied under Yitzhak Elchanan Spektor and Meir Simcha of Dvinsk. After the death of Rabbi Spektor his son established a yeshiva in memory of his father called Knesses Beis Yitzhak. Rabbi Rabinowitz became its first head. In 1904 after Rabbi Shkop left the Telshe Rabbinical College, Rabbi Rabinowitz was appointed the head there. He taught there for twenty six years where he became known as Reb Chaim Telzer. While there he developed his own method of Talmudic study.

Three volumes of his Talmudic lectures have been published by the Telz Yeshiva in Cleveland under the title of *Shiurei Rebbi Chaim MiTelz*.

Rabinowitz-Teomim, Eliyahu David (Aderet)

Rabbi Rabinowitz-Teomim, also know as the Aderet from his initials, was born in Pikeln, Kovno in 1845. He studied under his father. In 1873 he became the rabbi of Panavezys. After twenty years in this position he became the rabbi of Mir in Minsk. He later immigrated to Palestine and in 1901 he was made the assistant to Rabbi Samuel Salant, the chief rabbi of the Ashkenazi communities in Jerusalem. He was the father-in-law of Rabbi Abraham Isaac Kook.

He wrote over 120 books that included many novellae and Talmudic glosses. There have been recent efforts to collect these and re-publish them in groups. He died in 1905.

Rapoport, Solomon Judah Loeb

Solomon Judah Loeb Rapoport was born in Galicia in 1790. He first entered business but subsequently became the rabbi first of Tarnopol in 1837 and then of Prague in 1840.

He published biographies on Saadia Gaon, Nathan ben Jehiel, the author of Arukh, Hai Gaon, the payyatan Eleazar Kalir and others. He also wrote the first part of an encyclopedia. He died in Prague in 1867.

Reggio, Isaac Samuel (Yashar)

Isaac Samuel Reggio was an Italian-Austrian rabbi who was born in 1784 in Goritz, Illyria, which at that time was probably part of the Balkan states. He not only studied Hebrew and rabbinics from his father, Abraham Vita, the liberal rabbi of Goritz, but also studied many languages and mathematics. He followed a secular career firstly as a tutor in Trieste, then as a professor when Goritz came under French control. When Illyria came under Austrian control he was forced to resign and devoted himself to Jewish studies.

In the early 1820s he established a rabbinical assembly in Padua. In order to make the Bible available to the masses he translated it into Italian and added his own commentary. The bible was called *Sefer Torat Elohim* and the commentary was *HaTorah weha-Peusufiah*. He also wrote *Iggerot Yashar* that was a collection of exegetical, philosophical and historical treatises in the form of letters to a friend. He wrote many other smaller works. Rabbi Reggio died in 1855.

Reischer, Jacob ben Joseph (Backofen)

Jacob Reischer, also known as Jacob Backofen was an Austrian rabbi who was born in Prague in 1661 (1670). He first studied under Rabbi Aaron Simeon Spira in Prague and then under his son Benjamin Wolf Spira. He subsequently married Benjamin's daughter. Reischer's family was originally from Poland before immigrating to Bohemia. While still a young man Reischer became the dayan of the bet din of Prague. Later he was appointed as the Av Beth Din of Ansbach in Bavaria. In 1709 he became the head of the yeshiva there and in 1715 the Av Beth Din of Worms. In 1718 he was appointed the Av Beth Din and Rosh Yeshiva of Metz. He remained in this position for the rest of his life.

Rabbi Reischer's first work was written while still a young man in Prague in 1689 and titled *Minhat Ya'akov*. This work was divided into two parts: The first is an explanation of Moses Isserles' *Torat Hattat* and the second part is an exposition of the *Yoreh De'ah, Hilkhot Niddah* of the *Shulkhan Arukh*. He also wrote *Shevut Ya'akov* that consisted of a three-part collection of responsa. Rabbi Reischer died in Metz in 1733.

Reuben, Jacob ben

Jacob ben Reuben was a Karaite and a biblical scholar from the eleventh century. He wrote a brief commentary of the bible titled *Sefer HaOsher* which can be found in manuscript form in the library at Lyden. Previous manuscripts were known to be in St. Petersburg and Paris. The work was a compilation of other commentaries with additions by the author.

Reuben, Jacob ben

Jacob ben Reuben was a Spanish rabbi of the twelfth century. He wrote *Sefer Milhamot Adonai* ("Book of the Wars of the Lord") in response to the attacks by the convert Petrus Alphonsi. It is divided into twelve chapters and contains refutations of Christian arguments based on the Tanakh. It also has a criticism of the Gospels and the Acts of the Apostles and points out contradictions.

Reuven, Nissim ben, of Gerona (RaN)

Rabbi Nissim ben Reuven or RaN was born in Barcelona, Catalonia in 1320. It is thought that his father was his primary Talmudic teacher. He was also a physician and understood astronomy. His most important students were Isaac ben Sheshet (Rivash) and Hasdai Crescas.

His most important work for which he is known is his commentary and explanation of Alfasi's (the RIF's) *Halacoth* (Alfes). In this explanation he concentrates mainly on the practical aspects and only briefly discusses the theoretical aspects. The RaN is now printed alongside the RIF in most standard editions of the Talmud. The RaN also wrote a Talmud commentary, only part of which still exists. He also wrote responsa and a commentary on the Bible, that was recently published, a collection of sermons and a philosophical work. He died in 1380.

Rivkes, Moses ben Naftali Hertz

Rabbi Moses ben Naftali Hertz Rivkes was born in Vilna in the seventeenth century. He escaped the Chmielnicki massacres of 1648 and finally went to live in Amsterdam.

He was the author of *Be'er HaGolah* ("The Well of Exile" – a well name which is mentioned in the Mishnah, Erubin 10:14). It provides cross-references to the Talmud, the commentaries, codes of law and responsa. Some of the author's explanatory notes are added.

Rosanes, Judah ben Samuel

Rabbi Rosanes was born in 1657. He was taught by Samuel HaLevi and Joseph di Trani. He became the rabbi of Constantinople where he spent the remainder of his life.

He was the author of *Parashat Derakim* that was published the year he died. It was a work of midrashic and halakhic content and consisted of twenty six treatises on various subjects. He also wrote *Mishneh la-Melek* that were glosses and comments on Maimonides' *Yad HaHazakha* (*Mishneh Torah*). He died in 1727.

Rosen, Yosef (Rogatchover Gaon, Tzafnach Paneach)

Rabbi Rosen was born in Rogachev (now Belarus) in 1858. He was a part of the Kapuster Hassidim family. At the age of thirteen he went to study with Rabbi Chaim Soloveitchik, and after that with Rabbi Moshe Yehuda Leib Diskin (Maharil Diskin) in Shklov. He then became the rabbi of the Hassidic community in Dvinsk. Among his students whom he ordained were

Mordechai Savitsky of Boston, Zvi Olshwang of Chicago, Avrohom Elye Plotkin, the author of *Birurei Halachot* and Menachem Mendel Schneerson, the seventh Lubavitcher Rebbe.

He had a tremendous Torah knowledge, but rarely quoted authorities after the Rishonim.

His primary work consisted of a commentary on Maimonides' work, especially his *Guide for the Perplexed* (*Moreh Nevuchim*). It was published during his lifetime. He also wrote a five-volume set of responsa. His surviving works were smuggled out of Latvia during the second world war and were published many years after his death under the title of *Tzafnach Paneach* ("Decipherer of Secrets"). These works included responsa and novellae on the Talmud and Torah. They are very difficult to understand. Rabbi Menachem Kasher at Yeshiva University provided an explanatory commentary on some of them called *Mefa'aneach Tzefunoth*. He died in Vienna in 1936 following surgery.

Ruderman, Yaakov Yitzhak

Rabbi Ruderman was born in Dolhinov, Russia in 1901. He studied in the yeshiva at Slobodka under Rabbi Nosson Tzvi Finkel and Rabbi Moshe Mordechai Epstein. Rabbi Yaakov Kamenetsky and Rabbi Yitzhak Hutner were colleagues of his at the yeshiva.

He immigrated to America in 1930 and in 1933 he moved to Baltimore where he opened the Ner Yisroel Yeshiva. He led this yeshiva for fifty-four years until his death and built it into one of the largest yeshivas in the United States.

In 1926, he published his only work, *Avodas Levi*. After his death his students collected and published a two-volume set of his teachings, that were ethical insights into the weekly parsha, titled *Sichos Levi*. Another work, *Mas'as Levi* was a collection of his lectures on the nineteenth century work *Minchat Chinuch* of Yosef ben Moshe Babad, as well as other Talmudic and halakhic insights. Rabbi Ruderman died in 1987.

Saba, Avraham ben Yaakov

Avraham ben Yaakov Saba was born in Zamora, Spain in the early part of the fifteenth century. After the 1492 Spanish expulsions he settled in Portugal. He wrote *Tror Hamor* that was a commentary on the Pentateuch that had a kabbalistic inclination. He also authored *Eshkol Hakofer* that was a commentary on the book of Ruth. He died in 1508.

Sahula, Meir ben Solomon Abi

Meir Sahula was born in about 1260. He lived in Guadalajara in Spain. He was a famous kabbalist. Guadalajara was a center of kabbalah. His approach to kabbalah differed from Nahmanides (Ramban) and Solomon Aderet as well as from the *Zohar*.

He was the author of a commentary on *Sefer Yezirah*. Most of this is in manuscript form in the author's own handwriting and is in the Angelica Library in Rome.

Salanter, Israel Lipkin

Rabbi Israel Lipkin, known better as Yisroel Salanter was born in Zhagory, northern Lithuania in 1810. As a child he studied under Rabbi Tzvi Hirsch Braude of Salant. He then settled in Salant and continued his studies under Rabbis Hirsch Broda and Yosef Zundel. The latter was very influential in shaping Salanter's thoughts.

Rabbi Salanter went on to form the Mussar movement. In 1842 he was appointed Rosh Yeshiva of the Tomchai Torah yeshiva in Vilna. There he established another yeshiva. He also established his first Mussar society. He later moved back to Kovno, Lithuania where he established another yeshiva. Here ethical texts were studied. For health reasons he left Kovno and went to Prussia. He spent time in Berlin. While in Prussia he began a monthly publication devoted to rabbinical law and ethics called *Tevunah*. It only lasted one year. Many of these articles were collected and published in *Imrei Einah*. His *Iggeret HaMussar* ("Ethical Letter") was first published in 1858. Many of his letters were published in 1890 in *Ohr Yisrael*. His students collected his discourses and published them in *Even Yisrael* in 1853 and in *Etz Peri* in 1880. Rabbi Salanter died in 1883.

Samuel, Aaron ben

Aaron ben Samuel was born in Germany in about 1620. He was known primarily for his work *Bet Aharon* which was published in 1690. It was very well received by the rabbinic authorities. The book takes the verses in the Bible and correlates each one of these with the places in the Talmud, the Midrashim, the Zohar and many other rabbinic and kabbalistic works where these are quoted or explained. Among the predecessors upon whom he relied for resource material were Aaron of Pesaro, Jacob Sasportas and Menasseh ben Israel.

In 1701 he published a commentary on *Perek Shirah* ("A Chapter of Song"). This work of unknown authorship or attributed to King David is about how everything in the natural world teaches lessons in philosophy and ethics. This work was included in a prayer book published in Berlin that year.

Samuel, Eliezer ben, of Metz

Eliezer ben Samuel of Metz lived in the twelfth century. He was a Tosafist and the author of a work on halakha, titled *Sefer Yereim*. It was first published in Vilna in 1892. Benjamin ben Abraham Anaw wrote an abridged version of this work. Samuel died in 1175.

Samuel, Isaac ben, of Dampierre (Ri)

Isaac ben Samuel the Elder of Dampierre or the Ri lived in Ramerupt and Dampierre in the twelfth century. He was the grandson of Simhah ben Samuel of Vitry, and was a great-grandson of Rashi. He is often referred to as Isaac of Dampierre. In Dampierre he established a successful school.

Isaac completed the Talmud commentary of Rashi. He also compiled all Rashi's previous explanations under the title of *Tosefot Yeshanim*. He is very frequently quoted in the Tosefot as well as in other works, especially Baruch ben Isaac's *Sefer HaTerumah* and Isaac ben Moses' *Or Zarua*. He is also quoted as a biblical commentator. Rabbi Isaac died about 1200.

Samuel, Isaac ben (Hasefardi)

Isaac ben Samuel (Hasefardi) was born in Spain in the eleventh century. He appears to have lived in Palestine. He was a biblical interpreter. Among the authorities he quoted were several gaonim, Judah ibn Balaam and Nathan ben Jehiel. His commentary on the second book of Samuel is found in the British Museum.

Samuel, Judah ben, of Regensburg (He-Hasid)

Judah ben Samuel lived during the twelfth and thirteenth centuries. He was a descendant of a family of kabbalists from the East that had settled in Germany. He studied under his grandfather, Kalonymus. He left his birthplace of Speyer and settled in Regensburg, where he founded a yeshiva. Among its students were Eleazar of Worms (Rokeach), Isaac ben Moses of Vienna (Or Zarua) and Baruch ben Samuel of Mayence.

There were a number of legends associated with his life. He was an ethical writer and mystic. His writings therefore, also seemed to be steeped in this legend and obscurity. He wrote *Sefer Hasidim* ("Book of the Pious") and *Sefer Hakavod* ("Book of Glory"), although the latter has been lost. The former work contains ethical, ascetic and mystical descriptions combined with popular German beliefs. In the twentieth century Rabbi Avraham Aharon Price wrote a commentary on *Sefer Hasidim*, using the same title for his work. He is also thought to have composed piyyutim, but this is not at all certain. Isaac ben Samuel died in 1217.

Samuel, Meir ben (RAM)

Meir ben Samuel was born in France in Ramerupt about 1060. He studied in Lorraine under Isaac ben Asher HaLevi and Eleazar ben Isaac of Mainz. He married Rashi's second daughter, Yocheved, and had three sons, Samuel ben Meir (Rashbam), Isaac ben Meir (Ribam) and Jacob ben Meir (Rabbeinu Tam), He was one of the founders of the Tosafists of Northern France. His halakhic decisions were quoted by Rabbeinu Tam and other Tosafists. He changed the composition of the Kol Nidre prayer. He also wrote a commentary on a passage in the Gemara that can be found at the end of the first chapter of Menachot. He died just after 1135.

Samuel, Simha ben, of Speyer

Simha ben Samuel of Speyer was a thirteenth century rabbi and Tosafist. He was a participant in the rabbinical synod held in Mayence and was one of the signers of the regulations and decrees issued by that body.

He was the author of tosefot and novellae on the Talmud. *Seder Olam* was a work containing decisions and comments on Talmudic passages. It is quoted in *Haggahot Maimuniyot* of Jacob ben Isaac HaLevi (Jabez). Other decisions and responsa of his are mentioned in the collection of responsa of Meir of Rothenburg.

Samuel, Simhah ben, of Vitry

Simhah ben Samuel was an eleventh century French Talmudist. He was a pupil of Rashi. He compiled the *Vitry Mahzor*. It contains halakhic rules and responsa by Rashi and other authorities. There remain three manuscripts in existence, one in Reggio, one in the Bodleian Library at Oxford and one in the British Museum. In the British Museum copy there are a number of liturgical poems. These were later published under the title of *Contres HaPiyyutim*. There is also a published edition of the *Vitry Mahzor* that contains a commentary of *Pirke Avot* found in the British Museum manuscript. Simhah died in 1105.

Sardi (HaSardi, HaSefaradi), Samuel ben Isaac

Samuel ben Isaac HaSardi, also referred to as HaSefaradi, lived in Spain in the first half of the thirteenth century. He studied under Nathan ben Meir of Trinquetaille in Provence. He was a contemporary of Nahmanides.

He wrote in 1225 *Sefer HaTerumot* which were novellae on the civil laws of the Talmud. These were divided into sections called she'arim or gates that then were sub-divided into chapters.

Sarug, Israel

Israel Sarug lived in the sixteenth century. He was a student of Isaac Luria. After the latter's death he propagated his kabbalism. He had many followers in Italy and also lectured in Germany and Amsterdam.

He wrote a kabbalistic essay titled *Kabbalah*. He also wrote *Contres Ne'im Zemirot Yisrael*, a kabbalistic commentary on three of Luria's piyyutim for the Sabbath.

Saruq, Menahem ben Jacob ibn

Menahem ben Saruq was born in Tortosa, Spain in 920. At a young age he went to Cordoba. For a while he was an assistant to the Jewish statesman, Hasdai ibn Shaprut.

While still young he created an early dictionary of the Hebrew language. He titled it *Mahberet*. An alternative title was *Sefer HaPitronot*. Dunash ben Labrat opposed this work and wrote a criticism. However, the work prevailed and other scholars accepted it. Saruq died in 970.

Sasportas, Jacob ben Aaron

Jacob ben Aaron Sasportas was born in Oran, Algeria in 1610. When still young he became the rabbi of first Tlemcen, and then Morocco, Fez and Sali. After being captured by the Moorish king in 1646, he and his family escaped to Amsterdam. The Moroccan king invited him later to return. After undertaking a special mission for the king he went on to be the rabbi of the Portuguese community in London in 1664. He had previously accompanied

Menasseh ben Israel to London in 1655. With the outbreak of the plague in London in 1665 he went to Hamburg as the rabbi until 1673. He then went on to Amsterdam where he first became the head of the yeshiva there and then the rabbi of the Portuguese community.

Rabbi Sasportas wrote several works. *Toledot Yaacob* was an index of biblical passages found in the haggadic portion of the Jerusalem Talmud. It was similar to Aaron Pesaro's *Toledot Aharon* that was done for the Babylonian Talmud. *Ohel Yaacob* was a collection of responsa edited by his son, Abraham. *Zizat Nobel Zebi* was a polemical correspondence against Shabbetai Tzvi. This work was later abridged by Jacob Emden under the title of *Kizzur Zizat Nobel Zebi*. Rabbi Sasportas died in Amsterdam in 1698.

Schick, Moses (Maharam Schick)

Moses Schick was born in 1807 in the Slovakian part of the Austrian Empire. He was a student of Moses Sofer. He established a yeshiva at Hust, Hungary. He was a strong opponent of the Reform Movement, although he did believe that sermons could be preached in any language.

He wrote more than 1,000 responsa that are collected in his works *Maharam Schick* and *Derashot*. He died in 1879.

Schmelkes, Isaac

Isaac Schmelkes was a nineteenth century Rabbi living in Lemberg, Galicia, then part of Austria. He is known for his work *Bet Yitzhak* that contains responsa.

Schneerson, Levi Yitzhak

Levi Yitzhak Schneerson was born in Podrovnah, Ukraine in 1878. His father was Baruch Schneur and his great-great-grandfather was the Tzemach Tzedek. His son became the seventh and last Rebbe, Menachem Mendel Schneerson.

In 1909, he was appointed the rabbi of Yekatrinoslav. In 1939, he was captured by the Communists because of his opposition to the Party's efforts to eradicate Jewish study. He was tortured and exiled to the interior of Russia.

Levi Yitzhak was a recognized kabbalist. Some of his work has been published under the title of *Likkutei Levi Yitzhak*, but the majority of his writings were either burned by the Communists or confiscated by them. He died in exile in 1944.

Schneerson, Menachem Mendel (Tzemach Tzedek)

The first Menachem Mendel Schneerson, known as the Tzemach Tzedek ("Religious Scion"), was born in Liozna, Poland in 1789. His mother died when he was three and he was brought up by his maternal grandfather, Rabbi Shneur Zalman of Liadi. He married his first cousin, the daughter of Rabbi Dovber Schneuri. When both his father-in-law and uncle died he became the Lubavitch leader in 1831. He had seven sons and two daughters.

He had close ties with other Jewish leaders, including Rabbi Yitzhak of

Volozhin who was a major Mitnagid leader. They both opposed the Haskalah movement in Russia. This helped improve the relationship between the Mitnagdim and Hassidim.

His eponym the Tzemach Tzedek was from the title of his compendium of halakha, the *Shut Tzemach Tzedek*. His mystical explanation of the laws was titled *Derech Mitzvotecha* ("Way of Your Commandments"). He was the author of a philosophical work called *Sefer Chakira: Derech Emunah* ("Book of Philosophy: Way of Faith"). His other major work was *Ohr HaTorah* that consisted of Hassidic discourses. He also compiled the works of Rabbi Shneur Zalman of Liadi for publication, including *Siddur Mi'Kol HaShanah*, *Likutei Torah* and *Torah Ohr*. The Tzemach Tzedek died in 1866.

Schneerson, Menachem Mendel (The Lubavitcher Rebbe)

Menachem Mendel Schneerson, known as the Rebbe or the Lubavitcher Rebbe, the seventh and last spiritual leader of Chabad Lubavitch was born in Nikolaev, Ukraine in 1902. He was the eldest of three sons of Rabbi Levi Yitzhak Schneerson. His father was his main teacher. He was ordained as a rabbi by the Rogatchover Gaon, Rabbi Yosef Rosen. While growing up he was involved with communal and administrative duties, assisting his father. In 1928, he married Yosef Yitzhak Schneerson's daughter, Chaya Mushka, after studying in Berlin and Paris. He lived there after his marriage. In 1940, after the fall of Paris, he fled to Vichy and then in 1941 fled to the United States, going to Crown Heights, Brooklyn, New York where he joined his father-in-law. The following year he was appointed by Yosef Yitzhak as the director of the central Chabad organization. In 1952, a year after the passing of his father-in-law, he become the seventh Rebbe.

Schneerson placed great significance on bringing Jews into Orthodoxy and he made tremendous strides in outreach. He trained many rabbis and their wives to go all over the world to deliver the message of Chabad. He was also politically active. Although he never visited Israel, he was in contact with many of its leaders, including Zalman Shazar, Menachim Begin, Ariel Sharon and Benjamin Netanyahu.

When he turned eighty, the United States Congress awarded him the National Scroll of Honor. Posthumously he was awarded the Congressional Gold Medal for his "outstanding and enduring contributions toward world education, morality, and acts of charity". He was well-known for his scholarly work and Hassidic thoughts, especially on Rashi's Torah commentary. These comments were recorded by his aides. He also gave extensive regular discourses on the weekly Torah reading, which his aides also transcribed. These were later compiled in the *Likkutei Sichot* set of books. His thousands of responses to various questions were printed as *Igrot Kodesh* ('Letters from the Rebbe"). *Sefer HaSichot* was a ten-volume set of his talks between 1987 and 1992. *Sefer HaMa'amarim Melukot* was a six-volume set of Hassidic discourses.

After a prolonged illness, Menachem Mendel Schneerson died in 1994.

Schneerson, Shmuel (The Rebbe Maharash)

Rabbi Shmuel Schneerson was born in Lyubavichi, Russia in 1834. He was the seventh son of the Tzemach Tzedek. His first wife died shortly after marriage and his second wife was Rivkah, the daughter of Rabbi Dovber Schneuri, the Mitteler Rebbe. He had four sons and two daughters. He faced competition to head the Chabad Lubavitch Hassidic movement from three brothers. Each of them went on to form separate dynasties. He then became the fourth Rebbe.

He was not only active in community affairs but he was also an intellectual and wrote extensively on both religious and secular topics. Most were never published. Subsequently his discourses began to be published in 1945 under the title of *Likkutei Torat Shmuel*. To date twelve volumes have been published. The Rebbe Maharash died in Lyubavichi in 1882.

Schneerson, Sholom Dovber (Rebbe Rashab)

Sholom Dovber Schneerson was born in Lyubayichi in 1860. He was the second son of Shmuel Schneerson. His father died when he was only twenty-two years old and only ten years later did he fully assume the role as the fifth Rebbe of the Chabad Lubavitch Hassidic movement. In 1897, he established the first Chabad yeshiva, Tomchei Temimim and in 1911, he established one in Israel called Toras Emes. His third one was in Georgia in 1916.

He was very active in Jewish educational and organizational activities and met with and corresponded with other Chabad and non-Hassidic leaders. He was held in high regard by Israel Meir Kagan (the Chofetz Chaim). His teachings were such that he was responsible for the emergence of and emphasis on outreach programs as a major theme. He also promoted the development of Jewish agricultural settlements and employment opportunities for Jews. He was an opponent of Zionism.

In 1902, he visited Sigmund Freud who advised him to take long walks. These he did with his son, the sixth Rebbe. During these walks he related to his son dreams he had of his father who related Hassidic tales to him.

The Rebbe Rashab was responsible for developing Chabad Hassidic philosophy into an organized system. His most famous work, *Sefer HaMa'amarim* was a 29-volume set which became the introductory work to "oral" Chabad Hassidism (the "written" one being the Tanya). It is studied in Chabad yeshivas. He also wrote extensively on Chabad theology. *Kuntres HaTefilah* and *Kuntres HaAvodah* were in-depth explanations of Chabad Hassidic prayer. *Issa B'Midrash Tehillim* was on the mystical aspects of tefillin, a discourse that Chabad boys recite on their bar mitzvah.

During the first world war as the fighting approached Lyubayichi he moved to Rostov-on-Don. He remained there until his death in 1920.

Schneerson, Yosef Yitzhak (Rebbe Rayatz)

Rabbi Yosef Yitzhak Schneerson was born in Lyubavichi, Russia in 1880. At age fifteen he became the secretary and representative of his father, Rabbi Sholom Dovber Schneerson. He married at age seventeen. In 1898 he was appointed head of all the Tomchei Temimim yeshivas. He became an advocate for the Jews, particularly in trying to stop the pogroms and travelled in Europe for this cause.

After the death of his father he became the sixth rebbe of Chabad Lubavitch. It was the time of the Bolshevik Revolution. He became an outspoken opponent of the Communists anti-religious program. He was instrumental in creating religious schools. He was later imprisoned and sentenced to death, but a world outcry led the authorities to rescind this sentence and sent him to jail in the Urals for three years. He was finally allowed to leave Russia and went to Latvia. In 1930, he went to Palestine and then to the United states where he was received by President Herbert Hoover in the White House. He returned to Warsaw where he remained during the Nazi invasion. He was granted diplomatic immunity and arrived in New York City in 1940 where he settled in Crown Heights, Brooklyn. It was from here that, during the next decade, he began the process of rebuilding Orthodox Judaism in America. He began a campaign to build Jewish day schools and yeshivas for both boys and girls. He established printing houses and spread Jewish observance. His main work was *Sefer HaMa'amarim* He died in 1950 leaving no male heirs. His son-in-law, Menachem Mendel Schneerson, became the new Lubavitcher Rebbe.

Schneuri, Dovber (Mitteler Rebbe)

Dovber Schneuri was born in Liozna, Russia in 1773. His father was Rabbi Shneur Zalman of Liadi, the first Chabad Rebbe. Dovber was named after Shneur's teacher, Dov Ber of Mezritch, the successor to the Ba'al Shem Tov (Israel ben Eliezer), who founded the Hassidic movement. Dovber began the study of Talmud at age seven. His father taught him the Zohar as well as the teachings of the Ba'al Shem Tov. After his father's death, he moved to Lyubavichi together with many of his father's followers. There he established a yeshiva that was run by his son-in-law, Menachem Mendel. It was during this period that Czar Nicholas I restricted the Jews to the Pale, where opportunities were limited. Rabbi Schneuri encouraged the Jews to learn trades and encouraged the development of agriculture.

Rabbi Schneuri wrote works on Chabad philosophy and kabbalah as well as a commentary on the Zohar. His most famous work was *Sha'ar HaYichud* ("The Gate of Unity") that is a description of creation and the world according to kabbalah. His other important work was *Sha'arei Orah* on the festivals of Chanukah and Purim. His *Maamrei Admur HaEmtzei* consists of twenty volumes of Hassidic discourses on the Torah and the festivals.

Rabbi Schneuri died in 1827 and was succeeded by his son-in-law Menachem Mendel Schneerson.

Schotten, Samuel (Mharsheishoch)

Samuel Schotten HaKohen was born in Schotten in 1644. He moved to Frankfurt am Main in 1682. He became the Rosh Yeshiva there in 1685 and the Rabbi of the Grand Duchy of Hesse-Darmstadt. During his life he was considered the leading Talmud scholar in Frankfurt. He was the maternal grandfather of Moses Sofer (Schreiber), the Chatam Sofer.

He wrote a commentary on a number of passages of the Talmud, titled *Koss Hayeshu'ot* ("The Chalice of Salvation"). His collection of responsa was titled *Shut Mharsheishoch*. He died in 1719 in Frankfurt am Main.

Schwadron, Sholom Mordechai (Maharsham)

Sholom Mordechai Schwadron was born in Zloczow, Galicia in 1835. He studied under Rabbi Yoel Ashkenazy. He later became the rabbi in Berezhany. He was primarily known as a leading halakhic authority.

He was the author of a three-volume commentary on the Torah titled *Techeiles Mordechai*. However his main works were two collections of responsa titled *Shailos Uteshuvot Marsham* and *Daas Torah*. These latter two are widely used as sources of practical halakha. He died in Berezhany in 1911.

Segal, David ben Samuel HaLevi (Taz)

David ben Samuel HaLevi Segal was born in Ludmir, Volhynia in about 1586. His main teacher was his elder brother, Isaac. He married the daughter of Rabbi Joel Sirkes of Brest (the Bach) and lived with his father-in-law for several years while studying Torah. He then moved to Cracow. Later he was appointed the chief rabbi of Pollitsha. He later went to Posen and then in 1641 he became the rabbi in Ostrog, Volhynia where he established a famous yeshiva. It was while there that in 1646 he wrote his commentary on the *Yoreh De'ah* of the *Shulkhan Arukh*. Two years later he had to flee the Chmielnicki massacres of 1648-1649. He went to Steinitz, Moravia and later returned to Lemberg, Poland where he lived for the remainder of his life. His descendants were the Russian rabbinical family, Paltrowich, which produced thirty-three rabbis.

The Taz's most famous work was the *Turei Zahav* ("Rows of Gold") which is an important commentary on the *Shulkhan Arukh*. It consists of the commentary on the *Yoreh De'ah* plus a commentary on the *Orach Chaim*. An early publication of this work was combined with a similar commentary of the *Yoreh De'ah* by Rabbi Shabbatai Cohen (Shach) called the *Sifsei Cohen* ("Lips of Cohen"). The original text of the *Yoreh De'ah* was in the center and was flanked on either side by the work of the Taz and the Shach. In 1692 another publication by Shabbethai Bass was printed in conjunction with Abraham Abele Gombiner's *Magen Avraham*. David HaLevi Segal also wrote *Dibre David*, a super-commentary on Rashi. Rabbi David Segal died in 1667.

Sforno, Obadiah ben Jacob

Obadiah Sforno, born in Cesena, Italy in 1475, was a member of a well-known family of Italian rabbis. After studying Hebrew and rabbinic literature as well as secular subjects, he studied medicine in Rome, where he acquired a great reputation and was consulted by many rabbis.

He wrote a work on religious philosophy titled *Or Ammim* in which he tried to refute Aristotle's theory of the eternal nature of matter by using biblical arguments. He is best known for his commentaries on the Tanakh that were widely read and are still used by scholars and laymen. His commentaries appear in many Chumash publications together with those of Rashi, Ramban and Ibn Ezra. Rabbi Sforno died in Bologna in 1550.

Shabbethai, Kalonymus ben

Kalonymus ben Shabbethai was born in Rome about 1030. He established himself as a Talmudic authority and he received halakhic questions from many places. He became the rabbi of Worms in 1070, but with the persecutions in 1096 he appears to have been killed in them.

He wrote commentaries on the Talmud and the Tanakh, none of which are in existence but were quoted by Rashi, Jacob Tam, Samuel ben Meir, Eliezer ben Nathan and Joseph Kara.

Shahin, Jacob ben Nissim ibn (Rabbeinu Nissim, HaMafteach)

He was born in about 990 in Kairwan (Kairaouan) in Tunisia. His father was Jacob ben Nissim under whom he first studied. His father was the head of the yeshiva at Kairwan. When Hushiel ben Elhanan came to Kairwan he then studied under him. After Hushiel's death he became the head of the yeshiva. He maintained a constant correspondence on halakhic matters with Hai ben Sherira, the Gaon of Sura. He also corresponded with Samuel HaNagid in Granada.

Nissim devoted much of his time to the study of Talmud. His Talmudic method as shown in his writings not only included quoting references but he also expanded on commentaries by quoting from the Tosefta, Mekhilta, the Sifre and Sifra. His major work was *Sefer Mafteach Manu'ele HaTalmud* (or *HaMafteach*) ("Key to the Locks of the Talmud"), which was written in two parts. In the first part of this work he tried to simplify and explain the difficulties in the Talmud for people less knowledgeable. For his contemporaries and students he provided more extensive background Talmudic information. The second part of *Mafteach*, which is divided into fifty sections, contains halakhot from different sources in the Talmud.

His work, *Megillat Setarim* consisted of a collection of notes relating to halakhic decisions, explanations and midrashim. Only a few fragments of this have been preserved. He also wrote a collection of about sixty *Comforting Tales* based on the Mishnah, Baraita, the two Talmudim and the midrashic writings. He most likely wrote the Arabic commentary on the *Sefer Yezirah* that was translated into Hebrew by Moses ben Joseph. This Hebrew version is still extant in manuscript form. Nissim died in 1062.

Shakna, Shalom

Shalom Shakna was born in 1510. He was a pupil of Jacob Pollak, the founder of the Pilpul method of study of the Talmud. He established a yeshiva at Lublin. Moses Isserles, who was his son-in-law, and other great Acharonim studied there. It became a famous center of Talmudic study and kabbalah. He was succeeded by Solomon Luria (the Maharshal).

He wrote extensively, but his modesty prevented him from publishing his work. Only the treatise *Pesachim be-Inyan Kiddushin* was published. He died in Lublin in 1558.

Shapira (Szapira), Kalonymus Kalman

Kalonymus Kalman Shapira was born in Grodzisk, Poland in 1889. He came from a distinguished rabbinical family that included Elimelech of Lizhensk (Chozeh of Lublin) and the Maggid of Kozhnitz. He married Rachel Chaya Miriam and had two children. In 1909, he was appointed the rabbi of Piaseczno, near Warsaw. The main focus of his educational efforts was directed at children. He attempted to reverse the secularism that was taking hold among Eastern European Jewry. After the Nazis defeated Poland he was interned in the Warsaw Ghetto. After the Warsaw Ghetto uprising in 1943 he was taken to the Trawniki work camp where he was shot to death in November of 1943.

His most famous work was *Chovas haTalmidim* (The Student's Responsibility") where he discussed his theories on instilling education in children by not only imbuing the child with a vision of "his own potential greatness", but also that the teacher must learn to speak the language of the student. His other well-known work was written while in the ghetto. It was found in a canister at the end of the war and published in Israel in 1960 under the title of *Esh Kodesh*. It consists of the weekly sermons he gave to his students dealing with complex issues of faith in the face of the suffering of the Jews. He also wrote several other minor works.

Shapiro, Eliyahu ben Binyamin Wolf

Eliyahu Shapiro was born in Prague in 1660. He wrote a commentary to the *Shulkhan Arukh* called *Eliyahu Rabba*. He died in 1712.

Shapiro, Yehuda Meir

Yehuda Meir Shapiro was born on March 3, 1887, in Suczawa, Romania. He began his studies under his grandfather, Rabbi Samuel Yitzhak Schor. He became involved in Hassidism through his involvement with Dovid Moshe, the Chortkover Rebbe. In 1911, he became the rabbi of Galina and from there he went on to Sanok, Petrakov and Lublin. He is most well-known for having introduced the concept of Daf Yomi whereby on a daily basis one folio of the Talmud was studied each day with the aim to complete the cycle in seven and a half years. In the mid-nineteen twenties he established the famous Lublin Yeshiva where, as the Rosh Yeshiva, he spent the rest of his life. Later he was appointed the chief rabbi of Lodz, but died a few days after taking up this position.

Rabbi Shapiro wrote two important works. *Ohr HaMeir* consisted of a collection of responsa that dealt with halakha and philosophy mainly. *Imrei Daas* consisted of a collection of thoughts on the Torah, but it was lost during World War II. *Vortelach* consisted of a large series of short responsa, collected into a multi-volume set.

He died on October 27, 1933. In 1958, his remains were reburied in Jerusalem on Har HaMenuchot.

Sharabi, Shalom (Rashash)

Shalom Sharabi was born in Yemen in 1720. At an early age he went to Jerusalem, first visiting India, Baghdad and Damascus. In Israel he made a strong impression on the rabbinic sages there. He studied and worked at the Bet El Yeshiva. Within this yeshiva a group of twelve were chosen to specialize in kabbalah. Among his colleagues in this group were the Chida (Haim Yosef Azulai) and Yom-Tov Algazi. He eventually became the Rosh Yeshiva there. Under his leadership he initiated regulations, orders and kavanot for the daily prayers. It remains the center of kabbalistic study to this day. Although known primarily as a kabbalist he was also an acknowledged Torah and Talmud expert and his halakhic rulings had high authority, especially among Yemenite Jewry.

Sharabi created a kabbalistic siddur, *Sidur HaKavanot*, which is still used by kabbalists. In an abbreviated form it is also used by some Hassidim. He wrote three major kabbalistic works; *Emet va-Shalom*, *Rehovot Nahar* and *Nahar Shalom* in which he provides answers to questions by leading sages from Tunis. The *Nahar Shalom* became later a siddur which is known today as the *Siddur haRashash*. His *Minhagei Rashash* was a compilation of the minhagim of Yemenite Jews. He died in Jerusalem in 1777.

Shem Tov, Shem Tov ibn

Shem Tov ibn Shem Tov was born in Spain about 1390. He was a kabbalist and opposed rationalistic philosophy.

He wrote *Sefer HaEmunot* that was on religious dogmas. It was an attack on Aristotelian philosophy. He therefore also strongly opposed Maimonides. The book also strongly praised kabbalah. He also wrote a commentary on the Passover Haggadah. He died in about 1440.

Sherira, Hai ben, Gaon

Rav Hai ben Sherira was born in Babylonia in 939. He was the son of the most famous Gaon at Pumbedita. Hai was the last of the authoritative gaonim of Babylonia. He studied under his father, Sherira and while still young became his assistant in teaching. In his forties he became the Av Beth Din and issued decisions with his father. In 998 when Sherira was old and ill, he appointed Hai as Gaon. He remained in this position for the remainder of his life. Although he mastered Jewish law he was also familiar with the Koran and other secular subjects.

Rav Hai Gaon was best known for his many responsa. These affected the social and religious life of Jews in the Diaspora. There were over 800 dealing with civil law, explanations of certain halakhot and other Talmudic issues. They were mostly written in Arabic and have not been preserved. He also codified certain aspects of Talmudic law. These were later translated into Hebrew. He also wrote commentaries on the Mishnah. Hai ben Sherira died in 1038.

Sheshna, Amram ben, Gaon

He was a famous head of the academy of Sura in the ninth century. He was the author of a number of responsa, but is most famous for his liturgical contribution. He was the first person to arrange a complete liturgy for the synagogue. His prayer book, *Siddur Rab (Rav) Amram or Yesod HaAmrami*, was used and still many of the rites of prayer come from his work. It originated in the form of a responsum to the Jews of Barcelona.

The siddur is the oldest order of Jewish prayers still in existence. It covers prayers for the entire year as well as the laws and customs for different prayers. He used as his sources the Talmud as well as the works of the geonim and practices in the Babylonian academies. Three different manuscripts were found in the Cairo Genizah. The siddur was published in Warsaw in 1865. It was re-published several times in the late twentieth century. He died about 865.

Shkop, Shimon

Rabbi Shimon Shkop was born in Tortz, close to the borders of Poland and Lithuania, in 1860. He first studied at the Mir Yeshiva and then the Volzhin Yeshiva, where his teachers were Naphtali Tzvi Judah Berlin (Netziv) and Chaim Soloveitchik. In 1885 he went to teach at the Telze Yeshiva where he stayed until 1903. Following this he was appointed rabbi of Moltsh, then in 1907 of Bransk. In 1920 he became the Rosh Yeshiva of Sha'ar HaTorah in Grodno, making it one of the best yeshivot in Poland. In 1928 he went to the United States where he was persuaded to serve as Rosh Yeshiva at Rabbeinu Yitzhak Elchanan (RIETS) in New York. After one year he returned to Europe.

His most famous work was *Sha'arei Yosher* (The Gates of Honesty). It deals with the principles whereby laws are formulated. It was based on Aryeh Leib HaKohen's *Shev Shema'tata*. He wrote *Ma'arekhet haKinyanim* in 1936. He also wrote Talmudic novellae on Bava Kamma, Metzia and Basra that were published in 1947. He also wrote novellae on Nedarim, Gittin and Kiddushin that were published in 1952. These are still studied in many yeshivot.

Rabbi Shkop died in Grodno in 1940 as the Russian army approached.

Shor, Joseph ben Isaac Bekhor

Joseph ben Isaac Bekhor Shor was a French Tosafist who lived in the second half of the twelfth century in Orleans. He was a pupil of Jacob Tam, Joseph Kara and Samuel ben Meir (Rashbam). He wrote tosafot on most of the Talmud. He also wrote a literal commentary (peshat) of the Bible. In this latter he attempted to provide rational explanations to the stories that were associated with miracles. He authored a number of piyyutim.

Sirkis, Yoel (Bach)

Rabbi Yoel Sirkis was born in Lublin, Poland in 1561. At age fourteen he went to study at the yeshiva of Rabbi Solomon ben Judah, then went to the yeshiva of Rabbi Phoebus in Brest-Litovsk. At a young age he became the rabbi of Pruszany, near Slonim. After that he occupied a number of rabbinates in various centers, finally settling in a position in Cracow.

The Bach followed kabbalah, was against pilpul and also disagreed with those who followed only the *Shulkhan Arukh* for their halakhic decisions.

His most famous work is *Bayit Chadash* (Bach or "New House"). It is a significant commentary on the *Arba'ah Turim* of Jacob ben Asher. It elucidates basic and important principles of the Torah as they were recorded in the Mishnah, and both the Jerusalem and Babylonian Talmuds. He also wrote glosses titled *Hagahot Bach*, *Meshiv Nevesh*, that was a commentary on the Book of Ruth and responsa, known as *Teshuvos HaBach*. Rabbi Sirkis died in 1640 in Cracow.

Slonik (Solnik), Benjamin Aaron ben Abraham

Benjamin Aaron ben Abraham Slonik was born in Grodno, Poland in 1550. He studied under Nathan Spiro. He became the rabbi in Silesia and then in Podhajce. He also lived for some time in Cracow.

He was the author of *Masat Binyamin*, which consisted of 112 responsa and also on novellae on the *Shulkhan Arukh*. These reflected his independent mind and his opinions often differed from those of his colleagues. His decisions, however, were considered authoritative, both in his generation and for subsequent generations of Polish and German rabbis. They were often quoted by Shabbatai ben Meir HaKohen and Abraham Abele Gombiner. He also wrote a couple of other minor works. He died in 1619.

Sofer, Abraham Samuel Benjamin (Ksav Sofer)

Abraham Sofer was born in 1815. He was the son of Moses Sofer (Schreiber) or the Chatam Sofer. After his father's death, he took over as head of the yeshiva in Pressburg. This yeshiva was the dominant one in Hungary until the second world war. He was involved in the separation of the Jewish community in Hungary in 1868 into the reform and Orthodox denominations. He remained as the rabbi of Pressburg for thirty-three years. His main work was titled the *Ksav Sofer*. It is a commentary on the Torah. He also authored a four-volume collection of responsa. He died in 1871.

Sofer, Moses (Chatam Sofer)

Moses Sofer, who was also known in his own community as Moses Schreiber, was born in Frankfurt am Main (which was once an independent city state, and then became part of Germany), in 1762, during the Thirty Year War. His maternal grandfather was Samuel Schotten, the Marsheishoch.

When he was nine he went to study at the yeshiva of Nathan Adler in Frankfurt. He then became a pupil of Pinchas Horowitz. In 1776 he went to the yeshiva of Rabbi David Tebele Scheur in Mainz. Following this he went to Prostejov in Moravia, where he got married. He became the head of the Chevra Kadisha there and then the head of the yeshiva. In 1794, he became the rabbi of Straznice, then in 1797 the rabbi of Mattersdorf, where he established a yeshiva. There his most illustrious student was Meir Ash

Eisenstadt, the Maharam Ash. In 1806, he was called to Bratislava (then part of the Austrian Empire and now capital of Slovakia). There he also established a yeshiva that trained many famous rabbis of Hungarian Jewry. Under his influence Reform Judaism did not penetrate into Bratislava.

His first wife died in 1812. They were childless. He remarried, this time to the widow of Rabbi Akiva Eger. They had seven daughters and three sons. He was the author of many works, but he is known for his *Chatam Sofer* (Chiddushei Torat Moshe) ("Seal of the Tribe") that consisted of explanations of the Torah.

He died in 1839 in Bratislava. The grave survived the World War Two fascist regime as well as the communist era. In 1992, when Slovakia became an independent country, the tomb was reconstructed as the Mausoleum of Chatam Sofer, which also contains the remains of other famous rabbis.

Sofer, Yaakov Chaim (Kaf HaChaim)

Yaakov Chaim Sofer was born in Baghdad in 1870. His father was Yitzhak Baruch Sofer. He studied under a number of great sages, including Yosef Chaim (Ben Ish Chai) and Abdalla Somekh. In 1904, he visited Palestine and decided to remain there. In Jerusalem he first studied at the Bet El Yeshiva, known for the study of kabbalah. In 1909 he moved to the just created Shoshanim leDavid Yeshiva. It was here that he composed his works.

Rabbi Sofer's works of halakha and aggadah dealt with the original traditions of the Iraqi Jews. *Kaf HaChaim* is his great work. It is considered a classic for both Sephardi and Ashkenazi Jews. It discusses the halakha in the light of the commentaries of both the Rishonim and Acharonim. It covers the *Orach Chaim* and parts of the *Yoreh De'ah* of the *Shulkhan Arukh*. It is published in eight volumes. It is most often compared to the *Mishnah Berura* but Sofer's work uses quotations more extensively. He also wrote *Kol Yaakov* that dealt with the laws of writing Torah scrolls, tefillin and mezuzot. *Yagel Yaakov* was a collection of his sermons that he gave while in mourning for his father. *Yismach Yisrael* is a collection of novellae on the weekly Torah reading. Yaakov Sofer died in 1939.

Solomon, Menahem ben

Menahem ben Solomon lived in Italy in the twelfth century. He was the author of a book, *Sekel Kob* that was a midrashic compilation on the Pentateuch. His sources for this work were the Targumim, earlier Midrashic works as well as Geonic mystical literature. He also interpreted the halakhic authors especially Alfasi and Chananel ben Chushiel. It was a frequently quoted work. Currently only portions of the manuscript are still extant in the Bodleian Library.

Solomon, Samuel ben, of Falaise

Samuel ben Solomon of Falaise, also often designated in the literature by his French name, Sir Morel, was a twelfth and thirteenth century French Tosafist. He was a student of Judah Sir Leon of Paris and Isaac ben Abraham of Sens. He wrote tosafot to several Talmudic treatises. His ritual decisions were frequently quoted by Meir of Rothenburg.

Soloveitchik, Chaim (The Brisker Reb)

Rabbi Chaim Soloveitchik was born in Brest (Brisk in Yiddish), Belarus in 1853. He was a member of the Soloveitchik-family rabbinical dynasty. He is the founder of the Brisker method of Talmudic study, that is a highly analytical and exacting method of study, by focusing on the exact definition and categorization of Jewish law as dictated by the Torah. There is a heavy emphasis on the halakhic writings of Maimonides.

His two sons were also famous rabbis. Rabbi Yitzhak Zev Soloveitchik who went to live in Israel and Rabbi Moshe Soloveitchik who went to the United States of America and became the head of Yeshiva University. His three main students were his son, Yitzhak, Baruch Ber Leibowitz and Shimon Shkop.

Rabbi Soloveitchik's major work was *Chiddushei Rabbeinu Chaim* that was a work on insights on Maimonides' *Mishneh Torah*. In it he often would suggest an alternative understanding of the Talmud as well. His other work, *Chiddushei HaGRaCh Al Shas*, that covered his insights on the Talmud, was written from notes taken by his students. Chaim Soloveitchik died in 1918.

Soloveitchik, Joseph Ber (HaRav)

Joseph Ber Soloveitchik was born in 1903 in Pruszany, which was then a part of Russia. (It is now in Belarus). He was a descendant of a 200-year-old rabbinical dynasty. His grandfather was Chaim Soloveitchik. His father was Moshe Soloveichik, the head of the Rabbi Isaac Elchanan Theological Seminary (RIETS) at Yeshiva University.

Rabbi Joseph Soloveitchik had a traditional Talmud Torah education as well as a secular education, obtaining a Ph.D. in Germany in the early 1930s. While in Berlin he was a student of Rabbi Chaim Heller. A contemporary of his was Rabbi Yitzhak Hutner who became the Rosh Yeshiva at the Yeshiva Rabbi Chaim Berlin in Brooklyn, New York. While in Berlin he also met Rabbi Menachem Mendel Schneerson where they developed a strong friendship.

In 1932, he came to the United States and settled in Boston. In 1937, he established the Maimonides Hebrew Day School. Among his many innovations were teaching Talmud to combined boys and girls classes. He held other religious positions in Boston and lectured widely. He succeeded his father as the head of RIETS in 1941. His educational philosophy was a system of synthesis, whereby he combined the best of religious scholarship with that of Western secular scholarship. He became in his lifetime the greatest leader of Modern Orthodoxy in the twentieth century. He also was a pre-eminent pro-Zionist.

His children married prominent academics and Talmudic scholars. His daughter Atara married Rabbi Isadore Twersky who became the head of Jewish studies at Harvard University. His daughter, Tovah married Rabbi Aharon Lichtenstein, the Rosh Yeshiva of Yeshivat Har Etzion in Israel. His son Haim became a professor of Jewish studies at Yeshiva University.

Although he wrote a great number of smaller works and essays, his two most famous non-Talmudic works are *The Lonely Man of Faith* and the *Halakhic Man*. *The Lonely Man of Faith* is based on the contrasting aspects of the first two chapters of Genesis, He describes two types of Adam; Adam I, made in the image of God who masters the environment and Adam II who represents the lonely man of faith. In *Halakhic Man*, Soloveitchik provides a theological outlook on the centrality of halakha to Jewish thought. Other important works are *Fate and Destiny: From Holocaust to the State of Israel, Out of the Whirlwind: Essays on Mourning, Suffering and the Human Condition*, and *Days of Deliverance: Essays on Purim and Hanukkah*. Rabbi Soloveitchik died in 1993.

Soloveitchik, Yosef Dov (Beis HaLevi)

Yosef Dov Soloveitchik was born in Nesvizh, Belarus in 1820. In 1854 he became the co-Rosh Yeshiva of Volozhin Yeshiva with Naftali Tzvi Yehuda Berlin (Netziv). He stayed there for ten years and in 1865 he became the rabbi of Slutsk. Among his pupils was Yosef Rosen the Rogatchover Gaon and Zalman Sender Shapiro. Since he was an opponent of Maskilim he left Slutsk in 1874 and went to Warsaw. In 1877, he was offered the rabbinate of Brisk where he remained until his death. He was succeeded by his son, Chaim Soloveitchik.

His major work was *Beis HaLevi*. It covered his work on the *Mishneh Torah* of Maimonides and on the Torah. He died in 1892.

Somekh, Abdalla

Hakham Abdalla Somekh was born in Baghdad in 1831. He was the son of Abraham Somekh, a descendant of Nissim Gaon. He was the eldest of eight brothers and eight sisters. He was a student of Rabbi Yaakov Harofe. He became the Rosh Yeshiva of Yeshiva Midrash Abu Menashe. It was later renamed Midrash Beit Zilkha. Among his students were his brother-in-law Yosef Chaim (Ben Ish Chai) and Yaakov Chaim Sofer (Kaf HaChaim).

His major work was *Zivhei Tzedek* that provided rulings on the laws of *shechita* and *treifot*. It was widely used by Baghdad Jews as well as in the Far East. He was also the author of responsa on all parts of the *Shulkhan Arukh*. He died during a cholera epidemic in 1889.

Spektor, Yitzhak Elchanan

Yitzhak Spektor was born in Resh, Grodno, then a part of Russia, in 1817. His father, Israel Issar was the rabbi of Resh and his first teacher. After marriage at age thirteen he went to his parents-in-law in Vilkovisk where he studied first under Rabbi Elijah Schick and then under Benjamin Diskin. He became the rabbi of Sabelin in 1837 and then in 1839, Rabbi Jacob, one of the foremost rabbis of Russia, got him a position as the rabbi of Baresa. There he progressed rapidly. In 1846 he was appointed to the rabbinate of Nishvez. Five years later he became the rabbi of Novardok, Kovno. In 1864, he became the chief rabbi of Kovno, a position he held until his death

Over the ensuing years he became recognized as one of the foremost rabbinical authorities in Russia and corresponded widely with other rabbis and lay leaders in many parts of the world. He was active with Rabbi Yisrael Salanter in confronting and dealing with the Russian authorities on many issues affecting Russian Jewry. He was the author of *Be'er Yitzhak*, a collection of responsa, *Ein Yitzhak*, another collection of responsa and *Nachal Yitzhak* on the *Chosen Mishpat* part of the *Shulkhan Arukh*.

He died in 1896. A number of institutions were named after him, including the Rabbi Isaac Elchanan Theological Seminary (RIETS) of Yeshiva University.

Spira, Chaim Elazar

Chaim Elazar Spira was born in 1871 in Stryzow, in the kingdom of Galicia, which was then a part of the Austro-Hungarian Empire, but later became a part of Poland. He was one of the rebbes of the Munkacz (Munkatsh) Hassidic movement. His father was Rabbi Tzvi Hersh Spira.

From a young age he showed great potential. At age eleven he wrote his first book on halakha. In 1913, he became head of the Munkacz Hassidim. Under his leadership the movement grew tremendously. He established a vast network of charitable institutions that provided aid the needy. His yeshiva attracted students from around the world.

His most famous work was *Minchas Elazar*, which consisted of six volumes. He died in 1937 in Mukachevo, then part of Czechoslovakia after suffering from a grave illness.

Steinhardt, Aryeh Leib

Aryeh Leib Steinhardt lived in Jerusalem in the early twentieth century. He wrote a super-commentary on Nahmanides' (Ramban's) commentary on the Torah called *Kur Zahav*. It was published in 1936.

Steinhardt, Menahem Mendel ben Simeon

Menahem Mendel Steinhardt was born in Fuerth, Germany in 1768. He served as rabbi of Minden and then Hildesheim. When the kingdom of Westphalia was set up in 1808 he was approached by the government to formulate a constitution and theology for Judaism, similar to what Napoleon had done. Steinhardt's approach was to have a moderate form of Judaism. Later he became the rabbi of Warburg, then Pederhorn, where he lived for the remainder of his life. Steinhardt published in 1804 the collection of his responsa under the title of *Divrei Menahem*. He died in 1825.

Steinhart, Joseph ben Menachem

Joseph ben Menachem Steinhart was born in 1700 in the village of Steinhart in Germany. He first became the rabbi of Rizheim, then the chief rabbi of Upper Alsace, then of Nieder-Ehenheim in Lower Alsace and finally rabbi of Furth. He was considered the foremost Talmudist of his time. He took a very conservative approach.

He wrote an important work, *Zikron Yosef*, which consisted of responsa and rulings on the four parts of the *Shulkhan Arukh*. He also wrote *Mashbir Bar* that was a collection of commentaries on the Pentateuch and *Ko'ah Shor*, novellae to *Baba Batra*. He died in 1776.

Strashun, Samuel ben Joseph (Rashash)

Shmuel Strashun, known as the Rashash, was born in Zaskevich, a part of the government of Wilna, at that time a part of the Russian Empire, in 1794. He was educated by his father, married young and settled in his wife's village, Streszyn, from where he took his name. After the French army invasion of 1812, his father-in-law's distillery was destroyed and he moved to Wilna and established a new one. His wife ran the business while he studied and taught Talmud. He would give daily Talmud lectures at the Poplaves Street synagogue. These were well attended. He became well-known and respected throughout Russia.

His *Haggahot v'Chiddushei HaRashash* were the collection of annotations that came from the comments from these Talmud classes. These annotations are now incorporated into all recent editions of the Babylonian Talmud. He also wrote annotations to the *Midrashot Rabbot*. The Rashash died in Wilna in 1872.

Szapira, Elimelech

Rabbi Elimelech was born in Grodzisk Poland in 1823. He was the founder of the Grodzisk Hassidic dynasty, which eventually numbered ten thousand. His teachings were collected into two works, *Imrei Elimelech* and *Divrei Elimelech*. He died in 1892.

Taitazak, Joseph ben Solomon

Joseph Taitezak was born in Spain in the late fifteenth century. With his father and brothers he emigrated to Salonica in 1492. He was considered a leading Talmudic scholar of his time and was one of the most mysterious of the kabbalists. He is often quoted by other kabbalists.

He was the author of several, probably minor works, as well as many kabbalistic works.

Taubes, Aaron Moses ben Jacob

Aaron Moses Taubes was born in Lemberg, at that time a part of Poland, in 1787. He was a pupil of Jacob Ornstein. He became the rabbi of Sniatyn in Poland in 1820 and then of Jassy where he stayed until his death. He wrote *To'afot Re'em* that consisted of responsa on the four parts of the *Shulkhan Arukh*. *Karne Re'em* consisted of novellae on the Talmud. He died in 1852.

Tibbon, Moses ibn

Moses ibn Tibbon was born in Marseille in the thirteenth century. He was the son of Samuel ibn Tibbon and his son was Judah ibn Tibbon. He was a physician, translator and author. He wrote a number of works. Among these was a commentary on the Pentateuch. *Sefer Pe'ah* was an allegorical explanation of haggadic passages in the Talmud and Midrash, He also translated Maimonides' *Sefer HaMitzvot*. His translations were probably more important than his original works. Perhaps the most important were a number of Maimonides' other works in Arabic.

Tibbon, Samuel ben Judah ibn

Samuel ibn Tibbon was born in 1150 in Lunel, France. He received an education in rabbinic literature as well as in medicine and Arabic. After traveling around he settled in Marseilles.

He is best known for his translation into Hebrew of Maimonides' *Guide for the Perplexed* (*Moreh Nevuchim*). He consulted with Maimonides on the difficult passages. The latter was impressed with the quality of the translation. It was an accurate and faithful translation. He also translated several other works of Maimonides. He died in 1230.

Tolosa, Vidal di

Vidal di Tolosa was a fourteenth century Spanish rabbi. He lived in Catalonia. He is known for his work the *Maggid Mishneh*. It provides a complete explanation of Maimonides' rulings in six of the fourteen volumes of the *Mishneh Torah*. It traces these rulings back to their sources and provides an explanation for these rulings.

Torizer, Mordechai Gimpel Yaffe

Mordechai Yaffe was born in Lithuania in 1820. He subsequently moved to Palestine. He was the author of a super-commentary on Nahmanides' (Ramban's) commentary on the Torah, titled *Techeiles Mordechai*. He died in 1892.

Trabotto, Joseph Colon ben Solomon (Maharik)

Joseph Colon Trabotto was born about 1420 in Chambery, France. He studied mainly under his father, Solomon Trabotto. In the 1450s he went to live in Piedmont that was then a part of the Duchy of Savoy. He then went to Venice and following this became the rabbi of Bologna and Mantua He then went to Pavia following an argument with Judah Messer Leon.

He is best known for his responsa that are considered classics of rabbinic literature. These were collected by his son-in-law and pupils and published under the title of *The Responsa of Maharik*. He had a great influence on the subsequent development of halakha. It influenced particularly Ashkenazi halakha and was noted by Moses Isserles' glosses. It also formed the basis of Italian halakha for the next several centuries. He referred significantly to Maimonides' *Mishneh Torah*. He died in Padua in 1480.

Trani, Isaiah ben Mali di (RI'D)

He was a thirteenth century rabbi from Trani, Italy. He wrote the *Tosefot RI'D* that was a legal compendium summarizing and analyzing the laws found in the Talmud.

Treves (Tarfati), Abraham ben Solomon

Abraham ben Solomon Treves was a sixteenth century rabbi and scholar. He was born in Italy but lived in Turkey. There he officiated at German and Portuguese congregations in Adrianople. He preferred the Sephardi ritual and authored a work on the ritual titled *Birkat Abraham*.

Tukachinsky, Yechiel Michel

Rabbi Tukachinsky was a twentieth century Talmudist. He was born in Lyakhovichi, now in the Belarus, but also known as Lechovich that was a part of Lithuania in the early twentieth century. He immigrated to Jerusalem. He was famous and rendered opinions in a number of important areas. He wrote in the mid-twentieth century his classical work on death and mourning titled *Gesher HaChaim*. He also wrote *Bein HaShemashos*.

Twersky Family

The Twersky family originates from the Chernobyler Rebbe (Menachum Nachum Twersky) who lived in the eighteenth century and died in 1797. He took the name Twersky based on the city Teverya (Tiberias). This was based on a Midrash that stated that the Messiah would come from Teverya. The name "Teveryesky" therefore expressed the hope for the coming of the Messiah. One of the Twersky's of the Talner dynasty was a part of the Soloveitchik dynasty by marriage.

Rabbi David Twersky (1808-1882) was the first Talner Rebbe. He was the grandson of Rabbi Nochum Twersky the maggid of Chernobyl, who was a disciple of the Ba'al Shem Tov (Israel Eliezer). Rabbi Nochum Twersky became the head of Talner Hassidim in 1882, but died shortly thereafter. His son, Meshullam Twersky succeeded him. He in turn was succeeded by his son Isadore (Yitzhak) Twersky.

Among the current descendants are Rabbi Abraham Twerski, an accomplished psychiatrist and professional author, who writes extensively on Judaism and self-help. Professor Aaron Twerski was until 2007, dean and professor of tort law at Hofstra University School of Law.

Twersky, Isadore (Yitzhak)

Yitzhak Twersky was born in Boston in 1930 and died in 1997. He attended Boston Latin School and Boston Hebrew College (Hebrew Teacher's College). He graduated from Harvard University in 1952, then spent a year in Jerusalem studying under several famous scholars, including Harry Austryn Wolfson whom he ultimately succeeded as the Nathan Littauer Professor of Hebrew Literature and Philosophy at Harvard University. He succeeded his father as the Talner Rebbe for the last twenty years of his life. He was the son-in-law of Rabbi Joseph Soloveitchik (The Rav). His one son Moshe lives and teaches in Israel. His other son, Mayer, is the Leib Merkin Professor in Talmud and Jewish Philosophy at Yeshiva University.

Rabbi Twersky is best known for his seminal work *An Introduction to the Code of Maimonides* (*Mishneh Torah*) and his *A Maimonides Reader*.

Twersky, Menachem Nachum

Menachum Nachum Twersky of Chernobyl was born in Garynsk, Volhynia in 1730. He was the founder of the Chernobyl Hassidic dynasty. He was raised by his uncle Rabbi Nachum who sent him to an acclaimed yeshiva in Lithuania. He was a disciple of the Ba'al Shem Tov and subsequently of the Maggid of Mezritch.

He wrote and published one of the first books on Hassidic thought. *Me'Or Einayim* ("Light of the Eyes") contains a collection of his teachings on the weekly Torah portion and selections of the Talmud. It was a major work. He died in Chernobyl, Ukraine in 1797.

Tyrnau, Isaac

Isaac Tyrnau was born in Vienna, Austria and was active during the latter part of the fourteenth century and early fifteenth century. His teachers were Abraham Klausner of Vienna and Sar Shalom of Neustadt. He moved to Tyrnau in Austria.

Tyrnau is known for his important work *Sefer Minhagim* ("Book of Customs"), a compendium of the laws and customs of Ashkenazi Jews and is arranged according to the Jewish calendar. It is the first book that discusses in detail the Yahrzeit. He is quoted by Mordechai Jaffe in his *Levush Malkut*, which largely replaced Tyrnau's work. He probably died before 1427.

Tzahalon, Yom Tov ben Moshe (Maharitz)

Yom Tov Tzahalon was born in about 1559. His family originated in Spain. It is unknown where he was born. He studied under Moses di Trani and Moses Alshich.

He was the author of a commentary on the book of Esther, titled *Lekach Tov*. He was the author of a collection of responsa that was published. He wrote a commentary on *Abot deRabbi Natan* titled *Magen Avot*. He died in Safed in 1638.

Uzeda, Samuel de

Samuel de Uzeda was born in Safed in 1540. He was descended from a Spanish family from Uzeda. He studied under Isaac Luria (Ari) and Hayyim Vital. He was head of the academy in Safed where Talmud and kabbalah was studied. He is best known for his *Midrash Shmuel* that was a commentary on the tractate Avot. It is a compilation of the earlier commentaries on this tractate. It has undergone many printings. He also wrote a commentary on the book of Ruth, titled *Iggeret Shmuel*. He died in 1605.

Uziel, Ben-Zion Meir Hai

Ben-Zion Uziel was born in Jerusalem in 1880. He founded a yeshiva called Mahazikei Torah for young Sephardis. In 1923 he was appointed the Chief Rabbi of Tel-Aviv and in 1939 he was appointed the Sephardi Chief Rabbi of Palestine. He was very actively involved in communal and national affairs. He wrote *Mishpetei Ouziel* that was a collection of responsa. He died in 1953.

Veltz, Israel

Israel Veltz was a twentieth century rabbi who was the Av Beth Din of Budapest. He wrote an important booklet on the laws of Erev Pesach that begin on the Sabbath titled *Chok le-Yisra'el*.

Vidas, Eliyahu de

Eliyahu de Vidas was born in 1518. He lived in Palestine, first in Safed then in Hebron. He is known for his work on the kabbalah. He was a disciple of Moses ben Jacob Cordovero (Ramak) and of Isaac Luria (Arizal).

He was the author of the major work *Reshit Chochma* ("Beginning of Wisdom"), which is an important work on kabbalah, ethics and morality (Musar). It is based on the *Zohar*. It describes a method of meditation that is intended to inspire the reader with purity and holiness. It provides a pathway to enter the world of kabbalah. Vidas died in 1592.

Vital, Hayyim (Chaim) ben Joseph

Rabbi Hayyim Vital was born in Safed in 1543. As a child he was tutored by Moses Alshech. Little is known of his youth. Rabbi Joseph Caro was aware of the youth's talents. Vital also got to know Rabbi Lapidot Ashkenazi while still a teenager and the latter had a great influence on Vital. In 1570, he became a student of Isaac Luria (Arizal) and succeeded the Arizal when he died in 1572. Vital began the process of writing down all of Luria's teachings. Hayyim Vital is therefore best known as the scribe and editor of Luria's teachings. In 1577, he went to Egypt for a short while but then returned to Palestine and settled in Jerusalem. He became the rabbi there in 1584. A few years later he returned to Safed.

One of Vital's disciples, Rabbi Yehoshua obtained, through a bribe of Rabbi Vital's younger brother, all of his manuscripts. Yehoshua copied and widely disseminated these under the title of *Etz Hayyim* ("Tree of Life"). Vital maintained that most of the teachings in this work as well as his other mystic theories were derived from his teacher, the Arizal. This work consisted of eight sections. He also wrote several other minor works. In 1590, Vital received ordination from Rabbi Moshe Alshech. Four years later he went to Damascus and lectured on kabbalah. He died there in 1620.

Volozhin, Chaim ben Itzchok (Reb Chaim)

Chaim Volozhin, also known as Chaim Ickovits, Chaim Volozhiner or Chaim of Volozhin was born in 1749 in Volozhin. He studied under Rabbi Aryeh Leib Gunzberg (the author of *Shaagat Aryeh*) and later under Rabbi Raphael HaKohen (author of *Toras Yekusiel*). In 1774 he went to study under Rabbi Elijah ben Shlomo Zalman (the Vilna Gaon), where he became his most prominent disciple and ultimately followed his method of Torah, Mishnah and Talmud interpretation.

In 1803 Reb Chaim then opened the famous Volozhin Yeshiva where he applied the Vilna Gaon's methods. This yeshiva remained in operation for nearly 100 years when it was closed down in 1902. A major emphasis of study was to do penetrating analysis of the commentaries of the Rishonim. After his death, his son Isaac took over as the Rosh Yeshiva. A descendant of his is a President of Israel, Shimon Peres.

His major work was a kabbalistic one, titled *Nefesh HaChaim* ("Spirit of the Life"). Its purpose was to emphasize the power of Torah Study, to fulfill the commandments, and to worship with a pure heart in order to bring the Jew close to God. He also wrote *Ruach Chaim*, a commentary on *Pirkei Avot*. This includes mystical insights. Chaim Volozhin died in 1821.

Walden, Aaron

Aaron Walden was born in Warsaw in 1835. He was a follower of Hassidism. He was an editor and author. He is best known for his work *Shem HaGedolim HeHadash* that was published in 1864. It is a similar work to Haim Azulai's *Shem HaGedolim*. Like this work, Walden's work consists of two parts: *Ma'areket Gedolim* which is an alphabetical listing of the names of rabbis and authors, mostly who lived after Azulai, but also many seventeenth and eighteenth century ones not included in Azulai's work. These are listed according to the first name. *Ma'areket Sefarim* is an alphabetical listing of book titles. Another work of high quality was his *Mikdash Melek* that was a five-volume edition of the palms. Around these psalms are two major components. The first is *Bet HaMidrash* which was a collection of all the haggadot, referring to the psalms in the Talmud, midrashic literature, Targum and Zohar. The second is the *Bet HaKnesset* that is a collection of material taken from the most prominent ancient commentators. He died in 1912.

Walkin, Aaron

Aaron Walkin was born in 1863. He became the rabbi of Pinsk-Karlin in Lithuania. He wrote a collection of responsa in two parts titled *Zekan Aharon*. It is currently widely used. He died in Europe during World War II, presumably during the Holocaust.

Wallerstein, Abraham ben Asher

Abraham Wallerstein was an eighteenth century rabbi and scholar. He was the rabbi in Schnaittach, Bavaria. Rabbi Wallerstein was the author of several works. *Ma'amar Abraham* was a collection of his sermons in Hebrew covering the entire Pentateuch. *Zera Abraham* was an ethical work based on biblical and Talmudic principles. *Mahazeh Abraham* was an index to the four ritual codices, which was arranged alphabetically.

Weil Jacob ben Judah (Mahariv)

Jacob Weil flourished in the first half of the fifteenth century. He was a student of Jacob Moelin (Maharil) who ordained him. He was the rabbi of Erfurt. He was widely recognized and rendered many opinions. Only his collections of opinions and decisions survive, titled *She'elot u'Teshubot*. An appendix to this has been added, titled *She'elot u'Bedikot* that contains the regulations for the slaughtering and examination of slaughtered animals. It is considered an authoritative work, has gone through many editions and has been the subject of a number of commentaries.

Weil Jedidiah

Jedidiah Weil was born in Prague in 1721. He was the son of Nethaneel Weil. His father was his first instructor. He married the daughter of Jacob Eger of Prague in 1744. After the expulsion edict by Maria Theresa he went to Metz in 1745 where he studied under Jonathan Eybeschutz. In 1748, he returned to Prague and then in 1754 he became the rabbi of Wottitz in Bohemia, returning to Prague in 1758. In 1770 he succeeded his father as rabbi of Carlsruhe.

He published a commentary on the Passover Haggadah. He wrote a collection of responsa that were found in the collection of Ezekiel Landau, but in 1982 was independently published as *She'elot u'Teshubot*. Many novellae are preserved in manuscript form. He died in 1805.

Weil, Nethaneel ben Naftali Tzvi

Nethaneel Weil was born in the late seventeenth century. His father, Naftali Hirsch Weil, died when he was young and his mother took him to Prague where his uncle, Lippman Weil, adopted him. He attended the yeshiva of Prague and in 1708 married the niece of the Rosh Yeshiva, Rabbi Abraham Brod. Weil taught there and remained in Prague until 1744 when the edict of expulsion by Maria Theresa of Austria forced him to leave. He got a position of rabbi of the Black Forest, being located at Muhringen. He was there for five years during which he wrote most of his commentary on Asher ben Jehiel (Rosh). In 1750 he became the rabbi of Carlsruhe where he remained for twenty years. He completed his commentary that was published under the title of *Korban Netanel* in 1755. It was later printed with *Asheri* in editions of the Talmud.

He also wrote *Netib Hayyim* that consisted of critical notes on the *Shulkhan Arukh*, *Orach Chaim* and its commentaries *Ture Zahav* and *Magen Avraham*. He also wrote *Torat Netan'el* that consisted of a collection of responsa and halakhic derashot on the Pentateuch. These latter two works were published posthumously by his son, Simeon Hirsch Weil. Nethaneel died at Rostadt in 1769.

Weinberg, Yechiel Yaakov

Yechiel Weinberg was born in Poland in 1878. He studied at the Mir and Slabodka yeshivas. He served for seven years as the rabbi of Pilwishki. In 1914 he went to Germany where he obtained a Ph.D. on Masoretic Text. Later he became the Rosh Yeshiva at the Hildesheimer Rabbinical Seminary in Berlin. He spent his last twenty years in Montreaux, Switzerland.

He is best known for his halakhic work, *Seridei Eish* ("Remnants of the Fire"). It basically addresses issues of the modern world – technological, social and personal. It has become a classic of modern halakhic works. He also wrote *Mechkarim beTalmud* that are his studies in Talmudic methodology. It formed the basis for all his responsa. He died in 1966.

Weiss, Isaac Hirsch

Isaac Hirsch Weiss was born in Velke Mezirici, Moravia in 1815. At age eight he started his Talmud studies at the yeshiva of Moses Aaron Tichler. Later he studied at a yeshiva in Trebitsch, Moravia under Hayyim Joseph Pollak and then in Eisenstadt under Isaac Moses Perles.

In 1858, he settled in Vienna where after a few years he became a lecturer at the Bet HaMidrash of Adolf Jellinek, where he stayed until his death.

Soon after his appointment he worked on a Vienna edition of the Talmud that he annotated. He then wrote a compendium of laws and observances relating to the ritual, titled *Orah la-Zaddik* that was published by Schlossberg as a part of the *Seder Tefillat Ya'acob*. The following year he edited the Sifra with the commentary of Abraham ben David Posquierres (Ravad III), as well as providing a historical and linguistic introduction in nine chapters and also providing the text with critical notes, titled *Masoret HaTalmud*. He wrote a work, *Mishpat Leshon HaMishnah* on the language of the Mishnah.

However, his most important work and for which he is best known is his *Dor Dor we-Dorshaw*. It consists of five volumes and gives a history of the halakha from biblical times to the expulsion of Jews from Spain at the end of the fifteenth century. This work came to be accepted as the standard history of the oral tradition by the majority of the Haskalah scholars. Weiss died in 1905.

Weiss, Yitzhak Yaakov (Minchat Yaakov)

Rabbi Yitzhak Weiss was born in Dolynia, Galicia, then a part of Austria-Hungary in 1902 and died in 1989. His father was a well-known Hassidic rabbi. At the outbreak of World War I he moved to Munkacz, Hungary, which after the war fell under Czechoslovakia. By age twenty he had received s'micha and became Rosh Yeshiva there. During World War II he was in Romania and avoided deportation by going into hiding. After the war he emigrated to Manchester, England where he became the head of the Beth Din. He remained there until 1970 when he went to live in Jerusalem.

Rabbi Weiss was the author of a multi-volume set of responsa titled *Minchat Yaakov*, that addressed many contemporary issues of a social, economic and technical nature. His methodology in addressing these responsa was to review recent halakhic decisions and then trace these principles back to sources in the Talmud and Codes.

Wilovsky, Yaakov David (Ridvaz)

Yaakov Wilovsky was born in Kobrin, Russia in 1845. During his career he held multiple rabbinical posts in Izballin, Bobruisk, Vilna, Polotsk, Vilkomir and Slutsk. There he established a famous yeshiva in 1896. He appointed Rabbi Isser Zalman to run it. He made a number of trips to the United States to raise funds for the publication of his works. He later went to Safed where he established another yeshiva, Toras Eretz Yisrael.

After studying the Talmud Yerushalmi for over thirty years and working on his commentaries of these for many years, he began the publication of an edition of the Yerushalmi which contained both his own and all commentaries contained in former editions. There were two commentaries of his. *Chiddushei Ridvaz* was modeled on Rashi's commentaries on the Talmud Bavli. It explained the literal meaning of the text. *Tosafot HaRid* was modeled on the Tosefot. It compared and contrasted the significance of text with other Talmudic and halakhic texts.

His other works included *Migdal David* that were novellae on both the Yerushalmi and Bavli Talmuds, *Teshuvos Ridvaz*, a collection of responsa, and *Beis Ridvas* which was an explanation of Yisroel ben Shmuel Ashkenazi of Shklov's major work *Pe'at HaShulchan*. He died in 1913.

Yehuda, Eliezer ben, of Worms

Eliezer ben Yehuda was born in Germany in 1160. He wrote a code of ethical laws called *Rokeach* that also covered the liturgy and ritual. He intertwined aggadah, halakha and kabbalah. He died in 1237.

Yehuda, Gershon ben (Me'Or HaGolah)

Gershon ben Yehuda was born in Metz, France in 960. He was the Rosh Yeshiva in Metz. He established Ashkenazi traditions for readings and also wrote commentaries on the Talmud. Rashi included a number of these in his commentaries. His Talmud commentary was titled *Peirush Rabbeinu Gershom*. He died in Mainz, Germany in 1040.

Yitzhak, Baruch ben, of Worms

Yitzhak ben Baruch was born in Germany in 1170 and died in 1211. He wrote a code titled *Sefer HaTerumah* that consists of the laws according to the chapters of the various treatises of the Talmud. It was based on the teachings of Isaac ben Samuel of Dampierre (Ri). It became a widely used code in several European countries and was quoted by later authorities.

Yitzhaki, Shlomo (Rashi)

Rabbi Shlomo Yitzhaki was born in Troyes, Champagne in 1040. His name derives from that of his father, Yitzhak. He was an only child. There are a number of legends related to his birth. There are also claims that he is descended from King David through Rabban Gamliel the Elder, although Rashi made no such claim. His first Torah studies were probably taught by his father. He married at age seventeen and then went to study at the yeshiva of Rabbi Yaakov ben Yakar in Worms and then under Rabbi Isaac ben Eliezer HaLevi. These teachers in turn were students of Rabbeinu Gershom and Rabbi Eliezer HaGadol. He concentrated on Talmudic studies in Worms.

At age twenty five he returned to Troyes where within a short time he became the head of the Beth Din. In about 1070 he founded a yeshiva.

In 1096, the Crusade passed through Lorraine, killing in the process Rabbi Isaac ben Eliezer HaLevi's three sons. To commemorate this tragedy Rashi wrote several Selichot. One, *Adonai Elohei Hatz'vaot*, is still recited on the eve of Rosh Hashanah. Another, *Az Terem Nimtehu*, is recited on the fast of Gedaliyah.

Rashi wrote what was the first comprehensive commentary on almost the entire the Babylonian Talmud, covering thirty tractates. He provided a complete explanation of the words used as well as the logical structure of each passage. He commented on the Talmud literally phrase-by-phrase. These commentaries have been included in every edition of the Talmud since the first one was published in the fifteenth century. Portions of some of the tractates, for example Makkot, were published by his son-in-law, and Baba Batra by his grandson, Rashbam.

Rashi's commentary on the Tanakh, and particularly the Torah stand out as an equally essential commentary as that of the Talmud. His emphasis was to clarify the *peshat* or straight meaning of the text. His Torah commentary was first published in book form in 1475. For the rest of the Tanakh, he also published commentaries, except for Chronicles I and II. Many super-commentaries have been published on Rashi's work.

Rashi also wrote many responsa of which about 300 are extant. These were preserved by his students in works titled *Siddur Rashi*, *Sefer HaPardes* and *Sefer HaOrah*.

Rashi died in Troyes in 1105. The location of his grave was identified recently in the town square and a memorial has been placed there.

Yosef, Ovadia

Rabbi Ovadia Yosef was born in Basra, Iraq in 1920. He moved to Jerusalem with his family in 1924. He studied in the Porat Yosef Yeshiva and was taught by Rabbi Ezra Attiya. After the second world war he went to Cairo, Egypt as the head of the Beth Din. However, because of halakhic conflicts he resigned after two years and a short while later returned to Israel where he studied at the midrash Bnei Zion. In 1970, he was awarded the Israel Prize for Rabbinical literature. In 1973, he was elected the Chief Sephardic Rabbi of Israel.

He has published a number of works. He is most famous for his halakhic responsa. They are highly regarded and among some communities they are considered binding. These have been collected in two works titled *Yabia Omer* and *Yechavei Da'ath*. He published commentaries on the Talmud titled *Anaf Etz Avot* and *Maor Israel*. *Chazon Ovadia*, deals with the laws of Pesach. He completed Rabbi Chaim Sofer's work, *Kaf HaChaim* after the latter had died leaving it unfinished.

Yosef, Yitzhak

Yitzhak Yosef is the son of Ovadia Yosef. He is the author of *Yalkut Yosef* ("Collation of Yosef"). It is a twenty-seven volume collection of an authoritative contemporary collection of halakha derived from the *Shulkhan Arukh*. It is based on the rulings of Rabbi Ovadia Yosef. It is a practical guide for Jews of Sephardi and Oriental origin. It is also widely studied.

Zalman, Elijah ben Solomon (Vilna Gaon, Gra)

Rabbi Elijah ben Solomon Zalman was born in Vilna, Lithuania in 1720.

By the age of three he had memorized the Tanakh and by age seven he was studying the Talmud under Rabbi Moses Margalit. He had committed the Talmud to memory by age eleven. He also studied astronomy as a child. When a little older he travelled to Poland and Germany here he also studied there. He returned to Vilna in 1748.

He spent much time studying the Bible and Hebrew grammar. Because of his modesty he did not accept the rabbinate that was offered to him. When Hassidism took hold in Vilna, together with other rabbis, he tried to restrict its influence. In 1781, the Gaon excommunicated the Hassidim because of their proselytizing.

The Vilna Gaon restricted his teaching to a small select group of individuals in his Bet HaMidrash. An eminent student of his was Rabbi Chaim Volozhin, who founded a famous yeshiva.

He wrote extensively, writing commentaries on many of the older works. None of this was published during his lifetime. He wrote glosses on the Babylonian Talmud and the *Shulkhan Arukh*, titled *Biurei HaGra*. His commentary on the Mishnah was titled *Shenoth Eliyahu*. His comments on the Pentateuch are titled *Adereth Eliyahu*. The Gra died in 1797.

Zerah, Menahem ben Aaron ibn

Menahem Zerah was born in Estella, Spain in the first third of the fourteenth century. His father was forced to leave France in 1306 following the expulsion of Jews from that country. In 1328 his entire family was killed in the massacre of Estella. After this he studied under Joshua ibn Shu'aib and then went to Alcala to study Talmud and Tosefot under Judah ben Asher. He later became the rabbi of Alcala. After the civil war of 1368 he went to Toledo under the protection of Samuel Abravanel. This allowed him to study for the remainder of his life.

Zerah wrote *Zedak la-Derek* that was a specific type of halakhic code. It was aimed at wealthy Jews who associated with non-Jews and therefore had problems with following strict halakha. It contained only the most essential laws that might be overlooked. It was divided into five parts dealing with the ritual, forbidden foods, marriage laws, the Sabbath and festivals and fast and mourning days. This work stressed the ethical aspects. Menahem Zerah died in 1385.

Zerachiah HaYavani (The Greek) (Ra'Za'H)

Rabbi Zerachiah HaYavani lived in the thirteenth or fourteenth century in Greece. He was an ethicist and wrote a work on this subject titled *Sefer HaYashar*. It was for a time confused with Jacob Tam's halakhic work of the same name. It is divided into eighteen chapters and deals with the ethical relationship of man to God. It is similar to Bahya ibn Paquda's *Chovot HaLevavot*. Since its first publication in 1526 there have been a further twenty-three publications.

Zevi, Hillel ben Naphtali

Hillel ben Naphtali Zevi was born in Brest-Litovsk, Lithuania in 1615. He first studied under Hirsh Darshan and then continued his studies in Vilna. He stayed there until 1666 and then became the rabbi in several different Lithuanian towns. He later went as the rabbi to Altona and then Hamburg and finally in 1680 to Zolkiev.

Naphtali Zevi was the author of *Bet Hillel*. This was a commentary and novellae on the four parts of the *Shulkhan Arukh*. He died in 1690.

Zimra, David ben Solomon ibn Abi (Radbaz)

David ben Solomon ibn Abi Zimra was born in Spain about 1479. After the expulsions of 1492 he went with his parents to Safed where he studied under Joseph Saragossa. At the age of thirty-one he left Israel and went to Fez, Morocco where he was a member of the Beth Din. In 1517, he went to Cairo where he was appointed the chief rabbi, a position he held for forty years. He also became financially successful and founded a yeshiva, among whose students were Bezalel Ashkenazi and Isaac Luria.

At the age of ninety he retired and moved to Jerusalem and then back to Safed where he became a member of the Beth Din under Joseph Caro.

He wrote a number of minor works. His two major works were authoring more than 3,000 responsa that were published as a complete collection in Sudzilkow in 1836. He wrote *Yekar Tiferet* that was a commentary on Maimonides' *Mishneh Torah*. It complemented the *Maggid Mishneh* of Vidal of Tolosa. The Radbaz died in 1573, also stated to be in 1589.

Ziv, Simcha Zissel (Alter of Kelm)

Rabbi Ziv was born in Kelme, Lithuania in 1824. His father belonged to the Braude family and his mother was a descendant of the Chacham Zvi (Zvi Ashkenazi). After marrying he went to Kovno where he studied under Rabbi Yisrael Salanter, who was the founder of the Mussar movement. Rabbi Zvi spent his life furthering the teachings of Rabbi Salanter. While in Kovno he was sent to Zhagory to strengthen the Beit HaMussar that had been started there. Later he accompanied Kalmen Zev Wissotsky, the famous tea magnate and philanthropist, who had studied at the Volozhin Yeshiva, to Moscow. Rabbi Ziv then moved to St. Petersburg.

To overcome the growing influence of the Haskalah movement in Lithuania, Rabbi Ziv opened the Kelm Talmud Torah. It attracted many young students who were educated in the principles of the Mussar movement. He also introduced secular study there. Many of his students went to Israel and opened the Beis HaMussar in Jerusalem in 1892.

Rabbi Ziv wrote letters to his students. These were published as a two-volume set *Hokmah U-Mussar*. He died in 1898.

Section III

Works Of Authors And Classifications

Authors With Categorical Listing Of Their Works

This table provides the category of the work/s according to the alphabetical listing of the scholars. The classification system used is as previously tabulated. In some instances the work covers more than one category. Each category is listed according to the major section of classification and then the subdivision in each of these categories.

Author	Work	Category Of Work
A		
Aaron of Pesaro	Toledot Aharon	Biblical (Midrashic / Miscellaneous) / Talmud (General) / Other (Kabbalah)
Samuel ben Aaron of Schlettstadt	Kizzur Mordekai / Mordekai HaKaton	Talmud (Code of Law)
Solomon ben Kalman HaLevi Abel	Beit Shlomo	Talmud (General)
Isaac Aboab (Menorat HaMaor)	Menorat HaMaor, Aron HaEdut, Shulkhan HaPanim	Other (Ethics) Other (Ritual) Other (Liturgical)
Isaac Aboab	Super-Commentary to Nahmanides' Pentateuch Commentary Super-Commentary to Rashi's Pentateuch Commentary	Biblical (Super-Commentary) Biblical (Super-Commentary)
Samuel Aboab (Rasha)	Devar Shemuel Sefer HaZikranot	Talmud (Halakha) Other (Ethics)
Isaac ben Abraham of Dampierre (Riba)	Untitled Biblical commentaries Untitled Tosafot	Biblical (Commentary) Talmud (Tosafot)
Obadiah ben Abraham, of Bertinoro	Super-Commentary of Rashi's Pentateuch commentary Mishnah commentaries	Biblical (Super-Commentary) Talmud (Mishnah, Commentary)
Samson ben Abraham, of Sens	Commentary on Sifra Untitled Tosafot	Biblical (Midrashic) Talmud (Tosafot)
Isaac ben Judah Abravanel	Commentaries on Prophets Commentary on Torah	Biblical (Commentary) Biblical (Commentary)

Author	Work	Category Of Work
David ben Joseph ben David Abudraham	Sefer Abudraham (Tzibbur Perush HaBerakhot ve-ha-Tefillot)	Other (Liturgical)
Abraham ben Samuel Abulafia	Sefer HaYashar Sefer HaOt Imrei Shefer Sheba Netibot HaTorah Ozer Eden Ganuz Letter from the Grave Untitled Novellae	Kabbalah HaBrit Poem Talmud (Novellae)
Shmuel Aceda	Midrash Shmule	Talmud (Commentary)
Isaac Adarbi (Adribi)	Divrei Rivot Divrei Shalom	Talmud (Responsa) Biblical (Miscellaneous)
Solomon ben Joshua Adeni	Dibre Emet M'Lekhet Shlomo	Biblical (Super-Commentary) Talmud (Mishnah, Commentary)
Shlomo ben Aderet (Rashba)	Untitled Responsa Torat HaBayit	Talmud (Responsa) Talmud (Halakha)
Solomon Alami	Iggeret Mussar	Other (Ethics)
Moses ben Isaac Alashkar	Hassagot (Critical Notes) Untitled Responsa	Miscellaneous Talmud (Responsa)
Isaac ben Reuben Albargeloni	Talmud commentaries Azharot	Talmud Related Other (Piyyutim)
Joseph Albo	Ikkarim / Sefer HaIkarim	Other (Philosophy)
Abraham Alegri	Lev Sameach Lev Sameach	Halakha Commentary Talmud (Responsa)
Yitzhak ben Yaakov HaKohen Alfasi	Halacoth or Alfes or RIF Halakhot Ketanot	Talmud (Code of Law) Talmud (Code of Law)
Yom Tov Algazi	Untitled works on Jewish Law	Talmud (Halakha)
Judah ben Solomon Alharizi (al-Harizi)	Takhemoni	Other (Poetry)
Solomon ben Moses HaLevi Alkabetz	Lecha Dodi	Other (Kabbalah / Liturgical)

Author	Work	Category Of Work
Judah ben Solomon Chai Alkali	Goral la-Adonai Shalom Yerushalayim Minhat Yehuda	Miscellaneous Miscellaneous Other (Philosophy)
Joseph Almosnino	Edut bi-Yehosef	Talmud (Responsa)
Moses ben Baruch Almosnino	Yedeh Mosheh Pirkei Moshe Memmez Koah	Biblical (Commentary) Talmud Related Talmud (Commentary)
Moshe Alshich	Torat Moshe	Biblical (Miscellaneous)
Avraham Mordechai Alter	Imrei Emes	Biblical (Explanation)
Pinchas Menachem Alter	Pnei Menachem	Biblical (Explanation)
Simchah Bunim Alter	Lev Simcha	Biblical (Explanation)
Yehuda Aryeh Leib Alter (Sfas Emes)	Sfas Emes al HaTorah	Biblical (Explanation)
Israel Alter	Beis Israel	Biblical
Yitzhak Myer Alter	Chiddushei Harim	Biblical
Naphtali (Hirsch) ben Asher Altschul	Ayyalah SheluHah Imrei Shefer	Biblical (Commentary) Miscellaneous
David ben Aryeh Loeb Altshuler (Altshul)	Metsudot (Zion and David)	Biblical (Commentary)
Amnon of Mainz	U'netanneh Tokef	Other (Liturgical / Piyyutim)
Nathan ben Jehiel (Yechiel) Anaw (Anav)	Arukh	Miscellaneous
Zedekiah ben Abraham Anaw (Anav)	Shibbole HaLeket	Other (Piyyutim)
Abraham Ankava	Kerem Hemed	Talmud (Responsa)

Author	Work	Category Of Work
Isaac ben Moses Arama (Ba'al Akedah)	Sefer HaAkedah Yad Absholom	Biblical (Explanation) Biblical (Commentary)
Abba Arika	Untitled New Year Musaf Prayer	Other (Liturgical)
Yom Tov ibn Asevilli (Ritva)	Untitled	Talmud (Commentary)
Aaron ben Moses ben Asher	Aleppo Codex Sefer Dikdukei HaTe'amim	Biblical (Miscellaneous) Miscellaneous
Bayha ben Asher (Rabbeinu Behaye / Bachya)	Midrash Rabbeinu Bachya Kad HaKemah Shulkhan Arba Ohel Moed	Biblical (Commentary) Other (Ethics), Talmud (Halakha) Miscellaneous
Jacob ben Asher (The Tur)	Arba'ah Turim Sefer HaRemazim / Kitzur Piske HaRosh Rimze Ba'al HaTurim Perush al HaTorah	Talmud (Code of Law) Talmud (Commentary / Code of Law)
Rav Ashi	Editor Babylonian Talmud	Talmud (General)
Bezalel Ashkenazi	Shittah Mekubetzet	Talmud (Commentary / Glosses)
Gershon Ashkenazi	Avodat HaGershuni Tifferet HaGershuni Hiddushei HaGershuni	Talmud (Responsa) Biblical (Midrash) / Other (Kabbalah) Talmud (Code of Law)
Mordechai ben Hillel Ashkenazi	Sefer Hamordechai (The Mordechai) Selichot	Talmud (Commentary) Other (Liturgical)
Tzvi Hirsch ben Yaakov Ashkenazi (Chacham Tzvi)	Chacham Tzvi	Talmud (Responsa)
Yehuda ben Shimon Ashkenazi	Be'er Heitiv	Talmud (Code of Law)
Yisroel ben Shmuel Ashkenazi, of Shklov	Pe'at HaShulchan Beit Yisrael Nachalah u-Menuchah	Talmud (Code of Law) Talmud (Mishnah / Commentary) Talmud (Responsa)

Author	Work	Category Of Work
Yehuda Leib HaLevi Ashlag (Ba'al HaSulam)	Panim Meirot Umashirot Talmud Eser Sefirot HaSalem (Salem)	Other (Kabbalah) Other (Kabbalah) Other (Kabbalah)
Hayyim ibn Attar	Ohr HaChaim	Biblical (Commentary)
Menachem Mendel ben Meshulam Zalman Auerbach	Ateret Zekeinim	Talmud (Code of Law)
Shlomo Zalman Auerbach	Meorei Eish Ma'adnei Eretz Minchas Shlomo Minchas Shlomo Commentary on Shev Shema'tata	Talmud (Halakha) Talmud (Halakha) Talmud (Responsa) Talmud (Commentary) Talmud (Novellae)
Avraham of Tisk	Magen Avraham	Biblical (Miscellaneous)
Judah Ayyas	Lehem Yehuda Bet Yehuda Mateh Yehuda Shebbet Yehuda	Talmud (Code of Law) Talmud (Responsa) Talmud (Code of Law) Talmud (Code of Law)
Menachem Azaryah, of Fano	Assarah Maamarot	Other (Kabbalah)
Elazar ben Moshe Azikri (Ezkari)	Sefer Hareidim Divrei Kivushim On tractate Bezah Yedid Nefesh	Other (Ethics) Other (Ethics) Talmud (Commentary) Other (Piyyutim)
Abraham Azulai	Baalei Bris Avraham Chesed L'Avraham Ohr HaChachma Ohr HaGanuz Perush Yakar Al Shisha Sidrei Mishnah Perush Yakar Al HeLevush	Biblical (Commentary) Other (Kabbalah) Other (Kabbalah) Other (Kabbalah) Talmud (Mishnah Commentary) Talmud (Mishnah Commentary)
Haim Yosef David Azulai (Hida)	Shem HaGedolim Treatises on Kabbalah	Biblical (Explanation) / Miscellaneous Other (Kabbalah)

B

Author	Work	Category Of Work
Yosef ben Moshe Babad	Minchat Chinuch	Talmud (Halakha)

Author	Work	Category Of Work
Abraham Samuel Bachrach	Hut haShani	Talmud (Responsa)
Yair Chaim Bachrach	Havvot Yair Mekor Chaim	Talmud (Responsa) Talmud (Code of Law)
Isaac ben Sheshet Barfat (RiBaSH)	She'elot u-Teshuvot HaRibash Hahadashot Untitled Novellae	Talmud (Responsa) Talmud (Novellae)
Joseph ben Baruch (Joseph of Clisson)	Tosafot Piyyutim Selichot	Talmud (Tosafot) Other (Piyyutim) Other (Ritual)
Meir ben Baruch (Meir of Rothenburg) (MaHaRaM)	Tosafot (Yoma published) Untitled Responsa Hilkot Berakhot / Seder Berakhot Birkot MaHaRaM Hilkot Shehitah Hilkot Abelut / Hilkot Semahot Hilkot Pesukot Hilkot Erubin Hiddushim Commentary Sixth Mishnaic Order. Liturgical Poems	Talmud (Tosafot) Talmud (Responsa) Talmud (Halakha) Talmud (Halakha) Talmud (Halakha) Talmud (Halakha) Talmud (Halakha) Talmud (Halakha) Talmud (Novellae) Talmud (Mishnah Commentary) Other (Piyyutim)
Shneur Zalman Baruch (Borukovich), of Liadi (Alter Rebbe, GRaZ)	Tanya / Likkutei Amarim Shulchan Aruch HaRav Siddur Torah Or Likutei Torah	Other (Hassidic / Kabbalah / Philosophy) Talmud (Code of Law) Other (Liturgical) Biblical (Explanation)
Judah ben Barzillai	Sefer HaIttim	Talmud (Code of Law)
Shabbethai ben Joseph Bass	Sifte Yeshenim Sifsei Chachamim	Miscellaneous (Bibliographical) Biblical (Super-Commentary)
Behag	Halakhot Gedolot	Talmud (Code of Law)
Mordechai ben Abraham Benet	Biur Mordechai Magen Abot Parashot Mordechai Tekelet Mordechai	Talmud (Super-Commentary) Talmud (Halakha) Talmud (Responsa) Talmud (Commentary)

Author	Work	Category Of Work
Chaim Benveniste	Knesses HaGedolah	Talmud (Code of Law)
	Dina DeChaye	Talmud (Code of Law)
	Ba'ei Chaye	Talmud (Responsa)
	Chamra VeChaye	Talmud (Novellae)
	Pesach MeUvin	Talmud (Halakha)
Dov Ber (of Mezritch) (The Maggid)	Likkutei Amarim	Other (Hassidic)
	Likkutei Yesharim	Miscellaneous (Hassidic)
Aharon Berechyah of Modena	Maavar Yabok	Talmud (Halakha)
	Me'il Tzedakah	Other (Ritual)
	Bigdei Kodesh	Other (Ritual)
Sholom Noach Berezovsky	Nesivos Sholom	Miscellaneous
Isaiah ben Judah Loeb Berlin	Untitled Talmudic Glosses	Talmud (Glosses)
Naftali Tzvi Yehuda Berlin	HaEmek She'ela	Talmud (Commentary)
	Meishiv Davar	Talmud (Responsa)
	HaEmek Davar	Biblical (Commentary)
	Meromei Sadeh	Talmud (Commentary)
	HaEmek She'ela	Talmud (Commentary)
	Davar HaEmek	Biblical (Commentary)
Abraham ben Shem Tov Bibago	Derek Emunah	Other (Philosophy)
	Ez Hayyim	Other (Philosophy)
Isaac ben Moses Solomon Blaser (Rav Itzele Peterburger)	Peri Yitzhak	Talmud (Responsa)
Boruch of Kosov	Yesod HaEmunah	Other (Hassidic)
	Amud HaAvodah	Other (Hassidic)
Abraham ben Moses de Bouton	Lehem Mishneh	Talmud (Code of Law)
Shlomo ben Boya'a	Aleppo Codex	Biblical (Miscellaneous)
Israel Bruna	Teshuvot Mahari Bruna	Talmud (Responsa)
Solomon Buber	Pesikhta de-Rab Kahana	Biblical (Midrashic)

C

Isaac ben Jacob Campanton	Darche HaGemara / Darche HaTalmud	Talmud (General)

Author	Work	Category Of Work
Yehuda Leib ben Meir Channeles	Vayigash Yehuda	Talmud (Code of Law)
Joseph ben Ephraim Caro (Mechaber)	Beth Yosef	Talmud (Code of law)
	Shulkhan Arukh	Talmud (Code of law)
	Kesef Mishnah	Talmud (Code of law)
	Bedek HaBayit	Talmud (Code of law)
	Kelalei HaTalmud	Talmud (General)
	Maggid Mesharim	Other (Kabbalah)
	Derashot	Talmud (Responsa)
	Avkath Rochel	?Responsa
Jacob de Castro	Erek Lehem	Talmud (Novellae / Code of Law)
	Ohole Ya'akob	Other (Ritual)
	Kol Ya'acob	Biblical (Miscellaneous)
	Nazir	Talmud (Commentary)
	Erech HaShulchan	Talmud (Code of law / Glosses)
Aharon ibn Chaim	Korban Aharon	Biblical (Midrashic)
	Midos Aharon	Biblical (Midrashic)
Hakham (Chacham) Yosef Chaim (Ben Ish Chai)	Ben Ish Chai	Talmud (Code of Law)
	Me-Kabtziel	Talmud (Code of Law)
	Ben Yehovada	Talmud (Commentary)
	Rav Pe'alim	Talmud (Responsa)
	Torah Lishmah	
	Qanan-un-Nisa	Miscellaneous
Zvi Hirsch Chajes (Chayes) (The Maharatz Chajes)	Untitled	Talmud (Glosses)
	Torat Nevi'im	Talmud (Commentary)
	Darkhei Binah	Talmud (Halakha)
	Imrei Binah	Miscellaneous
	Minhat Kenaot	Miscellaneous
	Talmudic Glosses	Talmud (Glosses)
Abraham ibn Chananyah	Beit Avraham	Talmud (Code of Law)
Levi ben Jacob ibn Chaviv (Habib) (Ralbach)	She'elot u-Teshuvot	Talmud (Responsa)
	Kontres HaSemikah	Miscellaneous
	Perush Kiddush HaChodesh	Miscellaneous
Yaakov Ibn Chaviv (Habib)	Ayn Yaakov	Talmud (Commentary)
Yosef Chaviva	Nimukei Yosef	Talmud (Code of Law)

Author	Work	Category Of Work
Avraham Chayon	Amorot Tehorot	Other (Ethics)
Joseph Chayon	Milei DeAvot	Talmud (Commentary)
	Untitled Psalms Commentary	Biblical (Commentary)
Aron Chorin	Emek HaShaweh	Miscellaneous
	Nogah HaBedek	Other (Ritual)
Chananel ben Chushiel (Rabbeinu Chananel)	Untitled Torah Commentary	Biblical (Commentary)
	Untitled Talmud (Gemara)	Talmud (Commentary)
	Untitled Responsa	Talmud (Responsa)
Abigdor Cohen (of Vienna)	Untitled commentary on Pentateuch and Five Megillot	Biblical (Commentary)
	Tosafot on Ketuvot	Talmud (Tosafot)
Moses ben Jacob Cordovero	Pardes Rimonim ("Orchard of Pomegranates")	Other (Kabbalah)
	Ohr Yakar ("Precious Light")	Other (Kabbalah)
	Tomer Devorah ("Palm Tree Of Deborah")	Other (Kabbalah)
	Elimah Rabbati	Other (Kabbalah)
	Sefer Gerushim (The Book of Banishments")	Other (Kabbalah)
	Shiur Komah ("Measurement of Height")	Other (Kabbalah)
	Ohr Neerav ("A Pleasant Light")	Other (Kabbalah)
Hasdai ben Abraham Crescas	Or Adonai	Philosophy
	Refutation of Christian Principles	Miscellaneous
	Passover Sermon	Talmud (Halakha / Miscellaneous)
	Letter to Congregations of Avignon	Miscellaneous
Yaakov Culi	Me'am Loez	Biblical (Commentary)
	Simanim le'Oraita	Talmud (Halakha)

D

Author	Work	Category Of Work
Abraham ben Jehiel Danzig	Hayye Adam: Nishmat Adam ("The life of Man: the Soul of Man")	Talmud (Code of Law)
	Hokmat Adam: Binat Adam ("The Wisdom of Man: the Understanding of Man")	Talmud (Code of Law)
	Bet Abraham ("The House of Abraham")	Talmud (Halakha)

Author	Work	Category Of Work
Abraham ben Jehiel Danzig (cont)	Zikru Torat Moshe ("Be Mindful of the Teachings of Moses")	Talmud (Halakha)
	Toledot Adam	Other (Ritual)
	Sha'are Zedek ("The Gates of Justice")	Talmud (Halakha)
	Kitzur Sefer Hareidim	Miscellaneous
Samuel Danzig	Nehamot Ziyyon	Biblical (Commentary)
Abraham ben David (Ravad III)	Temim De'im	Talmud (Responsa)
	Orot Hayyim	Talmud (Responsa)
	Shibbole HaLeket	Talmud (Responsa)
	Sefer Ba'ale Nefesh	Miscellaneous
	Torath Kohanim	Talmud (Commentary)
	Glosses on Maimonides' Mishneh Torah	Talmud (Glosses)
	HaSagot haRaavad	Talmud (Code of Law)
Baruch ben David	Gedulah Mordechai	Talmud (Super-Commentary)
Mattithiah ben Solomon Delacrut	Perush	Other (Kabbalah)
Eliyahu Eliezer Dessler	Michtav me-Eliyahu	Miscellaneous
Hezekiah ben David DiSilo	Pri Chadash	Talmud (Code of Law)
Shabtai Donolo	Chachmuni	Biblical (Miscellaneous)
Simeon ben Zemah Duran (Rashbatz / Tashbetz)	Untitled	Talmud (Mishnah Commentary)
	Untitled	Talmud (Commentary)
	Piyyutim	Other (Piyyutim)
	Responsa	Talmud (Responsa)
Solomon ben Simon Duran (Rashbash)	Untitled	Talmud (Responsa)
Yehuda Meir Dvir	Untitled (from Torat Hashem Temima)	Biblical (Commentary)

E

Akiva Eger	Untitled	Talmud (Responsa)
	Untitled	Talmud (Glosses)

Author	Work	Category Of Work
David Solomon Eibenschutz	Lebushe Serad	Talmud (Code of Law)
	Ne'ot Deshe	Talmud (Responsa)
	Arbe Nahal	Biblical (Commentary)
Samuel Eidels	Hiddushei Halakhot	Talmud (Commentary / Novellae / Super-Commentary)
	Hiddushei Aggadot	Talmud (Commentary / Novellae)
Abraham Zevi Hirsch ben Jacob Eisenstadt	Pithei Teshuvah	Talmud (Code of Law) / Talmud (Responsa)
Benjamin Eisenstadt	Masot Binyamin	Talmud (Novellae)
Meir ben Iszak Eisenstadt (Meir Ash) (Maharam Ash / Panim Me'irot)	Panim Me'irot	Talmud (Responsa / Novellae)
	Or HaGanuz	Talmud (Novellae)
	Kotnot Or	Biblical (Commentary)
Meir Eisenstadter (Meir Ash) (Maharam Ash)	Imrei Esh	Talmud (Responsa)
	Imrei Yosher	Miscellaneous
	Imrei Binah	Talmud (Novellae)
Naftali Hertz ben Yaakov Elchanan (Bachrach)	Emeq HaMeleqh	Other (Kabbalah)
Abba Mari ben Elgidor	Commentary on Job	Biblical (Commentary)
Hillel ben Eliakim	Commentary to Midrash Sifra	Biblical (Midrash)
	Commentary to Midrash Sifre	
Tobiah ben Eliezer	Lekah Tob / Pesikta Zutarta	Biblical (Midrash)
Eliezer of Touques	Gilyon Tosafot / Tosafot Gillayon Tosafot Tuk	Talmud (Tosafot)
Perez ben Elijah (Rap / RaPaSh / MaHaRPaSh)	Sefer Peretz	Biblical (Miscellaneous)
Issachar ben Ellenberg	Tzeidah LaDerech	Biblical (Super-Commentary)
	Be'er Sheva	Talmud (Commentary)

Author	Work	Category Of Work
Jacob Israel ben Zvi Ashkenazi Emden (the Yabets)	Lehem Shamayim	Talmud (Mishnah / Commentary)
	She'elot Yabez	Talmud (Responsa)
	Siddur Tefilah	Other (Ritual)
	Mor u-Keziah	Talmud (Novellae)
	Zizim u-Ferahim	Other (Kabbalah)
Judah ben Enoch	Hinnuk ben Yehuda	Talmud (Responsa)
Moshe Chaim Ephraim of Sudilkov	Degel Machaneh Ephraim	Biblical (Miscellaneous) / Other (Hassidic)
Avraham Epstein	Ma'aseh Hageonim	Talmud (Halakha / Responsa)
Baruch HaLevi Epstein	Torah Temimah	Biblical (Commentary)
		Liturgy
	Baruch she-Amar	Other (Liturgical)
	Mekor Baruch	Miscellaneous
	Tosefet Berakhah	Talmud (Novellae)
Moshe Mordechai Epstein	Levush Mordechai	Talmud (Novellae)
Yechiel Michel HaLevi Epstein (the Aruch HaShulchan)	Aruch HaShulchan	Talmud (Halakha)
	Aruch HaShulchan he'Atid	Talmud (Halakha)
	Or li-Yesharim	Talmud (Commentary)
	Micah HaMayim	Talmud (Commentary / Super-Commentary)
	Leil Shimurim	Miscellaneous
Joseph Escapa	Rosh Yosef	Talmud (Code of Law / Novellae)
	Teshubot Rosh Yosef	Talmud (Responsa)
Yaakov Etlinger	Responsa Binyan Tzion	Talmud (Responsa)
	Aruch LaNer	Talmud (Mishnah Commentary)
Hayyim Judah Lob Ettinger	Untitled	Talmud (Responsa)
Isaac Aaron Ettinger	Untitled	Talmud (Responsa)

Author	Work	Category Of Work
Jonathan Eybeschutz	Ya'arot Devash	Miscellaneous
	Tiferet Yehonatan	Biblical (Miscellaneous)
	Taryag Mitzvot	Talmud (Commentary)
	Binah la-Ittim	Talmud (Halakha)
	Chiddushim al Hilkot Yom Tov	Talmud (Halakha)
	Shem Olam	Other (Kabbalah)
	Novellae to the Shulkhan Arukh	Talmud (Novellae)
Joseph ben Hanan ben Nathan Ezobi	Liturgical Poems	Other (Piyyutim)
Abraham ben Meir ibn Ezra (Abenezra)	Sefer HaYashar	Biblical (Commentary)
	Moznayim	Miscellaneous
	Sefer HaYesod	Miscellaneous
	Yesod Dikduk	Miscellaneous
	Iggeret Shabbat	Miscellaneous
	Yesod Mora	Biblical (Explanations)
	Mazhor Piyyutim	Other (Piyyutim)

F

Author	Work	Category Of Work
Samuel ben Uri Shraga Faibesh (Phoebus)	Beit Shmuel	Talmud (Code of Law)
Joshua ben Alexander (Katz) HaKohen Falk	Beit Israel	Talmud (Code of Law)
Moshe Feinstein (Reb Moshe)	Igrot Moshe	Talmud (Responsa)
	Dibros Moshe	Talmud (Novellae)
	Darash Moshe	Torah (Novellae)
Shneur Zalman Fradkin of Lublin	Toras Chesed	Other (Hassidic)
Solomon Bennett Freehof	The Responsa Literature	Talmud (Responsa)

Author	Work	Category Of Work
G		
Solomon ben Judah, ibn Gabirol (Gvirol)	Anak	Miscellaneous
	Mekor Chaim (Fons Vitae)	Other (Philosophy)
	Keter Malkut	Other (Piyyutim)
	Azharoth	Other (Piyyutim)
	Shir Hakavod	Other (Piyyutim)
	Shir Hayichud	Other (Piyyutim)
	Improvement of Moral Qualities / Ethics	Other (Ethics)
Abraham Galante	Yare'ach Yakar	Other (Kabbalah)
Solomon ben Joseph Ganzfried	Kitzur Shulkhan Arukh	Talmud (Code of Law)
	Kesses Hasofer	Talmud (Halakha)
	Pnei Shlomo	Talmud (Commentary)
	Toras Zevach	Talmud (Halakha)
Achai Gaon	Sheilot d'Rav Achai / Sheiltos	Biblical (Commentary) and Talmud (Commentary)
Hai Gaon	Untitled	Talmud (Commentary)
	Untitled	Talmud (Responsa)
Shem Tov ben Abraham ibn Gaon	Migdal Oz	Talmud (Halakha)
	Keter Shem Tov	Biblical (Super-Commentary)
Abraham Gediliyah	Bris Avraham	Biblical related
Yonah ben Avraham Gerondi (Rabbeinu Yonah)	Iggeret HaTeshuvah	Other (Ethics)
	Sha'are Teshuvah	Other (Ethics)
	Sefer HaYirah	Other (Ethics)
	Untitled Novellae	Talmud (Novellae)
Zerachiah ben Isaac HaLevi Gerondi (ReZaH, RaZBI, Ba'al HaMaor)	Sefer HaMaor	Talmud (Commentary)
	Sefer HaTsava	Talmud (Commentary)
	ReZaH	Miscellaneous
Levi ben Gershom (Gersonides, Ralbag)	Sefer Mikhamot Ha-Shem	Other (Philosophy)
	Sefer Ma'aseh Hoshev	Miscellaneous
	Perush al Sefer Iyob	Biblical (Commentary)
	Perush al Sefer HaTorah	Biblical (Commentary)
Isaac ben Judah ibn Ghiyyat (Ghayyat)	Sha'areh Simhah	Other (Ritual)
	Hilkot Pesahim	Other (Ritual)
	Sifte Renanot	Other (Piyyutim)

Author	Work	Category Of Work
Isaac ibn Gias	Meah Shearim (Yitzhak Yranan)	Talmud (Halakha)
Joseph ben Abraham Gikatilla (Joseph Ba'al HaNissim)	Ginnat Egoz Sha'areh Orah or Sefer Orah	Other (Kabbalah) Other (Kabbalah)
Louis Ginzberg	Commentary on Yerushalmi Legends of the Jews Geonica Responsa	Talmud (Commentary) Biblical and Talmudic (Midrashic) Miscellaneous / Talmudic (Responsa) Talmud (Responsa)
David Golinkin	Collection of Conservative Movement Responsa Untitled Responsa The Responsa of Professor Louis Ginzberg (edited) Responsa in a moment: Halakhic responses to contemporary issues	Talmud (Responsa) Talmud (Responsa) Talmud (Responsa Talmud (Responsa)
Abraham Abele ben Chaim HaLevi Gombiner (Magen Avraham)	Magen Avraham Zayit Ra'anan Tosafist Commentary	Talmud (Code of Law) Biblical (Midrashic) Talmud (Commentary)
Joseph ben Gorion	Sefer Yossipon	Miscellaneous
Eliezer David Greenwald	Keren L'david	Talmud (Responsa)
Chaim Ozer Grodzinski	She'elot uT'shuvot Achiezer	Talmud (Responsa)
Aryeh Leib ben Asher Gunzberg (Shaagat Aryeh)	Shaagat Aryeh Turei Even She'elot u-Teshuvot Shaagat Aryeh HaHadashot Gevurot Ari	Talmud (Halakha Talmud (Novellae) Talmud (Responsa) Talmud (Novellae)

H

Moses ibn Habib (Chaviv)	Get Pashut Ezrat Nashim Shammot ba-Arez Untitled Responsa	Talmud (Halakha) Talmud (Halakha) Talmud (Novellae) Talmud (Responsa)

Author	Work	Category Of Work
Moses HaDarshan	Yesod	Biblical (Midrashic)
Shimon ben Yitzhak HaGadol	Piyutei R' Shimon ben Yitzhak	Other (Liturgical / Piyyutim)
Jacob Hagiz	Lehem HaPannim	?
Moses Hagiz	Leket HaKemah	Talmud (Novellae)
	Eleh HaMitzvot	Talmud (Halakha)
Eleazar ben Eleazar HaKappar (Bar Kappara, Berebi)	Mishnah of Bar Kappara	Talmud (Mishnah)
Aaron ben Jacob ben David HaKohen	Ohrot Hayyim	Other (Ritual)
Abraham ben Eliezer HaKohen	Ori We-Yishi	Miscellaneous
Joseph ben Joshua Meir HaKohen	Emek Habachah (Valley of Weeping)	Miscellaneous
Meir Simcha Kalonymus HaKohen of Dvinsk	Ohr Somye'ach	Talmud (Novellae)
	Meshech Cochma	Biblical (Novellae) / Philosophy
Shabbatai ben Meir HaKohen (Shach)	Siftei Kohen (Shakh)	Talmud (Code of Law)
	Selichot	Other (Liturgical / Piyyutim)
	Gevurat Anashim	Talmud (Responsa)
Jose ben Halafta	Seder Olam Rabbah	Biblical
Chaim Halberstam of Sanz	Divrei Chaim	Other (Hassidic)
Aaron HaLevi, of Barcelona	Sefer HaChinuch (the Chinuch)	Talmud (Halakha)
Aaron Abraham ben Baruch Simeon HaLevi	Iggeret HaTe'amim	Other (Kabbalah)
Abraham ben David HaLevi (Abraham ibn Daud, Ravad I)	Al-akidah al-Rafiyah (Emunah Ramah)	Other (Philosophy)
Abraham ben Isaac HaLevi	Passover Piyyut	Other (Piyyutim)

Author	Work	Category Of Work
Aharon HaLevi (Ra'AH)	Bedek HaBayit	Talmud (Halakha)
Eliakim ben Meshulam HaLevi	Untitled Sabbath circumcision Piyyut	Talmud (Commentary) Other (Piyyutim)
Eliezer ben Joel HaLevi (Raviah)	Sefer HaRaviah (Avi HaEzri)	Talmud (Halakha)
Isaac ben Asher HaLevi (Riva)	Untitled Pentateuch Commentary Untitled Tosafot	Biblical (Commentary) Talmud (Tosafot)
Jacob ben Isaac HaLevi (Jabez)	Haggahot Maimuniyot	Talmud (Tosafot)
Judah ben Samuel HaLevi (RiHa'l)	Kuzari Various piyyutim	Other (Philosophy) Other (Piyyutim)
Isaac ben Eleazar HaLevi	Wedding Piyyutim	Piyyutim
David Weiss Halivni	Mekorot u'Mesorot Peshat and Derash: Plain and Applied Meaning in Rabbinic Exegesis Revelation Restored: Divine Writ and Critical Responses Introduction to Sources and Tradition Studies in the Formation of the Talmud, Mishnah and Gemara: The Jewish Predilection for Justified Law Breaking the Tablets: Jewish Theology After the Shoah	Talmud (Commentary) Talmud (Halakha) Miscellaneous Miscellaneous Talmud (Explanation) Miscellaneous
Judah HaNasi (Rabbeinu HaKadosh)	Editor of the Mishnah	Talmud (Mishnah)
Sherira ben Hanina, Gaon	Iggeret Rav Sherira Gaon	Talmud (General)
Ishtori ben Moses Haparchi (Kaftor Vaferech)	Sefer Kaftor Vaferech	Miscellaneous
Yedayah HaPenini	Bechinot Olam	Other (Philosophy)

Author	Work	Category Of Work
Zedekiah ben Avraham Anav HaRofei	Shibbole HaLeket	Talmud (Code of Law)
Joel Hayyim (Mahariah)	Hiddushei Mahariah	Talmud (Novellae / Super-Commentary)
Samuel Hayyun	Bene Shemuel	Talmud (Novellae / Responsa)
Yeshayah ben Mali Hazaken	Piskei HaRid	Talmud (Halakha / Novellae)
Jehiel ben Solomon Heilprin	Seder HaDorot Erke Kinnuyim	Miscellaneous Miscellaneous
Aryeh Leib HaKohen Heller (The Ketzos)	Ketzot HaChoshen Avnei Milluim Shev Shm'atata	Talmud (Code of Law) Talmud (Code of Law) Talmud (Halakha)
Yom Tov Lippman Heller (Tosefos Yomtov)	Tosefos Yomtov	Talmud (Mishnah, Commentary)
Abraham Herrero	Sha'ar HaShamayim Beit Elohim	Other (Kabbalah) Other (Kabbalah)
Abraham Joshua Heschel	Der Shem Hamefoyrosh: Mensch Man is Not Alone: A Philosophy of Religion God in Search of Man: A Philosophy of Judaism The Sabbath: It Meaning for Modern Man The Prophets Prophetic Inspiration After the Prophets: Maimonides and Others Torah min HaShamayim BeAspaklariya (Heavenly Torah: As Refracted Through the Generations)	Miscellaneous Other (Philosophy) Other (Philosophy) Other (Philosophy) Other (Philosophy) Miscellaneous Talmud (General)
Yaakov Yehoshua ben Zvi Hirsch (Jacob Joshua Falk)	Pene Yehoshua	Talmud (Commentary / Novellae)

Author	Work	Category Of Work
David Zevi Hoffmann	Untitled	Talmud (Responsa)
	Untitled	Talmud (Code of Law Commentary)
	Untitled	Talmud (Commentary)
Abraham ben Shabtai Sheftel Horowitz	Emek Berakhah Yesh Nohalin	Other (Ethics) Other (Ethics)
Isaiah HaLevi Horowitz (Shelah, Shaloh)	Shnei Luchos HaBris	Other (Ethics / Kabbalah / Ritual)
	Sha'ar HaShamayim	Other (Ritual)
Shabtai Sheftel Horowitz	Emek Berakhah (additions)	Other (Ethics)
	Vave Ammudim	Other (Ethics / Kabbalah)
	Zuwwa'ah	
	Sha'ar HaShamayim (additions)	Other (Ritual / Kabbalah)
		Other (Ethics / Ritual)
Judah Aryeh Loeb ben Joshua Hoschel	Torah Or	Talmud (Halakha)
Shabbethai Sheftel ben Akiba Hurwitz	Shef' Tal	Other (Kabbalah)
Yosef Yozel Hurwitz (Alter of Novardok)	Madragat HaAdam	Other (Ethics)
Yitzhak (Isaac) Hutner	Torat HaNazir	Miscellaneous
	Kovetz Ha'aros	Biblical (Midrashic)
	Pachad Yitzhak	Miscellaneous

I

Shemariah ben Elijah Ikriti of Negropont	Sefer HaMora	Other (Philosophy)
	Elef HaMagen	Biblical (Midrashic)
	Untitled	Other (Piyyutim)
Abraham ben Isaac of Narbonne (Raavad II)	HaEshkol	Talmud (Code of Law)
	Responsa	Talmud (Responsa)
Baruch ben Isaac	Sefer HaTerumah	Talmud (Code of Law)
	Tosafot on some treatises	Talmud (Tosafot)

Author	Work	Category Of Work
Elhanan ben Isaac, of Dampierre	Tikkun Tefillin Tosafot for several treatises Pizmonim for Passover	Miscellaneous Talmud (Tosafot) Other (Piyyutim)
Kalonymus ben Isaac	Tosafot (Hullin 47b) Responsum quote elsewhere	Talmud (Tosafot) Talmud (Responsa)
Samson ben Isaac, of Chinon (MaHaRShak)	Sefer Keritut Kontres Biur HaGet Super-Commentary (on Ibn Ezra's Pentateuch commentary)	Talmud (Commentary) Talmud (Commentary) Talmud (Halakha) Biblical (Super-Commentary)
Solomon ben Isaac	Responsa	Talmud (Responsa)
Israel of Krems	Haggahot Asheri	Talmud (Code of Law)
Menasseh ben Joseph ben Israel (MB'Y)	El Conciliador Humble Addresses Nishmat Hayim	Biblical (Explanation) Miscellaneous Miscellaneous
Israel ben Pethahiah Ashkenazi Isserlein	Terumat HaDeshen Pesakim u-Ketabim Super-Commentary on Rashi's Pentateuch	Talmud (Responsa) Talmud (Responsa) Biblical (Super-Commentary)
Moses ben Israel Isserles (Rema)	HaMapah Darkhei Moshe Torat Hattat (Issur we-Hetter) She'elot u-Teshubot	Talmud (Code of Law) Talmud (Code of Law) Talmud (Halakha) Talmud (Responsa)

J

Author	Work	Category Of Work
Jacob of Chinon	Tosafot (Sanhedrin, Gittin)	Talmud (Tosafot)
Menachem ben (Solomon ben Simson) Jacob	Synagogue service poems and Selichot	Other (Piyyutim)
Moses ben Jacob, of Coucy	Sefer Mitzvot Gadol (SeMaG)	Talmud (Code of Law)
Nissim ben Jacob (HaMafteach) (Rav Nissim Gaon)	HaMafteach Siddur Tefilah Megillat Setarim Ma'asiyyot HaHakhamim	Talmud (Commentary) Other (Liturgical) Talmud (Halakha) Miscellaneous
Yissachar Jacobson	Binah Mikrah Netiv Binah	Biblical (Explanation) Other (Liturgical)

Author	Work	Category Of Work
Mordechai ben Avraham Jaffe (Yoffe) (Ba'al HaLevushim)	Levush Malkhut Levush Orah Minor works	Talmud (Code of Law) Biblical (Super-Commentary) Various
Samuel ben Jacob Jam'a	Elef HaMagen (Agur) Novellae on Sanhedrin	Talmud (Code of Law) Talmud (Novellae)
Yonah ibn Janach (Merinos)	Sefer Hashorashim	Miscellaneous
Asher ben Jehiel (Rabbeinu Asher / Rosh)	Abstract of Talmudic law (see Piskei HaRosh) Orchot Chaim Mishnah commentaries, first and sixth Orders Untitled Tosafot	Talmud (Code of Law) Miscellaneous Talmud (Mishnah, Commentary) Talmud (Tosafot)
Jose bar Jose	Piyyutim	Other (Piyyutim)
Enoch Zundel ben Joseph	Commentary on Midrash Rabbah of Five Megillot and Pentateuch (Mibhar-Peninim) Olat HaChodesh Novellae on Haggadah of the Talmud	Biblical (Midrashic) Other (Liturgical) Talmud (Novellae)
Isaac ben Joseph of Corbeil	Ammude HaGolah / Sefer Mitzvot Katan (Semak)	Talmud (Code of Law)
Jehiel ben Joseph of Paris	Tosafot of many Tractates	Talmud (Tosafot)
Joshua Hoschel ben Joseph	Maginne Shelomoh She'elot u-Teshubot Pene Yehoshua	Talmud (Novellae) Talmud (Responsa)
Saadia ben Joseph, Gaon (Saadia Gaon)	Agron Emunot v'Deot Arabic translation of Bible Biblical exegesis Commentary on Sefer Yeziah Siddur Monographs of Responsa	Miscellaneous Other (Philosophy) Biblical (Miscellaneous) Biblical (Commentary) Miscellaneous Other (Liturgical) Talmud (Responsa)

Author	Work	Category Of Work
Samson ben Joseph, of Falaise	Tosafot – Shabbat, Erubin, Yebamot, Hulin	Talmud (Tosafot)
	Pesakim	Other (Ritual)
Daniel ben Judah	Yigdal Elohim Hai	Other (Piyyutim)
Gershom ben Judah (Rabbeinu Gershom)	Piyyutim for High Holydays	Other (Piyyutim)

K

Author	Work	Category Of Work
Israel Meir Kagan (HaKohen) (Chofetz Chaim)	Mishnah Berurah	Talmud (Code of Law / Glosses)
	Beiur Halacha	Talmud (Code of Law / Glosses)
	Sha'ar HaTziyyum	Talmud (Code of Law / Glosses)
	Ahavat Chesed	Miscellaneous
	Chafetz Chaim	Talmud (Halakha)
	Sh'mirat HaLashon	Miscellaneous
	Others	
Aaron Samuel ben Israel Kaidenover	Birkat HaZebah	Talmud (Commentary)
	Birkat Shemuel	Biblical (Miscellaneous)
	Emunate Shemuel	Talmud (Responsa)
	Tifferet Shemuel	Talmud (Novellae)
Zevi Hirsch Kaidenover	Kav Hayashar	Other (Ethics / Kabbalah)
Eleazar Kalir	Untitled for Festivals	Other (Piyyutim)
Zvi Hirsch Kalischer	Eben Bochan	Talmud (Code of Law)
	Sefer Moznyim la-Mishpat	Talmud (Code of Law)
	Glosses on Yoreh De'ah of Shulkhan Arukh	Talmud (Code of Law / Glosses)
	Sefer HaBerit	Biblical (Commentary)
	Sefer Yitziat Mitzrayim	Miscellaneous
	Sefer Emunah Yesharah	Other (Philosophy)
	Derishot Ziyyon	Miscellaneous
David ben Kalonymus, of Munzenberg	Untitled quoted elsewhere	Talmud (Responsa)
	Selichot	Other (Piyyutim)

Author	Work	Category Of Work
Eleazar ben Yehuda ben Kalonymus, of Worms (Rokeach)	HaRokeach	Talmud (Halakha / Ethics)
	Adderet Ha-Shem	Miscellaneous
	Sefer HaKapparot	Miscellaneous
	Sefer HaHayyim	Miscellaneous
	Sha'are HaSod HaYihud weha Emunah	Miscellaneous
	Various Kabbalistic works	Other (Kabbalah)
	Tosafot	Talmud (Tosafot)
	Piyyutim	Other (Piyyutim)
Elijah ben Kalonymus	Adderet Eliyahu	Biblical (Commentary)
Samuel ben Kalonymus (He-Hasid), of Speyer	Shir HaYihud	Other (Piyyutim)
	Tosafot for Tamid	Talmud (Tosafot)
Jacob Kamenecki (Yaakov Kamenetsky)	Emes leYaakov	Biblical, Talmud (Commentary)
	Iyunim BaMikra	Biblical (Commentary)
Abraham ben Abigdor Kara	Super-commentary to Rashi's Pentateuch	Biblical (Super-Commentary)
	Ana Elohe Abraham	Other (Piyyutim)
	Glosses to Arba'ah Turim	Talmud (Code of Law / Glosses)
Simeon Kara, of Frankfurt (HaDarshan)	Yalkut / Yalkut Shimoni	Biblical (Explanation / Commentary)
Karelitz, Abraham Isaiah (Chazon Ish)	Chazon Ish	Talmud (Code of Law)
Menachem Mendel Kasher	Torah Shelemah	Biblical (Miscellaneous) / Talmud (General)
	Divrei Menachem Responsa	Talmud (Responsa)
Jacob Joseph ben Tzvi HaKohen Katz, of Polonnoye	Toledot Ya'akov Yosef	Biblical (Commentary) / Other (Hassidic)
	Ben Porat Yosef	Biblical (Commentary) / Other (Hassidic)
	Tsafenat Pane'ah	Biblical (Commentary) / Other (Hassidic)

Author	Work	Category Of Work
Meir ben Isaac Katzenellenbogen (Maharam Padua)	She'elot u-Teshubot	Talmud (Responsa)
Simeon Kayyara	Halakot Gedolot	Talmud (Code of Law)
Samuel ben Naftali HaLevi Kelin	Mechatzit HaShekel	Talmud (Code of Law)
Joseph ben Isaac Kimchi	Sepher Zikkaron El Hasofer Sepher Haggulai	Biblical (Commentary) Biblical (Miscellaneous) Miscellaneous
Moses Kimchi	Mahalakh Shevile Hadda'ath	Miscellaneous
David Kimchi (RaDaK)	RaDaK Michlol Teshuvoth Lanotzrim El Hasofer	Biblical (Commentary) Miscellaneous Miscellaneous Biblical
Solomon ben Judah Aaron Kluger	Sefer HaHayyim Me Niddah Shenot Hayyim Sefer Setam Moda'a le-Bet Yisrael	Talmud (Code of Law, Commentary) Talmud (Novellae) Talmud (Responsa) Talmud (Responsa) Talmud (Responsa)
Abraham Isaac Kook (HaRaAYaH / HaRav)	Ayin Aiyah Igorot HaRaiyah Olat Raiyah	Talmud (Commentary) Miscellaneous Other (Liturgical)
Menachem Mendel ben Abraham Krochmal	Tzemach Tzedek	Talmud (Responsa)
Nachman Kohen Krochmal	Moreh Nebuke HaZeman	Other (Philosophy)

L

Author	Work	Category Of Work
Dunash HaLevi ben Labrat	Poetry – Drory Yikra Grammar Book	Other (Piyyutim) Miscellaneous
Yitzhak Hezekiah Lampronti	Pahad Yitzhak	Talmud (General)

Author	Work	Category Of Work
Landau Family		
Jacob ben Judah	Agur	Other (Ritual)
Israel Jonah	Me-on HaBerakhot	Talmud (Novellae)
Samuel Joseph	Mishkan Shiloh	Talmud (Novellae / Responsa)
Eleazar ben Israel		
Israel ben Ezekiel	Yad HaMelek	Talmud (Novellae)
Moses Israel	Hok Le-Yisrael	Talmud (Halakha)
Samuel ben Ezekiel	Marpe Lashon	Miscellaneous
	Shibat Ziyyon	Talmud (Responsa)
Ezekiel (Yechezkel) ben Judah Landau (Nodah B'Yehuda)	Nodah B'Yehuda	Talmud (Halakha / Responsa)
	Tziyyon Lenenfesh Hayyah	Talmud (Commentary)
	Dagul Merevavah	Talmud (Code of Law)
Yaakov Baruch ben Yehuda	Agur	Talmud (Halakha / Responsa)
Aaron ben Isaac Lapapa	Bnei Aharon	Talmud (Novellae / Responsa)
Boruch Ber Leibowitz	Birkas Shmuel	Miscellaneous
	Shiurei Reb Baruch Ber	Miscellaneous
Mordechai Leifer of Nadvorna	Gedulas Mordechai	Other (Hassidic)
Judah ben Isaac Messer Leon	Tosafot to most Talmudic tractates	Talmud (Tosafot)
	Responsa found in The Mordechai.	Talmud (Responsa)
Moses de Leon (Moshe ben Shem Tov)	Sefer HaRimonim	Other (Kabbalah / Ritual)
	HaNefesh HaHakhamah	Other (Kabbalah)
	Shekel HaKodesh	Other (Kabbalah)
	Mishkan HaEdut / Sefer HaSodot	Other (Kabbalah)
	Midrash de Rabban Shimon ben Yohai / Zohar	Other (Kabbalah)
Joseph ibn Lev	She'elot U'Teshubot R' Yosef ibn Lev	Talmud (Novellae / Responsa)

Author	Work	Category Of Work
Joshua Hoschel ben Elijah Zeeb Levin	Haggahot	Biblical (Midrashic)
	Ma'yene Yehoshua	Talmud (Commentary)
	Ziyyun Yehoshua	Talmud (General)
	Tosefot Sheni le-Ziyyon	Talmud (Mishnah Commentary)
	Dabar b'itti	Talmud (Halakha)
Shabbatai Carmuz Levita	Sefer HaYashar	Miscellaneous
Yerusham Levovitz	Daas Chochmah U'Mussar	Other (Ethics)
David Lida	Ir Miklat	Talmud (Halakha)
	Ir David	Talmud (Halakha)
	Sod Hashem VerSharvit HaZahav	Talmud (Halakha)
	Chalikei Avanim	Biblical (Super-Commentary)
Saul Lieberman	Al HaYerushalmi	Talmud (General)
	Tosefet Rishonim	Talmud (Commentary / Tosefet)
	Sifre Zuta	Biblical (Midrashic)
	Sheki'in	Miscellaneous
	Midreshei Teiman	Midrashic
Avraham Lieblein	Kesef Mezukak	Biblical (Super-Commentary)
Moses ben Isaac Judah Lima	Helkat Mehokek	Talmud (Code of Law)
Baruch Mordechai ben Jacob Lipschitz	Berit Ya'akob	Talmud (Responsa)
	Minhat Bikkurim	Talmud (Novellae)
	Untitled Novellae	Talmud (Novellae)
Hayyim ben Moses Lipschutz	Derek Hayyim	Other (Ritual)
Israel Lipschutz	Tiferet Israel	Mishnah (Commentary)
Moses ben Noah Isaac Lipschutz	Lehem Mishneh	Talmud (Mishnah, Commentary)
Noah ben Abraham Lipschutz (Noah Mindes)	Parpera'ot le-Hokmah	Other (Kabbalah)
	Nifla'ot Hadashot	Other (Kabbalah)

Author	Work	Category Of Work
Yosef (Yoselman) Loanz of Rosheim	Sefer HaMiknah	Other (Ethics / Other (Philosophy)
Samuel ben Nathan Loew	Machatsit HaShekel	Talmud (Super-Commentary)
Judah ben Bezalel Loew (Maharal / Maharal of Prague)	Gur Aryeh	Biblical (Super-Commentary)
	Gevurot Hashem	Other (Ritual)
	Divrei Negidim	Other (Ritual)
	Ner Mitzvah	Other (Ritual)
	Or Chadash	Other (Ritual)
	Chiddushei Aggadot	Talmud (Novellae)
	Derech Chaim	Talmud (Commentary)
	Kol Kitvei Maharal	Overall Collection
Menachem di Lonzano	Shtei Yadot	Miscellaneous
	Omer Man	Other (Kabbalah)
	Sefer Maasiyot	Talmud (General)
Jacob ben Jacob Moshe Lorberbaum, of Lisser (Ba'al HaNesivos / Lissa Rav)	Nesivos HaMishpat	Talmud (Code of Law)
	Derech Chaim	Talmud (Code of Law)
Meir ben Gedaliyah Lublin (Maharam)	Meir Einei Chachamim	Talmud (Novellae)
	Manhir Einei Chachamim	Talmud (Responsa)
Shlomo Ephraim Lunshitz (Kli Yakar)	Homolitic Works	Miscellaneous
	Ir Gibborim	
	Sifsei Daas	
	Orach LeChaim	
	Amudei Sheish	
	Kli Yakar	Biblical (Glosses)
Isaac Luria (Ashkenazi) (Ari, Arizal, He-Ari)	Untitled Sabbath Piyyutim	Other (Piyyutim)
Solomon Luria (Maharshal, Rashal)	Yam Shel Shlomo	Talmud (Commentary)
	Chochmat Shlomo	Talmud (Commentary) Commentary
	Yeri'ot Shlomo	Biblical (Super-Commentary)
	Amudei Shlomo	Talmud (Code of Law)
	Untitled	Talmud (Responsa)

Author	Work	Category Of Work
Moses Chaim Luzzatto (Ramchal)	Mesillat Yesharim Derekh Hashem Da'at Tevunoth Derekh Tevunoth	Other (Ethics / Kabbalah) Other (Philosophy) Other (Kabbalah) Talmud (General)

M

Author	Work	Category Of Work
Moses ben Maimon (Maimonides) (Rambam)	Commentary on the Mishnah (Perush Hamishnayot) Sefer HaMitzvot Mishneh Torah (Yad HaHazakha) Guide for the Perplexed (Moreh Nevuchim) Epistle to Yemen (Iggeret Teman) Scientific Works	Talmud (Mishnah, Commentary) Talmud (Halakha) Talmud (Code of Law) Other (Philosophy) Miscellaneous Miscellaneous
Hezekiah ben Manoah (Hizkuni / Chizkuni)	Hazzekuni	Biblical (Commentary) / Other (Kabbalah)
Abi Ezra Selig Margolis	Kessef Nivvar Hivvure Likkutim	Biblical (Commentary) Talmud (Novellae / Responsa)
Alexander Margolis	Teshubot HaRam	Talmud (Responsa)
Ephraim Zalman (Solomon) Margolis	Bet Hadash HaHadashot Bet Ephraim Yad Ephraim Sha'are Ephraim Shem Ephraim Mattei Ephraim Zera Ephraim	Talmud (Responsa) Talmud (Code of Law, Responsa) Talmud (Code of Law) Talmud (Halakha) Biblical (Commentary) Other (Ritual) Biblical (Midrashic)
Hayyim Mordechai Margolis	Sha'are Teshubah	Talmud (Code of Law)
Meir ben Zvi Hirsch Margolis	Meir Netivim Sod Yakin u-Voaz Derek HaTov veha-Yashar	Talmud (Novellae / Responsa) Other (Kabbalah) Talmud (Code of Law)
Abba Mari ben Moses ben Joseph Don Astruc of Lunel	Minhat Kenaot	Miscellaneous

Author	Work	Category Of Work
Yitzhak ben Abba Mari of Marseilles	Sefer HaIttur / Ittur Soferim	Talmud (Code of Law)
Jacob Tzvi Mecklenberg	Haketav (K'sav) V'ha-kabbalah	Biblical (Commentary)
Moses de Medina	Nefesh David	Biblical (Commentary) / Other (Kabbalah)
	Ruach David v'Nishmat David	Other (Kabbalah)
Samuel ben Moses de Medina (RashDaM)	Ben Shemuel Hiddushim Piske RashDaM	Miscellaneous Talmud (Novellae) Talmud (Responsa)
Shemaiah de Medina	Untitled Piyyutim	Other (Piyyutim)
Chaim Chizkiya Medini	S'Dei Chemed	Talmud (General / Halakha)
Isaac (Yitzhak) ben Meir (Rivam)	Untitled Tosafot	Talmud (Tosafot)
Jacob ben Meir (Tam) (Rabbeinu Tam)	Untitled Sefer haYashar Untitled Tosafot	Other (Piyyutim) Talmud (Novellae / Responsa) Talmud (Tosafot)
Moses ben Meir of Ferrara	Untitled – Appear in Haggahot Maimuniyyot	Tosafot
Samuel ben Meir (Rashbam)	Untitled Untitled Tosafot	Biblical (Commentary) Talmud (Tosafot)
Menachem ben Solomon Meiri (HaMeiri)	Beit HaBechirah Untitled Chibbur HaTeshuvah Kiryat Sefer	Talmud (Mishnah Commentary) Talmud (Novellae) Miscellaneous Biblical (Miscellaneous)
Isser Zalman Meltzer (Even HaEzel)	Even HaEzel	Talmud (Code of Law)
Menachem Mendel of Kotzk (Kotzker Rebbe)	Ohel Torah Emet Ve'emunah Amod HaEmet	Other (Hassidic) Other (Hassidic) Other (Hassidic)
Moses Mendelssohn	Biur Jerusalem	Biblical (Commentary) Other (Philosophy)

Author	Work	Category Of Work
Asher ben Meshullam	Hilcoth Yom-Tov Sefer HaMatanah	Talmud (Halakha) Talmud (Halakha)
Yerucham ben Meshullam	Meisharim Adam V'Chava	Talmud (Code of Law) Talmud (Code of Law)
Joshua Boaz Mevorakh / Joshua Boaz ben Simon Baruch (Shiltei Gibborim)	Masoret HaShas / Massoret HaTalmud Ein Mishpat Torah Ohr Neir Mitzvah Shiltei Gibborim / Sefer Makloket Siddur Mordechai Ve-Simanav / Siddur Dine Mordechai	Talmud (General) Talmud (Code of Law) Talmud (General) / Biblical (Miscellaneous) Talmud (Halakha) Talmud (Code of Law) Talmud (Code of Law) Talmud (Halakha)
Meir Leibush ben Jehiel Michel (Malbim)	HaTorah vehaMitzvah Untitled commentary Megillat Esther Mikra'ei Kodesh Artzoth HaChaim Artzoth HaShalom	Biblical (Commentary) Biblical (Commentary) Talmud (Novellae) Miscellaneous Miscellaneous
Joseph ben Meir HaLevi ibn Migash (Ri Migash)	She'elot uTeshuvot Ri Migash Untitled	Talmud (Responsa) Talmud (Novellae)
Abraham ben Judah HaLevi Minz	Seder Gittin ve-Halizah	Miscellaneous
Judah ben Eliezer HaLevi Minz (Mahari Minz)	Untitled	Talmud (Responsa)
Elijah Mizrachi (Re'em)	Sefer HaMizrachi Tosefte Semag	Biblical (Super-Commentary) Talmud (Novellae)
Samuel ben Moses di Modena (Maharshdam)	Untitled	Talmud (Responsa)
Jacob ben Moses Levi Moelin (Maharil)	Sefer HaMaharil / Minhagei Maharil / Minhagim	Talmud (Responsa)

Author	Work	Category Of Work
Isaac ben Mordechai of Regensburg (RiBaM)	Untitled Tosafot	Talmud (Tosafot)
Moses of Evreux	Tosafot of Evreux	Talmud (Tosafot)
Moshe Mos of Premysl	Matteh Moshe	Talmud (Halakha)
	Ho'il Moshe	
	Be'er Moshe	Biblical (Super-Commentary), Miscellaneous, Talmud (Novellae)
	Taryag Mitzvos	Talmud (Halakha)
Isaac ben Moses of Vienna (Or Zarua, Riaz)	Or Zarua	Talmud (Code of Law)
Joseph ben Moses	Leket Yosher	Talmud (Responsa)
Meshullam ben Moses	Multiple Piyyutim	Other (Piyyutim)
Meshullam ben Moses	Sefer HaHashalamah	Talmud (Code of Law)

N

Author	Work	Category Of Work
Nachman of Breslov	Likutei Moharan	Other (Hassidic)
	Sefer HaMiddot	Other (Hassidic)
	Tikkun HaKlali	Other (Hassidic)
	Sippurei Ma'asiyyot	Other (Hassidic)
Samuel ibn Naghrela (Samuel HaNagid)	Mavo HaTalmud	Talmud (General)
	Hilchata Gevurta	Talmud (Halakha)
	Ben Tehillim	Other (Piyyutim)
	Ben Koheleth	Other (Philosophy)
	Ben Mishlei	Miscellaneous
Moses ben Nahman (Nahmanides) (Ramban)	Untitled Torah Commentary	Biblical (Commentary)
	Untitled Talmudic Glosses	Talmud (Glosses)
	Mihamot Hashem	Talmud (Halakha)
	Minor Halakhic works	Talmud (Halakha)
	Torat Hashem Temima	Biblical (Miscellaneous)
Yehudai ben Nahman (Yehudai Gaon)	Halakhot Pesukot	Talmud (Halakha)
	Untitled	Talmud (Responsa)

Author	Work	Category Of Work
Abraham ben Nathan	HaMinhag (Minhag Olam)	Talmud (Responsa / Halakha)
Eliezer ben Nathan (Raavan)	Even HaEzer Untitled Piyyutim	Talmud (Halakha) Other (Piyyutim)
Judah ben Nathan (Riban)	Tosafot on Makkot, Nazir, Erubin, Shabbat, Yebamot	Talmud (Tosafot)
Joseph Saul Nathanson	Sho'el u-Meshiv	Talmud (Responsa)
Yitzhak Saggi Nehor (Isaac the Blind)	Bahir	Other (Kabbalah)
Meir ben Isaac Nehorai	Akdamut	Other (Piyyutim)

O

Author	Work	Category Of Work
Onkelos	Targum Onkelos	Biblical (Explanation)
Jacob Meshullam ben Mordechai Ze'ev Ornstein	Yeshuot Ya'acob Yeshuot Ya'acob	Talmud (Code of Law) Biblical (Commentary)

P

Author	Work	Category Of Work
Bahya ben Joseph ibn Paquda	Chovot HaLevavot	Other (Ethics)
Moshe Pellier of Kobrin	Imros Taharos	Other (Hassidic)
Joseph ibn Plat	Tikkun Soferim Untitled Treatises	Other (Ritual) Talmud (Halakha)
Meir Popperos	Etz Chaim Meorei Or Or Tzaddikim Or Rav	Other (Kabbalah) Other (Kabbalah) Other (Kabbalah) Other (Kabbalah)
Avraham Aharon Price	Mishnat Avraham Imrei Avraham Sefer Hasidim Mitzvot Gadol	Biblical (Miscellaneous) Biblical (Miscellaneous) Other (Ethics) Talmud (Code of Law)

Author	Work	Category Of Work
Q		
Yosef Quafih	Sepharid Rishonim Translations	Miscellaneous
	Siach Yerushalayim	Other (Ritual)
R		
Chaim Shalom Tuvia Rabinowitz (Reb Chaim Telzer)	Shiurei Rebbi Chaim MiTelz	Talmud (General)
Eliyahu David Rabinowitz-Teomim (Aderet)	Various Titles	Talmud (Novellae)
	Various Titles	Talmud (Glosses)
Solomon Judah Loeb Rapoport	Biographies	Miscellaneous
	Encyclopedia	Miscellaneous
Isaac Samuel Reggio (Yashar)	Sefer Torat Elohim	Biblical (Miscellaneous)
	HaTorah weha-Peusufiah	Biblical (Commentary)
	Iggerot Yashar	Miscellaneous
Jacob ben Joseph Reischer (Backofen)	Minhat Ya'akov	Talmud (Code of Law)
	Shevut Ya'akov	Talmud (Responsa)
Jacob ben Reuben	Sefer HaOsher	Biblical (Commentary)
Jacob ben Reuben	Sefer Milhamot Adonai	Miscellaneous
Nissim ben Reuven, of Gerona (RaN)	Commentary on Halacoth	Talmud (Code of Law)
	Untitled Talmud Commentary	Talmud (Commentary)
	Untitled Biblical Commentary	Biblical (Commentary)
	Untitled Responsa	Talmud (Responsa)
	Collection of Sermons	Miscellaneous
	Philosophy Work	Other (Philosophy)
Moses ben Naftali Hertz Rivkes	Be'er HaGolah	Talmud (General / Commentaries / Code of Law / Responsa)
Judah ben Samuel Rosanes	Parashat Derakim	Talmud (Halakha) / Biblical (Midrashic)
	Mishneh la-Melek	Talmud (Code of Law / Glosses)

Author	Work	Category Of Work
Yosef Rosen (Rogatchover Gaon, Tzafnach Paneach)	Commentary to Guide for the Perplexed Five Volume Set Responsa Tzafnach Paneach	Other (Philosophy) Talmud (Responsa) Torah and Talmud (Novellae), Talmud (Responsa)
Yaakov Yitzhak Ruderman	Avodas Levi Sichos Levi Mas'as Levi	Miscellaneous Biblical (Miscellaneous) / Other (Ethical) Talmud (Halakha)

S

Author	Work	Category Of Work
Avraham ben Yaakov Saba	Tror Hamor Eshkol Hakofer	Biblical (Commentary) Biblical (Commentary)
Meir ben Solomon Abi Sahula	Commentary on Sefer Yezirah	Other (Kabbalah)
Israel Lipkin Salanter	Imrei Binah Iggeret HaMussar Ohr Yisrael Even Yisrael Etz Peri	Talmud (Halakha) / Other (Ethics) Other (Ethics) Miscellaneous Other (Ethics) Other (Ethics)
Aaron ben Samuel	Bet Aharon Commentary on Perek Shirah	Biblical (Miscellaneous) Other (Ethics / Philosophy)
Eliezer ben Samuel of Metz	Sefer Yereim	Talmud (Halakha)
Isaac ben Samuel of Dampierre (Ri)	Tosefot Yeshanim Untitled Biblical Interpretation	Talmud (Tosafot) Biblical (Commentary)
Isaac ben Samuel (Hasefardi)	Untitled	Biblical Related
Judah ben Samuel of Regensburg (He-Hasid)	Sefer Hasidim Sefer Hakavod ?Piyyutim	Other (Ethical) / Miscellaneous Miscellaneous

Author	Work	Category Of Work
Meir ben Samuel (RAM)	Halakhic Decisions (untitled)	Talmud (Halakha)
	Commentary on Menachot	Talmud (Commentary)
	Altered Kol Nidre prayer	Other (Liturgy / Piyyutim)
Simah ben Samuel of Speyer	Untitled	Talmud (Tosafot / Novellae)
	Seder Olam	Talmud (Commentary)
	Vitry Mahzor	Talmud (Halakha / Responsa)
	Contre HaPiyyutim	Other (Piyyutim)
Simhah ben Samuel of Vitry	Vitry Mahzor	Talmud (Halakha, Responsa)
	Contre Piyyutim	Piyyutim
Samuel ben Isaac Sardi (HaSardi, HaSefaradi)	Sefer HaTerumot	Talmud (Novellae)
Israel Sarug	Kabbalah	Other (Kabbalah)
	Contres Ne'im Zemirot Yisrael	Other (Kabbalah)
Menahem ben Jacob ibn Saruq	Mahberet / Sefer HaPitronot	Miscellaneous
Jacob ben Aaron Sasportas	Toledot Yaacob	Biblical (Miscellaneous) / Talmud (General)
	Ohel Yaacob	Talmud (Responsa)
	Zizat Noble Zebi	Miscellaneous
Moses Schick (Maharam Schick)	Maharam Schick	Talmud (Responsa)
	Derashot	Talmud (Responsa)
Isaac Schmelkes	Bet Yitzhak	Talmud (Responsa)
Levi Yitzhak Schneerson	Likkutei Levi Yitzhak	Other (Kabbalah)
Menachem Mendel Schneerson (Tzemach Tzedek)	Shut Tzemach Tzedek	Talmud (Halakha)
	Derech Mitzvotecha	Other (Kabbalah)
	Sefer Chakira: Derech Emunah	Other (Philosophy)
	Ohr HaTorah	Other (Hassidic)
Menachem Mendel Schneerson (The Lubavitcher Rebbe)	Likkutei Sichot	Biblical (Explanation)
	Igrot Kodesh	Miscellaneous
	Sefer HaSichot	Miscellaneous
	Sefer HaMa'amarim Melukot	Other (Hassidic)

Author	Work	Category Of Work
Shmuel Schneerson (The Rebbe Maharash)	Lukkutei Torat Shmuel	Biblical (Miscellaneous) / Other (Ethics)
Sholom Dovber Schneerson (Rebbe Rashab)	Sefer HaMa'amarim Kuntres Hatefilah Kuntres HaAvodah Issa B'Midrash Tehillim	Other (Hassidic) Other (Hassidic) Other (Hassidic) Other (Hassidic)
Yosef Yitzhak Schneerson (Rebbe Rayatz)	Sefer Hama'amarim	Other (Hassidic)
Dovber Schneuri (Mitteler Rebbe)	Sha'ar HaYichud Sha'arei Orah Maamrei Admur HaEmtzei	Other (Kabbalah) Other (Ritual) Other (Hassidic) / Biblical (Miscellaneous)
Samuel Schotten (Mharsheishoch)	Koss Hayeshu'ot Shut Mharsheishoch	Talmud (Commentary) Responsa
Sholom Mordechai Schwadron (Maharsham)	Techeiles Mordechai Shailos Uteshuvot Marsham Daas Torah	Biblical (Commentary) Talmud (Halakha / Responsa) Talmud (Halakha / Responsa)
David ben Samuel HaLevi Segal (Taz)	Turei Zahav Dibre David	Code of Law Related Biblical (Super-Commentary)
Obadiah ben Jacob Sforno	Untitled Tanakh Commentaries Or Ammim	Biblical (Commentary) Other (Philosophy)
Kalonymus ben Shabbethai	Talmud and Tanakh Commentaries	Talmud (Commentary) / Biblical (Commentary)
Jacob ben Nissim ibn Shahin (Rabbeinu Nissim, HaMafteach)	HaMafteach (Sefer Mafteach Manu'ele HaTalmud) Megillat Setarim Comforting Tales Commentary to the Sefer Yezirah	Talmud (Commentary) Talmud (Halakha) / Midrash Talmud (Mishnah) / Midrash Other (Philosophy)
Shalom Shakna	Pesachim be-Inyan Kiddushin	Other (Kabbalah)

Author	Work	Category Of Work
Kalonymus Kalman Shapira (Szapira)	Chovas haTalmidim Esh Kodesh	Miscellaneous Miscellaneous
Eliyahu ben Binyamin Wolf Shapiro	Eliyahu Rabba	Talmud (Code of Law)
Yehuda Meir Shapiro	Ohr HaMeir Imrei Das Vortelach	Talmud (Responsa) Biblical (Explanation) Talmud (Responsa)
Shalom Sharabi (Rashash)	Sidur Hakavanot Emet va-Shalom Rehovot Nahar Nahar Shalom Siddur HaRashash Minhagei HaRashash	Other (Kabbalah / Liturgical) Other (Kabbalah) Other (Kabbalah) Other (Kabbalah) Other (Liturgical) Miscellaneous
Shem Tov ibn Shem Tov	Sefer HaEmunot Commentary on the Passover Haggadah	Other (Kabbalah) Other (Ritual)
Hai ben Sherira, Gaon	Untitled Untitled Untitled Untitled	Talmud (Responsa) Talmud (Code of Law) Talmud (Mishnah, Commentary) Talmud (Halakha)
Amram ben Sheshna Gaon	Siddur Rab Amram / Seder Rav Amram Untitled Responsa and halakha	Talmud (Responsa) / Other (Liturgical) Talmud (Responsa / Halakha)
Shimon Shkop	Has'arei Yosher Ma'arekhet haKinyanim Novellae to several Treatises	Talmud (Halakha) Miscellaneous Talmud (Novellae)
Joseph ben Isaac Bekhor Shor	Untitled Tosafot Untitled Untitled Piyyutim	Talmud (Tosafot) Biblical (Commentary) Other (Piyyutim)
Meir Simcha of Dvinsk	Ohr Somayach Meshech Chochma	Talmud (Novellae) Biblical (Novellae)

Author	Work	Category Of Work
Yoel Sirkis (Bach)	Bayit Chadash Hagahot Bach Meshiv Nefesh Teshuvos HaBach	Talmud (Code of Law) Talmud (Glosses) Biblical (Commentary) Talmud (Responsa)
Benjamin Aaron ben Abraham Slonik	Masat Binyamin	Talmud (Responsa / Novellae / (Code of Law)
Moses Sofer (Chatam Sofer)	Chatam Sofer	Biblical (Explanation)
Yaakov Chaim Sofer (Kaf HaChaim)	Kaf HaChaim Kol Yaakov Yagel Yaakov Yismach Yisrael	Talmud (Code of Law) Talmud (Halakha) Miscellaneous Novellae
Menahem ben Solomon	Sekel Kob	Biblical (Midrashic)
Samuel ben Solomon of Falaise	Talmud (Tosafot)	Talmud (Tosafot)
Chaim Soloveitchik (The Brisker Reb)	Chiddushei Rabbeinu Chaim Chiddushei HaGRaCh Al Shas	Talmud (Code of Law) Talmud (Commentary)
Joseph Ber Soloveitchik (HaRav)	The Lonely Man of Faith Halakhic Man Fate and Destiny Out of the Whirlwind Days of Deliverance	Other (Philosophy) Other (Philosophy) Other (Philosophy) Other (Philosophy) Other (Philosophy)
Yosef Dov Soloveitchik (Beis HaLevi)	Beis HaLevi	Biblical (Commentary) / Talmud (Code of Law)
Abdalla Somekh	Zivhei Tzedek Untitled Responsa	Talmud (Halakha) Talmud (Code of Law / Responsa)
Abraham Samuel Benjamin Sofer (Ksav Sofer)	Ksav Sofer Collection of Responsa	Biblical (Commentary) / Talmud (Responsa)
Yitzhak Elchanan Spektor	Be'er Yitzhak Ein Yitzhak Nachal Yitzhak	Talmud (Responsa) Talmud (Responsa) Talmud (Code of Law)

Author	Work	Category Of Work
Chaim Elazar Spira	Minchas Elazar	Other (Hassidic)
Aryeh Leib Steinhardt	Kur Zahav	Biblical (Super-Commentary)
Menahem Mendel ben Simeon Steinhardt	Divrei Menahem	Talmud (Responsa)
Joseph ben Menachem Steinhart	Zikron Yosef	Talmud (Code of Law / Responsa)
	Mashbir Bar	Bible (Commentary)
	Ko'ah Shor	Talmud (Novellae)
Samuel ben Joseph Strashun (Rashash)	Haggahot v'Chiddushei HaRashash	Talmud (General)
	Annotations to Midrashot Rabbot	Biblical (Midrashic)
Elimelech Szapira	Imrei Elimelech	Other (Hassidic)
	Divrei Elimelech	Other (Hassidic)

T

Author	Work	Category Of Work
Joseph ben Solomon Taitezak	Many works	Other (Kabbalah)
Aaron Moses ben Jacob Taubes	To'afot Re'em	Talmud (Code of Law / Responsa)
	Karne Re'em	Talmud (Novellae)
Eliyahu David Rabinowitz-Teomim (Aderet)	Untitled books of Glosses	Talmud (Glosses)
	Untitled Novellae	Talmud (Novellae)
Moses ibn Tibbon	Commentary on the Pentateuch	Biblical (Commentary)
	Sefer Pe'ah	Talmud (Commentary) / Biblical (Midrashic)
	Translated Maimonides' Sefer HaMitzvot	Talmud (Halakha)
	Translated Moreh Nevuchim	Other (Philosophy)
Samuel ben Judah ibn Tibbon	Translated Maimonides' Moreh Nevuchim	Philosophy
Vidal di Tolosa	Maggid Mishneh	Talmud (Code of Law)
Mordechai Gimpel Yaffe Torizer	Techeiles Mordechai	Biblical (Super-Commentary)

Author	Work	Category Of Work
Joseph Colon ben Solomon Trabotto (Maharik)	The Responsa of Maharik	Talmud (Responsa)
Isaiah ben Mali di Trani (RI'D)	Tosefot RI'D	Talmud (Tosafot)
Abraham ben Solomon Treves (Tarfati)	Birkat Abraham	Other (Ritual)
Yechiel Michel Tukachinsky	Gesher HaChaim Bein HaSemashos	Miscellaneous Miscellaneous
Isadore (Yitzhak) Twersky	An Introduction to the Code of Maimonides A Maimonides Reader	Talmud (Code of Law) Talmud (Code of Law)
Menachem Nachum Twersky	Me'or Einayim	Other (Hassidic)
Isaac Tyrnau	Sefer Minhagim	Talmud (Halakha)
Yom Tov ben Moshe Tzahalon (Maharitz)	Lekach Tov Untitled Magen Avot	Biblical (Commentary) Talmud (Responsa) Biblical (Midrashic)

U

Author	Work	Category Of Work
Samuel de Uzeda	Midrash Shmuel Iggeret Shmuel	Talmud (Commentary) Biblical (Commentary)
Ben-Zion Meir Hai Uziel	Mishpetei Ouziel	Talmud (Responsa)
Jonathan ben Uzziel	Targum Yonatan	Biblical (Explanation)

V

Author	Work	Category Of Work
Israel Veltz	Chok le-Ysra'el	Ritual
Eliyahu de Vidas	Reshit Chochma	Other (Kabbalah)
Hayyim ben Joseph Vital	Etz Hayyim	Other (Kabbalah)
Chaim ben Itzchok Volozhin (Reb Chaim)	Nefesh HaChaim Ruach Chaim	Other (Kabbalah) Talmud (Commentary)

Author	Work	Category Of Work

W

Aaron Walden	Shem HaGedolim heHadash	Miscellaneous
	Mikdash Melek	Biblical (Commentary)
Aaron Walkin	Zekan Aharon	Talmud (Responsa)
Abraham ben Asher Wallerstein	Ma'amar Abraham	Biblical (Miscellaneous)
	Zera Abraham	Other (Ethics)
	Mahazeh Abraham	Other (Ritual)
Jacob ben Judah Weil (Mahariv)	She'elot u'Teshubot	Responsa
	She'elot u'Bedikot	Talmud (Halakha)
Jedidiah Weil	Haggadah Commentary	Other (Ritual)
	She'elot u-Teshubot	Talmud (Responsa)
	Untitled Novellae	Talmud (Novellae)
Nethaneel ben Naftali Tzvi Weil	Korban Netanel	Talmud (Halakha)
	Netib Hayyim	Talmud (Code of Law)
	Torat Netan'el	Talmud (Responsa)
Yechiel Yaakov Weinberg	Seridei Eish	Talmud (Halakha)
	Mechkarim beTalmud	Talmud (General)
Isaac Hirsch Weiss	Vienna Edition of Talmud	Talmud
	Orah la-Zaddik	Other (Ritual)
	Sifre Edition (Masoret HaTalmud)	Talmud (Halakha)
	Mishpat Leshon HaMishnah	Mishnah
	Dor Dor we-Dorshaw	Talmud (Halakha)
Yitzhak Yaakov Weiss	Minchat Yaakov	Talmud (Responsa)
Yaakov David Wilovsky	Chiddushei Ridvaz	Talmud (Commentary)
	Tosafot haRid	Talmud (Commentary)
	Migdal David	Talmud (Novellae)
	Teshuvos Ridvaz	Talmud (Responsa)
	Beis Ridvaz	Talmud (Code of Law)

Y

Eleazar ben Yehuda of Worms	Rokeach	Talmud (Code of Law) / Other (Ethics)

Author	Work	Category Of Work
Gershon ben Yehuda (Me'Or HaGolah)	Peirush Rabbeinu Gershon	Talmud (Commentary)
Baruch ben Yitzhak of Worms	Sefer HaTerumah	Talmud (Code of Law)
Shlomo Yitzhaki (Rashi)	Untitled	Biblical (Commentary)
	Untitled	Talmud (Commentary)
	Selichot	Other (Piyyutim)
	Siddur Rashi	Talmud (Responsa)
	Sefer HaPardes	Talmud (Responsa)
	Sefer HaOrah	Talmud (Responsa)
Shimon bar Yohai (Rashbi)	Zohar	Other (Kabbalah)
Ovadia Yosef	Yabia Omer	Talmud (Responsa)
	Yechavei Da'ath	Talmud (Responsa)
	Anaf Etz Avot	Talmud (Commentary)
	Maor Israel	Talmud (Commentary)
	Chazan Ovadia	Talmud (Halakha)
Yitzhak Yosef	Yalkut Yosef	Talmud (Halakha)

Z

Author	Work	Category Of Work
Elijah ben Solomon Zalman (Vilna Gaon, Gra)	Biurei HaGra	Talmud (Glosses / Code of Law)
	Shenoth Eliyahu	Talmud (Mishnah Commentary)
	Adereth Eliyahu	Biblical (Commentary)
Menahem ben Aaron ibn Zerah	Zedal la-Derek	Talmud (Code of Law)
Zerachiah HaYavani (The Greek) (Ra'Za'H)	Sefer HaYashar	Other (Ethics)
Hillel ben Naphtali Zevi	Bet Hillel	Talmud (Code of Law / Novellae)
David ben Solomon ibn Abi Zimra (Radbaz)	Collection of Responsa	Talmud (Responsa)
	Yekar Tiferet	Talmud (Code of Law)
Simcha Zissel Ziv (Alter of Kelm)	Hokmah U-Mussar	Miscellaneous

Categorical Classification Of Works Listed By Author In Alphabetical Order

The purpose of this listing is to group all the authors who wrote work/s in a particular category of the classification. The title of the work is also listed. This allows the reader to have available the scope of literature in a particular field.

Structure

Category	Sub-Category	Page
A. Biblical		309
	1. Explanations	309
	2. Glosses	309
	3. Midrashic	309
	4. Commentaries	311
	5. Super-Commentaries	314
	6. Miscellaneous	314
B. Talmud		316
	1. Mishnah	316
	Mishnah Commentary	316
	2. Talmudic Specific Aspects	317
	General	317
	Glosses	318
	3. Talmud Commentaries	319
	Tosefot	321
	Super-Commentaries	323
C. Codes Of Law		323
	1. Codes and Commentaries	323
	2. Halakha Related	328
D. Responsa		332
E. Biblical And Talmudic Novellae		338
F. Other Traditional Scholarly Works		341
	1. Ethics	341
	2. Hassidic	342
	3. Kabbalah	343
	4. Liturgical	346
	5. Philosophy	347
	6. Piyyutim / Poetry	349
	7. Ritual	351
G. Miscellaneous		352

Category	Author	Work/s
A. Biblical		
1. Explanations		
	Avraham Mordechai Alter	Imrei Emes
	Pinchas Menachem Alter	Pnei Menachem
	Yehuda Aryeh Leib Alter (Sfas Emes)	Sefer Emes al HaTorah
	Yisrael Alter	Beis Yisrael
	Yitzhak Meir Alter	Chiddushei Harim
	Isaac ben Moses Arama (Ba'al Akedah)	Sefer HaAkedah Other works
	Haim Yosef David Azulai (Hida)	Untitled
	Shneur Zalman Baruch (Borukovich), of Liadi (Alter Rebbe, GRaZ)	Likutei Torah
	Abraham ben Meir ibn Ezra (Abenezra)	Yesod Morah
	Achai Gaon	Sheilot d'Rav Gaon / Sheiltos
	Menasseh ben Joseph ben Israel (MB'Y)	El Conciliador
	Yissachar Jacobson	Binah Mikrah
	Simeon Kara, of Frankfurt (HaDarshan)	Yalkut / Yalkut Shimoni
	Onkelos	Targum Onkelos
	Menachem Mendel Schneerson (The Lubavitcher Rebbe)	Likkutei Sichot
	Moses Sofer (Chatam Sofer)	Chatam Sofer
	Jonathan ben Uzziel	Targum Yonatan
2. Glosses		
	Shlomo Ephraim Lunshitz	Kli Yakar
3. Midrashic		
	Aaron of Pesaro	Toledot Aharon

Category	Author	Work/s
	Samson ben Abraham, of Sens	Sifra Commentary
	Gershon Ashkenazi	Tifferet HaGershuni
	Solomon Buber	Pesikhta de-Rab Kahana
	Aharon ibn Chaim	Korbath Aharon Midos Aharon
	Hillel ben Eliakim	Sifra and Sifre Commentaries
	Tobiah ben Eliezer	Lekah Tob / Pesikta Zutarta
	Louis Ginzberg	Legends of the Jews
	Abraham Abele ben Chaim HaLevi Gombiner (Magen Avraham)	Zayit Ra'anan
	Moses HaDarshan	Yesod
	Yitzhak Hutner	Kovet Ha'aros
	Shemariah ben Elijah Ikriti, of Negropont	Elef HaMagen
	Enoch Zundel ben Joseph	Commentary on Midrash Rabbah of Five Megillot Mibhar Mi-Peninim
	Joshua Hoschel ben Elijah Zeeb Levin	Haggahot on Midrash Rabbah
	Menachem Mendel Kasher	Torah Shelemah
	Saul Lieberman	Midreshei Teiman
	Ephraim Zalman Margolis	Zera Ephraim
	Judah ben Samuel Rosanes	Parashat Derakim
	Jacob ben Nissim ibn Shahin (Rabbeinu Nissim, HaMafteach)	Megillat Setarim (Comforting Tales)
	Menahem ben Solomon	Sekel Kob
	Samuel ben Joseph Strashun (Rashash)	Annotations to Midrashot Rabbot
	Moses ibn Tibbon	Sefer Pe'ah

Category	Author	Work/s
	Yom Tov ben Moshe Tzalon (Maharitz)	Magen Avot
4. Commentaries		
	Isaiah ben Judah Abravanel	On Prophets On the Torah
	Isaac ben Abraham, of Dampierre (RIBA)	Untitled
	Moses ben Baruch Almosnino	Yede Oshe
	Naphtali (Hirsch) ben Asher Altschul	Ayyalah SheluHah
	David ben Aryeh Loeb Altshuler (Altshul)	Metsudot (David and Zion)
	Isaac ben Moses Arama (Ba'al Akedah)	Yad Absholom
	Bahaya (Bachya) ben Asher (Rabbeinu Asher)	Midrash Rabbeinu Bachya
	Hayyim ibn Attar (Ohr HaChaim HaKadosh)	Ohr HaChaim
	Abraham Azulai	Baalei Bris Avraham
	Shabbethai ben Joseph Bass	Sifsei Chachamim
	Naftali Tzvi Yehuda Berlin	HaEmek Davar Davar HaEmek
	Joseph Chayon	Untitled on Psalms
	Chananel ben Chushiel (Rabbeinu Chananel)	Untitled on the Torah
	Abigdor Cohen, of Vienna	Untitled on the Pentateuch and Megillot
	Yaakov Culi	Me'am Loez
	Samuel Danzig	Nhamot Ziyyon
	Yehuda Meir Dvir	To Nahmanides' Torat Hashem Temima
	David Solomon Eibenschutz	Ne'Arba Nahal

Category	Author	Work/s
	Meir ben Iszak Eisenstadt (Meir Ash) (Maharam Ash / Panim Me'irot)	Kotnot Or
	Abba Mari ben Elgidor	Untitled on Job
	Baruch HaLevi Epstein	Torah Temimah
	Abraham ben Meir ibn Ezra (Abenezra)	Sefer HaYeshar
	Achai Gaon	Sheilot d'Rav Achai / Sheiltos
	Abraham Gediliyah	Bris Avraham
	Judah ben Gershom (Rabbeinu Gershom)	Untitled – written by his disciples
	Levi ben Gershom (Gersonides, Ralbag)	Perush al Sefer HaTorah Perush al Sefer Iyob
	Saadia ben Joseph Gaon	Arabic Translation of Bible
	Zvi Hirsch Kalischer	Sefer HaBrit
	Elijah ben Kalonymus	Aderet Eliyahu
	Jacob Kamenecki (Yaakov Kamenetsky)	Emes leYaakov Iyunim BaMikra
	Simeon Kara, of Frankfurt (HaDarshan)	Yalkut / Yalkut Shimoni
	Jacob Joseph ben Tzvi HaKohen Katz, of Polonnoye	Toledot Ya'akov Yosef Ben Porat Yosef Tsafenat Pane'ah
	David Kimchi (RaDaK)	RaDaK
	Joseph ben Isaac Kimchi	Untitled on the Pentateuch
	Hezekiah ben Manoah (Hizkuni / Chizkuni)	Hazzekuni
	Abi Ezra Zelig Margolis	Kesef Nivvar
	Ephraim Zalman Margolis	Shem Ephraim
	Jacob Tzvi Mecklenburg	HaKetav V'ha-kabbalah
	Moses Mendelssohn	Biur
	Moses de Medina	Nefesh David

Category	Author	Work/s
	Meir ben Leibush Jehiel Michel	Haftorah vehaMitzvah Mikra'ei Kodesh
	Moses ben Nahman (Nahmanides) (Ramban)	Torah Commentary
	Jacob Meshullam ben Mordechai Ze'ev Ornstein	Yeshuot Ya'acob
	Isaac Samuel Reggio (Yashar)	HaTorah weha-Pesufiah
	Jacob ben Reuben	Sefer HaOsher
	Nissim ben Reuven	Untitled Biblical Commentary
	Avraham ben Yaakov Saba	Tror Hamor Eshkol Hakofer
	Isaac ben Samuel (Hasefardi)	Untitled Biblical Commentary
	Sholom Mordechai Schwadron (Maharsham)	Techeiles Mordechai
	Obadiah ben Jacob Sforno	Tanakh Commentaries
	Kalonymus ben Shabbethai	Tanakh Commentaries
	Joseph ben Isaac Bekhor Shor	Bible Commentary
	Yoel Sirkis (Bach)	Meshiv Nefesh
	Abraham Samuel Benjamin (Sofer Ksav Sofer)	Ksav Sofer
	Yosef Dov Soloveitchik (Beis HaLevi)	Beis HaLevi
	Joseph ben Menachem Steinhart	Mashbir Bar
	Moses ibn Tibbon	Pentateuch Commentary
	Yom Tov ben Moshe Tzahalon (Maharitz)	Lekach Tov
	Samuel de Uzeda	Iggeret Shmuel
	Aaron Walden	Mikdash Melek
	Shlomo Yitzhaki (Rashi)	Tanakh Commentaries
	Elijah ben Solomon Zalman (Vilna Gaon, Gra)	Adereth Eliyahu

Category	Author	Work/s
5. Super-Commentaries		
	Isaac Aboab	On Rashi's Pentateuch Commentary On Nahmanides' Pentateuch Commentary
	Obadiah ben Abraham, of Bertinoro	Rabbotenu Ba'ale HaTosafot
	Shabbethai ben Joseph Bass	Sifsei Chachamim
	Yissachar ben Ellenburg	Tzeidah LaDerech
	Shem Tov ben Abraham ibn Gaon	Keter Shem Tov
	Samson ben Isaac, of Chinon (MaHaRShak)	On Ibn Ezra's Biblical Commentary
	Israel ben Pethahiah Ashkenazi Isserlein	On Rashi's Pentateuch Commentary
	Mordechai ben Avraham Jaffe (Yoffe) (Ba'al HaLevushim)	Levush Orah
	Abraham ben Abigdor Kara	On Rashi's Pentateuch Commentary
	David Lida	Chalukei Avanim
	Avraham Lieblein	Kesef Mezukak
	Judah ben Bezalel Loew (Maharal / Maharal of Prague)	Gur Aryeh
	Solomon Luria (Maharshal, Rashal)	Yeri'ot Shlomo
	Elijah Mizrachi (Re'em)	Sefer HaMizrachi
	Moshe Mos, of Premysl	Ho'il Moshe (first part)
	David ben Samuel HaLevi (Taz)	Dibre Torah
	Aryeh Leib Steinhardt	Kur Zahav
	Mordechai Gimpel Yaffe Torizer	Techeiles Mordechai
6. Miscellaneous		
	Aaron of Pisaro	Toledot Aharon

Category	Author	Work/s
	Isaac Adarbi (Adribi)	Divrei Rivot
	Solomon ben Joshua Adeni	Dibre Emet
	Moshe Alsich	Torat Moshe
	Aaron ben Moses ben Asher	Adaptation of Aleppo Codex
	Avraham of Trisk	Magen Avraham
	Shlomo ben Boya'a	Aleppo Codex
	Jacob de Castro	Kol Ya'acob
	Perez ben Elijah (Rap / RaPaSh / MaHaRPaSh)	Sefer Peretz
	Shabtai Donolo	Chachmuni
	Moshe Chaim Ephraim, of Sudilkov	Degel Machaneh
	Jonathan Eybeschutz	Tiferet Yehonatan
	Saadia ben Joseph, Gaon	Arabic translation of Bible
	Aaron Samuel ben Israel Kaidenover	Birkat Shemuel
	David Kimchi (RaDaK)	El Hasofer
	Menachem ben Solomon Meiri (HaMeiri)	Kiryat Sefer
	Joshua Boaz Mevorakh / Joshua Boaz ben Simon Baruch (Shiltei Gibborim)	Torah Ohr
	Avraham Aharon Price	Mishnat Avraham Imrei Avraham
	Isaac Samuel Reggio (Yashar)	Sefer Torat Elohim
	Yaakov Yitzhak Ruderman	Sichos Levi
	Aaron ben Samuel	Bet Aharon
	Jacob ben Aaron Sasportas	Toledot Yaacob
	Dovber Schneuri (Mitteler Rebbe)	Maamrei Admur HaEmtzei

Category	Author	Work/s
	Abraham ben Asher Wallerstein	Ma'amar Abraham

B. Talmud

1. Mishnah

Category	Author	Work/s
	Sherira ben Hanina.Gaon	Iggeret Rav Sheriria Gaon
	Eleazar ben Eleazar HaKappar (Bar Kappara, Berebi)	Mishnah of Bar Kappara
	Judah HaNasi (Rabbeinu HaKadosh)	Redactor of Mishnah
	Isaac Hirsch Weiss	Mishpat Leshon HaMishnah
Mishnah Commentary	Obadiah ben Abraham, of Bertinoro	In multiple sources
	Samson ben Abraham, of Sens	Untitled
	Solomon ben Joshua Adeni (M'Lekhet Shlomo)	M'Lekhet Shlomo
	Yisroel ben Shmuel Ashkenazi, of Shklov	Beit Israel
	Abraham Azulai	Perush Yakar Al Shisha Sidrei Mishnah Perush Yakar Al HaLevush
	Meir ben Baruch, of Rothenburg (MaHaRaM)	Untitled
	Simeon ben Zemah Duran (Rashbatz / Tashbetz)	Untitled, several tractates
	Jacob ben Zvi Ashkenazi Emden (Yabets)	Lehem Shemayim
	Yaakov Etlinger	Aruch LaNer
	Yom Tov Lipman Heller (Tosefos Yomtov)	Tosefos Yomtov
	Asher ben Jehiel (Rabbeinu Asher / Rosh)	Untitled
	Joshua Hoschel ben Elijah Zeeb Levin	Tosefot Sheni L-Ziyyon

Category	Author	Work/s
	Israel Lipschutz	Tifferet Yisrael
	Moses ben Noah Lipschutz	Lehem Mishneh
	Moses ben Maimon (Maimonides / Rambam)	Commentary on the Mishnah
	Jacob ben Nissim ibn Shahin (Rabbeinu Nissim, HaMafteach)	Comforting Tales
	Hai ben Sherira, Gaon	Untitled commentary
	Menachem ben Solomon Meiri (HaMeiri)	Beit HaBechirah
	Elijah ben Solomon Zalman (Vilna Gaon, Gra)	Shenoth Eliyahu
2. *Talmudic Specific Aspects*		
General	Aaron of Pesaro	Toledot Aharon
	Rav Ashi	Edited Babylonian Talmud
	Solomon ben Kalman HaLevi Abel	Beit Shlomo
	Isaac ben Jacob Campanton	Darche HaGemara / Darche HaTalmud
	Joseph ben Ephraim Caro (Karo) (Mechaber / HaMechaber)	Kelalei HaTalmud
	Yaakov ibn Chaviv (Habib)	Ayn Yaakov
	Sherira ben Hanina, Gaon	Iggeret Rav Sherira Gaon
	Abraham Joshua Heschel	Torah min HaShamayim BeAspaklariya shel Dorot
	Menachem Mendel Kasher	Torah Shelemah
	Yitzhak Hezekiah Lampronti	Pahad Yitzhak
	Joshua Hoschel ben Elijah Zeeb Levin	Ziyyun Yehoshua
	Saul Lieberman	Al HaYerushalmi
	Menachem di Lonzano	Sefer Maasiyot
	Moses Chaim Luzatto (Ramchal)	Derekh Tevunot

Category	Author	Work/s
	Chaim Chizkiya Medini	S'Dei Chemed
	Joshua Boaz Mevorakh / Joshua Boaz ben Simon Baruch (Shiltei Gibborim)	Masoret HaShas / Masoret HaTalmud
	Samuel ibn Naghrela (Samuel HaNagid)	Mavo HaTalmud
	Chaim Shalom Tuvia Rabinowitz (Reb Chaim Telzer)	Shiurei Rebbi Chaim MiTelz
	Moses ben Naftali Hertz Rivkes	Be'er HaGolah
	Jacob ben Aaron Sasportas	Toledot Yacob
	Samuel ben Joseph Strashun (Rashash)	Hagahot v'Chiddushei
	Samuel de Uzeda	Midrash Shmuel
	Yechiel Yaakov Weinberg	Mechkarim beTalmud
	Isaac Hirsch Weiss	Vienna Edition of the Talmud
Glosses	Bezalel Ashkenazi	Shittah Mekubetzet
	Isaiah ben Judah Loeb Berlin	Supplements to the Mesoret HaShas
	Zvi Hirsch Chajes (Chayes) (The Maharatz Chajes)	Untitled
	Jacob de Castro	Erech HaShulchan
	Abraham ben David (Ravad III)	On Maimonides' Mishneh Torah
	Akiver Eger	On the Mishnah and Shulkhan Arukh
	Israel Meir Kagan (HaKohen) (Chofetz Chaim)	Mishnah Berurah
	Zvi Hirsch Kalischer	On Yoreh De'ah of Shulkhan Arukh
	Abraham ben Abigdor Kara	On the Arba'ah Turim
	Solomon Luria (Maharshal, Rashal)	Chochmat Shlomo

Category	Author	Work/s
	Moses ben Nahman (Nahmanides) (Ramban)	On the Talmud
	Judah ben Samuel Rosanes	Mishneh la-Melex
	Eliyahu David Rabinowitz-Teomim (Aderet)	Various books
	Yoel Sirkis	Hagahot Bach
	Elijah ben Solomon Zalman (Vilna Gaon, Gra)	Biurei HaGra
3. *Talmud Commentaries*		
	Shmuel Aceda	Midrash Shmuel
	Isaac ben Reuben Albargeloni	On Ketubot
	Moses ben Baruch Almosnino	Pirkei Moshe
	Yom Tov ibn Asevilli (Ritva)	Untitled
	Jacob ben Asher (Tur)	Sefer HaRemazim / Kitzur Piskei HaRosh
	Bezalel Ashkenazi	Shittah Bekubetzet
	Mordechai ben Hillel Ashkenazi	Sefer Hamordechai
	Elazar ben Moshe Azikri (Ezkari)	On Bezah in the Jerusalem Talmud
	Mordechai ben Abraham Benet	Tekelet Mordechai
	Naphtali Tzvi Yehuda Berlin (Netziv)	HaEmek She'eila Meromeh Sadeh
	Jacob de Castro	Nazir
	Zvi Hirsch Chajes (Chayes) (The Maharatz Chajes)	Torat Nevi'im
	Yaakov ibn Chaviv (Habib)	Ayn Yaakov
	Joseph Chayon	Milei DeAvot
	Chananel ben Chushiel (Rabbeinu Chananel)	Untitled
	Abraham ben David (Ravad III)	Torath Kohanim

Category	Author	Work/s
	Simeon ben Zemah Duran (Rashbatz / Tashbetz)	Untitled, several tractates
	Samuel Eidels (Maharsha)	Hiddushei Halakhot Hiddushei Aggadot
	Yissachar ben Ellenburg	Be'er Sheva
	Yechiel Michel HaLevi Epstein (Aruch Hashulchan)	Micah HaMayim Or li-Yisharim
	Solomon ben Joseph Ganzfried	Pnei Shlomo
	Achai Gaon	Sheilot d'Rav Achai / Sheiltos
	Hai Gaon	Untitled
	Judah ben Gershom (Rabbeinu Gershom)	Untitled – by students
	Zerachiah ben Isaac HaLevi Gerondi (ReZaH, RaZBI, Ba'al HaMaor)	Sefer HaMaor Sefer HaTsava
	Louis Ginzberg	On Yerushalmi
	Abraham Abele ben Chaim HaLevi Gombiner (Magen Avraham)	Untitled
	Eliakim ben Meshullam HaLevi	Untitled
	Yaakov Yehoshua ben Zvi Hirsch (Jacob Joshua Falk)	Pene Yehoshua Kontres
	David Zevi Hoffmann	Untitled Commenatry (Midrashic)
	Samson ben Isaac, of Chinon (MaHaRShak)	Sefer Keritut
	Aaron Samuel ben Israel Kaidenover	Birkat HaZebah
	Abraham Isaac Kook (HaRaAYaH / HaRav)	Ayin Aiyah
	Ezekiel ben Judah Landau (Nodah B'Yehuda)	Tziyyon Lenefesh Hayyah
	Joshua Hoschel ben Elijah Zeeb Levin	May'yene Yehoshua

Category	Author	Work/s
	Saul Lieberman	Tosefot Rishonim
	Judah ben Bezalel Loew (Maharal / Maharal of Prague)	Derech Chaim
	Solomon Luria (Maharshal, Rashal)	Chochmat Shlomo Yam Shel Shlomo
	Jacob Kamenecki (Yaakov Kamenetsky)	Emes leYaakov
	Nissim ben Reuven, of Gerona (RaN)	Untitled
	Moses ben Naftali Hertz Rivkes	Be'er HaGolah
	Meir ben Samuel (RAM)	Commentary in Menachot
	Simha ben Samuel, of Speyer	Seder Olam
	Samuel Schotten (Mharsheishoch)	Koss Hayeshu'ot
	Kalonymus ben Shabbethai	Untitled
	Jacob ben Nissim ibn Shahin (Rabbeinu Nissim, HaMafteach)	HaMafteach Megillat Setarim
	Chaim Soloveitchik (The Brisker Reb)	Chiddushei HaGRaCh Al Shas
	Moses ibn Tibbon	Sefer Pe'ah
	Chaim ben Yitzhak Volozhin (Reb Chaim)	Ruach Chaim
	Yaakov David Wilovsky (Ridvaz)	Chiddushei Ridvaz Tosafot haRid
	Gershon ben Yehuda (Me'Or HaGolah)	Peirush Rabbeinu Gershon
	Shlomo Yitzhaki (Rashi)	Thirty Tractates Babylonian Talmud
	Ovadia Yosef	Anaf Etz Avot Maor Israel
Tosefot	Isaac ben Abraham (Riba)	Untitled
	Samson ben Abraham of Sens	Untitled

Category	Author	Work/s
	Joseph ben Baruch (Joseph of Clisson)	Untitled, quoted elsewhere
	Meir ben Baruch (Meir of Rothenburg) (MaHaRaM)	Yoma
	Abigdor Cohen of Vienna	For Ketuvot
	Eliezer of Toul	Untitled
	Eliezer of Touques	Gilyon Tosefot /Tosefot Gilyon Tosafot Tuk
	Isaac ben Asher HaLevi (Riva)	Tosefot Riva
	Jacob ben Isaac HaLevi (Jabez)	Haggahot Maimuniyot
	Baruch ben Isaac	Nashim, Nazir, Shabbat, Hullin
	Elhanan ben Isaac, of Dampierre	Untitled
	Kalonymus ben Isaac	Hullin 47b
	Solomon ben Isaac	Untitled
	Israel of Bramburg	For Mordechai Haggahot Mordechai
	Jacob of Chinon	Sanhedrin, Gittin
	Asher ben Jehiel (Rosh)	Untitled
	Jehiel ben Joseph of Paris	Untitled
	Samson ben Joseph of Falaise	Untitled
	David ben Kalonymus of Munzenberg	Untitled
	Eleazar ben Yehuda ben Kalonymus, of Worms (Rokeach)	Untitled
	Samuel ben Kalonymus (He-Hasid)	Tamid
	Judah ben Isaac Messer Leon	Untitled
	Saul Lieberman	Tosefet Rishonim
	Isaac (Yitzhak) ben Meir (Rivam)	Untitled

Category	Author	Work/s
	Jacob ben Meir (Tam) (Rabbeinu Tam)	In all editions of the Talmud
	Moses ben Meir, of Frerrara	Untitled, appear in Haggahot Maimuniyot.
	Samuel ben Meir (Rashbam)	Bava batra, Pesachim
	Isaac ben Mordechai of Regensburg (RiBaM)	Untitled, quoted by others
	Moses of Evreux	Tosafot of Evreux
	Judah ben Nathan (Riban)	Tosafot on Makkot, Nazir, Erubin, Yebamot, Shabbat
	Isaac ben Samuel, of Dampierre (Ri)	Tosefot Yeshanim
	Simha ben Samuel, of Speyer	Untitled
	Joseph ben Isaac Bekhor Shor	To most of the Talmud
	Samuel ben Solomon of Falaise	Untitled to several Talmudic treatises
	Isaiah ben Mali di Trani (RI'D)	Tosefot RI'D
Super-Commentaries	Mordechai ben Abraham Benet	Biur Mordechai
	Baruch ben David	Gedulah Mordechai
	Samuel Eidels (Maharsha)	Hiddushei Halakhot
	Yechiel Michel HaLevi Epstein (Aruch Hashulchan)	Or li-Yisharim
	Joel Hayyim (Mahariah)	Hiddushei Mahariah
	Samuel ben Nathan Loew	Machatsi HaShekel

C. Codes Of Law

1. Codes and Commentaries

	Samuel ben Aaron of Schlettstadt	Kizzur Mordekai / Mordekai HaKaton
	Yitzhak ben Yaakov HaKohen Alfasi	Halacoth / Alfes / RIF Halakhot Ketanot

Category	Author	Work/s
	Jacob ben Asher (Ba'al HaTurim / Tur)	Arba'ah Turim
	Gershon Ashkenazi	Hiddushe HaGershuni
	Yehuda ben Shimon Ashkenazi	Be'er Heitiv
	Yisroel ben Shmuel Ashkenazi of Shklov	Pe'at HaShulchan
	Menachem Mendel ben Meshulam Zalman Auerbach	Ateret Zekeinim
	Judah Ayyas	Lehem Yehuda
	Yair Chaim Bachrach	Mekor Chaim
	Shneur Zalman Baruch (Borukovich), of Liadi (Alter Rebbe, GRaZ)	Shulchan Aruch HaRav
	Judah ben Barzillai	Sefer HaIttim
	Behag	Halakhot Gedolot
	Chaim Benveniste	Knesses HaGedolah and Sheyarei Knesses HaGedolah Dina DeChaye
	Yehuda Leib ben Meir Channeles	Vayigash Yehuda
	Joseph ben Ephraim Caro (Karo) (Mechaber)	Beth Yosef Shulkhan Arukh Bedek – Bayit Kesef Mishna
	Jacob de Castro	Erech HaShulchan
	Abraham ibn Chananyah	Beit Avraham
	Yosef Chaviva	Nimukei Yosef
	Abraham ben Jehiel Danzig	Hayye Adam:Nishmat Adam Hokmat Adam:Binat Adam
	Abraham ben David (Ravad III)	HaSagot HaRaavad
	Hezekiah ben David DiSilo	Pri Chadash

Category	Author	Work/s
	David Solomon Eibenschutz	L'bushe Serad
	Abraham Zevi Hirsch ben Jacob Eisenstadt	Pithei Teshuvah
	Joseph Escapa	Rosh Yosef
	Samuel ben Uri Shraga Faibesh (Phoebus)	Beit Shmuel
	Joshua ben Alexander HaKohen Falk	Beit Israel
	Solomon ben Joseph Ganzfried	Kitzur Shulkhan Arukh
	Abraham Abele ben Chaim HaLevi Gombiner (Magen Avraham)	Magen Avraham
	Shabbatai ben Meir HaKohen (Shach)	Siftei Kohen (Shakh)
	Tzidkayah ben Avraham Anav HaRofei	Shibbole HaLeket
	Aryeh Leib HaKohen Heller (The Ketzos)	Ketot HaChoshen Avnei Milluim
	David Zevi Hoffmann	Untitled on the Shulkhan Arukh
	Abraham ben Isaac of Narbonne (Raavad II)	HaEshkol
	Baruch ben Isaac	Sefer HaTerumah
	Israel of Krems	Haggahot Asheri
	Moses ben Israel Isserles (Rema)	HaMapah Darkhei Moshe
	Moses ben Jacob, of Coucy	Sefer Mitzvot HaGadol (SeMaG)
	Mordechai ben Avraham Jaffe (Ba'al HaLevushim)	Levush Malkhut
	Samuel ben Jacob Jam'a	Elef HaMagen / Agur
	Asher ben Jehiel (Rabbeinu Asher, Rosh)	Abstract of Talmudic Law

Category	Author	Work/s
	Isaac ben Joseph of Corbeil	Ammude HaGolah / Sefer Mitzvot Katan (Semak)
	Israel Meir Kagan (HaKohen) (Chofetz Chaim)	Mishnah Berurah Beiur Halacha Sha'ar HaTziyyum
	Zvi Hirsch Kalischer	Eben Bochan Sefer Moznayim la-Mishpat
	Abraham Isaiah Karelitz (Chazon Ish)	Chazon Ish
	Simeon Kayyara	Halakot Gedolot / Halakot Rishonot
	Samuel ben Naftali HaLevi Kelin	Mechitzat HaShekel
	Solomon ben Judah Aaron Kluger	Sefer HaHayyim
	Ezekiel ben Judah Landau (Nodah B'Yehuda)	Dagul Merevavah
	Moses ben Isaac Judah: Lima	Helkat Mehokek
	Jacob ben Jacob Moshe Lorberbaum, of Lisser (Ba'al HaNesivos / Lissa Rav)	Nesivos HaMishpat Derech Chaim
	Solomon Luria (Maharshal, Rashal)	Amudei Shlomo
	Moses ben Maimon (Maimonides) (Rambam)	Mishneh Torah (Yad HaHazakha)
	Ephraim Zalman (Solomon) Margolis	Bet Ephraim Yad Ephraim
	Hayyim Mordechai Margolis	Sha'are Teshubah
	Meir ben Zvi Hirsch Margolis	Derek HaTov veha-Yashar
	Yitzhak ben Abba Mari, of Marseilles	Sefer HaIttur / Ittur Soferim
	Samuel ben Meir (Rashbam)	Untitled
	Isser Zalman Meltzer (Even HaEzel)	Even HaEzel

Category	Author	Work/s
	Yerucham ben Meshullam	Meisharim Adam V'Chava
	Joshua Boaz Mevorakh / Joshua Boaz ben Simon Baruch (Shiltei Gibborim)	Ein Mishpat Ner Mitzvah Shiltei Gibborim / Sefer Makloket
	Isaac ben Moses, of Vienna (Or Zarua, Riaz)	Or Zarua
	Meshullam ben Moses	Sefer HaHalachot
	Jacob Meshullam ben Mordechai Ze'ev Ornstein	Yeshuot Ya'acob
	Avraham Aharon Price	Mitzvot Gadol
	Jacob ben Joseph Reischer (Backofen)	Minhat Ya'akov
	Nissim ben Reuven, of Gerona (RaN)	Commentary on Alfasi's (RIF) Halacoth
	Moses ben Naftali Hertz Rivkes	Be'er HaGolah
	Judah ben Samuel Rosanes	Mishneh la-Melek
	Israel Lipkin Salanter	Imrei Binah Iggeret HaMussar Even Yisrael Etz Peri
	David ben Samuel HaLevi Segal (Taz)	Turei Zahav
	Eliyahu ben Binyamin Wolf Shapiro	Eliyahu Rabba
	Hai ben Sherira, Gaon	Untitled
	Yoel Sirkis (Bach)	Bayit Chadash (Bach)
	Benjamin Aaron ben Abraham Slonik	Masat Binyamin
	Yaakov Chaim Sofer (Kaf HaChaim)	Kaf HaChaim
	Chaim Soloveitchik (The Brisker Reb)	Chiddushei Rabbeinu Chaim

Category	Author	Work/s
	Yosef Dov Soloveitchik (Beis HaLevi)	Beis HaLevi
	Abdalla Somekh	Untitled Responsa to Shulkhan Arukh
	Yitzhak Elchanan Spektor	Nachal Yitzhak
	Joseph ben Menachem Steinhart	Zikron Yosef
	Aaron Moses ben Jacob Taubes	To'afot Re'em
	Vidal di Tolosa	Maggid Mishneh
	Isadore (Yitzhak) Twersky	An Introduction to the Code of Maimonides A Maimonides Reader
	Nethaneel ben Naftali Tzvi Weil	Netib Hayyim
	Yaakov David Wilovsky (Ridvaz)	Beis Ridvaz
	Eleazar ben Yehuda of Worms	Rokeach
	Baruch ben Yitzhak of Worms	Sefer HaTerumah
	Elijah ben Solomon Zalman (Vilna Gaon, Gra)	Biurei HaGra
	Menahem ben Aaron ibn Zerah	Zedak la-Derek
	Hillel ben Naphtali Zevi	Bet Hillel
	David ben Solomon ibn Abi Zimra (Radbaz)	Yekar Tiferet
2. Halakha Related		
	Samuel Aboab (Rasha)	Devar Shemuel
	Shlomo ben Aderet (Rashba)	Torat HaBayit
	Abraham Alegri	Lev Sameach
	Yom Tov Algazi	Several books
	Shlomo Zalman Auerbach	Me'orei Eish Ma'adnei Eretz
	Yosef ben Moshe Babad	Minchat Chinuch

Category	Author	Work/s
	Meir ben Baruch (Meir of Rothenburg) (MaHaRaM)	Hilkot Berakot / Seder Berakot Birkot MaHaRaM Hilkot Shehitah Hilkot Abelut / Hilkot Semahot Hilkot Pesukot Hilkot Erubin
	Mordechai ben Abraham Benet	Magen Abot
	Chaim Benveniste	Pesach MeUvin
	Aharon Berechyah of Modena	Maavar Yabok
	Zvi Hirsch Chajes (Maharatz Chajes)	Darkhei Binah
	Hasdai ben Abraham Crescas	Passover Sermon
	Yaakov Culi	Simanin le-Orieta
	Abraham ben Jehiel Danzig	Zikru Torat Moshe
	Avraham Epstein	Ma'aseh Hageonim
	Yechiel Michel HaLevi Epstein (the Aruch Hashulchan)	Aruch HaShulchan Aruch HaShulchan he'Atid
	Jonathan Eybeschutz	Binah La-Ittim Chiddushim al Hilkot Yom Tov
	Solomon ben Joseph Ganzfried	Kesses Hasofer Toras Zevach
	Shem Tov ben Abraham ibn Gaon	Migdal Oz
	Isaac ibn Gias	Meah Shearim (Yitzhak Yeranen)
	Aryeh Leib ben Ashur Gunzberg (Shaagat Aryeh)	Shaagat Aryeh
	Moses ibn Habib (Chaviv)	Get Pashut Ezrat Nashim
	Moses Hagiz	Eleh HaMitzvot
	Aaron HaLevi, of Barcelona	Sefer HaChinuch

Category	Author	Work/s
	Aharon HaLevi (Ra'aH)	Bedek HaBayit
	Eliezer ben Joel HaLevi (Raviah)	Sefer HaRaviah (Avi HaEzri)
	Yeshayah ben Mali Hazaken	Piskei HaRid
	Aryeh Leib HaKohen Heller (The Ketzos)	Shev Shema'atata
	Judah Aryeh Loeb ben Joshua Hoschel	Torah Or
	Samson ben Isaac of Chinon (MaHaRShak)	Biur HaGet
	Moses ben Israel Isserles (Rema)	Torat Hattat (Issur we-Hetter)
	Nissim ben Jacob (HaMafteach) (Rav Nissim Gaon)	Megillat Setarim
	Israel Meir Kagan (HaKohen) (Chofetz Chaim)	Chafetz Chaim
	Eleazar ben Yehuda ben Kalonymus of Worms (Rokeach)	HaRokeach
	Ezekiel ben Judah Landau (Nodah B'Yehuda)	Nodah B'Yehuda
	Yaakov Baruch ben Yehuda Landau	Agur
	Joshua Hoschel ben Elijah Zeeb Levin	Dabar b'itti
	David Lida	Ir Miklat Ir David Sod Hashem Ver-Sharvit HaZahav
	Moses ben Maimon (Maimonides) (Rambam)	Sefer HaMitzvot
	Ephraim Zalman (Solomon) Margolis	Sha're Ephraim
	Chaim Chizkiya Medini	S'Dei Chemed

Category	Author	Work/s
	Joshua Boaz Mevorakh / Joshua Boaz ben Simon Baruch (Shiltei Gibborim)	Siddur Mordechai Ve-Simanav / Siddur Dine Mordekai
	Moshe Mos, of Premysl	Matteh Moshe Taryag Mitzvos
	Samuel ibn Naghrela (Samuel HaNagid)	Hilchata Gevurta
	Moses ben Nahman (Nahmanides) (Ramban)	Mishpetei HaCherem Hilkhot Bedikah Torat HaAdam Sha'ar HaCherem Milhamot HaShem
	Yehudai ben Nahman (Yehudai Gaon)	Halakhot Pesukct
	Eliezer ben Nathan (Raavan)	Even HaEzer
	Joseph ibn Plat	Untitled treatises
	Judah ben Samuel Rosanes	Parashat Derakim
	Yaakov Yitzhak Ruderman	Mas'as Levi
	Israel Lipkin Salanter	Imrei Binah
	Eliezer ben Samuel of Metz	Sefer Yereim
	Meir ben Samuel (RAM)	Quoted in other Tosafists
	Simha ben Samuel, of Vitry	Vitry Mahzor
	Menachem Mendel Schneerson (Tzemach Tzedek)	Shut Tzemach Tzedek
	Sholom Mordechai Schwadron (Maharsham)	Shailos Uteshuvot Marsham Daas Torah
	Jacob ben Nissim ibn Shahin (Rabbeinu Nissim, HaMafteach)	HaMafteach Megillat Setarim
	Amram bar Sheshna, Gaon	Untitled
	Hai ben Sherira, Gaon	Untitled
	Shimon Shkop	Sha'arei Yosher
	Yaakov Chaim Sofer (Kaf HaChaim)	Kol Yaakov

Category	Author	Work/s
	Abdalla Somekh	Zivhei Tzedek
	Moses ibn Tibbon	Hebrew translation of Maimonides' Sefer HaMitzvot
	Isaac Tyrnau	Sefer Minhagim
	Jacob ben Judah Weil (Mahariv)	She'elot u'Bedikot
	Nethaneel ben Naftali Tzvi Weil	Korban Netanel
	Yechiel Yaakov Weinberg	Seridei Eish
	Isaac Hirsch Weiss	Masoret HaTalmud Dor Dor we-Dorshaw
	Ovadia Yosef	Chazon Ovadia
	Yitzhak Yosef	Yalkut Yosef
D. Responsa		
	Isaac Adarbi (Adribi)	Divrei Rivot
	Shlomo ben Aderet	Untitled
	Moses ben Isaac Alashkar	Untitled
	Abraham Alegri	Lev Sameach
	Joseph Almosnino	Edut bi-Yehosef
	Abraham Ankava	Kerem Hemed
	Tzvi Hirsch ben Yaakov Ashkenazi (Chacham Tzvi)	Chacham Tzvi
	Gershon Ashkenazi	Avodat HaGershuni
	Yisroel ben Shmuel Ashkenazi, of Shklov	Nachala u-Menucha
	Shlomo Zalman Auerbach	Minchas Shlomo
	Judah Ayyas	Bet Yehuda
	Abraham Samuel Bachrach	In the collected work, Hut haShani
	Yair Chaim Bachrach	Havaot Yair

Category	Author	Work/s
	Isaac ben Sheshet Barfat (RiBaSH)	She'elot u-Teshuvot HaRibash HaHadashot
	Meir ben Baruch (Meir of Rothenburg) (MaHaRaM)	Untitled
	Mordechai ben Abraham Benet	Parashot Mordechai
	Chaim Benveniste	Ba'ei Chaye
	Naftali Tzvi Yehuda Berlin	Meishav Davar
	Isaac ben Moses Solomon Blaser (Rav Itzele Peterburger)	Peri Yitzhak
	Israel Bruna	Teshuvot Mahari Bruna
	Joseph ben Ephraim Caro (Karo) (HaMechaber / Mechaber)	Avkath Rochel
	Levi ben Jacob ibn Chaviv (Habib) (Ralbach)	She'elot u-Teshuvot
	Chananel ben Chushiel	Untitled
	Abraham ben David (Ravad III).	Temim De'im Orot Hayyim Shibbole HaLeket
	Simeon ben Zemah Duran (Rashbatz / Tashbetz)	Untitled
	Solomon ben Simon Duran (Rashbash)	Untitled
	Akiva Eiger (Eger)	Untitled
	David Solomon Eibenschutz	Ne'ot Deshe
	Judah ben Enoch	Hinnuk ben Yehuda
	Abraham Zevi Hirsch ben Jacob Eisenstadt	Pithei Teshuvah
	Meir ben Iszak Eisenstadt (Meir Ash) (Maharam Ash / Panim Me'irot)	Panim Me'irot
	Meir Eisenstadter (Meir Ash) (Maharam Ash)	Imrei Esh

Category	Author	Work/s
	Jacob Israel ben Zvi Ashkenazi Emden (Yabets)	Pithei Teshuva
	Avraham Epstein	Ma'aseh Hageonim
	Joseph Escapa	Teshubot Rosh Yosef
	Yaakov Etlinger	Responsa Binyan Tzion
	Hayyim Judah Lob Ettinger	Untitled Responsa
	Isaac Aaron Ettinger	Responsa
	Moshe Feinstein	Igrot Moshe
	Solomon Bennett Freehof	The Responsa Literature Other works on Reform Responsa
	Hai Gaon	Untitled
	Louis Ginzberg	Geonica Untitled (The Responsa of Professor Louis Ginzberg)
	David Golinkin	Untitled Ed. – The Responsa of Professor Louis Ginzberg Responsa in a moment: Halakhic responses to contemporary issues
	Eliezer David Greenwald	Keren L'David
	Chaim Ozer Grodzinski	She'elot u'Teshuvot Achiezer
	Aryeh Leib ben Asher Gunzberg (Shaagat Aryeh)	She'elot u'Teshuvot Shaagat Aryeh HaHadashot
	Shabbatai ben Meir HaKohen (Shach)	Gevurat Anashim
	Samuel Hayyun	Bene Shemuel
	David Zevi Hoffmann	Untitled Halakhic
	Abraham ben Isaac, of Narbonne (Raavad II)	Untitled
	Kalonymus ben Isaac	Responsum

Category	Author	Work/s
	Solomon ben Isaac	Quoted in Sefer HaYashar
	Israel ben Pethahiah Ashkenazi Isserlein	Pesakim u-Ketabim Terumat HaDeshen
	Moses ben Israel Isserles (Rema)	She'elot u'Teshubot ReMA
	Joshua Hoschel ben Joseph	Maggine Shelomoh
	Saadia ben Joseph, Gaon	Untitled monographs
	Aaron Samuel ben Israel Kaidenover	Emunat Shemuel
	David ben Kalonymus, of Munzenberg	Untitled
	Menachem Mendel Kasher	Divrei Menachem
	Meir ben Isaac Katzenellenbogen (Maharam Padua)	She'elot u'Teshuvot
	Solomon ben Judah Aaron Kluger	Shenot Hayyim Sefer Satam Moda'a le-Bet Ysrael
	Menachem Mendel ben Abraham Krochmal	Tzemach Tzedek
	Samuel ben Ezekiel Landau	Shibat Ziyyon
	Samuel Joseph Landau	Mishkan Shiloh
	Ezekiel ben Judah Landau (Nodah B'Yehuda)	Nodah B'Yehuda
	Yaakov Baruch ben Yehuda Landau	Agur
	Aaron ben Isaac Lapapa	Bnei Aharon
	Judah ben Isaac Messer Leon	Untitled
	Joseph ibn Lev	She'elot U'Teshubot R' Yosef ibn Lev
	Baruch Mordechai ben Jacob Lipschitz	Berit Ya'akob
	Meir ben Gedaliyah Lublin (Maharam)	Manhir Einei Chachamim

Category	Author	Work/s
	Solomon Luria (Maharshal, Rashal)	Untitled
	Abi Ezra Selig Margolis	Hivvure Likkutim
	Alexander Margolis	Teshuvot HaRam
	Ephraim Zalman (Solomon) Margolis	Bet Ephraim
	Meir ben Zvi Hirsch Margolis	Meir Netivim
	Samuel ben Moses de Medina (RashDaM)	Piske RashDaM
	Jacob ben, Meir (Tam) (Rabbeinu Tam)	Sefer haYashar
	Joseph ben Meir HaLevi ibn Migash (Ri Migash)	She'elot uTeshuvot Ri Migash
	Judah ben Eliezer HaLevi Minz (Mahari Minz)	Untitled
	Samuel ben Moses di Modena (Maharshdam)	Untitled
	Jacob ben Moses Levi Moelin (Maharil)	Sefer HaMaharil / Minhagei Maharil / Minhagim
	Joseph ben Moses	Leket Yosher
	Yehudai ben Nahman (Yehudai Gaon)	Untitled
	Abraham ben Nathan	HaMinhag / Manhig Olam
	Joseph Saul Nathanson	Sho'el u-Meshiv
	Jacob ben Joseph Reischer (Backofen)	Shevut Ya'akov
	Nissim ben Reuven, of Gerona (RaN)	Collection of responsa
	Yosef Rosen (Rogatchover Gaon, Tzafnach Paneach)	Five volume collection
	Simhah ben Samuel of Vitry	Vitry Mahzor

Category	Author	Work/s
	Jacob ben Aaron Sasportas	Ohel Yaacob
	Moses Schick (Maharam Schick)	Maharam Schick Derashot
	Isaac Schmelkes	Bet Yitzhak
	Samuel Schotten (Mharsheishoch)	Shut Mharsheishoch
	Abraham Samuel Benjamin (Sofer Ksav Sofer)	Four volume untitled collection
	Sholom Mordechai Schwadron (Maharsham)	Shailos Uteshuvo- Marsham Daas Torah
	Hai ben Sherira, Gaon	Untitled
	Amram bar Sheshna, Gaon	Untitled Sidur Rav Amram / Yesod HaAmrami
	Yoel Sirkis (Bach)	Teshuvos HaBach
	Benjamin Aaron ben Abraham Slonik	Masat Binyamin
	Abdalla Somekh	Untitled to Shulkhan Arukh
	Yitzhak Elchanan Spektor	Be'er Yitzhak Ein Yitzhak
	Menahem Mendel ben Simeon Steinhardt	Divrei Menahem
	Joseph ben Menachem Steinhart	Zikron Yosef
	Aaron Moses ben Jacob Taubes	To'afot Re'em
	Joseph Colon ben Solomon Trabotto (Maharik)	The Responsa of Maharik
	Yom Tov ben Moshe Tzahalon (Maharitz)	Untitled
	Ben-Zion Meir Hai Uziel	Mishpetei Ouziel
	Aaron Walkin	Zekan Aharon
	Jacob ben Judah Weil (Mahariv)	She'elot u'Bedikot

Category	Author	Work/s
	Jedidiah Weil	She'elot u'Teshubot
	Nethaneel ben Naftali Tzvi Weil	Torat Netan'el
	Yaakov David Wilovsky (Ridvaz)	Teshuvos Ridvaz
	Shlomo Yitzhaki (Rashi)	Responsa Siddur Rashi Sefer HaOrah Sefer HaPardes
	Ovadia Yosef	Yabia Omer Yechavei Da'ath
	David ben Solomon ibn Abi Zimra (Radbaz)	Collection of Responsa

E. Biblical And Talmudic Novellae (Hiddushim)

	Author	Work/s
	Moses ben Todros HaLevi Abulafia	On the Talmud
	Shlomo Zalman Auerbach	Commentary on Shev Shema'atata
	Judah Ayyas	Mateh Yehuda Shebbet Yehuda
	Isaac ben Sheshet Barfat (RiBaSH)	Untitled Talmudic
	Chaim Benveniste	Chamra VeChaye
	Jacob de Castro	Erek Lehem
	Eleazar ben Yehuda Eidels (Maharsha)	Hiddushei Halakhot Hiddushei Aggadot
	Benjamon Eisenstadt	Masot Binyamin
	Meir ben Iszak Eisenstadt (Meir Ash) (Maharam Ash / Panim Me'irot)	Panim Me'irot Or HaGanuz
	Meir Eisenstadter (Meir Ash) (Maharam Ash)	Imrei Binah
	Jacob Israel ben Zvi Ashkenazi Emden (the Yabets)	Mor u-Kezi'ah

Category	Author	Work/s
	Baruch HaLevi Epstein	Tosefot Beracha
	Moshe Mordechai Epstein	Levush Mordechai
	Joseph Escapa	Rosh Yosef
	Jonathan Eybeschutz	On the Shulkhan Arukh
	Moshe Feinstein	Dibros Rabbi Moshe Lieberman Darash Moshe
	Yonah ben Avraham Gerondi	Untitled
	Aryeh Leib ben Asher Gunzberg (Shaagat Aryeh)	Turei Even Gevurot Ari
	Moses ibn Habib (Chaviv)	Shammot ba-Arez
	Moses Hagiz	Leket HaKemah
	Yeshayah ben Mali Hazaken	Piskei HaRid
	Meir Simcha Kalonymus HaKohen of Dvinsk	Ohr Someyach Meshech Chochma
	Joel Hayyim (Mahariah)	Hiddushei Mahariah
	Samuel Hayyun	Bene Shemuel
	Yaakov Yehoshua ben Zvi Hirsch (Jacob Joshua Falk)	Pene Yehoshua
	Samuel ben Jacob Jam'a	On Sanhedrin
	Enoch Zundel ben Joseph	On the Haggadah of the Talmud
	Joshua Hoschel ben Joseph	Maginne Shelomoh
	Aaron Samuel ben Israel Kaidenover	Tifferet Samuel
	Solomon ben Judah Aaron Kluger	Sefer HaHayyim Me Niddah
	Eleazar ben Israel Landau	Yad Melek
	Israel Jonah Landau	Me-on HaBerakhot
	Samuel Joseph Landau	Mishkan Shiloh
	Aaron ben Isaac Lapapa	Bnei Aharon

Category	Author	Work/s
	Joseph ibn Lev	She'elot U'Teshubot R' Yosef ibn Lev
	Baruch Mordechai ben Jacob Lipschitz	Minhat Bikkurim Untitled
	Judah ben Bezalel Loew (Maharal / Maharal of Prague)	Chiddushei Aggadot
	Meir ben Gedaliyah Lublin (Maharam)	Meir Einei Chachamim
	Abi Ezra Selig Margolis	Hivvure Likkutim
	Meir ben Zvi Hirsch Margolis	Meir Netivim
	Samuel ben Moses de Medina (RashDaM)	Hiddushim
	Jacob ben Meir (Tam) (Rabbeinu Tam)	Sefer haYashar
	Menachem ben Solomon Meiri (HaMeiri)	Untitled
	Meir Leibush ben Jehiel Michel (Malbim)	Artzoth HaChaim
	Joseph ben Meir HaLevi ibn Migash (Ri Migash)	Untitled Talmudic
	Elijah Mizrachi (Re'em)	Tosefte Semag
	Moshe Mos, of Premysl	Ho'il Moshe
	Eliyahu David Rabinowitz-Teomim (Aderet)	Many books
	Yosef Rosen (Rogatchover Gaon, Tzafnach Paneach)	Tzafnach Paneach
	Simah ben Samuel of Speyer	Untitled
	Samuel ben Isaac Sardi (HaSardi, HaSefaradi)	Sefer HaTerumot
	Shimon Shkop	Many tractates
	Benjamin Aaron ben Abraham Slonik	Masat Binyamin

Category	Author	Work/s
	Yaakov Chaim Sofer (Kaf HaChaim)	Yismach Yisrael
	Joseph ben Menachem Steinhart	Ko'ah Shor
	Aaron Moses ben Jacob Taubes	Karne Re'em
	Jedidiah Weil	Untitled collection
	Yaakov David Wilovsky (Ridvaz)	Migdal David
	Hillel ben Naphtali Zevi	Bet Hillel

F. Other Traditional Scholarly Works

1. Ethics

	Author	Work/s
	Isaac Aboab (Menorat HaMaor)	Menorat HaMaor
	Samuel Aboab (Rasha)	Sefer HaZikranot
	Solomon Alami	Iggeret Mussar
	Elazar ben Moshe Azikri (Ezkari)	Sefer Hareidim Divrei Kivushim
	Avraham Chayon	Amorot Tehorot
	Solomon ben Judah, ibn Gabirol (Gvirol)	The Improvement of Moral Qualities or Ethics.
	Abraham ben Shabtai Sheftel Horowitz	Emek Berakhah Yesh Nohalin
	Isaiah HaLevi Horowitz (Shelah, Shaloh)	Shnei Luchos HaBris (Shelah)
	Shabtai Sheftel Horowitz	Emek Berakhah (additions) Vave HaAmmudim Zuwwa'ah
	Yosef Yozel Hurwitz (Alter of Novardok)	Madragat HaAdam
	Zevi Hirsch Kaidenover	Kav Hayashar
	Yosef (Yoselman) Loanz, of Rosheim	Sefer HaMiknah
	Yerusham Levovitz	Daas Chochmah U'Mussar

Category	Author	Work/s
	Moses Chaim Luzzatto (Ramchal)	Mesillat Yesharim
	Bahya ben Joseph ibn Paquda	Chovot HaLevavot
	Avraham Aharon Price	Sefer Hasidim
	Yaakov Yitzhak Ruderman	Sichos Levi
	Israel Lipkin Salanter	Imrei Binah Iggeret HaMussar Even Israel Etz Peri
	Aaron ben Samuel	Commentary on Perek Shirah
	Judah ben Samuel, of Regensburg (He-Hasid)	Sefer Hasidim
	Shmuel Schneerson	Likkutei Torat Shmuel
	Abraham ben Asher Wallerstein	Zera Abraham
	Zerachiah HaYavani (The Greek) (Ra'Za'H)	Sefer HaYashar
	Eleazar ben Yehuda of Worms	Rokeach
2. Hassidic	Shneur Zalman Baruch (Borukovich), of Liadi (Alter Rebbe, GRaZ)	Tanya / Likkutei Amarim
	Dov Ber (Maggid of Mezritch)	Likkutei Amarim Likkutei Yesharim
	Boruch of Kosov	Yesod HaEmunah Amud HaAvodah
	Moshe Chaim Ephraim, of Sudilkov	Degel Machaneh Ephraim
	Shneur Zalman Fradkin, of Lublin	Toras Chesed
	Chaim Halberstam of Sanz	Divrei Chaim
	Jacob Joseph ben Tzvi HaKohen Katz, of Polonnoye	Toledot Ya'akov Yosef Ben Porat Yosef Tsafenat Pane'ah

Category	Author	Work/s
	Mordechai Leifer, of Nadvorna	Gedulas Mordechai
	Menachem Mendel, of Kotzk (Kotzker Rebbe)	Ohel Torah Emet Ve'emunah Amod HaEmet
	Nachman of Breslov	Likkutei Moharan Sefer haMiddot Tikkun HaKlali Sippurei Ma'asiyyot
	Moshe Pallier, of Kobrin	Imros Taharos
	Menachem Mendel Schneerson (Tzemach Tzedek)	Ohr HaTorah
	Menachem Mendel Schneerson (The Lubavitcher Rebbe)	Sefer Hama'amarim Melukot
	Sholom Dovber Schneerson (Rebbe Rashab)	Sefer HaMa'amarim Kuntres HaTefilah Kuntres HaAvodah Issa B'Midrash Tehillim
	Yosef Yitzhak Schneerson (Rebbe Rayatz)	Sefer Hama'amarim
	Dovber Schneuri (Mitteler Rebbe)	Maamrei Admur HaEmtzei
	Chaim Elazar Spira	Minchas Elazar
	Elimelech Szapira	Imrei Elimelech Divrei Elimelech
	Menachem Nachum Twersky	Me'Or Einayim
3. Kabbalah		
	Abraham ben Samuel Abulafia	Sefer HaYashar Sefer HaOt Imrei Shefer Sheba Netibot HaTorah
	Solomon ben Moses HaLevi Alkabetz	Lecha Dodi
	Gershon Ashkenazi	Tifferet HaGershuni

Category	Author	Work/s
	Yehuda Leib HaLevi Ashlag	Panim Meirot Umasbirot Talmud Eser Sefirot HaSulam (Sulam)
	Menachem Azaryah of Fano	Assarah Maamarot
	Abraham Azulai	Chesed L'Avraham Ohr HaChama Ohr HaGanuz
	Shneur Zalman Baruch (Borukovich), of Liadi (Alter Rebbe, GRaZ)	Tanya / Likkutei Amarim
	Joseph ben Ephraim Caro	Maggid Mesharim
	Moses ben Jacob Cordovero (Ramak)	Pardes Rimonim Ohr Yakar Tomer Devorah Elimah Rabbati Sefer Gerushim Shiur Komah Ohr Neerav
	Abraham ben Jehiel Danzig	Kitzur Sefer Hareidim
	Mattitiah ben Solomon Delacrut	Perush
	Naftali Hertz ben Yaakov Elchanan (Bachrach)	Emeq Hamelekh
	Jacob Israel ben Zvi Ashkenazi Emden (the Yabets)	Zizim u-Ferahim
	Jonathan Eybeschutz	Shem Olam
	Abraham Galante	Yare'ach Yakar
	Joseph ben Abraham Gikatilla (Joseph Ba'al HaNissim)	Ginnat Egoz Sha'are Orah / Sefer Orah
	Aaron Abraham ben Baruch Simeon HaLevi	Iggeret HaTe'amim
	Abraham Herrero	Sha'ar HaShamayim Beit Elohim
	Shabbethai Sheftel ben Akiba Hurwitz	Shefa' Tal

Category	Author	Work/s
	Isaiah HaLevi Horowitz (Shelah, Shaloh)	Shnei Luchos HaBris (Shelah)
	Zevi Hirsch Kaidenover	Kav Hayashar
	Eleazar ben Yehuda ben Kalonymus, of Worms (Rokeach)	Various Titles
	Moses de Leon (Moshe ben Shem Tov)	Sefer HaRimonim HaNefesh HaHakhamah Shekel HaKodesh Mishkan HaEdut / Sefer HaSodot Midrash de Rabban Shimon ben Yohai / Zohar
	Noah ben Abraham Lipschutz (Noah Mindes)	Parpera'ot le-Hokmah Nifla'ot Hadashot
	Menachem di Lonzano	Omer Mann
	Moses Chaim Luzzatto (Ramchal)	Mesillat Yesharim Da'at Tevunoth
	Hezekiah ben Manoah (Hizkuni / Chizkuni)	Hazzekuni
	Meir ben Zvi Hirsch Margolis	Sod Yakin u-Voaz
	Moses de Medina	Nefesh David Ruach David v'Nishmat David
	Yitzhak Saggi Nehor (Isaac the Blind)	Bahir
	Meir Popperos	Etz Chaim Meorei Or Or Tzaddikim Or Rav
	Meir ben Solomon Abi Sahula	Commentary on Sefer Yezirah
	Israel Sarug	Kabbalah Contres Ne'im Zemirot Yisrael
	Levi Yitzhak Schneerson	Likkutei Levi Yitzhak
	Menachem Mendel Schneerson (Tzemach Tzedek)	Derech Mitzvotecha

Category	Author	Work/s
	Dovber Schneuri (Mitteler Rebbe)	Sha'ar HaYichud
	Shalom Shakna	Pesachim be-Inyan Kiddushin
	Shalom Sharabi (Rashash)	Sidur Hakavanot Emet va-Shalom Rehovot Nahar Nahar Shalom Siddur haRashash
	Shem Tov ibn Shem Tov	Sefer HaEmunot
	Joseph ben Solomon Taitezak	Many Kabbalistic works
	Eliyahu de Vidas	Reshit Chochma
	Hayyim ben Joseph Vital	Etz Hayyim
	Chaim ben Itzchok Volozhin (Reb Chaim)	Nefesh HaChaim
	Shimon bar Yohai (Rashbi)	Zohar
4. Liturgical	Isaac Aboab (Menorat HaMaor)	Shulkhan HaPanim
	David ben Joseph Abudraham	Sefer Abudraham (Tzibbur Perush HaBerakhot ve-ha-Tefillot)
	Amnon of Mainz	U'netanneh Tokef
	Benjamin ben Abraham Anaw	Liturgical Poems
	Abba Arika	Musaph Prayer Rosh Hashanah
	Mordechai ben Hillel Ashkenazi	Selichot
	Shneur Zalman Baruch (Borukovich), of Liadi (Alter Rebbe, GRaZ)	Siddur Torah Or
	Aharon Berechyah of Modena	Me'il Tzedakah Bigdei Kodesh
	Baruch HaLevi Epstein	Baruch She-Amar
	Shimon ben Yitzhak HaGadol	Piyutei R'Shimon ben Yitzhak

Category	Author	Work/s
	Shabbatai ben Meir HaKohen (Shach)	Selichot
	Nissim ben Jacob (HaMafteach) (Rav Nissim Gaon)	Siddur Tefilah
	Yissachar Jacobson	Netiv Binah
	Enoch Zundel ben Joseph	Olat HaChodesh
	Gaon Saadia ben Joseph	Siddur
	Abraham Isaac Kook (HaRaAyaH / HaRav)	Olat Raiyah
	Shalom Sharabi (Rashash)	Sidur Hakavanot Siddur HaRashash
	Gaon Amram ben Sheshna	Yesod HaAmrami / Siddur Rav Amram
5. Philosophy		
	Joseph Albo	Ikkarim
	Israel ben Judah Abravanel	On the Sciences
	Yehuda Alkali	Minhat Yehuda
	Shneur Zalman Baruch (Borukovich), of Liadi (Alter Rebbe, GRaZ)	Tanya / Likkutei Amarim
	Abraham ben Shem Tov Bibago	Derek Emunah Ez Hayyim
	Abraham ibn Meir ibn Ezra (Abenezra)	Various Sources
	Solomon ben Judah, ibn Gabirol (Gvirol)	Mekor Chaim (Fons Vitae)
	Levi ben Gershom (Gersonides, Ralbag)	Sefer Milkhamot Ha-Shem
	Meir Simcha Kalonymus HaKohen, of Dvinsk	Meshech Chochma
	Abraham ben David (Abraham ibn Daud) HaLevi (Ravad I)	Al-akidah al-Rafiyah (Emunah Ramah)
	Judah ben Samuel HaLevi (RiHa'l)	Kuzari

Category	Author	Work/s
	Yedadayah HaPenini	Bechinat Olam
	Abraham Joshua Heschel	Man is Not Alone: A Philosophy of Religion God in Search of Man: A Philosophy of Judaism The Sabbath: Its Meaning for Modern Man The Prophets
	Shemariah ben Elijah Ikriti, of Negropont	Sefer HaMora
	Gaon Saadia ben Joseph	Emunot v'Deot
	Zvi Hirsch Kalischer	Sefer Emunah Yesharah
	Nachman Kohen Krochmal	Moreh Nebuke HaZeman
	Moses Chaim Luzzatto (Ramchal)	Derekh Hashem
	Yosef (Yoselman) Loanz of Rosheim	Sefer HaMiknah
	Moses ben Maimon (Maimonides) (Rambam)	Guide for the Perplexed (Moreh Nevuchim)
	Moses Mendelssohn	Jerusalem
	Samuel ibn Naghrela (Samuel HaNagid)	Ben Koheleth
	Nissim ben Reuven, of Gerona (RaN)	Philosophical work
	Yosef Rosen (Rogatchover Gaon, Tzafnach Paneach)	Commentary on Maimonides' Guide for the Perplexed (Moreh Nevuchim)
	Aaron ben Samuel	Commentary on Perek Shirah
	Meir ben Samuel (RAM)	Changed Kol Nidre
	Menachem Mendel Schneerson (Tzemach Tzedek)	Sefer Chakira:Derech Emunah
	Obadiah ben Jacob Sforno	Or Ammim
	Jacob ben Nissim ibn Shahin (Rabbeinu Nissim, HaMafteach)	Arabic Commentary to the Sefer Yezirah

Category	Author	Work/s
	Joseph Ber Soloveitchik (HaRav)	The Lonely Man of faith Halakhic Man Fate and Destiny Out of the Whirlwind Days of Deliverance
	Samuel ben Judah ibn Tibbon	Hebrew translation of Maimonides' Moreh Nevuchim
6. *Piyyutim / Poetry*		
	Isaac ben Reuben Albargeloni	Azharot
	Judah ben Solomon Alharizi (al-Harizi)	Takhemoni
	Amnon of Mainz	U'netannah Tokef
	Benjamin ben Abraham Anaw	Piyyutim found in the Roman Mahzor
	Elazar ben Moshe Azikri (Ezkari)	Yedid Nefesh
	Joseph ben Baruch (Joseph of Clisson)	Untitled
	Meir ben Baruch (Meir of Rothenburg) (MaHaRaM)	Liturgical Poems
	Joseph ben Hanan ben Nathan Ezobi	Untitled
	Moses ibn Ezra (HaSallah)	Untitled
	Solomon ben Judah, ibn Gabirol (Gvirol)	Keter Malkut Azharoth Shir Hakavod Shir Hayichud
	Isaac ben Judah ibn Ghiyyat (Ghayyat)	Sifte Renanot
	Shimon ben Yitzhak HaGadol	Piutei R'Shimon ben Yitzhak
	Shabbatai ben Meir HaKohen (Shach)	Selichot
	Abraham ben Isaac HaLevi	Untitled
	Isaac ben Eleazar HaLevi	Four Wedding Piyyutim
	Eliakim ben Meshullam HaLevi	Poem for Passover

Category	Author	Work/s
	Judah ben Samuel HaLevi (RiHa'l)	Piyyut for Sabbath Circumcision Piyyutim, Selichot, Kinot
	Shemariah ben Elijah Ikriti, of Negropont	Untitled
	Elhanan ben Isaac of Dampierre	Pizmonim for Passover
	Menachem ben (Solomon ben Simson) Jacob	For Synagogue Service
	Jose bar Jose	For New Year Day, Day of Atonement and Siddur
	Daniel ben Judah	Yigdal Elohim Hai
	Gershom ben Judah	Untitled Selichot
	Eleazar Kalir	Festivals
	Kalonymus Family	Various Holidays
	David ben Kalonymus	Selichot
	Samuel ben Kalonymus (He-Hasid), of Speyer	Shir HaYihud
	Abraham ben Abigdor Kara.	Ana Elohe Abraham
	Dunash HaLevi ben Labrat	Poetry – Dror Yikra
	Isaac Luria (Ashkenazi) (Ari, Arizal, He-Ari)	Untitled Sabbath
	Shemaiah de Medina	Untitled
	Jacob ben, Meir (Tam) (Rabbeinu Tam)	Untitled
	Meshullam ben Moses	Various
	Samuel ibn Naghrela (Samuel HaNagid)	Ben Tehillim
	Eliezer ben Nathan (Raavan)	Various
	Meir ben Isaac Nehorai	Akdamut
	Meir ben Samuel (RAM)	Changed Kol Nidre

Category	Author	Work/s
	Simhah ben Samuel, of Vitry	Contre HaPiyyutim
	Joseph ben Isaac Bekhor Shor	Untitled
	Shlomo Yitzhaki (Rashi)	Selichot
7. Ritual		
	Isaac Aboab (Menorat HaMaor)	Aron HaEdut
	Zedekiah ben Abraham Anaw	Shibbole HaLeket
	Avraham Azulai	Knaff Renanim
	Joseph ben Baruch (Joseph of Clisson)	Untitled
	Aharon Berechyah of Modena	Me'il Tzedakah Bigdei Kodesh
	Aron Chorin	Nogah HaBedek
	Chananel ben Chushiel	Sefer HaMikvaot
	Abraham ben Jehiel Danzig	Toledot Adam
	Jacob Israel ben Zvi Ashkenazi Emden (the Yabets)	Sefer Tefilah
	Isaac ben Judah ibn Ghiyyat (Ghayyat)	Sha'areh Simhah Hilkot Pesahim
	Aaron ben Jacob ben David HaKohen	Orhot Hayyim
	Isaiah HaLevi Horowitz (Shelah, Shaloh)	Shnei Luchos HaBris (Shelah) Sha'ar HaShamayim
	Shabtai Sheftel Horowitz	Additions to Sha ar HaShamayim
	Samson ben Joseph of Falaise	Pesakim
	Jacob ben Judah Landau	Agur
	Hayyim ben Moses Lipschutz	Derek Hayyim
	Judah ben Bezalel Loew (Maharal / Maharal of Prague)	Gevurot Hashem Divrei Negidim Ner Mitzvah Or Chadash

Category	Author	Work/s
	Ephraim Zalman (Solomon) Margolis	Matteh Ephraim
	Joseph ibn Plat	Tikkun Soferim
	Yosef Quafih	Siach Yerushalayim
	Dovber Schneuri (Mitteler Rebbe)	Sha'arei Orah Maamrei Admur HaEmtzei
	Shem Tov ibn Shem Tov	Commentary on Passover Haggadah
	Abraham ben Solomon Treves (Tarfati)	Birkat Abraham
	Israel Veltz	Chok le-Ysra'el
	Abraham ben Asher Wallerstein	Mahazeh Abraham
	Jedidiah Weil	Untitled commentary on Haggadah
	Isaac Hirsch Weiss	Orah la-Zaddek
G. Miscellaneous		
	Isaac Adarbi (Adribi)	Divrei Shalom
	Judah ben Solomon Chai Alkali	Goral la-Adonai Shalom Yerushalayim
	Naphtali (Hirsch) ben Asher Altschul	Imrei Shefer
	Moses ben Baruch Almosnino	Meammez Koah
	Nathan ben Jehiel (Yechiel) Anaw (Anav)	Arukh
	Aaron ben Moses ben Asher	Sefer Dikdukei HaTe'amim
	Bahya ben Asher	Kad HaKemah Shulkhan Arba Ohel Moed
	Sholom Noach Berezovsky	Nesivos Sholom
	Joseph ben Ephraim Caro	Derashot
	Chacham Yosef Chaim (Ben Ish Chai)	Qanan-un-Nisa

Category	Author	Work/s
	Zvi Hirsch Chajes (The Maharatz Chajes)	Imrei Binah Minhat Kenaot
	Levi ben Jacob ibn Chaviv (Habib) (Ralbach)	Kontres HaSemikah Perush Kiddush HaChodesh
	Aron Chorin	Emek HaShewah
	Hasdai ben Abraham Crescas	Or Adonai Refutation of Christian Principles Passover Sermon
	Abraham ben Jehiel Danzig	Bet Abraham
	Abraham ben David (Ravad III)	Sefer Ba'ale Nefesh
	Eliyahu Eliezer Dessler	Michtav me-Eliyahu
	Shabtai Donolo	Sefer HaYekar
	David Solomon Eibenschutz	Arbe Nahal
	Meir Eisenstadter (Meir Ash) (Maharam Ash)	Imrei Yosher
	Baruch HaLevi Epstein	Mekor Baruch
	Yechiel Michel HaLevi Epstein (the Aruch Shulchan)	Leil Shimurim
	Jonathan Eybeschutz	Ya'arot Devash
	Elazar ben Moshe Azikri / Ezkar_	Sefer Hareidim
	Abraham ben Meir ibn Ezra (Abenezra)	Moznayim Sefer Yesod Iggeret Shabbat
	Solomon ben Judah, ibn Gabirol (Gvirol)	Anak Ethics
	Sherira Gaon	Iggeret Rav Sherira Gaon
	Yonah ben Avraham Gerondi	Iggeret HaTeshuvah Sha'are Teshuvah Sefer HaYirah
	Zerachiah ben Isaac HaLevi Gerondi	ReZaH

Category	Author	Work/s
	Levi ben Gershom (Gersonides / Ralbag)	Sefer Ma'aseh Hoshev
	Louis Ginzberg	Geonica
	Joseph ben Gorion	Sefer Yossipon
	Abraham ben Eliezar HaKohen	Or We-Yish'i
	Joseph ben Joshua Meir HaKohen	Emek Habachah (Valley of Weeping)
	Haparchi, Ishtori ben Moses, (Kaftor Vaferech)	Sefer Kaftor Vaferech
	Jehiel Solomon Heilprin	Seder HaDorot Erke HaKinnuyim
	Abraham Joshua Heschel	Der Shem Hamefoyrosh Prophetic Inspiration After the Prophets
	Isaiah HaLevi Horowitz (Shelah, Shaloh)	Shnei Luchos HaBris (Shelah)
	Yitzhak (Isaac) Hutner	Torat HaNazir Pachad Yitzhak
	Elhanan ben Isaac of Dampierre	Tikkun Tefillin
	Menasseh ben Joseph ben Israel (MB'Y)	Humble Addresses Nishmat Hayyim
	Nissim ben Jacob (HaMafteach) (Rav Nissim Gaon)	Sefer Ma'asiyyot HaHakhamim
	Yonah ibn Janach (Merinos)	Sefer HaShorashim
	Asher ben Jehiel (Rosh)	Orach Chaim
	Gaon Saadia ben Joseph	Commentary on Sefer Yezirah
	Israel Meir Kagan (HaKohen) (Chofetz Chaim)	Ahavat Chesed Sh'mirat HaLashon
	Zvi Hirsch Kalischer	Sefer Yitzi'at Mizrayim Derishot Ziyyon

Category	Author	Work/s
	Eleazar ben Yehuda ben Kalonymus, of Worms (Rokeach)	HaRokeach Adderet Ha-Shem Sefer HaKapporet Sefer HaHayyim Sha'are HaSod HaYihud weha-Emunah
	Joseph ben Isaac Kimchi	Sepher Zikkaron Sepher Haggalui
	Moses Kimchi	Mahalakh Shevile Hadda'ath Sepher Tahbosheth
	David Kimchi (RaDaK)	Michlol / Sefer Miclol Teshuvoth Lanotzrim
	Abraham Isaac Kook (HaRaAyaH / HaRav)	Igorot HaRaiyah
	Dunash HaLevi ben Labrat	Grammar book
	Moses Israel Landau	Marpe Lashon
	Shabbatai Carmuz Levita	Sefer HaYashar
	Boruch Ber Leibowitz	Birkas Shmuel
	Saul Lieberman	Sheki'in
	Menachem di Lonzano	Shtei Yadot
	Shlomo Ephraim Lunshitz	Homiletic Works Ir Gibborim Sifsei Daas Orach LeChaim – Amudei Sheish
	Moses ben Maimon (Maimonides) (Rambam)	Epistle to Yemen (Iggeret Temam) Scientific works
	Abba Mari ben Moses ben Joseph Don Astruc, of Lunel	Minhat Kenaot
	Samuel ben Moses de Medina (RashDaM)	Ben Shemuel

Category	Author	Work/s
	Menachem ben Solomon Meiri (HaMeiri)	Chibbur HaTeshuvah
	Meir Leibush ben Jehiel Michel (Malbim)	Artzoth HaShalom
	Abraham ben Judah HaLevi Minz	Seder Gittin ve-Haliza
	Moshe Mos, of Premysl	Ho'il Moshe (Ba'er Heitiv)
	Samuel ibn Naghrela (Samuel HaNagid)	Ben Mishlei
	Eliezer ben Nathan (Raavan)	Even HaEzer
	Avraham Aharon Price	Mishnat Avraham Imrei Avraham
	Solomon Judah Loeb Rapoport	Biographies Encyclopedia
	Isaac Samuel Reggio (Yashar)	Iggerot Yashar
	Jacob ben Reuben	Sefer Milhamot Adonai
	Nissim ben Reuven, of Gerona (RaN)	Collection of sermons
	Israel Lipkin Salanter	Ohr Yisrael
	Judah ben Samuel of Regensburg (He-Hasid)	Sefer Hasidim
	Menahem ben Jacob ibn Saruq	Mahberet / Sefer HaPitronot
	Jacob ben Aaron Sasportas	Zizat Noble Zebi
	Menachem Mendel Schneerson (The Lubavitcher Rebbe)	Igrot Kodesh Sefer HaSichot
	Kalonymus Kalman Shapira (Szapira)	Chovas haTalmidim Esh Kodesh
	Shalom Sharabi (Rashash)	Minhagei haRashash
	Shimon Shkop	Ma'arekhet haKinyanim
	Yaakov Chaim Sofer (Kaf HaChaim)	Yagel Yaakov

Category	Author	Work/s
	Yechiel Michel Tukachinsky	Gesher HaChaim Bein HaShemashos
	Aaron Walden	Shem HaGedolim heHadash
	Eleazar ben Eleazar HaKappar (Bar Kappara, Berebi)	Mishnah of Bar Kappara
	Judah HaNasi (Rabbeinu Hakodesh)	Mishnah Editor / Redactor
	Simcha Zissel Ziv (Alter of Kelm)	Hokmah U-Mussar

Categorical Classification Of Works Listed By Century And Author

This table differs from the previous one in that the categorical listing of the works and the authors is further subdivided according to the century in which the work was produced. It therefore does not have the list categorized alphabetically, except within each century.

Structure

Category	Sub-Category	Page
A. Biblical		359
	1. Explanations	359
	2. Glosses	360
	3. Midrashic	360
	4. Commentaries	362
	5. Super-Commentaries	365
	6. Miscellaneous	366
B. Talmud		367
	1. Mishnah	367
	Mishnah Commentary	367
	2. Talmudic Specific Aspects	368
	General	368
	Glosses	370
	3. Talmud Commentaries	370
	Tosefot	373
	Super-Commentaries	375
C. Codes Of Law		375
	1. Codes and Commentaries	375
	2. Halakha Related	380
D. Responsa		384
E. Biblical And Talmudic Novellae		390
F. Other Traditional Scholarly Works		393
	1. Ethics	393
	2. Hassidic	394
	3. Kabbalah	396
	4. Liturgical	398
	5. Philosophy	400
	6. Piyyutim / Poetry	402
	7. Ritual	404
G. Miscellaneous		405

Works Of Authors And Classifications • 359

	Century	Work	Author
A. Biblical			
1. Explanations			
	First BCE - First CE	Targum Yonatan	Jonathan ben Uzziel
	First	Targum Onkelos	Onkelos
	Second	Seder Olam Rabbah	Jose ben Halafta
	Tenth	Aleppo Codex	Aaron ben Moses ben Asher
		Commentaries	Judah ben Gershom
	Eleventh	Untitled	Samuel ben Meir (Rashbam)
	Twelfth		
	Thirteenth	Super-Commentary on Ibn Ezra's Commentary on the Pentateuch	Abba Mari ben Elgidor
		Midrash Rabbeinu Bachya	Levi ben Gershom (Ralbag, Gersonides)
		Untitled	Samson ben Isaac of Chinon (MaHaRShak)
		Midrashim Rabbeinu Bachya	Bahya ben Asher
		Untitled	Isaac ben Abraham (RIBA)
	Fifteenth	Sefer HaAkedah Yad Absholom	Isaac ben Moses Arama (Ba'al Akedah)
	Sixteenth	Torat Moshe Levush Orah	Jacob de Castro
	Seventeenth	El Conciliador	Menasseh ben Joseph ben Israel (MB'Y)
		Ohr HaChaim	Hayyim ibn Attar
		Tifferet Yehonatan	Jonathan Eybeschutz
	Eighteenth	Aspects of Torah	Avraham Azulai (Hida)
		HaEmek Davar	Haim Yosef David Azulai
		Chiddushei Harim	Yitzhak Myer Alter

Century	Work	Author
Nineteenth	Likutei Torah	Shneur Zalman Baruch (Borukovich), of Liadi (Alter Rebbe, GRaZ)
	Binah Mikrah	Yissachar Jacobson
	Chatam Sofer	Moses Sofer (Chatam Sofer)
	Magen Avraham	Avraham of Trisk
	Imrei Emes	Avraham Mordechai Alter
	Sfas Emes al HaTorah	Yehuda Aryeh Leib Alter (Sfas Emes)
	Beis Yisrael	Yisroel Alter
	Untitled	Simchah Bunim Alter
	Or li-Yesharim	Yechiel Michel HaLevi Epstein
	Meshech Chochma	Meir Simcha Kalonymus HaKohen of Dvinsk
Twentieth	Likkutei Torat Shmuel	Shmuel Schneerson (The Rebbe Maharash)
	Pnei Menachem	Pinchas Menachem Alter
	Likkutei Sichot	Menachem Mendel Schneerson (The Lubavitcher Rebbe)
	Imrei Das	Yehuda Meir Shapiro

2. *Glosses*

Century	Work	Author
Sixteenth	Kli Yakar	Shlomo Ephraim Lunshitz

3. *Midrashic*

Century	Work	Author
Tenth	Megillat Setarim Comforting Tales	Jacob ben Nissim ibn Shahin (Rabbeinu Nissim, HaMafteach)
Eleventh	Commentary on Midrash Sifra Commentary on Midrash Sifre	Hillel ben Eliakim
	Lekah Tob / Pesikta Zutarta	Tobiah ben Eliezer

Century	Work	Author
	Yesod	HaDarshan
Twelfth	Commentary on the Sifra	Samson ben Abraham of Sens
	Sekel Kob	Menahem ben Solomon
Thirteenth	Elef HaMagen	Shemariah ben Elijah Ikriti of Negropont
	Sefer Pe'ah	Moses ibn Tibbon
Fifteenth	Toledot Aharon	Aaron of Pisaro
Sixteenth	Midos Aharon Korban Aharon	Aharon ibn Chaim
	Magen Avot	Yom Tov ben Moshe Tzahalon (Maharitz)
Seventeenth	Tifferet HaGershuni	Gershon Ashkenazi
	Zayit Ra'anan	Abraham Abele ben Chaim HaLevi Gombiner (Magen Avraham)
	Parashat Derakim	Judah ben Samuel Rosanes
Eighteenth	Zera Ephraim	Ephraim Zalman (Solomon) Margolis
	Annotations to Midrashot Rabbot	Samuel ben Joseph Strashun (Rashash)
Nineteenth	Pesikhta de-Rab Kahana	Solomon Buber
	Legends of the Jews	Louis Ginzberg
	Commentaries on the Midrash Rabbah of Five Megillot and the Pentateuch	Enoch Zundel ben Joseph
	Haggahot	Joshua Hoschel ben Elijah Zeeb Levin
	Torah Shelemah	Menachem Mendel Kasher
Twentieth	Kovet Ha'aros	Isaac Hutner
	Sifre Zuta Midreshei Teiman	Saul Lieberman

Century	Work	Author
4. Commentaries		
Eighth	Sheilot d'Rav Achai	Achai Gaon
Ninth	Arabic translation of Bible	Gaon Saadia ben Joseph
Tenth	Torah Commentary	Chananel ben Chushiel
Eleventh	Sefer HaYashar Yesod Mora	Abraham ben Meir ibn Ezra (Abenezra)
	Commentary on Pentateuch	Isaac ben Asher HaLevi (Riva)
	Sefer HaOsher	Jacob ben Reuben
	Untitled Tanakh Commentary	Kalonymus ben Shabbethai
	Commentary on the Tanakh	Shlomo Yitzhaki (Rashi)
Twelfth	Untitled	Isaac ben Abraham of Dampierre (RIBA)
	Torah and Five Megillot Commentary	Abigdor Cohen (of Vienna)
	Untitled Torah Commentary	Moses ben Nahman (Nahmanides) (Ramban)
	Untitled	Isaac ben Samuel (Hasefardi)
	Untitled Bible Commentary	Joseph ben Isaac Bekhor Shor
Thirteenth	Midrash Rabbeinu Bachya	Bahya (Bachya) ben Asher (Rabbeinu Behaye)
	Untitled on Job	Abba Mari ben Algidor
	Untitled (mostly lost)	Judah ben Gershom (Rabbeinu Gershom)
	Perush al Sefer HaTorah Perush al Sefer Iyob	Simeon Kara of Frankfurt
	RaDaK	David Kimchi (RaDaK)
	Untitled	Joseph ben Isaac Kimchi
	Hazzekuni	Hezekiah ben Manoah (Hizkuni / Chizkuni)

Century	Work	Author
	Tort Hashem Temima	Moses ben Nahman (Nahmanides) (Ramban)
	Commentary on the Pentateuch	Moses ibn Tibbon
Fourteenth	Untitled Biblical commentary	Nissim ben Reuven, of Gerona (RaN)
Fifteenth	Prophets	Isaac ben Judah Abravanel
	Untitled Psalms commentary	Joseph Chayon
	Tror Hamor Eshkol Hakofer	Avraham ben Yaakov Saba
	Untitled Tanakh Commentaries	Obadiah ben Jacob Sforno
Sixteenth	Yedeh Moshe	Moses ben Baruch Almosnino
	Ayyalah SheluHah	Naphtali (Hirsch) ben Asher Altschul
	Baalei Bris Avraham	Abraham Azulai
	Bris Avraham	Abraham Geciliyah
	Yalkut / Yalkut Shimoni	Simeon Kara of Frankfurt (HaDarshan)
	Meshiv Nevesh	Yoel Sirkis (Bach)
	Lekach Tov	Yom Tov ben Moshe Tzahalon (Maharitz)
	Iggeret Shmuel	Samuel de Uzeda
Seventeenth	Metsudot (David and Zion)	David ben Aryeh Loeb Altshuler (Altshul)
	Ohr HaChaim	Hayyim ibn Atar (Ohr HaChaim HaKadosh)
	Sifsei Chachamim	Shabbethai ben Joseph Bass
	Me'am Loez	Yaakov Culi
	Nehamot Ziyyon	Samuel Danzig
	Kotnot Or	Meir ben Iszak Eisenstadt (Meir Ash) (Maharam Ash / Panim Me'irot)

Century	Work	Author
Eighteenth	Adderet Eliyahu	Elijah ben Kalonymus
	Nefesh David	Moses de Medina
	Arbe Nahal Baalei Bris Avraham	David Solomon Eibenschutz
	Sefer HaBrit	Zvi Hirsch Kalischer
	Toledot Ya'akov Yosef Ben Porat Yosef Tsafenat Pane'ah	Jacob Joseph ben Tzvi HaKohen Katz, of Polonnoye
	Kesef Nivvar	Abi Ezra Selig Margolis
	Shem Ephraim	Ephraim Zalman (Solomon) Margolis
	HaKetav (K'sav) V'ha-kabbalah	Jacob Tzvi Mecklenburg
	Biur	Moses Mendelssohn
	Yeshuot Ya'acob	Jacob Meshullam ben Mordechai Ze'ev Ornstein
	Sefer Torat Elohim HaTorah weha-Pesufiah	Isaac Samuel Reggio (Yashar)
	Mashbir Bar	Joseph ben Menachem Steinhart
	Adereth Eliyahu	Elijah ben Solomon Zalman (Vilna Gaon, Gra)
Nineteenth	Davar HaEmek	Naftali Tzvi Yehuda Berlin
	Torah Temimah	Baruch HaLevi Epstein (the Aruch Hashulchan)
	HaTorah veh-haMitzvah Mikra'ei Kodesh	Meir Leibush ben Jehiel Michel (Malbim)
	Techeiles Mordechai	Sholom Mordechai Schwadron (Maharsham)
	Ksav Sofer	Abraham Samuel Benjamin (Sofer Ksav Sofer)
	Beis HaLevi	Yosef Dov Soloveitchik (Beis HaLevi)
	Mikdash Melek	Aaron Walden

Century	Work	Author
Twentieth	On Nahmanides' Torat Hashem Temima	Yehuda Meir Dvir

5. *Super-Commentaries*

Century	Work	Author
Thirteenth	Keter Shem Tov	Shem Tov ben Abraham ibn Gaon
	On Ibn Ezra's Pentateuch Commentary	Samson ben Isaac of Chinon
Fourteenth	Be'urim on Rashi's Pentateuch	Israel ben Pethahiah Ashkenazi Isserlein
Fifteenth	On Nahmanides' Commentary On Rashi's Commentary	Isaac Aboab
	On Rashi's Pentateuch	Obadiah ben Abraham of Bertinoro
	Sefer HaMizrachi	Elijah Mizrachi (Re'em)
Sixteenth	Tzeidah LaDerech	Yissachar Ber Ellenburg
	Levush Orah (Rashi's Pentateuch)	Mordechai ben Avraham Jaffe
	On Rashi's Pentateuch	Abraham ben Abigdor Kara
	Gur Aryeh	Judah ben Bezalel Loew (Maharal / Maharal of Prague)
	Yeri'ot Shlomo	Solomon Luria (Maharshal, Rashal)
	Ho'il Moshe (Be'er Moshe)	Moshe Mos of Premysl
	Dibre David	David ben Samuel HaLevi Segal (Taz)
Seventeenth	Sifsei Chachamim	Shabbethai ben Joseph Bass
	Chalukei Avanim	David Lida
	Kesef Mezukak	Avraham Lieblein
Nineteenth	Kur Zahav	Aryeh Leib Steinhardt
	Techeiles Mordechai	Mordechai Gimpel Yaffe Torizer

Century	Work	Author
6. *Miscellaneous*		
Ninth	Biblical translation to Arabic	Saadia ben Joseph, Gaon
Tenth	Sefer Dikdukei HaTe'amim	Aaron ben Moses ben Asher
	The Aleppo Codex	Shlomo Boya'a
	Chachmuni	Shabtai Donolo
Twelfth	Sefer Peretz	Perez ben Elijah (Rap / Rapash / Maharpash)
	El Hasofer	David Kimchi (Radak)
Thirteenth	Kiryat Sefer	Menachem ben Solomon Meiri (HaMeiri)
Fifteenth	Toledot Aharon	Aaron of Pissaro
Sixteenth	Divrei Shalom	Isaac Adarbi (Adribi)
	Torat Moshe	Moshe Alshich
	Kol Yacob	Jacob de Castro
	Torah Ohr	Joshua Boaz Mevorakh / Joshua Boaz ben Simon Baruch (Shiltei Gibborim)
Seventeenth	Dibre Emet	Solomon ben Joshua Adeni
	Tiferet Yehonatan	Jonathan Eybeschutz
	Birkat Shemuel	Aaron Samuel ben Israel Kaidenover
	Bet Aharon	Aaron ben Samuel
	Toledot Yaacob	Jacob ben Aaron Sasportas
Eighteenth	Degel Machaneh Ephraim	Moshe Chaim Ephraim of Sudilkov
	Sefer Torat Elohim	Isaac Samuel Reggio (Yashar)
	Maamrei Admur HaEmtzei	Dovber Schneuri (Mitteler Rebbe)
	Ma'amar Abraham	Abraham ben Asher Wallerstein

	Century	Work	Author
	Nineteenth	Magen Avraham	Avraham of Trisk
		Emes leYaakov Iyunim BaMikra	Jacob Kamenecki (Yaakov Kamenetsky)
		Mishnat Avraham Imrei Avraham	Avraham Aharon Price
	Twentieth	Sichos Levi	Yaakov Yitzhak Ruderman

B. Talmud

1. Mishnah

	Century	Work	Author
	Second	Systematized coding of halakha	Akiva ben Joseph (Rabbi Akiva)
		Redactor of the Mishnah	Judah HaNasi (Rabbeinu HaKadosh)
	Second-Third	Mishnah of Bar Kappara	Eleazar ben Eleazar HaKappar (Bar Kappara, Berebi)
	Tenth	Iggeret Rav Sherira Gaon	Sherira ben Hanina, Gaon
	Nineteenth	Mishpat Leshon HaMishnah	Isaac Hirsch Weiss
Mishnah *Commentary*	Tenth	Untitled	Hai ben Sherira, Gaon
		Comforting Tales	Jacob ben Nissim ibn Shahin (Rabbeinu Nissim, HaMafteach)
	Twelfth	Untitled	Samson ben Abraham of Sens
		Perush Mishnayot	Moses ben Maimon (Maimonides) (Rambam)
	Thirteenth	Untitled	Meir ben Baruch (MaHaRaM) (Meir of Rothenburg)
		Untitled	Asher ben Jehiel (Rabbeinu Asher / Rosh)
		Beit HaBechirah	Menachem ben Solomon Meiri (HaMeiri)

Century	Work	Author
Fourteenth	Untitled, several tractates	Simeon ben Zemah Duran (Rashbatz / Tashbetz)
Fifteenth	Untitled	Obadiah ben Abraham of Bertinoro
Sixteenth	Perush Yakar Al Shisha Sidre Mishnah Perush Yakar Al HaLevush	Abraham Azulai
	Tosefos Yomtov	Yom Tov Lippman Heller (Tosefos Yomtov)
	Lehem Mishneh	Moses ben Noah Lipschutz
Seventeenth	M'Lekhet Shlomo	Solomon ben Joshua Adeni
	Lehem Shamayim	Jacob Israel ben Zvi Ashkenazi Emden (the Yabets)
Eighteenth	Beit Yisrael	Yisroel ben Shmuel Ashkenazi, of Shklov
	Tifferet Yisrael	Israel Lipschutz
	Shenoth Eliyahu	Elijah ben Solomon Zalman (Vilna Gaon, Gra)
Nineteenth	Aruch LaNer	Yaakov Etlinger
	Tosefot Sheni L-Ziyyon	Joshua Hoschel ben Elijah Zeeb Levin

2. Talmud Specific Aspects

General

Century	Work	Author
Fourth	Edited Babylonian Talmud	Rav Ashi
Tenth	Iggeret Rav Sherira Gaon	Gaon Sherira ben Hanina
	Mavo HaTalmud	Samuel ibn Naghrela (Samuel HaNagid)
Fourteenth	Darche HaGemara / Darche HaTalmud	Isaac ben Jacob Campanton

Century	Work	Author
Fifteenth	Toledot Aharon	Aaron of Pesaro
	Kelalei HaTalmud	Joseph ben Ephraim Caro (Mechaber)
	Ayn Yaakov	Yaakov ibn Chaviv (Habib)
Sixteenth	Masoret HaShas / Massoret HaTalmud	Joshua Boaz Mevorakh (Shiltei Gibborim)
Seventeenth	Pahad Yitzhak	Yitzhak Hezekiah Lampronti
	Sefer Maasiyot	Menachem d. Lonzano
	Be'er HaGolah	Moses ben Naftali Hertz Rivkes
	Toledot Yaacob	Jacob ben Aaron Sasportas
Eighteenth	Derekh Tevunoth	Moses Chaim Luzzatto (Ramchal)
	Hagahot v'Chiddushei HaRashash	Samuel ben Joseph Strashun (Rashash)
Nineteenth	Beit Shlomo	Solomon ben Kalman HaLevi Abel
	Torah Shelameh	Menachem Mendel Kasher
	Ziyyun Yehoshua	Joshua Hoschel ben Elijah Zeeb Levin
	Al HaYerushalmi	Saul Lieberman (G'rash)
	S'Dei Chemed	Chaim Chizkiya Medini
	Shiurei Rebbe Chaim MiTelz	Rabinowitz, Chaim Shalom Tuvia (Reb Chaim Telzer)
	Mechkarim be Talmud	Yechiel Yaakov Weinberg
	Vienna Edition of the Talmud	Isaac Hirsch Weiss
Twentieth	Torah min HaShamayim BeAspaklariya shel HaDorot	Abraham Joshua Heschel

	Century	Work	Author
Glosses	Twelfth	Untitled	Abraham ben David (Ravad III)
		Untitled	Moses ben Nahman (Nahmanides) (Ramban)
	Fifteenth	Erech HaShulchan	Jacob de Castro
		Untitled	Abraham ben Abigdor Kara
	Sixteenth	Shittah Mekubetzet	Bezalel Ashkenazi
		Chochmat Shlomo	Solomon Luria (Maharshal, Rashal)
		Hagahot Bach	Yoel Sirkes (Bach)
	Seventeenth	Mishneh la-Melek	Judah ben Samuel Rosanes
	Eighteenth	Untitled	Isaiah ben Judah Loeb Berlin
		Untitled	Akiva Eger
		Untitled	Zvi Hirsch Kalischer
		Biurei HaGra	Elijah ben Solomon Zalman (Vilna Gaon, Gra)
	Nineteenth	Untitled	Zvi Hirsch Chajes (Chayes) (The Maharatz Chajes)
		Mishnah Berurah	Israel Meir Kagan (Ha-Kohen) (Chofetz Chaim)
		Untitled	Eliyahu David Rabinowitz-Teomim (Aderet)
3. Talmud Commentaries	Eighth	Sheilot d'Rav	Achai Gaon
	Tenth	Untitled	Chananel ben Chushiel (Rabbeinu Chananel)
		Untitled	Hai Gaon
		Peirush Rabbeinu Gershon	Gershon ben Yehuda (Me'Or HaGolah)
	Eleventh	Untitled	Isaac ben Reuben Albargeloni

Century	Work	Author
	Untitled	Eliakim ben Meshullam HaLevi
	Untitled, in Menachot	Meir ben Samuel (RAM)
	Untitled	Kalonymus ben Shabbethai
	Untitled on Babylonian Talmud	Shlomo Yitzhaki (Rashi)
Twelfth	Torath Kohanim	Abraham ben David (Ravad III)
	Sefer Has-Moar Sefer-Tsava	Zerachiah ben Isaac HaLevi Gerondi (ReZaH, RaZBI, Ba'al HaMaor)
Thirteenth	Untitled	Yom Tov ibn Asevilli (Ritva)
	Sefer HaRemazim / Kitzur Piskei HaRosh	Jacob ben Ashur (The Tur)
	Sefer HaMordechai	Mordechai ben Hillel Ashkenazi
	(Lost)	Judah ben Gershom (Rabbeinu Gershom)
	Sefer Keritut	Samson ben Isaac, of Chinon (MaHaRSHak)
	Seder Olam	Simha ben Samuel of Speyer
	Sefer Pe'ah	Moses ibn Tibbon
Fourteenth	Untitled, several tractates	Simeon ben Zemah Duran (Rashbatz / Tashbetz)
	Untitled	Nissim ben Reuven, of Gerona (RaN)
Fifteenth	Milei DeAvot	Joseph Chayon
Sixteenth	Midrash Shmuel	Shmuel Aceda
	Pirkei Moshe	Moses ben Baruch Almosnino
	Shittah Mikubetzet	Bezalel Ashkenazi

Century	Work	Author
	Untitled	Elazar ben Moshe Azikri (Ezkari)
	Nazir	Jacob de Castro
	Ayn Yaakov	Yaakov ibn Chaviv (Habib)
	Hiddushei Halakhot Hiddushei Aggadot	Samuel Eidels (Edels) (Maharsha)
	Be'er Sheva	Yissachar ber Ellenburg
	Derech Chaim	Judah ben Bezalel Loew (Maharal / Maharal of Prague)
	Chochmat Shlomo Yam Shel Shlomo	Solomon Luria (Maharshal / Rashal)
	Midrash Shmuel	Samuel de Uzeda
Seventeenth	Taryag Mitzvot	Jonathan Eybeschutz
	Untitled	Abraham Abele ben Chaim HaLevi Gombiner (Magen Avraham)
	Pene Yehoshua Kontres	Yaakov Yehoshua ben Zvi Hirsch (Jacob J. Falk)
	Birkat HaZebah	Aaron Samuel ben Israel Kaidenover
	Be'er HaGolah	Moses ben Naftali Hertz Rivkes
	Koss Hayeshu'ot	Samuel Schotten (Mharsheishoch)
Eighteenth	Tekelet Mordechai	Mordechai ben Abraham Benet
	Tziyyon Lenefesh Hayyah	Ezekiel ben Judah Landau (Nodah B'Yehuda)
	Ruach Chaim	Chaim ben Yitzhak Volozhin (Reb Chaim)
Nineteenth	HaEmek She'eila Meromei Sadeh	Naphtali Zvi Yehuda Berlin
	Torat Nevi'im	Zvi Hirsch Chajes (Chyes) (The Maharatz Chajes)

	Century	Work	Author
		Micah HaMayim Or li-Yesharim	Yechiel Michel HaLevi Epstein (the Aruch Hashulchan)
		Pnei Shlomo	Solomon ben Joseph Ganzfried
		On Yerushalmi	Louis Ginzberg
		Untitled	David Zevi Hoffmann
		Ayin Aiyah	Abraham Isaac Kook (HaRaAYaH / HaRav)
		May'yene Yehoshua	Joshua Hoschel ben Elizah Zeeb Levin
		Tosefot Rishonim	Saul Lieberman
		Chiddushei HaGra al Shas	Chaim Soloveitchik (The Brisker Reb)
		Chiddushei Ridvaz Tosafot haRid	Yaakov David Wilovsky
	Twentieth	Anaf Etz Avot Maor Israel	Ovadia Yosef
Tosefot	Eleventh	Tosafot Riva	Isaac ben Asher HaLevi (Riva)
		Untitled	Kalonymus ben Isaac
		Untitled	Isaac ben Meir (Rivam)
		Untitled	Samuel ben Meir (Rashbam)
		Untitled	Judah ben Nathan (Riban)
		Tosefot Yeshanim	Isaac ben Samuel, of Dampierre (Ri)
	Twelfth	Untitled	Isaac ben Abraham (Riba)
		Untitled	Samson ben Abraham of Sens
		Untitled	Joseph ben Baruch (Joseph of Clisson)
		Untitled	Abigdor Cohen, of Vienna
		Untitled	Baruch ben Isaac

Century	Work	Author
	Untitled	Elhanan ben Isaac, of Dampierre
	Untitled	Jacob of Chinon
	Untitled	Samson ben Joseph, of Falaise
	Untitled	Eleazar ben Yehuda ben Kalonymus, of Worms (Rokeach)
	Untitled	Samuel ben Kalonymus (He-Hasid), of Speyer
	Untitled	Judah ben Isaac Messer Leon
	Untitled	Jacob ben Meir (Rabbeinu Tam)
	Untitled	Isaac ben Mordechai, of Regensburg (RiBaM)
	Untitled	Joseph ben Isaac Bekhor Shor
	Untitled	Samuel ben Solomon, of Falaise
Thirteenth	Untitled	Meir ben Baruch, of Rothenburg (MaHaRaM)
	Gilyon Tosafot / Tosafot Gilyon	Eliezer of Touques
	Untitled	Asher ben Jehiel (Rabbeinu Asher / Rosh)
	Untitled	Jehiel ben Joseph, of Paris
	Untitled	Moses ben Meir, of Ferrara
	Tosefot of Evreux	Moses of Evreux
	Untitled	Simha ben Samuel, of Speyer
	Tosefot RI'D	Isaiah ben Mali di Trani (RI'D)
Nineteenth	Tosefot Rishonim	Saul Lieberman

	Century	Work	Author
Super-Commentaries		Emes leYaakov	Jacob Kamenecki (Yaakov Kamenetsky)
	Unknown	Gedulah Mordechai	Baruch ben David
	Sixteenth	Hiddushei Halakhot	Samuel Eidels (Maharsha)
	Eighteenth	Biur Mordechai	Mordechai ben Abraham Benet
		Hiddushei Mahariah	Joel Hayyim (Mahariah)
		Machatsi HaShekel	Samuel ben Nathan Loew
	Nineteenth	Or li-Yesharim	Yechiel Michel HaLevi Epstein (the Aruch Hashulchan)

C. Codes Of Law

1. Codes and Commentaries

	Century	Work	Author
	Second	Systematized coding of halakha in Mishnah	Akiva ben Joseph (Rabbi Akiva)
	Ninth	Halakhot Gedolot	Behag
		Halakot Gedolot / Halakot Rishonot	Simeon Kayyara
		Untitled	Hai ben Sherira, Gaon
	Tenth	Halacoth / Alfes / RIF	Yitzhak ben Yaakov HaKohen Alfasi
	Eleventh	Halakhot Ketonot	
		Sefer HaIttim	Judah ben Barzillai
	Twelfth	HaEshkol	Abraham ben Isaac of Narbonne (Raavad II)
		Elef HaMagen / Agur	Samuel ben Jacob Jam'a
		Sefer HaTerumah	Baruch ben Isaac
		Mishneh Torah (Yad HaHazakha)	Moses ben Maimon (Maimonides) (Rambam)
		Sefer HaIttur / Ittur Soferim	Yitzhak ben Abba Mari of Marseilles

Century	Work	Author
	Sefer HaHashalamah	Meshullam ben Moses
	Rokeach	Eleazar ben Yehuda of Worms
	Sefer HaTerumah	Baruch ben Yitzhak of Worms
Thirteenth	Sefer Mitzvot HaGadol (SeMaG)	Moses ben Jacob of Coucy
	Ammude HaGolah / Sefer Mitzvot Katan (Semak)	Isaac ben Joseph of Corbeil
	Shibbole HaLeket	Tzidkayah ben Avraham Anav HaRofei
	Abstract of Talmudic Law	Asher ben Jehiel
	Arba'ah Turim	Jacob ben Asher
	Meisharim Adam V'Chava	Yerucham ben Meshullam
	Or Zarua	Isaac ben Moses of Vienna (Or Zarua, Riaz)
Fourteenth	Kizzur Mordekai /Mordekai HaKaton	Samuel ben Aaron, of Schlettstadt
	Haggahot Asheri	Israel of Krems
	Commentary on Alfasi's (RIF) Halacoth	Nissim ben Reuven, of Gerona (RaN)
	Maggid Mishneh	Vidal di Tolosa
	Zedal la-Derek	Menahem ben Aaron ibn Zerah
Fifteenth	Beth Yosef Shulkhan Arukh Bedek-Bayit Kesef Mishna	Joseph ben Ephraim Caro (Karo) (Mechaber)
	Yekar Tiferet	David ben Solomon ibn Abi Zimra (Radbaz)
Sixteenth	Lehem Mishneh	Abraham ben Moses de Bouton

Century	Work	Author
	Vayigash Yehuda	Yehuda Leib ben Meir Channeles
	Erech HaShulchan	Jacob de Castro
	Rosh Yosef	Joseph Escapa
	HaMapah Darkhei Moshe	Moses ben Israel Isserles (Rema)
	Levush Malkhut	Mordechai ben Avraham Jaffe (Ba'al HaLevushim)
	Beit Israel	Joshua ben Alexander (Katz) HaKohen Falk
	Amudei Shlomo	Solomon Luria (Maharshal, Rashal)
	Turei Zahav	David ben Samuel HaLevi Segal (Taz)
	Bayit Chadash (Bach)	Yoel Sirkis (Bach)
	Masat Binyamin	Benjamin Aaron ben Abraham Slonik
	Bet Hillel	Hillel ben Naphtali Zevi
Seventeenth	Hiddushe HaGershuni	Gershon Ashkenazi
	Ateret Zekeinim	Menachem Mendel ben Meshulam Zalman Auerbach
	Lehem Yehuda	Judah Ayyas
	Mekor Chaim	Yair Chaim Bachrach
	Knesses HaGedolah Dina DeChaye	Chaim Benveniste
	Beit Avraham	Abraham ibn Chananyah
	Pri Chadash	Hezekiah ben David DiSilo
	Beit Shmuel	Samuel ben Uri Sharaga Faibesh
	Magen Avraham	Abraham Abele ben Chaim HaLevi Gombiner

Century	Work	Author
	Siftei Kohen (Shakh)	Shabbatai ben Meir HaKohen (Shach)
	Helkat Mehokek	Moses ben Isaac Judah Lima
	Minhar Ya'akov	Jacob ben Joseph Reischer (Backofen)
	Be'er HaGolah	Moses ben Naftali Hertz Rivkes
	Eliyahu Rabba	Eliyahu ben Binyamin Wolf Shapiro
	Netib Hayyim	Nethaneel ben Naftali Tzvi Weil
Eighteenth	Be'er Heitiv	Yehuda ben Shimon Ashkenazi
	Pe'at HaShulchan	Yisroel ben Shmuel Ashkenazi of Shklov
	Shulchan Aruch HaRav	Shneur Zalman Baruch (Borukovich), of Liadi (Alter Rebbe, GRaZ)
	Hayye Adam: Nishmat Adam Hokmat Adam: Binat Adam	Abraham ben Jehiel Danzig
	Ketzot HaChoshen Avnei Milluim	Aryeh Leib HaKohen Heller (The Ketzos)
	Lebushe Serad	David Solomon Eibenschutz
	Mechitzat HaShekel	Samuel ben Naftali HaLevi Kelin
	Sefer HaHayyim	Solomon ben Judah Aaron Kluger
	Dagul Merevavah	Ezekiel ben Judah Landau (Nodah B'Yehuda)
	Nesivos HaMishpat Derech Chaim	Jacob ben Jacob Moses Lorberbaum, of Lisser (Ba'al HaNesivos / Lissa Rav)

Century	Work	Author
	Bet Ephraim Yad Ephraim	Ephraim Zalman (Solomon) Margolis
	Sha'are Teshubah	Hayyim Mordechai Margolis
	Derek HaTov veha-Yashar	Meir ben Zvi Hirsch Margolis
	Yeshuot Ya'acob	Jacob Meshullam ben Mordechai Ze'ev Ornstein
	Zikron Yosef	Joseph ben Menachem Steinhart
	To'afot Re'em	Aaron Moses ben Jacob Taubes
	Biurei HaGra	Elijah ben Solomon Zalman (Vilna Gaon, Gra)
Nineteenth	Eben Bochan Sefer Moznayim la-Mishpat	Zvi Hirsh Kalischer
	Chazon Ish	Abraham Isaiah Karelitz
	Kitzur Shulkhan Arukh	Solomon ben Joseph Ganzfried
	Pithei Teshuvah	Abraham Zevi Hirsch ben Jacob Eisenstadt
	Ben Ish Chai	Chacham Yosef Chaim
	Untitled on Shulkhan Arukh	David Zevi Hoffmann
	Mishnah Berurah	Israel Meir Kagan (HaKohen) (Chofetz Chaim)
	Even HaEzel	Isser Zalman Meltzer (Even HaEzel)
	Kaf HaChaim	Yaakov Chaim Sofer (Kaf HaChaim)
	Chiddushei Rabbeinu Chaim	Chaim Soloveitchik (The Brisker Reb)

Century	Work	Author
	Beis HaLevi	Yosef Dov Soloveitchik (Beis HaLevi)
	Untitled responsa on Shulkhan Arukh	Abdalla Somekh
	Nachal Yitzhak	Yitzhak Elchanan Spektor
	Beis Ridvas	Yaakov David Wilovsky
Twentieth	Mitzvot Gadol	Avraham Aharon Price
	Introduction to the Code of Maimonides A Maimonides Reader	Isadore (Yitzhak) Twersky

2. Halakha Related

Century	Work	Author
Unknown	Ma'aseh Hageonim	Avraham Epstein
Eighth	Halakot Pesukot	Yehudai ben Nahman (Yehudai Gaon)
Ninth	Untitled	Amram br Sheshna Gaon
Tenth	Megillat Setarim	Nissim ben Jacob (HaMafteach) (Rav Nissim Gaon)
	Hilchata Givurt	Samuel ibn Naghrela (Samuel HaNagid)
	HaMafteach Megillat Setarim	Jacob ben Nissim ibn Shahin (Rabbeinu Nissim, HaMafteach)
	Various Halakhot	Hai ben Sherira, Gaon
Eleventh	Meah Shearim (Yitzhak Yeranen)	Isaac ibn Gias
	Even HaEzer	Eliezer ben Nathan (Raavan)
	Quoted by others	Meir ben Samuel (RAM)
	Vitry Mahzor	Simhah ben Samuel, of Vitry
Twelfth	Sefer HaRaviah	Eliezer ben Joel HaLevi (Raviah)

Century	Work	Author
	Piskei HaRid	Yeshayah ben Mali Hazaker
	HaRokeach	Eleazar ben Yehuda ben Kalonymus, of Worms (Rokeach)
	Sefer HaMitzvot Mishpetei HaCherem Hilkot Bedikah Torat HaAdam Sha'ar HaGemul	Moses ben Nahman (Nahmanides) (Ramban)
	Untitled	Joseph ibn Plat
	Sefer Yereim	Eliezer ben Samuel, of Metz
Thirteenth	Torat HaBayit	Shlomo ben Aderet
	Hilkot Berakot / Seder Berakot Mirkot MaHaRaM Hilkot Shehitah Hilkot Abelut / Hilkot Semahot Hilkot Pesukot Hilkot Erubin	Meir ben Baruch (Meir of Rothenburg) (MaHaRaM)
	Sefer HaChinuch / Chinuch	Aaron HaLevi (of Barcelona)
	Bedek HaBayit	Aharon HaLevi (Ra'AH)
	Migdal Oz	Shem Tov ben Abraham ibn Gaon
	Biur HaGet	Samson ben Isaac, of Chinon (MaHaRShak)
	Hilcoth Yomtov Sefer HaMatanah	Asher ben Meshullam
	Translated Sefer HaMitzvot	Moses ibn Tibbon
Fourteenth	Passover Sermon	Hasdai ben Abraham Crescas
	Sefer Minhagim	Isaac Tyrnau
Fifteenth	Devar Shemuel	Samual Aboab (Rasha)

Century	Work	Author
	Siddur Mordechai Ve-Simanav / Siddur Dine Mordekai	Joshua Boaz Mevorakh / Joshua Boaz ben Simon Baruch (Shiltei Gibborim)
	Agur	Yaakov Baruch ben Yehuda Landau
	She'elot u'Bedikot	Jacob ben Judah Weil (Mahariv)
Sixteenth	Maavor Yabok	Aharon Berechyah, of Modena
	Torat Hattat	Moses ben Israel Isserles (Rema)
	Matteh Moshe	Moshe Mos of Premysl
Seventeenth	Pesach MeUvin	Chaim Benveniste
	Simanim le-Oraita	Yaakov Culi
	Bina-La-Ittim Chiddushim al Hilkot Yom Tov	Jonathan Eybeschutz
	Shaagat Aryeh	Aryeh Leib ben Asher Gunzberg (Shaagat Aryeh)
	Get Pashut Ezrat Nashim	Moses ibn Habib (Chaviv)
	Eleh HaMitzvot	Moses Hagiz
	Ir Miklat Ir David Sod Hashem Versharvit HaZahav	David Lida
	Parashat Derakim	Judah ben Samuel Rosanes
	Korban Netanel	Nethaneel ben Naftali Tzvi Weil
Eighteenth	Magen Abot	Mordechai ben Abraham Benet
	Several books on law	Yom Tov Algazi
	Sha'are Zedek Zikru Torat Moshe	Abraham ben Jehiel Danzig

Century	Work	Author
	Shev Shema'atara	Aryeh Leib HaKohen Heller (Ketzos)
	Torah Or	Judah Aryeh Loeb ben Joshua Hoschel
	Nodah B'Yehuda	Ezekiel
	Sha'are Ephraim	Ephraim Zalman (Solomon) Margolis
	Shut Tzemach Tzedek	Menachem Mendel Schneerson (Tzemach Tzedek)
Nineteenth	Minchat Chinuch	Yosef ben Moshe Babad
	Darkhei Binah	Zvi Hirsch Chajes (Chayes) (The Maharatz Chajes)
	Aruch Hashulchan	Yechiel Michel HaLevi Epstein (Aruch Hashulchan)
	Kesses Hasofer Toras Zevachis	Solomon ben Joseph Ganzfried
	Chafetz Chaim	Israel Meir Kagan (Ha-Kohen) (Chofetz Chaim)
	Dabar b'itti	Joshua Hoschel ben Elijah Zeeb Levin
	S'Dei Chemed	Chaim Chizkiya Medini
	Imreih Bibah	Israel Lipkin Salanter
	Sha'arei Yosher	Shimon Shkop
	Shailos U'teshuvot Marsham Daas Torah	Sholom Mordechai Schwadron (Maharsham)
	Kol Yaakov	Yakkov Chaim Sofer (Kaf HaChaim)
	Zivhei Tzedek	Abdalla Somekh
	Seridei Eish	Yechiel Yaakov Weinberg
	Masoret HaTalmud Dor Dor we-Dorshaw	Isaac Hirsch Weiss

Century	Work	Author
Twentieth	Meorei Eish Ma'adnei Eretz	Shlomo Zalman Auerbach
	Mas'as Levi	Yaakov Yitzhak Ruderman
	Chazon Ovadia	Ovadia Yosef
	Yalkut Yosef	Yitzhak Yosef

D. Responsa

Century	Work	Author
Eighth	Untitled	Yehudai ben Nahman (Yehudai Gaon)
Ninth	Untitled	Amram Gaon
Tenth	Untitled	Chananel ben Chushiel
	Untitled	Hai Gaon
	Untitled	Judah ben Gershom
	Untitled	Hai ben Sherira, Gaon
Eleventh	She'elot uTeshuvot Ri Migash	Joseph ben Meir HaLevi ibn Migash (Ri Migash)
	Vitry Mahzor	Simhah ben Samuel of Vitry
	Siddur Rashi Sefer HaPardes Sefer HaOrah	Shlomo Yitzhaki (Rashi)
Twelfth	Untitled	David ben Kalonymus of Munzenberg
	Untitled	Kalonymus ben Isaac
	Untitled	Meir ben Todros HaLevi Abulafia
	Untitled	Abraham ben Isaac of Narbonne (Raavad II)
	Temim De'im Orot Hayyim Shibbole HaLeket	Abraham ben David (Ravad III)
	Found in the Mordechai	Judah ben Isaac Messer Leon
	Sefer haYashar	Jacob ben, Meir (Tam) (Rabbeinu Tam)

Century	Work	Author
	HaMinhag / Manhig Olam	Abraham ben Nathan
Thirteenth	Untitled	Shlomo ben Aderet
	Untitled	Meir ben Baruch (Meir of Rothenburg) (MaHaRaM)
Fourteenth	She'elot u-Teshuvot HaRibash HaHadashot	Isaac ben Sheshet Barfat (RiBaSH)
	Untitled	Simeon ben Zemah Duran (Rashbatz / Tashbetz)
	Pesakim u-Ketabim Terumat HaDeshen	Israel ben Petahaiah Ashkenazi Isserlein
	Sefer Maharil / Minhagei Maharil / Minhagim	Jacob ben Moses Levi Moelin (Maharil)
	Untitled collection	Nissim ben Reuven, of Gerona (RaN)
Fifteenth	Teshuvot Mahari Bruna	Israel Bruna
	Untitled	Moses ben Isaac Alashkar
	She'elot u-Teshuvot	Levi ben Jacob ibn Chaviv (Habib) (Ralbach)
	Untitled	Solomon ben Simon Duran (Rashbash)
	Sh'elot u-Teshubot	Meir ben Isaac Katzenellenbogen (Maharam Padua)
	Agur	Yaakov Baruch ben Yehuda Landau
	Untitled	Judah ben Eliezer HaLevi Minz (Mahari Minz)
	Leket Yosher	Joseph ben Moses
	The Responsa of Maharik	Joseph Colon ben Solomon Trabotto (Maharik)
	She'elot u'Teshubot	Jacob ben Judah Weil (Mahariv)

Century	Work	Author
Sixteenth	Collection of Responsa	David ben Solomon ibn Abi Zimra (Radbaz)
	Divrei Rivot	Isaac Adarbi (Adribi)
	Knaff Renanim	Avraham Azulai
	In the collected work, Hut haShani	Abraham Samuel Bachrach
	Avkath Rochel	Joseph ben Ephraim Caro (Karo) (HaMechaber / Mechaber)
	Teshubot Rosh Yosef	Joseph Escapa
	She'elot u-Teshubot ReMA	Moses ben Israel Isserles (Rema)
	She'elot u-Teshubot Pene Yehoshua	Joshua Hoschel ben Joseph
	Bene Shemuel	Samuel Hayyun
	She'elot U'Teshubot R' Yosef ibn Lev	Joseph ibn Lev
	Manhir Einei Chachamim	Meir ben Gedaliyah Lublin (Maharam)
	Untitled	Solomon Luria (Maharshal, Rashal)
	Piske RashDaM	Samuel ben Moses de Medina (RashDaM)
	Untitled	Samuel ben Moses di Modena (Maharshdam)
Seventeenth	Teshuvos HaBach	Yoel Sirkis (Bach)
	Masat Binyamin	Benjamin Aaron ben Abraham Slonik
	Lev Sameach	Abraham Alegri
	Edut bi-Yehosef	Joseph Almosnino
	Avodat HaGershuni	Gershon Ashkenazi
	Chacham Tzvi	Tzvi Hirsch ben Yaakov Ashkenazi
	Bet Yehuda	Judah Ayyas
	Havvot Yair	Yair Chaim Bachrach

Century	Work	Author
	Ba'ei Chaye	Chaim Benveniste
	Hinnuk ben Yehuda	Judah ben Enoch
	Panim Me'irot	Meir ben Iszak Eisenstadt (Meir Ash) (Maharam Ash / Panim Me'irot)
	She'elt Yaabez	Jacob Israel ben Zvi Ashkenazi Emden (the Yabets)
	Untitled	Hayyim Judah Lob Ettinger
	Gevurat Anashim	Shabbatai ben Meir HaKohen (Shach)
	Emunat Shemuel	Aaron Samuel ben Israel Kaidenover
	Tzemach Tzedek	Menachem Mendel ben Abraham Krochmal
	Bnei Aharon	Aaron ben Isaac Lapapa
	Shevut Ya'akov	Jacob ben Joseph Reischer (Backofen)
	Be'er HaGolah	Moses ben Naftali Hertz Rivkes
	Ohel Yaacob	Jacob ben Aaron Sasportas
	Shut Mharsheishoch	Samuel Schotten (Mharsheishoch)
	Untitled	Yom Tov ben Moshe Tzahalon (Maharitz)
	Torat Netan'el	Nethaneel ben Naftali Tzvi Weil
Eighteenth	Parashot Mordechai	Mordechai ben Abraham Benet
	Nachalah u-Menucha	Yisroel ben Shmuel Ashkenazi of Shklov
	Untitled	Akiva Eger (Eiger)
	Imrei Esh	Meir Eisenstadter (Meir Ash) (Maharam Ash)

Century	Work	Author
	Shenot Hayyim Sefer Satam Moda'a le-Bet Ysrael	Solomon ben Judah Aaron Kluger
	Nodah B'Yehuda	Ezekiel ben Judah Landau (Nodah B'Yehuda)
	Mishkan Shiloh	Samuel Joseph Landau
	Hivvure Likkutim	Abi Ezra Selig Margolis
	Teshuvot HaRam	Alexander Margolis
	Bet Hadash HaHadashot Bet Ephraim	Ephraim Zalman (Solomon) Margolis
	Meir Netivim	Meir ben Zvi Hirsch Margolis
	Divrei Menahem	Menahem Mendel ben Simeon Steinhardt
	Zikron Yosef	Joseph ben Menachem Steinhart
	To'afot re'em	Aaron Moses ben Jacob Taubes
	She'elot u'Teshubot	Jedidiah Weil
Nineteenth	Kerem Hemed	Abraham Ankava
	Meishiv Davar	Naftali Tzvi Yehuda Berlin
	Peri Yitzhak	Isaac ben Moses Solomon Blaser (Rav Itzele Peterburger)
	Pithei Teshuvah	Abraham Zevi Hirsch ben Jacob Eisenstadt
	Rav Pe'alim Torah Lishmah	Chacham Yosef Chaim (Ben Ish Chai)
	Responsa Binyan Tzion	Yaakov Etlinger
	Responsa	Isaac Aaron Ettinger

Century	Work	Author
	The Responsa Literature Various Reform Responsa	Solomon Bennett Freehof
	Geonica Untitled (The Responsa of Professor Louis Ginzberg)	Louis Ginzberg
	Keren L'David	Eliezer David Greenwald
	She'elot u'Teshuvot Achiezer	Chaim Ozer Grodzinski
	Untitled halakhic	David Zevi Hoffmann
	Divrei Menachem	Menachem Mendel Kasher
	Shibat Ziyyon	Samuel ben Ezekiel Landau
	Berit Ya'akob	Baruch Mordechai ben Jacob Lipschitz
	Sho'el u-Meshiv	Joseph Saul Nathanson
	Five volume collection	Yosef Rosen (Rogatchover Gaon, Tzafnach Paneach)
	Maharam Schick Derashot	Moses Schick (Maharam Schick)
	Bet Yitzhak	Isaac Schmelkes
	Shailos U'teshuvot Marsham Daas Torah	Sholom Mordechai Schwadron (Maharsham)
	Ohr HaMeir Vortelach	Yehuda Meir Shapiro
	Untitled to Shulkhan Arukh	Abdalla Somekh
	Untitled Four Volume Collection	Abraham Samuel Benjamin (Sofer Ksav Sofer)
	Be'er Yitzhak Ein Yitzhak	Yitzhak Elchanan Spektor
	Mishpetei Ouziel	Ben-Zion Meir Hai Uziel
	Zekan Aharon	Aaron Walkin

Century	Work	Author
	Teshuvos Ridvaz	Yaakov David Wilovsky
Twentieth	Minchas Shlomo	Shlomo Zalman Auerbach
	Ma'ase Hageonim	Moshe Feinstein
	Untitled Responsa in a Moment: Halakhic Responses to Contemporary Issues	David Golinkin
	Minchat Yaakov	Yitzhak Yaakov Weiss
	Yabia Omer Yechavei Da'ath	Ovadia Yosef

E. Biblical And Talmud Novellae (Hiddushim)

Century	Work	Author
Eleventh	Untitled – Talmudic	Joseph ben Meir HaLevi ibn Migash (Ri MIgash)
Twelfth	Untitled – Talmudic	Moses ben Todros HaLevi Abulafia
	Untitled – Talmudic	Yonah ben Avraham Gerondi (Rabbeinu Yonah)
	Piskei HaRid	Yeshayah ben Mali Hazaken
	Untitled – Talmudic	Samuel ben Jacob Jam'a
	Sefer haYashar	Jacob ben Meir (Tam) (Rabbeinu Tam)
Thirteenth	Untitled – Talmudic	Menachem ben Solomon Meiri (HaMeiri)
	Untitled – Talmudic	Simha ben Samuel, of Speyer
	Sefer HaTerumot	Samuel ben Isaac Sardi (HaSardi, HaSefaradi)
Fourteenth	Untitled – Talmudic	Isaac ben Sheshet Barfat (RiBaSH)
Fifteenth	Tosefte Semag	Elijah Mizrachi (Re'em)
Sixteenth	Erek Lehem	Jacob de Castro

Century	Work	Author
	Hiddushei Halkhot and Hiddushei Aggadot	Samuel ben Eliezer Judah Eidels (Maharsha)
	Rosh Yosef	Joseph Escapa
	Bene Shemuel	Samuel Hayyun
	Joshua Hoschel ben Joseph	Maginne Shelomoh
	Bnei Aharon	Aaron ben Isaac Lapapa
	She'elot U'Teshubot R' Yosef ibn Lev	Joseph ibn Lev
	Chiddushei Aggadot	Judah ben Bezalel Loew (Maharal / Maharal of Prague)
	Meir Einei Chachamim	Meir ben Gedaliyah Lublin (Maharam)
	Hiddushim	Samuel ben Moses de Medina (RashDaM)
	Parts of Ho'il Moshe	Moshe Mos, of Premysl
	Masat Binyamin	Benjamin Aaron ben Abraham Slonik
Seventeenth	Mateh Yehuda Shebbet Yehuda	Judah Ayyas
	Chamra VeChaye	Chaim Benveniste
	Panim Me'irot Or HaGanuz	Meir ben Iszak Eisenstadt (Meir Ash) (Maharam Ash / Panim Me'irot)
	Mor u-Kezi'ah	Jacob Israel ben Zvi Ashkenazi Emden (Yabets)
	Untitled on Shulkhan Arukh	Jonathan Eybeschutz
	Turei Even Gevurot Ari	Aryeh Leib ben Asher Gunzberg (Shaagat Aryeh)
	Shmot ba-Arez	Moses ibn Habib (Chaviv)
	Leket HaKemah	Moses Hagiz

Century	Work	Author
Eighteenth	One part of Pene Yehoshua	Yaakov Yehoshua ben Zvi Hirsch (Jacob Joshua Falk)
	Tifferet Shemuel	Aaron Samuel ben Israel Kaidenover
	Bet Hillel	Hillel ben Naphtali Zevi
	Hiddushei Mahariah	Joel Hayyim (Mahariah)
	Sefer HaHayyim Me Niddah	Solomon ben Judah Aaron Kluger
	Yad HaMelek	Eleazar ben Israel Landau
	Me-on HaBerakhot	Israel Jonah Landau
	Mishkan Shiloh	Samuel Joseph Landau
	Meir Netivim	Meir ben Zvi Hirsch Margolis
	Hivvure Likkutim	Abi Ezra Zelig Margolis
	Ko'ah Shor	Joseph ben Menachem Steinhart
	Karne Re'em	Aaron Moses ben Jacob Taubes
	Untitled	Jedidiah Weil
Nineteenth	Masot Binyamin	Benjamin Eisenstadt
	Tosefot Beracha	Baruch HaLevi Epstein
	Levush Mordechai	Moshe Mordechai Epstein
	Dibrot Moshe Darash Moshe	Moshe Feinstein (Reb Moshe)
	Ohr Someyach Meshech Chochma	Meir Simcha Kalonymus HaKohen of Dvinsk
	Untitled – Talmudic	Enoch Zundel ben Joseph
	Minhat Bikkurim Untitled – Talmudic	Baruch Mordechai ben Jacob Lipschitz
	Artzoth HaChaim	Meir Leibush ben Jehiel Michel (Malbim)

Century	Work	Author
	Multiple works	Eliyahu David Rabinowitz-Teomim (Aderet)
	Tzafnach Paneach	Yosef Rosen (Rogatchover Gaon / Tzafnach Paneach)
	Untitled – Talmudic	Shimon Shkop
	Yismach Yisrael	Yaakov Chaim Sofer (Kaf HaChaim)
	Migdal David	Yaakov David Wilovsky
Twentieth	Commentary on Shev Shema'tata	Shlomo Zalman Auerbach

F. Other Traditional Scholarly Works

1. Ethics

Century	Work	Author
Eleventh	The Improvement of Moral Qualities or Ethics.	Solomon ben Judah, ibn Gabirol (Gvirol)
	Chovot HaLevavot	Bahya ben Joseph ibn Paquda
Twelfth	Iggeret HaTeshuvah Sha'are Teshuvah Sefer HaYirah	Yonah ben Avraham Gerondi (Rabbeinu Yonah)
	Sefer Hasidim	Judah ben Samuel of Regensburg (He-Hasid)
	Rokeach	Eleazar ben Yehuda of Worms
Thirteenth	Sefer HaYashar	Zerachiah HaYavani (The Greek) (Ra'Za'H)
Fourteenth	Menorat HaMaor	Isaac Aboab (Menorat HaMaor)
	Iggeret Mussar	Solomon Alami
Fifteenth	Sefer HaZikranot	Samuel Aboab (Rasha)
	Amarot Tehorot	Avraham Chayon
	Sefer HaMiknah	Yosef (Yoselman) Loanz of Rosheim
Sixteenth	Sefer Hareidim Divrei Kivushim	Elazar ben Moshe Azikri (Ezkari)

Century	Work	Author
	Emek Berakhah Yesh Nohalin	Abraham ben Shabtai Sheftel Horowitz
	Shnei Luchos HaBris (Shelah)	Isaiah HaLevi Horowitz (Shelah, Shaloh)
	Emek Berakhah (additions) Vave HaAmmudim Zuwwa'ah Sha'ar HaShamayim (additions)	Shabtai Sheftel Horowitz
Seventeenth	Kav Hayashar	Zevi Hirsch Kaidenover
	Commentary on Perek Shirah	Aaron ben Samuel
Eighteenth	Mesillat Yesharim	Moses Chaim Luzzatto (Ramchal)
Nineteenth	Madragat HaAdam	Yosef Yozel Hurwitz (Alter of Novardok)
	Daas Chochmah U'Mussar	Yerusham Levovitz
	Imreih Binah Iggeret HaMussar Even Yisrael Etz Peri	Israel Lipkin Salanter
	Likkutei Torat Shmuel	Shmuel Schneerson (The Rebbe Maharash)
	Zera Abraham	Abraham ben Asher Wallerstein
Twentieth	Sefer Hasidim	Avraham Aharon Price
	Sichos Levi	Yaakov Yitzhak Ruderman

2. Hassidic

Century	Work	Author
Eighteenth	Likkutei Amarim Likkutei Yesharim	Dov Ber (Maggid of Mezritch)
	Tanya / Likkutei Amarim	Shneur Zalman Baruch (Borukovich), of Liadi (Alter Rebbe, GRaZ)
	Yesod HaEmunah Amud HaAvodah	Boruch of Kosov

Century	Work	Author
	Degel Machaneh Ephraim	Moshe Chaim Ephraim (of Sudilkov)
	Divrei Chaim	Chaim Halberstam of Sanz
	Toledot Ya'akov Yosef Ben Porat Yosef Tsafenat Pane'ah	Jacob Joseph ben Tzvi HaKohen Katz, of Polonnoye
	Ohel Torah Emet Ve'emunah Amod HaEmet	Menachem Mendel, of Kotzk (Kotzker Rebbe)
	Likutei Moharan Sefer HaMiddot Tikkun HaKlali Sippurei Ma'asiyyot	Nachman of Breslov
	Imros Taharos	Moshe Pallier, of Kobrin
	Ohr HaTorah	Menachem Mendel Schneerson (Tzemach Tzedek)
	Maamrei Admur HaEmtzei	Dovber Schneuri (Mitteler Rebbe)
	Me'Or Einyaim	Menachem Nachum Twersky
Nineteenth	Toras Chesed	Shneur Zalman Fradkin, of Lublin
	Gedulas Mordechai	Mordechai Leifer, of Nadvorna
	Sefer HaMa'amarim Kuntres HaTefilah Kuntres HaAvodah Issa B'Midrash Tehillim	Sholom Dovber Schneerson (Rebbe Rashab)
	Sefer Hama'amarim	Yosef Yitzhak Schneerson (Rebbe Rayatz)
	Minchase Elazar	Chaim Elazar Spira
	Imrei Elimelech Divrei Elimelech	Elimelech Szapira
Twentieth	Sefer HaMa'amarim Melukot	Menachem Mendel Schneerson (The Lubavitcher Rebbe)

Century	Work	Author
3. Kabbalah		
First	Zohar	Shimon bar Yohai (Rashbi)
Twelfth	Various Titles	Eleazar ben Yehuda ben Kalonymus, of Worms (Rokeach)
	Bahir	Yitzhak Saggi Nehor (Isaac the Blind)
Thirteenth	Ginnat Egoz Sha'are Orah / Sefer Orah	Joseph ben Abraham Gikatilla (Joseph Ba'al HaNissim)
	Sefer HaYashar Sefer HaOt Imrei Shefer Sheba Netibot HaTorah	Abraham ben Samuel Abulafia
	Sefer HaRimonim Hanefesh HaHakhamah Shekel HaKodesh Mishkan HaEdut / Sefer HaSodot Midrash de Rabban Shimon ben Yohai / Zohar	Moses de Leon (Moshe ben Shem Tov)
	Hazzekuni	Hezekiah ben Manoah (Hizkuni / Chizkuni)
	Commentary on Sefer Yezirah	Meir ben Solomon Abi Sahula
Fourteenth	Sefer HaEmunot	Shem Tov ibn Shem Tov
Fifteenth	Maggid Mesharim	Joseph ben Ephraim Caro
	Many works	Joseph ben Solomon Taitezak
Sixteenth	Lecha Dodi	Solomon ben Moses HaLevi Alkabetz
	Assarah Maamarot	Menachem Azaryah of Fano

Century	Work	Author
	Chesed L'Avraham Ohr HaChama Ohr HaGanuz	Abraham Azulai
	Pardes Rimonim Ohr Yakar Tomer Devorah Elima Rabbati Sefer Gerushim Shiur Komah Ohr Neerav	Moses ben Jacob Cordovero (Ramak)
	Iggeret HaTe'amim	Aaron Abraham ben Baruch Simeon HaLevi
	Kabbalah Contres Ne'im Zemirot Yisrael	Israel Sarug
	Perush	Mattithiah ben Solomon Delacrut
	Yare'ach Yakar	Abraham Galante
	Sha'ar HaShamayim Beit Elohim	Abraham Herrero
	Shnei Luchos HaBris (Shelah)	Isaiah HaLevi Horowitz (Shelah, Shaloh)
	Omar Man	Menachem di Lonzano
	Pesachim be-Inyan Kiddushin	Shalom Shakna
	Reshit Chochma	Eliyahu de Vidas
	Etz Hayyim	Hayyim ben Joseph Vital
Seventeenth	Tifferet HaGershuni	Gershon Ashkenazi
	Shefa' Tal	Shabbethai Sheftel ben Akiba Hurwitz
	Emeq HaMelekh	Naftali Hertz ben Yaakov Elchanan (Bachrach)
	Zizim u-Ferahim	Jacob Israel ben Zvi Ashkenazi Emden (the Yabets)
	Shem Olam	Jonathan Eybeschutz
	Kav Hayashar	Zevi Hirsch Kaidenover

Century	Work	Author
	Nefesh David Ruach David v'Nishmat David	Moses de Medina
	Etz Chaim Meorei Or Or Tzaddikim Or Rav	Meir Popperos
Eighteenth	Tanya / Likkutei Amarim	Shneur Zalman Baruch (Borukovich), of Liadi (Alter Rebbe, GRaZ)
	Kitzur Sefer Hareidim	Abraham ben Jehiel Danzig
	Parpera'ot le-Hokmah Nifla'ot Hadashot	Noah ben Abraham Lipschutz (Noah Mindes)
	Mesillat Yesharim Da'at Tevunoth	Moses Chaim Luzzatto (Ramchal)
	Sod Yakin u-Voaz	Meir ben Zvi Hirsch Margolis
	Derech Mitzvotecha	Menachem Mendel Schneerson (Tzemach Tzedek)
	Sha'ar HaYichud	Dovber Schneuri (Mitteler Rebbe)
	Sidur Hakavanot Emet va-Shalom Rehovot Nahar Nahar Shalom Siddur haRashash	Shalom Sharabi (Rashash)
	Nefesh HaChaim	Chaim ben Itzchok Volozhin (Reb Chaim)
Nineteenth	Panim Meirot Umasbirot Talmud Eser Sefirot HaSulam (Sulam)	Yehuda Leib HaLevi Ashlag
	Likkutei Levi Yitzhak	Levi Yitzhak Schneerson

4. *Liturgical*

Third	Musaph Prayer Rosh Hashanah	Abba Arika

Century	Work	Author
Ninth	Yesod Amram / Siddur Rav Amram	Gaon Amram ben Sheshna
	Siddur	Gaon Saadia ben Joseph
Tenth	U'netanneh Tokef	Amnon of Mainz
	Piutei R'Shimon ben Yitzhak	Shimon ben Yitzhak HaGadol
	Siddur Tefilah	Gaon Nissim ben Jacob
Eleventh	Changed Kol Nidre	Meir ben Samuel (RAM)
Thirteenth	Liturgical Poems	Benjamin ben Avraham Anaw
	Selichot	Mordechai ben Hillel Ashkenazi
	Liturgical Poems	Meir ben Baruch (Meir of Rothenburg) (MaHaRaM)
Fourteenth	Shulkhan HaPanim	Isaac Aboab (Menorat HaMaor)
	Sefer Abudraham	David ben Joseph ben David Abudraham
Sixteenth	Yedid Nefesh	Elazar ben Moshe Azikri (Ezkari)
	Me'il Tzedekah Bigdei Kodesh	Aharon Berechyah, of Modena
Seventeenth	Selichot	Shabbatai ben Meir HaKohen (Shach)
	Derek Hayyim	Hayyim ben Moses Lipschutz
Eighteenth	Siddur Torah Or	Shneur Zalman Baruch (Borukovich), of Liadi (Alter Rebbe, GRaZ)
Eighteenth	Sidur Hakavanot Siddur haRashash	Shalom Sharabi (Rashash)
Nineteenth	Olat HaChodesh	Enoch Zundel ben Joseph
	Baruch She-Amar	Baruch HaLevi Epstein
	Netiv Binah	Yissachar Jacobson

	Century	Work	Author
		Olat Raiyah	Abraham Isaac Kook (HaRaAyaH / HaRav)
5. Philosophy			
	Ninth	Emunot v'Deot	Gaon Saadia ben Joseph
	Tenth	Ben Koheleth	Samuel ibn Naghrela (Samuel HaNagid)
		Arabic commentary to Sefer Yezirah	Jacob ben Nissim ibn Shahin
	Eleventh	Various Sources	Abraham ben Meir ibn Ezra (Abenezra)
		Mekor Chaim (Fons Vitae)	Solomon ben Judah, ibn Gabirol (Gvirol)
		Kuzari	Judah ben Samuel HaLevi (RiHa'l)
	Twelfth	Al-akidah al-Rafiyah (Emunah Rama)	Abraham ben David (Abraham ibn Daud) HaLevi (Ravad I)
		Guide for the Perplexed (Moreh Nevuchim)	Moses ben Maimon (Maimonides) (Rambam)
		Translated into Hebrew Maimonides' Moreh Nevuchim.	Samuel ben Judah ibn Tibbon
	Thirteenth	Sefer Milkhamot Ha-Shem	Levi ben Gershom (Gersonides, Ralbag)
		Bechinat Olam	Yedadayah HaPenini
		Sefer HaMora	Shemariah ben Elijah Ikriti of Negropont
	Fourteenth	Ikkarim	Joseph Albo
		Untitled work	Nissim ben Reuven, of Gerona (RaN)
	Fifteenth	On the Sciences	Isaac ben Judah Abravanel
		Derek Emunah Ez Hayyim	Abraham ben Shem Tov Bibago
		Sefer HaMiknah	Yosef (Yoselman) Loanz of Rosheim

Century	Work	Author
	Or Ammim	Obadiah ben Jacob Sforno
Seventeenth	Commentary on Perek Shirah	Aaron ben Samuel
Eighteenth	Minhat Yehuda	Yehuda Alkalai
	Tanya / Likkutei Amarim	Shneur Zalman Baruch (Borukovich), of Liadi (Alter Rebbe, GRaZ)
	Sefer Emunah Yesharah	Zvi Hirsch Kalischer
	Moreh Nebuke HaZeman	Nachman Kohen Krochmal
	Derekh Hashem	Moses Chaim Luzzatto (Ramchal)
	Sefer Chakira: Derech Emunah	Menachem Mendel Schneerson (Tzemach Tzedek)
	Jerusalem	Moses Mendelssohn
Nineteenth	Commenatary on Maimonides' Guide for the Perplexed	Yosef Rosen (Rogatchover Gaon, Tzafnach Paneach)
	Meshech Chochma	Meir Simcha Kalonymus HaKohen of Dvinsk
Twentieth	Man is Not Alone: A Philosophy of Religion God in Search of Man: A Philosophy of Judaism The Sabbath: Its Meaning for Modern Man The Prophets	Abraham Joshua Heschel
	The Lonely Man of Faith Halakhic Man Fate and Destiny Out of the Whirlwind Days of Deliverance	Joseph Ber Soloveitchik (HaRav)

6. Piyuttim / Poetry

Century	Work	Author
Sixth	For Festivals	Eleazar Kalir
Eighth	For New Year, day of Atonement and for the siddur	Jose bar Jose
Tenth	U'netannah Tokef	Amnon of Mainz
	Untitled Selichot	Judah ben Gershom
	Poetry - Dror Yikra	Dunash HaLevi ben Labrat
	Piutei R'Shimon ben Yitzhak	Shimon ben Yitzhak HaGadol
	Ben Tehillim	Samuel ibn Naghrela (Samuel HaNagid)
	Selichot	Shlomo Yitzhaki (Rashi)
Eleventh	Azharot	Isaac ben Reuben Albargeloni
	Poem for Passover	Eliakim ben Meshullam HaLevi
	Untitled	Moses ibn Ezra (HaSallah)
	Keter Malkut Azharoth Shir Hakavod Shir Hayichud	Solomon ben Judah, ibn Gabirol (Gvirol)
	Sifte Renanot	Isaac ben Judah ibn Ghiyyat (Ghayyat)
	Four Wedding Piyyutim	Isaac ben Eleazar HaLevi
	Piyyut for Sabbath Circumcision Piyyutim Selichot Kinot	Judah ben Samuel HaLevi (RiHa'l)
	Various Holidays	Kalonymus Family
	Various	Meshullam ben Moses
	Various	Eliezer ben Nathan (Raavan)
	Akdamut	Meir ben Isaac Nehorai

Century	Work	Author
Twelfth	Changed Kol Nidre	Meir ben Samuel (RAM)
	Contres- haPiyyutim	Simhah ben Samuel of Vitry
	Takhemoni	Judah ben Solomon Alharizi (al-Harizi)
	Untitled	Joseph ben Baruch (Joseph of Clisson)
	Selichot	David ben Kalonymus of Munzenberg
	Untitled	Eleazar ben Yehuda ben Kalonymus of Worms (Rokeach)
	Shiur HaYihud	Samuel ben Kalonymus (He-Hasid) of Speyer
	Pizmonim for Passover	Elhanan ben Isaac of Dampierre
	For Synagogue Service	Menachem ben (ben Solomon ben Simson) Jacob
	For Sukkot, Shemini Azeret and others	Jacob ben Meir (Tam) (Rabbeinu Tam)
	Untitled	Joseph ben Isaac Bekhor Shor
Thirteenth	A Letter from the Grave	Meir ben Todros Abulafia
	Piyyutim, untitled	Benjamin ben Abraham Anaw
	Piyyutim, untitled	Meir ben Baruch, of Rothenburg (MaHaRaM)
	Piyyutim, untitled	Joseph ben Hanan ben Nathan Ezobi
	Untitled	Shemariah ben Elijah Ikriti of Negropont
Fourteenth	Untitled	Simeon ben Zemah Duran (Rashbatz / Tashbetz)
	Sefer Abudraham	David ben Joseph ben David Abudraham
	Untitled	Abraham ben Isaac HaLevi

	Century	Work	Author
		Yigdal Elohim Hai	Daniel ben Judah
	Sixteenth	Yedid Nefesh	Elazar ben Moshe Azikri (Ezkari)
		Ana Elohe Abraham	Abraham ben Abigdor Kara
		Untitled Sabbath	Isaac Luria (Ashkenazi) (Ari, Arizal), He-Ari
		Untitled	Shemaiah de Medina
	Seventeenth	Selichot	Shabbatai ben Meir HaKohen (Shach)
7. Ritual			
	Tenth	Sefer HaMikva'ot	Chananel ben Chushiel
	Eleventh	Sha'areh Simhah Hilkot Pesahim	Isaac ben Judah ibn Ghiyyat (Ghayyat)
	Twelfth	Selichot	Joseph ben Baruch (Joseph of Clisson)
		Pesakim	Samson ben Joseph, of Falaise
		Tikkun Soferim	Joseph ibn Plat
	Thirteenth	Shibbole HaLeket	Zedekiah ben Abraham Anaw
		Orhot Hayyim	Aaron ben Jacob ben David HaKohen
	Fourteenth	Aron HaEdut	Isaac Aboab (Menorat HaMaor)
		Commentary on the Passover Haggadah	Shem Tov ibn Shem Tov
	Fifteenth	Agur	Jacob ben Judah Landau
	Sixteenth	Shibbole HaLeket	Zedekiah ben Abraham Anaw
		Kenaff Renanim	Abraham Azulai
		Me'il Tzedakah Bigdei Kodesh	Aharon Berechyah of Modena

Century	Work	Author
	Gevurot Hashem Divrei Negidim Ner Mitzvah Or Chadash	Judah ben Bezalel Loew (Maharal / Maharal of Prague)
	Shnei Luchos HaBris (Shelah)	Isaiah HaLevi Horowitz (Shelah, Shaloh)
	Birkat Abraham	Abraham ben Solomon Treves (Tarfati)
Seventeenth	Siddur Tefilah	Jacob Israel ben Zvi Ashkenazi Emden (the Yabets)
	Derek Hayyim	Hayyim ben Moses Lipschutz
Eighteenth	Nogah HaBedek	Aron Chorin
	Toledot Adam	Abraham ben Jehiel Danzig
	Matteh Ephraim	Ephraim Zalman (Solomon) Margolis
	Sha'arei Orah Maamrei Admur HaEmtzei	Dovber Schneuri (Mitteler Rebbe)
	Mahazeh Abraham	Abraham ben Asher Wallerstein
	Commentary on Haggadah	Jedidiah Weil
	Or la-Zaddik	Isaac Hirsch Weiss
Twentieth	Siach Yerushalayim	Yosef Quafih
	Chok le-Ysra'el	Israel Veltz

G. Miscellaneous

Century	Work	Author
Ninth	Commentary on Sefer Yezirah	Gaon Saadia ben Joseph
Tenth	Sefer Dikdukei HaTe'amim	Aaron ben Moses ben Asher
	Sefer HaYekar	Shabtai Donolo
	Iggeret Rav Sherira Gaon	Sherira Gaon

Century	Work	Author
	Sefer Yossipon	Joseph ben Gorion
	Sefer Ma'asiyyot HaHakhamim	Nissim ben Jacob (HaMafteach)
	Sefer HaShorashim	Yonah ibn Janach (Merinos)
	Grammar book	Dunash HaLevi ben Labrat
	Ben Mishlei	Samuel ibn Naghrela (Samuel HaNagid)
	Mahberet / Sefer HaPitronot	Menahem ben Jacob ibn Saruq
Eleventh	Moznayim Sefer Yesod Iggeret Shabbat	Abraham ben Meir ibn Ezra (Abenezra)
	Anak Ethics	Solomon ben Judah, ibn Gabirol (Gvirol)
	Arukh	Nathan ben Jehiel Anaw, Anav)
	Even HaEzer	Eliezer ben Nathan (Raavan)
Twelfth	Tikkun Tefillin	Elhanan ben Isaac, of Dampierre
	Sefer Ba'ale Nefesh	Abraham ben David (Ravad III)
	ReZaH	Zerachiah ben Isaac HaLevi Gerondi
	HaRokeach Adderet Ha-Shem Sefer HaKapparot Sefer HaHayyim Sha'are HaSod HaYihud weha Emunah	Eleazar ben Yehuda ben Kalonymus, of Worms (Rokeach)
	Sepher Zikkaron Sepher Haggalui	Joseph ben Isaac Kimchi
	Mahalakh Shevile Hadda'ath Sepher Tahbosheth	Moses Kimchi

Century	Work	Author
Thirteenth	Michlol / Sefer Miclol Teshuvoth Lanotzrim	David Kimchi (RaDaK)
	Epistle to Yemen (Iggeret Temam) Scientific works	Moses ben Maimon (Maimonides) (Rambam)
	Sefer Hasidim	Judah ben Samuel of Regensburg (He-Hasid)
	Sefer Milhamot Adonai	Jacob ben Reuben
	Iggeret HaTeshuvah Sha'are Teshuvah Sefer HaYirah	Yonah ben Avraham Gerondi
	Orach Chaim	Asher ben Jehiel (Rosh)
	Sefer Ma'aseh Hoshev	Levi ben Gershom (Ralbag, Gersonides)
	Kad HaKemah Shulkhan Arba Ohel Moed	Bahya ben Asher
Fourteenth	Sefer Kaftor Vaferech	Haparchi, Ishtori ben Moses, (Kaftor Vaferech)
	Sefer HaYashar	Shabbatai Carmuz Levita
	Chibbur HaTeshuvah	Menachem ben Solomon Meiri (HaMeiri)
	Or Adonai Refutation of Christian Principles Passover Sermon	Hasdai ben Abraham Crescas
	Iggeret Mussar	Solomon Alami
	Minhat Kenaot	Abba Mari ben Moses ben Joseph Don Astruc of Lunel
	Untitled collection of sermons	Nissim ben Reuven, of Gerona (RaN)
Fifteenth	Toledot Aharon	Aaron of Pesaro
	Derashot	Joseph ben Ephraim Caro
	Emek Habachah (Valley of Weeping)	Joseph ben Joshua Meir HaKohen

Century	Work	Author
	Seder Gittin ve-Halizah	Abraham ben Eliezer HaLevi Minz
Sixteenth	Divrei Shalom	Isaac Adarbi (Adribi)
	Hassagot	Moses ben Isaac Alashkar
	Meammez Koah	Moses ben Baruch Almosnino
	Imrei Shefer	Naphtali (Hirsch) ben Asher Altschul
	Sefer Hareidim	Elazar ben Moshe Azikri (Ezkari)
	Shnei Luchos HaBris (Shelah)	Isaiah HaLevi Horowitz (Shelah, Shaloh)
	Shtei Yadot	Menachem di Lonzano
	Ben Shemuel	Samuel ben Moses de Medina (RashDaM)
	Ho'il Moshe (Ba'er Heitev)	Moshe Mos of Premysl
Seventeenth	Sifte Yeshenim	Shabbethai ben Joseph Bass
	Ya'arot Devash	Jonathan Eybeschutz
	Seder HaDorot Erke HaKinnuyim	Jehiel ben Solomon Heilprin
	Ori We-Yish'i	Abraham ben Eliezer Heilprin
	Humble Addresses Nishmat Hayim	Menasseh ben Joseph ben Israel (MB'Y)
	Zizar Nebel Zebi	Jacob ben Aaron Sasportas
Eighteenth		
	Shem HaGedolim	Haim Yosef David Azulai (Hida)
	Likkutei Amarim Likkutei Yeshirim	Dov Ber (Maggid of Mezritch)
	Emek HaShaweh	Aron Chorin
	Bet Avraham	Abraham ben Jehiel Danzig

Century	Work	Author
	Derishot Ziyyon	Zvi Hirsch Kalischer
	Marpe Lashon	Moses Israel Landau
	Biographies Encyclopedia	Solomon Judah Loeb Rapoport
	Iggerot Yashar	Isaac Samuel Reggio (Yashar)
	Minhagei haRashash	Shalom Sharabi (Rashash)
Nineteenth	Goral la-Adonai Shalom Yerushalayim	Judah ben Solomon Chai Alkali
	Qanan-un-Nisa	Chacham Yosef Chaim (Ben Ish Chai)
	Imrei Binah Minhat Kenaot	Zvi Hirsch Chajes
	Arbe Nahal	David Solomon Eibenschutz
	Geonica	Louis Ginzberg
	Ahavat Chesed Shmirat HaLashon	Israel Meir Kagan (Ha-Kohen) (Chofetz Chaim)
	Kontres HaSemikah Perush Kiddush HaChodesh	Levi ibn Chaviv (Habib)
	Michtav me-Eliyahu	Eliyahu Eliezer Dessler
	Mekor Baruch	Baruch HaLevi Epstein
	Leil Shimurim	Yechiel Michel HaLevi Epstein (Aruch Shulchan)
	Der Shem Hamefoyrosh Prophetic inspiration Inspiration After the Prophets	Abraham Joshua Heschel
	Artzoth HaShalom	Meir Leibush ben Jehiel Michel (Malbim)
	Igorot HaRaiyah	Abraham Isaac Kook (HaRaAyaH / HaRav)

Century	Work	Author
	Birkas Shmuel	Boruch Ber Leibowitz
	Ohr Yisrael	Israel Lipkin Salanter
	Chovas haTalmidim Esh Kodesh	Kalonymus Kalman Shapira (Szapira)
	Ma'arekhet haKinyanim	Shimon Shkop
	Yagel Yaakov	Yaakov Chaim Sofer (Kaf HaChaim)
	Shem HaGedolim heHadash	Aaron Walden
	Hokmah U-Mussar	Simcha Zissel Ziv (Alter of Kelm)
Twentieth	Torat HaNazir Pachad Yitzhak	Yitzhak (Isaac) Hutner
	Shev Shema'atata	Shlomo Zalman Auerbach
	Nesivos Sholom	Sholom Noach Berezovsky
	Sheki'in	Saul Lieberman
	Mishnat Avraham Imrei Avraham	Avraham Aharon Price
	Igrot Kadosh Sefer HaSichot	Menachem Mendel Schneerson (The Lubavitcher Rebbe)
	Gesher HaChaim Bein HaShemashos	Yechiel Michel Tukachinsky

Primary Works And Commentaries Of These

In the Biblical commentaries and particularly in the Talmudic commentaries there are a number of works that can be considered the primary interpretive work in a particular field. Of these, the Codes of Law form the largest and the most significant group. Following publication of these primary interpretive or explanatory works, a number of other scholars would subsequently analyze these primary works and write commentaries on them. Some of these primary works were of such signal importance that several authors would provide further commentary to the initial commentary of the primary work, the so-called super-commentary.

There is a large body of such work in the literature. In an attempt to summarize this in a chronological fashion, this table is divided into the three major sections where this type of analysis occurred – Biblical, Talmudic of which the Codes of Law form the largest portion, and Kabbalah. This classification is particularly helpful in the extensive Codes section where, over nine centuries, several primary codes were written. From the time of the first one in the ninth century until the last one in the eighteenth century, and then even beyond that, many commentaries and super-commentaries were written. This table shows the chronological sequence of these works. This is important because later authors would sometimes refer to earlier ones in their analyses.

The major sections and then the primary interpretive works are highlighted in bold.

Structure

Category	Primary Work	Page
Biblical Related		413
	Sefer HaYashar	413
	Rashi Pentateuch Commentary	413
	Torah Commentary	414
	Me'am Loez	415
	Pentateuch Commentary Nahmanides (Ramban)	416
Midrash		417
	Sifra	417
Mishnah Related		417
	Rashi Mishnah Commentary	417
	Tosefos Yomtov	417
Talmud Related		417
	Sefer HaMordecai (Mordecai)	417
Codes Of Law Related		418
	Halakot Gedolot	418

	Halacoth /Alfes / RIF	418
	Arukh	419
	HaEshkol	419
	Mishneh Torah (Yad HaHazakha)	419
	Arba'ah Turim (Tur)	420
	Sefer Mitzvot HaGadol (SeMaG)	422
	Abstract of Talmudic Law	423
	Shulkhan Arukh	423
	Hayye Adam: Nishmat Adam and Hokmat Adam: Binat Adam	431
	Levush Malkut	432
Halakha Related		432
	Torat HaBayit	432
	HaHalachot (Alfes)	432
	Sefer HaMitzvot (Book of Commandments)	433
	Sefer HaChinuch	433
	Torat Hattat	433
Kabbalah		433
	Sha'areh Orah / Sefer Orah Ginat Egoz	433
	Iggeret HaTe'amim	434
	Zohar	434
	Emeq Hamelqh	435
	Etz Chaim	435
	Luria's Sabbath Piyyutim	435

Category	Primary Work	Commentary	Super-Commentary	Century	Author
Biblical Related					
	Sefer HaYashar – Commentary on the Pentateuch			Twelfth	Abraham ben Meir ibn Ezra (Abenezra)
	Sefer HaYashar	Untitled		Thirteenth	Samson ben Isaac of Chinon
	Rashi Pentateuch Commentary			Eleventh	Shlomo Yitzhaki (Rashi)
	Rashi Pentateuch Commentary		Untitled Super-Commentary	Fifteenth	Samuel Aboab (Rasha)
	Rashi Pentateuch Commentary		Reprinted in the collective work "Rabbotenu Ba'ale HaTosafot"	Fifteenth	Obadiah ben Abraham of Bertinoro
	Rashi Pentateuch Commentary		Present in manuscript form (Be'urim)	Fifteenth	Israel ben Pethahiah Ashkenazi Isserlein
	Rashi Pentateuch Commentary		Sefer HaMizrachi	Fifteenth	Elijah Mizrachi (Re'em)
	Rashi Pentateuch Commentary	Be'er Sheva		Sixteenth	Yissachar Ber Ellenburg
	Rashi Pentateuch Commentary	Levush Orah		Sixteenth	Mordechai ben Avraham Jaffe (Yoffe) (Ba'al Ha-Levushim)

Category	Primary Work	Commentary	Super-Commentary	Century	Author
	Rashi Pentateuch Commentary		Untitled	Sixteenth	Abraham ben Abigdor Kara
	Rashi Pentateuch Commentary		Gur Aryeh	Sixteenth	Judah ben Bezalel Loew (Maharal / Maharal of Prague)
	Rashi Pentateuch Commentary		Yeri'ot Shlomo	Sixteenth	Solomon Luria (Maharshal, Rashal)
	Rashi Pentateuch Commentary		Ho'il Moshe (Be'er Moshe)	Sixteenth	Moshe Mos of Premysl
	Rashi Pentateuch Commentary		Sifsei Chachamim	Seventeenth	Shabbethai ben Joseph Bass
	Rashi Pentateuch Commentary		Levush Orah	Seventeenth	Mordechai ben Avraham Jaffe (Yoffe) (Ba'al Ha-Levushim)
	Rashi Pentateuch Commentary		Sod Hashem VerSharvit HaZahav	Seventeenth	David Lida
	Torah Commentary			Eleventh	Chananel ben Chushiel (Rabbeinu Chananel)

Category	Primary Work	Commentary	Super-Commentary	Century	Author
	Chananel ben Chushiel Torah Commentary	Midrash Rabbeinu Bachya – an extensive commentary on the Torah, based on Chananel ben Chushiel's work.		Thirteenth	Bahya (Bachya) ben Asher (Rabbeinu Behaye)
	Me'am Loez - Commentary on the Pentateuch			Seventeenth	Yaakov Culi
		Contributors to the Me'am Loez		Seventeenth	Yitzhak Bechor Agruiti Yitzhak Magriso Rachamim Menachem Mitrani Chiya Pontremoli
		Hebrew translation of Me'am Loez		Nineteenth	Shmuel Yerushalmi
		English translation of Me'am Loez		Twentieth	Aryeh Kaplan
	Based on the Teachings of the Ba'al Shem Tov	Degel Machaneh – Ephraim discusses the weekly Torah portion.		Eighteenth	Moshe Chaim Ephraim of Sudilkov

Category	Primary Work	Commentary	Super-Commentary	Century	Author
	Pentateuch Commentary Nahmanides (Ramban)			Twelfth	Moses ben Nahman (Nahmanides, Ramban)
	Pentateuch Commentary Nahmanides (Ramban)		Untitled	Fifteenth	Samuel Aboab (Rasha)
	Pentateuch Commentary Nahmanides (Ramban)		Kesef Mezukak	Nineteenth	Avraham Lieblein
	Pentateuch Commentary Nahmanides (Ramban)		Kur Zahav	Nineteenth	Aryeh Leib Steinhardt
	Pentateuch Commentary Nahmanides (Ramban)		Techeiles Mordechai	Nineteenth	Mordechai Gimpel Yaffe Torizer
	Moses ben Nahman (Nahmanides, Ramban) Torat Hashem Temima	Untitled		Twentieth	Yehuda Meir Dvir
	Yalkut. Yalkut Shimoni			Thirteenth	Simeon Kara of Frankfurt (HaDarshan)
	Yalkut / Yalkut Shimoni	Bris Avraham		Sixteenth	Abraham Gediliyah

Category	Primary Work	Commentary	Super-Commentary	Century	Author
Midrash					
	Sifra	Commentary		Twelfth	Samson ben Abraham of Sens
	Sifra	Korban Aharon Midos Aharon		Sixteenth	Aharon ibn Chaim
Mishnah Related					
	Rashi Mishnah Commentary				
	Rashi Mishnah Commentary	Commentaries found in all editions of the Mishnah		Fifteenth	Obadiah ben Abraham of Bertinoro
	Maimonides Commentaries				
	Samson ben Abraham of Sens				
	Tosefos Yomtov	Major commentary		Sixteenth	Abraham Azulai
Talmud Related					
	Sefer HaMordechai (Mordechai)			Thirteenth	Mordechai ben Hillel Ashkenazi's
	Sefer HaMordechai (Mordechai)		Gedulath Mordechai (The Greatness of Mordechai)	?	Baruch ben David

Category	Primary Work	Commentary	Super-Commentary	Century	Author
	Sefer HaMordechai (Mordechai)	Biur Mordechai		Eighteenth	Mordechai ben Abraham Benet
Codes Of Law Related					
	Halakot Gedolot – (One of first comprehensive codes of law)			Ninth	Simeon Kayyara
	Halacoth / Alfes / RIF (Practical rules which follow Mishnaic tractates)			Eleventh	Yitzhak ben Yaakov HaKohen Alfasi (RIF)
	Halakhot Ketonot – deals with other halakhot				
	Halacoth / Alfes / RIF	Sefer HaMaor		Twelfth	Zerachiah ben Isaac HaLevi Gerondi
	Halacoth / Alfes / RIF	HaSagot HaRaavad		Twelfth	Abraham ben David (Ravad III)
	Halacoth / Alfes / RIF	Sefer HaHashalamah		Twelfth	Meshullam ben Moses
	Halacoth / Alfes / RIF	Milhamot HaShem		Twelfth	Moses ben Nahman (Nahmanides) (Ramban)
	Halacoth / Alfes / RIF	Nimukei Yosef		Fourteenth	Yosef Chaviva

Category	Primary Work	Commentary	Super-Commentary	Century	Author
	Halacoth / Alfes / RIF	Untitled Commentary		Fourteenth	Nissim ben Reuven, of Gerona (RaN)
	Halacoth / Alfes / RIF	Shiltei Gibborim			
	Arukh			Eleventh	Nathan ben Jehiel
	Arukh	Elef HaMagen – Supplement to the Arukh		Twelfth	Samuel ben Jacob Jam'a
	HaEshkol – Practical code of law			Twelfth	Abraham ben Isaac of Narbonne (Raavad II)
	Mishneh Torah (Yad HaHazakha)			Twelfth	Moses ben Maimon (Maimonides) (Rambam)
	Mishneh Torah	Glosses		Twelfth	Abraham ben David
	Mishneh Torah	Maggid Mishneh		Fourteenth	Vidal di Tolosa
	Mishneh Torah	Yekar Tiferet		Fifteenth	David ben Solomon ibn Abi Zimra (Radbaz)
	Mishneh Torah	Lehem Mishneh		Sixteenth	Moses de Bouton

Category	Primary Work	Commentary	Super-Commentary	Century	Author
	Mishneh Torah	Kesef Mishneh		Sixteenth	Joseph ben Ephraim Caro (Mechaber)
	Mishneh Torah	Mishneh la-Melek		Seventeenth	Judah ben Samuel Rosanes
	Mishneh Torah	Lehem Yehuda		Seventeenth	Judah Ayyas
	Mishneh Torah	Binah la-Ittim		Eighteenth	Jonathan Eybeschutz
	Mishneh Torah	Even HaEzel		Nineteenth	Isser Zalman Meltzer (Even HaEzel)
	Mishneh Torah	Ohr Somayach		Nineteenth	Meir Simcha Kalonymus HaKohen of Dvinsk
	Mishneh Torah	Chiddushei Rabbeinu Chaim		Nineteenth	Chaim Soloveitchik (The Brisker Reb)
	Mishneh Torah	Beis HaLevi		Nineteenth	Yosef Dov Soloveitchik (Beis HaLevi)
	Mishneh Torah	Introduction to the Code of Maimonides A Maimonides Reader		Twentieth	Isadore (Yitzhak) Twersky
	Arba'ah Turim (Tur)			Thirteenth	Jacob ben Asher (Ba'al HaTurim)

Category	Primary Work	Commentary	Super-Commentary	Century	Author
	Arba'ah Turim (Tur)	Shibbole HaLeket – Glosses on the first part of the Tur		Thirteenth	Tzidkayah ben Avraham Anav HaRofei
	Arba'ah Turim (Tur)	Haggahot Asheri – Notes on Arba'ah Turim (Tur)		Fourteenth / Fifteenth	Israel of Krems
	Arba'ah Turim (Tur)	Leket Yosher – a collection of responsa and other halakhic material based on the Tur.		Fifteenth	Joseph ben Moses
	Arba'ah Turim (Tur)	Vayigash Yehuda		Sixteenth	Yehuda Leib ben Meir Channeles
	Arba'ah Turim (Tur)	Beth Yosef – Commentary on the Arba'ah Turim of Jacob ben Asher – see Shulkhan Arukh below) Bedek HaBayit – supplement to Beth Yosef		Sixteenth	Joseph ben Ephraim Caro (Karo) (Mechaber)
	Arba'ah Turim (Tur)	Rosh Yosef – Commentary and novellae on the Arba'ah Turim		Sixteenth	Joseph Escapa

Category	Primary Work	Commentary	Super-Commentary	Century	Author
	Arba'ah Turim (Tur)	Beit Israel – Commentary on the Tur, and the Shulkhan Arukh		Sixteenth	Joshua ben Alexander (Katz) Ha-Kohen Falk
	Arba'ah Turim (Tur)	Darkhei Moshe – Commentary on the Tur		Sixteenth	Moses ben Israel Isserles (Rema)
	Arba'ah Turim (Tur)	Bayit Chadash (Bach)		Sixteenth	Yoel Sirkis (Bach)
	Arba'ah Turim (Tur) (Orach Chaim)	Mor u-Kezi'ah		Seventeenth	Jacob Israel ben Zvi Ashkenazi Emden (the Yabets)
	Arba'ah Turim	Bet Yehuda		Seventeenth	Judah Ayyas
	Sefer Mitzvot HaGadol (SeMaG)			Thirteenth	Moses ben Jacob of Coucy
	Sefer Mitzvot HaGadol (SeMaG)	Sefer Mitzvot Katan / Ammudeh HaGolah (SeMaK)		Thirteenth	Isaac ben Joseph of Corbeil
	Sefer Mitzvot HaGadol (SeMaG)	Tosefte Semag		Fifteenth	Elijah Mizrachi (Re'em)
	Sefer Mitzvot HaGadol (SeMaG)	Amudei Shlomo		Sixteenth	Solomon Luria (Maharshal, Rashal)

Category	Primary Work	Commentary	Super-Commentary	Century	Author
	Sefer Mitzvot HaGadol (SeMaG)	Dina DeChaye		Seventeenth	Chaim Benveniste
	Sefer Mitzvot HaGadol (SeMaG)	Mitzvot Gadol		Twentieth	Avraham Aharon Price
Abstract of Talmudic law				Thirteenth	Asher ben Jehiel (Rosh)
	Abstract of Talmudic law	Piskei HaRosh		Thirteenth	Jacob ben Asher (Ba'al HaTurim)
Shulkhan Arukh – Abridgement of Beth Yosef which was a commentary on the Arba'ah Turim of Jacob ben Asher				Sixteenth	Joseph ben Ephraim Caro (Karo) (Mechaber)
	Shulkhan Arukh	Erech HaShulchan – Glosses to Shulkhan Arukh		Sixteenth	Jacob de Castro
	Shulkhan Arukh	Beit Israel – Commentary on the Tur, and the Shulkhan Arukh		Sixteenth	Joshua ben Alexander (Katz) HaKohen Falk
	Shulkhan Arukh	HaMapah – Glosses to the Shulkhan Arukh		Sixteenth	Moses ben Israel Isserles (Rema)

Category	Primary Work	Commentary	Super-Commentary	Century	Author
	Shulkhan Arukh	Turei Zahav – Commentary on both the Orach Chaim and the Yoreh De'ah		Sixteenth	David ben Samuel HaLevi Segal (Taz)
	Shulkhan Arukh	Masat Binyamin contained novellae on the Shulkhan Arukh		Sixteenth	Benjamin Aaron ben Abraham Slonik
	Shulkhan Arukh	Hiddushe HaGershuni, on the Even HaEzer and Choshen Mishpat		Seventeenth	Gershon Ashkenazi
	Shulkhan Arukh	Ateret Zekeinim		Seventeenth	Menachem Mendel ben Meshulam Zalman Auerbach
	Shulkhan Arukh	Mateh Yehuda Shebbet Yehuda		Seventeenth	Judah Ayyas
	Shulkhan Arukh-Even HaEzer	Beit Avraham		Seventeenth	Abraham ibn Chananyah
	Shulkhan Arukh	Pri Chadash		Seventeenth	Hezekiah ben David DiSilo

Category	Primary Work	Commentary	Super-Commentary	Century	Author
	Shulkhan Arukh	Beit Shmuel – Commentary on Even HaEzer chapter of Shulkhan Arukh		Seventeenth	Samuel ben Uri Shraga Faibesh (Phoebus)
	Shulkhan Arukh	Magen Avraham – Commentary on the Orach Chaim of the Shulkhan Arukh		Seventeenth	Abraham Abele ben Chaim HaLevi Gombiner (Magen Avraham)
	Shulkhan Arukh	Siftei Kohen (Shakh) – Commentary on the Yoreh De'ah and Choshen Mishpat of the Shulkhan Arukh		Seventeenth	Shabbatai ben Meir HaKohen (Shach)
	Shulkhan Arukh	Leket HaKemah – Novellae on the Shulkhan Arukh		Seventeenth	Moses Hagiz
	Shulkhan Arukh	Helkat Mehokek		Seventeenth	Moses ben Isaac Judah Lima
	Shulkhan Arukh	Shulkhan Arukh		Seventeenth	Jacob ben Joseph Reischer (Backofen)
	Shulkhan Arukh	Eliyahu Rabba		Seventeenth	Eliyahu ben Binyamin Wolf Shapiro

Category	Primary Work	Commentary	Super-Commentary	Century	Author
	Shulkhan Arukh	Netib Hayyim – Critical notes on the Orach Chaim and the Ture Zahav and Magen Avraham		Seventeenth	Nethaneel ben Naftali Tzvi Weil
	Shulkhan Arukh	Bet Hillel Commentary and novellae on the four parts		Seventeenth	Hillel ben Naphtali Zevi
	Shulkhan Arukh	Be'er Heitiv Summary of Halakhic rulings and responsa from the Shulkhan Arukh		Eighteenth	Yehuda ben Shimon Ashkenazi
	Shulkhan Arukh	Pe'at Hashulchan was a supplement to the Shulkhan Arukh		Eighteenth	Yisroel ben Shmuel Ashkenazi of Shklov
	Shulkhan Arukh	Glosses to the Shulkhan Arukh		Eighteenth	Akiva Eger
	Shulkhan Arukh	Lebushe Serad – Commentary on Shulkhan Arukh		Eighteenth	David Solomon Eibenschutz

Category	Primary Work	Commentary	Super-Commentary	Century	Author
	Shulkhan Arukh	Ketzot HaChoshen – Clarifies difficult sections of the Choshen Mishpat of the Shulkhan Arukh Avnei Milluim – Clarifies difficult passages of the Even HaEzer of the Shulkhan Arukh		Eighteenth	Aryeh Leib HaKohen Heller (Ketzos)
	Shulkhan Arukh	Eben Bochan – Commentary on aspects of Choshen Mishpat of Shulkhan Arukh Sefer Moznayim la-Mishpat – Commentary on entire Choshen Mishpat of Shulkhan Arukh Glosses to the Yoreh De'ah of the Shulkhan Arukh		Eighteenth	Zvi Hirsch Kalischer

Category	Primary Work	Commentary	Super-Commentary	Century	Author
	Shulkhan Arukh	Orach Chaim	Mechitzat Hashekel	Eighteenth	Samuel ben Naftali HaLevi Kelin
	Shulkhan Arukh	Sefer HaChaim - novellae on Orach Chaim		Eighteenth	Solomon ben Judah Aaron Kluger
	Shulkhan Arukh	Dagul Merevavah - Notes on the Shulkhan Arukh		Eighteenth	Ezekiel ben Judah Landau (Nodah B'Yehuda)
	Shulkhan Arukh	Magen Avraham and Shach (Yoreh De'ah section)	Machatsit HaShekel	Eighteenth	Samuel ben Nathan Loew
	Shulkhan Arukh	Nesivos HaMishpat Derech Chaim On the Orach Chaim		Eighteenth	Jacob ben Jacob Moses Lorberbaum, of Lisser (Ba'al HaNesivos / Lissa Rav)
	Shulkhan Arukh	Bet Ephraim - On the Yoreh De'ah Yad Ephraim - On the Orach Chaim		Eighteenth	Ephraim Zalman (Solomon) Margolis
	Shulkhan Arukh	Sha'are Teshubah - On the Orach Chaim		Eighteenth	Hayyim Mordechai Margolis

Category	Primary Work	Commentary	Super-Commentary	Century	Author
	Shulkhan Arukh	Derek HaTov veha-Yashar		Eighteenth	Meir ben Zvi Hirsch Margolis
	Shulkhan Arukh	Yeshuot Ya'acob – On the Orach Chaim, Yoreh De'ah, Even HaEzer		Eighteenth	Jacob Meshullam ben Mordechai Ze'ev Ornstein
	Shulkhan Arukh	To'afot Re'em – Were responsa on the four parts of the Shulkhan Arukh		Eighteenth	Aaron Moses ben Jacob Taubes
	Shulkhan Arukh	Mishnah Berura – Gloss of Orach Chaim of Shulkhan Arukh Beiur Halacha – Associated with Mishnah Berura Sha'ar HaTziyyum – Documents sources of laws in Mishnah Berurah		Nineteenth	Israel Meir Kagan (HaKohen) (Chofetz Chaim)

Category	Primary Work	Commentary	Super-Commentary	Century	Author
	Shulkhan Arukh	Chazon Ish – Commentary on aspects of the Shulkhan Arukh, mainly the Orach Chaim		Nineteenth	Abraham Isaiah Karelitz (Chazon Ish)
	Shulkhan Arukh	Pithei Teshuvah – Addresses certain aspects of three of the four sections of the Shulkhan Arukh		Nineteenth	Abraham Zevi Hirsch ben Jacob Eisenstadt
	Shulkhan Arukh	Kitzur Shulkhan Arukh – Summary of the Shulkhan Arukh		Nineteenth	Solomon ben Joseph Ganzfried
	Shulkhan Arukh	Berit Ya'akob – Responsa to the four parts of the Shulkhan Arukh Minhat Bikkurim – Novellae on the Shulkhan Arukh		Nineteenth	Baruch Mordechai ben Jacob Lipschitz

Category	Primary Work	Commentary	Super-Commentary	Century	Author
	Shulkhan Arukh Orach Chaim	Artzoth HaChaim – Novellae		Nineteenth	Meir Leibush ben Jehiel Michel (Malbim)
	Shulkhan Arukh Orach Chaim and parts of Yoreh De'ah	Kaf HaChaim		Nineteenth	Yaakov Chaim Sofer (Kaf HaChaim)
	Shulkhan Arukh	Nachal Yitzhak – On the Choshen Mishpat of the Shulkhan Arukh		Nineteenth	Yitzhak Elchanan Spektor
		Untitled		Nineteenth	David Zevi Hoffmann
	Shulkhan Arukh	Beis Ridvas – An explanation of Pe'at Hashulchan		Nineteenth	Yaakov David Wilovsky
	Shulkhan Arukh	Yalkut Yosef		Twentieth	Yitzhak Yosef
	Hayye Adam: Nishmat Adam and Hokmat Adam: Binat Adam – Both cover new additional material following the first two parts of the Shulkhan Arukh			Eighteenth	Abraham ben Jehiel Danzig

Category	Primary Work	Commentary	Super-Commentary	Century	Author
	Levush Malkut – Utilized the Tur and the Shulkhan Arukh to create a code of law for Eastern European Jewry.			Sixteenth	Mordechai ben Avraham Jaffe (Yoffe) (Ba'al Ha-Levushim)
Halakha Related					
	Torat HaBayit			Thirteenth	Shlomo ben Aderet
	Torat HaBayit	Bedek HaBayit – Critical notes to the Torat HaBayit of the Rashba		Thirteenth	Aharon HaLevi (Ra'AH)
	HaHalachot (Alfes)			Eleventh	Yitzhak ben Yaakov HaKohen Alfasi (RIF)
	HaHalachot (Alfes)	Nimukei Yosef		Fourteenth	Yosef Chaviv
	Mishnah	Perush Yakar Al HaLevush – Commentary on the Mishnah		Sixteenth	Abraham Azulai

Category	Primary Work	Commentary	Super-Commentary	Century	Author
	Talmud, Tosafot	Hiddushei Halakhot – Commentary on the Talmud, on Rashi, and mainly the Tosafot		Sixteenth	Samuel Eidels (Maharsha)
	Sefer Hamitzvot (Book of Commandments)			Twelfth	Moses ben Maimon (Maimonides) (Rambam)
	Sefer Hamitzvot	Lev Sameach		Sixteenth	Abraham Alegri
	Sefer HaChinuch			Thirteenth	Aaron HaLevi (of Barcelona)
	Sefer HaChinuch	Minchat Chinuch		Nineteenth	Yosef ben Moshe Babad
	Torat Hattat	Minhat Ya'akov		Seventeenth	Jacob ben Joseph Reischer (Backofen)
Kabbalah					
	Sha'areh Orah / Sefer Orah Ginat Egoz - Treatises on various names of God			Thirteenth	Joseph ben Abraham Gikatilla (Joseph Ba'al HaNissim)
	Sha'areh Orah / Sefer Orah	Perush		Sixteenth	Mattitiah ben Solomon Delacrut

Category	Primary Work	Commentary	Super-Commentary	Century	Author
	Iggeret HaTe'amim - On accents and Ten Sefirot			Sixteenth	Aaron Abraham ben Baruch Simeon HaLevi
	Iggeret HaTe'amim	Shefa' Tal		Seventeenth	Shabbethai Sheftel ben Akiba Hurwitz
	Zohar			First	Shimon bar Yohai (Rashbi)
	Zohar	Or HaChachma and Ohr HaGanuz		Sixteenth	Abraham Azulai
	Zohar	Ohr HaYakar		Sixteenth	Moses ben Jacob Cordovero
	Zohar	Ohr Yakar		Seventeenth	Moses ben Jacob Codovero (Ramak)
	Zohar	Yare'ach Yakar		Seventeenth	Abraham Galante
	Zohar	Or Rav		Seventeenth	Meir Popperos
	Zohar	HaSulam (Sulam)		Nineteenth	Yehuda Leib HaLevi Ashlag

Category	Primary Work	Commentary	Super-Commentary	Century	Author
	Emeq Hameleqh - Authoritative work on Lurianic Kabbalah			Seventeenth	Naftali Hertz ben Yaakov Elchanan (Bachrach)
	Etz Chaim	Etz Chaim – Derech Chaim – Pri Etz Chaim – Nof Etz Chaim		Seventeenth	Meir Popperos
	Luria's Sabbath Piyyutim			Sixteenth	Isaac Luria
	Luria's Sabbath Piyyutim	Contres Ne'im Zemirot Yisrael		Sixteenth	Israel Sarug
	Etz Chaim	Panim Meirot Umasbirot		Nineteenth	Yehuda Leib HaLevi Ashlag

Alphabetical Listing Of Titled Works And The Authors

This table is a comprehensive listing of all the manuscripts and books written by the authors included in this work. The list is alphabetically arranged according to the title of the work.

Work	Author
A	
Adam V'Chava	Yerucham ben Meshullam
Adderet Eliyahu	Elijah ben Kalonymus
Adereth Eliyahu	Elijah ben Solomon Zalman (Vilna Gaon, Gra)
Adderet Ha-Shem	Eleazar ben Yehuda ben Kalonymus, of Worms (Rokeach)
Agron	Saadia ben Joseph, Gaon (Saadia Gaon)
Agur	Yaakov Baruch ben Yehuda Landau
Agur or Elef HaMagen	Samuel ben Jacob Jam'a
Ahavat Zion	Ezekiel (Yechezkel) ben Judah Landau (Nodah B'Yehuda)
Ahavat Chesed	Israel Meir Kagan (HaKohen) (Chofetz Chaim)
Akdamut	Meir ben Isaac Nehorai
Al-akidah al Rafiyah (Emunah Ramah)	Abraham ben David (Abraham ibn Daud, Ravad I) HaLevi
Al HaYerushalmi	Saul Lieberman
Aleppo Codex	Aaron ben Moses ben Asher
Aleppo Codex	Shlomo ben Boya'a
Ammude HaGolah, or Sefer Mitzvot Katan (Semak)	Isaac ben Joseph of Corbeil
Amod HaEmet	Menachem Mendel of Kotzk (Kotzker Rebbe)
Amorot Tehorot	Avraham Chayon
Amud HaAvodah	Boruch of Kosov
Amudei Sheish	Shlomo Ephraim Lunshitz
Amudei Shlomo	Solomon Luria (Maharshal, Rashal)

Work	Author
Ana Elohe Abraham	Abraham ben Abigdor Kara
Anaf Etz Avot	Ovadia Yosef
Anuk	Solomon ben Judah ibn Gabirol (Gvirol)
Arba'ah Turim	Jacob ben Asher
Arbe Nahal	David Solomon Eibenschutz
Aron HaEdut	Isaac Aboab (Menorat HaMaor)
Aruch HaShulchan Aruch HaShulchan he-Atid	Yechiel Michel HaLevi Epstein (the Aruch HaShulchan)
Aruch LaNer	Yaakov Etlinger (Aruch LaNer)
Arukh	Nathan ben Jehiel (Yechiel) Anaw (Anav)
Artzoth HaChaim Artzoth HaShalom	Meir Leibush ben Jehiel Michel (Malbim)
Assarah Maamarot	Menachem Azaryah of Fano
Ateret Zikeinim	Menachem Mendel ben Meshulam Zalman Auerbach
Avi HaEzri (Sefer HaRaviah)	Eliezer ben Joel HaLevi (Raviah)
Avkath Rochel	Joseph ben Ephraim Caro (Karo) (HaMechaber / Mechaber)
Avnei Milluim	Aryeh Leib HaKohen Heller (The Ketzos)
Avodas Levi	Yaakov Yitzhak Ruderman
Avodat HaGershuni	Gershon Ashkenazi
Ayin Aiyah	Abraham Isaac Kook (HaRaAYaH / HaRav)
Ayn Yaakov	Yaakov ibn Chaviv
Ayyalah SheluHah	Naphtali (Hirsch) ben Asher Altschul
Azharot	Isaac ben Reuben Albargeloni
Azharoth	Solomon ben Judah ibn Gabirol (Gvirol)

B

Ba'ei Chaye	Chaim Benveniste
Bahir	Yitzhak Saggi Nehor (Isaac the Blind)

Work	Author
Baruch she-Amar	Baruch HaLevi Epstein
Bayit Chadash (Bach)	Yoel Sirkis (Bach)
Bechinat Olam	Yedadayah HaPenini
Bedek Bayit Beth Yosef	Joseph ben Ephraim Caro
Bedek HaBayit	Aharon HaLevi (Ra'AH)
Be'er HaGolah	Moses ben Naftali Hertz Rivkes
Be'er Heitiv	Yehuda ben Shimon Ashkenazi
Be'er Sheva	Yissachar Ber Ellenburg
Be'er Yitzhak	Yitzhak Elchanan Spektor
Bein HaShemashos	Yechiel Michel Tukachinsky
Beis HaLevi	Yosef Dov Soloveitchik (Beis HaLevi)
Beis Ridvaz	Yaakov David Wilovsky (Ridvaz)
Beit Avraham	Abraham ibn Chananyah
Beit Elohim	Abraham Herrero
Beit HaBechirah	Menachem ben Solomon Meiri (HaMeiri)
Beit Israel	Joshua ben Alexander (Katz) HaKohen Falk
Beit Shlomo	Solomon ben Kalman HaLevi Abel
Beit Shmuel	Samuel ben Uri Shraga Faibesh (Phoebus)
Beiur Halacha	Israel Meir Kagan (HaKohen) (Chofetz Chaim)
Ben Ish Chai Ben Yehovada	Chacham Yosef Chaim (Ben Ish Chai) (Joseph Hayyim ben Elijah Al-Hakam)
Ben Koheleth Ben Mishlei Ben Tehillim	Samuel ibn Naghrela (Samuel HaNagid)
Ben Porat Yosef	Jacob Joseph ben Tzvi HaKohen Katz, of Polonnoye
Ben Shemuel	Samuel ben Moses de Medina (RashDaM)
Bene Shemuel	Samuel Hayyun

Work	Author
Berit Ya'akob	Baruch Mordechai ben Jacob Lipschitz
Bet Abraham	Abraham ben Jehiel Danzig
Bet Aharon	Aaron ben Samuel
Bet Ephraim Bet Ephraim Bet Hadash HaHadashot	Ephraim Zalman (Solomon) Margolis
Bet Hillel	Hillel ben Naphtali Zevi
Bet Yehuda	Judah Ayyas
Bet Yitzhak	Isaac Schmelkes
Binah La-Ittim	Jonathan Eybeschutz
Binah Mikrah	Yissachar Jacobson
Birkas Shmuel	Boruch Ber Leibowitz
Birkat Abraham	Abraham ben Solomon Treves (Tarfati)
Birkat HaZebah Birkat Shemuel	Aaron Samuel ben Israel Kaidenover
Biur	Moses Mendelssohn
Biur HaGet	Samson ben Isaac, of Chinon (MaHaRShak)
Biurei HaGra	Elijah ben Solomon Zalman (Vilna Gaon, Gra)
Biur Mordechai	Mordechai ben Abraham Benet
Breaking the Tablets: Jewish Theology After the Shoah	David Weiss Halivni
Bris Avraham	Abraham Gediliyah

C

Work	Author
Chachmuni	Shabtai Donolo
Chafetz Chaim	Israel Meir Kagan (HaKohen) (Chofetz Chaim)
Chalukei Avanim	David Lida
Chamra VeChaye	Chaim Benveniste
Chatam Sofer	Moses Sofer (Chatam Sofer)
Chazzekuni	Hezekiah ben Manoah (Hizkuni / Chizkuni)

Work	Author
Chazon Ish	Abraham Isaiah Karelitz (Chazon Ish)
Chazon Ovadia	Ovadia Yosef
Chesed L'Avraham	Abraham Azulai
Chibbur HaTeshuvah	Menachem ben Solomon Meiri (HaMeiri)
Chiddushei Agadot	Judah ben Bezalel Loew (Maharal / Maharal of Prague)
Chiddushei Harim	Yitzhak Myer Alter
Chiddushei Mahariah	Joel Hayyim (Mahariah)
Chiddushei Rabbeinu Chaim Chiddushei HaGRaCh Al Shas	Chaim Soloveitchik (The Brisker Reb)
Chiddushei Ridvaz	Yaakov David Wilovsky (Ridvaz)
Chiddushim al Hilkot Yom Tov	Jonathan Eybeschutz
Chinuch, the (Sefer HaChinuch)	Aaron HaLevi (of Barcelona)
Chochmat Shlomo	Solomon Luria (Maharshal, Rashal)
Chok le-Ysra'el	Israel Veltz
Chosen (Hoshen) Mishpat section of Arba'ah Turim	Jacob ben Asher
Chovas HaTalmidim	Kalonymus Kalman Shapira (Szapira)
Chovot HaLevavot	Bahya ben Joseph ibn Paquda
Comforting Tales	Jacob ben Nissim ibn Shahin (Rabbeinu Nissim, HaMafteach)
Commentary on the Mishnah Torah (Perush Hamishnayot)	Moses ben Maimon (Maimonides) (Rambam)
Contres HaPiyyutim	Simhah ben Samuel of Vitry
Contres Ne'im Zemirot Yisrael	Israel Sarug

D

Daas Chochmah U'Mussar	Yerusham Levovitz
Daas Torah	Sholom Mordechai Schwadron (Maharsham)
Da'at Tevunoth	Moses Chaim Luzzatto (Ramchal)

Work	Author
Dabar b'itti	Joshua Hoschel ben Elijah Zeeb Levin
Dagul Merevavah	Ezekiel (Yechezkel) ben Judah Landau (Nodah B'Yehuda)
Darash Moshe	Moshe Feinstein (Reb Moshe)
Darche HaGemara / Darche HaTalmud	Isaac ben Jacob Campanton
Darkhei Binah	Zvi Hirsch Chajes (Chayes) (The Maharatz Chajes)
Davar HaEmek	Naftali Tzvi Yehuda Berlin
Darkhei Moshe	Moses ben Israel Isserles (Rema)
Days of Deliverance: Essays on Purim and Hanukkah	Joseph Ber Soloveitchik (HaRav)
Degel Machaneh Ephraim	Moshe Chaim Ephraim (of Sudilkov)
Der Shem Hamefoyrosh	Abraham Joshua Heschel
Derashot	Joseph ben Ephraim Caro
Derashot	Moses Schick (Maharam Schick)
Derech Chaim	Judah ben Bezalel Loew (Maharal / Maharal of Prague)
Derek Emunah	Abraham ben Shem Tov Bibago
Derek Hashem Derekh Tevunoth	Moses Chaim Luzzatto (Ramchal)
Derek Hayyim	Hayyim ben Moses Lipschutz
Derech Chaim	Jacob ben Jacob Moses Lorberbaum of Lisser (Ba'al HaNesivos / Lissa Rav)
Derek HaTov veha-Yashar	Meir ben Zvi Hirsch Margolis
Derech Mitzvotecha	Menachem Mendel Schneerson (Tzemach Tzedek)
Derishot Ziyyon	Zvi Hirsch Kalischer
Derush Lezion Derush Lehesped	Ezekiel (Yechezkel) ben Judah Landau (Nodah B'Yehuda)
Devar Shemuel	Samuel Aboab (Rasha)

Work	Author
Dibre David	David ben Samuel HaLevi Segal (Taz)
Dibros Moshe	Moshe Feinstein (Reb Moshe)
Dina DeChaye	Chaim Benveniste
Divrei Chaim	Chaim Halberstam of Sanz
Divre Emet	Solomon ben Joshua Adeni
Divrei Elimelech	Elimelech Szapira
Divrei Kivushim	Elazar ben Moshe Azikri (Ezkari)
Divrei Menachem Responsa	Menachem Mendel Kasher
Divrei Menahem	Menahem Mendel ben Simeon Steinhardt
Divrei Rivot	Isaac Adarbi (Adribi)
Divrei Shalom	
Dor Dor we-Dorshaw	Isaac Hirsch Weiss

E

Work	Author
Eben Bochan	Zvi Hirsch Kalischer
Edut bi-Yehosef	Joseph Almosnino
Ein Mishpat	Joshua Boaz Mevorakh / Joshua Boaz ben Simon Baruch (Shiltei Gibborim)
Ein Yitzhak	Yitzhak Elchanan Spektor
El Conciliador	Menasseh ben Joseph ben Israel (MB'Y)
El Hasofer	David Kimchi (RaDaK)
Elef HaMagen	Shemariah ben Elijah Ikriti of Negropont
Elef HaMagen or Agur	Samuel ben Jacob Jam'a
Eleh HaMitzvot	Moses Hagiz
Elimah Rabbati	Moses ben Jacob Cordovero
Eliyahu Rabba	Eliyahu ben Binyamin Wolf Shapiro
Emek Berakhah	Abraham ben Shabtai Sheftel Horowitz
Emek Berakhah (additions)	Shabtai Sheftel Horowitz
Emek Habachah (Valley of Weeping)	Joseph ben Joshua Meir HaKohen

Work	Author
Emeq Hamelekh	Naftali Hertz ben Yaakov Elchanan (Bachrach)
Emek HaShaweh	Aron Chorin
Emes leYaakov	Jacob Kamenecki (Yaakov Kamenetsky)
Emet va-Shalom	Shalom Sharabi (Rashash)
Emet Ve'emunah	Menachem Mendel, of Kotzk (Kotzker Rebbe)
Emunah Ramah (Al-akidah al-Rafiyah)	Abraham ben David (Abraham ibn Daud, Ravad I) HaLevi
Emunat Shemuel	Aaron Samuel ben Israel Kaidenover
Emunot v'Deot	Saadia ben Joseph, Gaon (Saadia Gaon)
Epistle to Yemen (Iggeret Temam)	Moses ben Maimon (Maimonides) (Rambam)
Erech HaShulchan Erek Lehem	Jacob de Castro
Erke HaKinnuyim	Jehiel ben Solomon Heilprin
Esh Kodesh	Kalonymus Kalman Shapira (Szapira)
Eshkol Hasofer	Avraham ben Yaakov Saba
Ethics	Solomon ben Judah, ibn Gabirol (Gvirol)
Etz Chaim	Meir Popperos
Etz Hayyim	Hayyim ben Joseph Vital
Etz Peri	Israel Lipkin Salanter
Even HaEzel	Isser Zalman Meltzer (Even HaEzel)
Even HaEzer	Eliezer ben Nathan (Raavan)
Even HaEzer section of Arba'ah Turim	Jacob ben Asher
Even Yisrael	Israel Lipkin Salanter
Ez Hayyim	Abraham ben Shem Tov Bibago
Ezrat Nashim	Moses ibn Habib (Chaviv)

Work	Author
F	
Fate and Destiny: From Holocaust to the State of Israel	Joseph Ber Soloveitchik (HaRav)
G	
Gedulah Mordechai	Baruch ben David
Gedulas Mordechai	Mordechai Leifer of Nadvorna
Geonica	Louis Ginzberg
Gesher HaChaim	Yechiel Michel Tukachinsky
Get Pashut	Moses ibn Habib (Chaviv)
Gevurat Anashim	Shabbatai ben Meir HaKohen (Shach)
Gevurot Ari	Aryeh Leib ben Asher Gunzberg (Shaagat Aryeh)
Gevurot Hashem	Judah ben Bezalel Loew (Maharal / Maharal of Prague)
Gilyon Tosafot / Tosafot Gillayon	Eliezer of Touques
Ginnat Egoz	Joseph ben Abraham Gikatilla (Joseph Ba'al HaNissim)
Glosses (Talmudic)	Isaiah Berlin
Glosses (Talmudic)	Zvi Hirsch Chajes (Chayes) (The Maharatz Chajes)
Glosses on Maimonides' Mishneh Torah	Abraham ben David (Ravad III)
God in Search of Man: A Philosophy of Judaism	Abraham Joshua Heschel
Goral l-Adonai	Judah ben Solomon Chai Alkali
Guide for the Perplexed (Moreh Nevuchim)	Moses ben Maimon (Maimonides) (Rambam)
Gur Aryeh	Judah ben Bezalel Loew (Maharal / Maharal of Prague)

Work	Author
H	
HaMaor HaGadol and HaMaor HaKatan (See Sefer HaMaor)	Zerachiah ben Isaac HaLevi Gerondi
HaEmek Davar HaEmek She'ela	Naftali Tzvi Yehuda Berlin
HaEshkol	Abraham ben Isaac of Narbonne (Raavad II)
Haggahot Bach	Yoel Sirkis (Bach)
Haggahot v'Chiddushei HaRashash	Samuel ben Joseph Strashun (Rashash)
Haggahot	Joshua Hoschel ben Elijah Zeeb Levin
Haggahot Asheri	Israel of Krems
Haggahot Maimuniyot	Jacob ben Isaac HaLevi (Jabez)
HaKetav (K'sav) V'ha-kabbalah	Jacob Tzvi Mecklenberg

Halachic Works:
  Hilkot Berakhot /
Seder Berakhot
  Birkot MaHaRaM
  Hilkot Shehitah
  Hilkot Abelut /
Hilkot Semahot
  Hilkot Pesukot
  Hilkot Erubin
Hiddushim
	Meir ben Baruch
	(Meir of Rothenburg)
	(MaHaRaM)

Halacoth or Alfes or RIF Halakhot Ketanot	Yitzhak ben Yaakov HaKohen Alfasi (RIF)
Halakhic Man	Joseph Ber Soloveitchik (HaRav)
Halakhot Gedolot	Behag
Halakot Gedolot	Simeon Kayyara
Halakhot Pesukot	Yehudai ben Nahman (Yehudai Gaon)
HaMafteach (Sefer Mafteach Manu'ele HaTalmud)	Jacob ben Nissim ibn Shahin (Rabbeinu Nissim, HaMafteach)
HaMapah	Moses ben Israel Isserles (Rema)

Work	Author
HaMinhag / Manhig Olam	Abraham ben Nathan
HaNefesh HaHakhamah	Moses de Leon (Moshe ben Shem Tov)
HaRokeach	Eleazar ben Yehuda ben Kalonymus, of Worms (Rokeach)
HaSagot HaRaavad	Abraham ben David (Ravad III)
HaSulam (Sulam)	Yehuda Leib HaLevi Ashlag
HaTorah veha-Mitzvah	Meir Leibush ben Jehiel Michel
HaTorah weha-Pesufiah	Isaac Samuel Reggio (Yashar)
Hayye Adam: Nishmat Adam Hokmat Adam: Binat Adam	Abraham ben Jehiel Danzig
Hazzekuni	Hezekiah ben Manoah (Hizkuni / Chizkuni)
Heavenly Torah: As Refracted Through the Generations	Abraham Joshua Heschel
Helkat Mehokek	Moses ben Isaac Judah Lima
Hiddushe HaGershuni	Gershon Ashkenazi
Hiddushei Aggadot Hiddushei Halakhot	Samuel Eliezer ben Judah Eidels (Maharsha)
Hiddushei Mahariah	Hayyim, Joel (Mahariah)
Hiddushim	Samuel ben Moses de Medina (RashDaM)
Hilchata Gevurta (Hilchos HaNagid)	Samuel ibn Naghrela (Samuel HaNagid)
Hilcoth Yom-Tov	Asher ben Meshullam
Hilkot Pesahi	Isaac ben Judah ibn Ghiyyat (Ghayyat)
Hilkhot Bedikah	Moses ben Nahman (Nahmanides) (Ramban)
Hinnuk ben Yehuda	Judah ben Enoch
Hivvure Likkutim	Abi Ezra Selig Margolis
Ho'il Moshe	Moshe Mos of Premysl
Hok Le-Ysrael	Israel ben Ezekiel Landau
Hokmah U-Mussar	Simcha Zissel Ziv (Alter of Kelm)

Work	Author
Hoshen Mishpat – see Choshen	
Humble Addresses	Menasseh ben Joseph ben Israel (MB'Y)

I

Work	Author
Iggeret Mussar	Solomon Alami
Iggeret HaMussar	Israel Lipkin Salanter
Iggeret HaTe'amim	Aaron Abraham ben Baruch Simeon HaLevi
Iggeret Shabbat	Abraham ben Meir ibn Ezra (Abenezra)
Iggeret Rav Sherira Gaon	Sherira ben Hanina, Gaon
Iggeret Shmuel	Samuel de Uzeda
Iggeret Temam	Moses ben Maimon (Maimonides) (Rambam)
Iggeret Teshuva	Yonah ben Avraham Gerondi (Rabbeinu Yonah)
Iggerot Yashar	Isaac Samuel Reggio (Yashar)
Igorot HaRaiyah	Abraham Isaac Kook (HaRaAYaH / HaRav)
Igrot Kodesh	Menachem Mendel Schneerson (The Lubavitcher Rebbe)
Igrot Moshe	Moshe Feinstein (Reb Moshe)
Ikkarim / Sefer HaIkarim	Joseph Albo
Imrei Shefer	Naphtali (Hirsch) ben Asher Altschul
Imrei Avraham	Avraham Aharon Price
Imrei Binah	Zvi Hirsch Chajes (Chayes) (The Maharatz Chajes)
Imrei Binah	Israel Lipkin Salanter
Imrei Binah Imrei Esh Imrei Binah	Meir Eisenstadter (Meir Ash) (Maharam Ash)
Imrei Das	Yehuda Meir Shapiro
Imrei Elimelech	Elimelech Szapira
Imrei Emes	Avraham Mordechai Alter
Imros Taharos	Moshe Pallier, of Kobrin

Work	Author
Introduction to the Code of Maimonides	Isadore (Yitzhak) Twersky
Introduction to Sources and Tradition	David Weiss Halivni
Ir David Ir Miklat	David Lida
Ir Gibborim	Shlomo Ephraim Lunshitz
Issa B'Midrash Tehillim	Sholom Dovber Schneerson (Rebbe Rashab)
Issur we-Hetter (Torat Hattat)	Moses ben Israel Isserles (Rema)
Ittur Soferim / Sefer HaIttur	Yitzhak ben Abba Mari, of Marseilles
Iyunim BaMikra	Jacob Kamenecki (Yaakov Kamenetsky)

J

Jerusalem	Moses Mendelssohn

K

Kabbalah	Israel Srug
Kad HaKemah	Bayha ben Asher (Rabbeinu Behaye)
Kaf HaChaim	Yaakov Chaim Sofer (Kaf HaChaim)
Karne Re'em	Aaron Moses ben Jacob Taubes
Knaff Renanim	Avraham Azulai
Kav Hayashar	Zevi Hirsch Kaidenover
Kelalei HaTalmud Kesef Mishnah	Joseph ben Ephraim Caro
Kerem Hemed	Abraham Ankava
Keren L'David	Eliezer David Greenwald
Kesef Mezukak	Avraham Lieblein
Kesef Nivvar	Abi Ezra Selig Margolis
Keter Malkut	Solomon ben Judah, ibn Gabirol (Gvirol)
Keter Shem Tov	Shem Tov ben Abraham ibn Gaon
Ketzot HaChoshen	Aryeh Leib HaKohen Heller (The Ketzos)

Work	Author
Kiryat Sefer	Menachem ben Solomon Meiri (HaMeiri)
Kitzur Sefer Hareidim	Abraham ben Jehiel Danzig
Kitzur Shulkhan Arukh Kesses Hasofer	Solomon ben Joseph Ganzfried
Kli Yakar	Shlomo Ephraim Lunshitz (Kli Yakar)
Knesses HaGedolah and Sheyarei Knesses HaGedolah	Chaim Benveniste
Ko'ah SHor	Joseph ben Menachem Steinhart
Kol Kitvei Maharal	Judah ben Bezalel Loew (Maharal / Maharal of Prague)
Kol Ya'acob	Jacob de Castro
Kol Yaakov	Yaakov Chaim Sofer (Kaf HaChaim)
Kontres	Samson ben Isaac, of Chinon (MaHaRShak)
Kontres HaSemikah	Levi ben Jacob ibn Chaviv (Habib) (Ralbach)
Korban Aharon	Aharon ibn Chaim
Korban Netanel	Nethaneel ben Naftali Tzvi Weil
Kos Hayeshu'ot	Samuel Schotten (Mharsheishoch)
Kotnot Or	Meir ben Iszak Eisenstadt (Meir Ash) (Maharam Ash / Panim Me'irot)
Kovetz Ha'aros	Yitzhak (Isaac) Hutner
Ksav Sofer	Abraham Samuel Benjamin (Sofer Ksav Sofer)
K'sav (Haketav) V'ha-kabbalah	Jacob Tzvi Mecklenberg
Kuntres HaAvodah Kuntres HaTefilah	Sholom Dovber Schneerson (Rebbe Rashab)
Kur Zahav	Aryeh Leib Steinhardt
Kuzari	Judah ben Samuel HaLevi (RiHa'l)

L

Lebushe Serad	David Solomon Eibenschutz

Work	Author
Legends of the Jews	Louis Ginzberg
Lehem HaPannim	Jacob Hagiz
Lehem Mishneh	Abraham ben Moses de Bouton
Lehem Mishneh	Moses ben Noah Isaac Lipschutz
Lehem Shamayim	Jacob Israel ben Zvi Ashkenazi Emden (the Yabets)
Lehem Yehuda	Judah Ayyas
Leil Shimurim	Yechiel Michel HaLevi Epstein (the Aruch Hashulchan)
Lekah Tob / Pesikta Zutarta	Tobiah ben Eliezer
Lekach Tov	Yom Tov ben Moshe Tzahalon (Maharitz)
Leket HaKemah	Moses Hagiz
Leket Yosher	Joseph ben Moses
Letter to Congregations of Avignon	Hasdai ben Abraham Crescas
Lev Sameach (Halakha) Lev Sameach (Responsa)	Abraham Alegri
Levush Malkhut Levush Orah	Mordechai ben Avraham Jaffe (Yoffe) (Ba'al HaLevushim)
Levush Mordechai	Moshe Mordechai Epstein
Likkutei Moharan	Nachman of Breslov
Likkutei Amarim / Tanya Likutei Torah	Shneur Zalman Baruch (Borukovich), of Liadi (Alter Rebbe, GRaZ)
Likkutei Amarim Likkutei Yesharim	Dov Ber (Maggid of Mezritch) Benjamin Eisenstadt
Likkutei Levi Yitzhak	Levi Yitzhak Schneerson
Likkutei Sichot	Menachem Mendel Schneerson (The Lubavitcher Rebbe)
Likkutei Torat Shmuel	Shmuel Schneerson (The Rebbe Maharash)

Work	Author
M	
Ma'amar Abraham	Abraham ben Asher Wallerstein
Maamrei Admur HaEmtzei	Dovber Schneuri (Mitteler Rebbe)
Ma'arekhet HaKinyanim	Shimon Shkop
Ma'ase Choshev	Avraham Azulai
Ma'aseh Hageonim	Avraham Epstein
Machatsit HaShekel	Samuel ben Nathan Loew
Madragat HaAdam	Yosef Yozel Hurwitz (Alter of Novardok)
Magen Abot	Mordechai ben Abraham Benet
Magen Avot	Yom Tov ben Moshe Tzahalon (Maharitz)
Magen Avraham	Abraham Abele ben Chaim HaLevi Gombiner (Magen Avraham)
Maggid Mesharim	Joseph ben Ephraim Caro
Maggid Mishneh	Vidal di Tolosa
Maginne Shelomoh	Joshua Hoschel ben Joseph
Mahalakh Shevile Hadda'ath	Moses Kimchi
Maharam Schick	Moses Schick (Maharam Schick)
Mahazeh Abraham	Abraham ben Asher Wallerstein
Mahberet (see Sefer HaPitronot)	Menahem ben Jacob ibn Saruq
Maimonides Reader	Isadore (Yitzhak) Twersky
Man is Not Alone: A Philosophy of Religion	Abraham Joshua Heschel
Manhig Olam / HaManhig	Abraham ben Nathan
Manhir Einei Chachamim	Meir ben Gedaliyah Lublin (Maharam)
Maor Israel	Ovadia Yosef
Mareh Yehezkel	Ezekiel (Yechezkel) ben Judah Landau (Nodah B'Yehuda)
Marpe Lashon	Moses Israel
Mas'as Levi	Yaakov Yitzhak Ruderman

Work	Author
Masat Binyamin	Benjamin Aaron ben Abraham Slonik
Mashbir Bar	Joseph ben Menachem Steinhart
Masoret HaTalmud	Isaac Hirsch Weiss
Masot Benyamin	Benjamin Eisenstadt
Massoret HaShas / Massoret HaTalmud	Joshua Boaz Mevorakh / Joshua Boaz ben Simon Baruch (Shiltei Gibborim)
Matte Ephraim	Ephraim Zalman (Solomon) Margolis
Matteh Moshe	Moshe Mos, of Premysl
Mateh Yehuda	Judah Ayyas
Mavo HaTalmud	Samuel ibn Naghrela (Samuel HaNagid)
Ma'yene Yehoshua	Joshua Hoschel ben Elijah Zeeb Levin
Me Niddah	Solomon ben Judah Aaron Kluger
Meah Shearim (Yitzhak Yeranen)	Isaac ibn Gias
Me'am Loez	Yaakov Culi
Meammez Koah	Moses ben Baruch Almosnino
Mechitzat HaShekel	Samuel ben Naftali HaLevi Kelin
Mechkarim beTalmud	Yechiel Yaakov Weinberg
Megillat Setarim	Jacob ben Nissim ibn Shahin (Rabbeinu Nissim, HaMafteach)
Meir Einei Chachamim	Meir ben Gedaliyah Lublin (Maharam)
Meir Netivim	Meir ben Zvi Hirsch Margolis
Meisharim	Yerucham ben Meshullam
Meishiv Davar Meromei Sadeh	Naftali Tzvi Yehuda Berlin
Me-Kabtziel	Chacham Yosef Chaim (Ben Ish Chai)
Mekor Baruch	Baruch HaLevi Epstein
Mekor Chaim (Fons Vitae)	Solomon ben Judah ibn Gabirol (Gvirol)
Mekorot u'Mesorot	David Weiss Halivni

Work	Author
Menorat HaMaor	Isaac Aboab (Menorat HaMaor)
Me-on HaBerakhot	Israel Jonah Landau
Me'Or Einayim	Menachem Nachum Twersky
Meorei Or	Meir Popperos
Meshech Chochma	Meir Simcha Kalonymus HaKohen, of Dvinsk
Meshiv Nefesh	Yoel Sirkis (Bach)
Mesillat Yesharim	Moses Chaim Luzzatto (Ramchal)
Metsudot (David and Zion)	David ben Aryeh Loeb Altshuler (Altshul)
Mibhar Mi-Peninim	Enoch Zundel ben Joseph
Micah HaMayim	Yechiel Michel HaLevi Epstein (the Aruch Hashulchan)
Michlol	David Kimchi (RaDaK)
Michtav me-Eliyahu / Strive for Truth	Eliyahu Eliezer Dessler
Midos Aharon	Aharon ibn Chaim
Midrash de Rabban Shimon ben Yohai / Zohar	Moses de Leon (Moshe ben Shem Tov)
Midrash Rabbeinu Bachya	Bayha ben Asher (Rabbeinu Behaye)
Midrash Shmuel	Shmuel Aceda
Midrash Shmuel	Samuel de Uzeda
Midreshei Teiman	Saul Lieberman
Migdal David	Yaakov David Wilovsky (Ridvaz)
Migdal Oz	Shem Tov ben Abraham ibn Gaon
Mikdash Melek	Aaron Walden
Mikra'ei Kodesh	Meir Leibush ben Jehiel Michel
Milei DeAvot	Joseph Chayon
Milhamot HaShem Mishpetei HaCherem	Moses ben Nahman (Nahmanides) (Ramban)

Work	Author
Minchase Elazar	Chaim Elazar Spira
Minhagei Mahril / Minhagim / Sefer Maharil	Jacob ben Moses Levi Moelin (Maharil)
Minhagei HaRashash	Shalom Sharabi (Rashash)
Minhat Bikkurim	Baruch Mordechai ben Jacob Lipschitz
Minchat Chinuch	Yosef ben Moshe Babad
Minchat Yaakov	Yitzhak Yaakov Weiss
Minhat Kenaot	Zvi Hirsch Chajes (Chayes) (The Maharatz Chajes)
Minhat Kenaot	Abba Mari ben Moses ben Joseph Don Astruc, of Lunel
Minhat Ya'akov	Jacob ben Joseph Reischer (Backofen)
Minhat Yehuda	Yehuda Alkalai
Mishkan HaEdut / Sefer HaSodot	Moses de Leon (Moshe ben Shem Tov)
Mishkan Shiloh	Samuel Joseph Landau
Mishnah Editor / Redactor	Judah HaNasi (Rabbeinu HaKadosh)
Mishnah of Bar Kappara	Eleazar ben Eleazar HaKappar (Bar Kappara, Berebi)
Mishnah Berurah	Israel Meir Kagan (HaKohen) (Chofetz Chaim)
Mishnat Avraham	Avraham Aharon Price
Mishneh la-Melek	Judah ben Samuel Rosanes
Mishneh Torah (Yad HaHazakha)	Moses ben Maimon (Maimonides) (Rambam)
Mishpat Leshon HaMishnah	Isaac Hirsch Weiss
Mishpetei Ouziel	Ben-Zion Meir Hai Uziel
Mitzvot Gadol	Avraham Aharon Price
M'Lekhet Shlomo	Solomon ben Joshua Adeni
Moda'a le-Bet Ysrael	Solomon ben Judah Aaron Kluger

Work	Author
Mor u-Kezi'ah	Jacob Israel ben Zvi Ashkenazi Emden (the Yabets)
Mordechai, the (See Sefer HaMordechai)	Hillel ben Mordechai Ashkenazi
Moreh Nebuke HaZeman	Krochmal, Nachman Kohen
Moreh Nevuchim (Guide for the Perplexed)	Moses ben Maimon (Maimonides) (Rambam)
Moznayim	Abraham ben Meir ibn Ezra (Abenezra)

N

Work	Author
Nachal Yitzhak	Yitzhak Elchanan Spektor
Nahar Shalom	Shalom Sharabi (Rashash)
Nazir	Jacob de Castro
Nefesh David	Moses de Medina
Nefesh HaChaim	Chaim ben Itzchok Volozhin (Reb Chaim)
Nehamot Ziyyon	Samuel Danzig
Ne'ot Deshe	David Solomon Eibenschutz
Ner Mitzvah	Judah ben Bezalel Loew (Maharal / Maharal of Prague)
Nesivos HaMishpat	Jacob ben Jacob Moses Lorberbaum, of Lisser (Ba'al HaNesivos / Lissa Rav)
Nesivos Sholom	Sholom Noach Berezovsky
Netiv Binah	Yissachar Jacobson
Netiv Hayyim	Nethaneel ben Naftali Tzvi Weil
Nifla'ot Hadashot	Noah ben Abraham Lipschutz (Noah Mindes)
Nimukei Yosef	Yosef Chaviva
Nishmat Hayim	Menasseh ben Joseph ben Israel (MB"Y)
Nodah B'Yehuda	Ezekiel (Yechezkel) ben Judah Landau (Nodah B'Yehuda)

Work	Author
Nogah HaBedek	Aron Chorin
Novellae on Sanhedrin	Samuel ben Jacob Jam'a
Novellae on the Shulkhan Arukh	Jonathan Eybeschutz
Novellae on the Talmud	Yonah ben Avraham Gerondi (Rabbeinu Yonah)

O

Work	Author
Ohel Moed	Bayha ben Asher (Rabbeinu Behaye)
Ohel Torah	Menachem Mendel, of Kotzk (Kotzker Rebbe)
Ohel Yaacob	Jacob ben Aaron Sasportas
Ohele Ya'acob	Jacob de Castro
Ohr HaChama (Light of the Sun) Ohr HaChachma Ohr Ha Ganuz.	Avraham Azulai
Ohr HaMeir	Yehuda Meir Shapiro
Ohr HaTorah	Menachem Mendel Schneerson (Tzemach Tzedek)
Ohr Neerav	Moses ben Jacob Cordovero
Ohr Somayach	Meir Simcha Kalonymus HaKohen, of Dvinsk
Ohr Yakar	Moses ben Jacob Cordovero
Ohr Yisrael	Israel Lipkin Salanter
Olat HaChodesh	Enoch Zundel ben Joseph
Olat Raiyah	Abraham Isaac Kook (HaRaAYaH / HaRav)
Omer Man	Menachem di Lonzano
Or Adonai	Hasdai ben Abraham Crescas
Or Ammim	Obadiah ben Jacob Sforno
Or Chadash	Judah ben Bezalel Loew (Maharal / Maharal of Prague)
Or HaGanuz	Meir ben Iszak Eisenstadt (Meir Ash) (Maharam Ash / Panim Me'irot)

Work	Author
Or Rav	Meir Popperos
Or Tzaddikim	
Or Zarua	Isaac ben Moses, of Vienna (Or Zarua, Riaz)
Orach LeChaim	Shlomo Ephraim Lunshitz
Orchot Chaim	Asher ben Jehiel (Rabbeinu Asher / Rosh)
Orhot Hayyim	Aaron ben Jacob ben David HaKohen
Ori W-Yish'i	Abraham ben Eliezer HaKohen
Or li-Yesharim	Yechiel Michel HaLevi Epstein (the Aruch Hashulchan)
Orach (Orah) Chaim (Hayyim) of the Arba'a Turim	Jacob ben Asher
Orah la-Zaddik	Isaac Hirsch Weiss
Orot Hayyim	Abraham ben David (Ravad III)
Out of the Whirlwind: Essays on Mourning, Suffering and the Human Condition	Joseph Ber Soloveitchik (HaRav)

P

Work	Author
Pachad Yitzhak	Yitzhak (Isaac) Hutner
Pahad Yitzhak	Yitzhak Hezekiah Lampronti
Panim Me'irot	Meir ben Iszak Eisenstadt (Meir Ash) (Maharam Ash / Panim Me'irot)
Panim Meirot Umasbirot	Yehuda Leib HaLevi Ashlag
Parashat Derakim	Judah ben Samuel Rosanes
Parashot Mordechai	Mordechai ben Abraham Benet
Pardes Rimonim	Moses ben Jacob Cordovero
Parpera'ot Hadashot	Noah ben Abraham Lipschutz (Noah Mindes)
Passover Letter	Hasdai ben Abraham Crescas
Pe'at HaShulchan	Yisroel ben Shmuel Ashkenazi, of Shklov
Peirush Rabbeinu Gershon	Gershon ben Yehuda (Me'Or HaGolah)

Work	Author
Pene Yehoshua	Yaakov Yehoshua ben Zvi Hirsch (Jacob Joshua Falk)
Peri Yitzhak	Isaac ben Moses Solomon Blaser (Rav Itzele Peterburger)
Perush	Mattithiah ben Solomon Delacrut
Perush al Sefer Iyob Perush al Sefer HaTorah	Levi ben Gershom (Gersonides, Ralbag)
Perush Hamishnayot (Commentary on the Mishnah)	Moses ben Maimon (Maimonides) (Rambam)
Perush Kiddush HaChodesh	Levi ben Jacob ibn Chaviv (Habib) (Ralbach)
Perush Yakar Al Shisha Sidrei Mishnah Perush Yakar Al HaLevush	Avraham Azulai
Pesach Me'Uvin	Chaim Benveniste
Pesakim	Samson ben Joseph, of Falaise
Pesachim be-Inyan Kiddushin	Shalom Shakna
Pesakim u-Ketabim	Israel ben Pethahiah Ashkenazi Isserlein
Peshat and Derash: Plain and Applied Meaning in Rabbinic Exegesis	David Weiss Halivni
Pesikhta de-Rab Kahana	Solomon Buber
Pesikta Zutarta / Lekah Tob	Tobiah ben Eliezer
Pirkei Moshe	Moses ben Baruch Almosnino
Piskei HaRid	Yeshayah ben Mali Hazaken
Piske RashDaM	Samuel ben Moses de Medina (RashDaM)
Pithei Teshuvah	Abraham Zevi Hirsch ben Jacob Eisenstadt
Piyutei R'Shimon ben Yitzhak	Shimon ben Yitzhak HaGadol
Pnei Menachem	Pinchas Menachem Alter
Pnei Sofer	Solomon ben Joseph Ganzfried
Pri Chadash	Hezekiah ben David DiSilo

Work	Author
Prophetic Inspiration After the Prophets	Abraham Joshua Heschel
The Prophets	

Q

Work	Author
Qanan-un-Nisa	Chacham Yosef Chaim (Ben Ish Chai)

R

Work	Author
Rabbotenu Ba'ale HaTosafot	Obadiah ben Abraham of Bertinoro
RaDaK	David Kimchi (RaDaK)
Rav Pe'alim	Chacham Yosef Chaim (Ben Ish Chai)
Refutation of Christian Principles	Hasdai ben Abraham Crescas
Rehovot Nahar	Shalom Sharabi (Rashash)
Reshit Chochma	Eliyahu de Vidas
Responsa Binyan Tzion	Yaakov Etlinger
Responsa Chacham Tzvi	Tzvi Hirsch ben Yaakov Ashkenazi (Chacham Tzvi)
Responsa Temim De'im Orot Hayyim Shibbole HaLeket	Abraham ben David (Ravad III)
Responsa	Shlomo ben Aderet
Responsa	Amram Gaon
Responsa	Hai Gaon
Responsa of Maharik	Joseph Colon ben Solomon Trabotto
The Responsa Literature	Solomon Bennett Freehof
Responsa in a moment: Halakhic responses to contemporary issues The Responsa of Professor Louis Ginzberg	David Golinkin (ed.)
Revelation Restored: Divine Writ and Critical Responses	David Weiss Halivni

Work	Author
ReZaH	Zerachiah ben Isaac HaLevi Gerondi
Rosh Yosef	Joseph Escapa
Rokeach	Eleazar ben Yehuda of Worms
Ruach David v'Nishmat David	Moses de Medina
Ruach Chaim	Chaim ben Itzchok Volozhin (Reb Chaim)

S

Work	Author
S'Dei Chemed	Chaim Chizkiya Medini
Seder Gittin ve-Halizah	Abraham ben Eliezer HaLevi Minz
Seder Olam	Simah ben Samuel, of Speyer
Seder Olam Rabbah	Jose ben Halafta
Seder HaDorot	Jehiel ben Solomon Heilprin
Sefer Ba'ale Nefesh	Abraham ben David (Ravad III)
Sefer Chakira: Derech Emunah	Menachem Mendel Schneerson (Tzemach Tzedek)
Sefer Dikdukei HaTe'amim	Aaron ben Moses ben Asher
Sefer Emes al HaTorah	Yehuda Leib Alter
Sefer Emunah Yesharah Sefer HaBerit Sefer Moznayim la-Mishpat Sefer Yitziat Mitzrayim	Zvi Hirsch Kalischer
Sefer Gerushim	Moses ben Jacob Cordovero
Sefer HaAkedah	Isaac ben Moses Arama (Ba'al Akedah)
Sefer HaChinuch (the Chinuch)	Aaron HaLevi (of Barcelona)
Sefer HaEmunot	Shem Tov ibn Shem Tov
Sefer HaIttur / Ittur Soferim	Yitzhak ben Abba Mari, of Marseilles
Sefer HaHalachot	Meshullam ben Moses
Sefer HaHayyim Sefer Setam	Solomon ben Judah Aaron Kluger

Work	Author
Sefer HaHayyim Sefer HaKapparot Sha'are HaSod HaYihud weha-Emmunah	Eleazar ben Yehuda ben Kalonymus of Worms (Rokeach)
Sefer HaIttim	Judah ben Barzillai
Sefer HaIkarim / Ikkarim	Joseph Albo
Sefer HaMa'amarim	Sholom Dovber Schneerson (Rebbe Rashab)
Sefer HaMa'amarim	Yosef Yitzhak Schneerson (Rebbe Rayatz)
Sefer HaMa'amarim Melukot	Menachem Mendel Schneerson (The Lubavitcher Rebbe)
Sefer HaMaor (See HaMaor HaGadol and HaMaor HaKatan) Sefer HaTsava	Zerachiah ben Isaac HaLevi Gerondi
Sefer HaMatanah	Asher ben Meshullam
Sefer HaMiddot	Nachman of Breslov
Sefer HaMiknah	Yosef (Yoselman) Loanz, of Rosheim
Sefer HaMitzvot	Moses ben Maimon (Maimonides) (Rambam)
Sefer HaMizrachi	Elijah Mizrachi (Re'em)
Sefer HaMora	Shemariah ben Elijah Ikriti, of Negropont
Sefer HaMordechai (See Mordechai)	Hillel ben MordechaiAshkenazi
Sefer HaOrah Sefer HaPardes	Shlomo Yitzhaki (Rashi)
Sefer HaOsher	Jacob ben Reuben
Sefer HaPitronot (See Mahberet)	Menahem ben Jacob ibn Saruq
Sefer HaRaviah (Avi HaEzri)	Eliezer ben Joel HaLevi (Raviah)
Sefer Hareidim	Elazar ben Moshe Azikri (Ezkari)
Sefer HaRimonim Sefer HaSodot / Mishkan HaEdut	Moses de Leon (Moshe ben Shem Tov)
Sefer HaShorashim	Yonah ibn Janach (Merinos)

Work	Author
Sefer HaSichot	Menachem Mendel Schneerson (The Lubavitcher Rebbe)
Sefer Hasidim	Judah ben Samuel, of Regensburg (He-Hasid)
Sefer Hasidim	Avraham Aharon Price
Sefer HaTerumah	Baruch ben Isaac
Sefer HaTerumah	Baruch ben Yitzhak, of Worms
Sefer HaTerumot	Samuel ben Isaac Sardi (HaSardi, HaSefaradi)
Sefer HaYashar	Abraham ben Samuel Abulafia
Sefer HaYashar	Abraham ben Meir ibn Ezra (Abenezra)
Sefer HaYashar	Shabbatai Carmuz Levita
Sefer HaYashar	Jacob ben, Meir (Tam) (Rabbeinu Tam)
Sefer HaYashar	Zerachiah HaYavani (The Greek) (Ra'Za'H)
Sefer HaYekar	Shabtai Donolo
Sefer HaYesod	Abraham ben Meir ibn Ezra (Abenezra)
Sefer HaYirah	Yonah ben Avraham Gerondi (Rabbeinu Yonah)
Sefer HaZikranot	Samuel Aboab (Rasha)
Sefer Kaftor Vaferech	Haparchi, Ishtori ben Moses, (Kaftor Vaferech)
Sefer Keritut	Samson ben Isaac, of Chinon (MaHaRShak)
Sefer Ma'aseh Hoshev	Levi ben Gershom (Gersonides, Ralbag)
Sefer Ma'asiyyot HaHakhamim	Nissim ben Jacob (HaMafteach) (Rav Nissim Gaon)
Sefer Mafteach Manu'ele HaTalmud (HaMafteach)	Jacob ben Nissim ibn Shahin (Rabbeinu Nissim, HaMafteach)
Sefer Maharil / Minhagei Maharil / Minhagim	Jacob ben Moses Levi Moelin (Maharil)
Sefer Makloket / Shiltei Gibborim	Joshua Boaz Mevorakh / Joshua Boaz ben Simon Baruch (Shiltei Gibborim)
Sefer Milkhamot Ha-Shem	Nissim ben Jacob (HaMafteach) (Rav Nissim Gaon)

Work	Author
Sefer Milhamot Adonai	Jacob ben Reuben
Sefer Minhagim	Isaac Tyrnau
Sefer Mitzvot Gadol (Semag)	Moses ben Jacob of Coucy
Sefer Mitzvot Katan (Semak) or Ammude HaGolah	Isaac ben Joseph of Corbeil
Sefer Orah or Sha'are Orah	Joseph ben Abraham Gikatilla (Joseph Ba'al HaNissim)
Sefer Pe'ah	Moses ibn Tibbon
Sefer Peretz	Perez ben Eliah (Rap / RaPaSh / MaHaRPaSh)
Sefer Torat Elohim	Isaac Samuel Reggio (Yashar)
Sefer Yadot	Menachem di Lonzano
Sefer Yereim	Eliezer ben Samuel of Metz
Sefer Yossipon	Joseph ben Gorion
Sepher Haggulai Sepher Zikkaron	Joseph ben Isaac Kimchi
Sekel Kob	Menahem ben Solomon
Selichot	Shabbatai ben Meir HaKohen (Shach)
Semag (Sefer Mitzvot Gadol)	Jacob of Coucy
Semak (Sefer Mitzvot Katan) or Ammude HaGolah	Isaac ben Joseph, of Corbeil
Seride Eish	Yechiel Yaakov Weinberg
Sfas Emes al HaTorah	Yehuda Aryeh Leib Alter (Sfas Emes)
Shaagat Aryeh She'elot u-Teshuvot Shaagat Aryeh HaHadashot	Aryeh Leib ben Asher Gunzberg (Shaagat Aryeh)
Sha'ar HaGemul	Moses ben Nahman (Nahmanides) (Ramban)
Sha'ar HaShamayim	Abraham Herrero
Sha'ar Hashamayim	Isaiah HaLevi Horowitz (Shelah, Shaloh)
Sha'ar Ha'shamayim (additions)	Shabtai Sheftel Horowitz

Work	Author
Sha'ar HaTziyyum	Israel Meir Kagan (HaKohen) (Chofetz Chaim)
Sha'ar HaYichud	Dovber Schneuri (Mitteler Rebbe)
Sha'are Ephraim	Ephraim Zalman (Solomon) Margolis
Sha'arei Orah	Dovber Schneuri (Mitteler Rebbe)
Sha'areh Simhah	Isaac ben Judah ibn Ghiyyat (Ghayyat)
Sha'are Teshuvah	Yonah ben Avraham Gerondi (Rabbeinu Yonah)
Sha'are Teshubah	Hayyim Mordechai Margolis
Sha'arei Yosher	Shimon Shkop
Sha'are Zedek	Abraham ben Jehiel Danzig
Shailos Uteshuvot Marsham	Sholom Mordechai Schwadron (Maharsham)
Shalom Yerushalayim	Judah ben Solomon Chai Alkali
Shammot ba-Arez	Moses ibn Habib (Chaviv)
Shebbet Yehuda	Judah Ayyas
She'elot u'Bedikot She'elot u'Teshubot	Jacob ben Judah Weil (Mahariv)
She'elot u-Teshubot	Meir ben Isaac Katzenellenbogen (Maharam Padua)
She'elot u'Teshubot	Jedidiah Weil
She'elot u-Teshuvot	Levi ben Jacob ibn Chaviv (Habib) (Ralbach)
She'elot uT'shuvot Achiezer	Chaim Ozer Grodzinski
She'elot u-Teshubot Pene Yehoshua	Joshua Hoschel ben Joseph
She'elot u-Teshubot ReMA	Moses ben Israel Isserles (Rema)
She'elot U'Teshubot R' Yosef ibn Lev	Joseph ibn Chaviv
She'elot uTeshuvot Ri Migash	Joseph ben Meir HaLevi ibn Migash (Ri Migash)
She'elot Yabez	Jacob Israel ben Zvi Ashkenazi Emden (the Yabets)
Shefa' Tal	Shabbethai Sheftel ben Akiba Hurwitz

Work	Author
Sheilot d'Rav Achai or Sheiltos	Achai Gaon
Shekel HaKodesh	Moses de Leon (Moshe ben Shem Tov)
Sheki'in	Saul Lieberman
Shem Ephraim	Ephraim Zalman (Solomon) Margolis
Shem HaGedolim	Haim Yosef David Azulai (Hida)
Shem HaGedolim heHadash	Aaron Walden
Shem Olam	Jonathan Eybeschutz
Shenoth Eliyahu	Elijah ben Solomon Zalman (Vilna Gaon, Gra)
Shenot Hayyim	Solomon ben Judah Aaron Kluger
Shev Shema'atata	Aryeh Leib HaKohen Heller (The Ketzos)
Shevut Ya'akov	Jacob ben Joseph Reischer (Backofen)
Shibat Ziyyon	Samuel ben Ezekiel Landau
Shibbole HaLeket	Zedekiah ben Abraham Anaw
Shibbole HaLeket	Abraham ben David (Ravad III)
Shibbole HaLeket	Tzidkayah ben Avraham Anav HaRofei
Shiltei Gibborim / Sefer Makloket	Joshua Boaz Mevorakh / Joshua Boaz ben Simon Baruch (Shiltei Gibborim)
Shir Hakavod Shir Hayichud	Solomon ben Judah, ibn Gabirol (Gvirol)
Shir HaYihud	Samuel ben Kalonymus (He-Hasid), of Speyer
Shiurei Reb Boruch Ber	Boruch Ber Leibowitz
Shiurei Rebbi Chaim MiTelz	Rabinowitz, Chaim Shalom Tuvia (Reb Chaim Telzer)
Shiur Komah	Moses ben Jacob Cordovero
Sh'mirat HaLashon	Israel Meir Kagan (HaKohen) (Chofetz Chaim)
Shnei Luchos HaBris (Shelah) (Shnei Luhot HaBrit)	Isaiah HaLevi Horowitz (Shelah, Shaloh)
Sho'el u-Meshiv	Joseph Saul Nathanson
Shtei Yadot	Menachem di Lonzano

Work	Author
Shulchan Aruch HaRav	Shneur Zalman Baruch (Borukovich), of Liadi (Alter Rebbe, GRaZ)
Shulkhan HaPanim	Isaac Aboab (Menorat HaMaor)
Shulkhan Arba	Bayha ben Asher (Rabbeinu Behaye)
Shulkhan Arukh	Joseph ben Ephraim Caro (Karo) (Mechaber)
Shut Mharsheisshoch	Samuel Schotten (Mharsheishoch)
Shut Tzemach Tzedek	Menachem Mendel Schneerson (Tzemach Tzedek)
Siach Yerushalayim	Yosef Quafih
Sichos Levi	Yaakov Yitzhak Ruderman
Sidur Hakavanot Siddur HaRashash	Shalom Sharabi (Rashash)
Siddur Rab Amram / Seder Rav Amram	Amram Gaon
Siddur Mordechai Ve-Simanav / Siddur Dine Mordekai	Joshua Boaz Mevorakh / Joshua Boaz ben Simon Baruch (Shiltei Gibborim)
Siddur Rashi	Shlomo Yitzhaki (Rashi)
Siddur Tefilah	Jacob Israel ben Zvi Ashkenazi Emden (the Yabets)
Siddur Tefilah	Nissim ben Jacob (HaMafteach) (Rav Nissim Gaon)
Siddur Torah Or	Shneur Zalman Baruch (Borukovich), of Liadi (Alter Rebbe, GRaZ)
Sifre Zuta	Saul Lieberman
Sifsei Chachamim	Shabbethai ben Joseph Bass
Sifsei Daas	Shlomo Ephraim Lunshitz
Siftei Kohen (Shakh)	Shabbatai ben Meir HaKohen (Shach)
Sifte Renanot	Isaac ben Judah ibn Ghiyyat (Ghayyat)
Sifte Yeshenim	Shabbethai ben Joseph Bass
Sippurei Ma'Asiyyot	Nachman of Breslov

Work	Author
Sod Hashem VerSharvit HaZahav	David Lida
Sod Yakin u-Voaz	Meir ben Zvi Hirsch Margolis
Strive for Truth / Michtav me-Eliyahu	Eliyahu Eliezer Dessler
Studies in the Formation of the Talmud, Mishnah and Gemara: Jewish Predilection for Justified Law	David Weiss Halivni
Sulam (HaSulam)	Yehuda Leib HaLevi Ashlag

T

Work	Author
Takhemoni	Judah ben Solomon Alharizi (al-Harizi)
Talmudic Glosses	Isaiah Berlin
Talmud Commentary	Hai Gaon
Talmud Eser Sefirot	Yehuda Leib HaLevi Ashlag
Targum Onkelos	Onkelos
Targum Yonatan	Jonathan ben Uzziel
Taryag Mitzvot	Jonathan Eybeschutz
Taryag Mitzvos	Moshe Mos of Premysl
Techeiles Mordechai	Sholom Mordechai Schwadron (Maharsham)
Techeiles Mordechai	Mordechai Gimpel Yaffe Torizer
Tekelet Mordechai	Mordechai ben Abraham Benet
Temim De'im	Abraham ben David (Ravad III)
Teshuvos HaBach	Yoel Sirkis (Bach)
Teshuvos Rodvaz	Yaakov David Wilovsky (Ridvaz)
Teshuvot HaRam	Alexander Margolis
Tehuvoth Lanotzrim	David Kimchi (RaDaK)
Teshuvot Mahari Bruna	Israel Bruna
Teshubot Rosh Yosef	Joseph Escapa
Terumat HaDeshen	Israel ben Pethahiah Ashkenazi Isserlein

Work	Author
The Lonely Man of Faith	Joseph Ber Soloveitchik (HaRav)
The Sabbath: Its Meaning for Modern Man The Prophets	Abraham Joshua Heschel
Tifferet HaGershuni	Gershon Ashkenazi
Tifferet Shemuel	Aaron Samuel ben Israel Kaidenover
Tiferet Yehonatan	Jonathan Eybeschutz
Tiferet Yisrael	Israel Lipschutz
Tikun Tefillin	Elhanan ben Isaac, of Dampierre
Tikkun HaKlali	Nachman of Breslov
Tikkun Soferim	Joseph ibn Plat
To'afot Re'em	Aaron Moses ben Jacob Taubes
Toledot Ya'akov Yosef	Jacob Joseph ben Tzvi HaKohen Katz, of Polonnoye
Toledot Adam	Abraham ben Jehiel Danzig
Toledot Yaacob	Jacob ben Aaron Sasportas
Torah Lishmah	Chacham Yosef Chaim (Ben Ish Chai)
Torah min HaShamayim BeAspaklariya (Heavenly Torah: As Refracted Through the Generations)	Abraham Joshua Heschel
Torah Or	Judah Aryeh Loeb ben Joshua Hoschel
Torah Ohr	Joshua Boaz Mevorakh / Joshua Boaz ben Simon Baruch (Shiltei Gibborim)
Torah Shelemah	Menachem Mendel Kasher
Toras Chesed	Shneur Zalman Fradkin of Lublin
Toras Zevach	Solomon ben Joseph Ganzfried
Torat HaAdam Torat Hashem Temima	Moses ben Nahman (Nahmanides) (Ramban)
Torat HaBayit	Shlomo ben Aderet

Work	Author
Torat HaNazir	Yitzhak (Isaac) Hutner
Torath Hattat (Issur we-Hetter)	Moses ben Israel Isserles (Rema)
Torath Kohanim	Abraham ben David (Ravad III)
Torat Netan'el	Nethaneel ben Naftali Tzvi Weil
Torat Nevi'im	Zvi Hirsch Chajes (Chayes) (The Maharatz Chajes)
Torah Temimah	Baruch HaLevi Epstein
Tosafot (Yoma published)	Meir ben Baruch (Meir of Rothenburg) (MaHaRaM)
Tosafot	Samson ben Joseph, of Falaise
Tosafot	Eliezer of Toul
Tosafot for Ketuvot	Abigdor Cohen, of Vienna
Tosafot for Nashim, Nazir, Shabbat, Hullin	Baruch ben Isaac
Tosafot for Nedarim, Megillah and Avodah Zarah	Elhanan ben Isaac, of Dampierre
Tosafot for Tamid	Samuel ben Kalonymus (He-Hasid), of Speyer
Tosafot haRid	Yaakov David Wilovsky (Ridvaz)
Tosafot of Evreux	Moses of Evreux
Tosafot Sheni le-Ziyyon	Joshua Hoschel ben Elijah Zeeb Levin
Tosafot Tuk	Eliezer of Touques
Tosafot Yeshanim	Isaac ben Samuel, of Dampierre (Ri)
Tosefet Berakhah	Meir ben Baruch (Meir of Rothenburg) (MaHaRaM)
Tosefot RI'D	Isaiah ben Mali di Trani (RI'D)
Tosefet Rishonim	Saul Lieberman
Tosefos Yomtov	Yom Tov Lippman Heller (Tosefos Yomtov)
Tror Hamor	Avraham ben Yaakov Saba

Work	Author
Tsafenat Pane'ah	Jacob Joseph ben Tzvi HaKohen Katz, of Polonnoye
Turei Even	Aryeh Leib ben Asher Gunzberg (Shaagat Aryeh)
Turei Zahav	David ben Samuel HaLevi Segal (Taz)
Tzafnach Paneach	Yosef Rosen (Rogatchover Gaon, Tzafnach Paneach)
Tzeidah La-Derech	Yissachar Ber Ellenburg
Tzemach Tzedek	Menachem Mendel Schneerson (third Rebbe)
Tzemach Tzedek (Zemah Zedek)	Menachem Mendel ben Abraham Krochmal
Tziyyon Lenefesh Hayyah	Ezekiel (Yechezkel) ben Judah Landau (Nodah B'Yehuda)

V

Work	Author
Vave HaAmmudim	Shabtai Sheftel Horowitz
Vayigash Yehuda	Yehuda Leib ben Meir Channeles
Vitry Mahzor	Simhah ben Samuel of Vitry
Vortelach	Yehuda Meir Shapiro

Y

Work	Author
Ya'arot Devash	Jonathan Eybeschutz
Yabia Oner	Ovadia Yosef
Yad Absholom	Isaac ben Moses Arama
Yad Ephraim	Ephraim Zalman (Solomon) Margolis
Yad HaHazakha (Mishneh Torah)	Moses ben Maimon (Maimonides) (Rambam)
Yad HaMelek	Eleazar ben Israel Landau
Yagel Yaakov	Yaakov Chaim Sofer (Kaf HaChaim)
Yalkut (Yalkut Shimoni)	Simeon Kara of Frankfurt (HaDarshan)
Yalkut Yosef	Yitzhak Yosef
Yam Shel Shlomo	Solomon Luria (Maharshal, Rashal)

Work	Author
Yare'ach Yakar	Abraham Galante
Yechavei Da'ath	Ovadia Yosef
Yedid Nefesh	Elazar ben Moshe Azikri (Ezkari)
Yekar Tiferet	David ben Solomon ibn Abi Zimra (Radbaz)
Yeri'ot Shlomo	Solomon Luria (Maharshal, Rashal)
Yeshuot Ya'acob (Shulkhan Arukh Commentary) Yeshuot Ya'acob (Pentateuch Commentary)	Jacob Meshullam ben Mordechai Ze'ev Ornstein
Yesod	Moses HaDarshan
Yesod Dikduk Yesod Mora	Abraham ben Meir ibn Ezra (Abenezra)
Yesod HaEmunah	Boruch of Kosov
Yesh Nohalin	Abraham ben Shabtai Sheftel Horowitz
Yideh Mosheh	Moses ben Baruch Almosnino
Yigdal Elohim Hai	Daniel ben Judah
Yismach Yisrael	Yaakov Chaim Sofer (Kaf HaChaim)
Yitzhak Yeranen (Meah Shearim)	Isaac ibn Gias
Yoreh De'ah section of Arba'ah Turim	Jacob ben Asher

Z

Work	Author
Zayit Ra'anan	Abraham Abele ben Chaim HaLevi Gombiner (Magen Avraham)
Zedak la-Derek	Menahem ben Aaron ibn Zerah
Zekan Aharon	Aaron Walkin
Zera Abraham	Abraham ben Asher Wallerstein
Zera Ephraim	Ephraim Zalman (Solomon) Margolis
Zivhei Tzedek	Abdalla Somekh
Zikron Yosef	Joseph ben Menachem Steinhart

Work	Author
Zikru Torat Moshe	Abraham ben Jehiel Danzig
Ziyyun Yehoshua	Joshua Hoschel ben Elijah Zeeb Levin
Zizat Noble Zebi	Jacob ben Aaron Sasportas
Zizim u-Ferahhim	Jacob Israel ben Zvi Ashkenazi Emden (the Yabets)
Zohar	Shimon bar Yohai (Rashbi)
Zohar / Midrash de Rabban Shimon ben Yohai	Moses de Leon (Moshe ben Shem Tov)
Zuwwa'ah	Shabtai Sheftel Horowitz

Section IV

Aspects Of The Authors

Period Lived By Sages, Rabbis And Scholars

This listing provides the dates of birth and death where both are known. If only the one is known then that is listed. Sometimes only the century in which the scholar lived is known and that is then listed. The listing is alphabetically arranged by the proper last name appearing first.

A

Aaron of Pesaro	c. 15th century
Aaron, Samuel ben, of Schlettstadt	Second half 14th century
Abba, Hiyya bar	b. middle 2nd century
Abba the Surgeon	Talmudic period
Abba, Samuel bar (Samuel of Nehardea)	c. 165 – 257
Abba, Tanhuma bar	c. 4th century
Abba, Yermiyahu bar	3rd century (1) and 4th century (2)
Abbahu	Late 3rd early 4th century CE
Abbahu, Hanina bar	2nd / 3rd century
Abbaye	c. 280 – 340 CE
Abel, Solomon ben Kalman HaLevi	1857 – 1886
Aboab, Isaac (Menorat HaMaor)	14th century
Aboab, Isaac	1433 – 493
Aboab, Samuel (Rasha)	1610 – 1694
Abraham, Isaac ben, of Dampierre (Riba)	d. 1210
Abraham, Jona ben	14th century
Abraham, Obadiah ben, of Bertinoro	d. 1500
Abraham, Samson of Sens	c. 1150 – c1230
Abravanel, Don Isaac ben Judah	1437 – 1508
Abuchatzeirah, Harav Israel	1890 – 1984
Abudraham, David ben Joseph ben David	14th – 15th century
Abulafia, Abraham ben Samuel	c. 1240 – c. 1290
Abulafia, Meir ben Todros HaLevi	1170 – 1244
Abuyah, Elisha ben	1st – 2nd century CE
Adarbi (Adribi), Isaac	c. 1510 – c. 1584
Aceda, Shmuel	1538 – 1602
Adeni, Solomon ben Joshua	17th century
Aderet, Shlomo ben (Rashba)	1235 – 1310
Ahavah, Adda bar	3rd century CE
Akavya ben Mahalel	2nd or 3rd century CE
Alami, Solomon	14th – 15th centuries
Alashkar, Moses ben Isaac	15th – 16th centuries
Albargeloni, Isaac ben Reuben	b. 1043
Albo, Joseph	c. 1380 – c. 1230
Alegri, Abraham	15th / 16th century – 1652

Alfasi, Yitzhak ben Yaakov HaKohen (RIF)	1013 – 1103
Algazi, Yom Tov	1727 – 1802
Alharizi (al-Harizi), Judah ben Solomon	1160 – 1230
Alkabetz, Solomon ben Moses HaLevi	c. 1505 – ?
Alkali, Judah ben Solomon Chai	1798 – 1878
Almosnino, Joseph B. Ludwig	1642 – 1689
Almosnino, Moses ben Baruch	c. 1515 – c. 1580
Alshich, Moshe	1508 – 1593
Alter, Avraham Mordechai	1866 – 1848
Alter, Pinchas Menachem (Pnei Menachem)	1926 – 1996
Alter, Simchah Bunim (Lev Simcha)	1898 – 1992
Alter, Yaakov Aryeh	1939 –
Alter, Yehuda Aryeh Leib (Sfas Emes)	1847 – 1905
Alter, Israel (Beis Israel)	1895 – 1977
Alter, Yitzhak Meir (See Imrei Emes)	1798 – 1866
Altschul, Naphtali (Hirsch) ben Asher	Late 16th – early 17th century
Altshuler, David ben Aryeh Loeb	Late 17th century
Amemar I	4th century
Amemar II	5th century
Ammi ben Nathan	3rd century
Amnon, of Mainz	c. 10th – 12th century
Anaw (Anav), Benjamin ben Abraham	Thirteenth century
Anaw (Anav) Anav, Nathan ben Jehiel (Yechiel)	1035 – 1106
Anaw (Anav), Zedekiah ben Abraham	13th century
Ankava, Abraham	19th century
Arach, Eleazar ben	1st century CE
Arama, Isaac ben Moses (Ba'al Akedah)	1420 – 1494
Arika, Abba (Rav)	d. 247
Asevilli, Yom Tov Ibn (Ritva)	2nd half 13th century – 1st half 14th century
Asher, Aaron ben Moses ben	d. c. 960
Asher, Baya ben (Rabbeinu Behaye)	mid 13th century – 1340
Asher ben Meshullam	2nd half 12th century
Asher, Jacob ben (Ba'al HaTurim, Tur)	1270 – 1343
Ashi, Hiyya bar	?2nd – 4th century
Ashi, Rav	352 – 427
Ashi, Tabyomi bar (Mar bar Rav Ashi)	5th century
Ashkenazi, Bezalel	16th century
Ashkenazi, Gershon	Early 17th century – 1693
Ashkenazi, Mordechai ben Hillel (or Mordechai ben Hillel)	1250 – 1298
Ashkenazi, Tzvi Hirsch ben Yaakov (Chacham Tzvi)	1656 – 1712
Ashkenazi, Yehuda ben Shimon	1730 – 1770
Ashkenazi, Yisroel ben Shmuel, of Shklov	c. 1770 – 1839
Ashkenazi, Yitzhak Luria (The ARI)	1534 – 1572

Ashlag, Yehuda Leib HaLevi	1885 – 1954
Assi, Rabbi	3rd and 4th centuries
Attar, Hayyim ibn (Ohr HaChaim HaKadosh)	1696 – 1743
Auerbah, Menachem Mendel ben Meshulam Zalman	1620 – 1689
Auerbach, Shlomo Zalman	1910 – 1995
Avin, Rabbi Yose bar	
Avina	3rd – 4th century
Avraham of Trisk	1802 – 1889
Avtalyon	d. 37 –30 BCE
Azai, Rabbi ben	
Ayyas, Judha	1690 – 1760
Azariah, Elazar ben	Late 1st to 2nd century CE
Azaryah, Menachem, of Fano	1548 – 1620
Azikri (Ezkari), Elazar ben Moshe	1533 – 1600
Azulai, Abraham	1570 – 1643
Azulai, Haim Yosef David (Hida)	1724 – 1806
Azzai, Shimon ben	2nd century

B

Baba, Judah ben	2nd century
Babad, Yosef ben Moshe	1801 – 1874
Bachrach, Abraham Samuel	1575 – 1615
Bacharach, Yair, Chaim	1639 – 1702
Barfat, Isaac ben Sheshet (RiBaSH)	1326 – 1408
Baruch, Joseph ben (Joseph of Clisson)	12th – 13th centuries
Baruch, Meir ben (Meir of Rothenburg) (MaHaRaM)	c. 1215 – 1293
Baruch (Borukovich), Shneur Zalman, of Liadi (Alter Rebbe, GRaZ)	1745 – 1812
Barzillai, Judah ben	late 11th century
Bass, Shabbethai ben Joseph	1641 – 1718
Behag	?7th – 10th centuries
Benet, Mordechai ben Abraham	1753 – 1829
Benveniste, Chaim	1603 – 1673
Ber, Dov of Mezritch, (The Maggid of Mezritch)	1710 – 1772
Berab, Jacob	1474 – 1546
Berechyah, Aharon, of Modena	d. 1639
Berzovsky, Sholom Noach	1911 – 2000
Berlin, Isaiah ben Judah Loeb	1725 – 1799
Berlin, Naftali Tvi Yehuda (The Netziv)	1817 – 1893
Bibago, Abraham ben Shem Tov	15th century
Blaser, Isaac ben Moses Solomon (Rav Itzele Peterburger)	1837 – 1937

Boruch of Kosov	d. 1782.
Bouton, Abraham ben Moses de	c. 1560 – c. 1605
Boya'a, Shlomo ben	10th century
Bruna, Israel	1400 – 1480
Buber, Solomon	1827 – 1906

C

Campanton, Isaac ben Jacob	1360 – 1463
Caro, Joseph ben Ephraim	1488 – 1575
Castro, Jacob de	d. 1610
Chaim, Aharon ibn	1560 – 1632
Chaim, Hakham (Chacham) Yosef (Ben Ish Chai)	1832 – 1909
Chajes, Zvi Hirsch (Maharatz Chajes)	1805 – 1855
Chama	4th century
Chama, Chanina bar	3rd – 4th centuries
Chama, Rami bar	4th century
Chaviv (Habib) (Ralbch), Levi ben Jacob ibn	c. 1480 – c. 1545
Chananyah Abraham ibn	1605 – 1651
Channeles, Yehuda Leib ben Meir	Early 1500s – 1596
Chaviv (Habib), Yaakov ibn	d. 1516
Chaviva, Yosef	late 14th century / early 15th century
Chayon, Avraham	d. 1510
Chayon, Joseph	1425 – early 16th century
Chisda (Hisda), Rav	died 308
Chorin, Aron	1766 – 1844
Chushiel, Chananel ben (Hushiel, Hananel ben)	990 – 1053
Cohen, Abigdor (of Vienna)	Twelfth century
Cordovero (also Kordovero), Moses ben Jacob (Ramak)	1522 – 1570
Crescas, Hasdai ben Abraham	c. 1340 – 1410 / 11
Culi, Yaakov	1689 – 1732

D

Danzig, Abraham ben Jehiel	1747 / 8 – 1820
Danzig, Samuel	17th century
David, Avraham ben (Ravad III)	1125 – 1198
David, Baruch ben	?
Delacrut, Mattithiah ben Solomon	mid 16th century
Dessler, Eliyahu Eliezer	1892 – 1953
DiSilo, Hezekiah ben David	1659 – 1698
Donolo, Shabtai	913 – c. 982
Dosa, Hanina ben	1st century CE

Duran, Simeon ben Zemah (Rashbatz / Tashbetz)	1361 – 1444
Duran, Solomon ben Simon (Rashbash)	c. 1400 – 1467
Dvir, Yehuda Meir	20th century

E

Eger (Eiger), Akiva	1761 – 1837
Eibenschutz, David Solomon	d. c. 1812
Eidels (Edels), Samuel Eliezar ben Judah (Maharsha)	1555 – 1631
Eisenstadt, Abraham Zwi Hirsch ben Jacob	1813 – 1875
Eisenstadt, Benjamin	1846 – 1920
Eisenstadt, Meir ben Iszak (Meir Ash) (Maharam Ash / Panim Me'irot)	1670 – 1744
Eisenstadter, Meir (Meir Ash) (Maharam Ash)	1780 – 1852
Elchanan (Bachrach) Naftali Hertz ben Yaakov	17th century
Eliakim, Hillel ben	11th – 12th centuries
Eliezer, Israel ben (Ba'al Shem Tov / Besht)	1698 – 1760
Eliezar, Tobiah ben	11th century
Eliezer of Toul	13th century
Eliezer of Touques	13th century
Elgidor, Abba Mari ben	13th century
Elijah, Perez ben (Rap / RaPaSh / MaHaRPaSh)	d. c. 1295
Elisha, Ishmael ben (Rabbi Ishmael)	90 – 135 CE
Ellenburg, Yissachar Ber	1570 – 1623
Emden, Jacob Israel ben Zvi Ashkenazi (Yabets)	1697 – 1776
Enoch, Judah ben	17th century – 18th century
Ephraim, Moshe Chaim (of Sudilkov)	1748 – 1800
Epstein, Avraham	?
Epstein, Baruch HaLevi	1860 – 1941
Epstein, Moshe Mordechai	1866 – 1933
Epstein, Yechiel Michel (the Aruch Hashulchan)	1829 – 1907
Escapa, Joseph	1572 – 1662
Etlinger, Yaakov (Aruch LaNer)	1808 – 1871
Ettinger, Hayyim Judah Lob	2nd half 17th century – 1739
Ettinger, Hayyim Aaron	1827 – 1891
Eybeschutz, Jonathan	1690 – 1764
Ezekiel, (Rav Yehuda)	220 – 229 CE
Ezobi, Joseph ben Hanan ben Nathan	13th century
Ezra	6th century BCE
Ezra, Abraham ben Meir ibn (Abenezra)	1092 / 3 – 1167
Ezra, Moses ibn (HaSallah)	1055 – 1060 – >1138

F

Faibesh, Samuel ben Uri Shraga (Phoebus)	b. 2nd half 17th century
Falk, Joshua ben Alexander (Katz) HaKohen	1555 – 1614
Feinstein, Moshe (Reb Moshe)	1895 – 1986
Fradkin, Shneur Zalman, of Lublin	1830 – 1902
Freehof, Solomon Bennett	1892 – 1990

G

Gabirol (Gvirol), Solomon ben Judah, ibn	1021 – 1058
Galante, Abraham	d. 1588
Gamliel I (The Elder) (Rabban)	1st century CE
Gamliel II (of Yavne)	1st – 2nd century CE
Gamliel III	3rd century CE
Gamliel IV	late 3rd century
Gamliel V	4th century
Gamliel VI	late 4th century
Gamliel, Shimon ben	c. 10 BCE – 70 CE
Gamliel II, Shimon ben	2nd century CE
Ganzfried, Solomon ben Joseph	1804 – 1886
Gaon, Achai	8th century
Gaon, Rav Hai	969 – 1038
Gaon, Shem Tov ben Abraham ibn	c. 1283 – 1330
Gediliyah, Abraham	1590 – 1672
Gerondi, Yonah ben Avraham (Rabbeinu Yonah)	d. 1263
Gerondi, Zerachiah ben Isaac HaLevi (ReZaH, RaZBI, Ba'al HaMaor)	1125 – 1186
Gershom, Levi ben (Gersonides, Ralbag)	1288 – 1344
Ghiyyat (Ghayyat), Isaac ben Judah ibn	1038 – 1089
Gias, Isaac ibn	1020 – 1089
Gikatilla, Joseph ben Abraham (Joseph Ba'al HaNissim)	1248 – after 1305
Ginzberg, Louis	1873 – 1953
Golinkin, David	1955 –
Gombiner, Abraham Abele ben Chaim HaLevi (Magen Avraham)	c. 1633 – c1683
Gorion, Joseph ben	10th century
Greenwald, Eliezer David	19th century – 1928
Grodzinski, Chaim Ozer	1863 – 1940
Gunzberg, Aryeh Leib ben Asher (Shaagat Aryeh)	1695 – 1785

H

Habib (Chaviv), Moses ibn	17th century

HaDarshan, Moses	11th century
HaGadol, Shimon ben Yitzhak	c. 950 - c. 1020
Hagiz, Jacob	1620 - 1670s
Hagiz, Moses	1671 - 1750
HaKanah, Nechunya ben (Nechunya HaGadol)	1st - 2nd century
HaKappar, Eleazar ben Eleazar (Bar Kappara, Berebi)	late 2nd century - early 3rd century
Hakinai, Hanina (Hananya) ben	2nd century
HaKohen, Aaron ben Jacob ben David	13th century
HaKohen, Abigdor ben Elijah	mid 13th century
HaKohen, Abraham ben Eliezer	17th - 18th centuries
HaKohen, Joseph ben Joshua Meir	1496 - 1577
HaKohen, Meir Simcha Kalonymus of Dvinsk	1843 - 1926
HaKohen, Shabbatai ben Meir (Shach)	1621 - 1662
HaLaban, Isaac ben Jacob	12th century
Halafta, Jose ben	2nd century CE
Halberstam, Chaim, of Sanz	1793 - 1876
HaLevi, Aaron (of Barcelona)	2nd half 13th century
HaLevi, Aaron Abraham ben Baruch Simeon	1st quarter 16th century
HaLevi, Abraham ben Isaac	d. 1393
HaLevi, Abraham ben David (Abraham ibn Daud, Ravad I)	c. 1110 - 1180
HaLevi, Aharon (Ra'AH)	1235 - c. 1290
HaLevi, Eliakim ben Meshullam	1030 - end of 11th century
HaLevi, Rav Eliezer ben Joel (Raviah)	1140 - 1225
HaLevi, Isaac ben Asher (Riva)	11th century
HaLevi, Isaac ben Eleazar	d. 1070
HaLevi, Jacob ben Isaac (Jabez)	12th century
HaLevi, Judah ben Samuel (RiHa'l)	c. 1075 - 1141
Halivni, David Weiss	1927 -
Hamnuna	3rd century
Hamnuna Saba (The Elder)	3rd century
HaNasi, Judah (Rabbeinu HaKadosh)	c. 135 - c. 220
Hanina Sherira ben, Gaon	10th century
Hannanya Joshua ben	1st - 2nd century CE
Haparchi, Ishtori ben Moses (Kaftor Vaferech)	1280 - 1345
Hapenini, Yedadayah	d. 1315
HaRofei, Tzidkayah ben Avraham Anav	1230 - 1300
Hayyim, Joel (Mahariah)	18th century
Hayyun, Samuel	16th century
Hazaken, Yeshayah ben Mali	1180 - 1260
Heilprin, Jehiel ben Solomon	c. 1660 - c. 1746
Heller, Aryeh Leib HaKohen (The Ketzos)	1745 - 1813
Heller, Yom Tov Lippman (Tosefos Yomtov)	1579 - 1654
Herrero, Abraham	1570 - 1635

Heschel, Abraham Joshua	1907 – 1972
Hillel, The Elder	1st century BCE – 1st century CE
Hillel, Son of Gamliel III	3rd century CE
Hillel II	4th century
Hillel, Shimon ben	1st century CE
Hirsch, Yaakov Yehoshua ben Zvi (Jacob Joshua Falk)	1680 – 1756
Hisda, Rav	d. 309
Hisma, Eleazar	First third 2nd century
Hoffmann, David Zevi	1843 – 1921
Horowitz, Abraham ben Shabtai Sheftel	16th century – 1615
Horowitz, Isaiah HaLevi (Shaloh, Shelah)	1565 – 1630
Horowitz, Shabtai Sheftel	c. 1590 – 1660
Hoschel, Judah Aryeh Loeb ben Joshua	18th century
Huna, Rav	3rd century
Hercanus, Eliezer ben (Hyrcanus) (Eliezer HaGadol)	1st and 2nd centuries
Hurwitz, Shabbethai Sheftel ben Akiba	Early 17th century
Hurwitz, Yosef Yozel (Alter of Novardok)	1849 – 1919
Hutner, Yitzhak (Isaac)	1906 – 1980

I

Ilai, Judah ben (Rabbi Judah)	2nd century
Ikriti, Shemariah ben Elijah, of Negropont	b. c. 1275
Isaac, Abraham ben, of Narbonne (Raavad II)	1110 – 1179
Isaac, Baruch ben	12th century
Isaac, Elhanan ben, (of Dampierre)	12th century
Isaac, Nahman bar (Yitzhak)	d. 356
Isaac, Kalonymus ben	d. 1127
Isaac, Samson ben, of Chinon (MaHaRShak)	1260 – 1330
Isaac, Solomon ben	12th century
Israel of Bramburg	Middle 13th century
Israel of Krems	14th – 15th centuries
Israel, Menasseh ben	1604 – 1657
Isserlein, Israel ben Pethahiah Ashkenazi	1390 – 1460
Isserles, Moses ben Israel (Rema, Ramo)	1520 – 1572

J

Jacob of Chinon	1190 – 1260
Jacob, Menachem ben (ben Solomon ben Simson)	12th century
Jacob Yaakov), Meshullam ben	12th century
Jacob, Moses ben, of Coucy	13th century
Jacob, Nahman bar	3rd – 4th centuries
Jacob, Nissim ben (HaMafteach, Rav Nissim Gaon)	990 – 1062

Jacobson, Yissachar	?
Jaffe (Yoffe), Mordechai ben Avraham (Ba'al HaLevushim)	c. 1530 – 1612
Jam'a, Samuel ben Jacob	12th century
Janach, Yonah ibn (Merinos)	983 – 1040
Jehiel, Asher ben (Rabbeinu Asher / Rosh)	1250 / 59 – 1328
Jehiel, Nathan ben	1035 – 1106
Jonah, (Rav)	4th century
Jose, Eliezer ben	2nd century
Jose, Jose bar	8th century
Joseph, Akiva ben (Rabbi Akiva)	c. 50 – 135
Joseph, Enoch Zundel ben	d. 1867
Joseph, Isaac ben, of Corbeil	13th century
Joseph, Joshua Hoschel ben	c. 1578 – 1648
Joseph, Jehiel ben, of Paris	d. 1286
Joseph, Moses ben, of Trani	1505 – 1585
Joseph, Saadia ben, Gaon (Saadia Gaon)	892 – 942
Joseph, Samson ben, of Falaise	12th century
Josiah (Yehoshiyyahu), Ahai (or Achai) ben	2nd century
Joshua (Yehoshua) (ben Chananyah)	1st century CE
Judah, Daniel ben	14th century
Judah, Gershom ben (Rabbeinu Gershom / Rabbeinu Gershom Me'Or HaGolah)	960 – 1040
Judah II	3rd century
Judah III	3rd century
Judah IV	4th century

K

Kagan, Israel Meir (HaKohen) (Chofetz Chaim)	1838 – 1933
Kahana, Rav	3rd – 4th centuries
Kaidanover, Aaron Samuel ben Israel	1614 – 1676
Kaidenover, Zevi Hirsch	17th century – 1712
Kalir, Eleazar	? 6th – 10th centuries
Kalischer, Zvi Hirsch	1795 – 1874
Kalonymus Family	Various
Kalonymus, David ben, of Munzenberg	12th – 13th centuries
Kalonymus, Eleazar ben Yehuda ben, of Worms (Rokeach)	c. 1176 – 1238
Kalonymus, Elijah ben	17th century
Kalonymus, Samuel ben (He-Hasid), of Speyer	12th century
Kamenecki, Jacob (Yaakov Kamenetsky)	1891 – 1986
Kara, Abraham ben Abigdor	d. 1542
Kara, Simeon, of Frankfurt (HaDarshan)	early 13th century

Karelitz, Abraham Isaiah (Chazon Ish)	1878 – 1953
Kasher, Menachem Mendel	1895 – 1983
Katz, Jacob Joseph ben Tzvi HaKohen, of Polonnoye	c. 1710 – c. 1784
Katzenellenbogen, Meir ben Isaac (Maharam Padua)	1482 – 1565
Kayyara, Simeon	9th century
Kelin, Samuel ben Naftali HaLevi	1724 – 1806
Kimchi, Joseph ben Isaac	c. 1100 – c. 1175
Kimchi, David (RaDaK)	1160 – 1235
Kluger, Solomon ben Judah Aaron	1783 – 1869
Kook, Abraham Isaac (HaRaAYaH / HaRav)	1865 – 1935
Krochmal, Menachem Mendel ben Abraham	c. 1600 – 1661
Krochmal, Nachman Kohen	1785 – 1840

L

Labrat, Dunash HaLevi ben	920 – 990
Lakish, Shimon ben (Resh Lakish)	b. c. 200
Lampronti, Yitzhak Hezekiah	1679 – 1756
Landau Family	Various
Landau, Ezekiel ben Judah (Nodah B'Yehuda)	1713 – 1793
Landau, Yaakov Baruch ben Yehuda	Early 1400s – 1493
Lapapa, Aaron ben Isaac	c. 1590 – c1674
Leibowitz, Boruch Ber	1870 – 1940
Leifer, Mordechai, of Nadvorna	d. 1895
Leon, Judah ben Isaac Messer	1166 – 1245
Leon, Moses de (Moshe ben Shem Tov)	1250 – 1305
Lev, Joseph ibn	1500 – 1580
Levi, Joshua ben	1st half 3rd century
Levin, Joshua Hoschel ben Elijah Zeeb	1818 – 1883
Levita, Shabbatai Carmuz	14th century
Levovitz, Yerusham	d. 1936
Lieberman, Saul (G'rash)	1898 – 1983
Lieblein, Avraham	19th century
Lida, David	1625 – 1698
Lima, Moses ben Isaac Judah	c.1615 – c. 1670
Lipschitz, Baruch Mordechai ben Jacob	c. 1810 – 1885
Lipschutz, Hayyim ben Moses	b. 1620
Lipschutz, Israel	1782 – 1860
Lipschutz, Moses ben Noah Isaac	16th century
Lipschutz, Noah ben Abraham (Noah Mindes)	d. 1797
Loanz, Yosef (Yoselman), of Rosheim	1480 – 1554
Loew, Samuel ben Nathan	c. 1720 – 1806
Loew, Judah ben Bezalel (Maharal / Maharal of Prague)	1525 – 1609

Lonzano, Menachem di — 16th century – early 17th century.
Lorberbaum, Jacob ben Jacob Moses, of Lisser (Ba'al HaNesivos / Lissa Rav) — 1760 – 1832
Lublin, Meir ben Gedaliyah (Maharam) — 1558 – 1616
Lunshitz, Shlomo Ephraim (Kli Yakar) — b. 16th century – d. 1619
Luria (Ashkenazi), Isaac (Ari, Arizal, He-Ari) — 1534 – 1572
Luria, Solomon (Maharshal, Rashal) — 1510 – 1574
Luzzatto, Moses Chaim (Ramchal) — 1707 – 1746

M

Maimon, Moses ben (Maimonides) (Rambam) — 1135 – 1204
Manoah, Hezekiah ben (Hizkuni / Chizkuni) — 13th century
Margolis, Abi Ezra Zelig — 18th century
Margolis, Alexander — d. 1802
Margolis, Ephraim Zalman — 1762 – 1828
Margolis, Hayim Mordechai — d. 1818
Margolis, Meir ben Zvi — d. 1790
Mari, Abba, ben Moses ben Joseph Don Astruc of Lunel — b. end 13th century
Mari, Abba, Yitzhak ben, of Marseilles — c. 1122 – c. 1193
Mecklenberg (Mecklenburg), Jacob Tzvi — 1785 – 1865
Medina, Moses de — Late 17th century
Medina, Samuel ben Moses de (RashDaM) — 1505 – 1589
Medina Shemaiah de Medina — d. 1648
Medini, Chaim Chizkiya — 1832 – 1904
Meir, Rabbi Ba'al HaNes (Nahori) — 2nd century
Meir, Isaac (Yitzhak) ben, (Rivam) — 1090 – 1130
Meir, (Tam) Jacob ben (Rabbeinu Tam) — 1100 – 1171
Meir, Moses ben, of Ferrara — 13th century
Meir, Samuel ben (Rashbam) — 1085 – 1158
Meiri, Menachem ben Solomon (HaMeiri) — 1249 – 1306
Meltzer, Isser Zalman (Even HaEzel) — 1870 – 1953
Mendel, Menachem of Kotzk (Kotzker Rebbe) — 1787 – 1859
Mendelssohn, Moses — 1729 – 1781
Meshullam, Asher ben — 12th century
Meshullam, Yerucham ben — 1280 – 1350
Mevorakh, Joshua Boaz / Joshua Boaz ben Simon Baruch (Shiltei Gibborim) — d. 1557
Michel, Meir Leibush ben Yechiel (Malbim) — 1809 – 1879
Migash, Joseph ben Meir HaLevi ibn, (Ri Migash) — 1077 – 1141
Minz, Abraham ben Judah HaLevi — Late 15th – 16th centuries
Minz, Judah ben Eliezer HaLevi (Mahari Minz) — c. 1408 – 1508
Mizrachi, Elijah (Re'em) — 1455 – 1525 / 6
Modena, Samuel ben Moses di (Maharshdam) — 1506 – 1590
Moelin, Jacob ben Moses Levi (Maharil) — 1365 – 1427

Mordechai, Isaac ben, of Regensburg — 12th century
Mos, Moshe, of Premysl — 1540 – 1606
Moses of Evreux — 13th century
Moses, Isaac ben, of Vienna (Or Zarua, Riaz) — c. 1200 – 1270
Moses, Joseph ben — 1423 – c. 1490
Moses, Meshullam ben — 11th century
Moses, Meshullam ben — 1175 – 1238

N
Nachman of Breslov — 1772 – 1808
Naghrela, Smauel ibn (Samuel HaNagid) — 993 – 1056
Nahman, Moses ben (Nahmanides) (Ramban) — 1194 – 1270
Nahman (Nahmani), Samuel ben — 3rd – early 4th century
Nahmani, Rabbah — c. 270 – c. 330
Nahman, Yehudai ben (Yehudai Gaon) — 8th century
Nappacha, Yochanan bar — d. c. 279
Nathan — 2nd century
Nathan, Abraham ben — Second half 12th century
Nathan, Eliezer ben (Raavan) — 1090 – 1170
Nathan, Judah ben (Riban) — 11th century
Nathanson, Joseph Saul — 1808 – 1875
Nehor, Yitzhak Saggi (Isaac the Blind) — c. 1160 – 1235
Nehorai, Meir ben Isaac — 11th century

O
Onkelos — 1st century CE
Ornstein, Jacob Meshullam ben Mordechai Ze'ev — c. 1839

P
Palaggi, Hayyim (Maharhaf, HaVif) — 1788 – 1869
Pappa, Rav — c. 00 – c. 375
Pappa, Chanina ben — 3rd – 4th century
Paquda, Bahya ben Joseph ibn — 1st half 11th century
Parta, Eleazar ben (Elazar ben Perata) — 2nd century
Pedat, Eleazar ben — d. 279
Paquda, Bahya ben Joseph ibn — First half 11th century
Pellier, Moshe, of Kobrin — 1784 – 1858
Plat, Joseph ibn — ?1198 – 1225
Popperos, Meir — 1624 – 1662
Price, Avraham Aharon — 1900 – 1994

Q
Quafih, Yosef — 1917 – 2000

R

Rabbah, Hoshayya (Roba, Berabi)	c. 200 CE
Rabinowitz, Chaim Shalom Tuvia (Reb Chaim Telzer)	1856 – 1930
Rabinowitz-Teomim, Eliyahu David (Aderet)	1845 – 1905
Rapoport, Solomon Judah Loeb	1790 – 1867
Rava (Abba bar Yosef bar Chama)	270 – c. 350
Ravina I	d. c. 470
Ravina II	d. 499
Reggio, Isaac Samuel (Yashar)	1784 – 1855
Reischer, Jacob ben Joseph (Backofen)	1661 (1670) – 1733
Reuben, Jacob ben	11th century
Reuben, Jacob ben	12th century
Reuven, Nissim ben, of Gerona (RaN)	1320 – 1380
Rivkes, Moses ben Naftali Hertz	17th century
Rosanes, Judah ben Samuel	1657 – 1727
Rosen, Yosef (Rogatchover Gaon, Tzafnach Paneach)	1858 – 1936
Ruderman, Yaakov Yitzhak	1901 – 1987

S

Saba, Avraham ben Yaakov	Early 1400s – 1508
Safra, Rav	4th century
Sahula, Meir ben Solomon Abi	b. 1260
Salanter, Israel Lipkin	1810 – 1883
Samuel, Eliezer ben, of Metz	d. 1175
Samuel, Aaron ben	b. c. 1620 – Early 18th century
Samuel, Isaac ben, of Dampierre (Ri)	d. c. 1200
Samuel, Isaac ben (Hasefardi)	11th – 12th centuries
Samuel, Judah ben, of Regensburg (He-Hasid)	d. 1219
Samuel, Meir ben (RAM)	c. 1060 – c. 1135
Samuel, Simha ben, of Speyer	13th century
Samuel, Simhah ben, of Vitry	d. 1105
Sardi HaSardi, (HaSefaradi), Samuel ben Isaac	13th century
Sarug, Israel	16th century
Saruq, Menahem ben Jacob ibn	920 – 970
Sasportas, Jacob ben Aaron	1610 – 1698
Schick, Moses (Maharam Schick)	1807 – 1879
Schmelkes, Isaac	19th century
Schneerson, Levi Yitzhak	1878 – 1944
Schneerson, Menachem Mendel (Tzemach Tzedek)	1789 – 1866
Schneerson, Menachem Mendel (The Lubavitcher Rebbe)	1902 – 1994

Schneerson, Shmuel (The Rebbe Maharash)	1834 – 1882
Schneerson, Sholom Dovber (Rebbe Rashab)	1860 – 1920
Schneerson, Yosef Yitzhak (Rebbe Rayatz)	1880 – 1950
Schneuri, Dovber (Mitteler Rebbe)	1773 – 1827
Schotten, Samuel (Mharsheishoch)	1644 – 1719
Schwadron, Sholom Mordechai (Maharsham)	1835 – 1911
Segal, David ben Samuel HaLevi (Taz)	1586 – 1667
Sforno, Obadiah ben Jacob	1475 – 1550
Shabbethai, Kalonymus ben	c. 1030 – 1096
Shahin, Jacob ben Nissim ibn (Rabbeinu Nissim)	c. 990 – 1062
Shakna, Shalom	1510 – 1558
Shammai	c. 50 BCE – 30 CE
Shamua, Elazar ben	2nd century
Shapira (Szapira), Kalonymus Kalman	1889 – 1943
Shapiro, Eliyahu ben Binyamin Wolf	1660 – 1712
Shapiro, Yehuda Meir	1887 – 1933
Sharabi, Shalom Mizrahi (Rashash)	1720 – 1777
Shem Tov, Shem Tov ibn	c. 1390 – 1440
Shemuel (Shmuel)	2nd – 3rd century
Sherira, Hai ben, Gaon	939 – 1038
Sheshet	3rd century
Sheshna, Rav Amram ben, Gaon	d. c. 865
Shila of Kefar Temarta	3rd century
Shimon, Elazar ben	2nd century – 3rd century
Shkop, Shimon	1860 – 1940
Sh'maya (Shemaiah)	1st century BCE
Shor, Joseph ben Isaac Bekhor	2nd half 12th century
Simlai	3rd century
Sirkis, Yoel (Bach)	1561 – 1640
Slonik (Solnik), Benjamin Aaron ben Abraham	1550 – 1619
Sofer, Abraham Samuel Benjamin (Ksav Sofer)	1815 – 1871
Sofer, Moses (Chatam Sofer)	1762 – 1839
Sofer, Yaakov Chaim (Kaf HaChaim)	1870 – 1939
Solomon, Menahem ben	12th century
Solomon, Samuel ben, of Falaise	12th – 13th century
Soloveitchik, Chaim (The Brisker Reb)	1853 – 1918
Soloveitchik, Joseph Ber (HaRav)	1903 – 1993
Soloveitchik, Yosef Dov (Beis HaLevi)	1820 – 1892
Somekh, Abdalla	1831 – 1889
Spektor, Yitzhak Elchanan	1817 – 1896
Spira, Chaim Elazar	1871 – 1937
Steinhardt, Aryeh Leib	19th century
Steinhardt, Menachem Mendel ben Simeon	1768 – 1825
Steinhart, Joseph ben Menachem	1700 – 1776

Strashun, Samuel ben Joseph (Rashash)   1794 – 1872
Szapria, Elimelech   1823 – 1892

T

Taitezak, Joseph ben Solomon	15th century
Tarfon	1st century CE – 2nd century
Taubes, Aaron Moses ben Jacob	1787 – 1852
Teradion (Teradyon), Hananyah (Hanina) ben	2nd century CE
Tibbon, Moses ibn	13th century
Tibbon, Samuel ben Judah ibn	1150 – 1230
Tolosa, Vidal di	14th century
Torizer, Mordechai Gimpel Yaffe	1820 – 1892
Trabotto, Joseph Colon ben Solomon (Maharik)	c. 1420 – 1480
Trani, Isaiah (ben Mali), di (RI'D)	13th century
Treves (Tarfati), Abraham ben Solomon	16th century
Tukachinsky, Yechiel Michel	20th century
Twersky, Isadore (Yitzhak)	1930 – 1997
Twersky, Menachum Nachum	1730 – 1797
Tyrnau, Isaac	14th century – 15th century
Tzadok	1st century CE
Tzahalon, Yom Tov ben Moshe (Maharitz)	c. 1559 – 1638

U

Ulla	3rd – 4th century CE
Uzeda, Samuel de	1540 – 1605
Uziel, Ben-Zion Meir Hai	1880 – 1953
Uzziel, Jonathan ben	1st century BCE

V

Veltz, Israel	20th century
Vidas, Eliyahu de	1518 – 1592
Vital, Hayyim ben Joseph	1543 – 1620
Volozhin, Chaim ben Itzchok (Reb Chaim)	1749 – 1821

W

Walden, Aaron	1835 – 1912
Walkin, Aaron Stallings	1862-3 – early 1940s
Wallerstein, Abraham ben Asher	18th century
Weil, Jacob ben Judah (Mahariv)	15th century
Weil, Jedidiah	1721 – 1805
Weil, Nethaneel ben Naftali Tzvi	late 17th century – 1769
Weinberg, Yechiel Yaakov	1878 – 1966

Weiss, Isaac Hirsch	1815 – 1905
Weiss, Yitzhak Yaakov	1902 – 1989
Wilovsky, Yaakov David	1845 – 1913

Y

Yehuda, Eliezer ben, of Worms	1160 – 1237
Yehuda, Gershon ben (Me'Or HaGolah)	960 – 1040
Yitzhak, Baruch ben, of Worms	1170 – 1211
Yitzhaki, Shlomo (Rashi)	1040 – 1105
Yohai, Shimon bar (Rashbi)	1st century CE
Yosef, Ovadia	1920 –
Yosef, Yitzhak	20th century

Z

Zadok, Eliezer bar	1st century CE
Zakai, Yochanan ben	c. 30 CE – 90 CE
Zalman, Elijah ben Solomon (Vilna Gaon, Gra)	1720 – 1797
Zerachiah HaYavani (The Greek) (Ra'Za'H)	13th or 14th century
Zerah, Menahem ben Aaron ibn	d. 1385
Zevi, Hillel ben Naphtali	1615 – 1690
Zimra, David ben Solomon ibn Abi (Radbaz)	c. 1479 – 1573 (?1589)
Ziv, Simcha Zissel (Alter of Kelm)	1824 – 1898

Chronology Of Selected Pre-Gaonic Sages

Since much of Talmudic discussion is based on precedent, this table provides a chronological listing of the rabbis. This is not exact since many of the rabbis' birthdates are not known. It also lists student and teachers where these are known.

Era	Century Lived / Generation	Name	Dates Lived	Colleagues / Relatives	Teachers	Students
Pre-Tannaitic						
	1st Cent. BCE	Avtalyon		Sh'maya (Shemaiah)	Judah ben Tabbai, Simon ben Shetach	Hillel
	1st Cent. BCE	Sh'maya (Shemaiah)		Avtalyon	Judah ben Tabbai	
	1st Cent. BCE – 1st Cent. CE	Gamliel I (Rabban)	d. 61 CE	Grandson of Hillel the Elder		
	End 1st Cent. BCE – 1st Cent. CE	Hillel the Elder		Shammai		
	End 1st Cent. BCE – 1st Cent. CE	Shammai	50 BCE – 30 CE	Hillel the Elder		
	End of 1st Cent. BCE – 1st Cent. CE	Shimon ben Gamliel		Son of Gamliel I		

Era	Century Lived / Generation	Name	Dates Lived	Colleagues / Relatives	Teachers	Students
	1st Cent.	Gamliel II (of Yavne)	d. c. 120 CE	Son of Shimon ben Gamliel	Yochanan ben Zakai	
Tannaitic						
	1st Cent. BCE – 1st Cent. CE	Jonathan ben Uzziel			Hillel the Elder	
	1st Cent.	Elish ben Abuyah				
	1st Cent.	Hanina ben Dosa			Yochanan ben Zakai	
	1st Cent.	Tzadok		Yochanan ben Zakai		
	2nd Gen.	Eleazar ben Arach			Yochanan ben Zakai	
	1st Cent.	Eliezer bar Zadok		Yochanan ben Zakai		
	1st Cent.	Yochanan ben Zakai	c. 30 CE – 90 CE		Hillel	
	1st to 2nd Cent.	Nechunya ben HaKanah			Yochanan ben Zakai	
	1st – 2nd Cent.	Joshua ben Hananiah		Eliezer ben Hyrcanus	Yochanan ben Zakai	
		Eliezer ben Hyrcanus (Eliezer HaGadol)			Yochanan ben Zakai	Rabbi Akiva

Era	Century Lived / Generation	Name	Dates Lived	Colleagues / Relatives	Teachers	Students
	Born c. 50 CE 1st – 2nd Cent.	Akiva ben Joseph (Rabbi Akiva)			Elizer ben Hyrcanus, Joshua ben Hananiah, Nahum of Ginzo	Jose ben Halafta, Judah ben Ilai, Rabbi Meir, Rabbi Nehemiah, Eleazar ben Shammai, Shimon ben Yohai
	2nd Gen.	Rabbi Meir Ba'al HaNes (Nahori)				
	?	Akavya ben Mahalel				
	3rd Gen.	Ishmael ben Elisha (Rabbi Ishmael)	90-135 CE	Joshua ben Hananiah		
	1st Cent. to 2nd Cent.	Shimon bar Yohai (Rashbi)			Rabbi Akiva	
	Late 1st - early 2nd Cent.	Tarfon		Rabbi Akiva, Simeon and Elazar ben Azaryah		
	Early 2nd Cent.	Eleazar ben Parta (Parata)		Hananyah ben Teradyon		

Aspects Of The Authors • 493

Era	Century Lived / Generation	Name	Dates Lived	Colleagues / Relatives	Teachers	Students
	2nd Cent.	Elazar ben Azariah		Eliezer ben Hyrcanus Joshua ben Hananiah Rabbi Akiva Rabbi Tarfon	Rabban Gamliel II	
	2nd Cent.	Shimon ben Azzai (Ben Azzai)				
	2nd Cent.	Judah ben Baba		Rabbi Akiva		Judah ben Ilai
	First third 2nd Cent.	Eleazar Hisma			Joshua ben Hananiah ?Rabbi Akiva	
	b. middle 2nd Cent.	Hiyya bar Abba		Judah I Uncle of Rav (Abba Arika)		
	3rd Gen. / 2nd Cent. (youth in Bar Kokhba Revolt)	Shimon ben Gamliel II		Gamliel II		
	2nd Cent.	Hanina ben Hakinai		Ben Azzai	Rabbi Akiva Rabbi Tarfon	

494 • Aspects Of The Authors

Era	Century Lived / Generation	Name	Dates Lived	Colleagues / Relatives	Teachers	Students
	2nd Cent., 4th Gen.	Jose ben Halafta			Rabbi Akiva	Yehuda HaNasi
	2nd Cent.	Judah ben Ilai (Rabbi Judah)			Rabbi Eliezer, Rabbi Akiva	
	2nd Cent.	Eliezer ben Jose			Rabbi Akiva	
	2nd Cent.	Elazar ben Shamua			Rabbi Akiva	Yehuda HaNasi
	2nd Cent.	Elazar ben Shimon		Judah HaNasi	Shimon bar Yohai (also father)	
	2nd Cent.	Hananyah ben Teradion				
	3rd Cent.	Nathan		Rabbi Judah		
Amoraic						
	2nd Cent.	Samuel bar Abba (Samuel of Nehardea)	c. 165 – 257	Abba Arika	Abba bar Abba (father)	

Aspects Of The Authors • 495

Era	Century Lived / Generation	Name	Dates Lived	Colleagues / Relatives	Teachers	Students
	?	Yirmiyahu bar Abba (#1)				
	1st Gen.	Chanina bar Chama		Joshua ben Levi, Rav Yochanan, Resh Lakish	Judah HaNasi, Chiya, Ismael bar R' Yossi, Bar Kappara	
	2nd – 3rd Cent., 1st Gen.	Hoshayya Rabbah (Roba, Berabi)				
	2nd – 3rd Cent., 1st Gen.	Shemuel (Shmuel)		Yehuda HaNasi Rav	Abba bar Abba (father)	Nahman bar Yaakov
	Early 3rd Cent.	Yochanan bar Nappacha		Simeon ben Lakish	Yehuda HaNasi, Oshaya Rabbah, Yannai, Chanina bar Chama	

496 • Aspects Of The Authors

Era	Century Lived / Generation	Name	Dates Lived	Colleagues / Relatives	Teachers	Students
	3rd Cent.	Abba Arika, (Rav)	d. 247	Samuel	Judah I (Yehuda HaNasi)	
	3rd Cent.	Eleazar ben Pedat	d. 279		Rav (Abba Arika), Samuel, Hoshayya Rabbah	
	3rd Cent.	Gamliel III			Judah I (Yehuda HaNasi) (father)	
	3rd Cent. 2nd Gen.	Adda bar Ahavah	250-290		Abba Arika Rav)	
	3rd Cent. 2nd Gen.	Judah ben Ezekiel (Rav Yehuda)	220-299		Abba Arika (Rav), Samuel	
	2nd Gen.	Rav Huna				Rav Chisda
	3rd Cent. 2nd Gen.	Shimon ben Lakish (Resh Lakish)	200 - 275	Yochanan bar Nappacha	Judah Nesi'ah (Judah II), ?Bar Kappara	

Era	Century Lived / Generation	Name	Dates Lived	Colleagues / Relatives	Teachers	Students
	3rd Cent.	Joshua ben Levi		Resh Lakish	Bar Kappara, Judah ben Pedaiah	
	3rd Gen.	Ammi ben Nathan		Rav Assi (Rav Assi ben Nathan), Abbahu, Hanina, Pappi, Isaac and Samuel ben Nahman Hiyya bar Abba	Hoshayya Rabbah, Rav Yochanan	
	3rd Gen.	Amemar I		Judah ben Ezekiel, Rav Sheshet		
	3rd Cent.	Hammuna Saba (The Elder)			Adda bar Ahavah, Judah ben Ezekiel, Ulla, Rav Chisda, Rav Huna	
	3rd Cent.	Hillel (son of Gamliel III)				

Era	Century Lived / Generation	Name	Dates Lived	Colleagues / Relatives	Teachers	Students
	3rd Cent.	Judah II (Son of Gamliel III)				
	3rd Cent.	Judah III (son of Gamliel IV and grandson Judah II)		Rav Ammi, Rav Assi	Yochanan	
	3rd Cent., 3rd Gen.	Sheshet		Nahman bar Jacob, Rav		
	3rd Cent.	Shila of Kefar Temarta				
	3rd Cent.	Simlai				
	Late 3rd Cent.	Gamliel IV			Rabbi Judah II (father)	
	3rd – 4th Cent., 3rd Gen.	Rabbi Assi		Rabbi Ammi	Rabbi Yochanan	
	3rd – 4th Cent., 3rd Gen.	Rav Chisda (Hisda)	d. c. 308	Rav Huna	Abba Arika	
	3rd – 4th Cent., 3rd Gen.	Nahman bar Jacob	d. 320		Mar Samuel	
	3rd – 4th Cent.	Rabbi Avina				

Era	Century Lived / Generation	Name	Dates Lived	Colleagues / Relatives	Teachers	Students
	3rd – 4th Cent.	Hammuna			Abba Arika (Rav)	
	Late 3rd Cent. to Early 4th Cent. / 3rd Gen.	Abbahu		Resh Lakish	Yochanan bar Nafcha (Nappah)	
	Late 3rd Cent. to Early 4th Cent. / 3rd Gen.	Abbaye	c. 280 – 340	Rava		
	3rd – 4th Cent.	Rav Kahana				Rav Ashi
	3rd Cent. – early 4th Cent.	Samuel ben Nahman (Nahmani)		Judah II	Jonathan ben Eleazar	
	3rd – 4th Cent.	Rabbah Nahmani	c. 270 – c. 330		Rav Huna, Judah ben Ezekiel	
	3rd – 4th Cent.	Chanina ben Pappa		Samuel ben Nahman, Abbahu, Isaac Napacha		
	3rd – 4th Cent.	Rava (Abba bar Yosef bar Chama)	270 – c. 350	Abbaye		

Era Century Lived / Generation	Name	Dates Lived	Colleagues / Relatives	Teachers	Students
3rd – 4th Cent.	Ulla			Eleazar II	Aba bar Adda
Late 3rd Cent. to Early 4th Cent. / 3rd Gen.	Abbaye	c. 280 – 340	Rava		
4th Cent., 3rd Gen.	Rami bar Chama (Hama)		Raba, Rav Nahman	Rav Chisda (Hisda)	
4th Cent.	Yirmiyahu bar Abba (#2)		Abbahu Ze'ira		
4th Cent. / 4th Gen.	Hanina bar Abbahu				
4th Cent.	Hillel II (Hillel HaNasi)	c. 330 – 360		Judah III (father)	
4th Cent.	Rav Chama (Hama)		Nahman bar Yitzhak		
4th Cent, 4th Gen.	Rav Jonah			Ze'era I, Rav Ela, Rav Yirmeyahu bar Abba	
4th Cent.	Gamliel V			Hillel II (father)	
5th Gen.	Nahman bar Isaac	d. 356		Nahman bar Jacob	

Aspects Of The Authors • 501

Era	Century Lived / Generation	Name	Dates Lived	Colleagues / Relatives	Teachers	Students
	4th Cent.	Safra			Abbaye, Amni ben Natan	
	4th Cent., 5th Gen.	Rav Pappa (Pappa bar Chanan)	c. 300 – c. 375	Rav Huna bar Rav Joshua	Rava, Abbaye	
	4th Cent.	Judah IV	d. c. 400			
	4th – 5th Cent.	Amemar II		Rav Ashi		
	4th – 5th Cent.	Rav Ashi	352 – 427	Rava	Rav Kahana	
	4th – 5th Cent.	Tabyomi bar Ashi (Mar bar Rav)			Rav Ashi (father)	
	4th – 5th Cent.	Gamliel VI	d. 425			
	5th Gen.	Tanhuma bar Abba			Huna bar Abin, Judah ben Shalom, R. Phinas	
	5th Gen.	Ravina I (Rav Avina)	d. c. 470	Rav Aha	Rav Ashi	
	5th Gen.	Ravina II (Ravina bar Huna)	d. 499	Rav Ashi		Ravina II

Chronological Listing Of Sages, Rabbis, Commentators And Scholars By Birthdate

Scholars are listed in two chronological ways. The first is by the century in which they lived. Then within each century, there is a chronological listing according to the actual or estimated birthdate. The century selected is by the known or presumed birth. The purpose of this way of listing is to provide a chronology of the scholars in particular time periods. In an indirect fashion it would indicate a progression of the analysis of the law, since later scholars may quote their predecessors. In each century the first group of names listed are for those individuals when the year of birth is not known.

Presented in this way the reader can evaluate the intensity of scholarly activity in a particular century. Furthermore it shows that from the eleventh century onwards, activity increased significantly. Thus, for example in the tenth century, there are sixteen scholars listed. In the thirteenth century there are forty-five listed and in the nineteenth century there are eighty scholars listed. This also clearly shows the ongoing vibrancy of traditional analysis and interpretation.

The list also indicates who were the contemporaries of a particular scholar.

Century / Date	Rabbi And Commentator
Sixth Century BCE	Ezra
First Century BCE	Avtalyon
	Sh'maya (Shemaiah)
First Centuries BCE / CE	Hillel the Elder (d. 20 CE)
	Shammai (50 BCE – 30 CE)
	Shimon ben Gamliel (c. 10 BCE – 70 CE)
	Shimon bar Yohai (Rashbi)
	Jonathan ben Uzziel
First Century CE	Abuyah, Elisha ben
	Eleazar ben Arach
	Joshua (Yehoshua) (ben Chananyah)
	Elazar ben Azariah (late into 2nd century)
	Gamliel I (The Elder) (Rabban)
	Hanina ben Dosa
	Tzadok
	Onkelos

Century / Date	Rabbi And Commentator

First Century CE	Eliezer bar Zadok
	Yochanan ben Zakai (c. 30 – 90)
	Akiva ben Joseph (Rabbi Akiva) (c. 50 – 135)
	Ishmael ben Elisha
	    (Rabbi Ishmael) (90 – 135)
	Joshua ben Hannanya (1st – 2nd century)
	HaKanah, Nechunya ben
	    (Nechunya HaGadol)
	Tarfon (1st – 2nd century)

Second Century CE	Akavya ben Mahalel Shimon ben Azzai Eleazar ben Eleazar HaKappar (Bar Kappara, Berebi) Gamliel II (of Yavne) Jose ben Halafta Judah ben Ilai (Rabbi Judah) Ahai (or Achai) ben Josiah (Yehoshiyyahu) Meir Ba'al HaNes (Nahori) Nathan Eleazar ben Parta (Elazar ben Perata) Elazar ben Shamua Hananyah (Hanina) ben Teradion (Teradyon) Judah HaNasi (Rabbeinu HaKadosh) (c. 135 – c. 220) Shemuel (Shmuel) Samuel bar Abba (Samuel of Nehardea) (c. 165 – 257)
Second / Third Century CE	Shimon ben Lakish (Resh Lakish) Adda bar Ahava Ammi ben Nathan Chisda (Hisda) Judah ben Baba Nahman bar Isaac Elazar ben Shimon
Third Century CE	Adda bar Ahavah Abba Arika ?Amemar I Hoshayaa Rabbah (Roba, Berabi)

Century / Date	Rabbi And Commentator
Third Century CE	Sheshet
	Shila of Kefar Temarta
	Simlai
	Judah ben Ezekiel (Rav Yehuda) (220 – 299)
	Rava (Abba bar Yosef bar Chama) (270 – c. 350)
	Abbahu (279 – 320)
	Abbaye (280 – 340)
	Assi
	Chanina bar Chama
	Gamliel III
	Gamliel IV
	Hamnuna
	Hamnuna Saba (The Elder)
	Hillel, son of Gamliel III
	Rami bar Chama
	Rav Hiyya bar Abba
	Judah II
	Judah III
	Kahana
	Joshua ben Levi
	Samuel ben Nahman (Nahmani)
	Ulla (3rd – 4th century)
	Yochanan bar Nappacha (d. c279)
	Eleazar ben Pedat (d. 279)
	Chanina ben Pappa (3rd – 4th century)
	Rabbah Nahmani (c. 270 – c. 330)
Fourth Century CE	Tanhumah bar Abba
	Hanina bar Abbahu
	Amemar II
	Chama
	Gamliel V
	Gamliel VI
	Hillel II
	Judah IV
	Rav Pappa (c. 300 – c. 375)
	Rav Ashi (352 – 427)
	Ravina I (d. c. 470)
	Safra

Century / Date	Rabbi And Commentator
Fifth Century CE	Tabyomi bar Ashi (Mar bar Rav Ashi) Ravina II (d. 499)
Sixth Century	Eleazar Kalir (?6th - 10th centuries)
Eighth Century	Achai Gaon Jose bar Jose Yehudai ben Nahman (Yehudai Gaon)
Ninth Century	Behag (?7th - 10th century) Simeon Kayyara Amram ben Sheshna, Gaon (d c865) Saadia ben Joseph, Gaon (Saadia Gaon) (892 - 942)

Tenth Century	Amnon of Mainz (?12th century)
	Shlomo ben Boya'a
	Sherira ben Hanina, Gaon
	Joseph ben Gorion
	Aaron ben Moses ben Asher (d. c. 960)
	Shabtai Donolo (913 - c. 982)
	Dunash HaLevi ben Labrat (920 - 990)
	Menahem ben Jacob ibn Saruq (920 - 970)
	Hai ben Sherira, Gaon (939 - 1038)
	Shimon ben Yitzhak HaGadol (c. 950 - c. 1020)
	Gershon ben Yehuda
	   (Me'Or HaGolah) (960 - 1040)
	Yonah ibn Janach (Merinos) (983 - 1040)
	Chushiel, Chananel ben
	   (Rabbeinu Chananel) (990 - 1053)
	Jacob ben Nissim ibn Shahin (Rabbeinu
	   Nissim, HaMafteach) (c. 990 - 1062)
	Samuel ibn Naghrela
	   (Samuel HaNagid) (993 - 1056)

Eleventh Century	Isaac ben Asher HaLevi (Riva) Moses HaDarshan Tobiah ben Eliezer Meshullam ben Moses Judah ben Nathan (Riban) Meir ben Isaac Nehorai

Century / Date	Rabbi And Commentator
Eleventh Century	Bahya ben Joseph ibn Paquda
	Isaac ben Samuel (Hasefardi)
	Jacob ben Reuben
	Solomon ben Judah, ibn Gabirol (1021 – 1058)
	Isaac ben Eleazar HaLevi (d. 1070)
	Yitzhak ben Yaakov HaKohen Alfasi (1013 – 1103)
	Simhah ben Samuel of Vitry (d. 1105)
	Hillel ben Eliakim (11th – 12th centuries)
	Isaac ibn Gias (1020 – 1089)
	Eliakim ben Meshullam HaLevi (1030 – end of 11th century)
	Kalonymus ben Shabbethai (c. 1030 – 1096)
	Nathan ben Jehiel Anaw (Anav) (1035 – 1106)
	Isaac ben Judah ibn Ghiyyat (Ghayyat) (1038–1089)
	Shlomo Yitzhaki (Rashi) (1040 – 1105)
	Isaac ben Reuben Albargeloni (b. 1043)
	Kalonymus ben Isaac (died 1127)
	Moses ibn Ezra (HaSallah) (1055 to 1060 – 1138)
	Meir ben Samuel (RAM) (c. 1060 – c. 1135)
	Judah ben Samuel HaLevi (RiHa'l) (c. 1075 – 1141)
	Joseph ben Meir HaLevi ibn Migash (Ri Migash) (1077 – 1141)
	Samuel ben Meir (Rashbam) (1085 – 1158)
	Isaac (Yitzhak) ben Meir (Rivam) (1090 – 1130)
	Eliezer ben Nathan (Raavan) (1090 – 1170)
	Abraham ben Meir ibn Ezra (Abenezra) (1092 / 3 – 1167)
Twelfth Century	Isaac ben Abraham (Riba)
	Joseph ben Baruch (Joseph of Clisson)
	Jacob ben Isaac HaLevi (Jabez)
	Abraham ben David (Abraham ibn Daud, Ravad I)
	Elhanan ben Isaac, of Dampierre
	Baruch ben Isaac
	Solomon ben Isaac
	Menachem ben (ben Solomon ben Simson) Jacob
	Meshullam ben Jacob (Yaakov)
	Samuel ben Jacob Jam'a

Century / Date	Rabbi And Commentator
Twelfth Century	Samson ben Joseph, of Falaise
	Samuel ben Kalonymus (He-Hasid) of Speyer
	Isaac ben Mordechai of Regensburg (RiBaM)
	Asher ben Meshullam (2nd half)
	Joseph ibn Plat
	Jacob ben Reuben
	Menahem ben Solomon
	Eliezer ben Samuel of Metz (d. 1175)
	Joseph ben Isaac Bekhor Shor (2nd Half)
	Isaac ben Samuel of Dampierre (Ri) (d. c. 1200)
	Jacob ben, Meir (Tam) (Rabbeinu Tam) (1100 - 1171)
	Joseph ben Isaac Kimchi (c. 1100 - c. 1175)
	Abraham ben Isaac of Narbonne (Raavad II) (1110 - 1179)
	Moses Kimchi (d. 1190)
	HaLevi (c. 1110 - 1180)
	Yitzhak ben Abba Mari of Marseilles (c. 1122 - c. 1193)
	Zerachiah ben Isaac HaLevi Gerondi (ReZaH) (1125 - 1186)
	Abraham ben David (Ravad III) (1125 - 1198)
	RaZBI, Ba'al HaMaor (1125 - 1186)
	Moses ben Maimon (Maimonides) (Rambam) (1135 - 1204)
	Judah ben Samuel of Regensburg (He-Hasid) (d. 1217)
	Samuel ben Solomon of Falaise (12th - 13th centuries)
	Eliezer ben Joel HaLevi (Raviah) (1140 - 1225)
	Abraham ben Nathan (Second half)
	Samson ben Abraham of Sens (1150-1230)
	Samuel ben Judah ibn Tibbon (1150 - 1230)
	Judah ben Solomon Alharizi (al-Harizi) (1160 - 1230)
	David Kimchi (RaDaK) (1160 - 1235)
	Yitzhak Saggi Nehor (Isaac the Blind) (c. 1160 - 1235)
	Eleazar ben Yehuda of Worms (1160 - 1237)
	Judah ben Isaac Messer Leon (1166 - 1244)
	Baruch ben Yitzhak of Worms (1170 - 1211)
	Meir ben Todros Abulafia (1170 - 1244)
	Meshullam ben Moses (1175 - 1238)
	Eleazar ben Yehuda ben Kalonymus of Worms (Rokeach) (c. 1176 - 1238)
	Yeshayah ben Mali Hazaken (1180 - 1260)
	Jacob of Chinon (1190 - 1260)
	David ben Kalonymus of Munzenberg (end of 12th century)
	Moses ben Nahman (Nahmanides) (Ramban) (1194 - 1270)

Century / Date	Rabbi And Commentator
Thirteenth Century	Simeon Kara of Frankfurt (HaDarshan)
	Benjamin ben Abraham Anaw
	Zedekiah ben Abraham Anaw
	Eliezer of Touques
	Joseph ben Hanan ben Nathan Ezobi
	Aaron ben Jacob ben David HaKohen
	Abigdor ben Elijah HaKohen
	Aaron HaLevi (of Barcelona)
	Moses ben Jacob of Coucy
	Isaac ben Joseph of Corbeil
	Shabbatai Carmuz Levita
	Hezekiah ben Manoah (Hizkuni / Chizkuni)
	Moses ben Meir of Ferrara
	Moses of Evreux
	Samuel ben Isaac Sardi (HaSardi, HaSefaradi)
	Simha ben Samuel of Speyer
	Moses ibn Tibbon
	Vidal di Tolosa
	Isaiah ben Mali di Trani (RI'D)
	Zerachiah HaYavani (The Greek) (Ra'Za'H)
	Isaac ben Moses of Vienna (Or Zarua, Riaz) (c. 1200 – 1270)
	Meir ben Baruch (Meir of Rothenburg) (MaHaRAM) (c. 1215 – 1293)
	Aharon HaLevi (Ra'AH) (1235 – c. 1290)
	Perez ben Elijah (Rap / RaPaSh / MaHaRPaSh) (d. c. 1295)
	Meir ben Solomon Abi Sahula (b. 1260)
	Yonah ben Avraham Gerondi (Rabbeinu Yonah) (d. 1263)
	Jehiel ben Joseph of Paris (died 1286)
	Tzidkayah ben Avraham Anav HaRofei (1230 – 1300)
	Abraham ben Samuel Abulafia (c. 1240 – c. 1290)
	Joseph ben Abraham Gikatilla (Joseph Ba'al HaNissim) (1248 – after 1305)
	Menachem ben Solomon Meiri (HaMeiri) (1249 – 1306)
	Mordechai ben Hillel Ashkenazi (1250 – 1298)
	Moses de Leon (Moshe ben Shem Tov) (1250 – 1305)
	Yedayah HaPenini (d. 1315)
	Asher ben Jehiel (Rabbeinu Asher / Rosh) (1250 / 59 – 1328)
	Bayha Asher (Rabbeinu Bahaya) (mid 13th century – 1340)
	Samson ben Isaac, of Chinon (MaHaRShak) (1260 – 1330)

Century / Date	Rabbi And Commentator
Thirteenth Century	Jacob ben Asher (Ba'al HaTurim, Tur) (1270 – 1343) Shemariah ben Elijah Ikriti of Negropont (b. c. 1275) Abba Mari ben Elgidor (13th – 14th centuries) Ishtori ben Moses Haparchi (Kaftor Vaferech) (1280 – 1345) Yerucham ben Meshullam (1280 – 1350) Shem Tov ben Abraham ibn Gaon (c. 1283 – 1330) Levi ben Gershom (Gersonides, Ralbag) (1288 – 1344) Abba Mari ben Moses ben Joseph Don Astruc of Lunel (b. end 13th century)
Fourteenth Century	Isaac Aboab (Menorat HaMaor) Solomon Alami Daniel ben Judah Israel of Krems (14th – 15th centuries) Nissim ben Reuven, of Gerona (RaN) (1320 – 1380) Menahem ben Aaron ibn Zerah (d. 1385) Isaac ben Sheshet Barfat (RiBaSH) (1326 – 1408) Crescas, Hasdai ben Abraham (c. 1340 – 1410 / 11) Samuel ben Aaron of Schlettstadt (2nd half) Isaac Tyrnau (latter part – d. before 1427) Isaac ben Jacob Campanton (1360 – 1463) Simeon ben Zemah Duran (Rashbatz / Tashbetz) (1361 – 1444) Jacob ben Moses Levi Moelin (Maharil) (1365 – 1427) Abraham ben Isaac HaLevi (d. 1390) Israel ben Pethahiah Ashkenazi Isserlein Joseph Albo (c. 1380 – c. 1430) Yosef Chaviva (Late 14th century) Shem Tov ibn Shem Tov (c. 1390 – 1440)
Fifteenth Century	Aaron of Pesaro Moses ben Isaac Alashkar Abraham ben Shem Tov Bibago Jacob ben Judah Weil (Mahariv) Obadiah ben Abraham (d. 1500) Avraham Chayon (d. 1510) Joseph ben Solomon Taitezak Solomon ben Simon Duran (Rashbash) (c. 1400 – 1467) Avraham ben Yaakov Saba (Early 1400s – 1508) Yaakov Baruch ben Yehuda Landau (Early 1400s – 1493) Judah ben Eliezer HaLevi Minz (Mahri Minz) (c. 1408 – 1508)

Century / Date	Rabbi And Commentator
Fifteenth Century	Isaac ben Moses Arama (Ba'al Akedah) (c. 1420 – 1494)
	Joseph Colon ben Solomon Trabotto (Maharik) (c. 1420 – 1480)
	Joseph ben Moses (1423 – c. 1490)
	Joseph Chayon (c.1425 – early 16th century)
	Isaac Aboab (1433 – 1493)
	Isaac ben Judah Abravanel (1437 – 1508)
	Elijah Mizrachi (Re'em) (1455 – 1525 / 6)
	Jacob Berab (1474 – 1546)
	Israel Bruna (1400 – 1480)
	Joseph ben Ephraim Caro (Mechaber) (1488 – 1575)
	Yaakov ibn Chaviv (d. 1516)
	Abraham ben Abigdor Kara (d. 1542)
	Abraham ben Judah HaLevi Minz (late 15th – 16th century)
	Obadiah ben Jacob Sforno (1475 – 1550)
	David ben Solomon ibn Abi Zimra (Radbaz) (c. 1479 – 1573 / 1589)
	Levi ben Jacob ibn Chaviv (Habib) (Ralbach) (c. 1480 – c. 1545)
	Yosef (Yoselman) Loanz of Rosheim (1480 – 1554)
	Meir ben Isaac Katzenellenbogen (Maharam Padua) (1482 – 1565)
	Joseph ben Ephraim Caro (1488 – 1575)
	Abraham ben Abigdor Kara (d. 1542)
	Joseph ben Joshua Meir HaKohen (1496 – 1577)
Sixteenth Century	Bezalel Ashkenazi
	Samuel Danzig
	Aaron Abraham ben Baruch Simeon HaLevi
	Mattithiah ben Solomon Delacrut
	Moses ben Noah Isaac Lipschutz
	Samuel Hayyun
	Israel Sarug
	Abraham ben Solomon Treves (Tarfati)
	Joshua Boaz Mevorakh / Joshua Boaz ben Simon Baruch (Shiltei Gibborim) (d. 1557)
	Abraham Galante (d. 1588)
	Menachem di Lonzano (d. early 17th century)
	Abraham ben Shabtai Sheftel Horowitz (d. 1615)
	Shlomo Ephraim Lunshitz (d. 1619)

Century / Date	Rabbi And Commentator
Sixteenth Century	Aharon Berechyah of Modena (d. 1639)
	Shemaiah de Medina (d. 1648)
	Joseph ibn Lev (1500 – 1580)
	Solomon ben Moses HaLevi Alkabetz
	(Born c. 1505 – Death not recorded)
	Moses ben Joseph of Trani (1505 – 1585)
	Samuel ben Moses de Medina (RashDaM) (1505 – 1589)
	Samuel ben Moses di Modena (Maharshdam) (1506 – 1590)
	Moshe Alshich (1508 – 1593)
	Yehuda Leib ben Meir Channeles (early 1500's – 1596)
	Isaac Adarbi (Adribi) (c. 1510 – c. 1584)
	Shalom Shakna (1510 – 1558)
	Solomon Luria (Maharshal, Rashal) (1510 – 1564)
	Moses ben Baruch Almosnino (1515 – 1580)
	Eliyahu de Vidas (1518 – 1592)
	Moses ben Israel Isserles (Rema) (1520 – 1572)
	Moses ben Jacob Cordovero (1522 – 1570)
	Judah ben Bezalel Loew
	(Maharal / Maharal of Prague) (1525 – 1609)
	Mordechai ben Avraham Jaffe (Yoffe)
	(Ba'al HaLevushim) (c. 1530 – 1612)
	Elazar ben Moshe Azikri (Ezkari) (1533 – 1600)
	Isaac Luria (Ashkenazi) (Ari, Arizal), He-Ari (1534 – 1572)
	Shmuel Aceda (1538 – 1602)
	Moshe Mos of Premysl (1540 – 1606)
	Samuel de Uzeda (1540 – 1605)
	Hayyim ben Joseph Vital (1543 – 1620)
	Menachem Azaryah of Fano (1548 – 1620)
	Benjamin Aaron ben Abraham Slonik (1550 – 1619)
	Samuel Eidels (Maharsha) (1555 – 1631)
	Joshua ben Alexander (Katz) HaKohen Falk (1555 – 1614)
	Meir ben Gedaliyah Lublin (Maharam) (1558 – 1616)
	Yom Tov ben Moshe Tzahalon (Maharitz) (c. 1559 – 1638)
	Abraham ben Moses de Bouton (c. 1560 – c. 1605)
	Aharon ibn Chaim (1560 – 1632)
	Yoel Sirkis (Bach) (1561 – 1640)
	Isaiah HaLevi Horowitz (Shelah, Shaloh) (1565 – 1630)
	Yissachar Ber Ellenburg (1570 – 1623)
	Abraham Herrera (1570 – 1635)
	Abraham Azulai (1570 – 1643)

Century / Date	Rabbi And Commentator
Sixteenth Century	Naphtali (Hirsch) ben Asher Altschul (late 16th – early 17th centuries) Joseph Escapa (1572 – 1662) Abraham Samuel Bachrach (1575 – 1615) Joshua Hoschel ben Joseph (c. 1578 – 1648) Yom Tov Lippman Heller (Tosefos Yomtov) (1579 – 1654) David ben Samuel HaLevi Segal (Taz) (1586 – 1667) Abraham Gediliyah (1590 – 1672) Shabtai Sheftel Horowitz (c. 1590 – 1660) Aaron ben Isaac Lapapa (c. 1590 – c. 1674)
Seventeenth Century	Solomon ben Joshua Adeni Moses Ashkenazi (Johann Peter Spaeth) Yair Chaim Bachrach Naftali Hertz ben Yaakov Elchanan (Bachrach) Judah ben Enoch Moses ibn Habib (Chaviv) Abraham ben Eliezer HaKohen Shabbethai Sheftel ben Akiba Hurwitz (early 17th century) Elijah ben Kalonymus Moses ben Noah Isaac Lipschutz Moses ben Naftali Hertz Rivkes Abraham Alegri (d. 1652) Menachem Mendel ben Abraham Krochmal (c. 1600 – 1661) Chaim Benveniste (1603 – 1673) Menasseh ben Israel (1604 – 1657) Abraham ibn Chananyah (1605 – 1651) Samuel Aboab (Rasha) (1610 – 1694) Jacob ben Aaron Sasportas (1610 – 1698) Gershon Ashkenazi (2nd decade 17th century – 1693) Aaron Samuel ben Israel Kaidenover (1614 – 1676) Moses ben Isaac Judah: Lima (c. 1615 – c. 1670) Hillel ben Naphtali Zevi (1615 – 1690) Hayyim ben Moses Lipschutz (1620 – ?) Menachem Mendel ben Meshulam Zalman Auerbach (1620 – 1689) Jacob Hagiz (1620 – 1670s) Hayyim ben Moses Lipschutz (b. 1620) Aaron ben Samuel (c. 1620 – early 18th century) Shabbatai ben Meir HaKohen (Shach) (1621 – 1662) Meir Popperos (1624 – 1662)

Century / Date	Rabbi And Commentator

Seventeenth Century	David Lida (1625 – 1698)
	Abraham Abele ben Chaim HaLevi Gombiner
	    (Magen Avraham) (c. 1633 – c. 1683)
	Joseph Almosnino (1642 – 1689)
	Samuel Schotten (Mharsheishoch) (1644 – 1719)
	Samuel ben Uri Shraga Faibesh
	    (Phoebus) (2nd half of century)
	Tzvi Hirsch ben Yaakov Ashkenazi
	    (Chacham Tzvi) (1656 – 1712)
	Zevi Hirsch Kaidenover (17th century – 1712)
	Judah ben Samuel Rosanes (1657 – 1727)
	Hezekiah ben David DiSilo (1659 – 1698)
	Hayyim Judah Lob Ettinger (2nd half 17th century – 1739)
	Jehiel ben Solomon Heilprin (c. 1660 – c. 1746)
	Eliyahu ben Binyamin Wolf Shapiro (1660 – 1712)
	Jacob ben Joseph Reischer (Backofen) (1661 / 70 – 1733)
	Meir ben Iszak Eisenstadt (Meir Ash)
	(Maharam Ash / Panim Me'irot) (1670 – 1744)
	Yitzhak Hezekiah Lampronti (1679 – 1756)
	Yaakov Yehoshua ben Zvi Hirsch
	    (Jacob Joshua Falk) (1680 – 1756)
	Yaakov Culi (1689 – 1732)
	Moses de Medina (Late 17th century)
	Nethaneel ben Naftali Tzvi Weil (late 17th century – 1769)
	Judah Ayyas (1690 – 1760)
	Jonathan Eybeschutz (1690 – 1764)
	Aryeh Leib ben Asher Gunzberg
	    (Shaagat Aryeh) (1695 – 1785)
	Hayyim ibn Attar (Ohr HaChaim HaKadosh) (1696 – 1743)
	Israel ben Eliezer (Ba'al Shem Tov / Besht) (1698 – 1760)
	Jacob Israel ben Zvi Ashkenazi Emden
	    (the Yabets) (1697 – 1776)

Eighteenth Century	Joel Hayyim (Mahariah) Abi Ezra Zelig Margolis Abraham ben Asher Wallerstein Boruch of Kosov (d. 1782) Meir ben Zvi Margolis (d. 1790) Noah ben Abraham Lipschutz (Noah Mindes) (d. 1797) Alexander Margolis (d. 1802) Hayyim Mordechai Margolis (d. 1818) Jacob Meshullam ben Mordechai Ze'ev Ornstein (d. 1839)

Century / Date	Rabbi And Commentator

Eighteenth Century	Joseph ben Menachem Steinhart (1700 – 1776)
	Moses Chaim Luzzatto (Ramchal) (1707 – 1746)
	Jacob Joseph ben Tzvi HaKohen Katz,
	    of Polonnoye (1710 – 1784)
	Dov Ber (Maggid of Mezritch (1710 – 1772)
	Ezekiel (Yechezkel) ben Judah Landau
	    (Nodah B'Yehuda) (1713 – 1793)
	Elijah ben Solomon Zalman
	    (Vilna Gaon, Gra) (1720 – 1797)
	Samuel ben Nathan Loew (c. 1720 – 1806)
	Shalom Sharabi (Rashash) (1720 – 1777)
	Jedidiah Weil (1721 – 1805)
	Haim Yosef David Azulai (Hida) (1724 – 1806)
	Samuel ben Naftali HaLevi Kelin (1724 – 1806)
	Isaiah ben Judah Loeb Berlin (1725 – 1799)
	Moses Mendelssohn (1729 – 1781)
	Yehuda ben Shimon Ashkenazi (1730 – 1770)
	Menachem Nachum Twersky (1730 – 1797)
	Shneur Zalman Baruch (Borukovich), of Liadi
	    (Alter Rebbe, GRaZ) (1745 – 1812)
	Aryeh Leib HaKohen Heller (The Ketzos) (1745 – 1813)
	Abraham ben Jehiel Danzig (1747 / 8 – 1820)
	Moshe Chaim Ephraim (of Sudilkov) (1748 – 1800)
	Chaim ben Itzchok Volozhin (Reb Chaim) (1749 – 1821)
	David Solomon Eibenschutz (d. c. 1812)
	Mordechai ben Abraham Benet (1753 – 1829)
	Jacob ben Jacob Moses Lorberbaum of Lisser
	    (Ba'al HaNesivos / Lissa Rav) (1760 – 1832)
	Akiva Eger (1761 – 1837)
	Ephraim Zalman Margolis (1762 – 1828)
	Moses Sofer (Chatam Sofer) (1762 – 1839)
	Aron Chorin (1766 – 1844)
	Menahem Mendel ben Simeon Steinhardt (1768 – 1825)
	Yisroel ben Shmuel, Ashkenazi of Shklov (c. 1770 – 1839)
	Nachman of Breslov (1772 – 1808)
	Dovber Schneuri (Mitteler Rebbe) (1773 – 1827)
	Meir Eisenstadter (Meir Ash) (Maharam Ash) (1780 – 1852)
	Israel Lipschutz (1782 – 1860)
	Solomon ben Judah Aaron Kluger (1783 – 1869)
	Moshe Pellier of Kobrin (1784 – 1858)
	Isaac Samuel Reggio (Yashar) (1784 – 1855)
	Krochmal, Nachman Kohen (1785 – 1840)

Century / Date	Rabbi And Commentator
Eighteenth Century	Jacob Tzvi Mecklenburg (1785 – 1865) Menachem Mendel of Kotzk (Kotzker Rebbe) (1787 – 1859) Aaron Moses ben Jacob Taubes (1787 – 1852) Hayyim Palaggi (Maharhaf, HaVif) (1788 – 1869) Menachem Mendel Schneerson (Tzemach Tzedek) (1789 – 1866) Solomon Judah Loeb Rapoport (1790 – 1867) Samuel ben Joseph Strashun (Rashash) Chaim Halberstam of Sanz (1793 – 1876) Zvi Hirsch Kalischer (1795 – 1874) Judah ben Solomon Chai Alkali (1798 – 1878)
Nineteenth Century	Isaac Schmelkes Avraham Lieblein Aryeh Leib Steinhardt Abraham Ankava Enoch Zundel ben Joseph (d. 1867) Mordechai Leifer of Nadvorna (d. 1895) Yitzhak Myer Alter (1798 – 1866) Yosef ben Moshe Babad (1801 – 1874) Avraham of Trisk (1802 – 1889) Solomon ben Joseph Ganzfried (1804 – 1886) Isaac Hirsch Weiss (1815 – 1905) Moses Schick (Maharam Schick) (1807 – 1879) Judah Aryeh Loeb ben Joshua Hoschel Yaakov Etlinger (1808 – 1871) Joseph Saul Nathanson (1808 – 1875) Meir Leibush ben Jehiel Michel (Malbim) (1809 – 1879) Baruch Mordechai ben Jacob Lipschitz (b. c. 1810 – 1885) Israel Lipkin Salanter (1810 – 1883) Abraham Zevi Hirsch ben Jacob Eisenstadt (1813 – 1875) Abraham Samuel Benjamin Sofer (Ksav Sofer) (1815 – 1871) Naphtali Tzvi Yehuda Berlin (1817 – 1893) Yitzhak Elchanan Spektor (1817 – 1896) Joshua Hoschel ben Elijah Zeeb Levin (1818 – 1873) Yosef Dov Soloveitchik (Beis HaLevi) (1820 – 1892) Mordechai Gimpel Yaffe Torizer (1820 – 1892) Elimelech Szapira (1823 – 1892) Simcha Zissel Ziv (Alter of Kelm) (1824 – 1898) Isaac Aaron Ettinger (1827 – 1891) Solomon Buber (1827 – 1906)

Century / Date	Rabbi And Commentator

Nineteenth Century	Shneur Zalman Fradkin of Lublin (1830 – 1902)
	Abdalla Somekh (1831 – 1889)
	Chacham Yosef Chaim (Ben Ish Chai) (1832 – 1909)
	Chaim Chizkiya Medini (1832 – 1904)
	Shmuel Schneerson (The Rebbe Maharash) (1834 – 1882)
	Sholom Mordechai Schwadron (Maharsham) (1835 – 1911)
	Aaron Walden (1835 – 1912)
	Isaac ben Moses Solomon Blaser
	   (Rav Itzele Peterburger) (1837 – 1907)
	Israel Meir Kagan (HaKohen) (Chofetz Chaim) (1838 – 1933)
	David Zevi Hoffmann (1843 – 1921)
	Meir Simcha Kalonymus of Dvinsk HaKohen (1843 – 1926)
	Eliyahu David Rabinowitz-Teomim (Aderet) (1845 – 1905)
	Yaakov David Wilovsky (1845 – 1913)
	Benjamin Eisenstadt (1846 – 1920)
	Yehuda Aryeh Leib Alter (Sfas Emes) (1847 – 1905)
	Yosef Yozel Hurwitz (Alter of Novardok) (1849 – 1919)
	Chaim Soloveitchik (The Brisker Reb) (1853 – 1918)
	Solomon ben Kalman HaLevi Abel (1857 – 1886)
	Yosef Rosen (Rogatchover Gaon,
	   Tzafnach Paneach) (1858 – 1936)
	Eliezer David Greenwald (d. 1928)
	Yerusham Levovitz (d. 1936)
	Chaim Shalom Tuvia Rabinowitz
	   (Reb Chaim Telzer) (1856 – 1930)
	Baruch HaLevi Epstein (1860 – 1941)
	Shimon Shkop (1860 – 1940)
	Sholom Dovber Schneerson (Rebbe Rashab)
	Chaim Ozer Grodzinski (1863 – 1940)
	Aaron Walkin (1863 – early 1940s)
	Abraham Isaac Kook (HaRaAYaH / HaRav) (1865 – 1935)
	Avraham Mordechai Alter (1866 – 1948)
	Moshe Mordechai Epstein (1866 – 1933)
	Isser Zalman Meltzer (Even HaEzel) (1870 – 1953)
	Yaakov Chaim Sofer (Kaf HaChaim) (1870 – 1939)
	Boruch Ber Leibowitz (1870 – 1940)
	Chaim Elazar Spira (1871 – 1937)
	Louis Ginzberg (1873 – 1953)
	Abraham Isaiah Karelitz (Chazon Ish) (1878 – 1953)
	Levi Yitzhak Schneerson (1878 – 1944)
	Yechiel Yaakov Weinberg (1878 – 1966)

Century / Date	Rabbi And Commentator
Nineteenth Century	Yosef Yitzhak Schneerson (Rebbe Rayatz) (1880 - 1950) Yehuda Leib HaLevi Ashlag (1885 - 1954) Ben-Zion Meir Hai Uziel (1880 - 1953) Yehuda Meir Shapiro (1887 - 1933) Kalonymus Kalman Shapira (Szapira) (1889 - 1943) Abuchatzeirah, Harav Yisrael (1890 - 1984) Kamenecki, Jacob (Yaakov Kamenetsky) (1891 - 1986) Eliyahu Eliezer Dessler (1892 - 1953) Solomon Bennett Freehof (1892 - 1990) Yisroel Alter (1895 - 1977) Menachem Mendel Kasher (1895 - 1983) Moshe Feinstein (Reb Moshe) (1895 - 1986) Simchah Bunim Alter (1898 - 1992) Saul Lieberman (1898 - 1983)
Twentieth Century	Yehuda Meir Dvir Israel Veltz Yechiel Michel Tukachinsky Avraham Aharon Price (1900 - 1994) Yaakov Yitzhak Ruderman (1901 - 1987) Menachem Mendel Schneerson (The Lubavitcher Rebbe) (1902 - 1994) Yitzhak Yaakov Weiss (1902 - 1989) Joseph Ber Soloveitchik (HaRav) (1903 - 1993) Yitzhak (Isaac) Hutner (1906 - 1980) Abraham Joshua Heschel (1907 - 1972) Shlomo Zalman Auerbach (1910 - 1995) Sholom Noach Berezovsky (1911 - 2000) Yosef Quafih (1917 - 2000) Ovadia Yosef (1920 -) Pinchas Menachem Alter (1926 - 1996) David Weiss Halivni (1927 -) Isadore (Yitzhak) Twersky (1930 - 1997) Yaakov Aryeh Alter (1939 -) David Golinkin (1955 -) Yitzhak Yosef

Geographical Location/s Of The Scholar

In this section and the next one there are two tables. The purpose is to show in detail the country and region/s where the various scholars were born and worked. This reveals several social and historical aspects. There are different time periods when various countries or regions demonstrated the peak of scholarly activity. Much of this was related to the periods when the Jews were either allowed to flourish or at least were tolerated in various countries and then subsequently when they were either persecuted or expelled from a region causing a migration elsewhere. The other important aspect shown is that just as in current times, there is great mobility of scholars, so too in earlier centuries, scholars often moved to one or more different cities or even countries. In this case it was more a function of opportunity and less so of persecution.

The first table is the more detailed of the two. It shows according to the country and the city or region of birth, where it is known, and then the place or places where the individual further studied and worked. It lists each of the latter place names. The second table in the next section summarizes this data according to centuries and a combination of countries and regions rather than the detailed individual country information. This type of summary is particularly useful in regions of central and Eastern Europe. In this region during the last several centuries individual countries or sections of a country were at various times independent or part of a larger country or empire. Change was almost the norm. Places like Poland, Lithuania, Galicia changed many times over the centuries. In the more central European sector the German, Czechoslovakian and surrounding regions also changed hands. The Austro-Hungarian Empire also had a large impact on individual countries. The migration and peak scholarly activity in various countries and regions is discussed in more detail before the second table.

Scholar	Geographical Location (Birthplace)	Additional Geographic Location/s	Century When Born
	Africa		
Solomon ben Simon Duran (Rashbash)	Algeria		Fifteenth
Judah Ayyas	North Africa	Algiers, Jerusalem	Seventeenth
Jacob ben Aaron Sasportas	Algeria, Oran	Tlemen, Morocco, Fez, Sali, London, Hamburg, Amsterdam	Seventeenth

Aspects Of The Authors • 519

Scholar	Geographical Location (Birthplace)	Additional Geographic Location/s	Century When Born
Jacob ben Nissim ibn Shahin (Rabbeinu Nissim, HaMafteach)	Tunisia	Kairouan	Eleventh
Samuel ben Jacob Jam'a		Kabez	Twelfth
Arabia			
Solomon ben Joshua Adeni (M'Lekhet Shlomo)	Saana	Aden, Palestine (Hebron)	Seventeenth
Austria			
Hayyim Judah Lob Ettinger		Hollesschau, Lemberg	Seventeenth
Moses Israel Landau			Late Eighteenth
Aryeh Leib HaKohen Heller (The Ketzos)	Galicia (Kalush)	Stry	Eighteenth
Nachman Kohen Krochmal	Galicia (Brody)	Zolkiev, Tamopol	Eighteenth
Eleazar ben Israel Landau	Galicia (Brody)		Eighteenth
Ephraim Zalman (Solomon) Margolis	Galicia (Brody)		Eighteenth
Meir ben Zvi Hirsch Margolis	Galicia (Brody)	Lemburg, Ostrog, Poland	Eighteenth
Zvi Hirsch Chajes (The Maharatz Chajes)	Galicia	Kalisz (Poland)	Nineteenth
Isaac Aaron Ettinger	Galicia (Lemberg)		Nineteenth
Mordechai Leifer of Nadvorna	Galicia (Nadvorna)		Nineteenth

Scholar	Geographical Location (Birthplace)	Additional Geographic Location/s	Century When Born
Joseph Saul Nathanson	Galicia (Berezhany)		Nineteenth
Isaac Schmelkes	Galicia	Lemberg	Nineteenth
Chaim Elazar Spira	Galicia (Stryzow)	Mukachevo	Nineteenth
Sholom Mordechai Schwadron (Maharsham)	Galicia (Zloczow)	Berezhany	Nineteenth
Isaac Samuel Reggio (Yashar)	Goritz (Illyria)	Padua	Eighteenth
Israel of Krems	Krems	Germany	Fourteenth
Israel ben Pethahiah Ashkenazi Isserlein	Neustadt	Italy, Neustadt	Late Fourteenth
Moses Schick (Maharam Schick)	Slovakia	Hust (Hungary)	Nineteenth
Yitzhak Yaakov Weiss (Minchat Yaakov)	Galicia	Munkacz (Hungary), Romania, Manchester, England, Jerusalem	Twentieth
Abigdor Cohen of Vienna	Vienna		Twelfth
Isaac Tyrnau	Vienna	Tyrnau	Fourteenth
Yom Tov Lippman Heller (Tosefos Yomtov)		Vienna, Prague, Nimerov, Ludmir, Krakow	Sixteenth
Menachem Mendel ben Meshulam Zalman Auerbach	Vienna		Seventeenth

Aspects Of The Authors • 521

Scholar	Geographical Location (Birthplace)	Additional Geographic Location/s	Century When Born
	Babylonia		
Simeon Kayyara			Ninth
Achai Gaon	Pumbedita		Eighth
Hai Gaon	Pumbedita		Tenth
Sherira ben Hanina, Gaon	Pumbedita		Tenth
Hai ben Sherira, Gaon			Tenth
Abba Arika (Rav)	Sura		Third
Yehudai ben Nahman (Yehudai Gaon)	Sura		Eighth
Gaon Amram ben Sheshna	Sura		Ninth
	Bavaria		
Joseph ben Moses	Hoechstaedt		Fifteenth
Judah ben Enoch		Pfersee	Seventeenth
Abraham ben Asher Wallerstein		Schaittach	Eighteenth
	Belarus		
Chaim Soloveitchik (The Brisker Reb)	Brest (Brisk)		Nineteenth
Chaim Ozer Grodzinski	Iuje (near Vilna)	Volozhin, Vilna	Nineteenth
Abraham Isaiah Karelitz (Chazon Ish)	Kosava	Vilna, Palestine	Nineteenth
Yechiel Michel Tukachinsky	Lyakhovichi	Jerusalem	Twentieth

Scholar	Geographical Location (Birthplace)	Additional Geographic Location/s	Century When Born
Isser Zalman Meltzer (Even HaEzel)	Mir (Lithuania)	Volozhin, Slobodka, Jerusalem	Nineteenth
Saul Lieberman (Gra'sh)	Motol	Slobodka, Kiev, France, Palestine, USA	Twentieth
Yosef Dov Soloveitchik (Beis HaLevi)	Nesvizh	Volozhin, Slutsk, Warsaw, Brisk	Nineteenth
Yosef Rosen (Rogatchover Gaon, Tzafnach Paneach)	Rogachev	Dvinsk	Nineteenth
Yisroel ben Shmuel Ashkenazi of Shklov	Shklov	Vilna, Palestine (Safed)	Eighteenth
Boruch Ber Leibowitz	Slutsk	Brest, Slobodka, Minsk, Kremenchug, Vilna	Nineteenth
Moshe Feinstein (Reb Moshe)	Uzda	Luban, USA	Late Nineteenth
Israel Meir (HaKohen) Kagan (Chofetz Chaim)	Zhetl (modern Belarus)	Vilna, Radun	Nineteenth

Bohemia

Scholar	Geographical Location (Birthplace)	Additional Geographic Location/s	Century When Born
Isaac ben Moses of Vienna (Or Zarua, Riaz)		France, Germany, Vienna Saxony	Thirteenth
Abraham ben Abigdor Kara			Fifteenth
David ben Aryeh Loeb Altshuler (Altshul)	?Prague	Prague	Seventeenth
Nethaneel ben Naftali Tzvi Weil		Prague, Muhringen, Carlsruhe	Seventeenth

Scholar	Geographical Location (Birthplace)	Additional Geographic Location/s	Century When Born
Meir Popperos	Prague	Jerusalem	Seventeenth
Jacob ben Joseph Reischer (Backofen)	Prague	Ansbach (Bavaria), Worms, Metz	Seventeenth
Samuel ben Nathan Loew	Kolin		Eighteenth
Jedidiah Weil	Prague	Metz, Wottitz, Carlsruhe	Eighteenth
Bulgaria			
Tobiah ben Eliezer	Castoria		Eleventh
Croatia			
Judah ben Solomon Chai Alkali		Jerusalem, Semlin	Nineteenth
Czechoslovakia			
Abraham ben Abigdor Kara	(Bohemia)		Fifteenth
David Weiss Halivni	Ruthenia	Sziget, Romania USA Israel	Twentieth
Isaiah HaLevi Horowitz (Shelah, Shaloh)	Prague	Jerusalem, Safed	Sixteenth
Mordechai ben Avraham Jaffe (Ba'al HaLevushim)	Prague	Venice, Grodno, Posen	Sixteenth
Meir Popperos	Prague (Bohemia)	Jerusalem	Seventeenth
Eliyahu ben Binyamin Wolf Shapiro	Prague		Seventeenth

Scholar	Geographical Location (Birthplace)	Additional Geographic Location/s	Century When Born
Meir Eisenstadter (Meir Ash) (Maharam Ash)	Sastin (Slovakia)	Eisenstadt, Ungvar	Eighteenth
Samuel ben Ezekiel Landau		Prague	Nineteenth
Denmark			
Jacob Israel ben Zvi Ashkenazi Emden (the Yabets)	Altona		Seventeenth
Egypt			
Bezalel Ashkenazi	(Palestine)	Egypt	Sixteenth
Jacob de Castro			Sixteenth
Saadia ben Joseph Gaon (Saadia Gaon)	Dilaz	Palestine, Sura	Tenth
Moses de Medina		?Turkey	Seventeenth
England			
Solomon Bennett Freehof		USA	Nineteenth
France			
Simhah ben Samuel, of Vitry			Eleventh
Isaac ben Abraham, of Dampierre			Twelfth
Joseph ben Baruch (Joseph of Clisson)		Paris, Palestine	Twelfth
Elhanan ben Isaac, of Dampierre			Twelfth
Jacob of Chinon		Chinon	Twelfth

Aspects Of The Authors • 525

Scholar	Geographical Location (Birthplace)	Additional Geographic Location/s	Century When Born
Joseph ben Isaac Bekhor Shor		Orlean	Twelfth
Samuel ben Solomon, of Falaise			Twelfth
Jacob ben Asher (Ba'al HaTurim)		Spain	Thirteenth
Hezekiah ben Manoah (Hizkuni / Chizkuni)			Thirteenth
Moses, of Evreux			Thirteenth
Abba Mari ben Moses ben Joseph Don Astruc, of Lunel		Perpignan	Late Thirteenth
Yedayah HaPenini		Provence	Thirteenth
Joseph ben Joshua Meir HaKohen	Avignon	Genoa	Late Fifteenth
Levi ben Gershom (Gersonides, Ralbag)	Bagnol (Languedoc)		Late Thirteenth
Joseph Colon ben Solomon Trabotto (Maharik)	Chambery	Piedmont, Venice, Bologna, Pavia, Padua	Fifteenth
Samson ben Isaac of Chinon (MaHaRShak)	Chinon		Thirteenth
Perez ben Elijah Rap, RaPaSh, MaHaRPaSh)	Corbeil		Thirteenth
Isaac ben Joseph, of Corbeil		Corbeil	Thirteenth
Moses ben Jacob, of Coucy		Coucy	Thirteenth
Samson ben Joseph of Falaise		Falaise	Twelfth

Scholar	Geographical Location (Birthplace)	Additional Geographic Location/s	Century When Born
Asher ben Meshullam	Lunel		Twelfth
Abraham ben Nathan	Lunel	Dampierre, Toledo	Twelfth
Samuel ben Judah ibn Tibbon	Lunel	Marseille	Twelfth
Moses ibn Tibbon	Marseille		Thirteenth
Gershon ben Yehuda (Me'Or HaGolah)	Metz	Mainz	Tenth
Eliezer ben Samuel of Metz	Metz		Twelfth
Abraham ben Isaac, of Narbonne (Raavad II)	Montpelier	Barcelona, Narbonne	Twelfth
Moses HaDarshan	Norbonne		Eleventh
David Kimchi (RaDaK)	Narbonne		Twelfth
Aaron ben Jacob ben David HaKohen	Norbonne	Majorca	Thirteenth
Mordechai ben Hillel Ashkenazi	Nuremberg		Thirteenth
Meshullam ben Jacob		Lunel	Twelfth
Judah ben Isaac Messer Leon	Paris		Twelfth
Jehiel ben Joseph, of Paris		Paris	Thirteenth
Joseph ben Hanan ben Nathan Ezobi	Perpignan		Thirteenth
Abraham ben David (Ravad III)	Provence	Lunel	Twelfth

Scholar	Geographical Location (Birthplace)	Additional Geographic Location/s	Century When Born
Yitzhak ben Abba Mari, of Marseilles	Provence	Marseilles	Twelfth
Meshullam ben Moses	Provence		Twelfth
Yitzhak Saggi Nehor (Isaac the Blind)	Provence		Twelfth
Ishtori ben Moses Haparchi (Kaftor Vaferech)	Provence	Spain, Egypt, Israel	Thirteenth
Yerucham ben Meshullam	Provence	Spain	Thirteenth
Menachem ben Solomon Meiri (HaMeiri)	Provence		Thirteenth
Isaac (Yitzhak) ben Meir (Rivam)	Ramerupt		Eleventh
Samuel ben Meir (Rashbam)	Ramerupt		Eleventh
Meir ben Samuel (RAM)	Ramerupt	Lorraine	Eleventh
Jacob ben, Meir (Tam) (Rabbeinu Tam)	Ramerupt		Twelfth
Isaac ben Samuel of Dampierre (Ri)	Ramerupt	Dampierre	Twelfth
Samson ben Abraham, of Sens	Sens		Twelfth
Eliezer of Toul	Toul		Thirteenth
Eliezer of Touques	Touques		Thirteenth
Judah ben Nathan (Riban)	Troyes		Eleventh

Scholar	Geographical Location (Birthplace)	Additional Geographic Location/s	Century When Born
Shlomo Yitzhaki (Rashi)	Troyes	Worms	
	Germany		
Eliakim ben Meshullam HaLevi			Late Eleventh
Eliezer ben Joel HaLevi (Raviah)			Twelfth
Simha ben Samuel of Speyer			Thirteenth
Jacob ben Moses Levi Moelin (Maharil)		Mayence	Fourteenth
Yosef (Yoselman) Loanz, of Rosheim		Alsace	Fifteenth
Jacob ben Judah Weil (Mahariv)		Erfurt	Fifteenth
Aaron ben Samuel			Seventeenth
Yehuda ben Shimon Ashkenazi			Eighteenth
Samuel ben Naftali HaLevi Kelin			Eighteenth
Israel Lipschutz		Dessau, Danzig	Eighteenth
Yissachar Jacobson			
Abi Ezra Selig Margolis		Palestine	Eighteenth
Jacob Tzvi Mecklenberg		Koenigsberg	Eighteenth
Yaakov Etlinger		Altona	Nineteenth
Jacob Israel ben Zvi Ashkenazi Emden (the Yabets)	Altona (see Denmark)		Seventeenth

Aspects Of The Authors • 529

Scholar	Geographical Location (Birthplace)	Additional Geographic Location/s	Century When Born
Isaac of Bamberg	Bamberg		Thirteenth
Samuel Danzig	?Danzig		Seventeenth
Abraham ben Jehiel Danzig	Danzig	Wilna (Lithuania)	Eighteenth
Aaron of Pissaro			Fourteenth
Simeon Kara, of Frankfurt (HaDarshan)		Frankfurt	Thirteenth
Moses Mendelssohn	Dessau	Berlin	Eighteenth
Menahem Mendel ben Simeon Steinhardt	Fuerth	Minden, Hildesheim. Warburg, Pederhorn	Eighteenth
Naftali Hertz ben Yaakov Elchanan (Bachrach)	Frankfurt		Seventeenth
Moses Sofer (Chatam Sofer)	Frankfurt au Main	Mainz, Prostwjov, Straznice, Mattersdorf, Bratislava	Eighteenth
Meir ben Isaac Katzenellenbogen (Maharam Padua)	Katzenellenbogen	Prague, Padua	Late Fifteenth
Israel Jonah Landau	Kempen, Posen (Prussia)		Eighteenth
Samuel Joseph Landau	Kempen		Eighteenth
Zvi Hirsch Kalischer	Lissa (Prussia)	Thorn	Nineteenth
Shimon ben Yitzhak HaGadol	Mainz (Mayence)		Tenth
Moses ben Kalonymus	Mainz (Mayence)		Eleventh

Scholar	Geographical Location (Birthplace)	Additional Geographic Location/s	Century When Born
Meshullam ben Moses	Mayence		Eleventh
Eliezer ben Nathan (Raavan)			Eleventh
Eleazar ben Yehuda ben Kalonymus, of Worms (Rokeach)	Mayence	Worms	Twelfth
David ben Kalonymus, of Munzenberg		Munzenberg	Late Twelfth
Samuel ben Aaron of Schlettstadt	Schlettstadt	Strasburg	Fourteenth
Samuel Schotten (Mharsheishoch)	Schotten	Frankfurt am Main	Seventeenth
Isaac ben Asher HaLevi (Riva)	Speyer		Eleventh
Kalonymus ben Isaac	Speyer		Eleventh
Samuel ben Kalonymus (He-Hasid), of Speyer	Speyer	Spain, France	Twelfth
Judah ben Samuel of Regensburg (He-Hasid)	Speyer	Regensburg	Twelfth
Joseph ben Menachem Steinhart	Steinhart	Rizheim, Upper and Lower Alsace, Furth	Eighteenth
Isaac ben Eleazar HaLevi	Worms		Eleventh
Meir ben Isaac Nehorai	Worms		Eleventh
Menahem ben (ben Solomon ben Simson) Jacob	Worms		Twelfth
Eliezer ben Yehuda, of Worms	Worms		Twelfth

Scholar	Geographical Location (Birthplace)	Additional Geographic Location/s	Century When Born
Baruch ben Yitzhak of Worms	Worms		Twelfth
Meir ben Baruch of Rothenburg (MaHaRaM)	Worms		Thirteenth
Baruch ben Isaac	Worms	Regensburg	Thirteenth
Asher ben Jehiel (Rabbeinu Asher / Rosh)		Worms, France, Spain	Thirteenth
Abraham Samuel Bachrach	Worms	Prague, Bohemia, Moravia, Worms	Sixteenth
Yair Chaim Bachrach	Worms	Metz	Seventeenth
Moses Ashkenazi		Vienna	Seventeenth
Isaiah Berlin			Eighteenth
Greece			
Hillel ben Eliakim			Eleventh
Zerachiah HaYavani (The Greek) (Ra'Za'H)			Thirteenth
Abba Mari ben Elgidor	Salonica		Thirteenth
Abraham ben Moses de Bouton	Salonika		Sixteenth
Tzvi Hirsch ben Yaakov Ashkenazi (Chacham Tzvi)	Salonica	Sarajevo, Germany, London, Lemberg	Seventeenth
Isaac Adarbi (Adribi)	Salonica		Sixteenth
Shemaiah de Medina	Salonica	Venice	Sixteenth
Moses ben Baruch Almosnino	Thessalonika	Constantinople	Sixteenth

Scholar	Geographical Location (Birthplace)	Additional Geographic Location/s	Century When Born
Samuel ben Moses de Medina (RashDaM)		Salonica	Sixteenth
Hungary			
Akiva Eger		Lissa (Poland), Posen	Eighteenth
Mordechai ben Abraham Benet	Csurgo, Stuhlweissenburg	Prague, Schossburg, Moravia	Eighteenth
Israel Veltz	Budapest		Twentieth
Solomon ben Joseph Ganzfried	Carpathia (now Ukraine) – Uzhorod (Ungvar)		Nineteenth
Abraham Samuel Benjamin Sofer (Ksav Sofer)	Pressburg		Nineteenth
Iraq			
Chacham Yosef Chaim (Ben Ish Chai)	Baghdad		Nineteenth
Yaakov Chaim Sofer (Kaf HaChaim)	Baghdad	Jerusalem	Nineteenth
Abdalla Somekh	Baghdad		Nineteenth
Ovadia Yosef	Basra	Jerusalem, Cairo	Twentieth
Italy			
Joseph ben Gorion			Tenth
Menahem ben Solomon			Twelfth
Abraham Ankava	?		

Aspects Of The Authors • 533

Scholar	Geographical Location (Birthplace)	Additional Geographic Location/s	Century When Born
Judah ben Eliezer HaLevi Minz (Mahari Minz)		Padua	Fifteenth
Yaakov Baruch ben Yehuda Landau			Fifteenth
Abraham ben Judah HaLevi Minz		Padua	Late Fifteenth
Jacob ben Judah Landau			Late Fifteenth
Abraham ben Solomon Treves (Tarfati)		Adrianople	Sixteenth
Menachem di Lonzano	?Turkey	Jerusalem	Sixteenth
Obadiah ben Jacob Sforno	Cesena	Rome, Bologna	Fifteenth
Menachem Azaryah, of Fano	Fano	Mantua	Sixteenth
Moses ben Meir, of Ferrara	?Ferrara	Ferrara	Thirteenth
Yitzhak Hezekiah Lampronti	Ferrara	Provencal, Padua, Ferrara	Seventeenth
Hezekiah ben David DiSilo	Livorno		Seventeenth
Kalonymus II ben Moses	Lucca		Tenth
Aharon Berechyah, of Modena	Modena		Sixteenth
Moses Chaim Luzzatto (Ramchal)	Padua	Amsterdam, Acre	Eighteenth

Scholar	Geographical Location (Birthplace)	Additional Geographic Location/s	Century When Born
Nathan ben Jehiel Anaw (Anav)	Rome	Sicily, Kerwan, Narbonne, Rome	Eleventh
Kalonymus ben Shabbethai	Rome	Worms	Eleventh
Tzidkayah ben Avraham Anav HaRofei	Rome		Thirteenth
Benjamin ben Abraham Anaw	Rome		Thirteenth
Zedekiah ben Abraham Anaw	Rome	Germany	Thirteenth
Shemariah ben Elijah Ikriti, of Negropont	Rome		Thirteenth
Jonah Abraham, of Gerona	Rome	Gerona	Fourteenth
Daniel ben Judah	Rome	Rome	Fourteenth
Abraham Galante	Rome	Safed	Sixteenth
Shabtai Donolo	Oria		Tenth
Joshua Boaz Mevorakh / Joshua Boaz ben Simon Baruch (Shiltei Gibborim)	Sabbineta	Savigliano	Sixteenth
Yeshayah ben Mali Hazaken	Trani		Twelfth
Isaiah ben Mali di Trani (RI'D)	Trani		Thirteenth

Scholar	Geographical Location (Birthplace)	Additional Geographic Location/s	Century When Born
Samuel Aboab (Rasha)	Venice	Verona	Seventeenth
Latvia			
Abraham Isaac Kook (HaRav)	Griva	Volozhin, Palestine	Late Nineteenth
Eliyahu Eliezar Dessler	Libau	Israel	Twentieth
Lithuania			
Aryeh Leib ben Asher Gunzberg (Shaagat Aryeh)			Seventeenth
Moses ben Isaac Judah Lima			Seventeenth
Jehiel ben Solomon Heilprin		Minsk	Seventeenth
Yerusham Levovitz			Nineteenth
Chaim Shalom Tuvia Rabinowitz (Reb Chaim Telzer)			Nineteenth
Mordechai Gimpel Yaffe Torizer		Palestine	Nineteenth
Aaron Walkin		Pinsk-Karlin	Nineteenth
Yechiel Michel HaLevi Epstein (Aruch HaShulchan)	Babruyak	Minsk, Novogrudok	Nineteenth
Moshe Mordechai Epstein	Bakst	Kovno, Slabodka, Palestine	Nineteenth

Scholar	Geographical Location (Birthplace)	Additional Geographic Location/s	Century When Born
Hillel ben Naphtali Zevi	Brest-Litovsk	Vilna, Altona, Hamburg, Zolkiev	Seventeenth
Meir Simcha Kalonymus of Dvinsk HaKohen	Butrimonys (Baltrimantz)	Bialystok, Dvinsk	Nineteenth
Kamenecki, Jacob (Yaakov Kamenetsky)	Kalushkove	Dolhinov, Minsk, Slobodka, New York	Nineteenth
Simcha Zissel Ziv (Alter of Kelm)	Kelme	Kovno, Zhagory, Moscow, St. Petersburg	Nineteenth
Louis Ginzberg	Kovno	USA	Nineteenth
Eliyahu David Rabinowitz-Teomim (Aderet)	Kovno (Pikelin)	Panavezys, Minsk, Jerusalem	Nineteenth
Shneur Zalman Baruch (Borukovich), of Liadi (Alter Rebbe, GRaZ)	Liozna	Liadi	Eighteenth
Isser Zalman Meltzer (Even HaEzel)	Mir (Belarus)	Volozhin, Slobodka, Jerusalem	Nineteenth
Solomon ben Kalman HaLevi Abel	Neustadt (Kovno)		Nineteenth
Baruch HaLevi Epstein	Novardok	Volozhin, Pinsk	Nineteenth
Elijah ben Solomon Zalman (Vilna Gaon, Gra)	Vilna	Poland, Germany	Eighteenth

Scholar	Geographical Location (Birthplace)	Additional Geographic Location/s	Century When Born
Isaac ben Moses Solomon Blaser (Rav Itzele Peterburger)	Vilna	St. Petersburg, Kovno (Kaunas), Jerusalem	Nineteenth
Chaim ben Itzchok Volozhin (Reb Chaim)	Volozhin		Eighteenth
Israel Lipkin Salanter	Zhagory	Salant, Vilna, Kovno, Prussia	Nineteenth
Majorca			
Simeon ben Zemah Duran (Rashbatz / Tashbetz)	Adar	Algiers	Fifteenth
Moravia			
Israel Bruna (Mahari Bruna)	Brno	Ratisbon (Bavaria)	Fifteenth
Aron Chorin	Weisskirchen (Hranice)	Mattersburg (Hungary), Prague, Arad	Eighteenth
Isaac Hirsch Weiss	Velke Mezirici	Trebitsch, Eisenstadt, Vienna	Nineteenth
Morocco			
Dunash HaLevi ben Labrat	Fez		Tenth
Yitzhak ben Yaakov HaKohen Alfasi (RIF)	Fez		Eleventh
Abraham Azulai	Fez	Palestine	Sixteenth
Aharon ibn Chaim	Fez	Cairo, Smyrna, Venice, Jerusalem	Sixteenth

538 • Aspects Of The Authors

Scholar	Geographical Location (Birthplace)	Additional Geographic Location/s	Century When Born
Jacob Hagiz	Fez	Italy, Jerusalem, Constantinople	Seventeenth
Hayyim ibn Attar (Ohr HaChaim HaKadosh)	Sale	Lovorno (Italy), Palestine	Late Seventeenth
Harav Yisroel Abuchatzeirah	Morocco	Israel	Twentieth
	Palestine / Israel		
Judah HaNasi (Rabbeinu HaKadosh)			Second
Jose ben Halafta			Second
Eleazar ben Eleazar HaKappar (Bar Kappara, Bereibi)			Late Second
Shmuel Aceda	?	Safed	Sixteenth
Israel Sarug			Sixteenth
Eliyahu de Vidas	?	Safed, Hebron	Sixteenth
Moses ibn Habib (Chaviv)			Seventeenth
Aryeh Leib Steinhardt	?	Jerusalem	Nineteenth
Eliezer David Greenwald	Europe	Jerusalem	Nineteenth
Solomon ben Moses HaLevi Alkabetz	Safed		Sixteenth
Elazar ben Moshe Azikri (Ezkari)	Safed		Sixteenth

Aspects Of The Authors • 539

Scholar	Geographical Location (Birthplace)	Additional Geographic Location/s	Century When Born
Moses ben Jacob Cordovero (Ramak)	?Spain	Safed	Sixteenth
Yom Tov ben Moshe Tzahalon (Maharitz)		Safed	Sixteenth
Hayyim ben Joseph Vital	Safed	Egypt, Jerusalem, Damascus	Sixteenth
Bezalel Ashkenazi	Palestine	Egypt	Sixteenth
Yitzhak Luria Ashkenazi (The ARI)	Palestine	Egypt	Sixteenth
Abraham Gediliyah	Jerusalem	Hebron, Leghorn	Sixteenth
Isaac Luria (Ashkenazi) (Ari, Arizal, He-Ari)	Jerusalem	Cairo, Safed	Sixteenth
Yaakov Culi	Jerusalem	Safed, Constantinople	Seventeenth
Moses Hagiz	Jerusalem	Italy, Amsterdam, Safed	Seventeenth
Yom Tov Algazi	Jerusalem		Eighteenth
Haim Yosef David Azulai (Hida / Chida)	Jerusalem	Cairo, North Africa, Europe	Eighteenth
Chaim Chizkiya Medini	Jerusalem	Turkey, Buchara, Crimea, Hebron	Nineteenth
Ben-Zion Meir Hai Uziel	Jerusalem	Tel Aviv	Nineteenth
Shlomo Zalman Auerbach	Jerusalem		Twentieth
Yitzhak Yosef	Jerusalem		Twentieth
Samuel de Uzeda	Safed		Sixteenth

Scholar	Geographical Location (Birthplace)	Additional Geographic Location/s	Century When Born
Aaron ben Moses ben Asher	Tiberias		Tenth
Shlomo ben Baya'a	Tiberias		Tenth
Poland			
Moses ben Noah Isaac Lipschutz			Sixteenth
Shalom Shakna		Lublin	Sixteenth
Samuel ben Urig Sharaga Faibesh (Fayvish, Phoebus)			Seventeenth
Meir ben Iszak Eisenstadt (Meir Ash) (Maharam Ash / Panim Me'irot)		Posen, Szydlowiec, Worms, Prossnitz, Eisenstadt	
Abraham ben Eliezar HaKohen			Late Seventeenth
Alexanders Margolis			Eighteenth
Hayyim Mordechai Margolis			Eighteenth
Shneur Zalman Fradkin, of Lublin		Polotsk, Lublin, Jerusalem	Nineteenth
Yechiel Yaakov Weinberg		Pilwishki, Berlin, Montreaux (Switzerland)	Nineteenth
Menachem Mendel Kasher		Palestine	Twentieth
Avraham Aharon Price		Berlin, Paris, Toronto	Twentieth

Scholar	Geographical Location (Birthplace)	Additional Geographic Location/s	Century When Born
Abraham Zevi Hirsch ben Jacob Eisenstadt	Bialystok	Grodno, Kovno	Nineteenth
Benjamin Eisenstadt	Utina		Nineteenth
Samuel Eliezer ben Judah Eidels (Edels) (Maharsha)	Cracow	Prague, Posen, Chelm, Lublin, Ostrog	Sixteenth
Moses ben Israel Isserles (ReMA, Ramo)	Cracow		Sixteenth
Abraham ben Shabtai Sheftel Horowitz	Cracow	Lvov	Sixteenth
Gershon Ashkenazi	Cracow	Prossnitz, Hanau, Nikolsburg, Vienna, Metz	Seventeenth
Yaakov Yehosua Ben Zvi Hirsch (Jacob Joshua Falk)	Cracow	Berlin	Late Seventeenth
Menachem Mendel ben Abraham Krochmal	Cracow	Moravia (Kremsir), Prossnitz, Nikolsburg	Seventeenth
Jonathan Eybeschutz	Cracow	Metz, Altona	Eighteenth
Abraham ben Chaim HaLevi Gombiner (Magen Avraham)	Gombin (Gabin)		Seventeenth
Yitzhak Myer Alter	Ger (Gora Kalwaria)		Late Eighteenth
Avraham Mordechai Alter	Ger (Gora Kalwaria)	Israel	Nineteenth
Yehuda Reyeh Leib Alter (Sfas Emes)	Ger (Gora Kalwaria)		Nineteenth
Yisrael Alter	Ger	Israel	Late Nineteenth

Scholar	Geographical Location (Birthplace)	Additional Geographic Location/s	Century When Born
Simchah Bunim Alter	Ger (Gora Kalwaria)	Israel	Twentieth
Menachem Mendel of Kotzk (Kotzker Rebbe)	Goray	Kotzk	Eighteenth
Benjamin Aaron ben Abraham Slonik	Grodno	Silesia, Podhajce, Cracow	Sixteenth
Kalonymus Kalman Shapira (Szapira)	Grodzisk	Piaseczno, Warsaw	Nineteenth
Elimelech Szapira	Grodzisk		Nineteenth
Shabbethai ben Joseph Bass	Kalisz	Prague, Amsterdam	Seventeenth
Moshe Pellier of Kobrin	Kobrin		Eighteenth
Solomon ben Judah Aaron Kluger	Komarow	Brody (Galicia), Rawa, Kulikow (Galicia), Jozefow (Lublin), Breznay	Eighteenth
Aaron Moses ben Jacob Taubes	Lemberg	Sniatyn, Jassy	Eighteenth
Avraham Lieblein	Lemberg		Nineteenth
Shlomo Ephraim Lunshitz	?Lenshitz	Lemburg, Prague	Sixteenth
Jacob ben Jacob Moses Lorberbaum, of Lisser (Ba'al HaNesivos / Lissa Rav)	Leszno (Lissa) / Posen	Kalish	Eighteenth
Menachem Mendel Schneerson (Tzemach Tzedek)	Liozna		Eighteenth
Yaakov Aryeh Alter	Lodz	Israel	Twentieth

Scholar	Geographical Location (Birthplace)	Additional Geographic Location/s	Century When Born
Elijah ben Kalonymus		Lublin	Seventeenth
Joshua ben Alexander (Katz) HaKohen Falk	Lvov (Lemberg)		Sixteenth
Meir ben Gedaliyah Lublin (Maharam)	Lublin	Cracow, Lemburg	Sixteenth
Yoel Sirkis (Bach)	Lublin	Brest-Litovsk, Cracow	Sixteenth
Moshe Chaim Ephraim of Sudilkov	Medzibizh	Sudilkov	Eighteenth
Nachman of Breslov	Medzibizh	Jerusalem, Zlatipolia, Bratslav	Eighteenth
Ezekiel ben Judah Landau (Nodah B'Yehuda)	Opatow	Brody, Jampol, Prague	Eighteenth
Hayyim ben Moses Lipschutz	Ostrog		Seventeenth
Yehuda Leib ben Meir Channeles	Posen		Sixteenth
Solomon Luria (Maharshal, Rashal)	Posen	Ostrog, Lublin	Sixteenth
Yissachar ben Ellenburg	Posen	Gorizia (Italy), Austerlitz (Czechoslovakia)	Sixteenth
Moshe Mos of Premysl	Premysl	Apta (Opatow)	Sixteenth
Yosef ben Moshe Babad	Przeworsk	Safed	Nineteenth
Chaim Halberstam of Sens	Tarnogrod	Sans	Eighteenth
Shimon Shkop	Tortz	Moltsh, Bransk, Grodno	Nineteenth

Scholar	Geographical Location (Birthplace)	Additional Geographic Location/s	Century When Born
Shabbatai ben Meir HaKohen (Shach)	Vilna	Cracow	Seventeenth
Aaron Samuel ben Israel Kaidenover	Vilna	Moravia (Austrian Empire), Frankfurt am Main, Cracow	Seventeenth
Zevi Hirsch Kaidenover	Vilna	Frankfurt am Main	Seventeenth
Moses ben Naftali Hertz Rivkes	Vilna	Amsterdam	Seventeenth
Noah ben Abraham Lipschutz (Noah Mindes)	Vilna		Eighteenth
Isaac Elijah ben Samuel Landau	Vilna		Nineteenth
Joshua Hoschel ben Elijah Zeeb Levin	Vilna	Volozhin, Praga, Paris	Nineteenth
Shabtai Sheftel Horowitz	Volhynia	Prague, Furth, Frankfurt am Main, Vienna	Sixteenth
Jacob Joseph ben Tzvi HaKohen Katz, of Polonnoye	Volhynia	Shargorod, Polonnoye	Eighteenth
Aaron Walden	Warsaw		Nineteenth
Pinchas Menachem Alter	Warsaw	Israel	Twentieth
Abraham Joshua Heschel	Warsaw	New York	Twentieth
Isaac Hutner	Warsaw	Palestine, New York	Twentieth

Scholar	Geographical Location (Birthplace)	Additional Geographic Location/s	Century When Born
David Lida	Zwolen	Lemburg, Lithuania, Mainz, Amsterdam	Seventeenth
Portugal			
Solomon Alami			Fourteenth
Avraham Chayon		Constantinople	Fifteenth
Joseph Chayon		Constantinople	Fifteenth
Menasseh ben Joseph ben Israel (MB'Y)	Madeira	Amsterdam	Seventeenth
Romania			
Yehuda Meir Shapiro	Suczawa	Poland	Nineteenth
Russia			
Naphtali (Hirsch) ben Asher Altschul		Poland, Constantinople	Sixteenth
Yehuda Leib HaLevi Ashlag (Ba'al HaSulam)	Lodz (Congress of Poland)	Jerusalem, England, Jaffa, Tel Aviv	Nineteenth
Yosef Yozel Hurwitz (Alter of Novardok)		Novardok	Nineteenth
Yaakov Yitzhak Ruderman	Dolhinov	Baltimore, USA	Twentieth
Yaakov David Wilovsky	Kobrin	Slutsk, Safed	Nineteenth
Jacob Meshullam ben Mordechai Ze'ev Ornstein	Galicia (Lemberg)	Zolkiev, Lemberg	Eighteenth
Solomon Judah Loeb Rapoport	Galicia	Tarnopol, Prague	Eighteenth

Scholar	Geographical Location (Birthplace)	Additional Geographic Location/s	Century When Born
Enoch Zundel ben Joseph			Nineteenth
Baruch Mordechai ben Jacob Lipschitz		Siedice (Poland)	Nineteenth
Solomon Buber	Lemberg		Nineteenth
David Solomon Eibenschutz		Buzhanov, Iasi (Romania)	Eighteenth
Dovber Schneuri (Mitteler Rebbe)	Liozna	Lyubavichi	Eighteenth
David ben Samuel HaLevi Segal (Taz)	Ludmir, Volhynia	Cracow, Pollitsha, Posen, Ostrog, Steinitz (Moravia), Lemberg	Sixteenth
Shmuel Schneerson (The Rebbe Maharash)	Lyubavichi		Nineteenth
Sholom Dovber Schneerson (Rebbe Rashab)		Rostov-on-Don	Nineteenth
Yosef Yitzhak Schneerson (Rebbe Rayatz)		Latvia, Warsaw, New York City	Nineteenth
Judah Aryeh Loeb ben Joshua Hoschel	Minsk		Eighteenth
Joseph Ber Soloveitchik (HaRav)	Pruszany	Berlin, Boston	Twentieth
Yitzhak Elchanan Spektor	Resh (Grodno)	Vilkovisk, Sabelin, Baresa, Nishvez, Novohordok, Kovno	Nineteenth

Scholar	Geographical Location (Birthplace)	Additional Geographic Location/s	Century When Born
Avraham of Trisk	Trisk		Nineteenth
Naftali Tzvi Yehuda Berlin (The Netziv)		Volozhin	Nineteenth
Dov Ber (Maggid of Mezritch)	Volhynia		Eighteenth
Menachem Nachum Twersky	Volhynia	Chernobyl	Eighteenth
Meir Leibush ben Jehiel Michel (Malbim)	Volochisk, Volhynia	Wreschen, Kempen, Constantinople, Paris, Kalisz, Mogilef, Konigsberg, Kiev	Nineteenth
Samuel ben Joseph Strashun (Rashash)	Zaskevich	Wilna	Eighteenth

Serbia

Scholar	Geographical Location (Birthplace)	Additional Geographic Location/s	Century When Born
Joseph Almosnino	Belgrade	Moravia	Seventeenth

Slovakia

Scholar	Geographical Location (Birthplace)	Additional Geographic Location/s	Century When Born
David Zevi Hoffmann	Verbo	Vienna, Berlin	Nineteenth

Spain

Scholar	Geographical Location (Birthplace)	Additional Geographic Location/s	Century When Born
Yonah ibn Janach (Merinos)			Tenth
Isaac ben Samuel (Hasefardi)		Palestine	Eleventh
Judah ben Barzillai			Late Eleventh / Twelfth
Judah ben Solomon Alharzi			Twelfth

Scholar	Geographical Location (Birthplace)	Additional Geographic Location/s	Century When Born
Joseph ben Isaac Kimchi		France (Narbonne)	Twelfth
Jacob ben Reuben			Twelfth
Joseph ibn Plat		Lunel, Rome	Twelfth
Shem Tov ben Abraham ibn Gaon			Thirteenth
Samuel ben Isaac Sardi (HaSardi, HaSefaradi)			Thirteenth
Isaac Aboab (Abuhab) (Menorat HaMaor)			Fourteenth
Hasdai ben Abraham Crescas			Fourteenth
Yosef Chaviva			Late Fourteenth
Shabbatai Carmuz Levita	?Spain		Fourteenth
Shem Tov ibn Shem Tov			Fourteenth
Isaac ben Jacob Campanton			Fourteenth
Isaac ben Moses Arama (Ba'al Akedah)			Fifteenth
Joseph ben Solomon Taitezak		Salonica	Fifteenth
David ben Solomon ibn Abi Zimra (Radbaz)		Safed, Fez, Cairo, Jerusalem, Safed	Fifteenth
Moses ben Jacob Cordovero (Ramak)	?Spain	Safed	Sixteenth

Aspects Of The Authors • 549

Scholar	Geographical Location (Birthplace)	Additional Geographic Location/s	Century When Born
Abraham Herrera		Italy, Raguza, Amsterdam	Sixteenth
Joseph Albo	Aragon		Fourteenth
Isaac ben Reuben Albargeloni	Barcelona		Eleventh
Shlomo ben Aderet (Rashba)	Barcelona		Thirteenth
Aaron HaLevi, of Barcelona	Barcelona		Thirteenth
Abraham ben Isaac HaLevi	Barcelona		Fourteenth
Nissim Ben Reuven, of Gerona (RaN)	Barcelona		Fourteenth
Joseph ben Ephraim Caro (Karo) (Mechaber)		Portugal, Adrianole, Safed	Late Fifteenth
Yonah ben Avraham Gerondi (Rabbeinu Yonah)	Catalonia	Toledo	Thirteenth
Vidal di Tolosa	Catalonia		Fourteenth
Elijah Mizrachi (Re'em)	Constantinople		Fifteenth
Moses ben Maimon (Maimonides) (Rambam)	Cordoba	Fez, Palestine, Forstat (Egypt)	Twelfth
Menahem ben Aaron ibn Zerah	Estella	Alcala, Toledo	Fourteenth
Zerachiah ben Isaac HaLevi Gerondi (ReZaH, RaZBI, Ba'al HaMaor)	Gerona	Provence, Lunel	Twelfth

Scholar	Geographical Location (Birthplace)	Additional Geographic Location/s	Century When Born
Moses ben Nahman (Nahmanides) (Ramban)	Gerona	Palestine	Twelfth
Aharon HaLevi (Ra'ah)	Gerona		Thirteenth
Moses ibn Ezra (HaSallah)	Granada		Eleventh
Moses de Leon (Moshe ben Shem Tov)	Guadalajara		Thirteenth
Meir ben Solomon Abi Sahula	Guadalajara		Thirteenth
Isaac ben Judah Ghiyyat (Ghayyat)	Lucena		Eleventh
Isaac ibn Gias	Lucena		Eleventh
Solomon ben Judah ibn Gabirol (Gvirol)	Malaga	Valencia	Eleventh
Joseph ben Abraham Gikatilla (Joseph Ba'al HaNissim)	Medinaceli		Thirteenth
Samuel ibn Naghrela (Samuel HaNagid)	Merida	Cordoba	Tenth
Bahya ben Joseph ibn Paquda	Saragossa		Eleventh
Bahya ben Asher (Rabbeinu Behaye)	Saragossa		Thirteenth
Abraham ben Samuel Abulafia	Saragossa	Greece, Malta	Thirteenth
Abraham ben Shem Tov Bibago	Saragossa	Huesca	Fifteenth

Scholar	Geographical Location (Birthplace)	Additional Geographic Location/s	Century When Born
Joseph ben Meir HaLevi ibn Migash (Ri Migash)	Seville (?Granada)	Lucena	Eleventh
Yom Tov ibn Asevilli (Ritva)	Seville		Thirteenth / Fourteenth
David ben Joseph ben David Abudraham	Seville		Fourteenth
Abraham ben David HaLevi (Abraham ibn Daud, Rabad / Ravad I)	Toledo		Twelfth
Isaac Aboab	Toledo	Porto (Portugal)	Fifteenth
Jacob Berab	Toledo	Jerusalem, Cairo	Fifteenth
Isaac ben Judah Abravanel	Toledo	Italy	Fifteenth
Meir ben Todros HaLevi Abulafia (Ramaah)	Toledo		Thirteenth
Menahem ben Jacob ibn Saruq	Tortosa	Cordoba	Tenth
Judah ben Samuel HaLevi (RiHa'l)	Tudela		Eleventh
Abraham ben Meir ibn Ezra (Ibn Ezra, Abenezra)	Tudela	Italy, North Africa, Palestine, Baghdad	Late Eleventh
Isaac ben Sheshet Barfat (RiBaSH)	Valencia	Barcelona, Saragossa, Algiers	Fourteenth
Isaac ben Moses Arama	Zamora	Tarragona, Aragon	Fifteenth
Levi Yaakov Chaviv (Habib)	Zamora	Salonika,	Fifteenth

Scholar	Geographical Location (Birthplace)	Additional Geographic Location/s	Century When Born
Levi ben Jacob ibn Chaviv (Habib) (Ralbach)	Zamora	Salonika, Jerusalem	Late Fifteenth
Avraham ben Yaakov Saba	Zamora	Portugal	Fifteenth
Tunisia			
Chananel ben Chushiel (Rabbeinu Chananel)			Late Tenth
Jacob ben Nissim ibn Shahin	Kirwan		Tenth
Turkey			
Moshe Alshich		Adrianople Israel	Sixteenth
Aaron ben Isaac Lapapa		Salonika, Constantinople, Manissa, Smyrna	Sixteenth
Menachem di Lonzano	?Italy	Jerusalem	Sixteenth
Abraham Alegri		Constantinople	Seventeenth
Chaim Benveniste		Constantinople, Smyrna	Seventeenth
Judah ben Samuel Rosanes		Constantinople	Seventeenth
Joseph ibn Lev (Labi)	Monastir	Salonica, Constantinople	Sixteenth
Samuel ben Moses di Modena (Maharshdam)	Salonika		Sixteenth
Abraham ibn Chananyah	Salonica (later Greece)	Jerusalem	Seventeenth

Scholar	Geographical Location (Birthplace)	Additional Geographic Location/s	Century When Born
Moses ben Joseph, of Trani	Salonica	Adrianople, Safed, Jerusalem	Sixteenth
Joseph Escapa	Uskap	Salonika, Smyrna	Sixteenth
Hayyim Palaggi (Maharhaf, HaVif)	Smyrna		Eighteenth
Ukraine			
Israel ben Eliezer (Ba'al Shem Tov / Besht)	Okopy	Carpathia	Eighteenth
Yaakov Yosef HaKohen of Polnoye			Eighteenth
Solomon Buber	Lemberg		Nineteenth
Boruch of Kosov	Kosov		Eighteenth
Yitzhak Schneerson	Podrovnah	Yekatrinoslav, Russian exile	Nineteenth
Menachem Mendel Schneerson (The Lubavitcher Rebbe)	Nikolaev	Berlin, Paris, New York	Twentieth
United States Of America			
David Golinkin		Israel	Twentieth
Isadore (Yitzhak) Twersky	Boston		Twentieth
Yemen			
Shalom Sharabi (Rashash)		Jerusalem	Eighteenth
Yosef Quafih	Sana'a	Palestine	Twentieth

Shifting Centers Of Output Over The Centuries

This table lists the combination of either a country or a region where the rabbi was born, but not where he worked. The main purpose of this table is to demonstrate the shifting centers of output over the centuries.

In the first to tenth century it was the Middle East where Rabbinic interpretation began in a serious and systematized fashion. Then the focus spread to France, Spain and North Africa. The latter region was active only for two centuries. France remained an important region until the thirteenth century while Spain and then Portugal was active until the late fifteenth century. This obviously corresponded with the Spanish Inquisition and expulsion.

Italy had a relatively small but constant output of traditional scholarly work starting as early as the tenth century and continuing through to the eighteenth century. Germany and the German provinces saw rabbinic output of interpretive work starting in the eleventh century and continuing through to the nineteenth century.

Although the term Central Europe is a twentieth century one, that region, covering Austria, Czechoslovakia, Hungary, Serbia and Croatia had scholars who produced works from the twelfth through to the twentieth centuries, with it reaching a peak in the seventeenth century. Technically Germany falls into this European zone, but has been dealt with separately.

It is interesting to note that Palestine became a very active center in the sixteenth century, mainly related to the development of Safed as a Kabbalistic center then. However, Palestine has remained relatively active through the twentieth century.

The most striking development was that of Eastern European output. Beginning in the sixteenth century, it reached its peak of productivity, unequalled by any other region before, in the nineteenth century, only to be cut short by the second world war and the Holocaust.

Finally the United States only saw activity beginning in the twentieth century.

Century	Regional Birthplace And Number Of Scholars
Second	Palestine 3
Eighth	Babylonia 2
Ninth	Babylonia 2
Tenth	Babylonia 3 France 1 Italy 1 North Africa 4 Palestine 2 Spain / Portugal 3

Century	Regional Birthplace And Number Of Scholars
Eleventh	France 6 Germany and Provinces 8 Italy 2 North Africa 3 Southeastern Europe 2 Spain / Portugal 11
Twelfth	Austria / Hungary 1 France 22 Italy 2 Germany and Provinces 8 Spain / Portugal 9
Thirteenth	Central Europe 1 France 20 Italy 4 Germany and Provinces 6 Southeastern Europe 2 Spain / Portugal 12
Fourteenth	Austria / Hungary 2 Germany and Provinces 3 Italy 2 Spain / Portugal 13
Fifteenth	France 2 North Africa 2 Central Europe 3 Germany and Provinces 3 Italy 5 Spain / Portugal 15
Sixteenth	Austria / Hungary 1 Central Europe 2 Eastern Europe 18 Germany and Provinces 2 Italy 5 North Africa 4 Palestine 13 Southeastern Europe 5
Sixteenth	Spain / Portugal 2 Turkey 7

Century	Regional Birthplace And Number Of Scholars
Seventeenth	Austria / Hungary 2 Central Europe 7 Denmark 1 Eastern Europe 17 Germany and Provinces 8 Italy 3 Middle East 1 North Africa 5 Palestine 3 Southeastern Europe 1 Spain / Portugal 1 Turkey 4
Eighteenth	Austria / Hungary 13 Central Europe 4 Eastern Europe 30 Germany and Provinces 13 Italy 1 Middle East 3 North Africa 1 Palestine 2 Turkey 1
Nineteenth	Austria / Hungary 10 Central Europe 3 Eastern Europe 56 England 1 Germany and Provinces 2 Middle East 1 Palestine 4 Southeastern Europe 2
Twentieth	Eastern Europe 10 Central Europe 3 North Africa 1 Palestine 2 USA 3

SELECTED REFERENCES

This list of reference sources includes most that are mentioned in the book as well as those used as the basis for drawing on the biographical material. The public domain information forms an important reference source.

1. Haim Azulai: Shem HaGedolim
2. Michael Berger: Rabbinic Authority (Ch 3)
   (pg 124), Oxford University Press, 1998
3. James Kugel: How to Read the Bible (pg 648), Free Press, 2007
4. Martin Goodman: Rome and Jerusalem (pg 180-182), Alfred A. Knopf, 2007
5. Global Jewish Data Base (The Responsa Project), Bar-Ilan University
6. The New Complete Works of Josephus: Kregel Publications, 1999
7. Catherine Hezser: Roman Law and Rabbinic Legal Composition; pg 160, The Cambridge Companion to The Talmud and Rabbinic Literature, 2007. Ed. By Charlotte Elisheva Fonrobert and Martin S Jaffee
8. Shaye Cohen: Judaean Legal Tradition and Halakhah of the Mishnah; pg 139-140. The Cambridge Companion to The Talmud and Rabbinic Literature, 2007. Ed. By Charlotte Elisheva Fonrobert and Martin S Jaffee
9. Zachary Kessin: Jewish Names in the World of Medieval Islam . PDF 2002-2003. (http://www.s-gabriel.org/names/yehoshua/jews_in_cairo/index.html)
10. Sarah Stroumsa: Maimonides in His World; Portrait of a Mediterranean Thinker. Princeton University Press. 2009.
11. Shulamis Frieman: Who's Who in the Talmud. Jason Aronson Inc. 1995
12. Alfred J. Kolatch: Masters of the Talmud; Their Lives and Views. Jonathan David Publishers. 2003
13. Charles Cutter: Judaica Reference Sources. A Selective Annotated Bibliographic Guide. Third Edition
14. Tzvi Rabinowicz: Chassidic Rebbes, Targum/Feldheim, 1989
15. Artscroll History Series: The Rishonim and The Early Acharonim. Compiled and Edited by Rabbi Hersh Goldworm
16. Solomon Freehof: The Responsa Literature. Varda Books, 2001
17. Heinrich Graetz: History of the Jews
18. Michael Brenner: A Short History of the Jews. Verlag C.H. oHG Munchen 2008, Princeton University Press, 2010
19. Michael Polonsky: A History of the Jews of Poland and Russia. The Littman Library of Jewish Civilization, 2010
20. Michael Berger: The Centrality of Talmud. In The Cambridge Guide to Jewish History, Religion, and Culture
21. Jacob Neusner: Rabbinic Literature: An Essential Guide. Abington Press, 2005
22. Mordechai Margolioth, Encyclopediyah le-Chachmei ha-Talmud ve-haGeonim (Encyclopedia of Talmudic and Geonic Literature, being A Biographical Dictionary of the Tanaim, Amoraim and Geonim)
23. Mordechai Margolioth, Encyclopedia le-Chachmei Yisrael (An Encyclopedia

of Great Men in Israel being A Biographical Dictionary of Jewish Sages and Scholars From the 9th to the End of the 18th Century)

Online

Stanford Encyclopedia of Philosophy
International Sephardic Leadership Council
Jewish Encyclopedia.com
Encyclopedia Judaica
Wikipedia

Electronic Aspects

Bibliography mentions a number of electronic web-based reference sources. Encyclopedia Judaica of 1906 is entirely web-based. Other reference sources can be found in PDF form

www.ingramcontent.com/pod-product-compliance
Lightning Source LLC
Chambersburg PA
CBHW080721230426
43665CB00020B/2568